# Rome and Jerusalem

# ROME AND JERUSALEM

## THE CLASH OF ANCIENT CIVILIZATIONS

MARTIN GOODMAN

ALFRED A. KNOPF · NEW YORK · 2007

THIS IS A BORZOI BOOK
PUBLISHED BY ALFRED A. KNOPF

Copyright © 2007 by Martin Goodman
All rights reserved. Published in the United States by Alfred A. Knopf,
a division of Random House, Inc., New York.
www.aaknopf.com

Originally published in Great Britain by Allen Lane,
an imprint of the Penguin Group, Ltd., London.

Knopf, Borzoi Books, and the colophon are
registered trademarks of Random House, Inc.

Library of Congress Cataloging in Publication Data
Goodman, Martin, [date]
Rome and Jerusalem : the clash of ancient civilizations / Martin Goodman—1st U.S. ed.
p.   cm.
"This is a Borzoi book"—T.p. verso.
Includes bibliographical references and index.
ISBN 978-0-375-41185-4
1. Jews—History—168 B.C.–135 A.D.  2. Jews—Palestine—Politics and government.
3. Jews—Rome—History.  4. Judaism—History—Post-exilic period, 586 B.C.–210 A.D.
5. Palestine—Kings and rulers.  I. Title.
DS121.7.G66 2007
933'.05—dc22   2007005267

Manufactured in the United States of America
First United States Edition

*for Sarah*

# CONTENTS

## PART THREE: CONFLICT

# ILLUSTRATIONS, FIGURES AND MAPS

## PHOTOGRAPHS

*Photographic acknowledgements are given in parentheses.*

## FIGURES

## MAPS

# ACKNOWLEDGEMENTS

Many friends, colleagues and students have contributed to this book over the years I have been teaching and writing on Jewish and Roman history. I am particularly indebted to Judith Lieu, Fergus Millar and Sacha Stern, who all read the manuscript at an early stage in its long evolution and gave me invaluable help. The remaining errors are entirely my responsibility.

The idea for the book came from Stuart Proffitt at Penguin, and I owe a great deal to his meticulous reading of the text and his wise advice. In the selection of images for illustration I have been much helped by Cecilia Mackay, Volker Heuchert and Janet Delaine. I am grateful to Amos Kloner for his expertise when I was drawing up the maps of Jerusalem. Neelum Ali has typed and altered the long typescript in its many revisions with remarkably good humour and forbearance. The text was expertly copyedited by Elizabeth Stratford. The maps were drawn by John Gilkes. The index was compiled by Margaret Binns.

A book that covers so wide a span of history has necessarily culled insights from much previous scholarship, and in the endnotes, which are intended only as a general guide to the reader, I have not been able to give a full acknowledgement of all the many works to which I am indebted. I have made much use of previous English versions of ancient sources, in particular Geza Vermes, *The Complete Dead Sea Scrolls in English* (London, 1997), Averil Cameron and Stuart G. Hall, *Eusebius, Life of Constantine* (Oxford, 1999) and a number of the translations published in the Loeb Classical Library, especially the translation by H. St.-J. Thackeray of Josephus, *The Jewish War*.

I am grateful to the Oxford Centre for Hebrew and Jewish Studies and to the Oriental Studies Faculty of the University of Oxford for financial support in preparing the book for publication, and to the British Academy for awarding me a Research Readership, without which I do not think it would have been possible to complete the task.

It is a great sadness that my father did not live to see the book, but he did enjoy the knowledge that it was on its way (and he liked the cover). I dedicate this book to my wife, Sarah, whose consistent enthusiasm for penguins has encouraged me to keep going.

*Martin Goodman*
Oxford and Birmingham
October 2006

# DYNASTY
# FAMILY TREES

# THE JULIO-CLAUDIAN DYNASTY

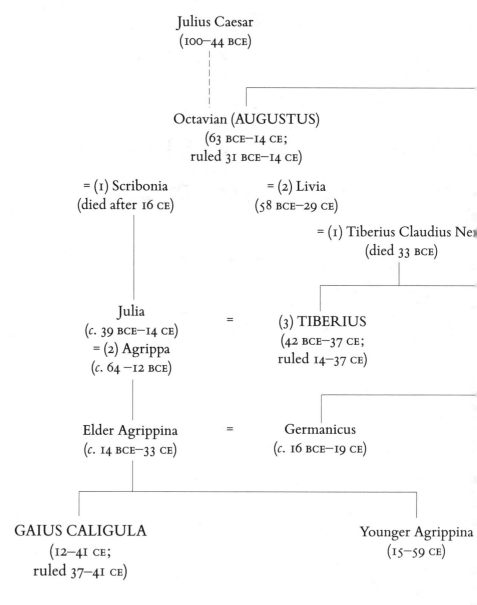

Julius Caesar
(100–44 BCE)

Octavian (AUGUSTUS)
(63 BCE–14 CE;
ruled 31 BCE–14 CE)

= (1) Scribonia
(died after 16 CE)

= (2) Livia
(58 BCE–29 CE)

= (1) Tiberius Claudius Nei
(died 33 BCE)

Julia
(c. 39 BCE–14 CE)
= (2) Agrippa
(c. 64 –12 BCE)

=

(3) TIBERIUS
(42 BCE–37 CE;
ruled 14–37 CE)

Elder Agrippina
(c. 14 BCE–33 CE)

=

Germanicus
(c. 16 BCE–19 CE)

GAIUS CALIGULA
(12–41 CE;
ruled 37–41 CE)

Younger Agrippina
(15–59 CE)

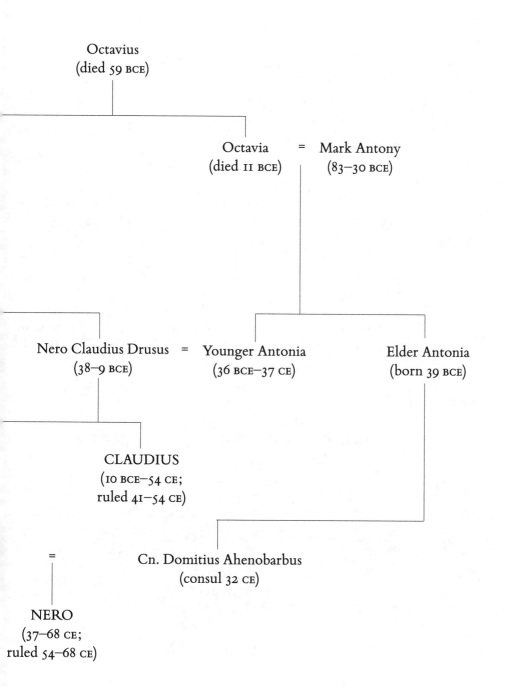

Octavius
(died 59 BCE)

Octavia     =     Mark Antony
(died 11 BCE)          (83–30 BCE)

Nero Claudius Drusus   =   Younger Antonia         Elder Antonia
(38–9 BCE)                (36 BCE–37 CE)           (born 39 BCE)

CLAUDIUS
(10 BCE–54 CE;
ruled 41–54 CE)

Cn. Domitius Ahenobarbus
(consul 32 CE)

=

NERO
(37–68 CE;
ruled 54–68 CE)

# THE HERODIAN DYNASTY

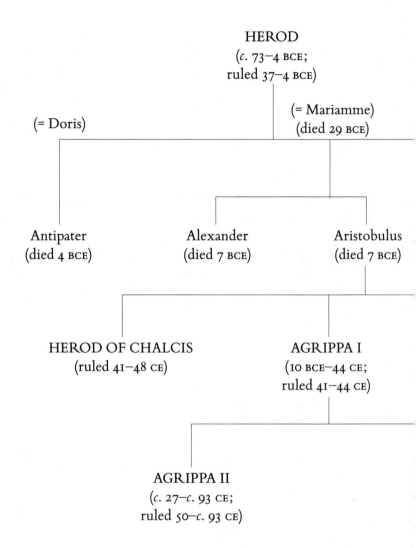

HEROD
(*c.* 73–4 BCE;
ruled 37–4 BCE)

(= Doris)

(= Mariamme)
(died 29 BCE)

Antipater
(died 4 BCE)

Alexander
(died 7 BCE)

Aristobulus
(died 7 BCE)

HEROD OF CHALCIS
(ruled 41–48 CE)

AGRIPPA I
(10 BCE–44 CE;
ruled 41–44 CE)

AGRIPPA II
(*c.* 27–*c.* 93 CE;
ruled 50–*c.* 93 CE)

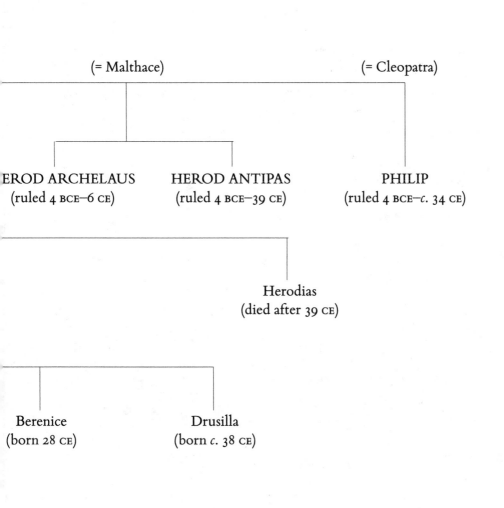

(= Malthace)                                                    (= Cleopatra)

HEROD ARCHELAUS       HEROD ANTIPAS           PHILIP
(ruled 4 BCE–6 CE)        (ruled 4 BCE–39 CE)     (ruled 4 BCE–*c.* 34 CE)

Herodias
(died after 39 CE)

Berenice               Drusilla
(born 28 CE)        (born *c.* 38 CE)

The destruction of Jerusalem is the only subject now remaining for an epic poem; a subject which, like Milton's *Fall of Man*, should interest all Christendom, as the Homeric War of Troy interested all Greece. There would be difficulties, as there are in all subjects; and they must be mitigated and thrown into the shade, as Milton has done with the numerous difficulties in the "*Paradise Lost*." But there would be a greater assemblage of grandeur and splendour than can now be found in any other theme . . . Here there would be the completion of the prophecies—the termination of the first revealed national religion under the violent assault of Paganism, itself the immediate forerunner and condition of the spread of a revealed mundane religion; and then you would have the character of the Roman and the Jew, and the awfulness, the completeness, the justice.

—Samuel Taylor Coleridge

# ROME AND JERUSALEM

# THE MAIN WITNESS

I N 70 CE the great city of Jerusalem, one of the most magnificent and renowned of its day, and, for Jews, the centre of all their aspirations, both religious and national, was devastated by Roman forces after a terrible siege. Over the following centuries Jews were pushed to the margins of Roman society. Rome came to be viewed by Jews as the epitome of evil power. Such polarization of two ancient cultures which had previously coexisted amicably was without parallel in the early Roman empire. This book seeks to explain why it occurred, and to examine its consequences to the present.

My original intention when I began to write this history was simply to examine the differences between the Jewish and Roman civilizations that shaped the world in which the controversial Jewish teacher Jesus lived and Christianity was formed. But it became clear that a static depiction of similarities and contrasts between the two peoples would be misleading. Pervading the history books, both ancient and modern, is an assumption that, because in 70 CE the conflict proved so dreadful, it must have been also inevitable. This interpretation of events, based on hindsight, seemed to me worth questioning. I therefore set out to examine whether the Jews of Jerusalem in the first half of the first century CE felt themselves to be the oppressed subjects of a hostile empire, as Judaean Jews clearly did a hundred years later, when the rebel leader Shimon bar Kosiba (known to later Jewish tradition as Bar Kokhba) led them in a second bloody revolt in 132–5 CE.

SCHOLARS TRYING to discover the truth about this unhappy story two thousand years ago can make use of a remarkable amount of contemporary

3

evidence. I shall discuss much of that evidence, and why it survives in such quantities, later in this book. But the reader should be introduced from the start to one ancient author whose copious writings will inevitably have more influence than any other on my reconstruction of the history of the Jews in the years immediately preceding 70 CE.

The Jerusalem priest Josephus (37–*c.* 100 CE) himself wrote an account of these years precisely in order to explain why such a disaster had befallen the Jews. He was in an outstandingly good position to know the answer, since he had himself participated in the war, first as a general on the side of the Jewish rebels and then (after his capture) as an observer inside the Roman headquarters. He composed the seven books of his *Jewish War* in Rome, as a Roman citizen and an acquaintance of the emperors, within a decade of the end of the conflict.[1]

Josephus was born into the ruling elite of Jerusalem and was much involved in the political intrigues of the city even before war broke out in 66. Just a few years before, in *c.* 61, he had travelled to Rome to appeal on behalf of some friends who had been sent there as prisoners by the governor of Judaea to render an account to the emperor Nero, and during that visit he had come into contact with the fringes of the imperial court. When he returned to Jerusalem he was caught up in the increasingly turbulent atmosphere and, once war appeared inevitable in October 66, joined the rebel government with responsibility for the defence of Galilee. As a general he was conspicuously unsuccessful and in spring 67 he was captured by Roman forces. According to his own account, he contemplated suicide to avoid falling into Roman hands but, persuaded by divine guidance in nightly dreams that God himself, who had created the Jewish people, had decided to break what he had made, and that a Roman victory was inevitable, he decided willingly to surrender to the Romans, taking God as witness that he was going "not as a traitor but as your minister."

In 69 Josephus' status as a prestige prisoner in the Roman camp was transformed by the revelation that he had prophesied, already in 67, the elevation of Vespasian, the general in command of the campaign in Judaea, to supreme power as emperor in Rome, an inspired prediction of considerable value to Vespasian in his bid for power against rival claimants to the purple. Josephus' later career depended entirely on this prophecy: in June 69 he was released from his bonds by Vespasian and in due course, when Vespasian was safely installed in the imperial palace in Rome in 70, Josephus was provided with lodgings in the city in the house which Vespasian himself had occupied before he became emperor. Honoured with Roman citizenship and granted a pension, Josephus settled down to write over the next thirty years or so a series of books about the Jews and Judaism, and the relationship of the Jews to the gentile world.

Josephus' vivid account of the events which led to the catastrophe of 70 CE was thus that of a participant and, in many cases, an eyewitness. He knew the terrain and the personalities of the leaders, and he understood the passions of both sides. But it would be unreasonable to expect him to be objective. He himself warned his readers that he would not try to suppress his private sentiments as he mourned the misfortunes of his native country, and his ability to exaggerate and distort his narrative to make a political or rhetorical point is revealed by some startling discrepancies between some passages in the *Jewish War* and parallel accounts in two of his later writings: the *Jewish Antiquities*, which in twenty books covered all of Jewish history from the beginnings of time to the outbreak of the war, and the *Life*, an autobiography published in 93 CE as a supplement to the *Antiquities*, in which he endeavoured to exculpate himself for having begun the war as a leader of the rebels.[2]

The whole of Josephus' narrative is permeated by the ambivalence which inevitably arose from this complex political career, first as defender of Jerusalem, then an apologist for the regime that had destroyed it. He himself claims that his change of sides was inspired by dreams sent from God. Later generations of Jews have been inclined to treat such claims as self-serving, as they undoubtedly were, but even if this judgement is correct, it should not detract from the value of his firsthand testimony, particularly when he is writing for Roman readers who had also witnessed the events he describes and could know when he is fabricating the story. To accept Josephus' often tendentious evaluation of the motives and characters of the Jews and Romans whose actions constitute his narrative would be rash, but to accept the details of his narrative, particularly when they contradict his own explanations of events, and so survive in the narrative only because they happened, is reasonable. As a result, the story of Jerusalem in the years up to 70 CE can be told in far more depth than that of any other city in the Roman empire at this time, apart from the story of Rome itself.

# THE DESTRUCTION OF JERUSALEM,

## 66–70 CE

I N MAY 66 CE, on 16 Iyyar, the Roman governor of Judaea, Gessius
Florus, who had been appointed to his post some two years earlier by
the emperor Nero, let loose his troops onto the upper market in Jerusalem
with instructions to kill all they met. The description of the ensuing mayhem, written just a few years later by Josephus, is chilling: "The
troops . . . not only plundered the quarter which they were sent to attack
but plunged into every house and slaughtered the inmates. There followed
a stampede through the narrow alleys, massacre of all who were caught,
every variety of pillage . . . The total number of that day's victims, including women and children—for they did not even abstain from infants—
amounted to about three thousand six hundred." It was the beginning of a
cycle of increasing violence that would end, just over four years later, in
the destruction of the whole city.[1]

Florus demanded that the inhabitants of Jerusalem should demonstrate
their submissiveness to his rule by going out in procession from the city
to greet two cohorts of Roman troops as they approached. It was political theatre, designed to humiliate, and when some of the Jews began to
shout abuse of the governor, the soldiers lashed out, with devastating
consequences:

In an instant the troops were round them, striking out with their clubs,
and on their taking flight the cavalry pursued and trampled them under
their horses' feet. Many fell beneath the blows of the Romans, a still
larger number under the pressure of their own companions. Around
the gates the crush was terrible; as each strove to pass in first, the flight

of all was retarded, and dreadful was the fate of any who stumbled; suf-
focated and mangled by the crowds that trod them down, they were
obliterated and their bodies so disfigured that their relatives could not
recognize them to give them burial.[2]

The leading Jewish moderates were led by Agrippa II (27–c. 93 CE),
great-grandson of Herod the Great (c. 73–4 BCE), who had been appointed
by the Romans both as king over various small territories north and east of
Judaea and as overseer responsible for the upkeep and operation of the
Jerusalem Temple. They tried to stem the flood of protest, but without
success. As Jerusalemites polarized between a peace party and a war party,
the captain of the Temple, a priest named Eleazar, described by Josephus as
"a very daring youth," forced the issue by persuading those officiating in
the Temple to refuse any further gifts or sacrifices brought by a foreigner.
"This action," wrote Josephus, "laid the foundation of the war with the
Romans," for it required an end to the long-standing custom of demonstrating loyalty by offering sacrifices in the Temple on behalf of the
emperor and Rome.[3]

In the first months of the ensuing conflict in Jerusalem the Romans
themselves were not directly involved. Factional strife within the Jewish
population led to heavy loss of life and the spectacular destruction of the
large town houses of some of the rich Jerusalemites who opposed revolt.
Among those in the peace party who were murdered was the former High
Priest Ananias, father of Eleazar. A Roman cohort of six hundred men,
garrisoned on the western edge of the city, struggled to provide support
for those still striving to avert a full-scale war, but they were besieged by
the rebels and confined to their headquarters in the former palace of Herod
the Great. By late August or early September, they were finally overcome,
and agreed to surrender their weapons in exchange for free passage out of
the city. Josephus, aware of the enormity of what happened next, named
the (otherwise unknown) Jews who gave on oath the necessary assurances:
Gorion son of Nicomedes, Ananias son of Sadok, Judas son of Jonathan.
Oaths taken, the Roman commander Metilius marched his men down
from their stronghold:

> So long as the soldiers retained their arms, none of the rebels molested
> them or gave any indication of treachery; but when, in accordance with

the covenant, they had all laid down their bucklers and swords and, with no suspicion remaining, were taking their departure, Eleazar's party fell upon them, surrounded and massacred them; the Romans neither resisting nor suing for mercy, but merely appealing with loud cries to "the agreements" and the "oaths." Thus, brutally butchered, perished all save Metilius; he alone saved his life by entreaties and promises to Judaize, even to the point of being circumcised. To the Romans this injury—the loss of a handful of men out of a boundless army—was slight; but to the Jews it looked like the prelude to their ruin. Seeing the grounds for war to be now beyond remedy, and the city polluted by such a stain of guilt as could not but arouse a dread of some visitation from heaven, if not of the vengeance of Rome, they gave themselves up to public mourning; the whole city was a scene of dejection, and among the moderates there was not one who was not racked with the thought that he would personally have to suffer for the rebels' crime.[4]

This much had occurred by the time that the Roman governor of Syria, Cestius Gallus, arrived from Antioch with a sizeable force at the feast of Tabernacles in the early autumn, a month or so later. Casual slaughter of civilians in his path, such as the fifty individuals left in Lydda after the rest of the population had gone to Jerusalem for the festival, and the burning of villages, made it clear that he intended to inflict corporate punishment on the Jews in retaliation for Roman losses. The rebel forces responded by rushing to attack him, with considerable success, killing five hundred and fifteen enemy for the loss of only twenty-two. Even at this late stage Agrippa tried to mediate a peaceful solution. He sent two friends to offer a treaty on behalf of Cestius. The terms (so Josephus claimed) were generous, reflecting Roman discomfiture in this first engagement and the Jews' control of the heights above the valleys where the Romans had taken up their temporary quarters. The rebels were offered pardon for their misdeeds if they would disarm and return to their allegiance. It was too late. The offer was greeted with such violence that one of Agrippa's emissaries was killed and the other wounded. Cestius therefore went on to Jerusalem, pitched his camp on Mount Scopus, which overlooked the Temple from the north-east, and eventually marched into the city, capturing the suburbs, setting fire to the "New City" of Bezetha to the north of the Temple precincts, and camping opposite the royal palace in the upper city in order to besiege the inner city and the Temple. Under the protection of a tortoise of shields, the soldiers began to undermine the wall and to set fire to the gate of the Temple. The besieged began to panic, and some, it was said, offered to open up the city to him.

And then, suddenly, Cestius stopped and, "without having suffered any reverse and contrary to all calculation, retired from the city."[5] Josephus alleges bribery, the natural explanation of inexplicable behaviour: Cestius' camp prefect had been corrupted by Gessius Florus and as a result diverted Cestius from the rapid victory he could so easily have obtained. Florus' motives were not mentioned, but Josephus gives the impression that the wicked governor was keen on any mayhem that might cover up the evidence of his crimes. In any case, the result was terrible: "Hence it came about that the war was so long protracted and the Jews drained the cup of irretrievable disaster."[6] In other words, a quick victory for Cestius Gallus then would have had far less serious consequences for the Jews than their eventual fate.

Perhaps Cestius thought he could stop because he had already achieved enough. He had demonstrated clearly the power of Rome by marching right up to the gates of the Temple, spreading devastation around him. The rebels were in disarray. There was no need to create further havoc, with the danger of further Roman losses. He could return to safer, more comfortable, quarters, where his supply lines would be more secure, and negotiate from there. If that was the calculation, it proved hopelessly misguided. Heavy infantry withdrawing through the narrow defiles leading from the hills round Jerusalem down towards the Mediterranean coast were extremely vulnerable. The light-armed Jewish rebels caused increasing casualties until the orderly march degenerated into a bloody rout. Cestius lost not only five thousand three hundred infantry and four hundred and eighty cavalry but also his heavy artillery—catapults, battering rams and other siege machines were abandoned along with the rest of the baggage train. After such a reverse there could be no more offers of peace. The Roman empire could counter so public a humiliation only by a full and thorough punishment of the rebellious city. Among the Jews who up to this juncture had gone on hoping for compromise and had stayed in Jerusalem to help broker a peace were included, remarkably, relatives and employees of King Agrippa. Now they fled to the Roman side.

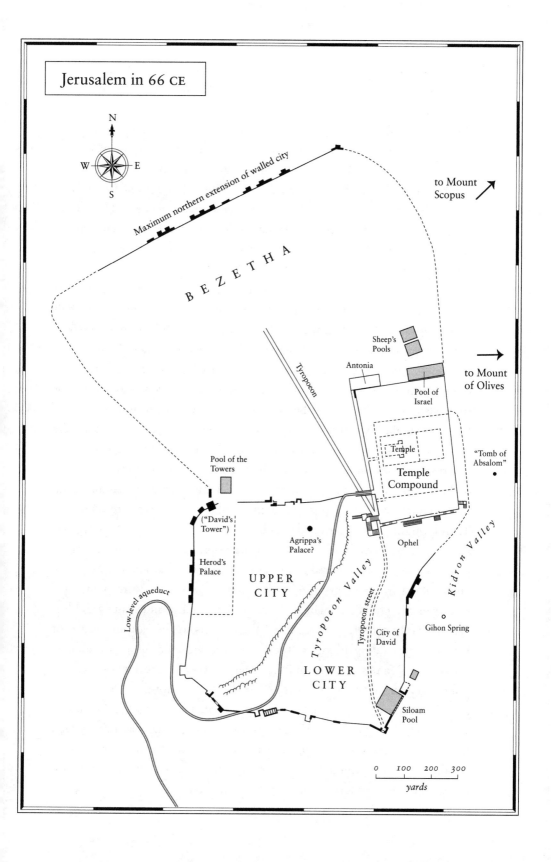

Jerusalem in 66 CE

N
W E
S

Maximum northern extension of walled city

to Mount
Scopus

B E Z E T H A

Tyropoeon

Sheep's
Pools

Antonia

to Mount
of Olives

Pool of
Israel

Pool of the
Towers

Temple

"Tomb of
Absalom"

Temple
Compound

("David's
Tower")

Agrippa's
Palace?

Ophel

Herod's
Palace

UPPER
CITY

Tyropoeon Valley

Kidron Valley

Low-level aqueduct

Tyropoeon street

City of
David

Gihon Spring

LOWER
CITY

Siloam
Pool

0    100    200    300

yards

Those who remained in Jerusalem set about organizing its defence, under the leadership of a former High Priest, Ananus son of Ananus. Generals were appointed for the different regions of the country, including Josephus, to take command of Galilee. In the capital, as Josephus reports, "all the powerful men who were not pro-Roman were busy repairing the wall and getting together much military equipment. In every part of the city missiles and suits of armour were being forged, masses of young men were undergoing training, and everything was full of uproar."[7] There were plenty of omens which could be taken by the pessimistic as evidence of the coming destruction, but those who had kindled the war found ways to interpret them favourably.

A full-scale siege of a city as well defended as Jerusalem was not to be undertaken lightly and, in the event, it was to be another three and a half years after the failure of Cestius Gallus before Roman troops again attacked the city walls. Cestius himself seems to have died in Syria quite early the following year—the Roman historian Tacitus (c. 56–c. 120) remarks unsympathetically that his death came about "in the course of nature or from vexation," although if he was sick the previous autumn that might help to explain his apparently incompetent generalship.[8] In any case, the command of the war in Judaea was entrusted instead by the emperor Nero to a reliable if uninspiring soldier, who had made his name in the conquest of Britain more than twenty years earlier. Titus Flavius Vespasianus, the future emperor Vespasian, spent months collecting a huge force. His son Titus brought a legion from Alexandria. The complement of three legions and a large body of auxiliary and allied troops, totalling altogether sixty thousand men, was gathered in Ptolemais (modern Akko) on the Mediterranean coast in early spring 67 CE. The next two years were spent cautiously gaining full control of the surrounding countryside—in 67 Galilee, Samaria and northern Judaea; in 68 the regions to the east and south of Jerusalem, including Idumaea (the region around Hebron) and the environs of the Dead Sea. But from June 68 any further progress was slowed by political uncertainty and ambition. The death that month of Nero threw into doubt Vespasian's formal right to prosecute the campaign. Then, in a year of political turmoil at Rome, two aspirants to imperial power each died in the early months of 69, a third was proclaimed by the legions in the German provinces, and in July Vespasian himself was acclaimed by his own troops. The siege of Jerusalem would have to wait.

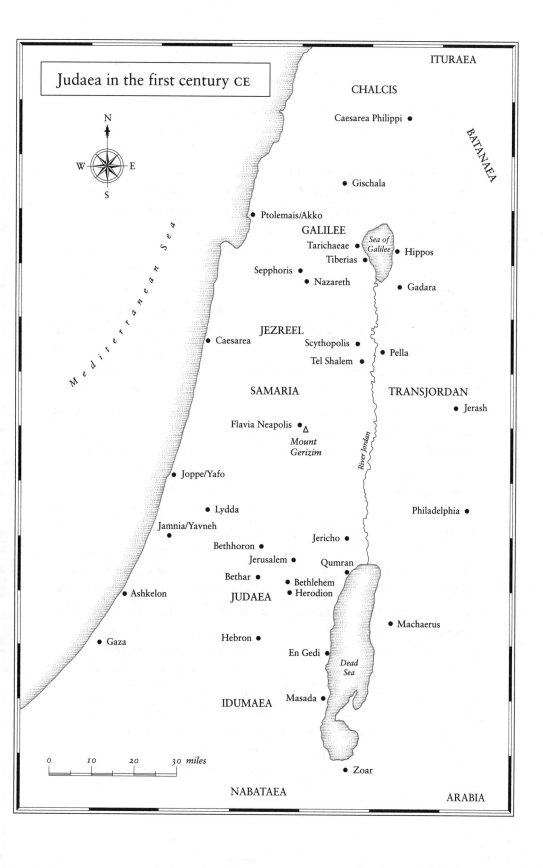

Judaea in the first century CE

N
W · E
S

ITURAEA

CHALCIS

Caesarea Philippi ●

BATANAEA

● Gischala

● Ptolemais/Akko

GALILEE

Taricheae ●
Sepphoris ●
● Nazareth

*Sea of Galilee*
Tiberias ●
● Hippos

● Gadara

*Mediterranean Sea*

JEZREEL

● Caesarea

Scythopolis ●
Tel Shalem ●

● Pella

SAMARIA

TRANSJORDAN

● Jerash

Flavia Neapolis ● △
*Mount Gerizim*

*River Jordan*

● Joppe/Yafo

● Lydda

Jamnia/Yavneh ●

Bethhoron ●
Jerusalem ●
Bethar ●

● Ashkelon

JUDAEA

● Gaza

Hebron ●

Philadelphia ●

Jericho ●

Qumran ●

Bethlehem ●
Herodion ●

● Machaerus

En Gedi ●
*Dead Sea*

IDUMAEA

Masada ●

0        10        20        30 *miles*

● Zoar

NABATAEA

ARABIA

It is hard to know to what extent news of these ramifications of Roman politics percolated to the rebels in Jerusalem. They were unlikely to appreciate the significance of such upheavals in the capital, not least because nothing like them had been experienced in the past hundred years. To the more optimistic, the failure of Roman troops to return to the city after the rout of Cestius Gallus may have seemed evidence that Rome had lost interest in or the will for reconquest, although the stories of devastation brought by refugees from the countryside served to remind the defenders of the terrors that the invading force might inflict.

The best evidence of the political ethos of the revolutionary government in Jerusalem can be gauged from the plentiful coinage they produced. It suggests a state proud of its independence and national freedom: although the rebels had access to Roman coinage, including the most valuable denominations (the *aurei* made of gold), they began to mint early in the conflict silver coinage of shekels and fractions of shekels and their own distinctive bronze small change. The silver content of the rather thick coins they produced was exceptionally pure. The legends on all the coins were in Hebrew rather than in Greek or Aramaic, the two languages most commonly found on inscriptions in Jerusalem in this period, and the palaeo-Hebrew script used was archaic, unfamiliar to most first-century Jews but redolent of antiquity. The slogans selected by the minting authorities—"Jerusalem is holy," "Freedom of Zion," "For the redemption of Zion," "Shekel of Israel"—proclaimed a political entity variously identified as Jerusalem or Israel or, on the bronze coins from the second to the fourth year of the revolt, as Zion. There was in general a remarkable degree of variation in types over the five-year period of the revolt: in particular, a chalice (referring to the Temple service) and a palm branch and citron, as carried in the celebration of the festival of Tabernacles, were frequently reproduced.[9]

It is clear that the authorities in Jerusalem believed themselves to be living in an independent and distinctive Jewish state centred on the Temple, for which the catchwords were "freedom" and "holiness." The coins contain no image reminiscent in any way of Rome, even in emulation or antagonistic opposition. The regular record on the coins of the progress of the new era ("Year One," "Year Two" and so on) proclaimed a self-consciously new state, with a self-consciously new name: not "Judah," which was too close to *Judaea* (the Roman name for the province), but "Israel."[10]

Documents in Hebrew and in Aramaic drawn up during this period of independence and discovered over the past fifty years in caves in Wadi Murabba'at in the Judaean desert, set out in some detail the terms of land sales between 67 and 69 in expectation of a settled future. The dating formulas follow a similar pattern in each document: "the fourteenth of Elul, year two to the redemption of Israel in Jerusalem," "on the twenty-first of Tishri, year four to the redemption of Israel in Jerusalem," "on the . . . day of Marheshvan, year three to the freedom of Jerusalem."[11]

This Jewish state was sufficiently untroubled by Roman attacks from 68 to early 70 for the city to be plagued by faction struggles, which were all the more violent because each faction was armed, ostensibly in readiness against the Romans. It seems to have been at this time, if not earlier, that the Christians of Jerusalem abandoned the city, "commanded by an oracle given by revelation before the war to those in the city who were worthy of it" (so, two and a half centuries later, wrote Eusebius, historian of the Church). According to one later tradition, they took refuge in the gentile city of Pella in Transjordan.[12]

The detailed history of this internal strife in independent Jerusalem can be traced only in the account of Josephus, who was not a wholly trustworthy witness of events inside the city, since by 68 he was a prisoner of Vespasian and knew about them only from rumours brought by deserters or prisoners. He will have been inclined to believe the worst of all those Jews who had not, like him, recognized the divine will and accordingly stopped opposing Rome, and it does not require sophisticated psychological analysis to suggest that his antagonism to his erstwhile fellow rebels was prompted by residual doubts over his own behaviour. In any case, by spring 68 the rebel government to which Josephus had attached himself in October 66 when he accepted appointment to the command in Galilee had lost power to rival groups. Josephus' former commander-in-chief, the ex–High Priest Ananus son of Ananus, on whom Josephus lavished inordinate praise as "a man on every ground revered and most just," was murdered by a coalition made up of insurgents from Idumaea and the Zealots, a faction based (by 68) in the inner court of the Temple; they were led by a group of priests, and built on the support both of refugees from the countryside of northern Judaea and of the Galileans who had followed to Jerusalem a certain John of Gischala, who a year earlier had been a political rival of Josephus when Josephus had held his Galilean command.[13] Hence the virulence of Josephus' description of the Zealots, full of abusive clichés standard in Roman political discourse in his day:

> With an insatiable lust for loot, they ransacked the houses of the wealthy; the murder of men and the violation of women were their sport; they caroused on their spoils, with blood to wash them down, and from mere satiety unscrupulously indulged in effeminate practices, plaiting their hair and attiring themselves in women's apparel, drenching themselves with perfumes and painting their eyelids to enhance their beauty. And not only did they imitate the dress, but also the passions of women, devising in their excess of lasciviousness unlawful pleasures and wallowing as in a brothel in the city, which they polluted from end to end with their foul deeds. Yet, while they wore women's faces, their hands were murderous, and approaching with mincing steps they would suddenly become warriors and whipping out their swords from under their dyed mantles transfix whomsoever they met.[14]

Josephus' judgements about specific Jewish rebel groups such as the Zealots may be of dubious value, but his general depiction of a city divided between competing factions with shifting allegiances is echoed in the account of Jerusalem just before its destruction written by his younger contemporary, Tacitus:

> There were three generals, three armies: the outermost and largest circuit of the walls was held by Simon, the middle of the city by John, known as Bargioras, and the Temple was guarded by Eleazar. John and Simon were strong in numbers and equipment, Eleazar had the advantage of position: between these three there was constant fighting, treachery and arson, and a great store of grain was consumed. Then John got possession of the Temple by sending a party, under pretence of offering sacrifice, to slay Eleazar and his troops. So the citizens were divided into two factions until, at the approach of the Romans, foreign war produced concord.[15]

Josephus himself distinguished the factions most clearly in his bitter retrospective summary of their violent characteristics, which he blamed for the disaster to come:

> Not only did he [John] put to death all who proposed just and salutary measures, treating such persons as his bitterest enemies among all the citizens, but he also in his public capacity loaded his country with evils innumerable, such as one might expect would be inflicted upon men by one who had already dared to practise impiety even towards God . . . Again, there was Simon, son of Gioras: what crime did not he commit? Or what outrage did he refrain from inflicting upon the persons of those very freemen who had created him a despot? Yet even their infatuation was outdone by the madness of the Idumaeans. For those most abominable wretches, after butchering the chief priests, so that no particle of religious worship might continue, proceeded to extirpate whatever relics were left of our civil polity, introducing into every department perfect lawlessness. In this the so-called Zealots excelled, a class which justified their name by their actions; for they copied every deed of ill, nor was there any previous villainy recorded in history that they failed zealously to emulate. And yet they took their title from their professed zeal for virtue, either in mockery of those they wronged, so brutal was their nature, or reckoning the greatest of evils good. Accordingly these each found a fitting end, God awarding due retribution to them all.[16]

These political divisions inside Jerusalem ended in spring 70, when a Roman army under Titus, son of the new emperor, finally arrived outside the walls of Jerusalem. In marked contrast to the hesitant policy of the previous year and a half, the siege, once begun, was prosecuted with exceptional speed and vigour. The force deployed by the Romans was huge. A fourth legion was added to the three earlier deployed by Vespasian, the contingents sent by allied kings were greatly strengthened and a large number of Syrian auxiliaries were drafted in. The change in Roman behaviour took the Jews by surprise. Men, women and children had gone up to the city from the surrounding villages to celebrate the Passover festival and were trapped by the surrounding army. Within days the squabbling Jewish factions agreed to place themselves under the command of a single general, Simon son of Gioras, who was to direct the defence of the city with great energy and skill over the coming months.

Josephus, from his vantage point in the Roman camp, was able to describe the siege of Jerusalem in gory detail, although his own part in the action was confined to pleading unsuccessfully with the defenders for them to surrender. In the course of the siege Titus ringed the city with a continuous stone wall manned by armed guards to cut off supplies and starve the population, a tactic reflected in a prophecy of Jesus as recorded in the Gospel of Luke: "And when he was come near, he saw the city, and wept over it . . . For the days shall come upon you when your enemies will cast a trench about you, and compass you round, and keep you in on every side."[17] Josephus' descriptions of the horrors of famine are lurid:

Many clandestinely bartered their possessions for a single measure—of wheat, if they were rich, of barley, if they were poor; then shutting themselves up in the most remote recesses of their houses, some in the extremity of hunger devoured the grain unground, others so baked it as necessity and fear dictated. Nowhere was any table laid; they snatched the food half-cooked from the fire and tore it in pieces. Pitiful was the fare and lamentable the spectacle, the stronger taking more than their share, the weak whimpering. Famine, indeed, overpowers all the emotions, but of nothing is it so destructive as of shame: what at other times would claim respect is then treated with contempt. Thus, wives would snatch the food from husbands, children from fathers, and— most pitiable sight of all—mothers from the very mouths of their infants, and while their dearest ones were pining in their arms they scrupled not to rob them of the life-giving drops . . . The famine became more intense and devoured the people by households and families. The roofs were thronged with women and babies completely exhausted, the alleys with the corpses of the aged; children and youths, with swollen figures, roamed like phantoms through the marketplaces and collapsed wherever their faintness overtook them. As for burying their relatives, the sick had not the strength, while those with vigour still left were deterred both by the multitude of the dead and by the uncertainty of their own fate. For many fell dead while burying others, and many went forth to their tombs before fate was upon them. And amidst these calamities there was neither lamentation nor wailing: famine stifled the emotions, and with dry eyes and grinning mouths these slowly dying victims looked on those who had gone to their rest before them.

The stories told by deserters to the Roman camp may well have been exaggerated:

Mannaeus, son of Lazarus, who sought refuge in those days with Titus, reported that there were carried out through a single gate, which had been entrusted to him, one hundred and fifteen thousand, eight hundred and eighty corpses, between the fourteenth of the month Xanthicus [the Hebrew month Nisan, in April], on which the general encamped before their walls, and the new moon of Panemus [the Hebrew month Tammuz, in June] . . . This refugee was followed by many eminent citizens, who reported that the corpses of the lower classes thrown out through the gates amounted in all to six hundred thousand; of the rest it was impossible to discover the number. They added that . . . a measure of corn had been sold for a talent, and that later when it was no longer possible to gather herbs, the city being all walled in, some were reduced to such straits that they searched the sewers and for old cow dung and ate the offal therefrom, and what once would have disgusted them to look at had now become food . . . Necessity drove the victims to gnaw anything, and objects which even the filthiest of brute beasts would reject they condescended to collect and eat: thus in the end they abstained not from belts and shoes and stripped off and chewed the very leather of their bucklers. Others devoured tufts of withered grass . . .[18]

The most appalling story of all involved a woman named Mary, daughter of Eleazar, who had fled to Jerusalem with the rest of the people from her home village of Bethezuba in Transjordan. Impelled by hunger and rage, wrote Josephus, she killed her son, "an infant at the breast," and roasted him. She had eaten part of the body and stored the rest for later consumption when she was betrayed by the smell of roasted meat.[19]

It might have seemed sufficient simply to wait for the resulting deprivation to take its toll and force the defenders to sue for peace, and Titus did

indeed allow the public crucifixion of those caught when they were driven
by hunger to try to escape the city, in "the hope that the spectacle might
perhaps induce the Jews to surrender for fear that continued persistence
would involve them in a similar fate. The soldiers out of rage and hatred
amused themselves by nailing their prisoners in different postures."[20] Titus
opted not to wait for surrender but to seek a more rapid victory by direct
assault. He began with an offensive against the northernmost wall of the
city, which, in contrast to the precipitous approaches on the other three
sides, lay on reasonably level land. On 7 Iyyar, in late April 70, after fifteen
days of siege, intensive fighting with heavy artillery, including catapults
and ballista balls, and the construction of three towers to enable archers,
javelin-men and stone throwers to harass the defence, the wall was
breached by a battering ram, which the Jews (according to Josephus) nicknamed (perhaps ironically) *Nikon*, "Victor."[21] The northern suburb of
Bezetha, which had been destroyed four years earlier by Cestius Gallus,
was now razed again. The Jews withdrew to a second wall which protected
the rest of the city against assault from the north, only for that wall also to
be breached after five days. Titus, with a thousand legionaries, entered the
narrow alleys where the wool-shops and clothes-market of the city were to
be found.

Titus seems to have hoped that this demonstration of power and purpose would be enough to induce the defenders to surrender. He forbade his
troops to kill indiscriminately or to set fire to the houses. The revolutionaries were given an opportunity freely to vacate the city and leave the general
populace unharmed—or so, in retrospect, claimed Josephus, who asserts
that Titus' paramount object at this stage of the siege was "to preserve the
city to himself and the Temple for the city."[22] The tactic failed through the
intransigence of the Jewish militants, who rejected Titus' terms and
counter-attacked, and it took a further four days of intensive fighting for
the second wall to be recaptured by Roman troops and demolished.

To discourage further opposition in the rest of the city, Titus attempted
to frighten the defenders by parading before them his impressive military
strength, as Josephus (an eyewitness) describes:

> The appointed day having arrived for the distribution of the soldiers'
> pay, he ordered his officers to parade the forces and count out the
> money to each man in full view of the enemy. So the troops, as was

their custom, drew forth their arms from the cases in which till now they had been covered and advanced clad in mail, the cavalry leading their horses which were richly caparisoned. The area in front of the city gleamed far and wide with silver and gold, and nothing was more gratifying to the Romans, or more awe-inspiring to the enemy, than that spectacle. For the whole of the old wall and the north side of the Temple were thronged with spectators, the houses across the wall were to be seen packed with craning heads, and there was not a spot visible in the city which was not covered by the crowd. Even the hardiest were struck with dire dismay at the sight of this assemblage of all the forces, the beauty of their armour and the admirable order of the men . . .[23]

A further weapon in psychological warfare was the deployment of Josephus himself to try to persuade the rebels to surrender, by talking to them in their native tongue, "thinking that perhaps they might yield to a fellow countryman." It must have been a hard speech to make. According to Josephus' own account, he had difficulty, as he went round the walls "repeatedly imploring them to spare themselves and the people," in approaching close enough to be heard while keeping out of range of missiles. The noise of derision and execration heaped on him by those on the ramparts cannot have helped. Josephus claims that his tearful appeal moved some of the ordinary inhabitants to desert the city, and that Titus allowed most such deserters to go wherever they wanted in the Judaean countryside, but the committed combatants were unmoved.[24] Preparation began for the next major assault against the central areas of the city.

In less than two weeks, the four legions had thrown up a rampart each, two against the upper city, on the western hill of Jerusalem, and two against the Antonia fortress, which lay to the north of the Temple enclosure, but the insurgents undermined them with tunnels and set them on fire. It was a serious setback for the Roman forces, not least because there was a severe shortage of local timber, but three weeks later four new wooden ramparts had been built. This time all four were directed against the wall around the Antonia. The battering rams got to work with devastating effect and in the middle of the night the wall subsided, only for it to become clear that the defenders had erected another wall behind it. As a temporary structure it would doubtless be far less strong than the wall that had just fallen, and the way to its summit was facilitated by the mounds of rubble, but it would require a brave man to lead the assault with scaling ladders.

On 3 Tammuz (in late June), Titus appealed for volunteers. One Sabinus, "a native of Syria, who showed himself both in might of hand and in spirit the bravest of men," was the first to rise to the challenge. Josephus describes his exploits with admiration:

Anyone seeing him before that day and judging from his outward appearance would not have taken him even for a common soldier. His skin was black, his flesh shrunk and emaciated; but within that slender frame, far too strait for its native prowess, there dwelt a heroic soul . . . With his left hand he extended his buckler over his head and with his right drew his sword and advanced towards the wall, almost exactly at the sixth hour of the day. He was followed by eleven others, who alone were found to emulate his gallantry; but the hero, impelled by some preternatural stimulus, far outstripped them all. From the ramparts the guards hurled their javelins at the party, assailed them from all quarters with showers of arrows, and rolled down enormous boulders which swept away some of the eleven; but Sabinus, facing the missiles and buried beneath the darts, yet never slackened his pace until he had gained the summit and routed the enemy. For the Jews, dumbfounded at his strength and intrepidity and, moreover, imagining that more had ascended, turned and fled . . . [But] at the moment when this hero had attained his object, he slipped and stumbling over a rock fell headlong upon it with a tremendous crash. The Jews, turning and seeing him alone and prostrate, assailed him from all sides. Rising upon his knee and screening himself with his buckler, he for a while kept them at bay and wounded many of those who approached him; but soon under his numerous wounds his arm was paralysed, and he was at length, before giving up his life, buried under the missiles: a man whose gallantry deserved a better fortune, but whose fall was in keeping with his enterprise.[25]

Sabinus' comrades were also killed or wounded, but the Antonia did not hold out much longer. Two days later a silent assault at the dead of night captured both the wall and the fortress, which was soon razed to the ground.

The Temple itself now lay open to attack, but it too was protected by strong external fortifications on all sides and by further walls between the outer court and the inner. An attempt to repeat the earlier tactic of a night attack with a small force was repulsed, and preparations were made for the erection of another four wooden ramparts and a full-scale artillery barrage. On 8 Ab, in late July 70, the final stages of the siege began. Great battering rams set to work on the western wall of the Temple enclosure but made no impression because of the size of the stones and their close fit. Attempts were made to undermine the foundations of the northern gate. It stood firm. "Finally," writes Josephus,

> despairing of all attempts with engines and crowbars, the Romans applied ladders to the porticoes. The Jews made no haste to prevent this, but as soon as they mounted vigorously attacked them. Some they thrust back and hurled down headlong, others who encountered them they slew; many as they stepped off the ladders they cut down with their swords, before they could shield themselves with their bucklers; some ladders, again, laden with armed men, they tilted sideways from above and dashed to the ground; not, however, without suffering considerable slaughter themselves. The Romans who had brought up the standards fought fiercely around these, deeming their loss a dire disaster and disgrace; yet, eventually, these ensigns also were taken by the Jews, who destroyed all who had mounted. The remainder, intimidated by the fate of the fallen, then retired . . . Titus, now that he saw that his endeavour to spare a foreign temple led only to the injury and slaughter of his troops, issued orders to set the gates on fire.[26]

Soon the porticoes around the outer court were ablaze.

A day later, on 9 Ab—a day filled with significance for the Jews since it marked the anniversary of the destruction by the Babylonians in 586 BCE of the first Temple, built by Solomon—a division of the Roman forces was deployed to extinguish the fire raging in the outer court and to clear a way to facilitate military access to the Temple for the final assault on the inner sanctuary. This day the insurgents remained behind the ramparts which protected the inner court, too exhausted and demoralized to venture out, but on 10 Ab some sallied forth to try to regain control of the outer precincts of the Temple, and were only forced to retreat back into the inner court through emergency assistance provided to the Roman troops by an elite cavalry unit.

Titus resolved that the following day he would attack the inner sanctuary itself at dawn with his whole force, but the plan was pre-empted by the spread of fire from the outer court to the inner and as a result his troops could enter unopposed. Josephus describes vividly the panic and confusion among the defenders:

> While the Temple blazed, the victors plundered everything that fell in their way and slaughtered wholesale all who were caught. No pity was shown for age, no reverence for rank; children and greybeards, laity and priests, alike were massacred; every class was pursued and encompassed in the grasp of war, whether suppliants for mercy or offering resistance. The roar of the flames streaming far and wide mingled with the groans of the falling victims; and, owing to the height of the hill and the mass of the burning pile, one would have thought that the whole city was ablaze. And then the din—nothing more deafening or appalling could be conceived than that. There were the war-cries of the Roman legions sweeping onward in a mass, the howls of the rebels encircled by fire and sword, the rush of the people who, cut off above, fled panic-stricken only to fall into the arms of the foe, and their shrieks as they met their fate. With the cries on the hill were blended those of the multitude in the city below; and now many who were emaciated and tongue-tied from starvation, when they beheld the sanctuary on fire, gathered strength once more for lamentations and wailing. Transjordan and the surrounding mountains contributed their echoes, deepening the din. But yet more awful than the uproar were the sufferings. You would indeed have thought that the Temple hill was boiling over from its base, being everywhere one mass of flame, but yet that the stream of blood was more copious than the flames and the slain more numerous than the slayers. For the ground was nowhere visible through the corpses; but the soldiers had to clamber over heaps of bodies in pursuit of the fugitives.[27]

The Temple site was now nearly empty of rebels and the Roman troops set up their standards within the court opposite the eastern gate and sacrificed to them, and "with rousing acclamations" hailed Titus as *imperator* ("commander-in-chief").[28] Some of the Temple priests were still taking refuge on the sanctuary wall, although at least two of them had chosen to end their lives spectacularly by plunging into the flames. On the fifth day those who were left were too hungry to hold out any longer. They surrendered themselves to the Romans, only to be put to death by Titus on the basis that "it is fitting for priests to perish along with their Temple."[29]

The capitulation of the rest of Jerusalem was rapid. Those parts of the lower city already under Roman control were deliberately set on fire. The erection of new towers to break down the walls of the upper city was completed on 7 Elul (in mid-August), and the troops forced their way in. By 8 Elul the whole city was in Roman hands—and in ruins. In recompense for the ferocious fighting they had been required to endure, the soldiers were given free rein to loot and kill, until eventually Titus ordered that the city be razed to the ground, "leaving only the loftiest of the towers, Phasael, Hippicus and Mariamme, and the portion of the wall enclosing the city on the west: the latter as an encampment for the garrison that was to remain, and the towers to indicate to posterity the nature of the city and of the strong defences which had yet yielded to Roman prowess. All the rest of the wall encompassing the city was so completely levelled to the ground as to leave future visitors to the spot no ground for believing that it had ever been inhabited."[30]

WHY HAD this disaster come about? Was there anything intrinsic in Jewish and Roman society that made it impossible for Jerusalem and Rome to coexist? Were the tensions which had so dramatic an effect in August 70 already apparent in 30 when Jesus preached in Jerusalem and died there on the order of a Roman governor? And, as early Christians began to carry their faith out from Jerusalem to the wider Roman empire, what was the effect of the conflict between Jews and Romans on the relations between Jews and Christians in a Roman world? It will be the task of this book to seek answers to these questions.

# PART ONE

# A Mediterranean World

CHAPTER ONE

# A TALE OF TWO CITIES

ROME AND JERUSALEM have existed for centuries in the Western imagination as opposite ideals of grandeur and sanctity. Rome, the "Eternal City," has long been conceived as the epitome of magnificent power imposed through military might and the force of law and as a warning of the dangers of moral corruption. The picturesque ruins of the imperial city have both fascinated and repelled, stimulating admiration for brilliant achievements by past generations and rumination on the fallibility of human desire for glory. Such images retain a hold even now in literature, art and cinema. In contrast, Jerusalem has been idealized as a holy place of revelations, miracles and spiritual intensity. The origins of these idealized images lie in the real history of these cities in the time of Jesus. At the beginning of the first millennium CE both cities were at the peak of their prosperity and grandeur, each famous throughout the Mediterranean world and beyond. They were two cities whose inhabitants came into close contact: Romans visited Jerusalem as soldiers, politicians, tourists; Jews came to Rome as suppliants, slaves or fortune-seekers. They were two cities with a culture partly shared, from the gleam of ceremonial white masonry in the summer sun to acceptance of Greek as a prestige language of the erudite and the influence of Greek architecture and philosophy. They were two cities that shared a political world fostered by friendships, alliances, patronage. But they were two cities which, as it turned out, came into conflict, with terrible results.

That a great deal can be said about both cities two thousand years ago is not entirely a matter of chance. Both Romans and Jews prized highly the art of writing, and produced large literatures. No less important, in both cases much of the literature survives to the present through a tradition of manuscript copying and preservation which was continuous from late antiquity to the Renaissance and the invention of printing. In the case of the Jews, Hebrew and Aramaic writings were preserved within the literary tradition of the rabbis, whose teachings, formulated in the first five centuries CE, laid the foundations of both medieval and modern orthodox Judaism. Jewish writings in Greek were ignored by the rabbis but preserved by Christians, who appropriated to themselves for religious edification a large number of Jewish texts composed before *c.* 100 CE, including the Septuagint (the Greek translation of the Hebrew Bible, with additional material now commonly found in English Bibles as the Apocrypha), the philosophical treatises of Philo, the histories of Josephus, and Greek versions of more mystical Jewish writings originally composed in Hebrew or Aramaic.

Christians were also responsible for the preservation of much of the literature of ancient Rome. From the fourth century CE Christians adopted the literature of pagan Greece and Rome as their own. Some pagans, like the emperor Julian (ruled 361–3), objected that Christians could not properly teach literature about the pagan gods if they did not believe in them, and the Christian St. Jerome (*c.* 347–420) worried that his devotion to Ciceronian style in his Latin prose made him less devoted to his faith, but during the fifth century the great works of Greek and Latin literature came to be seen by many Christians simply as a central element in the education of Christian Romans alongside the texts composed by Christians themselves. Thus many texts survive through the pious efforts of monks, from Cassiodorus in sixth-century Italy to the industrious scholars of Byzantium as late as the fifteenth century, who saw the reproduction of manuscripts as an act of devotion, almost regardless of their contents; and from many of the pagan writings they preserved, such as Vergil's *Aeneid* or the philosophical musings of Seneca, Christians would in time derive appropriate moral teachings.

The inhabitants of Jerusalem and Rome inevitably shared many experiences imposed upon them by the natural rhythms of the Mediterranean climate. For Jews, the Mediterranean was *haYam haGadol*, "the Great Sea"; *yama*, the word for "west" in Hebrew, reflected the view of the sea from Judaea. For the Romans, the Mediterranean was simply *mare nostrum*, "our sea," rather like the English view of La Manche as the English Channel.

Both cities sometimes experienced stifling heatwaves at the height of summer, although in Jerusalem, where snow is a great rarity, winters were milder than in Rome, where freezing temperatures are not unknown. Annual rainfall was less in Jerusalem than in Rome, and the summer drought, which could last from May to late November, was much longer and more complete, so that farmers in the Judaean hills relied more on the heavy dew precipitated by the sharp drop of air temperature at night. But in both cities people were all too aware of the potential effect of drought. In Jerusalem in 24 and 23 BCE drought led to food shortages and thus to plague, and to a dangerous lack of clothing in winter because flocks had died and there was "no wool or any other material to cover themselves." Livy, in the time of Augustus, thought it worth including in his history of Rome the information that the year 181 BCE, nearly two centuries before, had been "remarkable for drought and the failure of the crops. The story goes that for six months it did not rain at all."[1] Inhabitants of both cities imagined agricultural plenty in terms of wine, fruits and olives, grown on terraced hillsides, and pasturage, to supplement the grain crops cultivated on coastal plains and in valleys where the ground was sufficiently level for shallow ploughing. A Roman would have well understood the divine blessing that, if Israel will obey God's commandments, "I will give the rain for your land in its due season, the first rain and the latter rain, so that you may gather in your grain, and your wine, and your oil. And I shall send grass in your fields for your cattle," and the prophet Micah looking forward to the days when "they shall sit every man under his vine and under his fig tree, and none shall make them afraid."[2]

But away from the sea, the ecology of Judaea was very different from anything to be found in Italy and in some ways Jerusalem lay outside the Mediterranean sphere. The distinctive geography of the land of Israel is a result of the great rift valley which runs southwards from Syria towards Africa and includes the long stretch of the Jordan valley, ending in the region of the Dead Sea, many feet below sea level. Moving eastwards from Jerusalem, the terraced hillsides rapidly gave way in antiquity to semi-desert. As the road descended towards Jericho, the wholly arid terrain was punctuated only by rare oases such as Jericho itself, En Gedi, and the spring of En Feshqa, which fed the strange community of Jews who inhabited Qumran, the site near which the Dead Sea scrolls were found. Josephus with some reason extolled the extraordinary fertility of such parts of the

rift valley as could be sufficiently watered: on the borders of the Sea of
Galilee, he claimed, fruit trees bore their produce continuously throughout the year.[3]

Josephus had good reason to exaggerate the prosperity of the land of
Israel, both through natural patriotism and out of a desire to demonstrate
the impressive feats of his patrons, the emperors Vespasian and Titus, but
his geographical information can probably be trusted, and it is striking that
he divided the Jewish homeland not into two, Judaea and Galilee, but into
three: Judaea, Galilee and Peraea (which is Transjordan). Jewish territory
looked not just west, towards the sea, and north, towards Galilee, but also
east, towards the desert. The region east of the Jordan rises up to a basalt
plateau made sufficiently fertile by precipitation of rain coming from the
west to support a small number of cities in the Roman period—Philadelphia (on the site of modern Amman), Jerash and Pella among others—fed
by grain production and the raising of livestock, particularly cattle. Further east still lay the semi-desert, suitable only for the grazing of sheep and
goats (what the Bible called "small cattle"), and beyond the Peraea the Syrian desert itself, which was opening up precisely in the first century BCE
into a major highway for international trade from Mesopotamia. The success of the camel caravans was best illustrated by the growing prosperity of
the oasis of Palmyra, the trading centre known in the biblical texts as Tad-
mor. It was in the Roman period, particularly in the two and a half centuries after the imposition of Roman authority in *c.* 17 CE, that the oasis
reached the apogee of its wealth; many of the splendid tombs and temples
on which the Palmyrenes lavished their wealth, favouring a curious amal-
gam of Parthian, Greek, semitic and Roman artistic traits, can still be seen.[4]

Links to the east mattered to the inhabitants of Jerusalem. Josephus
even claims, in answer to the calumny that Jews could not have had a distinguished ancient history since the ancient Greeks did not write about
them, that "ours is not a country with a sea coast; neither commerce nor
the mixing which it enables with others has any attraction for us. Our cities
are built inland, remote from the sea . . ." Certainly Judaean Jews maintained close contact in the first century with their fellow Jews in Babylonia,
undeterred by the fact that Babylon was ruled by Parthia, outside the
sphere of Roman control. Herod the Great established in Batanaea, to the
east of the Sea of Galilee, a military colony of Babylonian Jews to provide
protection against brigandage for pilgrims coming to the Jerusalem Tem-

ple from Mesopotamia. According to Josephus, the first High Priest appointed by Herod after his capture of Jerusalem in 37 BCE was a certain Ananel, a Babylonian of inferior priestly origin. According to later rabbinic tradition, the great scholar Hillel, who flourished in Jerusalem in the early first century CE, also came originally from Babylon.[5]

On the other hand, if Judaea was not a wholly Mediterranean culture, neither did it easily fall into a category defined by the fertile crescent which links this region to Mesopotamia. The region shared the use of a language, Aramaic, which had originated in upper Mesopotamia and then spread to the Levant primarily through its adoption as the language of royal administration in the Persian empire during the fifth and fourth centuries BCE; but there is no evidence that inhabitants of the fertile crescent had a sense of common destiny such as was found among some communities on the shores of the Mediterranean, particularly the Greeks. Such a sense of belonging even to a smaller regional entity is not widely attested for communities in the Near East apart from the Jews until the imposition of Roman rule, and the regional identities which then emerged seem often to have been by adoption of Roman or Greek categories. During the first three centuries CE the Near East became increasingly Roman, both in the sense of a concentration of state military resources in the eastern part of the Roman empire and through the award to existing cities of the status of Roman colony, but in the early first century CE this process was still in its infancy. Viewed from the rest of the Mediterranean world, much of the fertile crescent, variously designated as Syria, Assyria or Arabia or by other exotic names, was still an undifferentiated region of little-known barbarism. To some extent, the unhappy fortune of Jerusalem under Roman rule was a result of the city's ambivalent position between the Mediterranean world and the Near East.[6]


DESPITE ALL the differences between the cultures of the two cities, a casual visitor to Rome and Jerusalem in the last decades of the first century BCE might have been more struck by similarities, since it was during these years that both cities metamorphosed from ramshackle agglomerations into shining testimonies to massive state expenditure. Rome, which up to the mid-first century BCE had been an unimpressive collection of brick buildings divided by winding alleyways, clustered around a small public area in the Forum and on the Capitoline hill, was remodelled with a series of new monumental public buildings and grand public spaces. Similarly, Jerusalem was expanded and transformed by Herod, to make it, as a Roman observer, the elder Pliny, proclaimed after its destruction in 70 CE, "by far the most famous city of the East." Both cities used the most up-to-date techniques of urban planning, borrowed architectural styles from the most impressive city of the previous generation, Alexandria in Egypt, and used vaulted arches to erect platforms out from the side of hills to form level public spaces. These two ancient cities were reborn at the same time and in similar ways, but the origin of the glory of Rome was wholly different from the foundation of the splendour of Jerusalem.[7]

# ROME

WHEN JOSEPHUS came to Rome from Jerusalem for his brief visit in the early 60s CE he found the city at the height of its opulence. The huge, sprawling city lay on the river Tiber, near the west coast of Italy and above the plain of Latium. By the first century, the true origins of the city had long been lost from collective memory, and speculation about its mythical foundation allowed free range to the imagination of poets and historians. Already by the early part of the first millennium BCE isolated villages, similar to others in the surrounding region of Latium, were in existence on the hills of the site that was to become Rome. These settlements grew in size and sophistication over the ensuing centuries, but the origins of the city as a single political unit are best dated to c. 600 BCE, when the Forum was laid out as a public meeting space in the valley between the hilltops. From then to the mid-first century BCE, the power of the city grew inexorably. Incorporation of all of Latium was followed by a gradual expansion of influence over the rest of Italy. In the third century BCE a long, bitter, but eventually successful struggle against the Phoenician trading city of Carthage, which lay on the north coast of Africa in modern Tunisia but also had many interests in Sicily and in Spain, left Rome in control of much of the coast of the western Mediterranean and, through use of a newly confident navy, of the sea routes between them. The conflict also left a residue of vocabulary and concepts to express hostility and contempt for a dangerous enemy, defined by their Punic language and customs as irremediably fickle. This early encounter was to have a formative effect on later Roman attitudes to bar-barians from the Syrian East.

Of Punic culture, or of the customs of the Celts to the north of Italy with whom Rome had already come into violent contact in the fourth cen-tury BCE, Rome adopted almost nothing. By contrast, Rome's conquest of the eastern Mediterranean from 200 BCE to the battle of Actium in 31 BCE changed the culture of the city markedly. We shall see in Chapter 2 how the imposition of Roman political power on the Greek cities of the Greek mainland paradoxically led to widespread Roman acceptance of the supe-riority of Greek art, architecture, literature and philosophy. The impact of Greek art on Roman taste can be traced further back to the first urbaniza-tion of the site in the early sixth century BCE, when Greek pots were already being imported into the city, and it is probable that a liking for Greek artefacts was promoted throughout the early period of Rome's his-tory through the similar cultural preferences found both among the more developed urban society of the Etruscans, whose cities lay to the north of Rome, and among the inhabitants of the Greek colonies in Italy, such as Neapolis (modern Naples); but there can be no doubt that Roman hege-mony over Greeks from the second century BCE much increased the avail-ability and attractiveness of Greek objects and ideas. During the conquest of the eastern Mediterranean Roman enthusiasm for Greek art could take the crudest of forms. In 146 BCE the Roman general who destroyed Corinth, Lucius Mummius, looted great quantities of art for display in Italy and especially in Rome.

As a result of almost continuous conquests Rome exercised political and military control by the mid-first century BCE over almost the whole of the Mediterranean world. Even Egypt, which was not formally brought under Roman rule until 30 BCE, was for some years before this treated by Roman aristocrats as a Roman protectorate—the last queen, Cleopa-tra VII, kept her throne only through manipulation of Roman politicians, most notably Julius Caesar and Mark Antony. The biggest danger to Rome came not from the subject peoples of the empire but from the personal ambitions of the Roman nobles themselves.

In 49 BCE the tensions between ambitious aristocrats, which had already escalated earlier in the century into sporadic civil war on the soil of Italy, erupted into an internecine struggle which was to involve almost every corner of the Mediterranean world as the arena for battles or in the supply of troops and money to the warring factions. The war began with a demand by one such aristocrat, Julius Caesar, to be permitted to assert his right to a share in power, but desire for glory after his victory over his enemies led to his proclamation in early 44 as perpetual *dictator*, and on the Ides of March of that year he was murdered by a large group of fellow senators, including some of his former friends. The ensuing years witnessed a struggle for Caesar's political legacy, dominated by the claims of his closest political ally, Mark Antony, and his young heir, his great-nephew Octavian.

The decisive battle took place near Actium, off the western coast of Greece, on 2 September 31. Octavian emerged as victor not only over his immediate rival Antony and his paramour Cleopatra, but over the whole system of shared power and authority on which the Roman state had been founded since the expulsion of the early kings some five centuries before. From 31 Rome was to be governed by sole rulers. Octavian described himself modestly as *princeps*, "chief," with the implication that he was only first among equals, and his example was followed by his successors for centuries. But the English word "emperor," derived from the acclamation of Roman generals as *imperator*, "commander," more accurately captures the nature of his autocratic rule, and the family name "Caesar," inherited (through adoption) from Julius, came to be used to designate any Roman monarch (whence *Kaiser* and *Tsar* in more recent societies). The remodelling of the city of Rome in the last decades of the first century BCE was thus ultimately the achievement of one man and his vision. By the time of Actium, prolonged war had left the Roman world exhausted and appalled. Contemporary literary references to the longing for peace within Italy, regardless of the cost of liberty, ring true. Octavian's rule, like that of all subsequent emperors, rested ultimately on his control of a military machine: he maintained a huge standing army, ensuring the loyalty of the army commanders by dispersing the legions to the frontier provinces to inhibit conspiracies between them. Nonetheless, the new regime saw value in a change of image to help offset public memory of the new ruler's bloody progress to power. The Senate in 27 BCE conferred on Octavian a new name, *Augustus*, "revered one," which was widely advertised on coins. An era of peace, prosperity and plenty was proclaimed. The city of Rome was transformed to become as magnificent as the greatest city of the Greek East, Alexandria, the capital of the erstwhile enemy queen, Cleopatra.

In Augustus' own summary and highly selective account of his achievements, he claimed to have repaired many temples in Rome—eighty-two in the year 28 alone—and to have built impressive new ones. His biographer Suetonius, writing a hundred years later, explained his motivation: "Since the city was not adorned as befitted the majesty of the empire, and was exposed to flood and fire, he beautified it to the extent that he could justly boast that he found it built of brick and left it in marble." Suetonius specified Augustus' most impressive building achievements: a new forum to house the increased population and the legal cases that had to be heard, the temple of Apollo on the Palatine, the shrine of Thundering Jupiter on the Capitol, the temple of Mars the Avenger, libraries for Latin and Greek books, colonnades and basilicas in honour of members of his family, the theatre of Marcellus. Nor was Augustus alone, since it was self-evident that flattering imitation of the princeps would be politically prudent. "Many such works were built at that time by many men: for example, the temple of Hercules of the Muses by Marcius Philippus, the temple of Diana by Lucius Cornificius, the Hall of Liberty by Asinius Pollio, the temple of Saturn by Munatius Plancus, a theatre by Cornelius Balbus, an amphitheatre by Statilius Taurus, and by Marcus Vipsanius Agrippa in particular many structures, and they were outstanding." Marcus Vipsanius Agrippa was Augustus' closest political ally, for the good reason that Augustus' victories in his rise to power had largely been owed to Agrippa's military competence, a skill that Augustus himself never acquired.[8]

The new Rome was indeed magnificent in the provision of public facilities as well as private indulgence. The public baths in the Campus Martius provided for the Roman people by Agrippa in *c.* 20 BCE were more luxurious and impressive than any previously known. Julius Caesar had already in his will left his gardens near the Tiber for the common use of the people; to these were now added the lavish gardens on the Esquiline of Maecenas, Augustus' close confidant and minister. Of private monuments, none outshone those of the imperial family, in particular the grandiose mound built by Augustus for his own mausoleum and, crowning the summit of the Palatine hill overlooking the Forum, the house of Augustus himself, a complex of buildings which from 12 BCE incorporated the shrine of Vesta, the goddess of the city's hearth. Over the next century the imperial residence was to increase in luxurious magnificence. By the late first century CE it had become the archetypical palace—the word "palace" itself derives from the hill on which it stood.[9]

The concentration of wealth and power in the city attracted a huge and heterogeneous population. War and the demands of empire brought about population movements in Italy in the last two centuries BCE on an unprecedented scale. This was a society accustomed to a great deal of human mobility. Migration into Rome from the rest of Italy had been common for well over a century before Augustus' rule, partly because of pressure on peasant smallholders caused by the agglomeration of landholdings by richer farmers able to take advantage of the demands for produce by the city market. To what extent such impoverished Italians retained in the late first century BCE a distinct sense of their identities as Etruscans, Samnites or others doubtless varied. Surviving evidence mostly concerns the rich, who maintained connections with their region of origin at the same time as embracing the life of urban aristocrats: Augustus' friend Maecenas was celebrated by his protégé, the poet Horace, as a descendant of Etruscan kings. But other groups were more easily identified within the crowds in the city. Syrians, Gauls, Germans, Spaniards, Africans, all took a full part in the life of Rome. They or their ancestors had come to the city as slaves but, once freed, they merged into the wider population while retaining their native customs and characteristics to varying extents. Not least visible among them was the local community of Jews (about whom more will be said in Chapter 10).

Rome in the first century thus had a multifarious, cosmopolitan population of perhaps a million people. Many of them lived in appalling poverty, dependent on regular imports of cheap food from the rest of Italy and, increasingly, from Sicily, and then from Egypt across the Mediterranean. The gap between the very rich in their grand town houses and the poor, crammed into high-rise apartment blocks (see p. 45 below) or left to beg on the streets, has its closest parallel in the great Third World cities of today. The city was a focus of excitement and squalor, power and despair. The wealthy enjoyed lives of extraordinary private luxury, served by hundreds of slaves, while immediately adjacent to their mansions the indigent starved. The whole unstable society was held in control by a large military force stationed, from the time of Augustus, just outside the city limits.

There was a constant danger from fire, about which little could be done. Augustus' establishment of a permanent semi-military force to deal with outbreaks could only be a partial solution when houses were packed so close, with so many inhabitants, in the heat of the Mediterranean summer. The great fire of 64 CE in the time of Nero, for which the government, seeking a scapegoat, blamed the Christians, was only the worst of numerous such disasters. The many aqueducts brought water in massive quantities from the Apennines, and the great drainage system which flushed the urban effluent into the Tiber was improved and repaired constantly throughout the early imperial period, but the city still stank from the presence of so many people.[10]

Despite all the disadvantages of overcrowding, a visitor to Rome in the early first century CE would have found much to admire. The Greek geographer Strabo, a native of Amaseia (modern Amasya, in Turkey), who made several journeys to Rome in the time of Augustus, notes that the position of Rome was not particularly advantageous—"neither was the site naturally strong, nor did it have enough land of its own in the surrounding territory to meet the requirements of the city"—but argues that this had been a blessing in disguise, deliberately adopted by the city's founders, who reasoned "that it was appropriate for the Romans to depend for their safety and general welfare, not on their fortifications, but on their arms and their own valour, in the belief that it is not walls that protect men but men that protect walls," as a result of which the Romans had early in their history been impelled to conquer the surrounding region. The result, notes Strabo, was that Rome in his time had access to exceptional supplies "not only in respect to food, but also in respect to timber and stones for the building of houses . . . a wonderful supply of materials provided by a plethora of mines and timber and the rivers which transport them." Besides these "blessings" which "the nature of the place provides to the city," Strabo remarks on the practical amenities in Rome provided by the foresight of the inhabitants:

for if the Greeks had a reputation for aiming particularly well in the founding of cities, in that they aimed at beauty, strength of position, harbours and productive countryside, these people [the Romans] had the best foresight in those matters of which those [the Greeks] took little account, the construction of roads and aqueducts and sewers able to

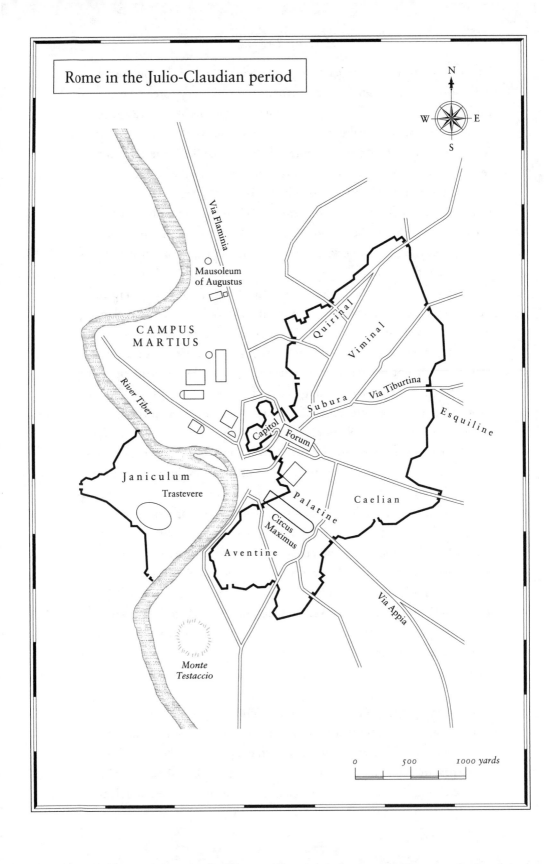

Rome in the Julio-Claudian period

Via Flaminia

Mausoleum
of Augustus

CAMPUS
MARTIUS

River Tiber

Quirinal

Viminal

Subura

Via Tiburtina

Esquiline

Capitol

Forum

Janiculum

Trastevere

Palatine

Caelian

Circus
Maximus

Aventine

Via Appia

Monte
Testaccio

N

W    E

S

0          500          1000 yards

wash out the filth of the city . . . They have so built the roads through the country, cutting through hills and banking up valleys, that their wagons can carry loads off the ships, and the sewers, vaulted with close-fitting stones, have in some places left room enough even for wagons loaded with hay to pass through them.[11]

A Greek contemporary of Strabo, the historian Dionysius of Halicarnassus, notes specifically that, in his opinion, "the three most magnificent works of Rome, from which the greatness of her hegemony is most apparent, are the aqueducts, the paved roads, and the construction of the sewers. I say this not only because of the usefulness of the work . . . but also because of the magnitude of the expense."[12]

In contrast an Italian contemporary, the poet Ovid (43 BCE–17 CE), picked on rather different aspects of Rome when he depicted the city from his involuntary exile in Tomi (modern Constantsa) on the Black Sea (not so very distant from Strabo's home in Amaseia). For Ovid, Rome was where he belonged, among the "advantages of city life," lamenting from far away the localities of the "beautiful city." His mind "surveys everything with eyes of its own. Now the fora, now the temples, now the theatres sheathed in marble, now every portico with its levelled ground comes before me; now the grass of the Campus [Martius] looking towards the beautiful gardens, and the pools and the canals."[13] Strabo had also not been immune from admiration for some of the Roman buildings he saw, but only for those recently erected: "the early Romans took but little account of the beauty of Rome, because they were occupied with other, greater and more necessary, matters, but the later Romans, and especially those of today and in my time, have . . . outdone all others in their zeal for buildings and in the expense incurred."[14] What this meant was that, to an outside observer like Strabo, accustomed to the gracious urban planning ubiquitous in his own Hellenistic world, the impressive monuments of Rome were primarily to be found in the new areas only recently incorporated within the city proper, such as the Campus Martius, which had lain outside the civic boundary until it was constituted as the ninth of the fourteen urban regions in the administrative reorganization carried out by Augustus:

The size of the Campus is remarkable since it affords space at the same time and without interference, not only for the chariot-races and every

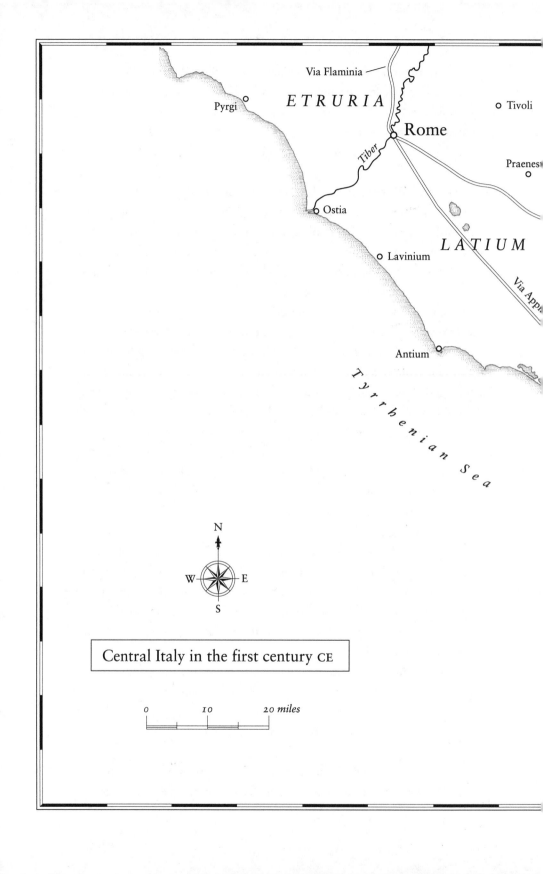

Via Flaminia

*E T R U R I A*

Pyrgi

○ Tivoli

Rome

Tiber

Praenest

○

Ostia

*L A T I U M*

Lavinium

Via App

Antium

*T y r r h e n i a n  S e a*

N

W ✳ E

S

Central Italy in the first century CE

0        10        20 *miles*

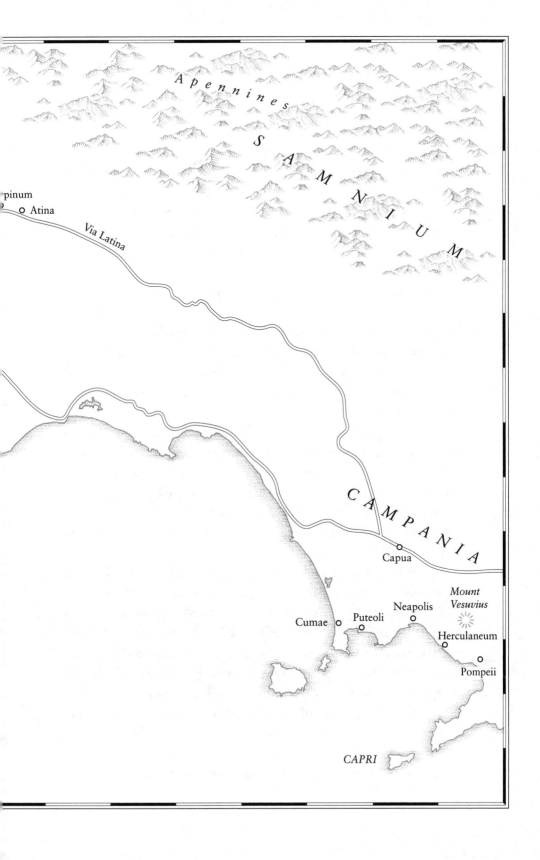

other equestrian exercise, but also for all that multitude of people who exercise themselves by ball-playing, hoop-trundling and wrestling; and the works of art situated around the Campus Martius, and the ground, which is covered with grass throughout the year, and the crowns of those hills that are above the river and extend as far as its bed, which present to the eye the appearance of a stage-painting—all this, I say, affords a spectacle that one could hardly draw away from. And near this campus is still another campus, with colonnades round about it in very great numbers, and sacred precincts, and three theatres, and an amphitheatre, and very costly temples, in close succession to one another, giving you the impression that they are trying, as it were, to declare the rest of the city a mere accessory.

The original religious and political heart of Rome, the Capitol, which housed the great temple of Jupiter, and the Forum where the Senate held its meetings, had been much adorned over the centuries, but their organic evolution had militated against a development as impressive as in areas outside the old city, even if periodic attempts were made to create new monumental public spaces alongside the old (a tendency which accelerated under the emperors, not least in the new forum built by Augustus himself). Strabo noted that "if, on passing to the old Forum [the *Forum Romanum*], you saw one forum after another ranged along the old one, and basilicas, and temples, and saw also the Capitolium and works of art there and those on the Palatine hill and in the promenade of Livia, you would easily forget the world outside."[15]

If Augustus incorporated suburban space within the new city boundary, there was a physical limit to the extent of urban sprawl without benefit of a modern transport system; when the elder Pliny noted in the 70s CE that it could be fairly claimed that "there had been no city in the whole world that could be compared to Rome for its size," he also noted that such a huge population was housed not just through settlement of a large area but, specifically, by density of occupation in high buildings.[16] A visitor to Rome, approaching on one of the fine paved roads flanked on either side by the funerary monuments of the aristocratic families of old, passed quite suddenly from countryside with peasant farms and grand villas surrounded by gardens to a dense *mélange* of winding streets and apartment blocks. The architect and engineer Vitruvius, who wrote in the time of Julius Caesar or in the very early years of Augustus' rule, noted rather optimistically that

> with this greatness of the city and the unlimited crowding of citizens, it is necessary to provide very numerous dwellings. Therefore since a level site could not receive such a multitude to dwell in the city, circumstances themselves have compelled the resort to raising the height of buildings. And so by means of stone pillars, walls of burnt brick, party walls of rubble, towers have been raised, and these being joined together by frequent board floors produce upper storeys with fine views over the city to the utmost advantage. Therefore walls are raised to a great height through various storeys, and the Roman people has excellent dwellings without hindrance.[17]

The height of tenement buildings was to increase dramatically in later centuries, when buildings of three storeys became standard and blocks of five or six storeys not uncommon.

A good idea of the standardized architecture of these blocks, with the ground floor dedicated to shops or perhaps the living quarters of a single rich family and the upper floors crammed with tenants in conditions of unsanitary squalor, can be gauged from buildings of the imperial period excavated at Ostia, the port through which passed the imports that supplied Rome. The gracious living evident in the more relaxed environment of first-century-CE Pompeii and Herculaneum, where evidence of the lives of the inhabitants has been preserved for posterity by the eruption of Vesuvius in 79, was possible only for the few in the heart of the capital of empire, where rents were exceptionally high. For the ordinary inhabitants of Rome, enduring a dark, smelly, smoky apartment, the roar of the city's trades in the day and the rumble of wagons at night, lugging water from aqueducts through the narrow streets and up the stairs for washing and cooking, venturing out at night in the unlit alleyways at peril of robbery or worse, gazing with envy at the blank walls surrounding the luxurious houses of the rich, congregating with friends in taverns or the all too public communal latrines, constituted an urban way of life that might sometimes provoke disgust or tedium but which evidently appealed sufficiently for hundreds of thousands to wish to live in Rome, turning their minds (like Ovid) to the happier aspects of the city—the temples, forums, gardens, and the great river Tiber flowing through the midst of the bustle, only occasionally transformed by heavy rainfall into a dangerous source of floods.

The magnificence of the city and its vast size were attributable directly and only to political power achieved through military conquest. Rome was not particularly well placed to profit from trade, although (as Strabo notes) goods could be transported easily enough into the city along the busy Tiber. The natural trading centres of the region lay further downstream on the Mediterranean coast, and the port of Ostia flourished in the imperial period. Rome enjoyed the benefit of no special mineral resources, and the Latian plain provided agricultural produce only for a local market. The massive population, which far exceeded that of most other contemporary cities, survived and continued to expand only through continuous exploitation of the rest of the empire. Much of the exploitation was direct. Provincial subjects of Rome paid to the state regular taxes fixed by the size of their landholdings as established by regular censuses. Of the sums thus raised, a large proportion was expended on the army on which the emperor's personal power depended, but much of the surplus went to Rome for expenditure on the city's inhabitants. The jibe by the satirist Juvenal (c. 67–c. 130), that "the people longs anxiously for only two things: bread and circuses," reflected all too accurately state spending in the capital city.[18] Subsidies ensured a regular supply of free grain for those adult male citizens resident in Rome who were registered on an official list which entitled them to tickets exchangeable for the corn dole. The number who benefited was limited by Augustus in 2 BCE to around two hundred thousand, and, since the tickets themselves could be sold, many of the poorer inhabitants were not helped by the scheme; but the emperors appointed prefects to keep a watchful eye on grain prices and, if necessary, to intervene in the market if shortages led to too drastic a price rise and potential disorder. The ability of a strong ruler to ensure regular food supplies was a major factor in the popularity of imperial rule among the ordinary people of Rome.

State expenditure also provided a great deal of employment at different levels, for shippers and other middlemen, and for dockers, porters, wagoners and other labourers. Excavation has revealed huge warehouses for grain and other products in the city, in the suburbs and in Ostia. Some acted as general stores, but others were more specialized, dedicated to specific types of merchandise, such as the buildings on the Esquiline used for the storage of papyrus and parchment. Inscriptions reveal the extraordinary variety of imported goods for sale and also the great variety of Roman tradesmen, many of them apparently self-employed, offering their skilled services as tanners, ropemakers, carpenters or caulkers, or simply their physical prowess as building workers or stevedores or in other menial tasks. That more than a hundred and fifty trades can be listed is partly the result of the custom (helpful for later historians) of Roman craftsmen organizing themselves into corporations, and the tendency of such corporations to advertise their existence on stone inscriptions, which still survive in large numbers. The urban economy thrived through the local provision of goods and services by the inhabitants of Rome to each other, fuelled by the regular and predictable influx of grain, raw materials and luxury goods from elsewhere in the empire.[19]

Imperial munificence ensured that public entertainments in Rome far outstripped in their splendour anything to be found elsewhere in the empire. Such entertainments were genuinely available to all, although the best seats were naturally reserved for those of high status. The numerous construction projects financed both by the state and by politicians, grown wealthy not least from their terms as provincial governors, provided employment for many of the poor. Rome in the early empire may not always have been the pleasantest place to live, but there was no doubt that the city offered excitement and, especially when the emperor and his entourage were in residence, glamour.

## JERUSALEM

THE RATIONALE of Rome, the grandiose capital city of a huge empire in which the boastful architecture of triumphal arches celebrating human achievements competed with the numerous temples and shrines that housed the images of many gods, could hardly have been more different from that of the Temple city of Jerusalem. Jerusalem too was reliant on an income far beyond the resources of its immediate environs, but the sources of its wealth and importance lay not in conquest but in religious enthusiasm.

Remains of structures from the early Bronze Age indicate that settlement began near the Gihon spring (which provided Jerusalem with its only

reliable water supply) as early as the fourth millennium BCE, long before
the coagulation, far away across the Mediterranean, of the villages that
were to become Rome. By the end of the second millennium the site had
become a stronghold, the natural defence of the rugged terrain enhanced
by well-fortified walls. This was the city that, according to the later, idealized, biblical account, King David conquered in *c.* 1000 BCE to make the
capital of his two realms, which stretched from the borders of Egypt to the
Euphrates, so that from David's reign to its destruction by the Babylonians
in 586 BCE Jerusalem was a major political and cultural centre. But David (it
was said) had also shrewdly transferred from its previous obscure lodging
to Jerusalem the Ark of the Covenant, the symbol of God's relation with
his people, and when Solomon, his son and successor, erected in the city
the first Temple as a fitting place for the Ark to rest permanently and as the
sole sacred site for the people of Israel to come together in communal worship through the performance of sacrifices, the future of Jerusalem as a
focus for religious cult was sealed.

The gravest blow to this future was dealt in 586 BCE when the city was
conquered by the Babylonians, the Temple was destroyed and many of the
inhabitants of Jerusalem were carried off into exile. But in 539 BCE the
Babylonian empire itself fell to the Persian king Cyrus, and soon after
the Jews were allowed to return to their homeland and to rebuild. Progress
on the rebuilding of the Temple itself seems to have been slow, but, since
Jerusalem was now at the centre of a rather unimportant Persian province
rather than a royal capital, this religious role gradually became the city's
most important function, and the priests who served in the Temple came
gradually to dominate the life of its inhabitants. In 331 BCE this Temple city
was one of the less impressive places to fall under the control of the Macedonian Alexander the Great (356–323) in the course of his extraordinary
conquest of the Near East up to the borders of India. There was a popular
legend that Alexander visited Jerusalem and was much impressed by the
cult of the Jewish God. From that date the city lay securely within the
political orbit of imperial powers that operated in the Greek language and
treated Greek culture as prestigious. The impact of Greek ideas and values
on the Jews of Jerusalem was to be as profound as the parallel process in
Rome.

Alexander died while still in his early thirties and his kingdom was
rapidly dismembered at the hands of the dynasties founded by the gener-

als who succeeded him. During the third century BCE Judaea was ruled from Egypt by the Ptolemaic dynasty, whose last representative was to be the Cleopatra who fought against Octavian at Actium. In a series of campaigns against the Ptolemies, the Seleucid kings, descendants of another of Alexander's generals, who ruled Syria and Mesopotamia from 301 BCE, attempted to wrest control of the southern Levant, and in 198 BCE Antiochus the Great, the most dynamic of the Seleucid kings, finally succeeded.

The transfer of Jerusalem to rule by a new dynasty, albeit another of Graeco-Macedonian origins, was to have dangerous results: Josephus records that Antiochus the Great guaranteed the inhabitants of Jerusalem that their ancestral cult would be safeguarded and that the priests would receive extensive privileges, but his son, Antiochus IV Epiphanes, tried to end worship of the Jewish God altogether, and provoked a revolt in 167 BCE. The precise reasons for Antiochus' behaviour are hard to reconstruct. The contemporary Greek historian Polybius, who had known Antiochus as a fellow hostage in Rome, claimed that the king was generally thought to be not *epiphanes*, "god-incarnate," but *epimanes*, "crazy."[20] The Jewish author of 1 Maccabees, composed perhaps a generation after the events, blamed compliant Jews who sought to assimilate into the world of Greek culture. Some non-Jewish authors attributed Antiochus' actions to his need to acquire easy money by looting the Jerusalem Temple after his ambitions to conquer Egypt were thwarted by Roman intervention. But whatever Antiochus' motivation, his attack on their worship prompted a robust defence by a number of Jews, and led to guerrilla warfare by Judas Maccabee and his brothers (later to be named, in honour of a distant ancestor, the Hasmonaeans), until in 164 BCE the Temple was rededicated to the Jewish God. It has been argued, with some justification, that the whole traumatic experience of opposing the desecration of the Temple by Antiochus Epiphanes was decisive in ensuring that over the following centuries Jews, unlike some other Near Eastern peoples, retained their ancestral customs intact.[21]

Over the course of the remainder of the second century BCE the Hasmonaeans capitalized on the glory they acquired by Judas' opposition to Antiochus, although Judas himself achieved no more than the liberation and purification of the Temple, and never seems to have held any formal office of pre-eminence in Jewish society: in 161 he fell in battle against

Seleucid forces and his place as leader of the Jews was taken over by his brother Jonathan. By manipulation of the interests of competing aspirants to the Seleucid throne, Jonathan in *c.* 152 elicited from one of those aspirants, Alexander Balas, nomination as High Priest. By the 120s Jonathan's nephew John Hyrcanus was exercising power in Jerusalem as independent ruler over the city and the rest of the hill country of Judaea, and in 104 his son Aristobulus was the first Hasmonaean to take for himself the title of king. The emergence of the Hasmonaean state as an independent force and, by the early first century BCE, as the dominant regional power, was facilitated by the gradual break-up of the Seleucid state, which in turn was much hastened by Roman interference in Seleucid affairs, although the Hasmonaeans themselves naturally stressed the internal Jewish factors in their rise to power. They saw themselves as the righteous champions of the Jewish God against the wicked gentiles and those Jews who had been prepared to give way to them. The book of 1 Maccabees, which narrates the political history of Judaea from 175 to 134, is a remarkably blatant example of dynastic propaganda dressed up as piety.[22]

The Hasmonaeans were not without opponents, not least because some Jews doubted their right to usurp the High Priesthood. The festival of Hanukkah, still celebrated today for eight days from 25 Kislev, around mid-December, originated as a commemoration of the victory of the Maccabees over the forces of the Seleucid king in the 160s BCE, but during the period of Hasmonaean rule it also provided an opportunity for all citizens of the Jewish state to demonstrate their loyalty in public; the essence of the demonstration was the exhibition of lighted wicks in a position where they could be seen by the public. Visibility of the lights was crucial: a rabbi quoted in the Mishnah (a collection of rabbinic legal opinions compiled in *c.* 200 CE) ruled that a shopkeeper would generally be liable for the damage to a camel-load of produce if it caught fire in the street because lighted lamps had been left outside the shop, but made an exception for the lamps lit for Hanukkah, when the danger of naked flames on the street was outweighed by the religious duty to proclaim the miraculous victory achieved by Judas Maccabee. What it felt like for an opponent of the Hasmonaean regime to be forced to protest his loyalty in this public way can readily be imagined.[23]

By the early first century BCE the political behaviour of Alexander Jannaeus, over twenty-seven years (103–76 BCE) the most aggressive and expansionist of the Hasmonaean rulers of Judaea, was much like that of other monarchs in the Hellenistic world. His was a personal monarchy like that of the Ptolemies and Seleucids before him. He used mercenary troops to increase his dominions, conquering cities on the coastal plain, including Ptolemais (ancient Akko) and Gaza, and the cities of Transjordan, many of which, such as Gadara and Pella, had long been centres of Greek culture. Alexander's aim seems to have been glory for its own sake: these newly conquered regions were not incorporated into the Jewish polity as Idumaea had been by his father, John Hyrcanus, in the 120s or 110s, and Galilee by his brother Aristobulus I in 104–103, but were ruled as vassal states, with the result that their inhabitants resented him and his successors as tyrants. He resided in magnificent palaces designed and decorated in Greek style, including a winter palace built in Jericho to take advantage of the special climate of the Dead Sea region.[24]

Alexander Jannaeus' kingdom was a distinctively Jewish state in which Hebrew remained the language most in public use, and he himself would have appeared at his most magnificent not in the garb of a king or a general but when he served in the Jerusalem Temple as High Priest, particularly when he wore the gorgeous vestments reserved for use on the most solemn day of the ritual year, the Day of Atonement in the early autumn, when the whole nation fasted in penitence for their sins and the High Priest performed an elaborate sacrificial ceremony to ensure that their repentance be acceptable to God. On the other hand the Hasmonaeans were sufficiently secularized by the first century BCE to be able to envisage political power being exercised separately from religious authority. Under the terms of his will, Alexander Jannaeus was succeeded on his death in 76 BCE by his widow, Salome, known in rabbinic tradition as Shelomzion. As a woman, Salome was debarred from the role of High Priest, so she devolved the post to her elder son, Hyrcanus, with the intention that he should become sole ruler when she died. These plans were already being challenged before her demise at an advanced age in 67 BCE, and within a short time after her death her younger son Aristobulus had defeated Hyrcanus in a battle near Jericho and seized for himself both priestly and royal power. Hyrcanus was initially inclined to acquiesce in his loss of position, but, egged on by his advisers, he made an attempt to recover his kingdom and his leading role in the Temple.

This fraternal dispute was to prove fatal to the fortunes of the dynasty.[25] By the 60s BCE Roman power had spread to almost every land neighbouring the eastern Mediterranean, and each brother recognized that his fortune depended on Roman support. Roman intervention during the second century BCE had fatally weakened the Seleucid empire which had once stretched from Anatolia to Iran. The power vacuum had been filled in the early first century BCE by an alliance of two dynasts, Mithradates of Pontus and Tigranes of Armenia, whose territorial ambitions were challenged by successive Roman generals in a series of campaigns. By 66 BCE both kings had been decisively defeated. In 64 Syria had become a Roman province, and Aristobulus and Hyrcanus competed in the level of bribes they were prepared to pay to the Roman general Pompey, who was based there. In 63 Pompey took these approaches as an invitation to intervene in the affairs of the Jews and marched on Jerusalem, ostensibly in support of Hyrcanus. Much of the city fell without resistance, but the Temple itself was stoutly defended for three months by Aristobulus' supporters until its capture in the late autumn. A massacre ensued. Thousands of captives were enslaved and taken to Rome. In 61 Aristobulus himself was made to walk, as representative of his defeated nation, in Pompey's triumphal procession through the streets of Rome. Hyrcanus was restored to the High Priesthood, but without the title of king, and with a much reduced territory to rule. In any case, his power was nominal. Jerusalem and its territory were required to pay tribute to Rome. The comments of Josephus were apt:

> For this misfortune which befell Jerusalem, Hyrcanus and Aristobulus were responsible because of their dissension. For we lost our freedom and became subject to the Romans, and the territory which we had gained by our arms and taken from the Syrians we were compelled to give back to them, and in addition the Romans exacted from us in a short space of time more than two thousand talents, and the royal power which had formerly been bestowed on those who were high priests by birth became the privilege of commoners.[26]

Josephus' opinion reflected his views not just as a Jew but as a Jerusalem priest. For over a century after 63 the political influence of the Temple authorities was to be diminished as rule was concentrated in the hands of secular authorities appointed by Rome. The power exercised by Hyrcanus in the 50s BCE was circumscribed by frequent interference in Judaea by the Roman governors of Syria, whose attention was drawn to the country by a series of insurrections led by Aristobulus and his sons, all of whom had escaped from Roman custody. In 57 Judaea was placed by one governor of Syria, Aulus Gabinius, into the care of a number of regional councils. Hyrcanus was left with only the custody of the Temple to his charge, but his astute support for Julius Caesar during the civil war against Pompey was temporarily effective in enhancing his own role in Jerusalem. The murder of Caesar in 44 threw all political calculation back into turmoil. Taking advantage of the distractions which beset the Roman elite, in 40 a Parthian army invaded northern Syria. Its commanders were persuaded by Aristobulus' son Antigonus, who had made many efforts during the preceding years to unseat Hyrcanus, to march south to Jerusalem to win for him the throne of Judaea. Hyrcanus was captured and taken by the Parthians as a prisoner to their power base in Babylonia, where his ears were cut off to render him ritually unfit for ever to serve as High Priest in the Jerusalem Temple. Antigonus' rule with Parthian support proved to be brief. It was ended in 37 by the Roman reconquest of Jerusalem with the aid of one of Hyrcanus' most long-standing and energetic henchmen, the Idumaean adventurer Herod the Great.

The Roman Senate chose Herod to become king of Judaea only for lack of a better option. Normal Roman practice in the subversion and control of countries which fell into their orbit was to hand over control to a selected scion of the native dynasty, on the grounds that gratitude would ensure the rulers' loyalty to Rome and inherited prestige would ensure authority over the subject population. Precisely such a policy had kept Hyrcanus in his post as High Priest in Jerusalem from 63 to 40. But in 40, when Herod appeared before the senators to seek their help, no adult male Hasmonaean remained alive for Rome to endorse, apart from Hyrcanus, who was in captivity in Mesopotamia, and Antigonus, the nominee of the enemy Parthians. If Rome was to recover influence in Judaea, normal practice would have to be waived; in 40, in the middle of upheaval in Rome, this would only be one policy innovation among many. As it turned out, from the point of view of Rome the choice of Herod proved inspired. Herod's paternal ancestry from Idumaea, an area some way to the south of Jerusalem whose inhabitants had been forcibly converted to Judaism only in the late second century BCE, was not best calculated to bring him prestige in the eyes of his fellow Jews—the Hasmonaean Antigonus is said to have described him, with a sneer, as a "half-Jew." In Roman eyes, his lack of local support made him all the more reliable in the interests of the Roman state. His rule in Jerusalem depended on Roman power from the moment in 37 that Roman legions conquered the city on his behalf and were with difficulty bribed not to indulge their natural instinct to loot and destroy as a reward for victory.[27]

At the point in 40 BCE when the Senate took its fateful decision to appoint him king of Judaea, Herod's main patron within the Roman aristocracy was Mark Antony, once the close lieutenant of Julius Caesar and now both colleague and rival to Caesar's heir, Octavian (the future emperor Augustus). Over the following years Herod maintained his friendship with Antony, not least through the judicious presentation of gifts, so it was no mean feat to change sides in 31 when Antony was defeated by Octavian at Actium. Herod had at least the good fortune, or had deliberately ensured through careful calculation, that he was not present at the battle itself, having duties nearer home. He endeared himself to Octavian with the prudent and effective promise that he would prove as loyal a servant to Octavian as he had been to his defeated rival.

Thus, just as Octavian, in his new incarnation as Augustus after 27 BCE, set himself to transform Rome, so Herod, in flattering imitation, devoted himself to rebuilding Jerusalem to reflect the magnificence of his ambitions. When Augustus' friend Marcus Vipsanius Agrippa visited Herod in Jerusalem in 15 BCE, he would have been confronted by a city still in some places a building site, but already partly transformed into a showpiece of modern architecture. Jerusalem was of course much smaller than Rome, not least because Jerusalem had no equivalent to the Apennines or the river Tiber: the Gihon spring had already proved inadequate in Hasmonaean times, and further water supplies had to be brought great distances by aqueduct. The narrow, twisting streets, following the natural contours, could not be redesigned without mass clearances, which Herod did not attempt, but in some places gleaming new pavements overlay the worn pathways of Hasmonaean times and new forts and towers, each named after one of Herod's family or, like the Antonia by the Temple site, after one of his friends, loomed over the city at strategic points, their perfect rectangular blocks shaming the rustic, rough-hewn masonry of earlier times. A few miles from Jerusalem, at Herodium, the site of a skirmish in 40 BCE, Herod prepared for himself a monumental tomb on a natural hill whose summit was levelled to create an outline as striking as Augustus' mausoleum, already constructed in Rome. Herod's own palace was dedicated to luxury, as Josephus described:

> In extravagance and equipment no building surpassed it. It was completely enclosed within a wall thirty cubits high, broken at equal distances by ornamental towers, and contained immense banqueting-halls and bed-chambers for a hundred guests. The interior fittings are indescribable—the variety of the stones (for species rare in every other country were here collected in abundance), ceilings wonderful both for the length of the beams and the splendour of their surface decoration, the host of apartments with their infinite varieties of design, all amply furnished, while most of the objects in each of them were of silver or gold. All around were many circular cloisters, leading one into another, the columns each being different, and their open courts all of greensward; there were groves of various trees intersected by long walks, which were bordered by deep canals, and ponds everywhere studded with bronze figures, through which the water was discharged, and around the streams were numerous cots for tame pigeons . . .

In, or close by, Jerusalem itself there was a theatre, adorned with inscriptions honouring Augustus, and "in the plain" was an amphitheatre. By the 60s CE the city also boasted a hippodrome and a monument known as the Memorial of Herod, although whether these were built in Herod's time or later is uncertain. But dwarfing all these impressive constructions was by far the most ambitious building project of all, the rebuilding of the Temple. Herod almost completely dismantled the existing building and erected a magnificent new edifice in its place. Work began late in 20 or early in 19 BCE and was to continue for decades. In part, Herod must have wished to impress his Roman patrons, as with all his other buildings, but the rebuilding of the Temple was also a monument to his piety and his bid for acceptance by his Jewish subjects.[28]

Already in the mid-second century BCE a Jew from Alexandria in Egypt who wished to impress upon his gentile readers the marvels of Jerusalem had stressed the domination of the earlier Temple over the rest of the city. The author of the *Letter of Aristeas* disguised his Jewish identity and presented himself as a gentile courtier of the Ptolemaic king, in order to give a greater impact to his profession of admiration for the sacred texts and laws of the Jews. He claimed to have been part of the embassy sent to Jerusalem by the Ptolemaic king to bring back to Alexandria learned translators to render the Jewish law into Greek. He offers his readers a description of the whole countryside near Jerusalem: "When we approached near the site, we saw the city lying in the midst of the whole land of the Jews, upon a mountain which rises to a great height. On the top of the hill the Temple had been constructed most splendidly." There follows an effusive account of the accoutrements of the building, then of the water supply system which served it, the unremitting work of the priests, who operate in reverent silence. Some have suspected, with good reason, that the author of this work had never actually visited the land of Israel and was simply repeating the fantasies of diaspora Jews. The notion that the Jordan "never dries up . . . As the river rises, like the Nile, about the time of harvest, it waters much of the land . . ." is, sadly, far from the truth, which is why water supply has often been a major political issue in the region. The perception that Jerusalem was essentially a Temple city is all the more striking. It was a perception shared by a gentile contemporary, the historian Polybius, who referred to the renown of "the Temple called Jerusalem" and the Jews who dwell around it.[29]

Thus if Herod wished to make his mark on his capital city of Jerusalem, it would be most effective to do so by a striking contribution to its central institution, the Temple, and, once his position was secure, he accordingly devoted himself to the embellishment of the Temple buildings on a scale and to a level of magnificence that would shed glory on his name for generations to come. Josephus' report, both of what Herod achieved and of his motivation, is not beyond criticism, not least because Josephus' main source of information was Herod's court historian, the gentile polymath Nicolaus of Damascus, who later decamped to the court of Augustus, but the sentiments recorded ring true:

It was at this time, in the eighteenth year of his reign . . . that Herod undertook an extraordinary work, the reconstructing of the Temple of God at his own expense, enlarging its precincts and raising it to a more imposing height. For he believed that the accomplishment of this task would be the most notable of all the things achieved by him, as indeed it was, and would be great enough to assure his eternal remembrance. But since he knew that the populace was not prepared for or easy to enlist in so great an undertaking, he thought it best to predispose them to set to work on the whole project by making a speech to them first, and so he called them together and spoke as follows. "So far as the other things achieved during my reign are concerned, my countrymen, I consider it unnecessary to speak of them, although they were of such a kind that the prestige which comes from them to me is less than the security which they have brought to you . . . But that the enterprise which I now propose to undertake is the most pious and beautiful one of our time I will now make clear. For this was the Temple which our fathers built to the most great God after their return from Babylon, but it lacks sixty cubits in height, the amount by which the first Temple built by Solomon exceeded it . . . But since, by the will of God, I am now ruler and there continues to be a long period of peace and an abundance of wealth and great revenues, and—what is of most importance—the Romans, who are, so to speak, the masters of the world, are loyal friends, I will try to remedy the oversight caused by the necessity and slavery of that earlier time, and by this act of piety make full return to God for the gift of this kingdom."[30]

The response of the people was dismay at the thought that the king might tear down the Temple and lack the means to complete its rebuilding, but their lack of confidence proved unwarranted. The building was a marvel,

built of hard, white stones, each of which was about twenty-five cubits in length, eight in height and twelve in width . . . The entrance-doors, which with their lintels were equal [in height] to the Temple itself, he adorned with multicoloured hangings . . . Above these, under the cornice, spread a golden vine with grape-clusters hanging from it, a marvel of size with artistry to all who saw with what costliness of material it had been constructed. And he surrounded the Temple with very large porticoes, all of which he made in proportion, and he surpassed his predecessors in spending money, so that it was thought that no one else had adorned the Temple so splendidly.[31]

The huge stones, fixed with iron clamps invisible from the outside, enclosed a great courtyard with the Royal Portico on the south, a crowning monument almost as impressive as the Temple shrine proper. The Temple, with its altar, and the Holy of Holies, into which only the High Priest was permitted to enter (and even he only on one day a year), was dedicated to God, but the Royal Portico, along the southern flank of the Temple court-yard, was the place where Herod could enjoy the fruits of his munificence, giving him a central presence in the Temple even though he could never himself act as a priest:

> It was a structure more noteworthy than any under the sun. For while the depth of the ravine was great, and no one who bent over to look into it from above could bear to look down to the bottom, the height of the portico standing over it was so great that if anyone looked down from its rooftop, combining the two elevations, he would become dizzy and his vision would be unable to reach the end of so measureless a depth. Now the columns [of the portico] stood in four rows, one opposite the other all along—the fourth row was attached to a wall built of stone—and the thickness of each column was such that it would take three men with outstretched arms touching one another to envelop it.

For Herod in Jerusalem, as for Augustus in Rome, expenditure ostensibly donated for the glory of the deity was also a way to bring glory to the ruler.[32]

The routines of the Temple shaped life for everyone in the city, not least because of the noise of the constant supply of animals for slaughter and the smell of the livestock and raw meat. Each day a huge staff attended to the sacrifices from dawn to dusk, dealing with both the regular daily communal offerings and the many thousands of animals brought by individuals to mark events in their private lives. The priests who officiated, and the Levites who assisted them, were divided into twenty-four "courses" which succeeded each other, a week at a time, in providing teams to perform the rites. Each course was associated with a specified section of the lay population, and a delegation from that population was designated to stand by the public sacrifices to witness them on behalf of the nation as a whole when the service was being carried out by the priests of the course to which they were attached. The Temple was a place of constant activity, often crammed with worshippers. The rabbis remarked over a century after the building had been destroyed that the "miracles wrought for our fathers in the Temple" included the alleged facts that "no woman miscarried through the smell of the flesh of the offerings, no flesh of the offerings ever turned putrid, no fly was seen in the shambles . . . [and the people] stood pressed together yet bowed themselves at ease." The mass of private offerings required the attentions of thousands of priests and attendants, particularly during the major festivals. The Temple was the main meeting-place of the city, the site of public gatherings of many different kinds, but it was also a place of, and for, intense religious emotion.[33]

The presence of the Temple turned Jerusalem into a magnet for Jews not just from the Judaean countryside but from all over the Jewish world. "There were dwelling at Jerusalem Jews, devout men, out of every nation under heaven . . . Parthians, and Medes, and Elamites, and the inhabitants of Mesopotamia, and Judaea, and Cappadocia, of Pontus, and Asia, of Phrygia and Pamphylia, of Egypt and the parts of Libya around Cyrene, and visitors from Rome, both Jews and proselytes, Cretans and Arabians," each, as the author of Acts noted, using their own language. International pilgrimage was encouraged by the ease and comparative safety of transport around the Mediterranean world ensured by Roman power, particularly after Pompey's campaign in 67 had denied to pirates their former bases in coastal Cilicia, and thus reduced dramatically the safe havens from which they could operate against shipping. Pilgrims brought with them some of the wealth they had accumulated in other countries and spent it in Jerusalem as an act of piety. The result was a population as culturally heterogeneous as the rainbow population of the city of Rome, with one major difference. Almost everyone in Jerusalem, apart from the small Roman garrison, was religiously committed to the Jewish God. Such commitment could take many different forms, as will be seen, but everyone in Jerusalem knew that this was a Jewish city.[34]

The population of first-century-CE Jerusalem was also economically heterogeneous, with the very poor living side by side with the very rich. Peasants moved from the villages to seek more lucrative employment, though not always with success. Some took to begging, but Josephus describes also the pressures placed in the 60s CE on Agrippa II to create jobs for eighteen thousand men in Jerusalem whose income had depended on their work on the Temple edifice: now that the building was finally complete, their services were redundant, and Agrippa, in a form of state aid, paid for them to be employed instead on repaving the city streets. At the other extreme of wealth were rich expatriates like Queen Helena of Adiabene, a pious proselyte whose munificence to the populace was famed. Helena, with the rest of the ruling dynasty of Adiabene, a small kingdom in northern Mesopotamia, had converted to Judaism, and she had moved to Jerusalem as an expression of her devotion to her new religion. Her palace and tomb became noted landmarks in the city. Her funerary monument, which consisted of three pyramids, was so famous that the Greek writer Pausanias in the mid-second century CE mentions it in the same breath as the famous tomb of Mausolus: "I know many wonderful graves, and will mention two of them, the one at Halicarnassus and one in the land of the Hebrews. The one of Halicarnassus was made for Mausolus, king of the city, and it is of such vast size and so notable for all its ornament that the Romans in their great admiration of it call remarkable tombs in their country 'Mausolea.' The Hebrews have a grave, that of Helena . . . in the city of Jerusalem, which the Roman emperor razed to the ground." Pausanias goes on to describe a mechanism which permitted the stone door to the grave to be opened only at a particular hour on a particular day each year. The monument is almost certainly to be identified with the Tombs of the Kings which can still be seen in Jerusalem.[35]

The total size of the settled population of the city is altogether more difficult to gauge. Estimates vary wildly, not least because both the methods and the data used vary. Some scholars have suggested a total of thirty-five thousand inhabitants in Herod's reign, others seventy thousand. All are agreed that numbers are likely to have increased over the following decades, when the city expanded, but there is less agreement on the extent of the increase. One method of calculating the population is to measure the size of the inhabited area, but this procedure is prejudiced by uncertainty about the density of settlement, particularly in the suburb of Bezetha in the north of the city which only began to be built up in the mid-first century CE, when Agrippa I, Herod's grandson, began work on the new northern defensive wall which would be the first to be breached by Titus in 70 CE. Other scholars have derived population figures from the amount of the water supply brought into the city, noting that this had to be increased during the first century CE when the governor Pontius Pilate ran into trouble with the local population by using sacred money to finance the building of an aqueduct. But here too there are uncertainties, not least over the extent to which water might be used extravagantly in a society influenced by Roman enthusiasm for bathing.[36]

Even if the permanent population was only in the tens of thousands (which in ancient terms would already constitute a large city), the numbers of people in Jerusalem exploded three times each year, when pilgrims came from all over the Jewish world. In the spring, early summer and early autumn, at the festivals of Passover, Pentecost and Tabernacles, Jerusalem was packed. In his account of the last days of the Temple in 70 CE, Josephus states that the total number of those who perished during the siege of Jerusalem was one million one hundred thousand. Of these the greater number were Jews but not native to the city,

> for, having assembled from the whole country for the feast of unleavened bread [Passover], they found themselves suddenly enveloped in the war . . . That the city could contain so many is clear from the count taken under Cestius. For he, being anxious to convince Nero, who held the nation in contempt, of the city's strength, instructed the chief priests, if at all possible, to take a census of the population. Accordingly, on the occasion of a feast called Passover, at which they sacrifice from the ninth to the eleventh hour, and a little fraternity, as it were, gathers round each sacrifice, of not fewer than ten men (feasting alone not being permitted), while the companies often include as many as twenty, the victims were counted and amounted to two hundred and fifty-five thousand six hundred; allowing an average of ten diners to each victim, we obtain a total of two million seven hundred thousand.

Josephus' arithmetic (or the text) is at fault, since the total should be two million five hundred and fifty-six thousand, and it is not unlikely either that he exaggerated the numbers or that the manuscripts have been corrupted, or both, but the implication of his story is clear enough: the number of pilgrims was staggeringly large. Since women and children also attended the festivals, albeit in smaller numbers, the size of the temporary population on these occasions will have been even greater. These pilgrims came from all over the Jewish world: according to the Jewish philosopher Philo, "countless men from countless cities."[37]

Thus Jerusalem, like Rome, housed a large proportion of impoverished inhabitants living alongside the very rich, with a community dependent on wealth imported from outside the country in order to maintain itself; but Jerusalem had as an added source of instability the periodic influx of great numbers of temporary residents, who brought with them economic opportunities but could also cause political and social unrest. As later in Mecca, the pilgrim festivals were the "harvest of the city," the residents of Jerusalem profiting from fellow Judaeans as well as diaspora Jews. The Mishnah describes how the first fruits were brought in procession to the city from all over the land of Israel:

> They that are near [to Jerusalem] bring fresh figs and grapes, and those that are far off bring dried figs and raisins. Before them goes the ox, having its horns overlaid with gold and a wreath of olive-leaves on its head. The flute is played before them until they come near to Jerusalem. When they came near to Jerusalem they sent [messengers] before them and bedecked their first fruits. The rulers and the prefects and the treasurers [of the Temple] go forth to meet them. According to the honour due to them that came in used they to go forth. And all the craftsmen in Jerusalem rise up before them and greet them, saying, "Brethren, men of such-and-such a place, you are welcome."[38]

Pilgrimage ensured that Jerusalem was an international city despite its distance from the sea and its isolation from the main land trade route. The countryside around Jerusalem was undoubtedly farmed intensively, but such agriculture was hardly in itself the basis of the city's astonishing prosperity in the century preceding its destruction in 70 CE. Jerusalem's greatness in the time of Jesus was the result not of victory in war or success in commerce, political intrigue or the harnessing of natural resources, but of the religious fervour of millions of Jews living throughout much of the eastern part of the Roman empire and beyond.

## CHAPTER TWO

# ONE WORLD UNDER ROME

## POLITICAL UNITY IMPOSED

LEAST PUZZLING in the unfolding of the events which led to the destruction of Jerusalem was the simple fact that political change in Italy could have such an impact so far away in Judaea. In political terms, the Mediterranean world was more unified under Rome in the first two centuries CE than it had ever been before and than it has ever been since. The brutal reality of the Roman empire was that the power of the emperor could reach almost every corner of this world. Decisions taken in Spain could affect the inhabitants of Turkey; unrest in Italy or Greece could change the lives of people in Syria and the northern coast of Africa.

In a dramatic scene just before the outbreak of revolt in Jerusalem in spring 66 CE, King Agrippa II stood with his sister Berenice on the roof of his palace and delivered a passionate speech, pleading with his fellow Jews not to bring disaster on their heads. According to the version preserved by Josephus, he reminded his Jewish audience in detail of the extraordinary military might that Rome had displayed in conquering, and retaining control of, so much of the known world:

Passing to your present passion for liberty, I say that it comes too late. The time is past when you ought to have striven never to lose it . . . There was, to be sure, a time when you should have strained every nerve to keep out the Romans; that was when Pompey invaded this country. But our forefathers and their kings, though in wealth and in vigour of body and soul far your superiors, yet failed to withstand a small fraction of the Roman army; and will you, to whom thraldom is hereditary, you who in resources fall so far short of those who first tendered their submission, will you, I say, defy the whole Roman empire? Look at the Athenians . . . Look at the Spartans . . . Look at the Macedonians . . . Myriads of other nations, swelling with greater pride in the assertion of their liberty, have yielded. And will you alone disdain to serve those to whom everything is subject? What is the army, what are the weapons, on which you rely? Where is your fleet to sweep the Roman seas? Where is your treasury to meet the cost of your campaigns? Do you really suppose that you are going to war with Egyptians or Arabs? Will you shut your eyes to the might of the Roman empire? Will you not measure your own weakness? Have not our forces been often defeated even by the neighbouring nations, while theirs have never met with a reverse throughout the whole inhabited world? Even that world has not sufficed for their ambition. For, not content with having for their frontiers on the east the Euphrates, on the north the Ister [the Danube], on the south Libya explored into the uninhabited regions, on the west Gades, they have sought a new world beyond the ocean and carried their arms as far as the Britons, previously unknown to history. I ask you, then, are you wealthier than the Gauls, stronger than the Germans, more intelligent than the Greeks, more numerous than all the peoples of the world? What is it which inspires you with confidence to defy the Romans?

There follows a survey of the empire, region by region, with details in each case of the minimal force needed to keep even the most rebellious peoples in check:

The Dalmatians, too, who have so often reared their heads for liberty, whose constant defeats have only led them to muster their forces for a fresh revolt, do they not now live in peace under a single Roman legion? . . . Again, consider what a wall of defence had the Britons, you who put your trust in the walls of Jerusalem: the ocean surrounds them, they inhabit an island no less in extent than the part of the world in which we live; yet the Romans crossed the sea and enslaved them, and four legions now secure that vast island.[1]

The rhetorical structure of this powerful speech, as it is reported, will have been the work not of Agrippa but of Josephus, since in ancient historiography rhetorical elaboration of speeches actually delivered, and even of speeches which should have been delivered but were not, was considered an important element of the historian's task. Nor is it unlikely that Josephus culled his detailed information about Roman administrative arrangements from an official Roman source rather than any account of what Agrippa in fact said as he faced an angry and excitable crowd of rebellious Jews. But, whether Agrippa's invention or Josephus', the speech encapsulates perfectly both the cultural variety of the Roman world and the firm imprint upon all of it imposed by Rome. There were a few remote regions where Roman power could not reach very effectively, such as the mountains of Rough Cilicia (Cilicia Tracheia) in what is now south-eastern Turkey, but in general Rome controlled her huge empire through sheer military might. The political unity of the empire thus depended ultimately more on control from the centre, and the consent (forced or voluntary) of disparate societies to subject themselves to that control, than on any sense among Rome's subjects that they belonged to a single organic society. In the mid-second century CE the Greek orator Aelius Aristides implied, somewhat optimistically, that Rome should be seen as the queen of a constellation of separate but mutually beneficent city-states organized along the same lines as the federal leagues long traditional among the Greeks, but a façade of local freedom was hard to maintain in many parts of the empire, particularly in the first century CE, when provincial revolts all too often punctured the Roman peace.[2]

The underlying fragility of political unity imposed by brutal force was most blatant on the geographical edges of the empire. As the sailor journeys east on the Black Sea, he reaches the point, as the historian Arrian put it in the mid-second century CE, "where Roman power ends."[3] Despite periodic campaigns to rectify such matters, Romans were well aware that the Parthians in the East and barbarians of various kinds in Germany and elsewhere remained free from the Roman yoke. It was less easy to admit publicly to lack of political control closer to the centre of empire. Most provincial revolts were hidden from public view by a state unwilling to advertise unwelcome news. Of the many rebellions known—from career-inscriptions of Roman soldiers, incidental remarks in literary texts, and other such scattered evidence—to have taken place in the first two centuries of the empire, only a handful were noted in government propaganda. If Rough Cilicia could not be captured—or, more accurately, was too impoverished to be worth capturing—the state could simply ignore it altogether. The regime ruled regions to which access was often very difficult, so that, in the absence of a free press and investigative journalists, parts of the Roman world could be proclaimed as Roman without any need to take any military action at all. Hence the fate of Armenia, ruled by a local dynasty of Iranian origin which managed with remarkable success to persuade the Roman state of its friendship while remaining on good terms with Parthia. The political fiction was willingly accepted by successive Roman emperors, not least because of the immense difficulties involved in any military campaign in the Armenian mountains. When, in the time of Augustus, the Armenian people assassinated their king Artaxias and accepted the Roman protégé Tigranes in his stead, Augustus' coins proclaimed ARMENIA CAPTA or ARMENIA RECEPTA even though Roman forces had in fact done nothing.[4]

In the eyes of most of Rome's subjects, the empire was embodied by the emperor. It had not always been so. Before the victory at Actium in 31 BCE of the future emperor Augustus, the public face of the Roman Republic was sometimes rather nebulous outside the city of Rome itself. The individual senators with whom provincials came into contact might represent the political will of only one faction in a divided ruling class. *Senatus Populusque Romanus*, "The Senate and people of Rome," did not always speak with a single voice even before breakdown into nearly continuous civil strife in the mid-first century BCE. Local elites in Greek cities in the eastern Mediterranean, long accustomed to negotiations with kings, attributed a personality to the new power which controlled their political lives by worshipping the personification of Rome as a divinity. The practice was helped more than a little by the coincidence that the name of Rome in Greek means "strength." But soon after Actium worship shifted to "Rome and Augustus," and when Augustus died it was his divinity that was celebrated alone. The imperial cult, the worship of emperors dead and alive, rapidly became one of the most powerful forces towards the unification of the Roman world.

The image of the emperor dominated the most pervasive medium for the propagation of slogans for the state, the coinage. Not only were coins

issued in huge quantities, but coin types varied greatly, in each case reflecting a decision by some official within the administration of the state, but,
whatever might appear on the other side of the coin, the heads of the
emperors or (less frequent, but still common) members of their families
were ubiquitous. All the emperor's subjects knew his appearance within
months of his accession to power—or, more accurately, the appearance
that he and his advisers wished him to have in his subjects' eyes. The
emperor's bust, whether placed to be worshipped in a temple among the
other gods or admired on a commemorative relief, was instantly recognizable even without the iconographic convention that, from the time of
Augustus, only an emperor could be depicted wearing a laurel wreath, traditionally in the Republic the privilege of a victorious general. A back-
woods provincial who sought asylum in times of personal danger by
clasping the emperor's statue might see in the imperial image the embodi-
ment of the state: in Nicomedia (modern Izmit) in Bithynia in the early
second century CE, when a certain Callidromus escaped from the bakers
who had kept him as a captive employee, he successfully took refuge before
one of Trajan's statues and in due course was able to tell his story to the
local magistrates and the governor of the province.[5]

Thus the personality of the emperor, or in some cases his contrived
public persona, mattered even to those who lived in the furthest reaches of
the Roman world. The tyranny of Gaius (Caligula) from 37 to 41 or Nero
from 54 to 68 could be deplored, or the beneficence of Trajan from 98 to
117 celebrated, even by provincials never remotely likely to see any members of the imperial family in the flesh. It seems likely that the qualities of
the emperor that the citizens chose to praise derived, at least in part, from
the qualities he and his regime chose to stress, although a study of the fre-
quency of the representation of individual imperial virtues on *denarii* over
the whole period from 69 to 235 reveals surprisingly infrequent reference
to such standard virtues as *clementia* and *iustitia*, and a strong emphasis on
*aequitas* ("fairness," probably referring to the just administration of the
mint), *liberalitas* (celebrating the emperor's generosity), and, on coins fea-
turing portraits of female members of the imperial family, *pudicitia*,
"chastity." A partial explanation of this pattern may lie in the frequent
employment, on a fifth of all coins, of the helpfully ambiguous concept
*pietas*, an old Roman virtue which referred in general to devotion, respect
and duty, whether to the gods, to parents, or to dependants.[6]

The Roman world in 14 CE

Occasionally events at the centre of empire produced reverberations in the provinces that the emperor is unlikely to have entirely welcomed. In 19 CE Germanicus, nephew and adopted son of the emperor Tiberius, died in Syria, convinced (probably without justification) that he had been poisoned by Gnaeus Calpurnius Piso, the governor of Syria, with whom he had serious public disagreements, leading to a formal breaking of their friendship. Germanicus was in his early thirties when he died. His affability was immensely popular, not least because of its contrast to the distant aristocratic style preferred by the elderly Tiberius. There is evidence that this popularity was not wholly welcome to Tiberius, and it was widely believed that the emperor's professions of grief at Germanicus' death were insincere. Nonetheless, in 20 CE Tiberius permitted the prosecution of Piso in the Senate. Piso protested his innocence, but, seeing the case going against him, committed suicide to protect other members of his family from harassment should he be condemned. The recent discovery in Spain of at least six copies of the text of the Senate's deliberations after Piso's trial and death shows that even quite small details of these events among the political elite were distributed widely throughout the provinces, in accordance with the Senate's own wish that "this decree of the Senate, inscribed on bronze, should be set up in the most frequented city of each province and the most frequented place in that city."[7]

In the 70s CE provincials in the eastern parts of the empire expressed equal enthusiasm for another youthful, charismatic emperor, lending support to a series of individuals who claimed, fraudulently, to be the emperor Nero returning to resume his imperial inheritance. The downfall of the real Nero, who (as we shall see in Chapter 11) had in fact died ignominiously in 68, had begun in part because soldiers in distant Gaul were disgusted at his reputation as a matricide. What emperors did was the stuff of gossip, like that in tabloid journalism. The stories in parables found in Jewish texts are sometimes located in royal courts which bear a general resemblance to the imperial court in Rome. Such stories reflected the semi-mythical status of the emperors in the eyes of outsiders from far away. Their impact on the imagination might be no less effective for being imprecise.[8]

Just occasionally elite politics impinged much more directly on provincials, most obviously in times of civil war, such as the ruinous struggle for power between Pompey and Julius Caesar from 49 BCE and then, from 44 to 31, between Caesar's political heirs, and, as we have seen in Vespasian's conduct of the campaign in Judaea, the attempts by a series of army commanders to seize and retain power in the tumultuous year following the death of Nero in 68 CE. In such times of turmoil provincial aristocrats had to make hard choices, not just whether to support Rome at all but which Romans to support. For a provincial actually to see the emperor would be rare, unless he were sent to Rome on an embassy on behalf of his local community. Few emperors travelled much outside Italy except to go to the frontiers to campaign for the glory of the state, and even campaigning could often be left to competent subordinates. Those emperors who took the field in person generally did so because their military capabilities were so in doubt that they deemed a personal appearance necessary: the emperor Claudius led the invasion of Britain in 43 CE in order to be able to claim, on an inscription of 51, probably set up on a triumphal arch, that he had received there "the surrender of eleven British kings without loss," asserting that "he was the first to subject to the rule of the Roman people barbarian peoples across the Ocean."[9]

The exception to the general rule that emperors preferred a comfortable life in Rome was Hadrian, emperor from 117 to 138. Hadrian set himself to tour the provinces, systematically setting to rights the affairs of his subjects, proclaiming his benevolence as he did so. Other emperors were content to restrict their interventions to those issues raised with them by the provincials themselves, many of whose numerous petitions for favours, if the outcome was successful, were memorialized on inscriptions: so, for instance, an inscription set up in the town of Sabora in Spain in 78 CE by the two chief magistrates, who had it inscribed on bronze "at public expense," recorded the greetings of Vespasian to the leading citizens: "Since you inform me that your weakness is beset by many difficulties, I permit you to build the town under my name in the plain, as you wish."[10] Provincial governors also tended to wait for prompts from below. The list of Jewish privileges preserved by Josephus in the fourteenth and sixteenth books of his *Jewish Antiquities* seems to derive from a dossier of inscriptions set up in the cities of Asia Minor to record favourable Roman decrees which had been issued in response to Jewish petitions. He cites a decree of the people of Ephesus:

Whereas the Jews in the city have petitioned the proconsul Marcus
Junius Brutus, son of Pontius, that they might observe their Sabbaths
and do all those things which are in accordance with their native customs without interference from anyone, and the governor has granted
this request, it has therefore been decreed by the council and people
that, as the matter is of concern to the Romans, no one shall be prevented from keeping the Sabbath days nor be fined for doing so, but
they shall be permitted to do all those things which are in accordance
with their own laws.[11]

The far more active approach of Hadrian, widely advertised by the minting of a series of coins to celebrate his arrival in each province, and commemorated in each of those provinces by the founding of cities and
erection of buildings, was in stark contrast.[12]

For many provincials the local representatives of the empire were
Roman soldiers, with whom relations naturally varied. On 6 May 124, a
centurion named Magonius Valens in the military camp which bordered
the date-palm groves in En Gedi by the Dead Sea made an emergency
short-term loan to a Jew named Judah at an interest rate of twelve per cent
per annum. A Roman soldier receiving regular pay, but with no opportunity to spend his money enjoyably in a secluded posting like En Gedi,
might well find himself with spare cash and the temptation to put his
money to use by lending to the provincials for a good return. In any such
transaction the upper hand was inevitably with the soldier. In the document recording the loan to Judah, the outer text (the text visible without
unsealing the document) stated that Judah would receive sixty *denarii*, but
the inner text was altered during the drawing-up of the agreement, with
the original reference to forty *denarii* erased and replaced by the addition
between the lines of the word "sixty." It seems possible that Judah was the
victim of skulduggery of some kind. At any rate, it would be naive to
assume that such evidence of social contact indicated friendly relations.[13]

Not all parts of the Mediterranean world were equally militarized.
Most Roman troops were stationed in frontier provinces, ostensibly either
to defend them against cross-border raids or in preparation for offensives to
expand the limits of Roman power. In practice, many troops would have
passed their entire careers without ever embarking on a campaign. Some
provinces had very few troops at all. Corresponding in *c.* iii CE with the

emperor Trajan during his governorship of Pontus and Bithynia, the younger Pliny raised a series of issues over the deployment of an extraordinarily small number of soldiers, such as whether to allow the procurator Maximus an extra six men to help with his special mission to collect corn from Paphlagonia (the response was that Maximus should hold on to the six soldiers until his mission was finished, after which "the two soldiers you have assigned him should be enough, plus the same number from Virdius Gemellinus, my procurator under whom he serves"). Where troops were to be found, they often formed a separate society of their own within which soldiers and their families might spend their whole lives, bringing up their children *in castris,* "within the camp." Their entry into the lives of individual provincials could be dramatically disruptive. In Apuleius' novel *The Golden Ass,* which in many respects reflects the reality of life in the empire of the second century when it was written (except that not many hapless young men can have been turned into asses by magic), the course of the narrative is suddenly altered when a soldier meets the ass and its owner and commandeers the ass for state business.[14]

For protection against such arbitrary action by the agents of the state, a Roman citizen could appeal to the emperor, as did Paul in *c.* 60 before the Roman governor of Judaea, Festus, when the latter wanted to send him to Jerusalem to be tried by the Jewish authorities.[15] It was evidently at Festus' discretion whether to allow the appeal; non-citizens did not even have such a right, and in the early imperial period only a few inhabitants of the empire held Roman citizenship. For them, redress had to be sought from the governor. In practice, the governor was the emperor's local representative, even though he was only sometimes directly nominated by the emperor—in other cases, appointment of governors lay in the hands of the Senate in Rome. Within their provinces, governors had immense power. The governor before whom a provincial brought his petition would look and behave like a regal figure, seated on a tribunal above the disputing parties in a court case, beholden to no one apart from the emperor and Senate, who might often seem far too far away to matter. The description by the Jewish philosopher Philo of the degeneration of communal relations between Jews and Greeks in Alexandria in Egypt in the 30s CE is full of unreliable animus against the governor Flaccus, who (in Philo's view) failed to stem the violence sufficiently to favour the Jews, but there is no reason to doubt Philo's picture of the practical obstacles which faced the Jewish community when it tried to make direct contact with the emperor in Rome: when the Jews wished to send a flattering message to Gaius, Flaccus would not allow them to convey it by an embassy and, despite his promises, failed to dispatch it himself on their behalf.[16]

Corrupt governors could hope with some justification to escape any punishment, since a prosecution of a governor of senatorial rank would have to be brought in most cases by a fellow senator, and bringing a charge against a colleague in whom emperor or Senate had shown sufficient confidence to appoint him in the first place might not be politically astute. Only those politically vulnerable for some other reason, or those who had committed crimes of particular culpability, might fear trial on completion of their office. The younger Pliny told his friend Caecilius Macrinus how he had allowed himself in 100 CE to be persuaded by the people of Baetica (in Spain) to act as counsel on their behalf in the Senate in their complaint about a certain Caecilius Classicus, who had been their governor. His initial reluctance was overcome by his natural feeling of gratification that his fellow senators wished him to take on this difficult public task, but also, crucially, "an additional influence was the fact that Classicus was now dead, which removed the most painful feature in this type of case— imperilling a senator. I saw then that I should win the same thanks for taking on the case as if he were alive, but without giving any offence." Pliny evidently saw nothing peculiar in such reasoning, since he included this letter in the selection of his correspondence which he himself edited for publication; but in his last book of letters, which seems to have been published after his death and which certainly presents a less highly polished picture of his political and literary personas, he (perhaps inadvertently) gives readers an even better insight into the problems he himself faced when, at the end of his career, he found himself governor of Pontus and Bithynia. In his letters to Trajan, between congratulating the emperor on his birthday, asking for patronage for friends and colleagues and checking on the deployment of troops, Pliny asks for advice on such knotty issues as the legal status of foundlings, and complains about the problems he faces in imposing his will on the province.[17]

For a governor like Pliny, with very few soldiers at his disposal and a huge region to control, a constant cause of difficulty was lack of manpower and a shortage of reliable information about what was happening within his province. He had no civil service to give advice. For administrative help he relied on the staff of domestic slaves and ex-slaves, members of his own household, who had accompanied him from Italy. When he wanted an expert to advise on the feasibility of a major construction project, the digging of a canal to link to the sea a large lake near Nicomedia, he asked Trajan to send him a qualified expert from Rome. Trajan replied by agreeing to send someone out, but also by suggesting that Pliny might ask the governor of a neighbouring province for an engineer. Pliny's earlier request for a land surveyor to inspect public works in Bithynia had been met by a blank refusal: "As for land surveyors, I have scarcely enough for the public works in progress in Rome or in the neighbourhood, but there are reliable surveyors to be found in every province and no doubt you will not lack such experts if you will take the trouble to investigate diligently."[18]

## POLITICAL UNITY EMBRACED

GOVERNMENT WITHOUT bureaucracy could operate successfully only if it was government by consent—even if the motivation for consent was ultimately the fear of extreme violence by the state as penalty for open opposition. Much administration, such as the collection of taxes at the local level, was in effect carried out on behalf of the state by local urban elites in return for Roman support of their local status. The success of government thus depended upon acceptance by provincial aristocrats of the value of honours and titles bestowed by local people and recognized by Rome. Much of the extant evidence for this "empire of honour" appears to confirm such a consensus. Inscriptions on monuments from all over the empire boast about the status of local magistrates and the favours granted to them, and through them to their communities, by governors and emperors. Such evidence suggests an integrated society of provincials willingly cooperating with a benevolent and responsive state. But of course only those individuals who accepted and benefited from the system will have paid for such monuments to be erected.[19]

It is also hard to know how effectively the widespread imperial cult, which involved worship both of emperors and of Rome itself, produced a general sense of unity among participants. Some of the temples and altars dedicated to this worship were set up on local initiative, and can be seen as a means for provincials to make religious sense of the irruption of Roman power into the lives of their communities, but in other places (and particularly in the western regions of the empire), the worship of emperors was imposed by the state and may have been viewed by Rome's subjects just as another type of subjection.

More significant than such overt recognition by provincials of their place in the Roman system of power was the nearly universal practice of patronage to give individuals of all backgrounds a sense of connection, however tenuous, between themselves and the emperor. Almost everyone in the Roman empire knew someone who knew someone who might be able to intervene, through however many links in the chain of patronage, at the centre of power in the state. Numerous inscriptions attest to such interventions by patrons on behalf of communities. Favours might be elicited by writing letters, and thousands of such written requests survive, from the blunt petitions of peasants to officials in Roman Egypt, the original copies preserved on papyrus, to the highly polished epistles of the younger Pliny, asking for favours for his friends from fellow senators or from the emperor. But for the provincials far away from the locus of power in Rome, the most effective invocation of patronage ties was achieved either by travelling to Rome in person or by sending an embassy. Josephus, as we have seen, visited Rome in the early 60s CE to seek the release of a group of priests from Jerusalem, friends of his, "very excellent men," who "on a slight and trifling charge" had been sent to Rome in bonds to "render an account to Caesar." After an adventurous voyage, which (if Josephus has not embellished his account in order to impress his readers) included a shipwreck in the Adriatic, Josephus landed safely at Puteoli in Italy. On arrival he rapidly formed a friendship with Aliturus, an actor, "Jewish as to race and a special favourite of Nero." Through Aliturus, Josephus engineered for himself an introduction to Poppaea, Nero's (current) wife, and through her secured the liberation of the two imprisoned priests, returning to Jerusalem laden with large gifts from his new patroness.[20]

The role of patronage, derived ultimately from the emperor in bringing to power the local leaders on whom Rome so heavily relied, was particularly blatant in the remarkable career of Agrippa I, the father of the Agrippa who tried so strenuously and ineffectively to ward off revolt in Jerusalem in 66 CE. Agrippa I was appointed king of Judaea in 41 by the emperor Claudius. His colourful career at the centre of political life both in Jerusalem and in Rome in the 30s and 40s of the first century CE exemplifies so strikingly the close interrelationship between the realities of power in both cities, and the impact of events in one part of the Mediterranean world on another, that it is worth recounting here in some detail. That this can be done is a result primarily of the interest shown in Agrippa by Josephus, who may well have had access to information in Rome from members of his household, including his son, Agrippa II. The early rabbis wrote about Agrippa I as a pious king; by contrast, early Christians remembered him as "Herod the King" who "killed James the brother of John with a sword" and imprisoned Peter in Jerusalem. Agrippa was equally at home in Rome and Jerusalem. His parents marked his Roman status from the start by giving him, at his birth in 10 BCE, a full Roman name, Marcus Iulius Agrippa, which commemorated the emperor Augustus' closest colleague, Marcus Vipsanius Agrippa, who had died two years previously. But Agrippa was also a Jew: his grandfather was Herod the Great and his grandmother the Hasmonaean princess Mariamme, whom Herod had both loved and, in an excess of jealousy, killed.[21]

Agrippa's reputation for piety by the time he became king of Judaea in 41 was not accidentally acquired. The Mishnah preserves an account of his methods of currying approval among Jews in the Jerusalem Temple when he carried out the duty of performing a ceremonial reading of the book of Deuteronomy, a task which it fell to the king to carry out every seven years:

> They make for him in the Temple court a platform on which he sits . . . The minister of the assembly takes a scroll of the Law and gives it to the chief of the assembly, and the chief of the assembly gives it to the prefect, and the prefect gives it to the High Priest, and the High Priest gives it to the king, and the king receives it standing and reads it sitting. [But] King Agrippa received it standing and read it standing, and for this the sages praised him. And when he reached [the passage in Deuteronomy which states] "You may not put a foreigner over you who is not your brother," his eyes flowed with tears [because he was a descendant of proselytes]; [but] they said to him, "Do not worry, Agrippa. You are our brother! You are our brother! You are our brother!"[22]

Such acceptance by acclamation, however artificially contrived, was a major achievement for an adventurer who had come to power mainly through exploitation of his personal contacts in the imperial court.

Agrippa I was descended both from Hasmonaean and from Herodian royalty, but he was separated from any real hope of influence or position in his homeland when his father Aristobulus was executed in 7 BCE by his own father, Herod, on a charge of treason. His liminality was accentuated by his upbringing. From the age of six or so, he was sent to live in Rome in close contact with the younger members of the imperial court, where his mother was a close friend of Antonia, the daughter of Mark Antony and Octavia, the sister of Augustus. Agrippa became close to the young Drusus, son of the future emperor Tiberius: the two boys were the same age. After 14 CE, when Augustus died, Drusus was heir apparent to Tiberius alongside Germanicus (evidently on the assumption that the two would somehow share power), and, following the untimely death in 19 of Germanicus (which, as we have seen, was widely publicized across the empire), Agrippa's friend looked set to inherit supreme power from his already elderly father Tiberius. But Agrippa's link to influence at the heart of empire was tenuous precisely because it was so personal. In 23 Drusus himself died in his mid-thirties, and Agrippa left Rome to face an uncertain future back in the land of his birth. The adventures which followed were governed by Agrippa's need to fund an extravagant lifestyle for which he had no regular income. He was dogged by scandal, including accusations of bribery, imprisonment for debt, and public tensions both in his relations with his uncle Herod Antipas (ruled 4 BCE–39 CE), who had been given authority by Rome over a part of Herod's former kingdom, and in his relations with Roman bureaucrats in a number of different provinces in the eastern Mediterranean. Eventually he managed to raise in Alexandria, from Alexander "the Alabarch," a sufficiently large loan for his purposes: Alexander, a pious Jew who was brother to the philosopher Philo, in fact refused to give the money to Agrippa himself, fearing (with good reason) his prodigality, but he gave it to Agrippa's wife Cypros "because he marvelled at her love for her husband and all her other good qualities." Armed with this cash, in the spring of 36 Agrippa sailed back to Italy.[23]

The political life of Rome had largely stagnated during the thirteen years of Agrippa's absence, which had seen the rise and fall of Tiberius' confidant Sejanus, who had been his prefect of the praetorian guard until, as will be described in Chapter 9, Tiberius' abrupt and damning accusation of treachery in a dramatic denunciation before the Senate brought Sejanus' instant overthrow and execution. Tiberius himself was by now old, and had been living in seclusion on the island of Capri for some nine years, showing little interest in affairs in Rome and taking no action in relation to the rest of the empire. It was a testament to Agrippa's real friendship with Tiberius' son Drusus long ago that his letter requesting permission to pay court to the emperor on Capri was received favourably and that he was welcomed to the island. It was perhaps even more a testimony to Antonia's fondness for Agrippa and his mother that, when Agrippa's failure to pay off a huge debt owed to one of the emperor's agents threatened his return to favour, she loaned him all three hundred thousand drachmas. Tiberius asked Agrippa to look after his teenage grandson Tiberius Gemellus, the son of Agrippa's old friend Drusus, who had died thirteen years before.

Since the emperor had appointed Tiberius Gemellus as one of the two heirs to his property, and since the old man could not last much longer, Agrippa might reasonably congratulate himself on his return to the centre of power in the empire. But relationships were rarely simple in the torrid atmosphere in Capri in the last months before Tiberius' death on 16 March 37. Designated as co-heir with Tiberius Gemellus was Gaius, son of the much lamented Germanicus and grandson of Agrippa's patroness Antonia. Gaius, in his mid-twenties and patently ambitious, seemed certain to eclipse his younger cousin if Tiberius were to die soon, and Agrippa devoted himself to courting his friendship. Once again the expense was considerable, but on this occasion a freedman of the emperor, of Samaritan origin, made him a loan of a million drachmas. Clearly Agrippa's prospects looked good enough to make his future worth the investment. Precisely how Agrippa and Gaius cemented their friendship can only be speculated. Josephus mentions only time spent together at dinner or out riding together in Agrippa's chariot, but the secrecy surrounding court life on Capri encouraged gossip, and Gaius' bizarre tastes, revealed when he eventually succeeded to power, suggest a fairly dissolute lifestyle. According to the hostile biography by Suetonius, Gaius "outdid in reckless extravagance the prodigals of all times in ingenuity . . . for he would bathe in hot or cold perfumed oils, drink pearls of great price dissolved in vinegar, and set before his guests loaves and meats of gold. . . ." His sexual exploits—heterosexual, homosexual and incestuous—were notorious. At the very least, it is difficult to imagine Agrippa trying to act as a good Jew in such company, restricting himself to kosher food or observing the regulations of the Sabbath.[24]

Indulgence of Gaius' megalomaniac ambitions proved dangerous. In flattery of the young man, Agrippa expressed a wish that Tiberius would soon cease to be emperor so that Gaius could take over in his place. Unfortunately for Agrippa, the conversation was overheard by one of his freedmen, a chariot driver called Eutychus—it reveals much about attitudes to such domestic staff that Josephus describes the remark as having been made when Agrippa and Gaius were alone, even though Eutychus was seated at their feet. In due course the story came out because Eutychus ran away from Agrippa's household after stealing some of his master's clothes, and, on being arrested and brought before the city prefect, tried to secure his release by offering his secret to Tiberius. The emperor's habitual dilatoriness delayed the revelation, but, when the truth was revealed by the disgruntled freedman, Agrippa was thrown into the custody of the praetorian guard and bound with chains.

Notwithstanding Agrippa's public punishment for speculating so rashly on the impending change of regime, in practice everyone surrounding the emperor must have been making plans for what would happen when he died. According to Josephus, Macro, the prefect of the praetorian guard, was slow to carry out Tiberius' order to make the arrest. It would be unwise to maltreat a friend of Gaius if Gaius might indeed soon be in power. Agrippa was permitted special privileges in custody—a daily bath, visits from his freedmen and friends, his favourite food, proper clothing, a comfortable bed, all provided with the connivance of Macro and his soldiers. In six months Tiberius was dead, aided at the last, according to rumour, by Macro, who was said to have ordered that the old man be finished off by suffocation. Agrippa's tribulations now turned to his advantage. Gaius, as the new emperor, waited for the sake of decency a few days after Tiberius' funeral before ordering his friend's release, appointing him king of the region that had been ruled, until his death in 34 CE, by Agrippa's uncle Philip, and presenting him with a gold chain of a weight equal to the iron chain with which he had been bound. Agrippa celebrated by dedicating the golden chain to the Temple in Jerusalem. As Josephus comments sententiously, "All were surprised to see him in his royal state. He was an object lesson in demonstrating the great power of fortune over mankind to those who beheld him and speculated on the contrast between his former distress and his present prosperity."[25]

It is significant that Agrippa was in no hurry to go in person to settle the affairs of his kingdom when he was first appointed in the spring of 37 CE, and that, when he did go, in 38, it was not for long. Royal status brought him prestige and an income, but to exercise real power and influence it was best to be in Rome. On the other hand, as Gaius showed increasing signs of irrational despotism, the imperial court was a dangerous place to be, even for a friend of the emperor. Whether Gaius was unhinged by power was already debated in antiquity. There was general agreement that the first year, perhaps more, of his rule was good, but also a belief that his cruelty and viciousness were innate. Some of his stranger exploits in later years may be susceptible to rational explanation. Even his insistence that he be worshipped as divine may have served a real political purpose. Unlike his predecessors Julius Caesar, Augustus and Tiberius, he could boast of no military conquests whatsoever. The unearthing of a conspiracy by an army commander in the winter of 39–40 confirmed his vulnerability. All he could stress was the undoubted aristocracy of his lineage, which was underlined by the extravagant honours accorded to his sisters, above all Drusilla, with whom he was rumoured to have had incestuous relations; on her untimely death in 38 in her early twenties she was consecrated as the goddess Panthea. It was reasonable for Gaius to hope that, by depicting himself as above mortal politics while still alive, he might strengthen the authority of his regime, and it is not at all impossible that among some of his subjects he was successful.[26]

Not so, however, among Jews, who reacted with horror at Gaius' plan to have a statue of himself placed for worship in the Temple in Jerusalem. Gaius petulantly refused to accept the claims of the Jews that their unwillingness to worship him as a god did not signify any disloyalty, and this suggests that his insistence on being accorded divine honours had become for him by 40 a matter of principle, regardless of the political impact of his policy. Petronius, the governor of Syria, to whom this desecration of the Temple had been delegated, tried hard to dissuade the emperor from a policy so unnecessarily inflammatory, risking his own life in the process. Gaius' tough response, a refusal to back down or indeed compromise in any way, revealed a despot insistent on imposing his will regardless of the consequences.

When the two sides of Agrippa's double life among Romans and Jews were thus thrown into conflict, he seems to have reacted with a firm and unselfish resolve which it would have been hard to predict from his previous adventurous career. His friendship with Gaius, of which the strength had so recently been tested and found firm, gave him a unique opportunity to help his fellow Jews at a time of immense danger to their central shrine. Despite the danger to himself, Agrippa did not shirk it. His contemporary Philo, the brother of the wealthy Alexandrian whose loan had enabled him to sail for Italy a few years before, was in Rome at the time of the crisis, engaged on an embassy on behalf of Alexandrian Jews, and described Agrippa's intervention at length in an account written a few years later, in which he gave the text of Agrippa's letter to the emperor:

> I, as you know, am by birth a Jew, and my native city is Jerusalem in which is situated the sacred shrine of the most high God. It fell to me to have for my grandparents and ancestors kings, most of whom had the title of High Priest, who considered their kingship inferior to the priesthood, holding that the office of High Priest is as superior in excellence to that of king as God surpasses men. For the office of one is to worship God, of the other to have charge of men. As my lot is cast in such a nation, city and temple I beseech you for them all . . . This temple, my Lord Gaius, has never from the first admitted any figure wrought by men's hands, because it is the sanctuary of the true God. For the works of painters and modellers are representations of gods perceived by sense but to paint or mould a likeness of the invisible was held by our ancestors to be against their religion. Your grandfather Agrippa visited and paid honour to the temple and so did Augustus . . . Your great-grandmother too . . .

The letter noted with fulsome gratitude the benefits that Agrippa had received from the emperor, but then asserted: "I exchange all for one thing only, that the ancestral institutions be not disturbed. For what would be my reputation among either my compatriots or all other men? Either I must seem a traitor to my own or no longer be counted your friend as I have been; there is no other alternative . . ."[27]

Friendship or flattery may well have induced Philo to exaggerate Agrippa's part in saving the Temple from desecration: Philo's nephew married Agrippa's daughter. But for Agrippa to have disagreed at all with a tyrant as wilful as Gaius required considerable courage. And (even more remarkably) Gaius acceded to the request and had a letter sent to Petronius with instructions that nothing was to be changed in Jerusalem. Soon afterwards Gaius changed his mind, but that Agrippa succeeded even temporarily demonstrated the close personal ties that bound him to the most powerful individual in the Roman world. Early in 41 Agrippa's power through such ties was to be demonstrated even more dramatically. His connections were temporarily to put him into a position of extraordinary influence not only over the future of Judaism but over the fate of the whole Roman empire.

In January 41 Gaius' increasing arrogance led him to indulge in a final, fatal series of jests. Asked, as their commander-in-chief, to set the password for the guards to use for the day, he ensured the enmity of Cassius Chaerea, a tribune of a cohort of the praetorian guard, by choosing insulting terms such as "Priapus" or "Venus" in order to mock Chaerea's alleged softness and effeminacy. Chaerea and his fellow conspirators attacked him as he was leaving the Palatine games through a narrow covered passage. Gaius was taken by surprise and his German bodyguards were of little use against the well-armed praetorians. The emperor died on the spot, and his wife and daughter were killed soon after. The state was thrown into confusion. The senators, meeting on the Capitol, announced the restoration of the Republic under the aristocratic leadership of elected consuls, and an end to domination of the state by one man. It appears that the praetorian troops who had killed Gaius had themselves no plans for any successor. It was enough to have done away with the tyrant. But for those like Agrippa, whose career had been so dependent on the favour of individual dynasts, a division of power at the centre of the state between competing aristocrats, a political system that had ended in disastrous bloodshed a century earlier, was not obviously desirable.

In the turmoil after Gaius' assassination, Agrippa led a squad of the praetorian guard to the palace, where Gaius' uncle, the disabled scholar Claudius, was found hiding in fear of his life. Agrippa knew Claudius well: he was the youngest brother of Germanicus, the son of Agrippa's family friend and patroness Antonia, and, being roughly the same age as the Jewish prince, had grown up with him in Rome in the last years of Augustus' rule. At Agrippa's instigation, the praetorians proclaimed Claudius the new emperor. Agrippa may have reminded them that it was in their interest to have an imperial patron if they were to secure their livelihoods: without an emperor, there would be no need for a praetorian guard. It was Agrippa who went to the senators, still locked in conclave, to advise them that they would be wise to abandon talk of restoring Republican rule when so fine a new emperor, already acclaimed by the armed praetorians who surrounded the Senate meeting, awaited their enthusiastic endorsement. Common sense rapidly prevailed, and Claudius was acclaimed as the new ruler of the Roman world.[28]

Agrippa's reward was handsome. Claudius added to his existing territory Judaea and Samaria, so that he became sovereign over a Jewish kingdom as large as had once been ruled by his grandfather Herod. Within his own realm he had absolute power, free of interference by governors of the neighbouring Roman provinces. At the same time, as Cassius Dio records in his *Roman History*, composed in the early third century CE, Claudius "bestowed on Agrippa of Palestine . . . the rank of consul, and to his brother Herod gave the rank of praetor and a principality [in Chalcis, in Lebanon]. And he permitted them to enter the Senate and to express their thanks in Greek." Agrippa was a great foreign king, and a treaty between him and the Senate and people of Rome was ratified formally in the middle of the Forum in the city of Rome. According to his biographer Suetonius, Claudius liked to ratify such treaties in the ancient Roman way with the sacrifice of a pig. We do not know what Agrippa would have thought about the choice of such an offering.[29]

Nonetheless, with his new status Agrippa seems to have decided that his future should be not in Rome but in Jerusalem, his new capital, and he set out almost immediately for Judaea. Within months he was engaged in a project to extend the defensive walls of Jerusalem to enclose within the city the new northern suburbs. Agrippa's ambitions were patent—and, for fellow Romans in the region, a cause of envy and concern. In any case, during the three years of Agrippa's rule in Jerusalem, a series of complaints were made to the emperor by Vibius Marsus, governor of Syria, who professed concern that Agrippa was growing too powerful. Claudius, despite all that he owed to his friend, paid heed to the warnings sufficiently to call a halt to work on the walls. Even more public was Marsus' intervention when Agrippa called a convention, in Tiberias in Galilee, of five fellow kings: Antiochus of Commagene, Sampsigeramus of Emesa, Cotys of Lesser Armenia, Polemon of Pontus and Herod of Chalcis. With all these kings Agrippa had ties of blood or marriage—Herod of Chalcis was his brother—but Marsus chose to interpret their meeting not as a celebration of Agrippa's elevated status but as a conspiracy: "He assumed that agreement among so many dynasts was not advantageous to Roman interests." The kings were summarily dismissed back to their territories. The suspicion that Agrippa might wish to break away from Roman protection was hardly plausible, but, as a member of Claudius' inner circle of friends, he had ties to the emperor far closer than those of most governors, including Vibius Marsus, and his ambitions might prove difficult to control.[30]

Agrippa's death soon after these events in 44 was premature and sudden. He appeared in public in Caesarea looking so splendid in his sparkling silver robes that the people shouted in flattery that he was like a god. Instead of responding to the blasphemy with horror, Agrippa appeared pleased, and (it was later believed) divine retribution was swift. Within days he was dead from an intestinal complaint: in the words of the author of the Acts of the Apostles, "the angel of the Lord smote him, because he gave not to God the glory: and he was eaten of worms, and gave up the ghost." On an inscription set up after his death in the western foothills of the Hauran, Agrippa was described as "Great King, Friend of Caesar, Pious, and Friend of Rome." Coins issued in Caesarea during his rule bear his image and the superscription "Great King Agrippa, Friend of Caesar." Agrippa's intermediary status, between the Jews who revered him in the Temple as their king and the Romans who saw him as an instrument of state control, is a striking example of the general process of patronage through personal friendships which cemented relationships right across the Roman world.[31]

Few people had the contacts, skills or charm to manipulate the system to their advantage as successfully as Agrippa, but, as we have seen, through village or city or some other communal authorities, almost everyone could in theory try to be heard and have their grievances settled or requests fulfilled. Only when Jews in the second century CE became so marginalized in the Roman world that they lacked any entrée into this network of friendships and obligations did it come about that pious Jews who sought help against arbitrariness or injustice in the Roman state would find no patron, not even a friend of a friend of a friend, to represent them at the imperial court. It is impossible to imagine a descendant of Agrippa I representing the interests of Judaism to Hadrian in the 130s CE in the way that Agrippa had braved the wrath of Gaius on behalf of his people and his religion just under a hundred years before.

# A Common Market

THE MEDITERRANEAN world was to a considerable extent an economic as well as a political unity in the first century CE, even though most of its inhabitants at that period were peasants, and most economic activity was directed to the production of foodstuffs for local consumption. Prosperity, fertility, life itself depended on the orderly progression of the seasons. There hung above everyone in the ancient world, to an extent difficult now for people in the developed world to appreciate, the threat of famine when the rains did not come during hot, dry summers, and the threat was only partly alleviated by the possibility of importing grain from elsewhere in the Mediterranean world to lessen the impact of disaster. But the influence of these shared rhythms, arising from a Mediterranean climate, on attitudes to the world and on the shaping of societies should not be exaggerated. Modern tourists, whisked from one site of sun-bleached ruins to another, past endless rocky beaches set against a sparkling blue sea, may feel that the Mediterranean world differs little from Gibraltar to Alexandria or Byzantium, but the impression of continuity is a delusion. The sea and its hinterland comprise a mass of diverse ecologies, which require very different methods of exploitation, a fact disguised by long generations of human interference in the natural landscape. The Mediterranean region is best envisaged as a network of local areas linked by the sea but in other respects remarkably varied in their way of life: there were, in proximity to the sea, areas of woodland exploited for fruit, timber and animal husbandry, as in southern Spain; flood plains whose wetlands produced a constant supply of reeds, as in the delta of the Ebro; fishing bays all along the coast providing a generally reliable harvest from the sea; mountain communities, as in the central Apennines in Italy, flourishing on local grain supplies and (sometimes) long-distance transhumance; even, in Egypt, where it was possible to rely on the annual flooding of the Nile, an irrigation economy requiring state intervention to ensure the best possible distribution of water to the fields.

What unified the Mediterranean economy in the early Roman empire was thus less the climate than the comparative ease with which goods could be traded throughout the region. In his huge and heterogeneous *Natural History*, the elder Pliny (uncle of the younger Pliny, whose correspondence is so revealing about the vicissitudes of life as a provincial governor) described in the 70s CE a great variety of artefacts and manufacturing processes from all over the Roman world and beyond its borders. He could tell his readers about the cutting of marble into thin slabs for use as veneers, "effected apparently by iron, but actually by sand, for the saw merely presses the sand upon a very thinly traced line, and then the passage of the instrument, owing to the rapid movement to and fro, is in itself enough to cut the stone," or the mining of gold "in our part of the world—not to speak of the Indian gold obtained from ants or the gold dug up by griffins in Scythia—obtained in three ways: in the detritus of rivers . . . by sinking shafts; or in the fallen debris of mountains." He could describe in detail industrial processes from all over the Roman world, such as the making of glass, which had recently undergone major changes:

A fire of light, dry wood is used for preparing the melt, to which are added copper and soda, preferably Egyptian soda. Glass, like copper, is melted in a series of furnaces, and dull black lumps are formed . . . After being reduced to lumps, the glass is again fused in the workshop and is tinted. Some of it is shaped by blowing, some machined on a lathe and some chased like silver . . . This was the old method of producing glass. Now, however, in Italy too a white sand which forms in the River Volturnus is found along six miles of the seashore between Cumae and Liternum. Wherever it is softest, it is taken to be ground . . . mixed with three parts of soda . . . melted . . . and forms pure glass . . . There is a story that in the reign of Tiberius there was invented a method of blending glass so as to render it flexible. The artists' workshop was completely destroyed for fear that the value of metals such as copper, silver and gold would otherwise be lowered.

But, Pliny adds, this last story "has for a long time been more frequent than certain."

Despite his willingness to believe in the possibility of Indian gold ants and Scythian griffins, Pliny's account of industries closer to home was based on a great deal of knowledge. He is also a reliable guide to the nature of the exotic products imported from outside the empire's frontiers:

Frankincense after being collected is conveyed to Sabota [in Yemen] on camels . . . At Sabota a tithe estimated by measure and not by weight is

taken by the priests for the god they call Sabis . . . It can only be
exported through the country of the Gebbanitae, and accordingly a tax
is paid on it to the king of that people as well. Their capital is Thomna,
which is 1,487½ miles distant from the town of Gaza in Judaea on the
Mediterranean coast; the journey is divided into sixty-five stages with
halts for camels. Fixed portions of the frankincense are also given to the
priests and the king's secretaries . . . Indeed all along the route they
keep on paying . . . and then again payment is made to the tax farmers
of our empire. Consequently the price of the best frankincense is six, of
the second best five, and of the third best three denarii a pound.

At any rate, it is clear that both for luxury products and for those of moderate value, production on a large scale and long-distance distribution
proved often to be worthwhile.[32]

Even a brief glance at the archaeological record of the Mediterranean
world in the first two centuries CE confirms Pliny's assertions about the
high volume of trade. The hazards of survival favour pottery above other
materials—it is quite difficult to destroy a pot so thoroughly that no trace
of its original appearance can be detected. From millions of potsherds
archaeologists have traced the distribution of fine red Samian wares from
their manufacturing bases in Italy and southern Gaul to many places
around the Mediterranean and into northern Europe. The increased inci-
dence of shipwrecks in this period is testimony to the large volume of
seaborne trade, unless (as is unlikely) ships were either much less seaworthy
or more unlucky. In some cases, traces of their varied cargoes survive to
reveal tellingly the ambitions of their owners: quarried marble, amphorae
stacked in layers in their thousands, filled with oil or wine, mixing bowls
from Italy, amphorae from Rhodes filled with figs, and amphorae of a different kind, probably from Africa, containing dates. Transport by land was
far more expensive, but evidently worthwhile for high-value goods and (as
is clear from the distribution of the archaeological remains) even for
cheaper products, like mass-produced pottery lamps, if they were not too
heavy or bulky.

The contribution of pan-Mediterranean trade to the total economy of
the early Roman empire was considerable, but it should not be exaggerated. It remains the case that fluctuations in the price of traded goods are
best understood if the Roman world is analysed not as a single market but

as a series of linked local markets. Most Mediterranean cities relied on production from the immediate vicinity to feed their populations; in this respect, the city of Rome itself was an exception. Much trade was with neighbouring regions. Most shipping hugged the coast and rarely strayed more than a few days from their home port. Navigable rivers were an important means of distribution: the Greek historian Dionysius of Halicarnassus noted in the time of Augustus that the trees which grew on Mount Sila (in modern Calabria) were so densely intertwined that they "keep the mountain in shadow throughout the whole day," and were "sufficient in quantity to serve all Italy for shipbuilding and the construction of houses . . . What grows nearest to the sea and rivers is felled at the root and taken down in full lengths to the nearest harbours . . . What grows inland from the sea and remote from rivers is cut up in sections . . . and is carried out on men's shoulders."[33]

But another Greek observer, Strabo, describing part of southern Spain at roughly the same time as Dionysius wrote about Italy, knew of trade on a genuinely international scale:

> All the trade of the country [around Seville] is carried on with Italy and Rome. There is good sailing [on the Atlantic] up to the Pillars [the Strait of Gibraltar] . . . and also on our sea [the Mediterranean]; for the sea routes all pass through a zone of fair weather, particularly if the sailor keeps to open sea, a fact helpful to merchant freighters. And, further, the winds on the open sea are regular. And added is the present state of peace, with piracies broken up, so that the sailor can be totally at ease.

For Strabo, from the far eastern end of the Mediterranean, near the Black Sea, to claim the Mediterranean at its extreme west as "our sea" is itself an illustration of the perceived unity of the Mediterranean world in his day. When he stressed the importance of the suppression of piracy on the Mediterranean, achieved by Roman generals in a series of campaigns in the first century BCE, he had perhaps ruefully in mind the continuing prevalence of piracy on the Black Sea near his own home city of Amaseia:

> These peoples [the Achaei, Zygi and Heniochi] live by robberies at sea. Their boats are slender, narrow, and light, holding only about twenty-

five people, though in rare cases they can hold thirty in all . . . At any rate, by equipping fleets . . . and sailing sometimes against merchant vessels and sometimes against a country or even a city, they hold the mastery of the sea. And they are sometimes assisted even by those who hold the Bosporus, the latter supplying them with mooring-places, with a marketplace, and with means of disposing of their booty. And since, when they return to their own land, they have no anchorage, they put the boats on their shoulders and carry them to the forests where they live and where they till a poor soil. And they bring the boats down to the shore again when the time for navigation comes. And they do the same thing in the countries of others, for they are well acquainted with wooded places; and in these they first hide their boats and then themselves wander on foot night and day for the sake of kidnapping people. But they readily offer to release their captives for ransom, informing their relatives after they have put out to sea. Now in those places which are ruled by local chieftains the rulers go to the aid of those who are wronged, often attacking and bringing back the boats men and all. But the territory that is subject to the Romans affords but little aid, because of the negligence of the governors who are sent there.[34]

Some of the ships used for trans-Mediterranean trade were up to four hundred tonnes, a size similar to the merchant vessels used in Europe in the sixteenth to eighteenth centuries. They could sail on most quarters of the wind, but they could be held up for long periods by bad weather and they never sailed in winter. Investment in a cargo was intrinsically risky, and Roman law facilitated the spread of both risk and profit by companies in which individuals might buy shares. These were complex operations requiring substantial capital. In some cases this was facilitated by the legal capacity of a freedman or slave to negotiate on behalf of his master or former master, but on most inscriptions which refer to merchants (*negotiatores* in Latin, *emporoi* in Greek), the individuals concerned are ex-slaves, and it is most likely that the effort and risk involved in these transactions appealed most to the upwardly mobile, although there is plenty of evidence that richer Romans might try to add to their fortunes by lending money on interest to such enterprises.

Quantification of trade in different products is necessarily only very rough. Huge amounts of olive oil, used not just for food but for lighting and as an ingredient in soaps, cosmetics and medicines, were exported from the western Mediterranean to central Italy despite competition with local Italian olive production. Similarly large quantities of higher-quality wine were shipped to the larger cities all over the empire. The surviving amphorae found in the central Italian town of Pompeii suggest an even more flourishing business importing to Italy gallons of *garum*, fermented fish sauce, used as a condiment. Trade in these products can be traced from the pots in which they were stored, but pottery itself was also worth transporting to distant markets, probably most often as a subsidiary rather than a main cargo. The elder Pliny notes the popularity in his day of pottery from different manufacturing centres: "Among table services, Samian is still praised. This reputation is also retained by Arretium [Arezzo] in Italy . . . Also Tralles in Asia Minor and Mutina [Modena] in Italy have their respective products, since even thus are peoples made famous and these products from the distinguished workshops of the potter's wheel are carried to and fro across seas and land."[35] Goldsmiths, silversmiths and other craftsmen in towns and cities all over the empire relied on supplies of metals, both precious and base, transported by private shippers. The trade in marble elicited moralizing reflections from Pliny:

> Mountains, however, were made by nature for herself to serve as a kind of framework for holding firmly together the inner parts of the earth, and at the same time to enable her to subdue the violence of rivers, to break the force of heavy seas and so to curb her most restless elements with the hardest material of which she is made. We quarry these mountains and haul them away for a mere whim; and yet there was a time when it seemed remarkable even to have succeeded in crossing them. Our forefathers considered the scaling of the Alps by Hannibal and later by the Cimbri to be almost unnatural. Now these selfsame Alps are quarried into marble of a thousand varieties. Headlands are laid open to the sea, and nature is flattened. We remove the barriers created to serve as the boundaries of nations, and ships are built specially for marble. And so, over the waves of the sea, Nature's wildest element, mountain ranges are transported to and fro . . . When we hear of the prices paid for these vessels, when we see the masses of marble that are being conveyed or hauled, we should each of us reflect, and at the same time think how much more happily many people live without them. That

men should do such things, or rather endure them, for no purpose or pleasure except to lie amid spotted marbles, just as if these delights were not taken from us by the darkness of night, which is half our life's span![36]

Pliny had rather more sympathy for the extensive trade in papyrus from Egypt, "since our civilization, or at all events our memory, depends very largely on the employment of paper." Wooden slats, wax tablets and animal skins were also used as writing materials, but papyrus was preferred, and hence liable to shortages: "as early as the principate of Tiberius," writes Pliny, "a shortage of paper led to the appointment of judges to supervise its distribution, since otherwise life was in chaos."[37] In contrast, the flourishing slave-trade was less likely to be affected by a dearth than by a glut, when the market was flooded by prisoners of war. A more regular supply was provided by breeding from existing slaves, the sale of children unwanted by their parents, and the importing of "barbarians" from across the frontiers of the empire, as on the Black Sea, where Strabo notes that Tanais "was a common emporium, partly of the Asiatic and the European nomads, and partly of those who navigated the lake from the Bosporus, the former bringing slaves, hides and such other things as nomads possess, and the latter giving in exchange clothing, wine and the other things that belong to civilized life."[38] Some indication of the size of the market in slave sales can be gauged from Cassius Dio's report of the imposition by Augustus in 7 CE of a tax on each transaction: "as there was need of more money for the wars and for the support of the night-guards, he introduced the tax of a fiftieth on the sale of slaves."[39]

The flow of trade was affected above all by the overwhelming size of the consumer market in the city of Rome and the rest of Italy. Monte Testaccio, a huge artificial hill near the Tiber south of the Aventine, consists entirely of pieces of broken pottery from vessels which once contained goods transported to the city, mostly from Spain, between the first and the mid-third centuries CE. Strabo notes that the sheep and pigs of Gaul "supply an abundance of cloth and salt meats not only to Rome but also to most parts of Italy."[40] The success of specialist olive production on a large scale in Tripolitania (in western Libya) was achieved by using local techniques for the management of scarce water resources, but the incentive for such production came from access to the market in imperial Rome. Not that free trade benefited all. Strabo notes that competition has slowed down mining around Vercelli in the Po valley, once a major source of gold: "as for the mines, at the present time they are not being worked as seriously as before—perhaps on account of the fact that those in the country of the Transalpine Celts and in Iberia are more profitable."[41] The state showed little interest in protectionism, or indeed in any interference in the operation of the economy, except in so far as it affected the income of the state itself. Suetonius records that the emperor Domitian once "issued an edict forbidding anyone to plant more vines in Italy and ordering that the vineyards in the provinces be cut down, or at most just half of them be left standing."[42] It is interesting that Italy received preferential treatment, but the reason was probably more political than economic, since it was in the city of Rome that emperors sought public acknowledgement of their popularity and power. In any case, the incentive for the edict was moral: it had been occasioned by the coincidence of a bumper wine harvest with a shortage of grain, which prompted ruminations on the need to get back to old Roman values of sobriety. In practice, the measure was never put into effect.

Most trans-Mediterranean trade was carried out by individual entrepreneurs using private capital, but it would be misleading to underestimate the impact of the demands of the state in promoting the transfer of goods. The literary sources have most to say about the corn trade, which at the height of the empire involved fleets of ships carrying grain to Rome from Sicily, North Africa and Egypt to ensure the food supply of the city, but the predominance of evidence about this particular state intervention reflects its political as much as its economic significance. It may well be that the efforts of the state to extract metals for coinage and marble for public building projects had no less of an impact on the economy. Traces of ancient gold-mining methods from the hills of Spain and Portugal, revealing the operation of water power to extract ore by crushing rocks beneath water released from pent-up streams, attest to the efficiency with which the government built aqueducts over miles of mountainous terrain in order to redirect water supplies to the places where they could operate to the greatest commercial advantage. Thousands of ostraca excavated at Mons Claudianus, a fortified village in the eastern desert mountains of Egypt, reveal a huge operation in the exploitation of the imperial quarry in the first three centuries CE, including the supply of granite columns to Rome in the early second century CE for the new forum built by the emperor Trajan.[43]

Even if it is impossible to know what proportion of the empire's economy was fuelled directly by state expenditure or direction, and how much depended on the decisions taken by the thousands of individuals who turned the political unity of the Roman world to their commercial advantage, the cumulative effect on the Mediterranean world of all this industrial activity has been illuminated, rather surprisingly, by discoveries far to the north, in the Arctic Circle. Analysis of the ice floes, which have accreted annually since antiquity, has shown that the level of metal residues released into the world's atmosphere reached a peak in the first two centuries CE which was not to be equalled again in volume until the Industrial Revolution.[44] To some extent productivity was encouraged, if not instigated, by the discovery of new technologies. Fascination with technical advances shines through the pages written on architecture by Vitruvius in the early years of Augustus, or the works on the aqueducts of the city of Rome and on military stratagems composed a century later by the distinguished senator Sextus Iulius Frontinus. Vitruvius' treatise, in ten books, covers not just architecture but many other topics in science and engineering (with an odd admixture of mathematics, astronomy, medicine, meteorology and philosophy), and it includes some detailed descriptions of complex machines, such as a set of pulleys which operated rather like a crane, and could be used to load and unload ships—"a machine ingenious enough and suitable for speedy use; but only skilled workmen can deal with it. Three sets of men working without a capstan quickly draw a load to the top. This kind of machine is called *polyspaston* [a compound pulley], because within its many pulleys it is very easy and quick to work."[45] Suetonius, in his biography of the emperor, tells the story of an engineer who promised Vespasian that he would haul columns up to the Capitol at minimal expense, presumably by making use of some sort of machine. According to Suetonius, Vespasian rejected the scheme on the grounds that it would render too many workmen unemployed, but he rewarded the engineer for his invention, and Suetonius' telling of the anecdote suggests that refusal to take advantage of technical progress was unusual rather than the norm.[46]

All these specific private and public initiatives flourished in a world in many respects economically unified by the political will of the Roman state. Economic unity was symbolized by the use of a currency standard common to almost all parts of the empire. The mints at Rome and Lyons were responsible for producing the gold coinage (*aurei*) for the whole empire, and silver *denarii* and bronze fractions of the *denarii* for the western provinces. In the eastern Mediterranean, provincial mints produced silver coins to a drachma standard which was closely equivalent to the standard of the *denarii* issued in Rome, and local city mints produced bronze coins valued at fractions of the drachma. It is curious that in the early empire there *were* such local mints, with distinctive local designs, but in economic terms what mattered was that all these coins could in principle be freely traded and their values understood. The relationship between the gold, silver and bronze coins minted in Rome was redefined differently at intervals by different emperors—Nero devalued the amount of gold to be found in an *aureus* and the amount of silver in a *denarius*. Only Egypt seems to have had a wholly separate monetary system, based on the Alexandrian tetradrachm, although local systems of measurement remained in many other places. Above all, the safe transport of goods throughout much of the Roman world was afforded by the protection of Roman arms. Seafaring could never be wholly safe despite the cessation of larger-scale piracy in the eastern Mediterranean after Pompey's campaigns in the 60s BCE, and banditry was endemic in many mountainous areas throughout the imperial period, but Roman military roads, primarily intended for the safe passage of troops, became major trading arteries. The merchants who benefited from the expenditure and efforts of the state could feel appropriately grateful as they read the commemorative milestones which still survive in abundance even in quite obscure places. A traveller by the Danube would be reminded, by an inscription cut into the natural rock near Orşova in Romania, that "the emperor Caesar Nerva Trajan Augustus Germanicus . . . had this road built by cutting through mountains and levelling irregularities."[47]

The army also stimulated economic productivity in less obvious ways. In the provinces where units were stationed the presence of a group of consumers with a guaranteed substantial income from the state encouraged local production to meet their requirements, a process particularly noticeable in northern parts of the empire, where legionary forts in places like Chester, originally walled off from the local population, came in time to be surrounded by shanty towns housing camp followers. The state's need to pay the soldiers required efficient extraction of a high level of taxation income, and that in turn stimulated the tax-paying provincials into greater production in order to continue to support themselves while also paying their dues to Rome. Payments to and by soldiers ensured both a large total supply of coin and its wide distribution from the empire's centre to the frontier provinces. The comparative safety of transport links encouraged the emergence of trans-regional businesses. According to the elder Pliny, "six owners were in possession of one half of the province of Africa at the time when the emperor Nero had them put to death."[48] These were absentee landlords, exploiting the ready market in the city of Rome for grain from Africa and other cash crops, notably olive oil; many, like the emperor himself, will have been Italian. The property of Augustus' friend Marcus Vipsanius Agrippa included the whole Thracian Chersonese, which passed on his death into the emperor's private domain. In almost every province the emperor and his family were by far the largest landowners, with huge estates entrusted to local agents, who might exploit agricultural land by leasing to tenants, or mines and quarries by the direct employment of slaves. In all such cases, control of local management could be sporadic. An inscription from Suk-el-Khemis in the Medjerba valley in Algeria records a petition to the emperor Commodus in the early 180s by tenants of an imperial estate in North Africa. The tenants alleged that the emperor's agent had colluded with the chief lessees against the tenants' interests by making them offer more free labour than they should:

> Please help us, and—since we are poor rustic men sustaining life by the toil of our hands and unequal, in our relations with your agents, to the lessee, who stands very high in their favour because of his lavish gifts and is well known to each of them in succession by virtue of the lease— please have pity on us, and deign to instruct by your sacred rescript that we are to perform no more service than we are obliged to . . . that is, three periods of two days' work per man.[49]

Judaea was in many ways integrated into this wider economic world, not least through the wealth imported into the country by pilgrims or sent to the Temple as offerings. From early in the first century CE the balsam groves of En Gedi by the Dead Sea were a lucrative private estate of the emperor, just as they had previously been the private property of Herod the Great (and, before him, briefly, Cleopatra, the queen of Egypt). An estate around Jamnia near the Mediterranean coast passed by bequest from

Salome, one of Herod's wives, to Livia, Augustus' consort; from her, it passed to her son, the emperor Tiberius, following which it remained the property of successive emperors. This particular imperial estate was to play a crucial role in the political history of Judaea. It was Tiberius' agent in Jamnia, a certain Capito, who nearly succeeded in imprisoning Agrippa I as a debtor of the emperor in the mid-30s CE. Some thirty years later Jamnia became the place of detention for aristocratic Jews who deserted Jerusalem in the last months of the revolt against Rome. In the early 70s, so it was later alleged, it was the site of the most influential rabbinic academy of the day, so that its Hebrew name, Yavneh, became synonymous in later rabbinic tradition with the period of rabbinic reconstruction of Judaism after the destruction of the Temple.

Since Judaea lacked any exceptional natural resources apart from the balsam groves, investment by foreign landowners other than the emperor is unrecorded and unlikely. Apart from exploitation of the balsam, there will have been few opportunities to specialize effectively in the production of cash crops for the wider Mediterranean market. The elder Pliny and other non-Jewish observers noted a few specialties of the region: the salt fish of Tarichaeae on the Sea of Galilee; the asphalt harvested from the Dead Sea, which had medicinal uses; the remarkably sweet juicy dates produced by Judaean palms. (It is probably significant that a common pictorial symbol of Judaea on coins issued both by Rome and by the independent Jewish state in 66–70 was a date palm.) In a document drawn up on 2 December 127, at a government office in Rabbat, east of the Dead Sea, four date groves in Maoza were registered by their owner, as part of a provincial census ordered by the Roman governor. Each grove was precisely defined and described: "within the boundaries of Maoza a date orchard called Bethphaaraia, the area of sowing twenty sata of barley . . . abutting [the property of] Tamar daughter of Thamous, and a road." Most of the tax to be paid on these date orchards was to be delivered in kind: "paying as tax, in dates . . . three kaboi, 'splits' two koroi, and for crown tax eight 'blacks' and forty-five sixtieths."[50]

## A CULTURAL CONTINUUM

DESPITE THE POLITICAL and economic force of the Roman state, the underlying cultural unity of the Mediterranean world was less Roman than Greek. From the third century BCE to the second century CE, the civilization of classical Athens in the fifth and fourth centuries BCE represented the pinnacle of human achievement to many inhabitants of the Mediterranean world, even though by the first century CE Athens was a political backwater, and admirers of Greek culture might never visit, or even have any historical connection with, Greece itself. The impetus for the spread of Greek culture in the Near East following the conquests of Alexander the Great had been political, since Alexander and his successors gave preferential treatment to those in local elites who openly espoused Greek culture. As the Athenian orator Isocrates (436–338 BCE) put it, rather fulsomely, in the generation before Alexander, "our city [Athens] has so much surpassed the rest of mankind in thought and in speech that her students have become the teachers of the rest of humanity, and she has made the name of the Hellenes [Greeks] to seem to be no more the name of the race but of a way of thought, so that those who share our education, more than those who share a common nature, are to be called Hellenes."[51]

Much of this shared Greek culture seems so natural now to those educated in the European tradition that only contrast with quite radically different societies—in China, for instance, or in New Guinea—can bring home properly the distinctive characteristics, such as the high value assigned to logical argument, which have endured in Western society since antiquity. Classical Athens had a highly politicized culture, in which rhetoric, spoken or written, was prized not least as a tool of political persuasion. Visual arts celebrated the external appearance of the idealized human form. Drama and poetry sought to encapsulate the dilemmas of individuals in extreme circumstances, most notably when duties to family or community came into conflict with each other, and philosophers strove to find a logical basis for the moral and political structures of societies.

It was in Athens that Plato and Aristotle had taught in the fourth century BCE, and after the death of Alexander the Great the city became home to distinguished philosophers from all over the Greek world who set up schools there. Plato's own school at the Academy moved away from his interests to deal mainly with ethics and, from the mid-third century BCE, to preach rejection of all kinds of dogmatism. The Lyceum, where Aristotle had taught, became a centre for scientific research. Epicurus (341–270) founded a close community which sought pleasure derived from imperturbability, to be achieved by the realization that the universe runs of its own volition and that man is simply a collection of atoms, and by avoidance of any activity which might arouse emotion. Most influential of all was Zeno (335–263), whose school of Stoics was named after the *stoa poikile*, "painted hall," where they met. Stoicism developed considerably during the Hellenistic period as it gained popularity, but it was always based on the tenet that the only good lies in virtue, which means living in accordance with the will of nature. The ideas of these philosophers spread throughout the Greek-speaking world, as did the more idiosyncratic scepticism taught by Pyrrhon of Elis (*c.* 365–275), who advocated a refusal to make any positive judgements at all, and the diatribes against the vanity of human pretensions preached by wandering Cynics, who all took their inspiration from the distinctive unconventional life ascribed to Diogenes of Sinope (*c.* 412–*c.* 321), even if their specific doctrines often diverged considerably.

From this varied legacy the search for rationality, explanations, order and beauty became integral, at least in very general terms, to all later European civilizations. All of the different societies in the Mediterranean world under Roman rule adopted and used aspects of this Greek culture in one way or another, even if in the West it was generally mediated through Latin. Hellenism proved very adaptable. The Greek pattern of education, which placed a high premium on teaching children to read and write and, at secondary level, on the exposition of literary texts, was followed in cities and towns throughout the Roman world. The main elements of the literary canon were generally accepted in the Greek world by the first century: the poems of Homer above all, then the tragic plays of Euripides, the comedies of Menander and the speeches of Demosthenes; but children also studied other epic poems, drama and lyric poetry and (although less) the prose of historians (especially Thucydides) and the moral fables of Aesop and Babrius. In the West a parallel canon of Latin writings took the place of the Greek. The rather tedious teaching methods revealed in schoolbooks found in Roman Egypt seem to have been standard. A great deal of learning was done by recitation and constant repetition, and by committing lists to heart: in appreciation of the *Iliad*, a child might be asked "which gods were favourable to the Trojans?" (expected answer, in alphabetical order, "Aphrodite, Apollo, Ares, Artemis, Leto, Scamander") or "who was the king of the Trojans?" (answer: "Priam").[52] Sciences and mathematics were taught, but literary studies were accorded much greater attention in a society that valued highly the written word (including the preservation of

huge numbers of commemorative texts on stone). At the same time Greek
rhetorical education, which involved training both in the evolution of
coherent arguments and in public declamation, served a purpose in urban
political life at many levels, not least because oral presentation of petitions
played a major role in the relationship between inhabitants of the empire
and the representatives of the state. Greek philosophy was less commonly
studied as part of the ordinary school curriculum—such higher education
was the preserve of the wealthy—but philosophical ideas were popularized
in the commonplaces inscribed on gravestones, with their references to the
concepts of the soul, fortune and fate, or to a lifetime as a thread spun by
the divine, or to death as the repayment of a life which had only ever been
on temporary loan. In the towns of Roman Spain, a schoolboy might be
unwittingly educated in the basics of Stoic and Platonic notions about the
world soul and its relation to the individual simply through study of the
speech of Anchises to his son Aeneas in Vergil's epic poem.

This was a culture shared across the Mediterranean sea: no half-
educated person in this world could be unaware of the stories in Homer's
*Iliad* and *Odyssey*. At the same time, the poems of Homer could be revered
by millions without imposing a Homeric value system or lifestyle on those
who treated them as founts of wisdom. On the contrary—and in this
respect there is a close parallel to the use of the Bible in medieval Europe—
no one in the first century CE wished to live literally in the moral universe
of Achilles or Odysseus.

The cultural consensus in according prestige to Greek culture ensured
that provincial aristocrats in all parts of the Mediterranean world in the
first century CE could be certain of much common ground with their
counterparts elsewhere. As one travelled from one urban centre to another,
from Spain to Syria, most of the cities looked and felt very much alike:
small towns, with rarely more than ten thousand inhabitants, with the
standard accoutrements of marketplace, temples, theatres, and often gym-
nasia and baths; local elites committed to participation in local government
based on shared responsibility exercised through a city council and elected
magistrates; monumental columnar façades and porticoes which continued
to make much use of the traditional Greek orders of architecture (Doric,
Ionic and Corinthian). Even in the West, where Latin was the lingua franca,
it was possible to get by as a trader with Greek as your only language, as
seems also to have been the case among early Christians in Rome and in

Gaul. Indeed the remarkable cosmopolitanism of the early Christian movement is in itself a testimony to the ubiquity of Hellenism. Paul, who came from Cilicia (in modern Turkey), could expect the complex arguments expressed in his letters, composed in a sophisticated Greek, to be comprehensible to fellow believers not just in Asia Minor, Syria and Greece but in Rome and Jerusalem too.

Nevertheless, the prestige of Greek culture, and the widespread adoption of much Greek lifestyle and ways of thinking, did not mean that everyone in the first-century-CE Mediterranean world thought of themselves as Greek. On the contrary, a surface Greek culture might disguise a variety of underlying local cultural patterns, whose nature might indeed sometimes be described most elegantly in Greek: in the mid-first century CE the Egyptian priest Chaeremon of Alexandria wrote in Greek about Egyptian religion and customs in order to educate both fellow Egyptians and the outside world. The adoption of Greek culture provided opportunities for such people not to abandon their native traditions but to express them in different ways. The *Phoenician History* of Philo of Byblos, apparently written at the beginning of the second century CE, claims (spuriously) to be a translation for a Greek readership of a work on the Phoenician gods written by a certain Sanchuniathon some time before the Trojan War, but most of his account of the nature and origins of the gods and his adventurous etymologies (often relating to Greek names) seems to have been a product of his Greek education and a desire to make sense in Greek terms of practices not properly understood by Phoenicians themselves.[53]

The relation of Romans and Jews to Greek culture was not dissimilar to that of these other Mediterranean peoples, and Rome and Jerusalem would have provided good examples of the adoption and adaption of Hellenism around the first century CE even if they did not have a special claim on our interest. Thus Rome was never conquered by Greeks but, as Horace puts it, "Greece captured has taken captive the savage victor and brought the arts to rustic Latium": the image is of a beautiful slave-girl, a prisoner of war, who captures the boorish heart of her master and teaches him refinement.[54] From at least the late third century BCE, Romans tended to see themselves, and all the world, through Greek categories of historiography, ethnography and myth. Their art, architecture, sculpture, poetry, drama, rhetorical techniques, philosophical traditions and even some of their religious practices had all been borrowed to some extent from Greece. Romans knew this well, and that it had come about largely because in the process of conquering the Greek world from the late third century BCE Roman aristocrats had become uneasily aware of the poverty of their own martial, agrarian culture in contrast to a complex civilization which had matured during centuries of settled urban prosperity.

By the first century CE the Romans themselves debated only the extent to which Hellenization had enhanced or swamped traditional Roman values, and whether Greek influence was to be welcomed or rejected. The great moralist Cato the Censor, the archetypical "antique Roman," who dominated the political and cultural life of Rome in the first half of the second century BCE, had argued fiercely against the infiltration of foreign ideas which might sap the moral fibre of his countrymen, but he did so with the aid of rhetorical techniques which had themselves been learned from the Greeks, and he was the first, in his *Origines*, to bring into the field of Latin prose literature the Greek art of historiography. Hostility combined with acceptance was a recurring pattern, although sometimes Greek customs were adopted as Roman without Romans noticing quite what had happened. The historian Livy (59 BCE–12 CE) knew that the god Apollo had long been worshipped in Greece before cult was first accorded to him in Rome in the fifth century BCE, when a temple was vowed to him "on behalf of the health of the people," but once Livy's contemporary Augustus had adopted Apollo as his special god, dedicating a new temple to him on the Palatine close to the imperial palace, the Apollo cult came to be seen as entirely Roman.[55]

The attitude of Jews to the Greek culture they adopted and adapted was equally ambivalent. Distaste for Greeks, inspired by political realities in the world order after Alexander the Great's conquests, spilled over in the last chapter of the biblical book of Daniel, composed in the second century BCE, into rhetoric about the incipient fall of the Greek empire, the last of the four kingdoms envisaged in God's plan as revealed to the seer. The vituperation, found in many Jewish texts, against all gentile practices as constitutive of actual or incipient pagan worship, may sometimes have had specifically Greek gentiles in mind, although, even at the height of Jewish awareness of the dangers posed to Judaism by Greek culture around the time of the revolt of the Maccabees (see Chapter 1), the gentile customs lambasted by Jewish authors tended to be generic. The specific gentiles singled out for hostility by the author of 1 Maccabees were such neighbouring people as Ammonites and Gileadites. The author of the Wisdom of Solomon, a work (now found in the Apocrypha) composed by a philosophically minded Jew probably in the second century BCE, reserved his polemic for the animal gods of the Egyptians: "Miserable are they, and in dead things are their hopes, who called them gods, which are the works of men's hands, gold and silver, to show art in, and resemblances of beasts . . ."[56]

For more specific attacks by Jews on Greeks for their cultural traits, the earliest specific testimony is to be found only in the apologetic treatise *Against Apion*. This was Josephus' last literary work, written in the mid-90s CE to refute misconceptions in the Greek and Roman world about Jews and Judaism and as a polemic against those Greek authors who peddled such lies. Josephus portrays Greeks as fickle, prone either to forget or to change their laws, sexually immoral, unduly enthusiastic about innovation, inclined to value rhetorical style above historical accuracy, unable to put their fine words into practice, lacking any real regard even for their own nation's writings, and contradicting each other even about their own history. As Josephus puts it, picking up an internal Greek critique to be found in the writings of Plato, "among the Greeks, everything is new, dating, so to speak, from yesterday and the day before." The list of Greek vices seems to owe more to the catalogue of Roman sneers against Greeks than anything Josephus is likely to have picked up from his Jewish literary heritage. In metropolitan Rome in Josephus' day, provincial intellectuals competed fiercely for the attention of the imperial court and other wealthy patrons. The trading of insults between individual writers, and between one group and another, was endemic. The same caricatures of Greeks which had surfaced three centuries earlier in the polemic of Cato the Censor could still be espoused, now in a satirical poem, by the Latin author Juvenal (himself from Spain), and only partly in jest: "There is a race of men which the very wealthiest among us find highly acceptable socially, but which I avoid above all others. About this race I am eager to speak, and no shyness shall stand in my way. Citizens, I cannot bear a Rome that has become a Greek city. And yet, what portion of the dregs in our city comes from Greece?" The reasons for Juvenal's venom about Greeks as glib and brash may have been personal, but he expected his Roman readers to appreciate his sentiments.[57]

Both Jews and Romans wanted the best of both worlds. They wanted to adopt and borrow from Greek culture whatever they liked, while despising the Greeks. In Greek literature written by Jews the audacious

claim was sometimes made that the best things in Greek culture came from
the Jews. A Jewish writer of the mid-second century BCE named Eupolemus picked up the tradition, well known to Greeks, that Greeks learned
their alphabet from the Phoenicians, but added the novel twist that the
Phoenicians in turn got their alphabet from the Jews. Artapanus, probably
a contemporary of Eupolemus, attributes to Moses—"he was called Mou-
saios by the Greeks; this Moses became teacher of Orpheus"—the invention of "ships, and machines for lifting stones . . . and philosophy." One
might imagine from Josephus' rude comments about Greeks in *Against
Apion* that he would wish to distance Jews from responsibility for what
Greeks had achieved, but, rather inconsistently, he portrays Plato as having
followed to some degree the example of Moses. The bizarre idea that
Plato's philosophical system was only an elaboration of the Jewish law
underlay the whole voluminous religious and philosophical agenda of
Philo, the aristocratic Jew from Alexandria who had acted as an ambas-
sador for his community before Gaius in the crisis of 40 CE and who was
described by Josephus as "not inexperienced in philosophy."[58]

No such claim to priority over the Greeks was made by any Roman.
Some Romans enthusiastically adopted the notion, enshrined in and to
some degree stimulated by Vergil's *Aeneid*, that the foundation of Rome
had been bound up with the heroic history of early Greece, when Aeneas
escaped from the sacked city of Troy at the end of the Trojan War. Jews also
occasionally linked their own origins to Greeks in similar fashion, notably
with the curious assertion, found in 1 Maccabees, that Jews and Spartans
shared a common ancestry, an idea rendered no less implausible by the
apparent willingness of the Spartans to agree with it in a letter sent to
Judaea at the time of the Maccabean revolt in response to a Jewish embassy:
"Areus, king of the Spartans to Onias, the great priest, greeting: 'It has been
found in a writing about the Spartans and Jews that they are brethren and
that they are of the family of Abraham.' " Neither Jews nor Romans were
unusual in the Mediterranean world in their search into Greek prehistory
for such links to their origins. Many people besides the Romans claimed a
link to Troy, and claims of Spartan ancestry were quite common.[59]

Lacking in either the Jewish or the Roman evidence is any sign of a serious concern, after the first generations of cultural fusion in the second century BCE, that adoption of Greek culture would eradicate native traditions.
Among the Romans the polemical tone of Cato was dropped in favour of

the language of adaptation: there was no need for Romans to reject Hellenism, but they had to ensure that it did not infringe values that Romans held dear. In the process the Romans constructed some contrasts which for centuries afterwards retained a strong hold on their self-image, such as the notion—found in the juxtaposition by Cicero (106–43 BCE) of the theoretical scientific achievements of the Greeks compared to Roman expertise in engineering—that Greeks were interested only in ideas whereas Romans were practical.

By the first century CE much the same ambivalence towards Greek culture was true also of the Jews. The struggles before and during the Maccabean revolt in the second century BCE had produced a stronger rhetoric against Greek culture than in Rome. The traumatic persecution by Antiochus Epiphanes was portrayed both by Jews and by gentiles as an attempt to impose Greek culture on a native population unwilling to change ancestral customs—according to the Roman historian Tacitus, Antiochus Epiphanes had "tried to give to the Jews the customs of the Greeks"; for the Jewish author of 2 Maccabees, an emotional retelling of the story of the revolutionary struggle intended to edify diaspora Jewish readers of later generations, the struggle was between two abstract concepts, *ioudaismos* ("Jewishness" or perhaps "Judaean-ness"), a neologism by the author of 2 Maccabees, and *hellenismos*, the ways of the Greeks.[60] But the opposition to Greek ways within Jewish society, which had been part of the rallying cry of the Maccabees, did not last long. The author of 2 Maccabees attacked Jason, the High Priest who had been replaced by the Maccabees, because he

took delight in establishing a gymnasium right under the citadel itself, and induced the finest of the young men to wear the *petasos* hat [the special broad-brimmed felt hat used by athletes]. Such was the acme of Hellenism . . . No longer were the priests interested in the service of the altar. Despising the Temple and neglecting the sacrifices, they would hasten to participate in the unlawful exercises of the palaestra as soon as the summons came for the discus-throwing. They valued as nothing the customs their fathers honoured, and coveted only the Greek honours as worthy of attainment. Because of this, dire calamity fell upon them . . .

But, in contrast to the horror expressed by the author of this text at such "new customs forbidden by the law," by the late second century BCE the

Hasmonaean dynasty had itself incorporated Greek culture sufficiently for
Aristobulus I, who ruled from 104 to 103, to style himself a philhellene,
"lover of things Greek." The dynastic tombs of the Hasmonaeans were
entirely Hellenistic in their architectural style. Many of the coins of
Alexander Jannaeus, who ruled from 103 to 76, bore a Hebrew legend on
one side, "of king Alexander" in Greek on the other. After a brief flurry of
open antagonism to Greek culture, Jews, like Romans, adapted it for their
own purposes and treated it as entirely natural.[61]


THUS THE LONG-HELD notion that there was a conflict between Judaism
and Hellenism in the time of Jesus has been a product less of the ancient
Jewish evidence than of other issues: attempts by nineteenth-century
thinkers to establish the foundations of European culture, the self-
definition of Jews in the period of emancipation in Europe, and the history
of early Christianity. Heinrich Heine wrote in 1840 that "all men are either
Jews or Hellenes," claiming that two types of human nature are intrinsically opposed: the gloomy, ascetic, intellectual spiritualism of the Jews
contrasted to the cheerful, practical, realistic, life-affirming sensuality of
the Greeks. The contrast was picked up, modified and popularized in En-
gland by the poet Matthew Arnold, who believed that European civilization would be perfected when Hebraism and Hellenism, which had always
been in tension through the ages, finally existed in harmony: "The uppermost idea with Hellenism is to see things as they really are; the uppermost
idea with Hebraism is conduct and obedience." But Arnold was not interested in real Jews at all, except those of the remote past, and Heine's attitude to Judaism was complicated by his ambivalence towards his own
Jewishness, which continued to matter to him throughout his life despite
his conversion to Christianity. For both men, the study of ancient history
was of importance precisely because of what it meant for the present. In
the course of the late eighteenth and nineteenth centuries, "Hellenism"
came to stand for different cultural stances in different European countries,
often idealized and romanticized, not least in Germany. Jewish intellectuals, as they gained political freedoms and began to see themselves as part of
wider European culture, resurrected with gusto the language of conflict,
either among the "orthodox" (a new term in the nineteenth century) to
warn against any involvement with the modern world, or as a symbol of

modernity for secular Jews for whom the Jew who wanted to live must be liberated from Judaism and become a Greek—an Athenian in Jerusalem. The contrast continues now within the rhetoric of debates about the true nature of Jewish identity in the modern state of Israel.[62]

Among some Christian scholars the contrast between Judaism and Hellenism sometimes masked a crude antisemitism: Christianity had to be rescued from its Jewish origins; the Church had captured the hearts of the Roman empire only because Pauline Christianity was a Hellenized and not a Jewish phenomenon. Kant had already in 1793 argued that Judaism was not a real religion and that Christianity was born from a "Greek mind." In fact, however, the contrast between Judaism and Hellenism does not seem to have been a major issue among early Christians any more than it was among other first-century Jews. Paul wrote sometimes as if Jews and Greeks were opposites, like masculine and feminine, but the term "Greek" in his letters means simply "gentile": "There will be tribulation and anguish, upon every soul of man that does evil, of the Jew first, and also of the Greek; but glory, honour, and peace, to every man that works good, to the Jew first, and also to the Greek."[63] The same use of "Greek" to mean "gentile" is found also in the writings of Josephus later in the first century CE. But by the first century the culture of Jews in Judaea as much as in the diaspora incorporated so many elements from the Greek world that it too has been rightly termed "Hellenistic Judaism."[64] All Jews, in Jerusalem as much as elsewhere, were acculturated to some extent to Greek language, art, commerce, philosophy and literature. Precisely the apparent lack of self-consciousness of Jews after the Maccabean period about the relationship of Judaism to Greek culture made Hellenization easy. The enigmatic passages in the Mishnah and later rabbinic texts about attempts to limit the teaching of Greek and Greek wisdom to Jewish children are exceptional in a history of general acceptance. All that can validly be asked is whether some Jews imbibed Greek culture more than others, and to what extent variations can be traced between places and over time.[65]

THE IMPACT on the Mediterranean world of the specifically Roman adaptation of Hellenism was limited primarily by the use of Latin rather than Greek in much Roman literature. The spread of Latin, the language of the army and of Roman jurists, into the eastern Mediterranean was minimal.

Ambitious provincials hoping to enter the Roman Senate needed to acquire enough of it to get by, but in the early imperial period such a career was possible only for a minuscule part of the population. In most respects the official language used by the Roman state in all parts of the empire east of the Balkans was Greek. This fact is in itself testimony to the extraordinary prestige of Greek culture; it is hard to think of many other states which have privileged the language of a subject people in this way. Roman treatment of Greek contrasts with the universal use of Latin in the western parts of the empire, where native languages such as Celtic or Punic, still spoken in the early first century CE, were ignored by the state. Nonetheless some aspects of Roman rather than just general Greek culture did become widespread throughout the Mediterranean world in this period. New Roman architectural techniques such as vaulting spread quite soon all round the Roman world, as did other technological advances, such as blown-glass production (invented, probably in Syria, in the first century BCE) and hypocausts, used especially to heat baths. Public baths in the Roman style were widely adopted in eastern as much as western provinces, and often, in the East, treated as a particularly luxurious version of a Greek gymnasium. The provision by aqueducts of adequate water supplies for such purposes was a striking benefaction of the Roman state to many of its subjects: aqueducts impressed both by what they achieved and by their visibility on the landscape as evidence of Roman power and beneficence. But the most distinctively Roman element in the common culture of the Mediterranean was the celebration of the imperial cult, with gladiatorial games, a specifically Roman form of entertainment, enthusiastically adopted throughout the Mediterranean world in the first two centuries CE: in the western provinces specially constructed amphitheatres were common from the late first century BCE, while in the eastern Mediterranean theatres were often adapted for the purpose. The notion once widely held that Greeks could have had no taste for the barbaric spectacles characteristic of Rome does not stand up to scrutiny.[66]

## SOCIAL TIES

TO A REMARKABLE extent, men and women from one part of this unified Mediterranean world came into contact with people from other areas at all levels of society—the very rich as landowners and state officials; others as soldiers, merchants and slaves. Roman provincial administrators could expect to visit places hundreds, or even thousands, of miles apart in the course of their careers. A certain Titus Haterius Nepos, who came originally from Fulginiae in Umbria, was posted in the reign of Trajan to Britain to help with the provincial census in the early second century CE, then to Armenia, then, after a spell organizing public games and other official activities in the city of Rome, to Egypt, where he became governor under Hadrian: an inscription records that on 18 February 121 he heard the sound emitted by the statue of Memnon at Thebes, a favourite tourist attraction. Important officials like him would have got to know local rich landowners, both because it was in their political interest to become his friend and because, although he would have a main residence in the province, a governor and his staff needed to rely on the hospitality of locals when travelling around on assizes.

Further down the social scale, the main agent for the transfer of men across the empire in huge numbers was the army. Recruits were expected to serve in areas distant from their homeland. Following the extensive legionary movements under Augustus, it gradually became normal during the first century CE for legions to stay in one place for many years, but soldiers were still often attached to units stationed in areas far away from where they were recruited, especially after 70, and individuals were sometimes uprooted by their specialist units being posted for service elsewhere: hence, in 136–7, the presence on Hadrian's Wall in Britain of auxiliary troops from Syria, the "first cohort of Hamian archers." The family of a soldier might move with him: the tombstone of Titus Flavius Virilis, who died in the early third century CE in Lambaesis in Africa at the age of seventy after he had served forty-five seasons, was erected by his wife, whose name, Lollia Bodicca, suggests that they were married while he was stationed in Britain. The prestige status in provincial society of soldiers, with their guaranteed salaries from the state, gave every encouragement for mixing. "The provincials were accustomed to live with the soldiers, and enjoyed association with them; in fact, many civilians were bound to the soldiers by ties of friendship and marriage," wrote the historian Tacitus, describing the legions in Syria in 69.[67] Conversely, the fact that Jews, unless they abandoned their Jewish customs, did not become soldiers in the Roman army will have hindered such processes of social integration. There is a striking lack of evidence for Jews joining the Roman army voluntarily, probably because they objected to the requirement to participate in the pagan religious ceremonies, especially sacrifice to the military standards, which were normal for Roman troops as demonstration of their loyalty to their commander-in-chief, the emperor. Josephus reports Roman governors taking seriously a claim by the Hasmonaean ruler Hyrcanus II in 43 BCE that Jews "cannot undertake military service because they may not bear arms or march on the days of the Sabbath; nor can they obtain the native foods to which they are accustomed."[68]

If, nonetheless, Jews came into contact with many other peoples in the Mediterranean world of their day, the reason lay in the existence of a far-flung and well-established Jewish diaspora whose origins lay in earlier centuries. By the early first century CE Jews were already to be found in many coastal cities of the eastern Mediterranean, in the countryside in Egypt and in Syria around Antioch, on the Anatolian plateau in modern-day Turkey, and in many other places. The nucleus of some of these diaspora communities lay in the settlement of captives after wars on the territory of Palestine either in the very distant past, as was the case for the Jews whose ancestors had been brought to Babylonia in 586 BCE (see Chapter 1) or in the Hellenistic period: in the mid-second century BCE the author of the *Letter of Aristeas* recorded, probably correctly, that Jews had been taken as prisoners to Egypt by Ptolemy Soter in the late fourth century BCE. By the mid-first century CE, Agrippa I, as cited by Philo, could claim with exaggerated rhetoric: "The holy city . . . is the mother city not of one country Judaea but of most of the others in virtue of the colonies sent out at various times to the neighbouring lands . . . as well as the lands lying far away . . . most of Asia up to Bithynia and the corners of Pontus, similarly also in Europe . . . And not only are the mainlands full of Jewish colonies but also the most highly esteemed of the islands . . . I say nothing of the countries beyond the Euphrates."[69]

Other Jews must have travelled to the diaspora voluntarily in search of a living, what we would now call economic migrants, compelled to leave their homeland by over-population caused not least by the distinctive Jewish antipathy to abortion and infanticide. Their choice of destination will have been determined in large part by distance: the biggest diaspora communities were in Egypt and Syria, the regions closest to Judaea. Many must have been attracted by the prospect of joining existing Jewish communities which might offer charitable help, a religious framework, a social base or employment. Papyri from the Egyptian countryside in the Ptolemaic period (from 301 to 30 BCE) reveal Jews as shepherds, farmers, vine-dressers, potters and weavers. Philo referred to Jewish traders in 38 CE whose merchandise was seized by Greeks when they put in to harbours on the Nile, and to the artisans in Alexandria whose workshops were ransacked by a Greek mob in the same year. According to the Acts of the Apostles, Aquila, a Jew from Pontus who lived for a while in Rome before moving to Corinth, was, like Paul of Tarsus, a tent-maker by trade. In pre-Roman times, Jews also sold their services as mercenaries in Egypt to the Persian state, and later in both Egypt and Cyrene to the Ptolemies, while the Seleucids used them for the same purpose in Asia Minor. Hellenistic kings had good reason to believe that Jews would be "faithful and excellent guards," as Josephus described them, and not only "because of their piety to their God . . . their good faith and zeal in doing what they are asked": Jews in such alien places depended for their own security on the support and protection of the state, and the state could therefore in turn rely upon their loyalty. Jews were thus spread widely across the eastern Mediterranean world by the first century CE—indeed, to the angry emperor Claudius, attempting in a stern letter to the city of Alexandria dated 10 November 41 to bring to an end intercommunal disturbances between Jews and Greeks, Jews seemed to be everywhere.[70]

As the Alexandrian case demonstrated all too clearly, living in the same city did not necessarily lead to good neighbourly relations. Jews were notorious for abstaining from the two main means of social intercourse with non-Jews. In the early second century CE Tacitus put it with characteristic succinctness: Jews stay "separate in their meals [and] apart in their beds . . . [and] abstain from sleeping with foreign women." It was a caricature that was largely, but not totally, true. For pious Jews to eat with non-Jews, sharing a convivial table, was possible, but difficult. "Aristeas" depicted the seventy-two sages who translated the Jewish Law into Greek in Alexandria as seated at dinner with the king, Ptolemy, to whom each provided an individualized soundbite of sage advice. Clearly they are depicted as sharing the king's dining room, but, as the author makes clear, the royal food was specially kosher for the occasion by order of the king: "Everything . . . will be served in compliance with your habits; and for me also along with you." But such pragmatic and irenic solutions to Jewish food taboos cannot have been the norm—if they were, it would be hard to understand the issues at stake in the early Christian community in Antioch according to Paul's accusation of Peter: "For before certain people came from James, he ate with the gentiles. But when they came, he withdrew and separated himself, fearing those who were of the circumcision." The pious Jewish author of *3 Maccabees*, writing probably in Egypt in the late second century BCE, wrote of the Jews that "reverencing God and conducting themselves according to his law, they kept themselves apart in the matter of food, and for this reason they appeared odious to some." In a thoroughly hostile account of the Jews incorporated into a narrative of the relationship of the Hasmonaeans to the Seleucid king Antiochus Sidetes in the late 130s BCE, the historian Diodorus Siculus asserted in the mid-first century BCE that "the Jews had made their hatred of mankind into a tradition, and on this account had introduced outlandish laws: not to share a table with any other race, nor to show any good will at all." It seems unlikely that many Jews contrived commensality with their gentile neighbours by taking the vegetarian option at civic banquets.[71]

The issue of intermarriage is rather more complex, since it was not in fact the case, despite the perceptions of both Jews and gentiles, that marriage links between Jewish and gentile families could not take place. Best attested of such marriages are those of political import, such as the spouses selected by Herod the Great for his offspring from the families of rulers of nearby kingdoms. The political significance of the marriage to the daughter of Aretas IV, king of the Nabataeans, of Herod Antipas, ruler of Galilee from 4 BCE to 39 CE (described by Jesus as "that fox" according to the Gospel of Matthew), became horribly apparent when he repudiated her out of passion for his brother's wife Herodias. Aretas unsurprisingly bore a grudge at the slight done to his daughter, and in 36 CE used a boundary dispute as an excuse for war, in which Antipas' army was comprehensively defeated. Such intermarriage was disguised within the normal Jewish practice of endogamy by the legal fiction of conversion to Judaism (on which more in Chapter 4). Exactly what a gentile woman had to do in order to become Jewish is uncertain, but the conversion of a gentile man contemplating a mixed marriage must have required, at the least, circumcision, since this sometimes proved a problem. The two daughters of Agrippa I both married kings from other parts of the Roman Near East: Berenice's husband was Polemon of Cilicia, and Drusilla married Azizus of Emesa. Both gentile kings submitted to circumcision for the sake of their marriages. In the case of Azizus, he won his wife only because her first betrothed, a son of Antiochus of Commagene, "was not willing to convert to Jewish customs." Both marriages nevertheless fell to pieces. Berenice pursued a series of notorious love affairs, first (it was rumoured) with her brother Agrippa II, then quite publicly with the Roman general and future emperor Titus. Drusilla forsook Azizus and married the ex-slave Felix, who had become the Roman governor of Judaea through his brother's influence over the emperor Claudius. Josephus expressed particular disgust at this last liaison, although whether he objected to Felix as ex-slave, or as gentile, or as seducer of married women, is unclear:

> Drusilla's marriage to Azizus was dissolved under the impact of the following circumstances. At the time when Felix was procurator of Judaea, he saw her, and, inasmuch as she surpassed all women in beauty, he conceived a passion for her. He sent to her one of his friends, a Cyprian Jew named Atomus, who pretended to be a magician, in an effort to persuade her to leave her husband and to marry Felix. Felix promised to make her supremely happy if she did not disdain him. She, being unhappy and wishing to escape the malice of her sister Berenice . . . was persuaded to transgress the ancestral laws and to marry Felix.

Josephus adds a sad postscript. Felix and Drusilla produced a son, whom she named Agrippa, presumably in memory of her father. The young man and his wife disappeared during the eruption of Vesuvius which engulfed Pompeii in 79 CE.[72]

The legal fiction of conversion which enabled Herodian princesses to marry gentiles was equally available to other Jews, but how many took advantage of it cannot be known. The lack of specific evidence for such marriages outside the Herodian dynasty does not prove that they did not take place, since not all proselytes may have wished to advertise on their funerary inscriptions or on their other documents their previous status as gentiles. Some Jews, of course, must have married out of the faith altogether, such as the Jewish mother of the Timothy mentioned in the Acts of the Apostles, whose father, according to Acts, was a Greek, but again, it is difficult to trace such mixed marriages in the surviving evidence except when, as we shall discuss in Chapter 4, the child of the union was consid-

ered Jewish. What strikes most is the concurrence of Jews and gentiles that
Jewish endogamy was the rule. Philo warned: "Do not enter into a partnership of marriage with a foreigner, lest, defeated by warring customs,
you one day give in and inadvertently miss the road to piety by turning
into a place that has no roads."[73]

MUCH THUS encouraged a sense of unity among those who inhabited the
Mediterranean world in the first century CE. Economic relations, social ties
and threads of a shared culture ensured that those who lived in Spain would
recognize as similar to their own many aspects of the lives of people in
Greece, Asia Minor, Syria or Judaea. Reinforcing this sense of unity was
the stark fact of political domination by one individual, the emperor in
Rome. And yet, as will emerge in the next chapter, behind this façade of
unity existed a great number of diverse societies whose values and lifestyles
were often at variance with the norm.

CHAPTER THREE

# DIVERSITY AND TOLERATION

## THE VIEW FROM ABOVE

THE HISTORIAN APPIAN, writing in the second century CE about the wars waged by Rome in the first century BCE, provided an unusually full description of the triumphal procession through the streets of Rome in 59 BCE which celebrated the defeat by Pompey of Mithradates Eupator, king of Pontus.

> He was awarded a triumph exceeding in brilliancy any that had gone before . . . It occupied two successive days, and many nations were represented in the procession, from Pontus and Armenia, and Cappadocia and Cilicia and all Syria, and Albanians and Heniochi and Achaeans of Scythia and Eastern Iberians . . . In the triumphal procession were . . . litters laden with gold . . . and a multitude of captives and bandits, none of them bound, but all arrayed in their native costumes. Before Pompey himself, at the head of the procession, went the leaders, sons and generals of the kings against whom he had fought . . . to the number of 324 . . . There were carried in the procession images of those who were not present . . . and images, and ornaments of barbarian gods in the fashion of their countries.[1]

Few public occasions captured as well as the triumph Roman assumptions about the nature of the empire they had conquered. The triumph was a theatrical representation of the victory commemorated. Its organization reflected the beliefs of Roman politicians as to which facts about foreign peoples and their conquest would most impress the urban populace. Most to be admired was naturally the evidence of wealth taken as booty, and testimonies to courage and daring, but, after that, attention was drawn above all to the spectacular and the unusual. Romans knew that their empire was a mosaic of varied peoples and cultures, and they gloried in that variety. Vergil wrote of Augustus portrayed on the shield of Vulcan reviewing the gifts of the nations as they passed before him: "The conquered peoples move in long array, as diverse in fashion of dress and arms as in their tongues."[2]

Romans classified the varied peoples they ruled by dividing the empire's space into provinces and allotting a name to each region and each ethnic group. If no native name was available, or if it was unknown to Roman administrators, or if it did not fit strategic boundaries, a new name could be imposed (and, if desired, changed): in the time of Augustus, the geographer Strabo noted that the name of the Lusitanians in Spain had previously been applied to those now called Callaicans, north of the river Durius, but that "Lusitania" was nowadays used specifically to denote the region further to the south.[3] Such naming could be arbitrary, so it is all the more remarkable how often the names of ancient peoples and regions adopted by local people themselves reflected the decisions of Roman administrators. Thus, for instance, when Pompey in the mid-60s BCE defeated Mithradates, a proud descendant of a Persian noble family which had received a kingdom on the shores of the Black Sea in the sixth century BCE, the Romans created a new province of Pontus to encompass his lands, but the designation imposed by Rome was artificial: "Pontos," in Greek, means simply "sea," so to use it as a name for a land area was strange. Strabo, who himself came from the region—Amaseia lies in the hills above the southern coast of the Black Sea in modern Turkey—and was born just at the time that the Roman province was created, wrote of "those who live close to the Euxine [the Black Sea], whom they now call Pontici." For the author of the Acts of the Apostles, the Christian Aquila, who met St. Paul in Corinth after his expulsion from Rome, was "a Jew, Pontic by race."[4]

Such impact on provincials' self-identity was only a by-product of a system designed not for their benefit so much as to avoid clashes of authority between Roman administrators. Each governor was allotted either by emperor or Senate a specific task, and in its original sense the Latin word *provincia* referred simply to that task, usually but not always in connection with a military campaign. But by the late Republic the term was sometimes used to refer to a specific geographical area under Roman rule, and by the first century CE this meaning was standard. Each province came to be endowed in Roman eyes with a distinctive personality that could be encapsulated visually. The emperor Hadrian issued an extensive series of coins to commemorate his travels, in each case depicting the province as an idealized female form distinguished by some particular local attribute. Egypt appears reclining on the ground against a large basket filled with corn-ears and fruit (referring to the fecundity of the province), and holding in her right hand a *sistrum*, the national musical instrument of the country as well as of the goddess Isis. In marked contrast is Britannia, who sits, draped, supporting her head on her right hand and holding a spear in her left, by her side a large shield with a decorated rim and a large spike in the centre. Mauretania is usually portrayed as a female figure holding one or two javelins and accompanied by a horse, an image presumably reflecting the military reputation of the region, although a variant coin type in which she wears an elephant headdress and holds two corn-ears seems to refer to the natural productivity of Mauretania both in grain and in elephants.[5]

Romans could also attribute personalities to individual peoples within provinces, as has become clear from publication of a remarkable series of relief sculptures excavated in Aphrodisias in modern Turkey in the late 1970s. The reliefs were part of the decoration of a temple complex, the Sebasteion, dedicated by the local inhabitants to Aphrodite and the Julio-Claudian emperors. A series of sculptures depicting the imperial family was also found at the site. In these sculptures a series of peoples were depicted as carefully individualized standing, draped women, each differentiated by pose, clothing, hairstyle, head type and attributes: it is likely that the iconographic conventions for each nation were borrowed from Rome, where Augustus was said to have made a portico "in which he had placed images of all the peoples; this portico was called 'To the Nations.'" The extant statue bases include one for "the people of the Jews," but the statue that personified them sadly does not survive.[6]

The choice of peoples for representation in the Aphrodisias Sebasteion almost certainly reflected the claims of conquest by Augustus in the memoir of his achievements published after his death in 14 CE:

> I extended the frontiers of all the provinces of the Roman people on whose boundaries were peoples not subject to our empire. I pacified the

Gallic and Spanish provinces and Germany . . . I pacified the Alps, from the region nearest to the Adriatic as far as the Tuscan Sea, without unjustly making war against any people. The Cimbri, the Charydes, the Semnones and other German peoples of the same region through their envoys sought my friendship and that of the Roman people. At my command and under my auspices two armies were led, at almost the same time, into Ethiopia and into Arabia which is called Felix . . . Into Ethiopia a penetration was made as far as the town of Napata, which is next to Meroe; in Arabia the army advanced into the territory of the Sabaeans to the town of Mariba. I added Egypt to the empire of the Roman people. Although I might have made Greater Armenia into a province when its king Artaxes was assassinated, I preferred to hand over this kingdom to Tigranes . . . I conquered and subjected to the empire of the Roman people the Pannonian tribes, to which before my principate no army of the Roman people had ever penetrated . . . and I extended the frontier of Illyricum to the bank of the river Danube.[7]

The peoples depicted at Aphrodisias included some which were fairly obscure: the Andizeti, Callaeai, Iapodes, Piroustae, Bessi, Dardani, Rhaeti and others. The selection of outlandish peoples seems to have been intended to stress the extraordinary range and variety of peoples under Roman rule. Many of the nations came from the edges of the empire, but the purpose of portraying them was not, or not only, to show the might of Rome. More significant was the implication of Rome and the emperor as benefactors to all these places and peoples. This sort of representation of Roman rule remained in essence unchanged in the group of reliefs made a century later for the temple of Hadrian in the Campus Martius in Rome, where a series of standing draped women again represented the different regions of the empire, but by this date it was apparently not thought necessary to label the figures, who were more clearly differentiated from each other in their clothing than those at Aphrodisias.[8]

Romans were fairly imprecise about geography: the elder Pliny made an error of about four hundred Roman miles when he tried to calculate the length of Italy. Geographical certainties were only possible where the army had built roads which systematically measured the distances between towns or staging posts. Many Roman officials treated the empire essentially as a series of civilized urban centres and military forts linked by roads to be traversed as rapidly as possible, and had only the most general idea of the lives of the inhabitants of the countryside away from the main roads. However, the need to know more about the nature of the peoples of and near the empire seems to have been sufficient to stimulate ethnographers, particularly but not only within what was then the literary genre of geography, in the late Republic and early imperial period.[9] Hence the writings of the Stoic polymath Posidonius, originally from Apamea on the Orontes in Syria, but for many years a teacher in Rhodes, and an influential visitor to Rome in the 80s BCE.

Only fragments of Posidonius' writings survive, but it is almost certain that his descriptions of native peoples, especially the Celts, underlie the analyses of these nations by later authors, including Julius Caesar (in his *Gallic Wars*) and Strabo. He wrote in full awareness of Roman conquests in Celtic lands in Spain and Gaul in the late Republic, even before the conquests of Caesar, and evidently himself visited Celtic regions, presumably in the wake of such conquests. Thus Strabo wrote that, although Posidonius was initially upset at the sight of human heads nailed up at the entrances to the houses of aristocratic Celts, he got used to it in time. Such firsthand information does not seem to have discouraged Posidonius from propagating a stylized analysis of Celtic society which took little account either of change over time or of differences between one group of Celts and another. He described Celtic society as strictly hierarchical, with large retinues of clients accompanying aristocrats who subscribed to a fierce code of honour and dispensed extravagant largesse; the power of warrior leaders was offset by the influence of bards, seers and, above all, druids, who provided moral and religious leadership, dispensed justice, and preached a philosophy in some respects akin to Stoicism, pronouncing that "men's souls and the universe are indestructible." The work of such Greek ethnographers was the product of Roman imperialism, but also informed Roman conceptions of the new societies they controlled: Posidonius' younger Latin contemporary, Marcus Terentius Varro (116–27 BCE), a scholar with a range to rival Posidonius, was said by Jerome to have studied Celtic society. On the other hand, Roman politicians could select from scholarly ethnography what suited policy: the learned Cicero could denigrate the inhabitants of Transalpine Gaul quite freely in a law court speech when his client, Marcus Fonteius, had been accused by them of corruptly accepting bribes.[10]

Posidonius or Varro may have given Caesar the information that helped him to understand the society he undertook to conquer in his campaign in Gaul, but more closely tied than either of them to the realities of Roman power were the geographical writings of Strabo himself, pupil and much younger acquaintance of Posidonius and apologist for the autocratic rule of Augustus. Despite his origins in Anatolia, to which he seems to have returned at the end of his life, Strabo was widely travelled and sufficiently acquainted with the city of Rome, which he visited on a number of occasions, to be able to write about the empire with awareness of the concerns of the Roman state. His final comments at the end of his *Geography*, composed in the early years of Tiberius' rule, show a keen awareness of the methods of Roman control in practice:

> Of this whole country which is subject to the Romans, some is ruled by kings, some they rule directly under the designation "provincial" territory, sending governors and tax collectors. There are also some free cities, some of which attached themselves to the Romans as friends from the outset, whereas to others the Romans themselves granted freedom as a mark of honour. There are also some dynasts, tribal chieftains and priestly rulers subject to the Romans; these people regulate their lives in accordance with certain ancestral laws. But the provinces, which have been differently divided at different times, are arranged at the present time as Caesar Augustus laid down. For when his native land entrusted him with supreme authority in the empire and he became established as lord for life of war and peace, he divided the whole territory into two parts, assigning one to himself, the other to the people. The part he assigned to himself was whatever has need of a military garrison: that is, the barbarian territory bordering on the peoples that have not yet been subdued, or poor territory that resists cultivation, so that, making up with plenty of strongholds for its lack of other resources, it is restless and disobedient. To the people he assigned the remainder, all that is peaceful and easy to govern without force.[11]

Strabo's impressively sober compendium of information about places, much of it (like the analysis of Celtic society inherited from Posidonius) culled from earlier sources, eschewed tales of wonders but picked out the special characteristics of the society of each region. Some of the peoples he described evidently struck him as particularly exotic, for all that they were integral to the Roman world of his time, as in his description of the inhabitants of parts of Africa:

Although most of the country inhabited by the Maurusians is so fertile, yet even to this time most of the people persist in living a nomadic life. But nevertheless they beautify their appearance by braiding their hair, growing beards, wearing golden ornaments, and also by cleaning their teeth and paring their nails. And only rarely can you see them touch one another in walking, for fear that the adornment of their hair may not remain intact. Their horsemen fight mostly with a javelin, using bridles made of rush, and riding bareback; but they also carry daggers. The foot-soldiers hold before them as shields the skins of elephants, and clothe themselves with the skins of lions, leopards, and bears, and sleep in them . . . The Pharusians mingle only rarely even with the Maurusians when passing through the desert, since they carry skins of water fastened beneath the bellies of their horses. Sometimes, however, they come even to Cirta, passing through certain marshy regions and over lakes. Some of them are said to live like Troglodytes, digging homes in the earth. And it is said that here too the summer rains are prevalent, but that in winter there is a drought, and that some of the barbarians in this part of the world use also the skins of snakes and fish both as wraps and as bed-covers. And the Maurusians [a mistake for "Pharusians"?] are said by some to be the Indians who came thither with Heracles.[12]

Strabo, like Posidonius, was a Greek outsider writing for the Roman elite. The *Germania* of Tacitus was, by contrast, a product from within the elite itself. Cornelius Tacitus' family originated almost certainly as provincial aristocracy in the region of Gaul south of the Alps. The historian appears to have been the first in the family to enter public life in Rome as a senator, rising, by virtue of his remarkable qualities as an orator, to the consulship in 97 CE. He wrote with some sympathy about the customs of the Germani of central Europe, describing the geography of the region they inhabited, the origins of their name ("modern and newly introduced"), their physical characteristics ("all have fierce blue eyes, red hair, huge frames, fit only for sudden exertion"), their military tactics, government, religion, dress, houses, social customs and so on. Whenever Germans are not fighting, "they pass much of the time in hunting, and still more in idleness, giving themselves up to sleep and to feasting . . . Almost alone among barbarians they are content with one wife, except a very few among them . . . A liquor for drinking is made out of barley or other grain and fermented into a certain resemblance to wine . . . If you indulge their love of drinking by supplying them with as much as they desire, they will be overcome by their own vices as easily as by the arms of an enemy." They are addicted to gambling, prone to feuds and extravagant in hospitality. To some extent, the treatise functioned as a mirror to Roman society, in which comparisons between Romans and Germans threw light on the vagaries of Roman behaviour: "lending money on interest and increasing it by usury are unknown among them—a more effective safeguard than if it were prohibited . . . Silver and gold the gods have refused to them, whether in kindness or in anger I cannot say . . . For the prostituted chastity of a woman there is no pardon . . . No one there laughs at vice, nor do they call it the 'spirit of the age' to corrupt and to be corrupted." But the long description of specific German tribes which takes up the second half of the treatise has no obvious moral purpose, and was most probably included simply for ethnographic interest.[13]

A reader of the first part of Tacitus' *Germania* might easily get the impression that these noble savages lived in a society wholly separate from the Roman senator, but both Tacitus and his contemporary readers knew this to be untrue. In his analysis of the institutions of the separate German tribes, Tacitus makes explicit mention of the Ubii (in modern Cologne), who "have earned the distinction of being a Roman colony and prefer to be called Agrippinenses" but are still proud of their German origin, and of the Batavi, who

> occupy an island within the Rhine and but a smaller portion of the bank. Formerly a tribe of the Chatti, they were forced by internal dissension to migrate to their present settlements and there become a part of the Roman empire. They still retain the honourable badge of an ancient alliance, for they are not insulted by tribute, nor ground down by the tax-gatherer. Free from the usual burdens and contributions, and set apart for fighting purposes, like a storehouse of weapons, we reserve them for our wars.

Leading figures from German tribes had been earning Roman citizenship and imperial approval, not least as commanders of specialist auxiliary forces attached to the legions, for almost a century by the time that Tacitus was writing. When in 9 CE Arminius, son of Sigimer, chief of the Germanic Cherusci, led his countrymen into a revolt which successfully destroyed three Roman legions and freed all Germany across the Rhine from the yoke of Roman taxation, he was a Roman citizen and had himself long served in the Roman army, reaching the status of a knight, *eques:* the man whom Tacitus described in his *Annals* as "beyond doubt the liberator of Germany" had been for years a warrior on behalf of Rome. The custom of using alongside and within the Roman army an array of ethnic auxiliary forces who made use of their distinctive weaponry and fighting methods itself constituted recognition of the advantages of diversity within Roman society. German and Gallic cavalrymen, Arab camel-riders and Syrian archers possessed skills that complemented the tactics of the main forces of the army, the massed infantry ranks of the legionaries.[14]

Thinking Romans were fascinated by the variety of peoples, places and natural phenomena within the borders of their huge empire and, although most of the extant early imperial works of paradoxography, collections of stories about strange marvels of all kinds culled from geography, botany and zoology as well as from human behaviour, are in Greek—Isigonus, who flourished in the time of Augustus, came from Nicaea, and Phlegon, a freedman of the emperor Hadrian, was from Tralles—they had Roman readers. Phlegon told bizarre stories of ghosts, giants, centaurs and similar phenomena, confirming the accuracy of some of his tabloid stories by claiming personal knowledge:

> A hippocentaur was found in Saune, a city in Arabia, on a very high mountain that is groaning with a deadly drug . . . The hippocentaur was captured alive by the king, who sent it to Egypt together with other gifts for Caesar. Its food was meat. But it did not tolerate the change of air, and died, so that the prefect of Egypt embalmed it and sent it to Rome . . . Its face was fiercer than a human face, its arms and fingers were hairy and its ribs were connected with its front legs and its stomach. It had the firm hooves of a horse and its mane was tawny . . . Anyone who does not believe can investigate for himself, since, as I said above, it has been embalmed and lies in the emperor's storehouse.[15]

Emperors may not always have been all that keen to receive such well-meaning gifts:

> Apollonios the grammarian reports that in the time of Tiberius
> Nero there was an earthquake and many notable cities of Asia Minor
> utterly disappeared, which Tiberius subsequently rebuilt at his own
> expense . . . In the cracks in the earth huge bodies appeared which the
> local inhabitants were hesitant to move, although as a sample they sent
> to Rome a tooth of one. It was not just a foot long but even greater
> than this measure. The ambassadors showed it to Tiberius and asked
> him if he wished the hero to be brought to him. Tiberius devised a
> shrewd plan such that, while not depriving himself of a knowledge of
> its size, he avoided the sacrilege of the robbing of the dead. He sum-
> moned a certain geometer, Pulcher by name, a man of some renown,
> whom he respected for his skill, and ordered him to fashion a face in
> proportion to the size of the tooth. The geometer estimated how large
> the entire body as well as the face would be by means of the weight of
> the tooth, speedily made a construction, and brought it to the emperor.
> Tiberius, saying that the sight of this was sufficient for him, sent the
> tooth back to where it had been brought from.[16]

The literary genre of paradoxography does not seem to have been as much adopted by Latin authors, although Gaius Licinius Mucianus, the powerful governor of Syria in 69 CE whose political support in the civil war was crucial in raising Vespasian to supreme power, wrote a book on geographical curiosities, entitled *Mirabilia*, "Wonders," based on data he had collected as a provincial administrator. But a general feeling that the more Romans know about the world as a result of conquest, the more remarkable that world is revealed to be, emerges also in the more sober descriptions of the world by the polymaths Varro and the elder Pliny. Pliny reported that he had seen the Arabian hippocentaur to which Phlegon referred, preserved in honey, but he was sceptical about the Egyptian phoenix exhibited to the Roman public in 47 CE. The historian Tacitus, arch-cynic in his analysis of the political motivations of politicians, reported doubts about the authenticity of a phoenix which appeared in Egypt in the time of Tiberius, but none about the generic phoenix myth, "on which there is agreement":

Those who have depicted it agree that its head and markings of its plumage distinguish it from other birds . . . When its years are complete and death is close, it is said to make a nest in its own country and shed over it a procreative substance, from which springs a young one. Its first function once it is mature is the burial of its father . . . The details are disputed and embellished by myths. But that the bird occasionally appears in Egypt is unquestioned.[17]

Much the most influential of these Roman literary observers of the variegated world in which they lived was the elder Pliny, some of whose observations on industrial processes and long-distance trade have already been cited.[18] His encyclopaedic *Natural History* included in its thirty-seven books the summation of contemporary knowledge: "my subject is the nature of things, that is, life." He claimed to provide his readers with twenty thousand important facts which he had learned from two thousand books. His work is a mine of information, some real, some imagined, some garbled. It is Pliny who describes in helpful detail the production of balsam in Judaea—the three varieties, the taste of balsam-seed ("very much like wine, with a red colour and a rather greasy consistency"), the collection of the juice (*opobalsamum*) from the bark in small horns by means of tufts of wool, the boiling down of twigs from the trees to make perfumes, how to test whether the balsam has been adulterated, the prices paid for different balsam products; but it is also Pliny who relates the less credible story of a stream in Judaea which, presumably in sympathy with the notorious religious scruples of the natives, dries up once a week on the Sabbath. The account of his scholarly habits written by his nephew reveals a man self-consciously seeking near-universal knowledge. He wasted no moment of the day, rising while it was still dark to work by lamplight. After his official duties "he devoted any spare time to his work . . . In the country, the only time he took from his work was for his bath, and by bath I mean his actual immersion, for while he was being rubbed down and dried he had a book read to him or dictated notes. When travelling he felt free from other responsibilities to give every minute to work; he kept a secretary at his side with book and notebook." Such working methods evidently impressed contemporaries (although they must have made the scholar rather poor company). Checking the truth of the information he transmitted to his readers from his own voluminous knowledge was neither possible nor, it seems, viewed by Pliny as particularly important. The audience for whom he wrote was as willing to accept marvels at face value as the onlookers who, according to his account over a century later, came to see the skeleton of the sea monster to which, according to the myth, Andromeda was exposed by her father Cepheus to assuage the wrath of the god Poseidon. Brought from the town of Joppe in Judaea, the skeleton, presumably of a whale, was shown in Rome among the rest of the marvels during Scaurus' year as aedile in the city: "it was forty foot long, the height of the ribs exceeding the elephants of India, and the spine being one foot and six inches thick." It was characteristic of Pliny to give the statistics. He was better at transmitting data than evaluating the plausibility of the information he so enthusiastically relayed.[19]

A similar approach informed Pliny's analysis of human societies. If all we knew about the habits of Jews was what survives in Pliny's *Natural History*, we would know that a branch of magic derived from them and that there is a kind of fish sauce, made from fish without scales, which is dedicated to Jewish rituals, but not much more, and even the information about the fish sauce looks peculiar in the light of the express injunction in Leviticus against the eating of fish without scales. It is rather striking that when Pliny came in the 70s CE to describe the geography of Judaea and its environs in the fifth book of his *Natural History*, he mentioned the source of the river Jordan, the Sea of Galilee and the Dead Sea ("the bodies of animals do not sink in its waters, even bulls and camels floating"), and gave the administrative division of Judaea into ten regions, but had nothing to say about Jewish society, despite a reference in passing to the impact of the recent war, noting the region of Oreine "in which Jerusalem was [note the past tense] by far the most famous of cities of the East, not only of Judaea." He chose instead to dwell on the curious customs of the Essenes:

> To the west [of the Dead Sea] the Essenes have put the necessary distance between themselves and the insalubrious shore. They are a people unique of its kind and admirable beyond all others in the whole world, without women and renouncing love entirely, without money, and having for company only the palm trees. Owing to the throng of new-comers, this people is daily re-born in equal number; indeed, those whom, wearied by the fluctuations of fortune, life leads to adopt their customs, stream in in great numbers. Thus, unbelievable though this

may seem, for thousands of centuries a race has existed which is eternal yet into which no one is born: so fruitful for them is the repentance which others feel for their past lives!

It is an interesting question whether Pliny or his source thought of these Essenes as Jews. He did not say so explicitly, and by calling them "a people unique of its kind and admirable beyond all others in the whole world," he might seem to imply the opposite: the Essenes were an eternal race "into which no one is born." On the other hand, the passage ends with "This is the limit of Judaea," distinguished from Phoenicia, Idumaea, Syria, Arabia and Egypt, which suggests that the region was that inhabited by Jews, whoever the Essenes might be taken to be. It is reasonable to understand Pliny's comments as an outsider's account of the Essene branch of Judaism described in glowing terms by Josephus and Philo, who emphasized both their asceticism and their philosophical bent. But if this was indeed the group to which Pliny intended to refer, his few rapturous words reveal more about the willingness of a Roman gentleman to believe that quite remarkable people existed within the Roman empire in his own day than they do about the real nature of the Essenes themselves.[20]

## ON THE GROUND

IT IS JUST as well for the modern investigator of the Roman world that an interest in the diverse cultures of that world was to be found at the centre, for otherwise history would have little to record about the lives of many of these peoples apart from what can be culled from the archaeological record of the material remains they left behind. The provincials themselves, in most parts of the empire, never composed any account of their own societies comparable to the histories of the Jews written by Josephus—or, if they did, these histories do not now survive. It would thus be too optimistic to expect that a snapshot of three provincial societies—Spain, Greece and Egypt—might provide contrasts for the first centuries CE as rich as the picture to be found in the Jewish literary tradition, but the accounts which can be pieced together do at least provide a clear indication that local cultural diversity continued in these places under Roman rule.

Pliny's evaluation of Spain, as second only to Italy in the wealth of its material resources, with inhabitants superior to those of Gaul in "the hardiness of body and eagerness of heart" displayed, is matched by no native literature to express the views of those inhabitants themselves. This is not because writers from Spain were not to be found in the early principate. On the contrary, a number of major Latin writers of the first century CE came from one Cordoban family: the orator Lucius Annaeus Seneca; his son, the philosopher, who bore the same name; and his grandson, Marcus Annaeus Lucanus, author of (among other works) an epic poem on the civil wars of the late Republic. The fact that Florus, author in the mid-second century CE of a drastically abbreviated version of Livy's history of Rome, praises Spain occasionally in the course of his narrative more than might be expected, probably indicates some connection with the province. The agricultural writer Columella was born in Cadiz, the poet Martial was from Bilbilis (modern Calatayud), and Quintilian, the doyen of rhetorical theorists, came from Calagurris (modern Calahorra). It is all the more remarkable that none of the extant writings by these Spanish authors has for its subject either Spain or its inhabitants, and that none appears aimed at a Spanish readership. Instead, the focus of their literary attentions was the city of Rome, which is where most of them spent most of their working lives.[21]

Pre-Roman Spain had been home to a number of different cultural influences—local, Celtic, Phoenician and Greek. The Pyrenees were inhabited by indigenous Iberians who have retained a non-Indo-European language, Basque, to modern times. Celts had invaded Spain over the Pyrenees during the fourth century BCE and settled in the south and east of the peninsula. Waves of Punic settlement from early times through to the time of Hannibal had left a strong Phoenician mark in the southernmost areas. Strabo wrote that the majority of the towns in Turdetania (the area around modern Seville and Cordoba) in the time of Augustus were inhabited by Phoenicians. Investigation of urban sites shows a contrast between quintessentially Roman centres, such as Italica, the birthplace near Seville of the emperors Trajan and Hadrian, and the indigenous communities like Baelo (modern Bolonia), where there was huge monumental development in the first century CE, and Carteia (near modern San Roque), where excavations show much continuity in the appearance of the town from its Punic period down to early imperial times. Finds of jewellery and sculpture, and excavation of private houses and countryside villas with fine mosaic floors, reveal a preference for Roman tastes among the wealthy, at least when they thought about interior decoration and comfort in their houses—such wealth derived from the Mediterranean trade in wine, olive oil, fish sauce, fine tablewares and metals (particularly gold, silver, lead, copper, tin and iron) from the mines and building stone from quarries. But hints that at least some of the inhabitants of the central and more northern regions continued to think in local Celtic terms rather than as Romans, despite the world empire of which they had become a part, can be traced in early imperial Latin inscriptions which record individuals from northern and central Spain as part of social groups defined as a "people" (*gens, gentilitas* or *cognatio*) or sometimes designated either by referring to the group in the genitive plural or by use of a symbol rather like a horseshoe lain on its side. No one knows quite what sort of organization was signified by these terms, but it is probable that they denote Iron Age ethnic identities or other indigenous relationships within social groups from pre-Roman times, and that the Latin terms were borrowed by the locals to refer to groupings which had so patent a function to them that there was no need to spell out their nature in the epigraphic record. Punic speakers are attested on inscriptions in imperial times, and at Gades (modern Cadiz), some twenty-eight per cent of the names recorded in the corpus of Latin inscriptions have some kind of Punic connection. Excavations of urban cemeteries reveal that the rich set up high-quality monuments to themselves close to the entrances of towns in the Roman style, and that, as in much of the western Roman empire, there was a shift from cremation to inhumation in many areas by the second century CE. There is little evidence about the religious beliefs of these people beyond the names they gave their gods and the construction of their sanctuaries: in the cave sanctuary at Murcia near Carthago Nova, painted texts reveal worship in one place of indigenous nymphs along with Roman and eastern gods.[22]

It is evident from the careers of Seneca and his relations that Spanish intellectuals could write Latin of a high quality, and the archaeological evidence shows a complex Spanish society in which heterogeneous cultures mingled with Roman in a multitude of ways, so it is a curious question why almost no literary expression of native Spanish culture survives. One, rather exceptional, text may help to provide an explanation: the geographical work of Pomponius Mela constitutes precisely such a provincial's view of the world, a distinctively Spanish viewpoint of the Mediterranean in the early imperial period, whose work "can shed light on the world of Roman provincial life in a way that a thousand artefacts cannot."[23]

Pomponius Mela was born in Tingentera (modern Algeciras) in the province of Baetica in southern Spain, probably in the Augustan period. His one extant writing, almost certainly from the reign of Claudius, to whose campaign in Britain in 43 CE he seems to refer, is a three-volume work *De Chorographia* ("On Places"), an account of the world in the form of descriptions of voyages along coasts: the lands facing the Mediterranean; a journey round the islands inside the Mediterranean and Black Sea; finally an account of farther-flung coasts, from the Atlantic shores of Spain, Portugal and northern Europe to the eastern edge of Asia and the southern coast of Africa, and back to Spain. Pomponius' main sources were necessarily Greek, since that was the language of most previous geographical writing, but he showed no enthusiasm for the Greek classics. Nor did he have much to write about Rome and Italy. What interested him instead was his own cultural background in Tingentera, "in which live Phoenicians who were transported from Africa and whence we ourselves are." Pomponius' view of the world concentrated on his Phoenician heritage and his Spanish place of birth. Hence his positive references to the glorious past of Tyre and Sidon, ignoring their more recent history as centres of specifically Greek learning, and the fact that he gives greater space to the description of the North African regions once controlled by Phoenician Carthage than to Greece and Italy in total. When Mela, in describing the North African coast east of Carthage, states that "the shores are inhabited by people socialized according to our custom," "our custom" means Phoenician custom. The small islands opposite the Gulf of Syrtis are described as "memorable for a Roman disaster," meaning not a Roman defeat, but the decisive victory by the Romans over Carthage in the First Punic War.[24]

If Mela's cultural outlook was Phoenician, his local patriotism was directed at Spain, about which he wrote more than about any other area except Africa. Not that Mela wrote in much detail about any region, but when it came to his native land, he provides more information than in his description of other places. "Spain is also abundant with men, horses, iron, lead, copper, silver and gold, and it is so fertile that wherever it changes and is barren for lack of water, it still supports flax or wild field grass." This was an up-to-date, if brief, guide to Mela's home country. Mela comments on the presence of Rome, but only in selected form. Thus he has nothing about Roman colonies, armies, forts and roads, the visible signs of imperialism, and instead there are references to the religious institutions—altars and temples—which linked provincials to Rome and, when it came to literary products, he identifies with other writers in Latin (as opposed to Greek) as "our authors." This provincial from Spain wished to have the best of both worlds, stressing both continuing pride in a Phoenician past and appreciation of the benefits of a Roman present. Frequent reference to Hercules, traditionally identified with the Phoenician god Melqart, linked the Pillars of Hercules, where Mela's geography began and ended, with the ancient culture of Tyre and Sidon at the other end of the Mediterranean:

> Gades [Cadiz] is on the strait. That island is separated from the continent by a narrow space, as if by a river, and has an almost straight bank where it lies nearer to the mainland. Where the island faces Ocean it reaches into the sea with two promontories, and the shoreline in between recedes. On one horn it supports an opulent city of the same name, on the other horn lies a temple of Egyptian Hercules famous for its founders, its cult, its age and its wealth. The Tyrians founded it, and Hercules' bones, buried there, show why the place is sacred. The temple began its existence in the Trojan era, and time has fed its wealth.

It seems that Mela's original readership consisted of his fellow provincials in southern Spain. They could identify with his final reference at the end of the third book to the "end of this work and of the Atlantic shore," which lies at "the promontory of Ampelusia, as it turns towards our strait, whence we made our start." "Our strait" is the Strait of Gibraltar. Mela was appealing to a common identity; his readers were also his neighbours.

Why, then, did the local literature of this Spanish author survive, while that of others did not? The most likely explanation for the copying of Mela's text by a certain Rusticius Helpidius Domnulus in sixth-century Ravenna (from whose copy all the extant manuscripts ultimately derive), and then by monks in different parts of Europe, is that it was not just about Spain but constituted a rare attempt at a world geography in Latin, more accessible to readers than the excerpts of Greek geographical traditions found in encyclopaedic works such as Pliny's *Natural History*. That is to say, Mela's work survived largely because later generations did not recognize it as a reflection of local Spanish pride.[25]

The widespread use of inscriptions in the early imperial period suggests considerable literacy throughout the empire, at least among the urban elite.

It is deeply implausible that the literary tastes of all these provincials were wholly confined to the products of authors writing in Rome or for a Roman audience. If most of their work for local audiences has been lost over the past two thousand years—and we shall see some exceptions in the remainder of this chapter—it is much more likely that this reflects the tastes and interests of scribes before the invention of printing than a dearth of literary invention. The contrast with the survival of Jewish literature from late antiquity should not be taken as evidence that other provincials clung on to their distinctive cultural identities less fiercely than did the Jews. In this respect at least—the survival of so much of their literature through a continuous literary tradition since antiquity—the Jews were a peculiar people.

PECULIAR, but not unique. Special conditions of their own led also to the survival of much evidence for how the Greeks saw themselves in the first two centuries CE. Their writings were preserved alongside the literature of the Latin-speaking Roman elite, since, in the eyes of those who copied out the ancient texts in the Middle Ages, there was no great difference between the texts produced in Athens or Asia Minor in the second century CE and those written seven centuries earlier at the height of the classical period—a failure to distinguish which was more than a little encouraged by the classicizing tendencies of Greeks in the first and second centuries CE. The extraordinary success of Hellenism as the prestige culture of much of the Mediterranean world in the first two centuries allowed the inhabitants of the Greek heartlands—mainland Greece and the west coast of Turkey— an acknowledged cultural superiority at precisely the time when their power to control their own political fortunes was at its lowest ebb. Phil-hellene Roman emperors might attend the Olympic games and even, in the case of Nero, perform in them. Nero's enthusiasm culminated on 28 November 67 CE with an announcement at a special celebration of the Isthmian games in Corinth that Greece would henceforth be free from Roman administration and taxation, as a surviving inscription of the Greek text of the speech he delivered on the occasion attests: "Other leaders have liberated cities, only Nero a province." But freedom that relies on the whim of a Nero is no real freedom. What could be given could as easily be taken away (and was, by Vespasian). The cities which had given birth to the art of politics centuries earlier had now become little more than conduits for the demands of the Roman state. As the moralist Plutarch (*c.* 50–*c.* 120) remarks in his *Precepts of Statecraft*, in his time an ambitious young man in Greece could not hope to lead in war or overthrow a tyranny; he would have to seek glory in public lawsuits or by going on an embassy to the emperor.[26]

Plutarch himself demonstrated in his own career one way in which Greeks could come to terms with the loss of political autonomy. People all over the Mediterranean world might adopt Greek culture, but they could not simply by an act of self-definition become Athenians or Spartans (or Thebans, Ephesians, Smyrnaeans, Pergamenes, or natives of any of the other proud cities of ancient Greece). Plutarch came from Chaeronea, a city in Boeotia, to the north-west of Athens. A member long ago of the Boeotian Confederacy, Chaeronea had been the site of the great battle in 338 BCE in which the Macedonian king Philip II, father of Alexander the Great, gained dominion over the Greeks. In Plutarch's time the city was a backwater of minimal political importance. Nonetheless, although Plutarch was a Roman citizen, held office within the Roman administration and was a man of considerable status in Roman terms, it was the Greek rather than the Roman side of his identity that he chose to emphasize in his writings. His parallel lives of Greeks and Romans were designed to set the qualities of Greek individuals of the classical era alongside similar great figures of the Roman past. Both sets of biographies examine character flaws as much as strengths. The comparison at the end of nineteen of the twenty-three pairs of lives makes clear his purpose, to extract from the careers of great men in two separate traditions examples of virtue and vice in practice. He was well acquainted with powerful Romans, including the senior senator Lucius Mestrius Florus whose Roman name he bore, and, according to some late sources, he was awarded by Trajan the same honorary rank of ex-consul (*ornamenta consularia*) that the Jewish king Agrippa I had received from Claudius sixty or so years before. But for the last thirty years of his life he was a priest at Delphi, and his philosophical dialogues are full of the names of members of his family in Chaeronea, such as his grandfather Lamprias and his father Autobulus. This was a man who looked to his home culture for inspiration, in marked contrast to the Roman perspectives adopted by his contemporaries among the intellectuals from Spain.[27]

The proud history of Plutarch's home town Chaeronea was insignificant in comparison with Athens, the greatest of the fabled cities of Greece before the world was changed by Alexander the Great. The cultural renaissance of Athens reached its peak in the early second century CE, when Hadrian transformed the city's appearance with a lavish building programme. Hadrian became an honorary citizen of the city and was treated by the Athenians as a second founder (with the creation of a thirteenth Athenian tribe named "Hadrianis"), and, at the request of the Athenians, he redrafted through his jurists the ancients laws of Draco and Solon which governed not only the ordinary civil and criminal laws but also the constitution itself. Hadrian's beneficence was the culmination of a series of gifts to the city by Roman senators and emperors keen to pay tribute to Athens' glorious past. The eastern part of the agora, the civic centre, had been remodelled by Julius Caesar and Augustus as a market. Augustus' friend Marcus Vipsanius Agrippa had paid for an odeum (a hall for musical competitions) to reflect the importance of Athenian culture, and a series of libraries had been erected. These Roman benefactors naturally sought their own glory alongside that of Athens. The colossal temple of Zeus Olympius, which had been begun in the sixth century BCE, was completed in magnificent style by Hadrian. It was approached through an arch that separated the "new Athens built by Hadrian" from the old Athens of Theseus. All this external reverence undoubtedly helped to bolster Athenian pride. Philostratus, who composed in the early third century CE his "Lives of the Sophists," reported, as evidence of the arrogance of the orator Polemo of Laodicea, who "conversed with cities as his inferiors, emperors as not his superiors, and the gods as his equals," that, "since he well knew that the natures of the Athenians need to be held in check rather than encouraged, this was his introductory speech: 'They say, Athenians, that you are wise hearers of words. I shall find out.' "[28]

By contrast, the pride of the Spartans lay in their claims to a distinctive way of life which had bred their legendary military prowess. During the first century CE, they "revived" many of the old customs, although "revival" often consisted in the invention of tradition and spurious attribution to the traditional founder of the Spartan lifestyle, Lycurgus. Partly for Roman tourists in the early empire, but increasingly for Greeks seeking self-affirmation in the second century CE, Spartans stressed to themselves and to the outside world their archaic traditions, from their heroic endurance in the Persian wars to their "Lycurgan" customs. Their local patriotism was strongly endorsed by other Greeks. Plutarch wrote a biography of Lycurgus, a man about whom little can now or could then be said with any certainty; turning him into a philosophical and political seer, Plutarch admitted that the treatment of helots, the underclass in classical Sparta, was notoriously inequitable and cruel, and he deemed it therefore not really Spartan: "for I cannot persuade myself to ascribe to Lycurgus so abominable a measure . . . judging of his character from the gentleness of his disposition and his justice upon all other occasions." In general the special qualities of lifestyle boasted by the Spartans seem often to have touched only the surface of their lives, which in many aspects resembled that elsewhere in Roman Greece; it is noticeable, for instance, that Spartan women are praised in inscriptions for their moderation, their love of their husbands, their dignity and their decorum, in contrast to the notorious independence of Spartan women in classical times. But remaining distinctive (or possibly revived in the Roman period) was the Spartan system of rearing youths. Civic overseers organized contests in song, dance, athletics and military exercises. A large series of dedicatory inscriptions from the temple of Artemis Orthia shows that such training was organized by age group, and that from the late first century CE each group was subdivided into "herds," or teams, providing, if the evidence of the surviving inscriptions is indicative, an intense sense of team identity. A "contest of endurance" in which Plutarch saw a boy die seems to have been a particularly violent event involving the youths making an attack on the altar of Artemis Orthia, which was defended by men bearing whips. Claims about the antiquity of these customs were rendered more plausible by the use of archaic terminology and, in dedications to the goddess, a Doric dialect of Greek.[29]

Greek local patriotism and its basis in memories of a distant past more glorious than the present emerge clearly from the *Description of Greece* written by Pausanias in the mid-second century CE. Pausanias was himself from the city of Magnesia in Lydia (modern Turkey), but his tourist guide covered the main regions of the Greek mainland: Attica, Megara, the whole of the Peloponnese, Boeotia and Phocis (including Delphi)—all the Roman province of Achaia of his time apart from the mountainous region of Aetolia and the islands. He wrote enthusiastically about the sculpture and painting of the archaic and classical periods that were still to be seen in the ancient cities of Greece, but made only occasional reference to the artistic benefactions of Roman emperors and others in his own time, and showed little interest in the period of decline which had preceded the Roman conquest. Learned comments about the historical background to the monuments he described, and about the religious cults and rituals to be witnessed by a leisurely traveller through these ancient cities, bear witness to the sense of identification with the Greek past shared even by those from across the Aegean. For Pausanias, the history of Greece that mattered was the story of the glorious years between the Persian wars in the early fifth century BCE and the Roman conquest three hundred years later: "Miltiades, son of Cimon, overcame in battle those of the barbarian invaders who had landed at Marathon, stayed the advance of the Medes, and so became the first benefactor of all Greece, just as Philopoemen, son of Craugis [leader of the Achaean League in the late third and early second centuries BCE] was the last." Pausanias noted that "after this, Greece ceased to bear good men." It is probable that Pausianias' intended readership lay among other Greeks from Asia Minor like himself, for whom the names of Athens, Sparta, Delphi and Olympia, all of which feature prominently in the *Description*, resonated with heroic glory.[30]

By the time Pausanias was writing in the second century, rhetorical displays harking back to the classical past had become mass entertainment. The brilliant speeches of orators who conjured up the spirit of Pericles or Demosthenes in set pieces before admiring crowds set the tone of the culture of Greek cities. A successful professor of rhetoric might win applause by declaiming "in the character of Aristogeiton demanding the right to denounce Demosthenes for conspiring with Persia and Aeschines for conspiring with Philip," or on the theme "Hypereides, when Philip is at Elatea, pays heed only to the counsels of Demosthenes." The shared Hellenic culture of the city elites was consolidated by the internationalism of the traditional athletic games at Olympia and elsewhere, and by institutions such as the Worldwide Guild (*Synodos*) of the Artists of Dionysus, who provided professional entertainment at the great religious festivals. All this nostalgia for the glorious past prompted much expenditure by the urban elite on their native cities, sometimes in the erection of archaizing monuments, as in Athens, or by minting their own base-metal coinages on which local traditions were loyally recalled. The designs used on the coinage of Nysa in the late first century CE in Asia Minor referred mostly to the cult of Pluto and Kore because an important shrine to these divinities lay close to the city; the coins of Pergamum in the same period referred to the local cults too, in this case Asclepius and Athena, but they also included types showing the head of the eponymous hero Pergamos, alleged founder of the city. Antiquarian designs became more common during the second century CE. But even more lasting than coins or buildings was the literary record. The orators of the "Second Sophistic," so fulsomely described by Philostratus (who coined the term in his "Lives of the Sophists" in order to assert a link between itinerant professors of higher education in the Greek world in the fifth century BCE and the public teachers of rhetoric who flourished in the Greek world between *c.* 60 and 230 CE), produced between them a rich literature on classical themes, from the speeches of Dio Chrysostom and Aelius Aristides to Plutarch's biographies and the history of Alexander the Great composed by the historian and philosopher Arrian of Nicomedia. Much of our picture of the world of classical Greece has been coloured by these accounts, written with wistful hindsight in a world now dominated by Rome.[31]

The career of Arrian (*c.* 86–160) may help to explain the preservation of so much of this literature in contrast to the loss of writings produced by and for provincials elsewhere in the empire. As a young aristocrat in Bithynia, Arrian held a magistracy in his home town and devoted himself to the study of philosophy with the Stoic Epictetus, who in the 90s CE had set up a school in Nicopolis, on the western coast of Greece. While engaged on such intellectual pursuits Arrian became friendly, some time between 108 and 112, with the future emperor Hadrian, ward of the emperor Trajan and by this date a senator of consular rank, who shared his enthusiasms, including a passion for hunting. The friendship brought him into political prominence once Hadrian succeeded to power in 117. Arrian was made a senator, gained the consulship, and from 131 to 137 served as governor of Cappadocia. He wrote about his own contemporary career in the style of his classical predecessors. His Greek style was a conscious imitation of Xenophon and other classical historians, and even while fulfilling his duties in Cappadocia he managed to write an *Essay on Tactics* and a geographical essay about the coasts of the Black Sea. His *Order of Battle Against the Alans* recounted, in the style of Xenophon, how he had repelled an attack on his province by the nomadic Alans, who had tried to infiltrate south from the Caucasus. Arrian's prominence in Roman terms thus in no way conflicted with his self-perception as an inheritor of the traditions of classical Greece.

On the contrary, the more Greek his behaviour, the more favour he was likely to receive from Hadrian, whose own devotion to Greek studies led to him being called *Graeculus,* "little Greek." Among the last works Arrian is known to have produced are the eight books of *Bithyniaca,* which gave the history of Bithynia from the very beginnings down to its annexation by Rome.[32]

What was life like for these Greeks under Roman rule? Of the peasants who cultivated the countryside, we know little: an apparently realistic picture of self-sufficient isolated farmers in southern Euboea, who survived, poor but happy, by keeping away from the nearest town, was composed by the philosopher Dio Chrysostom in the late first century CE, not as an ethnographic description but as a moral lesson for those who preferred luxury to simplicity. The culture espoused by Greeks who were conscious of their Greekness was urban.[33]

That urban culture had changed a good deal from the city life of the classical period. Inhabitants of cities which had long been political rivals were now, under the Roman peace, deprived of the opportunity to attack each other, except at the courts of Roman governors. Deeply aware of this loss of the political freedom which had once provided the focus of civic life, Greeks threw their energy and resources instead into beautifying and enjoying the public spaces of their cities.

What such cities usually looked like, and the function they usually fulfilled, is evident from the sneers of Pausanias about Panopeus, a city in central Greece, which failed to live up to expectations—"if one can give the name of city to those which possess no government offices, no gymnasium, no theatre, no marketplace, no water descending to a fountain, but live in bare shelters just like mountain cabins."[34] Richer Greeks spent their surplus wealth less on private luxuries and sumptuous rural villas than on the erection of such buildings to win the approbation of their fellow citizens. Local civic identity was as strong in Greece under Roman rule in the first century CE as it had ever been. Numerous inscriptions attest to the continuing importance of the traditional associations of boys, young men and elders which gave an individual Greek male a sense of his place in civic society. But civic pride was combined with a sense of solidarity with other Greeks in contrast to the Roman outsider. Panhellenic celebrations, above all the Olympic games, held in Olympia in the north-western Peloponnese, were more popular than ever before in Greek history, and star performers in athletics, as in oratory, drama and song, gained renown across the Greek world. The Roman state gave positive support to such manifestations of cultural solidarity: in 43 and 48–9 CE the emperor Claudius confirmed the privileges, previously granted by Augustus, of the Worldwide Guild of Crowned Victors in the Sacred Contests of Dionysus and their Fellow Competitors, the stage artists whose performances packed theatres all over the Greek world.[35]

OF ALL the provincials ruled by Rome, only the Greeks could hope to have their contemporary literature treated as prestigious and preserved by and through the Roman elite. If evidence about local attitudes to their world survived elsewhere, that was the result of luck. In this respect the luck of the Egyptians lay in the climate and environment of the Nile valley, which preserved thousands of texts on papyrus for posterity to read.

The roots of Egyptian culture lay millennia in the past, a fact well known to almost every educated person in the ancient world. For any Greek ignorant of the facts, the Egyptian priest Manetho wrote in the third century BCE an orderly account in Greek of the dynastic history of the early Pharaohs. During the Hellenistic period the transference of political control to a Greek elite encouraged the adoption of Hellenism by Egyptians as happened elsewhere in the countries once ruled by Alexander, but the exclusive racism of the ruling Ptolemaic dynasty rendered native achievement of political power difficult: the Ptolemies preferred to entrust all authority to Macedonians and Greeks so far as they could. In the administrative changes imposed by Rome after Egypt was "added to the empire of the Roman people" by Augustus, racial distinctions were strengthened still further and the inferior status of Egyptians remained enshrined in administrative law. But despite the predominance of Greek as the language of Egyptian papyri in the first two centuries CE, it remains possible to say a great deal about the attitudes and beliefs not just of the Greek elite but also of ordinary Egyptians, whose cultural background, even in Greek documents, is often betrayed by their names: "Petosiris," "Nephersorchos," "Teteimouthis," "Taychis." The papyri show Egyptians continuing in some social practices wholly contrary to normal Roman behaviour, most strikingly in approval of brother-sister marriages. Such unions had been found both among the Pharaohs and the Ptolemies, and Diodorus Siculus remarked in the mid-first century BCE that "the Egyptians . . . made a law, they say, contrary to the general custom of mankind, permitting men to marry their sisters." There is much evidence in census records, marriage contracts, deeds of divorce, private letters and other documents from the Roman period that the custom was widespread not only among the Egyptian peasantry but also among the Greek elite in Egypt. An archive of sixty-nine documents relating to a certain Kronion, spanning the years from 107 to 53, reveals that two of his five children—his eldest son, also called Kronion, and his daughter Taorsenouphis—married and produced offspring of their own. A census document of 173–4 CE listing the property and families of four brothers, Pantbeus, Tithoennesis, Phalakris and Haronoesis, records that two of the brothers had married their own sisters. Roman citizens were forbidden such unions, and this must have been one of the local customs that came most under strain when Roman citizenship was conferred on the inhabitants of Egypt in 212: brother-sister marriage was eventually forbidden throughout the empire by an imperial edict in 295.[36]

At the same time as they upheld traditional customs, Egyptians were quite capable of using the Roman administration to their advantage when law and order were needed, as they were by a villager, Orsenouphis, whose detailed complaint to the local police chief in 28 CE is recorded on a papyrus:

In the month Mesore of the past fourteenth year of Tiberius Caesar Augustus I was having some old walls on my premises demolished by the builder Petesouchus son of Petesouchus, and while I was absent from home to gain my living, Petesouchus in the process of demolition discovered a hoard which had been secreted by my mother in a little box as long ago as the sixteenth year of [Augustus] Caesar, consisting of a pair of gold earrings weighing four quarters, a gold crescent weighing three quarters, a pair of silver armlets of the weight of twelve drachmas of uncoined metal, a necklace with silver ornaments worth eighty drachmas, and sixty silver drachmas. Diverting the attention of his assistants and my people, he had them conveyed to his own home by his unmarried daughter, and after emptying out the aforesaid objects he threw away the box empty in my house, and he even admitted finding the box, though he pretends that it was empty. Wherefore I request, if you approve, that the accused be brought before you for the consequent punishment.[37]

The documents, archaeological as much as papyrological, also show religious accommodation to Roman rule. The walls of the great Egyptian temples still visited by tourists today bear prayers for the well-being of Roman emperors as much as, sometimes more than, Egyptian Pharaohs. Sculptured reliefs show the emperor Augustus sacrificing to the animal gods in the Egyptian style. But religion also provides one of the best touchstones for the continuation of local culture through the period of Roman rule. Numerous documents attest to the effort, personnel and expense devoted to worship of distinctively Egyptian gods: Thoeris, Isis, Sarapis, Horus, Anubis, Apis, Osiris. Such worship did not preclude veneration also of Greek and Roman gods. At Oxyrhynchus, Egyptian divinities worshipped included Zeus-Ammon, Hera-Isis, Sarapis, Osiris and Thoeris; Greek gods included Demeter, Kore, the Dioscuri, Dionysus, Hermes and Apollo; among Roman gods were Jupiter Capitolinus and Mars. Precisely what significance the professed and explicit overlap between the identities of different gods held for worshippers is unclear.[38]

Despite such complexities it is evident that traditional Egyptian religion remained strong. The political status and financial standing of the Egyptian priestly caste were markedly diminished under Roman rule compared to their privileged position under the Ptolemies, but they continued to function (and earn privileges from the state). A papyrus of 107 CE refers to the work of five hieroglyph cutters in Oxyrhynchus, although they swore specifically that five was all there were in their district:

To Claudius Menandrus, basilicogrammateus [royal scribe], from Teos . . . and Asklas . . . both of the city of Oxyrhynchus, hieroglyphic carvers, who have been delegated by their fellow-carvers: list of ourselves and the said fellow-carvers of hieroglyphics for the present 11th year of Traianus Caesar the lord, as follows: . . . Total 5 men. And we swear by the emperor . . . that we have honestly and truthfully presented the foregoing list, and that there are no more than these, and that we have no apprentices or strangers carrying on the art down to the present day . . .[39]

The priests at Socnopaiou Nesos in the mid-second century CE celebrated in their temples a total of one hundred and fifty-three festival days each year. That much of the ordinary populace continued to believe in the Egyptian gods, depicted wholly or partly in animal form, seems undeniable. All this could be deduced even without the chance survival of fragments of a treatise on Egyptian religion by Chaeremon of Alexandria, who included among his pupils the young Nero. Writing from within the Egyptian tradition, Chaeremon presented native customs with a Stoic philosophical gloss to a sometimes sceptical outside world, as a much later writer reported:

> Chaeremon the Stoic tells in his exposé about the Egyptian priests, who, he says, were considered also as philosophers among the Egyptians, that they chose the temples as the place to philosophise . . . They renounced every employment and human revenues, and devoted their whole life to contemplation of the divine . . . They were always seen near the gods, or rather their statues. And each of the acts was no empty gesture, but an indication of some allegorical truth . . . Their way of walking was disciplined, and they took care to have a quiet look, so that they did not blink when they wanted to do so. They seldom laughed . . . They were not allowed to touch foods or drinks that were produced outside Egypt . . . They abstained from all kinds of fish, and from such quadrupeds as had uncloven hoofs or had toes or had no horns, and also from such birds as were carnivorous . . . The periods of purification and fasting observed by all priests were clean. This was the period when they were to perform something pertaining to the sacred rites. Then they spent a number of days in preparation . . . and during this time they abstained from all animal food, from all vegetables and pulse, but above all from sexual intercourse with women, for (needless to say) they never at any time had intercourse with males . . . Such are the things testified about the Egyptians by a man who was a lover of truth and an accurate writer, and who was among the Stoics a very clever philosopher.[40]

The use of hieroglyphs and hieratic script for writing was confined to the Egyptian priesthood, who used them only in religious and ceremonial contexts, but the Egyptian language expressed in other scripts was widely used in business documents and the private correspondence of ordinary people, even if not on the same scale as Greek. The shift from use of demotic script, extensively employed in the Ptolemaic period and the first century of Roman rule, to Coptic script, which began to appear in Christian documents towards the end of the third century CE, reveals the impact of Greek literacy: Coptic is essentially Egyptian written in Greek characters (with a few extra letters for those Egyptian sounds for which Greek does not adequately provide). The eventual emergence of Coptic Christianity is in itself testimony to the continuing vitality of the Egyptian language as a medium not just for mundane transactions but for thought and literary invention. Many of the surviving texts of demotic literature were copied in the early Roman period. Although the composition of most should probably be dated to Ptolemaic times, it is not impossible that some of these writings were still being devised in the first century CE. A demotic papyrus now in the British Museum has a copy in handwriting dated to the Roman period of the story of Setne Khamwas and his visit to the underworld, where he witnesses the blessed existence of the just and the tortures of the wicked:

> Setne said: "My son Si-Osire, many are the marvels that I have seen in the netherworld. Now let me learn what is happening to those people who are plaiting ropes while donkeys chew them up" . . . Si-Osire said: "In truth, my father Setne, those people whom you saw plaiting ropes while donkeys were chewing them up, they are the kind of people on earth who are under the curse of the god. They labour night and day for their livelihood, while their women rob them behind their backs, and they find no bread to eat. When they came to the netherworld in their turn, their misdeeds were found to be more numerous than their good deeds. It was ordered that what had happened to them on earth should happen to them in the netherworld."

A demotic papyrus from the first century CE now in Leiden contains a series of wisdom instructions which were evidently quite popular, since a number of other copies also survive in fragmentary form: "The teaching to be measured in everything, so as to do nothing but what is fitting . . . Do not be a glutton, lest you become the companion of poverty . . . The teaching not to be a fool, so that one does not fail to receive you in the house ... The teaching of knowing the greatness of the gods so as to put it in your heart." During the second and third centuries CE some of these Egyptian literary works were translated or adapted into Greek, rather in the same way as Jews like Josephus adapted Jewish history from the Bible. The legend of Tefnut, which involved the mission of Thoth to conciliate Tefnut, who as a result of a quarrel had withdrawn to the Nubian desert and taken on the form of a lioness, is known both from a demotic papyrus of the second century CE and also from a literary version in Greek found on a third-century papyrus in the British Museum, in which Thoth is named Hermes. There was clearly a demand for such translations in this period. Other extant texts of this kind include an invocation of Isis and a Life of Imuthes-Asclepius.[41]

Abundant evidence thus shows Egyptians tenacious in their own culture, but also willing to accept and adapt cultural imports from both Greece and Rome. Nowhere does this emerge more clearly than in the huge number of surviving mummy portraits. The care of the dead, which had been so conspicuous a feature of Egyptian culture for millennia, continued under Roman rule. Tomb paintings and shrouds depict Osiris and the jackal-headed Anubis, the god who presided over the processes of mummification. But the portraits of the dead are painted realistically in the Roman style, often charming pictures which probably provide an idealized picture of the deceased.

The survival of all this material through archaeological chance, rather than by virtue of approval from those critics who thought some literature worthy to be copied through the Middle Ages, when other works were lost, also makes more likely than elsewhere in the empire the preservation of evidence of native opposition to Roman rule. The Roman sources refer to only one native uprising which required suppression, by the *boukoloi* ("herdsmen") who rebelled in the Egyptian delta in 172 CE; they mention nothing about the reasons for dissent. Copies of the nationalist demotic prophecy called the *Oracle of the Potter*, originally composed against the Ptolemies in the second century BCE to predict the future glory of Memphis and the demise of the city of Alexandria "when Egypt will see the foreigners fall like leaves from the branch," was still circulating in Greek versions in the second and third centuries CE. But much the most virulent anti-Roman literature preserved from Roman Egypt is, perhaps surprisingly, not Egyptian but Greek. The Greeks of the city of Alexandria, who felt that their authority in the country where they had held privileged sway under the Ptolemies had been fatally compromised by the imposition of Roman rule, produced a literary compilation of narratives describing heroic opposition to emperors, ranging from Tiberius in the first to Commodus in the late second century CE, by Alexandrian dissidents, sometimes portrayed as the leading citizens of the city. These martyr acts take the form of reports of genuine trials, and some are based on real events, including the struggle between Jews and Greeks in the city in the 30s and 40s CE which had brought Philo on his embassy to Rome to appeal to Gaius in 40 and had embroiled Agrippa I, as we saw in Chapter 2. In one text, preserved in a number of fragmentary papyri, a certain Isidorus is shown protesting to the emperor Claudius: "My lord Caesar, what do you care for a two-penny-halfpenny Jew like Agrippa? . . . I accuse them [the Jews] of wishing to stir up the entire world . . . They are not of the same nature as the Alexandrians, but live rather after the fashion of the Egyptians . . . I am neither a slave nor a girl-musician's son, but gymnasiarch of the glorious city of Alexandria, but you are the cast-off son of the Jewish Salome!" The literary genre of opposition to Rome by Alexandrian Greeks was to remain popular, if the date and number of copies of extant papyri is a good guide, into the third century CE, even though by then real political opposition was negligible.[42]

ELSEWHERE IN the empire the evidence for the continuation of local cultures under Roman rule has to be pieced together from less direct indications: the language used in inscriptions, artistic styles, names of people and places. In many parts of the empire Greek or Latin were the languages of public display regardless of the languages in general use, much as Latin was used on monuments throughout Europe in early modern times. A distinctive local culture, like that of diaspora Jews, could express itself through the medium of Greek, just as Pomponius Mela propagated his Phoenician viewpoint in a work composed in Latin; so nothing can be learned from the absence of epigraphic evidence for a local language, although a decision to use such a language was likely to be significant. Recognition of the significance of native artistic preferences is in some ways even harder, since much of the surviving archaeological evidence is found on pottery, not an obvious type of artefact for the expression of political sentiment in antiquity any more than now. The study of names may seem more promising. A father who gave his son a wholly Roman-sounding name, such as the father of Marcus Iulius Agrippa (the full name of the Jewish king Agrippa I), did not thereby deny his native culture, but the choice of a distinctive local name is likely to have signified cultural pride. In the Jerusalem over which Agrippa I ruled, the names of the high priests were notably Jewish. Ananus son of Sethi, himself High Priest in 6 CE, had five sons who each held the high priesthood for a while. They were called Eleazar, Jonathan, Theophilus, Matthias and Ananus: in some contexts, it seems, to give your child a Greek or Roman name did not seem appropriate. Evidence of the strength of local cultures comes also from place names—not so much the names foisted on cities by Roman authorities, which changed with the vagaries of the regime (much like the transmutations of St. Petersburg during the twentieth century), but the names that survived antiquity. It probably says something about the tribal identity of the Parisii in whose territory it lay that the town of Lutetia, laid out as a standard Roman town with forum, temples and regular street plan, is now known as Paris, rather than Lutèce.

Despite such limitations of evidence, enough material survives to confirm that multifarious local cultures existed in the empire. Local languages persisted from pre-Roman times to re-emerge as Welsh or Basque in the Middle Ages. The native language of North Africa, written in a distinctive alphabet of its own, left traces on inscriptions written in the early centuries CE in places from the Atlantic coast to eastern Tunisia. Ovid remarked on the Getic and Sarmatian spoken by the locals in the Black Sea region to which he had been banished by his erstwhile patron Augustus. Bilingualism must have been common, and trilingualism (in Greek, Latin and some local language) not unusual: the great Roman lawyer Ulpian (died 223 CE) came from Tyre and would presumably have been conversant with Phoenician and Greek, the languages used for inscriptions in the city before it became a Roman colony during his lifetime, before he devoted himself to an administrative career in Rome and the composition of juristic works in Latin. A number of different local languages continued in use in Anatolia, most strikingly evidenced in the numerous neo-Phrygian inscriptions in Greek letters of the first to third centuries CE on funerary texts and religious dedications to the Anatolian god Men and to abstract divinities of moral qualities such as holiness and justice. But most languages were probably not written down. Nothing in the archaeological record survives of the language of the people of Lystra who in the first century CE witnessed the miraculous healing of a cripple by Paul, according to Acts: "And when the people saw what Paul had done, they lifted up their voices, saying in the speech of Lycaonia, 'The gods are come down to us in the likeness of men.' "[43]

One provincial at least took solace from this variety of customs. Bar Daisan, a speculative Christian philosopher at the court of Abgar VIII of Edessa (modern Urfa, in south-eastern Turkey), wrote a treatise in Syriac *On Fate, or the Book of the Laws of Countries* in the late second century CE, in which he argued against astrological determinism by showing (not altogether accurately) how the customs of peoples differ:

> Now listen, and try to understand that not all people over the whole world do that which the stars determine by their Fate and in their sectors, in the same way. For men have established laws in each country by that liberty given them from God . . . Among the Romans, everyone who has stolen some trifle is scourged then set free. On the further side of the Euphrates, towards the East, no man called a thief or a murderer will become very angry. But if a man is accused of having had sexual intercourse with boys, he revenges himself and does not even shrink from murder . . . In the North, however, on the territory of the Germans and their neighbours, the boys who are handsome serve the men as wives, and a wedding feast, too, is held then . . . Among the Britons, many men together take one wife . . .

From such evidence, argued Bar Daisan, it is clear that man controls his own fate, and that life is controlled neither by the stars nor by geography. The same argument is bolstered by evidence that people can change their customs, most strikingly and effectively, according to Bar Daisan, when they become Christians.[44]

The Roman world, it seems, was what we would call today multicultural, as was acknowledged by both rulers and ruled. Observation of the kaleidoscope of customs within the empire elicited at different times moralizing, humour, disdain, distaste or admiration, but not surprise. Everyone knew that the peoples of the Roman world followed distinctive local traditions, and apparently took it for granted that such variety was inevitable.

## TOLERATION

IN GENERAL, the Romans were happy to allow their provincial subjects to continue to live in such idiosyncratic ways. The tolerance of the state in allowing provincials to retain non-Roman lifestyles is all the more striking when the Romans knew well the practical advantages which could accrue to the state from cultural change. The historian Tacitus claimed that his father-in-law Agricola spent the winter of 78–9 CE during his governorship of Britain attempting "to induce a people, hitherto scattered, uncivilized and therefore prone to fight, to grow pleasurably inured to peace and ease." This was achieved, according to Tacitus, by encouraging the building of temples, marketplaces and large houses, and by promoting the Latin language and the wearing of a toga, leading on to "the amenities that make vice agreeable," such as baths and banquets.[45] As has long been noted, so conscious an imposition of Roman culture by a single governor in so short a space of time could not possibly work, and Tacitus is not in this instance to be trusted. Nevertheless, a long-term policy along the lines ascribed to Agricola would have been perfectly sensible and feasible, and if urbanization in Roman Britain was slow and patchy over the first two centuries CE, as can be amply demonstrated from the archaeological evidence from numerous sites, this was the result of the policy not being followed even though Romans knew it might have worked. In other words, the normal attitude of the state to provincial culture was laissez-faire.

But laissez-faire did not imply that in the eyes of Romans all cultures were equally valuable. Romans were not racially prejudiced in the sense of believing that some peoples were inherently inferior, but they had a clear notion of the barbarian as the opposite to civilized society and outside the bounds of true humanity. The whole concept of the barbarian, borrowed from its original Greek use where it denoted those who spoke languages other than Greek (thus, ironically, including the Latin-speaking Romans), provided a useful mechanism to distance the acceptable culture of the civilized metropolis from its implied antithesis. Barbarians could occasionally be held up for admiration by the cynic deploring the decline in Roman morals; hence the praise of aspects of simple German society in the *Germania* of Tacitus. But more often the barbarian was seen as benighted, rescuable (if at all) only by incorporation into the civilized world of Rome. Both language about barbarians and the physical depiction of them could be extremely violent. On the column of Trajan in Rome, which celebrated the emperor's victories in Dacia in 101–2 and 105–6, a series of images carved in relief record the operation of the Roman army on the Danube. The scenes depicted, evidently preserved for the admiration of the general Roman public (even if not all the details could be fully appreciated from the ground), show the mass murder of the enemy, the enslavement of women and children, even the display of severed heads as trophies. Extermination of such enemies could be celebrated in chilling terms. According to the historian Cassius Dio, when the annihilation of the Nasamones in Africa in 85–6 included the destruction of all the non-combatants, the emperor Domitian announced triumphantly to the Senate, "I have forbidden the Nasamones to exist."[46] Peoples and groups might be defined as "internal barbarians" in this way only by certain individuals at particular times or for specific purposes, but the language and concept were dangerously available for their isolation and denigration. National caricatures based on "science," such as the astrological geography of the great astronomer Claudius Ptolemaeus (Ptolemy), who wrote in the mid-second century CE, could easily degenerate into systemic hostility:

The remaining parts of the quarter, situated around the middle of the whole inhabited world, Idumaea, Coele-Syria, Judaea, Phoenicia, Chaldaea, Orchinia and Arabia Felix, which are situated towards the north-west of the whole quarter, have additional familiarity with the north-western triangle, Aries, Leo and Sagittarius, and, furthermore, have as co-rulers Jupiter, Mars and Mercury. Therefore these peoples are, in comparison with the others, more prone to trade and exchange; they are more unscrupulous, and despicable cowards, and treacherous, and servile, and totally fickle, on account of the stars mentioned standing in mutual opposition. Of these, again the inhabitants of Coele-Syria, and Idumaea, and Judaea are more closely familiar to Aries and Mars, and therefore these peoples are in general bold, and godless, and scheming.[47]

It could take a long time for Romans to reach the conclusion that any specific behaviour fell outside the bounds of civilized acceptability as they defined it. The practices of the druids in Gaul and in Britain were outlawed in the time of Tiberius, and the emperor Claudius took action to suppress them. The Roman sources which report these actions by the state express revulsion at druidic barbarity: Suetonius records of Claudius that "he utterly abolished the cruel and inhuman religion of the druids among the Gauls, which under Augustus had been forbidden only to [Roman] citizens." The elder Pliny, who was living somewhat closer to the time described, in his discussion of the ubiquity of magic throughout the world attributed the change to Tiberius: "Magic certainly found a home in the Gallic provinces, and that down to living memory. For the principate of Tiberius Caesar did away with their druids and this tribe of seers and medical men . . . It is impossible to calculate how great is the debt owed to the Romans, who swept away the monstrous rites, in which to kill a man was a most religious act and for him to be eaten was most conducive to health."[48] Whether or not such charges were false in whole or in part, Roman disgust had evidently been slow to manifest itself. Some hundred years before Claudius, both Cicero and Julius Caesar had established close and friendly ties with the Aeduan druid Divitiacus, and Caesar seems to have found nothing problematic about druidism during his conquest of Gaul in the 50s BCE.

Such prohibitions of provincial customs were highly unusual in the first century CE, and it is significant that Pliny tried to justify the suppression of druids by accusing them of cannibalism, a charge not infrequently adduced against any group deemed hostile to normal society. It is likely that the real problem posed to Rome by druids lay in their popular following among ordinary Gauls, which threatened to undermine the authority of the rich local aristocrats to whom Rome had devolved power in the province. When no such political issues arose, provincials could act how they liked, as they did when siblings married each other in Egypt.

The main impulse to acceptance of Roman *mores* by provincials thus came not through imposition from above but as a result of the ambitions of the provincials themselves. The Roman elite was remarkably willing to accept into its ranks capable men of almost any background, provided that they lived in a Roman way. Under Nero, most Roman senators came from Italy, although there were already quite a few from southern Spain and southern Gaul, but by the late first century CE there were numerous members of the senatorial order from the Greek-speaking regions of the empire, mostly from the province of Asia in western Turkey, and in the early second century there began to be many senators whose families derived from the northern coast of Africa. By the mid-second century CE, when a certain Tiberius Claudius Gordianus, the earliest senator to derive from Tyana in Cappadocia on the very eastern limit of Roman rule, entered the Roman elite, there were few regions of the empire not represented in the body which was still seen by Romans as the central organ of the state.[49]

The Romans knew well, of course, that individuals had skins of different colour, and remarks are scattered through Latin literature expressing aesthetic judgements on black-skinned "Ethiopians" and the pale faces and "excessive" height of northern Europeans, but these were matters of taste rather than moral or social significance, and ethnic origins could be ignored if someone was sufficiently talented. Thus a telling omission in the description by the Roman senator Tacitus of Tiberius Iulius Alexander, prefect of Egypt in the 60s CE and in due course chief of staff to the future emperor Titus during his prosecution of the siege of Jerusalem in 70, is any mention of his Jewish origin. Tiberius Alexander was in fact the son of one of the most prominent members of the Alexandrian Jewish community. His father Marcus, who had held a powerful administrative role for Rome as *alabarch* (a position which probably involved superintendence of customs collection on the Arabian side of the Nile), was famous for his gift of gilded gates to the Jerusalem Temple. He was the benefactor whose loan to Agrippa I in the mid-30s CE had enabled the Jewish king to restart his political career in Rome. Tiberius' brother (also called Marcus, like his father) had been married to Agrippa's daughter, the Jewish princess Berenice. His uncle was Philo, the great Jewish philosopher who had been one of the leaders of the embassy sent to the emperor Gaius in 40 CE to plead on behalf of the Jews of Alexandria.[50] Tiberius Alexander had himself been sent in 46 by Claudius as governor of Judaea, presumably on the assumption that his Jewish background would give him an advantage in ruling over Jerusalem, as it had done for his brother's father-in-law, Agrippa I. And yet, despite all these Jewish connections, Tacitus describes Tiberius Alexander, when he was an officer on the staff of the Roman general Corbulo in Armenia in 63, just as "a distinguished Roman knight." Even more remarkably, having just informed his readers at the beginning of his *Histories*, which cover the years 69 to 96, that in 69 "the war against the Jews was being directed with three legions by Flavius Vespasianus," he immediately proceeds to describe the government of Egypt, "managed from the time of the deified Augustus by Roman knights in place of their former kings . . . At this time the governor was Tiberius Alexander, of that same nation [i.e. an Egyptian]." The satirist Juvenal, writing at about the same time as Tacitus, mocks Tiberius Alexander, against whose triumphal statue "it is permissible not only to pee," as "some Egyptian Arabarch or other," referring to the post held by Tiberius' father. For both Roman authors, Tiberius Alexander's origins as a Jew were apparently irrelevant. His career exemplified the willingness of the Roman elite to ignore the ethnic and racial origins of provincials who sought to be treated as Roman, provided only that the individual in question adopted Roman customs in full.[51]


WHEN SUCH diverse societies flourished unchecked without interference, why should the life of Jerusalem have been deemed so much more inimical to Rome than others in the empire? We must now seek an answer by examining the differences between Roman and Jewish attitudes to the world they shared.

# PART TWO

# ROMANS AND JEWS

# CHAPTER FOUR

# IDENTITIES

## BEING ROMAN AND BEING JEWISH

THE RELATIONSHIP BETWEEN Rome and Jerusalem was complicated by the fact that a Roman could be Jewish and a Jew could be Roman. Thus, according to the Acts of the Apostles, in the late 50s CE the apostle Paul, a Jew from the city of Tarsus in Cilicia, could ensure (at least temporarily) his physical inviolability when arrested in Jerusalem by letting slip his status as a Roman citizen:

> The tribune commanded him to be brought into the barracks and ordered that he should be examined by flogging so that he might find out why they cried so much against him. And as they bound him with thongs, Paul said to the centurion that stood by: "Is it lawful for you to scourge a man that is a Roman, and uncondemned?" When the centurion heard that, he went and told the tribune, saying, "Be careful what you do: for this man is a Roman."[1]

A few sceptics have doubted the story, but without justification: the whole narrative of the last section of Acts hinges on this status of Paul, as a result of which he ended up being sent as a prisoner to Rome to plead his case before the emperor. The account by the author of Acts of the reaction of others to Paul's revelation about himself is instructive. They are much surprised: it is not to be expected that a diaspora Jew who has got himself into trouble, as Paul has done, will turn out to be a Roman. On the other hand, it turns out that Paul is not the only Roman present. The tribune informs him that he too has Roman citizenship, "bought with a great sum." Paul, by contrast, affirms that he was born a Roman citizen.

Roman identity depended ultimately on recognition as a citizen by the Roman state. There were clear rules. A male Roman citizen could only produce legitimate citizen offspring if his spouse was either herself Roman or from a community within the empire which was specifically acknowledged by the Roman state to have the right of *conubium*, intermarriage, with Romans. A female Roman citizen could not secure citizen rights for her newborn children if her husband was not Roman. But senior Roman magistrates could, and did, grant citizenship to individual non-Romans in the provinces of the empire as a privilege, either for services rendered or (less respectably) in response to a bribe (such as had evidently been offered for this purpose by the tribune who spoke to Paul). In a cosmopolitan city like Jerusalem, one never knew who was Roman and who was not. Neither appearance, nor dress, nor language, nor name was a certain guide. There were many strange Romans about. Their number, and the variety of their origins, were more than ever in a state of change at the time of Paul's arrest.[2]

The liberality of Romans with their citizenship was very unusual in the ancient world. Despite the physical expansion of Rome by the first century CE, only a very small proportion of the total population of the empire could ever be housed there. No matter: although the main way to become a Roman citizen was to be born one, already in the earliest days of the Republic, in the fifth century BCE, the Romans incorporated some of their Latin neighbours into their polity. By the early first century BCE the process of incorporation included all of Italy. Once the step had been taken to accept as citizens people who had no physical or familial connection to the city of Rome, it was easy to extend citizenship further, first to privileged individuals among the subject communities, then to whole peoples and regions. Legally, the process required in each case the approval of the political organs of the Roman state, but, in practice, by the mid-first century BCE the power to grant citizenship was often devolved to the most powerful magistrates. The advantage gained by particular politicians as patrons of new citizens, or the unsuitability of specific individuals for citizen status, occasionally caused controversy, but the general principle that Romanness might spread indefinitely does not seem to have been doubted by anyone. In a speech in 62 BCE on behalf of the poet Archias, whose right to Roman citizenship had been questioned on technical grounds by political enemies, Cicero could urge in aid of his client's (legally dubious) claim even the nebulous achievement that he had written poetry "to celebrate the fame and glory of the Roman people."[3]

Among the most remarkable demonstrations of this liberality was the acceptance as citizens of ex-slaves. The enormity of the transfer of status this entailed is hard to grasp. Slaves of Roman citizens were not legally persons. They were things, property, like animals or inanimate objects in the modern world. But even they could become Roman citizens. All that was required was a formal ceremony before a Roman magistrate to mark liberation from servile status and incorporation into the Roman people. Sometimes the procedure could be even simpler, with freedom, and full citizen rights, granted by the will of a deceased owner.

Romans were well aware of the value of such grants of citizenship, and some slaves might be manumitted informally without citizenship rights, either because the owner wished to regain control over whatever the freed slave earned or because the owner deemed him or her unworthy. It remained true, and astonishing, that decisions about which slaves should become Roman citizens lay to such an extent in the remit of the individual owner, male or female. A Roman woman, who could not herself vote, could give that right to her male slave, by the simple procedure of granting him his liberty in the presence of a magistrate. In the time of Augustus a series of laws was passed to try to regulate the freeing and enfranchisement of huge numbers of slaves at one time by the testaments of exceptionally wealthy owners wishing to deprive their heirs of this part of their property, and the granting of citizen rights to slaves who had previously been punished as criminals either by their owners or by the state. A century later, Suetonius interestingly attributed such laws to a desire "to keep the people pure and unsullied by any taint of foreign or servile blood," which was not at all their effect: only criminal slaves were totally debarred from citizenship, and there remained no limit to the number of slaves a man or woman could free in his or her lifetime. The ethnic diversity of the slave inhabitants of the city of Rome in the late Republic and early empire thus, within only a few generations, transformed the ethnic composition of the citizen population. Quite a few of these freed slaves were Jews.[4]

Outside Italy, grants of citizenship to favoured individuals were more common in the western part of the empire than in the east during the first century BCE, but over the following two centuries eastern provincials benefited increasingly, until finally, in 212 CE, the emperor Caracalla granted citizenship to all the inhabitants of the Roman world. Caracalla's immediate motivation was said to have been to increase the tax revenues of the state, but the universal grant of citizenship was the culmination of a process that had taken many centuries. The dialogue of Paul with his captors, as recorded in Acts, suggests that, for these provincials, Roman citizenship was worth acquiring for its practical benefits, rather like a passport, rather than as a statement of Roman identity, but such benefits, tangible enough in the case of Paul when he was arrested, do not seem to have involved much more than the right to appeal to the emperor against arbitrary action by the Roman and provincial authorities, and the value of such a right was diluted as citizenship spread. By the time of Hadrian, the state was making distinctions about the entitlement to legal protection of Roman citizens from different levels of society. More lenient penalties were to be applied to those who were richer, "more honourable"; a humbler person convicted for the same offence could expect more degrading, often corporal, punishment. It is not clear how "Roman" any of these humbler citizens came to feel—or, indeed, how clear a notion they had of what it meant to be Roman. Plutarch, as we have seen, became a Roman but stayed a Greek. Such continuing loyalty to a non-Roman identity was common. But attitudes in any one region or group could change over time. Some inhabitants of the Apennine mountain ranges had felt sufficiently opposed to Roman culture to set up their own state of Italia in 90 BCE, but within less than sixty years of their defeat in 87 they were to be fully embroiled as citizens in the purely Roman civil conflict between Antony and Octavian: many of the supporters of Octavian in the wars of the 30s, and beneficiaries of the reconstituted Roman state he proclaimed in 27 BCE, were just such Italians.

A proportion of the inhabitants of the city of Rome in the first century CE were foreigners or slaves, and thus not Roman citizens, and their attitudes and social relations in many respects were distinct from those of citizens and to a large extent unknown, but even in trying to establish the attitudes of citizens this fluidity of Roman identity creates problems for historians trying to establish Roman attitudes to their world. It is not just that in any complex society there are bound to be varied opinions and thus discovering a majority or standard view is necessarily impressionistic without the evidence of opinion polls. The more intractable problem is that opinions expressed by a Roman writer may not reflect his views as a Roman so much as (one of) his non-Roman identities. The letters of Paul constitute a notable example. They are in some sense Roman literature, expressing the point of view of a Roman author, but to extract from them generalizations about Roman religion and culture would be patently absurd. The same can be said, to a greater or lesser extent, of all Roman texts written in Greek in the early empire. It is probable that Cassius Dio, author, in the early third century CE, of a multivolume history of Rome, thought of himself as a Roman if only because he was a senator and twice consul, even though his history was composed in Greek; but the same cannot be said with confidence of his Bithynian namesake from over a century earlier, Dio Cocceianus (later called Chrysostom, "golden-mouthed"), despite the length of time he spent as orator and philosopher in Rome under the Flavians and his later friendship with the emperor Trajan. Citizens might feel their Roman identity more strongly at some times in their lives, less strongly at others. Context was crucial. In the army, where Latin was the language of command, but also the language used on the tombstones of soldiers, a legionary might identify more fully with Rome, regardless of his place of origin, than did his non-military relatives. Latin-speaking legionaries settled in Phoenicia by Augustus in 15 BCE to create the new Roman colony of Berytus (modern Beirut) might see themselves as bastions of Roman culture in an alien world: it was not accidental that Berytus became in the third century CE a great centre for the study (in Latin) of Roman law, attracting Greek-speaking provincials from all over the Roman Near East. Conversely, a Greek-speaking Roman citizen in the city of Rome might feel all the more strongly his Greek origin because of the Italian sea in which he found himself swimming.

Acknowledgement of fuzzy boundaries does not make the search for Roman attitudes impossible, just more difficult. There is always a danger of describing ideal types rather than real people, but that may not be altogether a bad thing. Societies need ideal types by which to judge their own performance. Even if many Romans, like Paul and Josephus, usually judged themselves by criteria culled from far outside normal Roman assumptions, it will still be worthwhile trying to find out how they may have thought of themselves in the interludes when the personas they adopted were Roman.*

"Who is a Jew?" The question was as difficult to answer in the early Roman empire as it is now. Indeed, the lack of clear boundaries to define Jewishness makes the contemporary world—or, more accurately, the world in which European and American Jews have lived since the emancipation of European Jews began in the eighteenth and nineteenth centuries—more similar to the multicultural society of the pagan Roman empire than to any intervening period of Jewish history. Throughout the Middle Ages, under both Christian and Muslim rule, the limits of Jewish communities were generally agreed both by the Jews themselves and by the states in which they lived. In the Roman world in the first century CE, there was no such clarity. Jewish identity was then, as now, both religious and ethnic, and the root cause of uncertainty was, for Jews as for Romans, the liberal extension of this identity to outsiders. Precisely when and why Jews began to believe that gentiles who came to join them and took up their customs should be treated not just as tolerated strangers but as Jews in their own right is uncertain. However, the notion of such proselytes was well entrenched in the text of the Septuagint, the Greek translation of the Hebrew Bible, and it is therefore reasonable to suppose that gentile conversions to Judaism were taken for granted by Greek Jews in the third and second centuries BCE, when the Septuagint was completed. There is much in favour of the hypothesis that this Jewish concept was adopted in response to the universalism of Hellenism. Just as anyone who wished to do so could become Greek by behaving in a Greek fashion, so too anyone who wished to do so could become a Jew by following the customs of the Jews.[5]

Conversion to Judaism was not just a theoretical possibility. The names of individuals identified as proselytes are preserved on inscriptions from

---

* Since my aim is to describe in the following chapters what was specifically Roman about Roman culture, I shall be conservative in the use of evidence produced by those with dual identity. I shall use writings composed in Greek only when they emanated from individuals who can be shown to have thought of themselves as Roman, and, as far as possible, my analysis will depend either on evidence from or about the city of Rome itself, or on the literature and inscriptions of the Romans who used the distinctive language of Rome, namely Latin.

different parts of the Jewish world of late antiquity. For most such converts, the precise mechanism by which they became Jewish is not known,
but in the unique case of the conversion of Izates, king of Adiabene in
northern Mesopotamia, and of his mother Helena, a quite full and illumi-
nating narrative was preserved by Josephus—partly, no doubt, because
Helena (as we saw in Chapter 1) became a well-known personality in
Jerusalem in the years when Josephus was a child and teenager.[6]

The story as told by Josephus has elements of romance. Izates, offspring
of an incestuous union between siblings, was marked out in advance by a
divine voice which spoke to his father while he was still in the womb: the
baby "by the providence of God had had a fortunate start and would also
attain a fortunate end." Already thus his father's favourite, Izates was sent
off to the court of a neighbouring king, Abennerigus of Spasinou Charax,
which lies near the mouths of the Tigris and the Euphrates. While he was
there a Jewish merchant named Ananias visited the royal harem and
"taught them to worship God after the manner of the Jewish tradition. It
was through their agency that he was brought to the notice of Izates,
whom he similarly won over with the cooperation of the women." On
Izates' return to Adiabene, Ananias accompanied him home. "It so happened, moreover, that Helena [his mother] had likewise been instructed by
another Jew and had been brought over to their laws"—a fact unknown to
Izates when it happened, but "when he learned that his mother was very
much pleased with the customs of the Jews, he was zealous to convert to
them himself." At this point in the story there was an impasse:

Since he considered that he would not be securely a Jew unless he was
circumcised, he was ready to act accordingly. When his mother learned
of his intention, however, she tried to stop him by telling him that it
was a dangerous move. For, she said, he was a king; and if his subjects
should discover that he was devoted to rites that were strange and foreign to themselves, it would produce much disaffection and they would
not tolerate the rule of a Jew over them. Besides this advice she tried by
every other means to hold him back. He, in turn, reported her arguments to Ananias. The latter expressed agreement with the king's
mother and actually threatened that if he should be unable to persuade
Izates, he would abandon him and leave the land. For he said that he
was afraid that if the matter became universally known, he would be

punished, in all likelihood, as personally responsible because he had instructed the king in unseemly practices. The king could, he said, worship the Divine even without being circumcised if indeed he had fully decided to be a devoted adherent of the ancestral practices of the Jews, for it was this that counted more than circumcision. He told him that God Himself would pardon him if, constrained thus by necessity and by fear of his subjects, he failed to perform this rite.

At the time, the king was apparently convinced by Ananias' arguments, but it did not last:

Afterwards, however, since he had not completely given up his desire, another Jew, named Eleazar, who came from Galilee and who had a reputation for being extremely strict when it came to the ancestral laws, urged him to do the deed. For when he came to him to pay him his respects and found him reading the law of Moses, he said: "In your ignorance, O king, you are guilty of the greatest offence against the law and thereby against God. For you ought not merely to read the law but also, and even more, to do what is commanded in it. How long will you continue to be uncircumcised? If you have not yet read the law concerning this matter, read it now, so that you may know what an impiety it is that you commit." Upon hearing these words, the king postponed the deed no longer. Withdrawing into another room, he summoned his physician and had the prescribed act performed. Then he sent for both his mother and his teacher Ananias and notified them that he had performed the rite. They were immediately seized with consternation and fear beyond measure that . . . they themselves would be in jeopardy since the blame for his action would be attributed to them. It was God who was to prevent their fears from being realized. For although Izates himself and his children were often threatened with destruction, God preserved them, opening a path to safety from desperate straits. God thus demonstrated that those who fix their eyes on Him and trust in Him alone do not lose the reward of their piety.[7]

In the eyes both of Josephus and of the later rabbis, Izates and Helena thus became not just gentile worshippers of the Jewish God, "Godfearers," but authentic Jews. This is all the more impressive because the conversion narrative itself gives no indication at all by whose authority they had become Jewish. It was not apparently through either Eleazar (who plays no further part in the narrative after his uplifting speech) or Izates' teacher Ananias, who expresses horror at the news of the king's circumcision. The act of circumcision is carried out in private, by the court physician, who is not described as a Jew. Stories of the mass conversion to Judaism of the Idumaeans in the 120s BCE, or of Ituraeans in Galilee in 104–103, presuppose that the High Priest, who was responsible for the proselytization of these gentiles, had the power to turn them by fiat into Jews. One can imagine that a local Jewish community, or its leaders, or a learned Jewish sage, might do the same. In later periods of Jewish history, the task has fallen to a tribunal of rabbis. But no priest, rabbi, sage or local Jewish community seems to have been involved in Adiabene when Izates was circumcised in a secluded part of his palace. Unlike Roman identity, Jewish identity was, it seems, to some extent a matter of personal self-identification. In essence, Izates was a Jew primarily because he thought of himself as a Jew.[8]

The lack of any single external authority to define who was a Jew had most impact in such cases of conversion from gentile to Jewish status, but it also affected some of those Jews—the vast majority—whose Jewishness came not from choice but from birth. Most Jews, in antiquity as now, were born Jews, and for most of them their status was unequivocal. The offspring of a legal union between Jewish spouses was a Jew. But the position was more complex if only one parent was Jewish. For Jews in the first century CE there was no clarity like the rules for Roman citizenship. On the contrary, it appears that over the course of centuries from the third century BCE through to the third century CE, a general assumption that only the Jewish status of the father mattered gradually gave way to a belief that the maternal one is decisive. The early biblical narrative told of Jewish heroes marrying non-Jewish women and producing with them legitimate Jewish offspring. The births of Manasseh and Ephraim to the patriarch Joseph are celebrated in the book of Genesis without the slightest evidence of embarrassment that their mother was Asenath, the daughter of Potipherah, priest of On. At the end of the first century CE, Josephus still noted specifically the conversion of the gentile men who married Herodian princesses, but he had nothing to say about the Jewish status of the gentile women who married Herodian princes, which should have counted for more if the Herodian family thought that the matrilineal principle was what mattered most. By contrast, a discussion in the Tosefta, a collection of rabbinic legal opinions, similar to the Mishnah, which was compiled in the mid-third century CE, can be read to imply that the child of a Jewish woman and a gentile father is a Jew, and this view became standard in rabbinic law by the fourth century CE. A period of uncertainty during the shift from a patrilineal to a matrilineal system may be reflected in a mixed marriage recorded in the Acts of the Apostles. When Paul came to Derbe and to Lystra in Asia Minor, "a disciple was there, named Timothy, the son of a Jewish woman who was a believer; but his father was a Greek. He was well spoken of by the brethren of Lystra and Iconium. Paul wanted Timothy to accompany him; and he took him and circumcised him because of the Jews that were in those places, for they all knew that his father was a Greek."9 "Ambrosiaster," an anonymous commentator on the Pauline epistles from the mid-fourth century, argued that the author of Acts implied in this passage that Paul must have thought that Timothy was a Jew because his mother was Jewish, since Paul was famously adamant that non-Jews did not need to undergo circumcision.10 It is worth imagining the difficulties faced by the priests in the Temple confronted by crowds of pilgrims eager to enter the Court of the Israelites. It was their duty to exclude those who were not Jews, but how were they to tell?

At least it could be taken for granted that those who went up to Jerusalem for the festivals wanted to assert their Jewish identity. Outside Jerusalem, Jewishness was not always of prime significance in the way Jews saw themselves and the world any more than their Roman identity was always central to the lives of all Romans (or than Jewish identity is central to all Jews now). When revolt broke out in Jerusalem in 66 CE, the Jews of Scythopolis (Beth Shean, just south of Galilee) chose to side not with their compatriots in Jerusalem but with their fellow Scythopolitans. The story told by Josephus was of dual loyalties at a time of crisis brought to a head by events in Judaea over which the Scythopolitan Jews had no effective control:

Thus far the Judaeans had been faced with aliens only, but when they invaded Scythopolis they found the Jews there in arms against them; for the Jews in this district ranged themselves on the side of the Scythopolitans, and, regarding their own security as more important than the ties of blood, met their own countrymen in battle. However, this excess of ardour brought them under suspicion: the people of Scythopolis feared that the Jews might attack the city by night and inflict upon them some grave disaster, in order to make amends to their brethren for their defection. They, therefore, ordered them if they wished to confirm their allegiance and demonstrate their fidelity to those of a foreign nation, to betake themselves and their families to the adjoining grove. The Jews obeyed these orders, suspecting nothing. For two days the Scythopolitans made no move, in order to lull them into security, but on the third night, watching their opportunity when some were off their guard, and others asleep, they slaughtered them all to the number of upward of thirteen thousand and pillaged all their possessions.

The Jerusalemite Josephus, who at this stage of the revolt had been firmly on the side of the Judaean rebels, expressed no understanding of the dilemma of these Scythopolitan Jews. He blamed them for putting their own security first, and he showed only little sympathy for their eventual fate. Their behaviour shows with tragic clarity that the political attitudes of the Jews of Jerusalem were not shared by all Jews elsewhere, even in the land of Israel.[11]

What evidence, then, can we use to understand the attitudes of Jews in Jerusalem in the time of Jesus? Whatever Josephus wrote was obviously possible for a Jerusalemite Jew to think, although, as we have seen, his views may have been slanted to reflect his own tortuous career and to appeal to his non-Jewish readers. The writings of Philo can be used, but only with care, since he lived in the diaspora and may have visited Jerusalem only once. The earliest texts in the corpus of rabbinic literature date to the early third century CE and most were copied down much later, so there is a danger that they reflect a world much changed from the first century, while there is no way of knowing for certain whether the *Psalms of Solomon* (written in the mid-first century BCE) and the apocalyptic prophecy of *4 Ezra* (composed in the late first century CE) and other such Jewish religious texts preserved only through the Christian tradition reflected mainstream Jewish opinion or only minority attitudes which happened to be useful for Christians as they developed their own distinctive theology. The danger that evidence has been selected to fit the agenda of later religious movements, whether rabbinic or Christian, does not apply to the Jewish writings discovered by chance in manuscripts unearthed in the Judaean desert, such as the Dead Sea scrolls found at Qumran and the private legal documents found in caves in Wadi Murraba'at and elsewhere, but the very fact that they were found in isolated places may suggest that they were produced by Jews from outside the mainstream.[12]

So can we at least regard the injunctions of the Hebrew Bible as a solid foundation of the lives of all Jews in the first century CE? Not entirely. All Jews agreed that the Bible, and particularly the Pentateuch, incorporated the law which should govern everything they did and thought, but that did not mean that in practice they did exactly what the biblical text enjoined. On the contrary, Jews varied in their ways of interpreting the Bible more in the first century CE than in any other time in Jewish history until the emergence of Reform and Liberal Judaism in Europe in the nineteenth century. One example will suffice to illustrate this variation, even if the biblical law in question may strike us as not entirely central to the Jewish lifestyle. The biblical book of Deuteronomy explicitly requires all Jews to carry with them at all times a spade for excavating a latrine: "And you shall have a place also outside the camp, and you shall go out to it. And you shall have a stick among your weapons, and it shall be, when you will ease yourself outside, you shall dig with it, and shall turn back and cover up your excrement. For the Lord your God walks in the midst of your camp, to deliver you, and to give up your enemies before you; therefore shall your camp be holy."[13] One Jewish group, the Essenes, evidently did exactly what the Torah commanded in this respect, as Josephus reports:

> Those desiring to join the sect are not immediately admitted. For one year, during which the postulant remains outside the fraternity, they prescribe for him their own rule of life, presenting him with a small hatchet . . . They dig a hole a foot deep with a mattock—such is the nature of the hatchet which they present to the new disciples—and, wrapping their mantle about them . . . squat above it. They then replace the excavated soil in the trench. For this purpose they select the more retired spots. And though this discharge of excrement is a natural function, they make it a rule to wash themselves after it, as if defiled.[14]

Since this particular aspect of the Essene lifestyle was, unlike others, no more than an acceptance of the plain meaning of the biblical text, it is disconcerting to find that Josephus describes it as a bizarre idiosyncrasy. Evidently other contemporary Jews did not carry shovels with them as the Essenes did. Philo, rather than keeping the ruling literally, extracted an allegorical meaning from the biblical passage: " 'Let there be to you . . . a shovel upon your girdle, and you shall dig with it,' that is to say, reason shall be in control of passion, digging it out, tucking it up, not suffering it to clothe you about. For God would have us gird up our passions, not wear them flowing and loose."[15] Two rabbinic teachers of the first half of the second century CE were reported to have raised the law in the context of the nature of the manna eaten by the children of Israel in the wilderness: if manna is angelic food, and angels do not excrete, why did the Israelites who ate manna need spades to dig latrines with? (The answer: they must have bought other foodstuffs from travelling merchants of other nations.)[16] A different rabbinic reading of the biblical text elicited, in the context of a homily against rumour-mongering, a message for modern readers by wilfully altering the vocalization of the Hebrew text to read "Let there be a plug in your ears," with the implication that the law was required "so that you cannot hear tittle-tattle."[17]

First-century Judaism was thus very varied, but one assumption shared by all types of Jew was that Jerusalem was the ideal sanctuary for the worship of God. It was denial of this one tenet that ensured that Samaritans were not Jews, either in their own eyes or in the eyes of other Jews. On the Samaritan side, the issue was simple. They never called themselves Jews (*ioudaioi* in Greek, *yehudim* in Hebrew). They were the "Israelites who worship God on Mount Gerizim." For them, *yehudi* meant "Judaean," and denoted someone from the province of Judaea, *Yehud*, which was distinct in the Persian and Hellenistic periods from Samaria to the north. But for Jews, it was their devotion to their rival sanctuary on Mount Gerizim in Samaria that put Samaritans beyond the pale. The issue seems to have been that the Samaritans were believed to be breaking biblical commands by preferring to offer sacrifices to God in places other than Jerusalem. Jews knew that fellow Jews might have other temples without thereby seceding from their Jewish identity, and Josephus indeed describes in some detail a Jewish temple in Heliopolis in the delta in Egypt, which was used by Jews from the mid-second century BCE to its closure by the Romans soon after the fall of Jerusalem in 70 CE—Josephus, a Jerusalem priest, was not exactly enthusiastic about it, but neither did he condemn it as un-Jewish.

The Samaritans, however, were excluded from being Jews by their claim that their temple should be seen not as an addition to the Jerusalem cult but as its legitimate replacement: in their eyes, Mount Gerizim, not Jerusalem, was the place where God had chosen to be worshipped. The sense of hostility and suspicion between the two peoples, and the mutual feeling that, despite their similarities, they had separate destinies, emerges well from a snide aside written by Josephus about the Samaritans: "They alter their attitude according to circumstance and, when they see the Jews prospering, call them kinsmen . . . but, when they see the Jews in trouble, they say that they have nothing whatever in common with them, nor do they have any claim of friendship or race, and they declare themselves to be foreign settlers of another race."[18] Acceptance of the pre-eminence of Jerusalem was an essential part of being a Jew.

## THE SIGNIFICANCE OF PLACE

IN A DIFFERENT way the city of Rome was as central to Roman identity as Jerusalem was for Jews. Romans were to be found all over the empire in the first century CE, but what mattered to them above all were events in the city, in Rome itself. On a political level, emperors demonstrated the centrality of the city by parading there, before the Senate and people, the public face of their power and through investing much of the surplus wealth of empire in the glorification of the city. The city's population was privileged: Rome was the capital of the world.

And from the time of Augustus the world itself was thought of as Roman, tamed by the might of empire. Cicero, a generation earlier, had popularized among Romans the Greek notion that the *orbis terrarum*, "the circle of the countries"—in Greek, the *oikoumene*, "the inhabited region"—was "only a small island surrounded by the body of water which you on earth call either the Atlantic, or the Great Sea, or Ocean."[19] In the early empire both Strabo and Pomponius Mela tried to show that by their day this world had been completely circumnavigated. Very few places remained for exploration and conquest, northwards from Germany, or southwards from Egypt, where the Nile rises, or the semi-mythical land of "Thule," said to lie six days' sail to the north of Britain. Thule was the place on earth furthest from civilized life, but even this remote country

A typical brick-faced apartment block from Ostia, the port of Rome. The ground floor was used for shops opening on to the street, with the apartments in domestic use above. In Rome itself three-story blocks were common, and remains have been discovered of buildings constructed in the second century CE which rose to five or six stories by using the steep hillsides for support.

The Colosseum, the first monumental amphitheatre, was built in Rome. Dedicated by Titus in June 80 CE for performances of a variety of sports, it could hold an audience of around fifty thousand.

*Columned courtyard of the House of the Silver Wedding in Pompeii. Excavation of such houses in Pompeii has revealed much about the private tastes of rich Romans in the first century* CE.

*Interior of a fine house in the Upper City of Jerusalem destroyed in 70* CE. *The use of stone vessels by the inhabitants reflects their concern about purity.*

*Augustus began work on his monumental mausoleum (above) on the Campus Martius soon after his victory at Actium in 31 BCE. Herod's tomb at Herodium (below), constructed soon afterwards near Bethlehem, has the same circular structure.*

*The southern edge of the Temple Mount in Jerusalem, looking east towards the Kidron Valley and the Mount of Olives. Excavation has uncovered remains of the impressive flight of steps which led up, through great gates and broad stepped tunnels built underneath Herod's royal portico, to the platform on which the Temple stood.*

*Remains of the western wall of the Temple enclosure built by Herod. The Dome of the Rock, built in the seventh century CE, now stands in the center of the Temple Mount.*

*Inscribed reliefs on pedestals from the Sebasteion in Aphrodisias (in modern Turkey). The "nation of Jews" (top left) was just one of fifty peoples and places personified in relief, along with Dacians (top right) and the islands of Crete (bottom left) and Cyprus (bottom right). The personification of the nation of the Jews does not survive.*

Hadrian celebrated the distinctive characteristics of the provinces of the empire in a series of coins. Egypt (top left) reclines on the ground against a large basket filled with grain, facing an ibis. Britannia (top right) sits in an attitude of vigilance, wearing native dress and holding a spear and a large shield. The coins celebrating the visits of the emperor to Mauretania (bottom left) and Judaea (bottom right) belong to a standard type issued to commemorate his arrival in each province. In both coins the emperor raises his right hand in greeting while the personification of the province stands facing him, holding a libation bowl above an altar. Mauretania wears military dress and holds a standard, probably in recognition of the military reputation of soldiers from the area. Judaea is depicted as a veiled woman in normal Graeco-Roman clothing. None of her attributes is noticeably Jewish, and the imagery may well have alluded to the benefits brought to the province by the establishment of the new Roman colony of Aelia Capitolina.

*Funerary portrait of a young woman from Egypt (second century* CE*). The realistic conventions of Roman portraiture have been adapted for a traditional Egyptian purpose.*

*The so-called Tomb of Absalom in the Kidron valley, close to the eastern wall of the Temple enclosure in Jerusalem. The tomb, built in the first century CE, combines Greek architectural styles (Ionic columns and a Doric frieze) with an Egyptian cornice. The burial chamber is in the lower, square structure.*

was seen (so they claimed) by a Roman fleet towards the end of the first century CE.

"Ocean" was an endless mass of water in which currents of frightening force were generated by the huge ebb and flow of the unchecked sea. The image doubtless reflected the perceptions of Mediterranean peoples confronted by the awesome size of the Atlantic. Navigation so close to the edge of the earth was unpredictable: around Thule, "the sea is sluggish and heavy to the oar and does not rise with the wind as other seas do."[20] All the more striking that Augustus claimed as one of his great achievements that his fleet "sailed through Ocean from the mouth of the Rhine to the region of the rising sun as far as the borders of the Cimbri."[21] How much the Roman populace understood of the geography of these distant places is uncertain, but the rhetorical meaning of the emperor's boasts was easier to interpret. Ovid obligingly expressed it succinctly: "The land of other nations has a fixed boundary; the space of Rome is the space of the world."[22]

But the centrality of Rome in this Roman geography was contingent on the fact of Roman power. The centrality of Jerusalem for Jews, by contrast, was a fact of religious certainty. Already in the Septuagint Jerusalem was described as the world's navel (as Delphi was for Greeks). Jewish behaviour and law both confirmed an understanding of the world in which the most pure, holy and important place is the Holy of Holies in the Temple, into which only the High Priest was permitted to enter, on just one day each year, and even then only after intense ritual purification over a week. Less holy than the Holy of Holies was the Court of the Priests, then the Court of the Israelites, the Court of Women, the Court of Gentiles, Jerusalem outside the Temple, the land of Israel outside Jerusalem, and, finally, the rest of the world. Such notions had real consequences. There was a riot in *c.* 26 CE when Pontius Pilate brought into the holy city of Jerusalem military standards which Jews had received without concern while they were kept elsewhere in Judaea. Gentiles, welcomed into the outer courts of the Temple, were threatened with instant death if they ventured closer than permitted to the Holy of Holies.[23] Declaration of the borders of the land of Israel likewise had practical consequences because some commandments, notably those regarding tithing of agricultural produce and the observance of the sabbatical year, applied only in the land and not in the rest of the world.

The biblical boundary texts, such as the description in Numbers of the borders of Canaan given by God to Moses just before the conquest of this land, provided a framework for later Jews to use, but they were contradictory, some encompassing much more territory than others, and reconciling them with the real world required ingenious interpretation. In the *Genesis Apocryphon,* an elaboration of Genesis composed probably in the second century BCE and preserved among the Dead Sea scrolls, God showed Abraham the land as defined to its greatest extent, from the Nile to the Euphrates: "The next morning I went up to Ramath Hazor and from that high place I beheld the land from the River of Egypt to Lebanon and Senir, and from the Great Sea to Hauran, and all the land of Gebal as far as Kadesh, and all the Great Desert to the east of Hauran and Senir as far as the Euphrates. And He said to me, 'I will give all this land to your seed and they shall possess it for ever.' "[24] By contrast the rabbis formulated a series of less ambitious definitions of the boundaries of the land. In a discussion of Deuteronomy 11:24, "Every place whereon the sole of your foot shall tread shall be yours; from the wilderness, and Lebanon, from the river, the river Euphrates, even unto the hinder sea shall be your border," the midrashist in *Sifre on Deuteronomy,* redacted probably in the third century, came up with a list of "the boundaries of the Land of Israel as seized by those who came up from Babylonia," which encompassed a much smaller area: "The Ashkelon junction, the walls of Strato's Tower, Dor, and the walls of Acco . . . upper Tarnegola of Caesarea [Philippi] . . . the Garden of Ashkelon, and the great road leading to the wilderness."[25] These seem to be the names of real places surrounding the areas in which Jews were, or had been, a majority of the inhabitants in recent centuries. In this world-view, the land of Israel had a special status and required to be treated with the respect due to its holiness as if in itself it possessed a personality: "Defile not yourself in any of those things, for in all these the nations are defiled which I cast out before you . . . that the land vomit not you out also, when you defile it, as it vomited out the nation that was before you."[26]

Unlike Romans, whose ethnographical interests were stimulated by the needs of imperial rule, Jews were not much encouraged to speculate about the geography of the rest of the world, which was often lumped together in rabbinic thought as simply "abroad," "outside the land." The world of the gentiles ( *goyim,* "peoples") was largely undifferentiated, and rabbinic ethnography of other peoples rarely rises above the level of caricature: Persians "eat and drink like a bear, their flesh is swollen like a bear, they grow long hair like a bear, and they are restless like a bear." Jews in this period did not apparently produce a geographical literature like that in contemporary Greece and Rome. The geographical excursuses in the histories of Josephus provided, in the manner of Polybius, sufficient geographical information for the reader to follow the historical narrative, but did not survey the geography of the world for its own sake, as Herodotus, the father of Greek historiography, had done.[27]

What did sometimes lead Jews to formulate their own notions about the geography of the world was the need to interpret the biblical texts in the context of their day. Sometimes literal reading of the biblical texts led to geographical nonsense: because Jews seeking justice are urged in Deuteronomy to "arise, and go up to the place which the Lord your God will choose," the author of *Sifre on Deuteronomy* deduced that the Temple must be the highest place in the land of Israel, and the land of Israel higher than the rest of the world.[28] But other Jews succeeded in correlating the biblical texts to the prevailing geographical notions of the Greeks. The base biblical text for interpretation was the list of the nations of the world to be found in chapter 10 of Genesis, "the families of the sons of Noah, after this generation, in their nations; and by these were the nations divided in the earth after the flood."[29] The author of *Jubilees* in the mid-second century BCE pictured the world, as Romans did, as a roughly circular land mass surrounded by Ocean, but for him the centre was Zion, the extreme east the Garden of Eden, and the extreme west the Straits of Gibraltar. The relative positions of all the peoples mentioned in the Genesis account were delineated with care. The notion that the sons of Noah had solemnly agreed to these land-divisions implied that all conquest of territory was counter to the divine will. The conquest of the land of Israel by the Jews, which might therefore seem of dubious morality, was justified (tacitly) by the assertion that Canaan, to whom North Africa had been assigned, had violently seized the Levant, which had been allotted by God to Arpachshad, the ancestor of Abraham.[30] The geographical rationalization of the same biblical text by Josephus concentrated more on an antiquarian effort to match up the biblical names with modern equivalents: "Chethimos [biblical Kittim] held the islands of Chethima, the modern Cyprus, whence the name *Chethim* given by the Hebrews to all islands and to most maritime countries; here I call to witness one of the cities of Cyprus which has succeeded in preserving the old appellation, for even in its Hellenistic form Cition [on the site of Larnaka] is not far removed from the name of Chethimos." Josephus' geography may of course have been atypical for a Jew because he was writing for sophisticated non-Jewish readers within the Greek tradition of investigating the origins of people. He had to note for his Greek readers that in Hebrew the termination of proper names is always the same, unlike in Greek, so that "Nochos is called [in Hebrew] Noe [Noah]." He was well aware that identities had been imposed on many native peoples in the Hellenistic period: "It is the Greeks who are responsible for this change of nomenclature; for . . . they appropriated even the glories of the past, embellishing the nations with names which they [the Greeks] could understand."[31]

Neither Josephus nor other Jewish authors have as much to say as Romans about the edges of the earth. When Jews, like the author of *1 Enoch,* did speculate, they seem to have thought that at the outer limits of the world beyond Ocean lay chaos and darkness, although just on the edge was paradise: "And from there I went to the ends of the earth and I saw there large animals, each different from the other, and also birds (which) differed in form, beauty, and call—each different from the other. And to the east of these animals, I saw the ends of the earth on which heaven rests, and the open gates of heaven. And I saw how the stars of heaven come out, and I counted the gates out of which they came, and wrote down all their outlets . . ."[32]

## MEMORY, TIME AND MAKING SENSE OF THE PAST

SHARED IDENTITIES are the product of shared history, not in the unverifiable sense that the genetic ancestors of all members of a community played a part in remembered past events, but in the present reality that everyone in the community thinks of those past events as relevant to themselves. So too among both Romans and Jews.

Knowledge of the very distant past of Rome was embarrassingly hazy by the early empire, despite the efforts of historians since the third century BCE to fill in the lack of memory, if necessary by ingenious and learned invention. The origins of the city were traced back to two main legends. The common story of Romulus told of his childhood suckled by a she-wolf; his quarrel with his twin Remus over the site of the city; the slaying of Remus when he leaped over the wall that Romulus had marked out; and the transformation of Romulus into the guardian god of the city, under the name of Quirinus. A rival legend linked the foundation of the city to the travels of Aeneas, a Trojan warrior thought to have come to Latium after traversing much of the Mediterranean following the defeat of Troy by the Greeks: in earlier versions of the story, Aeneas founded Rome itself, but, in what became the canonical account, Vergil's *Aeneid,* he was portrayed as founder of a different city, Lavinium, from whose ruling family, his descendants, Romulus in time would spring. The two legends were both separately well entrenched by the third century BCE but by the late Republic were often combined. Romulus came to be reckoned the first of a series of Roman kings, and, using inherited stories about the number of kings and the length of their reigns, the learned Varro was enabled in the first century BCE to assign the city's foundation to a date equivalent to 753 BCE.

When Octavian, the future emperor Augustus, re-established peace in Rome after the turmoil of the late Republic, "some expressed the opinion that he ought to be called Romulus as if he too was the founder of the city,"[33] but the Aeneas story was to have greater impact on the early empire, not least because of the power of Vergil's poem, which had become vastly popular by the time of the poet's death on 20 September 19 BCE. "Pious Aeneas" became a type to emulate: always devoted to duty, serious and determined, he had battled against great odds to win through in the end with the help of the gods. Such stories presupposed that the distant past had been glorious, a view encouraged by the contrast with the uncertainties and crises of the late Republic. The rustic simplicity of earlier generations was a recurrent theme in the imagination of the historian Livy, Vergil's contemporary. Ancient Romans had been straightforward, honest farmers, who had rushed to war only to defend the fatherland when it was in peril, like the hero Horatius, "the one-eyed," who, five centuries before Livy wrote, had held the bridge over the Tiber into Rome against the invading army of the Etruscan Lars Porsenna, until the bridge was destroyed and the city was safe.

Every Roman schoolboy knew the exploits of these distant heroes. In the political maelstrom of the late Republic, reference in political speeches to glorious episodes in past epochs could be guaranteed an audience able to appreciate the significance of the examples selected. When Cicero sought to refer in the course of a speech to the best possible case of a religious act carried out by a totally responsible politician, all he had to do was to mention Marcus Horatius Pulvillus, who "though many men were moved by jealousy to interfere with his actions on false pleas of religious hindrances, still stood his ground and with unfaltering resolution dedicated the Capitol." The whole story, believed to have taken place in the first year of the Republic nearly five centuries before, was known to all: according to Livy, as Horatius was in the act of dedicating the temple of Jupiter on the Capitol, his enemies announced to him the death of his son, but "he was only so far distracted by the information as to order that the body should be buried."[34]

References more specifically to family and ancestral achievements were a normal part of political discourse, and presupposed general awareness of the history of Rome's rise to greatness. The obstinacy of the younger Cato, who committed suicide at Thapsus in Africa in April 46 BCE rather than fall into the power of his political opponent Julius Caesar, was based in part on the reputation of his great-grandfather, Cato the Censor, who was famous (or notorious) for his image of unbending rectitude. The communal memory of wars and political struggles over centuries had partly been preserved by the adoption in the middle Republic of Greek notions of historiography, but also partly by precisely this assumption by politicians that ancestral achievements provided inspiration, justification, and sometimes warnings of value in the maelstrom of contemporary politics. Such appeals to the distant past are not uncommon in other societies, however artificial they may seem when the political quarrels of earlier centuries have little in common with modern problems.[35]

This high evaluation of the achievements of past heroes encouraged politicians to seek commemoration of their own. Cicero, eager to ensure that the memory of his heroism during his consulship in 63 BCE be preserved for posterity, offered to send the raw material to a friend contemplating composition of a history of the period. Agreement that history mattered encouraged falsification, or at least tendentious emphasis, in the way politicians portrayed their own careers. Julius Caesar's account of his actions in the civil war which brought him to supreme power in 46 BCE was designed to exculpate him from accusations of illegality and overweening ambition. The histories of his contemporary Sallust, whose own political career had ended in ignominy on charges of malpractice as governor of Africa, were designed to bring to light the moral decline of the venal nobility who had rejected him. These political stories enabled Romans to populate the past with figures and achievements which made sense of the present. Schoolboys did not learn lists of dates, but the history of Livy was organized in the form of annals, each year dated by its consuls. Much information had been culled originally from the *annales maximi*, the annual record of the names of magistrates and of public events such as eclipses, although by Livy's time the annalistic tradition of historiography had been established in Rome for two centuries and he could use the earlier annalistic narratives of Fabius Pictor, Cato and others. These lists of the consuls for each year gave a basic chronology—even if it was not foolproof, since sometimes consuls of the same name could hold the consulship many years apart.

In other respects, Romans were fascinated by the measurement of time. The original annual calendar in Rome, which ensured regular performance of religious rites at particular times each year, required intercalations to ensure synchronicity with the seasons, but this was done incompetently in the second and first centuries BCE to such an extent that when Julius Caesar, as *pontifex maximus* ("chief priest"), reformed the system in 46, he had to intercalate such a long period that the year totalled four hundred and forty-five days. Within each month some days were lucky and others most definitely not, but taboos on action on bad days could be ignored if inconvenient without incurring censure (except for rashness). Inscribed calendars, of which a number survive in Italy from the early imperial period painted on plaster or inscribed on stone, distinguished days on which official law court business could be done from those on which such activity should not take place: "The festivals are days dedicated to the gods; on the working days people may transact private and public business; and the inbetween days are shared between gods and humans." So wrote the learned Macrobius in the fifth century CE, attributing this distinction between days to Numa, the legendary second king of Rome.[36]

The public display of calendars suggests that these divisions of time were important in structuring Roman lives, but the great test of the strength of calendrical taboos lies in time of war. Macrobius wrote of days, such as those during the festival of the Saturnalia, when it was religiously forbidden (*nefas*) to make war, but he also noted specifically that, in a crisis, anything could be done to defend the state or individual on a forbidden day. If events turned out favourably, that proved that the decision had been right. If everything went wrong, that was evidence of the gods' displeasure. When, in the late Republic, the general Lucullus engaged the Armenian Tigranes in battle on such a day, "some of his officers advised him to beware of the day, which was one of the unlucky days, which they call 'black.' For on that day Caepio and his army were destroyed in a battle with the Cimbri. But Lucullus answered with the memorable words: 'Indeed, I shall make this day, too, a lucky one for the Romans.' "[37]

SUCH TABOOS were paid far more attention by the Jews of Jerusalem. Indeed, the seriousness with which Jews took the demands of their calendar was notorious in the ancient world. Josephus reports the ridicule their scrupulous observance of the Sabbath during the defence of their city attracted from the historian Agatharchides of Cnidus in the mid-second century BCE:

> Those called Jews, who inhabit the most strongly fortified of cities, which happens to be called by the natives Jerusalem, have a custom of abstaining from work every seventh day; on those occasions they neither bear arms nor take any agricultural operations in hand, nor engage in any other form of public service, but pray with outstretched hands in the temples until the evening. Consequently, because the inhabitants, instead of protecting their city, persevered in their folly, Ptolemy, son of Lagus, was allowed to enter with his army; the country was thus given over to a cruel master, and the defect of a practice enjoined by law was exposed. That experience has taught everyone else, except those people, the lesson not to resort to dreams and traditional fancies about the law, until its difficulties are such as to baffle human reason.[38]

The same issue was picked up in the treatise *On Superstition* attributed to Josephus' younger contemporary Plutarch: "But the Jews, because it was the Sabbath day, sat in their unwashed clothes, while the enemy were planting ladders against the walls and capturing the walls, and they did not get up, but remained there, bound fast in their superstition as in one great net."[39] For Jews, the calendar was not just a means for men to organize their activities and their relationship to the gods. It was a divine instruction, given by God to Israel. Changing it, or ignoring its requirements, would be a gross infringement of God's law. The Jewish calendar gave a precise shape to life day by day, week by week, and month by month. Worship must be performed within certain specified time-constraints each day, as is illustrated by the opening sentence of the Mishnah, which concerns the time in the evening when the Shema, the declaration of the unity of God, should be recited: " 'From the time when the priests enter [the Temple] to eat of their heave-offering until the end of the first watch.' The words of Rabbi Eliezer. But the Sages say: 'Until midnight.' " And the whole institution of the week was a side effect of the Sabbath, when total rest from labour was ordained. Naturally enough, there was much dispute over what precisely constituted total rest, but the principle of the Sabbath and its concomitant timetable were unquestioned.[40]

This weekly pattern was superimposed on an annual calendar, based for most Jews on the lunar cycles, whose timing dictated the regular festivals, in particular the three great pilgrim feasts of Passover, Pentecost and Tabernacles. Passover marked the beginning of the barley harvest and commemorated the exodus of the children of Israel from Egypt; Pentecost celebrated the conclusion of the barley and the beginning of the wheat harvest; Tabernacles, during which worshippers were required to dwell in temporary booths, marked the final ingathering of the crops. It is remarkable, in the light of the importance of the calendar, that at least two different calendrical systems existed among Jews in the late Second Temple period, during the last two centuries BCE and the first century CE: the sectarians who produced the Dead Sea scrolls used a solar calendar at variance with the lunar system used by the Temple authorities and later by the rabbis. The rabbinic texts themselves reveal the calendar as an issue of intense debate, particularly over the date of Pentecost, which was fixed, according to the Bible, fifty days after the first *omer* (the ceremonial offering of a sheaf of the first fruits of the harvest), which in turn took place following the celebration of Passover: "And you shall count for yourselves from the morrow after the Sabbath, from the day that you brought the sheaf of the wave offering; seven weeks shall there be complete." How then to interpret "the morrow after the Sabbath"? Different religious groups came to different

conclusions. One such group, the Sadducees, took the view that the day of
the *omer* should be the Sunday after the first Sabbath following the Passover
offering: "Sabbath" meant "Sabbath." Other groups, including Pharisees
and the rabbis, understood "the Sabbath" to be the day of the Passover
offering itself, a reading also presupposed in the Septuagint and by Philo
and Josephus. Since Pharisees and Sadducees shared the one Temple, some
of them will often have found themselves being required to celebrate Pentecost on what they believed to be the wrong day. Unlike other issues of
biblical interpretation, which might be a matter for private conscience
only, the correct computation of the calendar had major public impact. If
in the eyes of some Jews, like the members of the Dead Sea sect, the High
Priest in Jerusalem ate and drank on what they believed to be the Day of
Atonement, the most sacred fast day of the year, they could not consider
him an appropriate religious leader of his people.[41]

Discussion, dispute and disagreement about the divinely ordained divisions of the annual calendar contrast to Jewish vagueness about longer-
term chronology. The biblical text divided time into periods of seven
years, of which the last, the sabbatical year, was to be marked by the cessation of agricultural work on the land. After seven sabbatical year cycles, the
fiftieth year was to be a Jubilee: "And you shall hallow the fiftieth year, and
proclaim liberty throughout the land to all its inhabitants . . . You shall
return every man to his property, and you shall return every man to his
family." In a document cited by Josephus, Julius Caesar, reiterating privileges granted by previous rulers, refers to the exemption of Jerusalem from
tax "in the seventh year, which they call the sabbatical year, because in this
time they neither take fruit from the trees nor do they sow," and there are
scattered references to the seven-year cycle as a recognized method of dating in later Jewish writings. An Aramaic text written on a papyrus found in
the Judaean desert records an admission of a debt incurred in "the second
year of the emperor Nero," 55 or 56 CE, with the proviso that "I will pay it
to you with an added fifth, and that will be until I have repaid it entirely,
even if it is a sabbatical year." A whole tractate of the Mishnah was devoted
to expounding the practical issues which arose from the need to avoid
working the land during this year or profiting from produce grown in defi-
ance of the law.[42]

The Jubilee cycle formed the chronological base of the rewriting of the
biblical book of Genesis by the author of *Jubilees*, which was composed

probably at some time in the second century BCE, and Josephus writes enthusiastically about the Jubilee as part of "the code of laws which Moses . . . learnt from the mouth of God and transmitted in writing to the Hebrews," without any hint that this example of Jewish dedication to social justice is any different from the institution of the sabbatical year. It is therefore surprising to discover that by his time the Jubilee, unlike the sabbatical year, seems to have fallen into disuse—if, indeed, it had ever been put into practice. No extant source from the late Second Temple period dates any particular year by its place in the Jubilee cycle, which was forgotten as a way of shaping memories of the recent past. Indeed, Josephus' reckoning of long periods is often inconsistent, so that what he wrote about the number of years in one part of his history is incompatible with his assertions elsewhere. It seems that Jews had a good sense of the passage of time over the past decade or so, but that earlier history, except for what was written in the Bible, was less differentiated.[43]

Thus Jews of the first century CE ended up strikingly less well informed about the past three hundred years than their Roman contemporaries, despite knowing, or thinking that they knew, far more about the distant past and the origins of their people. From the second century BCE a few Jews, under the influence in part of Greek models of historiography, wrote recent political history, much like their Roman contemporaries, although the author of 1 Maccabees preferred to follow a sober narrative style in imitation of the historical books in the Hebrew Bible, perhaps in the hope that this would make his account appear more portentous to Jewish readers. Most other Jewish writing about the past in the late Hellenistic and early Roman periods concentrated on rewriting the biblical narratives for religious edification or rhetorical effect. Occasionally the story of more recent events might be narrated in dramatic tones to illustrate the role of divine providence in protecting the Jews, either in the "pathetic" history of 2 Maccabees, which invited readers to imagine and empathize with the emotions of the leading characters, or in the tales of tyranny defeated and punished to be found in Philo's writing and rewriting of the traumatic struggle between Jews and Greeks in Alexandria in which he himself had participated. Biographical narratives like the Gospels, which present insights into the psychological dramas and complex motivations of ordinary people set against the background of wider political events, were not standard among Jews any more than among Greeks or Romans; the popularity of the genre among early Christians as a way of spreading the word about Jesus' life and teaching may be ascribed in part precisely to the novelty of this sort of writing. The only Jewish historians specifically known to have tackled recent history with (at least in large part) the aims of Greek and Roman historiography, to explain the causes of political events and especially of wars, were Josephus and Justus of Tiberias, who both wrote about the great revolt against Rome.

The claim that Jews in general did not write history of the Graeco-Roman type is of course vulnerable, as are all arguments from silence, and the fragments which survive in Greek of rewritings of biblical stories by Jewish writers show that they, like the Roman annalists, tried to reconcile native traditions with the "scientific" historiography of the Greeks. Around the mid-second century BCE Moses was equated by the historian Artapanus with Musaeus. A contemporary of Artapanus, known only as Pseudo-Eupolemus, asserted that "Atlas and Enoch are the same." Another contemporary, Cleodemus the prophet, "also called Malchus," a writer quoted by Josephus from the learned compilation of Alexander Polyhistor in the mid-first century BCE but himself of unknown origin, claimed that the offspring of Abraham colonized Assyria and Africa. The fact that the subject matter of all these fragments was biblical rather than more recent history partly reflects the limited interests of the authors, but partly also the concerns of those who preserved what they wrote: most of the extant passages of these writers survive because they were cited by Christian authors, particularly Clement of Alexandria (in the late second and early third century) and Eusebius of Caesarea (in the early fourth century), and both these Christian theologians had a far greater interest in the biblical stories than in the later history of the Jews.[44]

In any case, it is striking that the authors cited by Josephus in his narrative of the previous three hundred years in the last eight books of his twenty-volume *Jewish Antiquities* tended to be gentile, and that he relied heavily on the gentile historian Nicolaus of Damascus for his account of the end of the second century and most of the first century BCE. Nicolaus presumably had more to say about Jews than other Greek intellectuals of his time because he served at the court of Herod the Great. It seems that Jews themselves had little more to go on than oral traditions. The rabbinic texts of the second century CE and later reveal an extraordinary ignorance about events between Ezra and Nehemiah in the fifth century BCE and the great rabbinic sages of the first century CE. The historical outlook encapsulated in the classic account in the Mishnah of the transmission of tradition from Moses down to the present shows neither knowledge of, nor interest in, the postbiblical centuries, except for names of (a very few) sages:

> Moses received Torah from Sinai and transmitted it to Joshua, and Joshua to elders, and elders to prophets; and prophets transmitted it to the men of the Great Assembly . . . Shimon the Just was of the remnants of the Great Assembly . . . Antigonus, a man of Sokho, received [Torah] from Shimon the Just . . . Yose b. Yoezer, a man of Zeredah, and Yose b. Yohanan, a man of Jerusalem, received from them . . . Joshua b. Perahyah and Nittai the Arbelite received from them . . . Judah b. Tabbai and Shimon b. Shetah received from them . . . Shemaiah and Abtalion received from them . . . Hillel and Shammai received from them.

Some have suggested that rabbinic reticence about the Hasmonaeans reflects political or religious hostility to the dynasty, but ignorance is a better explanation: some Hasmonaeans, notably Salome, who ruled from 76 to 67 BCE, were treated by the rabbis with approval.[45]

It seems likely, then, that Josephus' attempt in the late first century CE to write a detailed account of postbiblical Jewish history in his *Antiquities* was pioneering. The books of the Hebrew Bible provided him with information for a more or less coherent narrative of the fortunes of the Jews from the beginning to the fifth century BCE, but for the fourth and for much of the third century he could rely on almost no evidence at all from Jewish sources, so he wove what narrative he could out of the minimal material at his disposal, such as the story in the *Letter of Aristeas* about the translation of the Septuagint in Alexandria. Great swathes of the history of Judaea in the not very distant past were simply unknown—a fact that Josephus was at pains to hide because he felt it did not reflect well on the Jews. Josephus knew that the biblical account finished long ago in the reign of Artaxerxes in the Persian period, before Alexander the Great, but, he asserted, "from Artaxerxes to our own time the complete history has been written, but has not been deemed worthy of equal credit with the earlier records because the exact succession of the prophets has not happened." About the diaspora even less was known. Josephus was aware that Jews had been in Babylonia since the exile of 586 BCE, but he could provide only an occasional vignette of what had happened to the Babylonian Jews since then, such as the success of a robber state ruled by the Jewish brothers Asinaeus and Anilaeus in the region of Nehardea on the Euphrates in the time of Tiberius, when they broke away from Parthian rule for several decades.[46]

Ignorance about more recent centuries contrasted with Jewish certainty about the distant past, since, as Josephus states, the surviving accounts were believed to be full, coherent, consistent and divinely inspired:

> It therefore naturally, or rather necessarily, follows (seeing that with us it is not open to everybody to write the records, and that there is no discrepancy in what is written; seeing that, on the contrary, the prophets alone had this privilege, obtaining their knowledge of the most remote and ancient history through the inspiration which they owed to God, and committing to writing a clear account of the events of their own time just as they occurred) that we do not possess myriads of inconsistent books, conflicting with each other. Our books, those which are justly trusted, are but two and twenty, and contain the record of all time.

For Josephus, lack of disagreement could be taken as evidence of veracity. Jews could point to a long native written record of their origins, with detailed stories of glorious (and less glorious) kings and other leaders. For Jews, as for Romans, these narratives of distant figures could be taken as lessons for present behaviour. Philo explicitly interpreted the life of each patriarch as a symbolic allegory of a moral lesson: " 'And the Lord said unto Abraham, Depart out of thy land, and out of thy kindred, and out of thy father's house' . . . 'Land' or 'country' is a symbol of body, 'kindred' of sense-perception, 'father's house' of speech." The Dead Sea sectarians took the prophecies of Habakkuk as ciphers for the travails of the Teacher of Righteousness to whose leadership they ascribed their own special relationship to God: " 'Because of the blood of men and the violence done to the land, to the city, and to all its inhabitants.' Interpreted, this concerns the Wicked Priest whom God delivered into the hands of his enemies because of the iniquity committed against the Teacher of Righteousness and the men of his Council." Biblical names were frequent choices for Jewish boys in the Second Temple period: there were many men called Shimon, Judah, Joseph, Joshua and Jonathan (although it is curious to note that Aaron, David, Solomon and Elijah, names popular in other periods of Jewish history, were rarely used, and that for girls, only the biblical names Salome and Mariamme were common). It was a remarkable fact, equalled by few other ancient peoples, that Jews possessed a continuous historical account of their past from the creation of the world down to *c.* 400 BCE.[47]

Despite Jews' pride about their ancient history, there was a curious timelessness about their attitude to the past. Events were rarely dated by a common Jewish era. Jewish legal documents used secular, gentile dates: the year of the emperor's rule, the names of the consuls for the year in Rome, the Seleucid era which continued to be popular in the Near East until the Middle Ages. No Jewish era was used in chronological writings like *Jubilees* or *Seder Olam*, which gave lengths of time between events from the creation of the world to the revolt of Bar Kokhba. What interested these chronographers was the relationship of events to each other, not any sense of absolute time. It may well be significant that rabbinic discussions of the right time for religious ceremonies treat always of the time of day as experienced by everyone (such as the time in the morning when "one can distinguish between blue and white"). Jews do not seem to have had much use for precise measurements of time, such as was provided by the great sundial of Augustus in the Campus Martius at Rome. For Jews, what mattered, after all, was that, through Moses on Mount Sinai, Jews had received the Law by which they lived their lives. What had happened between Moses and now might be of interest, particularly in discussions with gentile critics who cast doubt on the antiquity and therefore the value of Jewish customs, but in itself it was not very important.

It has indeed been plausibly argued that those Jews who thought and wrote in Hebrew and Aramaic in this period had no notion of time as an entity which might be spent or wasted, or which might flow, fly or pass slowly, as it does in English and Greek, and as it did in early imperial Rome.[48] Vergil could write that "time flies and cannot be repaired" and Seneca wrote a whole letter on the value of time: "Time is the one loan which even a grateful recipient cannot repay." By contrast, the idea of time as a flow, agent, resource or commodity, as opposed to specific points in time when things happen, is hard to find in the Hebrew Bible, early rabbinic literature, or the Dead Sea scrolls. The Jewish writings in which the

personification of time does appear are those composed in Greek with
Greek literary pretensions, like Josephus in *Against Apion*, writing for a
Greek and Roman readership: "Now, since time is reckoned in all cases the
surest test of worth, I would call time as witness of the virtue of our lawgiver [Moses] . . . [Critics] reviled our lawgiver as an insignificant person,
but his virtue has found a witness of old in God, and after God, in time."[49]

Jews in the first century CE shared with Romans a nostalgia for the distant past. Earlier generations had been better men than the present, as a
story in the Tosefta neatly expressed:

> When the latter prophets died, that is, Haggai, Zechariah and Malachi,
> then the Holy Spirit came to an end in Israel. But even so, they made
> them hear through an echo [a *bat kol*]. It once happened that the sages
> gathered together in the upper room of the house of Guria in Jericho,
> and a *bat kol* came out and said to them, "There is a man among you
> who is worthy to receive the Holy Spirit, but his generation does not
> deserve such an honour."

The prophets no longer functioned as they used to. The oracular Urim and
Thummim no longer revealed the divine will by the way they sparkled on
the High Priest's breastplate: according to Josephus, they "ceased to shine
two hundred years before I composed this work because of God's displeasure at the transgression of the laws," although the Mishnah dated their
cessation to "when the first prophets died."[50]

But it is striking that most nostalgia after 70 CE was precisely for the last
years of the Second Temple, not for a past whose memory was lost in the
mists of antiquity: "Since the day that the Temple was destroyed there has
been no day without its curse; and the dew has not fallen in blessing and
the fruits have lost their savour." The theory that history consisted in the
unfolding of God's plan for his people, and that Israel would be rewarded
for obedience and punished for sin, made sense of the sufferings of the distant past, notably the destruction of the Temple of Solomon in 586 BCE
and the exile to Babylonia, but Jews did not feel themselves to be suffering
in any such way before 70 CE. Far from being deprived of a Temple in the
reign of Herod and in the early years of Roman rule, Jews could bask in the
glory of the sanctuary rebuilt to a magnificence equal to the time of
Solomon himself. The notion that Jews in the late Second Temple period

saw themselves as sinners permanently punished by God and in need of salvation from the sufferings of exile and Roman domination is a myth expressed particularly by New Testament scholars in order to provide a theological grounding for the mission of Jesus to Israel. The most that can be said is that some wicked actions, like the internecine struggles and other sins of the Hasmonaeans in the 60s BCE, could be interpreted, as in the contemporary *Psalms of Solomon,* as having brought about specific national disasters such as the capture of Jerusalem by Pompey in 63 BCE:

> God exposed their sins to the sun; the whole earth came to know the righteous judgements of God . . . There was no sin they left undone in which they did not surpass the gentiles. Therefore God mixed them spirit to mislead, and gave them a cup of undiluted wine to make them drunk. He brought one from the end of the earth, one who smites mightily; he declared war against Jerusalem, and her land . . . He took possession of the fortified towers and the wall of Jerusalem, for God led him in securely while they went astray. He killed their leaders and every man wise in counsel, he poured out the blood of the inhabitants of Jerusalem like unclean water.

To be sure, the end of the Hasmonaean dynasty had been a time of disasters, as had the capture of Jerusalem in 37 BCE by Herod, but it was hard to say the same of the next hundred years to 70 CE, during which, despite occasional alarums, the city prospered and grew.[51]


## EXPECTATIONS

No ONE KNOWS where it is all going to end, either for the nation, or, indeed, for all humanity. Speculation may seem worthless or worse, agnosticism the only sensible policy. The Epicurean Lucretius (*c.* 94–*c.* 51 BCE) offered the consolation that nothing matters: "Some peoples increase even as others diminish, and the generations of living things are changed in a brief span of time; and like runners, they pass on the torch of life." So too the Jewish author of Ecclesiastes, probably in the third century BCE: "Vanity of vanities, says the preacher, vanity of vanities. All is vanity. What profit has a man of all his labour at which he toils under the sun? One generation passes away, and another generation comes, but the earth abides for ever." But none of these pessimistic philosophical musings prevented the growth of doctrines of hope in both societies.[52]

Philosophical Romans like the Stoic Seneca might imagine a time when Rome would disappear, noting that "of all the cities that have ever held dominion . . . men will some day ask where they were, and they will be swept away by various kinds of destruction: some will be ruined by wars, others will be destroyed by idleness and a peace that ends in sloth, or by luxury, the bane of those of great wealth," but others, like Vergil, might imagine that the golden age of the distant past would return, and, already in the time of Augustus, both Tibullus and Ovid referred to Rome as the "eternal city." A silver *denarius* minted under Vespasian bore the legend ROMA PERPETUA, and ROMA AETERNA appears on imperial coins from the time of Hadrian. The general assumption in Roman society was that the city and its empire would be around for ever.[53]

Confirmation of this assumption about the future lies in the steps taken by individuals to preserve the memory of themselves and their achievements for future generations to admire. Such steps presupposed both that there would indeed be such future generations and that the values and assumptions of those to come would resemble those of the present. Many Romans in the early imperial period demonstrated confidence in the future by an extraordinary explosion of the epigraphic habit: the inscription on stone of many thousands of honorific texts and epitaphs showed an expectation among ordinary Romans that their descendants, or others with whom they had once been connected, would read the words in hundreds of years' time.

By contrast, most Jews in the first century CE had a clear notion of the end of history. At some time, of God's choosing, the world would come to an end. Quite what that would be like, and when it would happen, were matters for speculation, but that it would happen in some form was widely accepted. It would not always be tactful to spell out for gentiles the implications of this belief for the eventual fate of the Roman empire. Josephus recounts in his *Antiquities* the prophecy of Daniel to Nebuchadrezzar, king of Babylonia from 605 to 565 BCE, that his dream, about a statue made of different metals, meant that his Babylonian realm would fall to the Medes and Persians, who in turn would be conquered by Alexander the Great, whose power would finally be ended "by still another, like iron, that will have dominion for ever through its iron nature." Daniel's knowledge of the future was remarkable and proves

> how mistaken are the Epicureans, who exclude Providence from life and refuse to believe that God governs its affairs or that the universe is directed by a blessed and immortal Being to the end that the whole of it may endure, saying that the world runs by its own movement without knowing a guide or another's care . . . For if it were the case that the cosmos goes on by some automatism, we should not have seen all these things happen in accordance with his prophecy.[54]

All the more striking, then, that Josephus elected not to explain for his readers the prophecy of Daniel that the statue of different metals was crushed to pieces by a stone: "Then was the iron, the clay, the brass, the silver, and the gold, broken to pieces together, and became like the chaff of the summer threshing floors; and the wind carried them away, so that not a trace of them could be found."[55] Daniel interpreted this to refer to the setting up of God's kingdom which shall never be destroyed. But Josephus was reticent:

> And Daniel also revealed to the king the meaning of the stone, but I have not thought it proper to relate this, since I am expected to write of what is past and done and not of what is to be; but if there is anyone who has so keen a desire for exact information that he will not stop short of enquiring more closely but wishes to learn about the hidden things that are to come, let him take the trouble to read the Book of Daniel, which he will find among the sacred writings.[56]

Jews seem to have envisaged this forward progression of history less as a straight march to a known final destination than a spiral towards a summit always (so far) out of sight. The spiral progress of history explained the repetition of significant events on particular days of the year. The Mishnah recorded the events which had befallen Israel on specific days: "Five things befell our fathers on . . . 9 Ab [July or August, depending on the year] . . . On 9 Ab it was decreed against our fathers that they should not enter into the Land [of Israel], and the Temple was destroyed the first and the second time, and Bethar was captured and the city was ploughed up. When Ab comes in, gladness is diminished." Josephus dated the destruction of the Temple in his own days to 10 Ab, a day later, but he too saw this later date, "the fated day, the tenth of the month . . . the day on which of old it had been burnt by the king of Babylon," as significant:

> Deeply as one must mourn for the most marvellous edifice which we have ever seen or heard of, whether we consider its structure, its magnitude, the richness of its every detail, or the reputation of its holiness, yet may we draw very great consolation from the thought that there is no escape from Fate, for works of art and places any more than for living beings. And one may well marvel at the exactness of the cycle of Destiny; for, as I said, she waited until the very month and the very day on which in bygone times the Temple had been burnt by the Babylonians.[57]

Before the last days there would be a struggle between good and evil, although about its precise nature Jews had no consensus. A nineteen-column scroll from Cave 1 at Qumran described "The war of the Sons of Light against the Sons of Darkness." The Sons of Light, recruited from the tribes of Levi, Judah and Benjamin, and aided by angels, will confront the army of Belial, led by the Kittim and their allies (Edomites, Moabites, Ammonites and Philistines) and "the ungodly of the covenant," that is, bad Jews. The *War Rule* lays down details of the battle timetable, the standards to be carried by the troops, the regulations for battle divisions and clothing, the need to ensure the purity and holiness of the army: "All these shall pursue the enemy to destroy him in an everlasting destruction in the battle of God." Fragments of copies of the same text from Cave 4 suggest that speculation on these bloody preliminaries to the final victory of Israel was common within the sect.[58] But other Jewish texts suggest a variety of quite different images hard to reconcile with this rather down-to-earth military account. So, in *4 Ezra*, composed soon after 70 CE:

> Sown places shall suddenly appear unsown, and full storehouses shall suddenly be found empty; and the trumpet shall sound aloud, and when all hear it, they shall suddenly be struck with fear. At that time [friends shall make war on friends like enemies], and the earth [and

those who inhabit it] shall be stricken with fear, and the springs of the fountains shall stand still, so that for three hours they shall not flow. And it shall be that whoever survives after all that I have foretold to you shall be saved and shall see my salvation and the end of my world. And they shall see the men who were taken up, who from their birth have not tasted death. Then shall the heart of the earth's inhabitants be changed and converted to a different spirit. For evil shall be blotted out, and deceit shall be extinguished; faithfulness shall flourish, and corruption shall be overcome, and truth, which has been so long without fruit, shall be revealed.[59]

The seer in *4 Ezra* envisaged a hostile multitude gathered together from all over the world to attack Mount Zion. The destruction of such hostile powers will sometimes be inflicted directly by God himself, sometimes by an intermediary. Victory will be followed by the establishment of a new and glorious Jerusalem. The dispersed of Israel will travel from all over the diaspora to return to Jerusalem, as envisaged in the *Psalms of Solomon* in the mid-first century BCE:

Sound in Zion the trumpet to summon the saints; announce in Jerusalem the voice of one bringing good news, for the God of Israel has been merciful in watching over them. Stand on a high place, Jerusalem, and look at your children, from the east and the west gathered together by the Lord. From the north they come in the joy of their God; from far distant islands God has gathered them. He flattened high mountains into a plain for them; the hills fled at their coming. The woods shaded them as they passed by: God made every fragrant tree to spring up for them; so that Israel might pass by at the visitation of the glory of their God. Jerusalem, put on the garments of your glory, prepare the robe of your holiness, for God has spoken well of Israel for ever and ever. May the Lord do what he has spoken about Israel and Jerusalem; may the Lord lift up Israel in his glorious name. May the mercy of the Lord be upon Israel for ever and ever.[60]

Finally, the kingdom of heaven will be established in the holy land, as the daily prayers preserved in the rabbinic tradition request: "Take from us sor-

row and sighing, and reign over us, you Lord alone, in grace and mercy."
This new kingdom will be full of joy and happiness for the righteous and
disaster for the wicked, as the book of *Jubilees* proclaimed:

> And they will drive out their adversaries, and the righteous will see and
> give praise, and rejoice for ever and ever with joy, and they will see
> all of their judgements and all of their curses on their enemies. And
> their bones will rest in the earth, and their spirits will have much joy,
> and they will know that the Lord is an executor of judgement; but he
> will show mercy to hundreds and to tens of thousands, and to all who
> love him.[61]

In the special feast to celebrate, the dishes to be served will include the
mythical beast Leviathan.[62]

It is not at all a matter of chance that the composite picture of Jewish
beliefs about the last days given above has been compiled from a variety of
sources composed in different times and places. There is no evidence of an
agreed coherent eschatology within any ancient Jewish group. It is, however, striking that expectation of some dramatic change in the world was
so widespread. Even the philosopher Philo, whose interpretation of the
Torah generally focused firmly on the psychological need of the individual
worshipper to concentrate on the higher meaning of the laws, still let slip
an uncharacteristic hope that God would one day bring to an end "the
enmity of wild beasts which is activated by natural antipathy" and produce
an age in which nature will be at peace: "When that time comes I believe
that bears and lions and panthers and the Indian animals, elephants and
tigers, and all others whose vigour and power are invincible, will change
their life of solitariness and isolation for one of companionship, and gradually in imitation of the gregarious creatures show themselves tame when
brought face to face with mankind . . . Then too the tribes of scorpions
and serpents and the other reptiles will have no use for their venom." Philo
did derive a moral message from the analogy between these wild beasts and
the wild beasts within the soul, but it seems likely that this idealized picture, so close to the prophecy in Isaiah of the lion lying down with the
lamb, owed more than a little to popular conceptions of the perfect time
when the last days arrive.[63]

In some Jewish texts the central figure in these events of the last days is called the Messiah, "the anointed." Some texts, like the *Psalms of Solomon*, describe the Messiah as a human figure, descended from David:

> Behold, Lord, and raise up for them their king, the son of David, to
> reign over your servant Israel in the time which you did foresee, O
> God. Gird him with strength to destroy unrighteous rulers, and purge
> Jerusalem from the nations who trample her down to destruction . . .
> And he will be a righteous king over them, taught by God. There will
> be no unrighteousness among them in his days, for all shall be holy, and
> their king shall be the anointed Lord.[64]

In other texts, however, the Messiah is described as a supernatural figure, as befits the events in which he is involved. So the author of *2 Baruch*, a description of a series of visions alleged to have been experienced by Baruch, amanuensis of the prophet Jeremiah, but in fact composed by a Jew, probably in Hebrew, in the late first century CE and now preserved only in Christian translations into Syriac and Arabic:

> And it will happen after these things when the time of the appearance
> of the Anointed has been fulfilled and he returns with glory, that then
> all who sleep in hope of him will rise. And it will happen at that time
> that those treasuries will be opened in which the number of the souls of
> the righteous were kept, and they will go out and the multitudes of the
> souls will appear together, in one sole assembly, of one mind . . . The
> souls of the wicked, on the contrary, will waste away completely when
> they shall see all these things.[65]

Among the Dead Sea sectarians are to be found varied and conflicting ideas about the nature of the Messiah. Sometimes the scrolls envisage just one royal, Davidic, triumphant Messiah, but sometimes a Messiah of Israel was contrasted to a Messiah of Aaron, who in turn was differentiated from "the Prophet": "They shall depart from none of the counsels of the Law to walk in all the stubbornness of their hearts, but shall be ruled by the first precepts in which the men of the Community began to be instructed until there shall come a prophet and the Messiahs of Aaron and Israel."[66] In the *Assumption of Moses*, an address said to have been delivered by Moses to Joshua just before the former's death, a description is given of the last days

in which no Messiah appears at all. The same is true also of the detailed battle described in the *War Rule* from Qumran—there victory is achieved not
through a royal Messiah but by the intervention of the archangel Michael.
The Mishnah, the foundation document of early rabbinic Judaism, has so
little to say about the Messiah that it has been described as presenting
"Judaism without Messiah." That is an exaggeration, since in fact a few
mentions are found—and the scarcity of messianic references may owe
more to the genre of the Mishnah, a compilation of legal opinions, than it
does to the wider outlook of those who compiled it. It is hardly surprising
that the concept of the Messiah is assumed rather than elaborated in such a
work.[67]

Despite the eventual emergence of Christianity from late Second Temple Judaism, the figure of the Messiah is either missing or unimportant in
many Jewish religious texts of this period. Christian interest in messianism
may explain why much more is to be found about the figure of the Messiah
at the end of days in the early Jewish literature preserved by Christians than
in the Jewish literature of the second and third centuries CE preserved by
the rabbis. However, the eschatological emphasis of some of the writings
produced by the Dead Sea sect, all of which survive through chance alone,
and the appearance in many different Qumran documents of references to
a Messiah or to messianic qualities ("son of David"), demonstrate that messianic speculation was also common among groups of Jews about whom
the later Christian tradition was apparently ignorant. What remains significant is the lack of coherence in the picture of the expected Messiah which
emerges even from the Jewish writings which Christians used as texts of
religious value. One would have expected the early Church to emphasize
all the literature they could find which showed Jews to be engrossed in
messianic speculation, since the only Jewish group in the first century CE
which came to define itself by its devotion to a Messiah was the Christians
themselves, whose name "Christians" means "enthusiasts for *Christos*,
Messiah." The fact that the picture of the Messiah which emerges from all
the literature they did preserve is so confused, fragmentary and contradictory indicates that this confusion was indeed standard among Jews.

Expectation of the end of history discouraged the creation by Jews of
monuments for later generations. Unlike the impressive funerary markers
and honorific inscriptions favoured by those Romans who could afford it,
the ossuaries used by many Jews in Herodian Jerusalem to contain the

bones of relatives are marked with the name of the deceased but provide no information on his or her achievements in life. Inscriptions recording donations and honours are almost unknown in first-century CE Judaean society, where the epigraphic habit never became popular (as it did among diaspora Jews in later centuries). Much Jewish literature in the Second Temple period, including all the Dead Sea sectarian texts, is presented either anonymously or in the name of a fictitious author, usually a figure from the distant past: the real authors of these works were presumably more interested in disseminating their ideas than in recording anything about themselves as individuals. The early rabbis, by contrast, professed a concern to preserve a record of the name of the originator of each of the legal traditions they passed on, but in the first two centuries CE they rarely preserved much more than the name: the record of the character and achievements of individual rabbis in the earliest stratum of rabbinic literature is so scanty that it is impossible to write even a bare biography of most of them.

One exception to this lack of interest in the preservation of memory was Herod the Great. Josephus attributed explicitly to Herod's concern for his reputation with posterity his huge expenditure on the rebuilding of the Temple. Just before his death Herod summoned before him the Jewish leaders and recounted "all his strenuous efforts on their behalf, and told them at what great expense to himself he had constructed the Temple . . . He had also, he said, adorned [the Temple] with notable dedicatory offerings, and for these reasons he cherished the hope that even after his death he would leave behind a memorial of himself and an illustrious name." Herod's tomb at Herodium was intended to impress and preserve his memory, just as the tombs of the biblical patriarchs in Hebron, which he himself beautified by the erection of a magnificent new enclosure which still stands, kept alive the memory of their significance to the Jewish people. Some other wealthy Jews also spent money on impressive tomb markers in the vicinity of Jerusalem, particularly in the Kidron valley. But most seem to have been satisfied with a final resting place in a discreet stone ossuary hidden away within a warren of corridors and ledges excavated into the Judaean hillside. It is tempting to ascribe the attitude of Herod to the Roman side of his identity—or, more specifically, to emulation of his Roman patron Augustus.[68]

If most Jews were more concerned with a divinely engineered change

in the world order than they were with the views of future human generations, this was because the main human story in which they were interested, in the future as in the past, was the drama of Israel's relationship
with God. Just as in the past national fortunes had been shaped by the
attempts of Israel to fulfil the covenant with God, so too in the future. As
Josephus wrote at the beginning of his monumental *Jewish Antiquities*,
"the main lesson to be learned from this history by any who care to peruse
it is that men who follow the will of God and do not dare to contravene all
the laws that have been excellently laid down, prosper in all things beyond
belief, and happiness is their reward from God; but in so far as they depart
from strict attention to those laws, what was possible becomes impossible,
and whatever good thing they are eager to do is turned to irretrievable
disasters."[69]

MUCH JEWISH eschatology was thus otherworldly, and could be understood by sympathetic Romans as a return to the lost golden age, as when
Jews hoped for a time when gentiles will pay homage to the Messiah
because they will recognize that God has given him power: "[The Lord]
shall have mercy on all the nations who reverently stand before him,"
according to the eschatological vision of the author of the *Psalms of Solomon*
in the mid-first century BCE.[70] At other times Jewish expectations for the
other nations of the world were more black, particularly in the shadow of
recent disaster:

> When the nations are troubled and the time of my Anointed comes, he
> will call all nations, and some of them he will spare, and others he will
> kill. These things will befall the nations which will be saved by him.
> Every nation which has not reigned over Israel and which has not trod-
> den down the seed of Jacob will live ... All those, now, who have
> ruled over you, or have known you, will be delivered up to the sword.[71]

But this all lay in the distant future. In any case, some of the eschatological
hopes of some Jews included a role for good gentiles, with the prediction
that in the end times all humanity would recognize the sovereignty of the
Jewish God. Isaiah had long ago written:

It shall come to pass in the last days that the mountain of the Lord's house shall be established in the top of the mountains, and shall be exalted above the hills, and all nations shall flow to it. And many people shall go and say, "Come, and let us go up to the mountain of the Lord, to the house of the God of Jacob; and he will teach us of his ways, and we will walk in his paths; for out of Zion shall go forth the law, and the word of the Lord from Jerusalem."[72]

The New Jerusalem for which Jews yearned was a heavenly city only loosely related to that on earth. It would be revealed by God when he deemed fit. In the meantime Jews could only describe visions about its remarkable appearance: the report of an angel's detailed measurements of the gates, avenues and houses of the eschatological city, found in a first-century-CE Aramaic writing of which fragments were discovered in five different caves at Qumran, follows the same pattern as the vision recorded by the prophet Ezekiel many years before. Jews continued to harbour such hopes over the centuries after the end of antiquity during which they lived in peace while they were ruled by other peoples. In principle they could have retained their eschatological expectations while living in peace also under Roman rule.[73]

# CHAPTER FIVE

# COMMUNITIES

## *RES PUBLICA* AND *THEOKRATIA*

*DULCE ET DECORUM EST PRO PATRIA MORI.* "Sweet it is, and fitting, to die for the fatherland."[1] So wrote Horace, in uncharacteristically sombre mood, about old Roman virtues of endurance, courage, independence and reticence. Thus were the great heroes of the past remembered, those who had died for Rome. The glorious Jewish dead, by contrast, were believed to have given up their lives for God, as in the dreadful tortures inflicted, it was said, during the persecutions which preceded the revolt of the Maccabees in the 160s BCE:

> It came to pass also, that seven brothers with their mother were arrested, and compelled by the king to taste swine's flesh forbidden by the law, and were tormented with scourges and whips. But one of them made himself their spokesman, and said, "What do you intend to ask and learn of us? We are ready to die, rather than to transgress the laws of our fathers." Then the king, being in a rage, commanded pans and cauldrons to be made hot . . . [2]

Nonetheless, Jews as much as Romans envisaged their nation as a person. Rome was a goddess, *Dea Roma*, much worshipped outside Rome but also within the city itself from the time of Hadrian. To see Israel or Jerusalem as similarly divine was of course impossible for Jews, but Israel was envisaged as the spouse of God within the covenant between God and Israel brokered, according to the account in Exodus, by Moses and sealed on Mount Sinai, or as the wayward child of a loving father. In both societies the body politic could be understood through metaphors of health and disease. Sallust described the collapse of morals in Rome during the late Republic: "At first these vices grew slowly; now and then they were punished; finally, when the disease had spread like a deadly plague, the state was changed, and a government second to none in equity and excellence became cruel and intolerable."[3] So too Josephus, writing about the state of Judaean society before the outbreak of war and perhaps reflecting, like Sallust, the historiographic influence of Thucydides: "That period had become somehow so prolific of crime of every description among the Jews that no deed of iniquity was left unperpetrated . . . Thus everyone, both in private and in public, was sick." In the 50s CE, as soon as one group of disorders was reduced in Judaea "another part flared up again, as in a sickening body." Josephus addressed himself rhetorically to Jerusalem in the middle of the Roman siege, when the blood of corpses formed pools in the courts of God: "What misery to equal that, most wretched city, have you suffered at the hands of the Romans, who entered to purge with fire your internal pollutions?"[4]

The differences between Romans and Jews lay in conceptions of what the state is for. Neither society indulged as much as Greeks had done in the classical and Hellenistic periods in abstract political philosophy and analyses of the structure of the perfect state, but their shared Greek background ensured that some Jews and some Romans reflected on such matters at least a little, and the vocabulary and rhetoric conventional in each society revealed much about their political conceptions. Among Romans, more extended political philosophizing was not unknown, but in the imperial period it tended to take the form, as in Seneca's writings, of personal advice to rulers on ethical conduct and advice to subjects on how to maintain both dignity and morality when deprived of power. Cicero's treatise *On the Republic*, written in the political chaos of the late Republic, contained an analysis of the constitution of the ideal state along the lines standard in Plato and Aristotle, favouring a constitution which combined monarchy, oligarchy and democracy, an analysis which owed much to his judgement about earlier Roman history and the political turmoil of his own times, but such theoretical discussions were not much favoured under the benevolent rule of the emperors.

For Romans, the state was *res publica*, literally "the public affair," an agglomeration of individuals united for the common good but permitting the greatest possible freedom of private ownership and individual political action, especially among the political elite. This was the nature of the "Republic" which Augustus claimed, on his coins issued in 27 BCE, to have restored following the long years of civil war. An objective observer, with the benefit of hindsight, might see Augustus' rule as the restoration of monarchy, which was indeed how the historian Cassius Dio described it in the early third century CE, but Augustus' portrayal of his regime as conservative and traditional precluded any images of revolutionary change. Hence the contrast between Augustus' own boast in the memoir of his achievements that he "refused to accept any office offered [to him] which was contrary to the traditions of our ancestors' and Dio's statement that

> the power of both people and Senate passed entirely into the hands of Augustus, and from this time there was, strictly speaking, a monarchy; for monarchy would be the truest name for it, even if two or three men later held the power at the same time. Now, the Romans so detested the name of monarchy that they called their emperors neither dictators nor kings nor anything of this sort. Yet, since the final authority for the government devolves upon them, there needs must be kings.[5]

Dio's cynicism reflects the hindsight of the two hundred and fifty years of imperial rule which had passed by the time he was writing. In the first century CE the ostentatious deaths of senatorial "martyrs," who preferred to die rather than compromise their rights to a somewhat spurious liberty which, in essence, involved little more than the right to speak their mind in public, show that some in the political elite continued to keep memories alive of the old ideals of an aristocracy dedicated to the state and prepared to share political power for the sake of the common good. The third element of the mixed constitution envisaged by Cicero, democracy, was hardly an issue at all in the imperial period, even though popular assemblies continued to meet to elect consuls (in normal conditions during the Republic the senior magistrates of the state, with two in office at any one time) and other senior magistrates and to pass laws. In his panegyric of the emperor Trajan, the younger Pliny praised the emperor for the seriousness with which he seemed to take the process of canvassing at the elections, but by his time, the end of the first century CE, the elections were a charade, the results in effect being decided by the favour of the emperor, with real choice delegated only to senators, and even then not for election to the most senior posts. What was left was no more than the vocabulary of democracy. Decisions were taken "by the Senate and people of Rome." Emperors gloried in their role as tribunes of the plebs, using the years of their tribunician power as the criterion for dating their reigns. Winning popular approval in the hippodrome or in other arenas where emperors appeared in public was sufficiently important for the imperial image to justify immense expense on bread and circuses; only a rash emperor would deliberately provoke the people's hostility as Gaius did when he cried in anger, "I wish the Roman people had only one neck." The formalities of democracy, which at times had given real power to the assemblies during the power struggles of the Republic, functioned now only as a façade for autocracy under the rule of emperors.[6]

Josephus, influenced by Thucydides, praised Ananus son of Ananus, the former High Priest who became commander-in-chief of the rebels in Jerusalem in autumn 66 CE, as uniquely a lover of freedom and enthusiast for democracy, but neither individual liberty nor the popular mandate of a majority vote carried the same weight for Jews as for Greeks and Romans. It has even been claimed that the concept of individual freedom is nowhere to be found in the Hebrew Bible, except in the narrow sense of release from slavery. The national freedom created by the Exodus from Egypt turned the Israelites from slaves of Pharaoh into a nation of servants of God. Jews had no formal public assemblies to match those in Rome, and the public assemblies which gave a semblance of authority to leaders in times of crisis did so not in conformity to any national constitution but simply as enthusiastic crowds, vocal in support of their favoured politicians: in 140 BCE the Hasmonaean Simon sought ratification from a "great congregation of the priests, and people, and rulers of the nation, and elders of the country" for his family's usurpation of the high priesthood; Herod in 12 BCE assembled the people in Jerusalem to present to them his three sons, who would be his heirs, although the only function of the crowd was to listen to the speech in which he expressed his affection and hopes for his offspring. Mass meetings seem to have played a significant role in the shifts of power between ambitious politicians during the intrigues in the inde-

pendent city from 66 to 70 CE, but in all cases the power of the massed people was a brutal political fact rather than an ideal. For Jews, all ideals for the
perfect state were expressed in terms of religion and subservience to God.[7]

Josephus' apologetic treatise *Against Apion* contained an analysis of
Judaism which came as close as a Jew ever came to political theorizing
about the nature of such a perfect state:

> Some peoples have entrusted the supreme political power to monar-
> chies, others to oligarchies, yet others to the masses. Our lawgiver,
> however, was attracted by none of these forms of polity, but gave to his
> constitution the form of what—if a forced expression be permitted—
> may be termed a "theocracy," placing all sovereignty and authority in
> the hands of God. To him he persuaded all to look, as the author of all
> blessings, both those which are common to all mankind, and those
> which they had won for themselves by prayer in the crises of their
> history.[8]

Josephus seems to have been responsible for inventing in this passage the
word "theocracy" (*theokratia*), which has since had a long history, adapted
to many European languages. The term is less easy to translate into classical
Hebrew, but both the Bible and Jewish liturgy refer frequently to the
image of God as king, and the opposition voiced in the biblical book
I Samuel to the people of Israel's demand for "a king to govern us like all
the nations" was based explicitly on the conflict between rule by a human
monarch and rule by God: "And the Lord said to Samuel, 'Hearken to the
voice of the people in all that they say to you: for they have not rejected
you, but they have rejected me from being king over them . . .' "[9] In his
discussion of the Jewish constitution in *Against Apion*, Josephus makes it
clear that for Jews the rule of God is ideally to be mediated through priests,
and especially the High Priest: "Could there be a finer or more equitable
polity than one which sets God at the head of the universe, which assigns
the administration of its highest affairs to the whole body of priests, and
entrusts to the supreme High Priest the direction of the other priests?"
Elsewhere, at the end of his *Jewish Antiquities*, Josephus called this rule by
High Priests an aristocracy: "After the death of these kings [Herod and
Archelaus], the constitution was an aristocracy, while the High Priests
were entrusted with the leadership of the nation." The terminology may

have had an apologetic intent for his gentile readers, since "aristocracy" means "the rule of the best," and in his description of Moses' legislation, in the fourth book of the *Antiquities*, Josephus, not yet apparently having thought of "theocracy," had called the Mosaic constitution an aristocracy: "Aristocracy, with the life that is lived thereunder, is indeed the best: let no craving possess you for another polity, but be content with this, having the laws for your masters and governing all your actions by them; for God is sufficient to be ruler."[10]

Josephus did not claim that Jews had in fact always lived under this ideal constitution. On the contrary, he was well aware that they had come under many different forms of government over the years, as he laid out at the beginning of his narrative of the Second Temple period, from the return by some Jews to Jerusalem from exile in Babylonia in the late sixth century BCE to the destruction of the Temple in 70 CE:

> They dwelt in Jerusalem under a form of government that was aristoc-
> racy with oligarchy. For the High Priests were at the head of affairs
> until the descendants of the Hasmonaean family came to rule as kings.
> Before the captivity and deportation they were ruled by kings, begin-
> ning first with Saul and David, for five hundred and thirty-two years,
> six months and ten days; and before these kings the rulers who gov-
> erned them were the men called judges and monarchs, and under this
> form of government they lived for more than five hundred years after
> the death of Moses and Joshua the general.[11]

A priestly aristocracy mediating the commands of God had thus not always been achieved by Jews—indeed, with the Temple destroyed it was no longer in operation at the time when Josephus was writing—but it was the Jewish ideal. The Jewish constitution was sufficiently distinctive to have come to the attention of the sympathetic Greek scholar Hecataeus of Abdera in the time of Alexander the Great, in the late fourth century BCE:

> He [Moses] picked out the men of most refinement and with the great-
> est ability to head the entire nation, and appointed them priests; and he
> ordained that they should occupy themselves with the Temple and the
> honours and sacrifices offered to their God. These same men he
> appointed to be judges of the most important law cases, and entrusted

to them the guardianship of the laws and customs. For this reason there is never a king of the Jews, and the leadership of the people is regularly given to whichever priest is regarded as superior to his colleagues in wisdom and virtue. They call this man High Priest, and believe that he acts as a messenger to them of God's commandments. It is he, so they say, who in their assemblies and other gatherings announces what is ordained, and the Jews are so docile in such matters that straightway they fall to the ground and do reverence to the High Priest when he expounds the commandments to them. Added to the end of their laws it is even written that Moses, having heard these things from God, declares them to the Jews.[12]

It is clear that, for Josephus at least, this role of priests in the mediation of God's rule to his people was crucial, for he was vituperative about the followers of a certain Judas the Galilean who in 6 CE "incited his country-men to revolt, upbraiding them as cowards for consenting to pay tribute to Romans and after God tolerating mortal lords. This man was a sophist who founded a school of his own which had nothing in common with the oth-ers."[13] As we shall see in Chapter 11, the accuracy of Josephus' picture of Judas' "Fourth Philosophy," its origins, influence and relation to other types of Judaism, is questionable, since his two brief accounts of its doc-trines contain blatant contradictions and are supported by evidence from no other source, but his lack of confidence in unmediated divine rule emerged also in his condemnation of the Zealots when in 68 CE they appointed a new High Priest by lot rather than hereditary succession,

asserting that in old days the High Priesthood had been determined by lot; but in reality their action was the abrogation of established practice and a trick to make themselves supreme by getting these appointments into their own hands . . . By chance the lot fell to one who proved a sig-nal illustration of their depravity . . . such a country rustic that he scarcely knew what the High Priesthood meant. At any rate they dragged their reluctant victim out of the country and, dressing him up for his assumed part, as on the stage, put the sacred vestments upon him and instructed him how to act in keeping with the occasion. To them this monstrous impiety was a subject for jesting and sport, but the other priests, beholding from a distance this mockery of their law, could not restrain their tears and bemoaned the degradation of the sacred honours.

Despite Josephus' denial of the Zealots' justification for this procedure by citing ancient custom, the use of the lot may have seemed to them a pious means to place the choice in the hands of God.[14]

In many periods of Jewish history in antiquity this reliance on divine rule mediated through priests coexisted with acceptance of monarchic rule. The Bible describes how Samuel grumbled at the request of the elders of Israel to "appoint us a king to govern us like all the nations," but still acceded to their demand, however unwillingly.[15] The power of the High Priest, even as described by Josephus, was quasi-monarchical, as was that of the patriarch or *nasi* within the rabbinic movement of the third and fourth centuries CE, and that of the *maskil,* the Guardian or Master, who presided over the strictly hierarchical assembly of the congregation which both constituted and governed the Dead Sea sect. For over half a century the Hasmonaean High Priests actually arrogated to themselves the title of "King," partly, no doubt, in imitation of contemporary rulers of other Hellenistic states. Jews were presumably capable of justifying such monarchical rule by reference to the virtue of the monarch, along the same lines as Stoic arguments in defence of kingship: thus Philo praises Moses as leader of all those who joined the Exodus from Egypt on the grounds that he had been "invested with this office and kingship, not like some of those who thrust themselves into positions of power by means of arms and engines of war and strength of infantry, cavalry and navy, but on account of his goodness and his nobility of conduct and the universal benevolence to all which he never failed to show. Further, his office was bestowed upon him by God, the lover of virtue and nobility, as the reward due to him."[16] But such explicit justification for monarchy was rare. Rule by one man seems to have occurred in Jewish society, as in Roman, not as a product of ideology but as a by-product of the thirst for power by individuals—the priestly Hasmonaeans, the Herodians from Idumaea, and the "tyrants," John of Gischala, Eleazar son of Simon, and Simon son of Gioras, whose internecine scheming for control of Jerusalem in the heady days of independence before the spring of 70 CE Josephus described with horrified distaste, until, as we have seen, the external pressures of the Roman siege forced even the most ambitious into an alliance for the common good, too late to avoid disaster.[17]

How were these two very different societies structured? Were the contrasting rationales for Rome and Jerusalem as civic communities in practice reflected in the social ties which mattered for ordinary Jews and Romans? And where differences existed, were they in any way responsible for the hostility which destroyed Jerusalem?

# KINSHIP

If the individuals who expressed sentiments on tombstones and other monuments are any guide to the affectionate relationships which really matter, what people cared most about in imperial Rome was the nuclear family. An epitaph might of course be commissioned only out of a sense of duty to the deceased by a relative or a beneficiary of the estate, but many inscriptions reveal real affection during life between spouses, children, parents and siblings.

The close relationship between spouses is striking, because the legal framework within which Roman marriages operated was quite loose. Marriage was not a sacrament. Technically, all that was required for a man and woman to become husband and wife was for them to cohabit, with each regarding the other as a spouse, and marriages could be contracted and broken with little practical upheaval. On the other hand, as modern experience shows, emotional responses could be more complex. The beginning of a marriage union was marked by elaborate celebrations, at least among the upper classes, and by appeals to the many divinities who surrounded the new couple, to ensure their felicity and fertility. After a ceremony, in which bride and groom had sat, garlanded with flowers, on chairs tied together with wool and covered with the skin of the sheep that had been sacrificed to the gods that morning, and then enjoyed the wedding feast and endured the wedding speeches, they might have to remind themselves that the essence of the day was the witnessing and sealing of a contract which could always be dissolved. On the other hand, the proud boast on some tombstones that a woman had been *univira*, "a one-man woman," suggests that it was common to have more than one partner in a lifetime, both because of high mortality among young adults and because divorce was easy and evoked little or no public disapproval. Again, the technicalities of divorce were simple: all that was required was for either husband or wife to announce to their partner that they no longer wished to live together within marriage. In the late Republic and early empire, divorce was so common among aristocrats that Roman practice appears less like monogamy than serial polygamy, one spouse at a time, but it would be wrong to assume as general in the wider Roman population behaviour that, at times at least, was generated more by political than domestic concerns: for instance, in 12 BCE the future emperor Tiberius was required by Augustus to divorce his wife Vipsania Agrippina, of whom he was fond, in order to marry Augustus' daughter Julia.[18]

On divorce, children stayed with their father. The effect on Roman children of separation from their mother can only be speculated upon, but Romans were well aware of the importance of maternal affection. Literary accounts portray the ideal mother as moral educator of sons. Roman mothers may have had less close relationships with their children than in modern Western societies, particularly if the baby was handed over to a wet-nurse and the child to a *paedagogus* (child-minder), but there is much evidence of mothers retaining affection and respect through a child's adolescence and into the mother's old age. Seneca wrote of his mother's generosity to him when he started in public life, and when he consoled a certain Marcia for her son, prematurely deceased, he stressed their close ties: "He was left a fatherless ward in the care of guardians until his fourteenth year, but his mother's guardianship lasted all of his life."[19]

The perfect nuclear family of father, affectionate wife and mother, and just the right number of healthy children, was a Roman dream, but only rarely a Roman reality. Roman poets often expressed a wish that man and wife might grow old together. Thus Martial in a gentle epigram: "May she love him when once he is old, and may she herself, even when she is old, not seem to be so to her husband." In fact, however, a typical marriage was likely to end after fewer than twenty years through the death of one of the couple, if it had not ended before through divorce. Since remarriage was common, many children grew up living with stepparents. In Latin literature, the wicked stepmother was often demonized. Conflict generally concerned property: the younger Pliny delivered one of his finest court-room speeches (according to his own estimation) in support of an aristocratic woman "disinherited by her eighty-year-old father ten days after he had fallen in love and brought home a stepmother for his daughter . . . Fathers, daughters and stepmothers all anxiously awaited the verdict . . . The stepmother, who had been left under the will a sixth of the estate, lost her case." But many examples are also attested of cordial relations between children and both stepmothers and stepfathers. There is a striking lack of reference in the sources to conflict between step- and half-siblings, perhaps precisely because it was so normal for children with such relationships to grow up together.[20]

The willingness of Romans to pay less attention to genetic inheritance than to a legally defined familial relationship, apparent in the number of families with step-relationships, emerges also in the willingness of men to treat their offspring conceived by their female slaves as slaves, and in the common use, at least within the elite, of adoption. Adoption was a practice long established in Rome and regulated by law: a private ritual performed before a magistrate put the adopted person into a legal relationship to the adopter identical to that of a natural child born within wedlock, and on entering the new family the child took on the name and rank of his or her new father and came under the legal power of a new *paterfamilias*, family head. Much of the surviving evidence for adoption concerns the adoption of adults—the adoptive father might consider this a sensible move since he would be spared the uncertainties of childhood survival and would have a good idea what sort of person he was taking into his family. Augustus himself was adopted by Julius Caesar, albeit posthumously through a stipulation in his will, and the whole series of imperial successions from Nerva in 96 CE to Lucius Verus in 161 was shaped by a series of adoptions by emperors of younger men deemed appropriate successors.

The adoption of adult males suggests that the motivation of the adopter was generally the transfer and control of property or power. Even a Roman citizen who was a bachelor could adopt a son. There is little to suggest that a Roman would wish to adopt a baby for the pleasure of raising a family, as in some modern societies. Some families might house foster-children, known as *alumni* in the inscriptions, but sometimes only temporarily, and perhaps more for help around the house than to fill an emotional need or create a sentimental attachment: among the many sad epitaphs from Rome which record the piety of sons and daughters of the deceased, almost none were set up by foster-children. Some of those brought up by foster-parents will have been foundlings exposed by their natural parents at birth, and some of them will have lived in their new homes as slaves. Whether the treatment of such babies as slaves was approved by the law was one of the problems put to the emperor Trajan by the younger Pliny, who wanted to know how to decide cases in the province he was governing when the foundlings asserted their right to freedom; an added question was whether foundlings declared free should be required to refund to their former owners the costs incurred in their upbringing. Trajan replied that the issue "has often been discussed"; it was evidently a real problem. In practical terms, a free-born foundling and a slave foundling might live very similar lives as children in a poor household.[21]

In all but the poorest families, there would always be at least some slaves, and they would be treated as much as part of the family unit as the free children, even if their right to be spared physical abuse was legally inferior. Many Roman writers take for granted the administration of corporal punishment to children, if not by parents then by a slave nurse or *paedagogus* or, indeed, any adult who felt it would be good for a child's education to be chastised. Seneca's assertion, in an essay on anger (and how to control it), "that it is of the utmost importance that children be raised in the correct manner even if this means harsh punishment," would have won broad assent among fellow Romans.[22] Roman children were treated as vulnerable and in need of protection but also as unformed beings to be controlled, shaped and socialized to prepare them for the adult world. Romans saw childhood, as we do now, as a separate stage of life associated with particular rituals and emotions, although the divisions they made within childhood differed from those familiar in the modern world; they do not, for instance, seem to have recognized adolescence as a special and difficult time for unmarried girls, despite awareness that boys in the period of their *iuventus*, youth, need to be given greater freedom outside the house. An *infans* ("non-speaking" person) was any child under seven—there is no Latin word that translates simply as "baby." A newborn was bathed, then swaddled limb by limb to mould it into shape: physical care for the very young inevitably took priority over other concerns when at least half of those children who survived to their first birthday would be dead before they were ten. Few households seem to have been multigenerational, since most grandparents died before their grandchildren reached an age that permitted them to establish close ties, but few households consisted simply of a nuclear family. Slaves, freedmen, stepchildren and others related in one way or another to the father and mother of the family all cohabited and contributed to the life of the house.

The term *familia* in Latin was quite frequently used to mean the household of slaves on whose work the running of the household depended, but *familia* could also mean, more formally, either all those in the legal power of one *paterfamilias*, whether they were relatives or slaves, or all the other blood relations through the male line who at one time had been in his power. In many ways the most distinctive feature of the law governing the private life of Roman citizens was the extraordinarily broad legal power wielded over his extended family by this family head, whose control reached down through the generations and could affect the fortunes of relatives who lived apparently quite separate lives. Any Roman male citizen not himself within the power of an older male relative was by definition himself a *paterfamilias* with power over all his descendants through his male children. The system ensured a great deal of social stability regardless of the fluidity of marriage relationships and the setting up of independent households. When it came to important decisions, the *paterfamilias* was in charge. He had total control over those within his jurisdiction: technically, they did not own anything at all, and if they "acquired" anything it passed immediately into his possession. The relationship was lifelong, unless the *paterfamilias* chose to emancipate a child, or a girl was transferred, as sometimes happened, to the jurisdiction of her husband's *paterfamilias* when she was married. Marriage was only permitted with his consent and he could insist on a divorce.

Thus all adult Roman citizen women and some adult Roman citizen men spent their entire lives without winning full control over their own destinies. That this was not even more common for adult men was the result of low life expectancy: since far more adults died between the ages of twenty and forty than in modern societies, and survival through to the sixties and beyond was rare, twenty-year-olds might find themselves without older male relatives to exercise legal constraint over their lives. When young adult males did find themselves still without power to make their own decisions about marriage or money, tensions between the generations could become acute. Romans were well aware of this possibility, which provided stock situations in Roman exercises in the techniques of oratory, as in a knotty problem posed for students by the elder Seneca at the start of his *Controversiae*:

Children should support their parents, or be imprisoned. Two brothers quarrelled among themselves. One had a son. The uncle fell on hard times. Although his father forbade him to do so, the young man supported his uncle; for this reason, his father disinherited him, and he did not protest. His uncle adopted him. His uncle received an inheritance and became wealthy. His father began to fall on hard times. Although his uncle forbids him to do so, the young man supports his father. His uncle is now disinheriting him.

What arguments could the young man use to justify what he had done?[23]

In legal theory a *paterfamilias* had far more extreme powers of life and death, and Romans told stories of their virtuous ancestors who had executed their sons in the interests of the state. Even in the first century CE Augustus' marriage laws permitted a *paterfamilias* in very specific circumstances to kill his daughter if he caught her in an act of adultery. But by the early empire such legally condoned violent exercise of control belonged mostly in the realm of folk memory, tempered by ties of affection and gentler custom, except in one case which was still common: it was the *paterfamilias* whose decision about a newborn infant decreed whether it should be raised or left to die (about which more in Chapter 6). For a Roman to beat his spouse and children as he felt free to beat his slaves was evidently, though legal in the name of "discipline," not normal. Romans took pride in being good, gentle fathers and husbands. In the mid-second century BCE Cato the Censor "used to say," according to his biographer Plutarch, "that the man who struck his wife or child laid hands on what was most holy and sacred."[24] Clearly such treatment was conceivable but it was not, it seems, socially respectable. For most teenage or adult Romans, more real than physical violence was the possibility of disinheritance. A *paterfamilias* had wide rights to dispose of his property as he pleased by testament and could explicitly disinherit a son in his will: by the early empire, a son could appeal to a magistrate against such a will as "undutiful," but without certainty of success.

The *familia*—siblings, cousins, uncles, nephews, nieces on the male side of the family—provided the social base for most Roman citizens, from which they could expect, even if they did not always receive, support and patronage. Wider kinship ties, though formally recognized, had less impact on social relationships. A Roman citizen belonged by definition to a *gens* or clan which provided a central element to his or her name: hence the emperors were Iulii, Claudii and Flavii during the first century CE, signifying their membership of the Julian, Claudian and Flavian *gentes*. Aristocratic Romans who shared membership of a particular *gens* might occasionally in the late Republic call on each other for support, believing themselves descended from a common ancestor and linked by communal cults or shared burial places: "The bonds of common blood hold men fast through good-will and affection; for it means much to share in common the same family monuments, to use the same sacred rites, to have common tombs."[25] This was what Cicero wrote, but in Rome a century later there is little evidence that those who shared the name of a *gens* shared anything more than the name itself. It did not help that freedmen took the name of their former masters and that newly enfranchised citizens were free to choose what name they liked, often opting for the name of the ruling emperor—hence huge numbers of Romans with Julius, Claudius or Flavius in their names.

Those born as Roman citizens also inherited membership of one of the Roman tribes. In the early Republic, allocation to a tribe had been by virtue of place of residence, with Roman territory divided by the mid-third century BCE between four urban and thirty-one rustic tribes, but from 241 BCE, as citizenship was extended throughout Italy and beyond, no new tribes were created, new citizens being assigned to existing tribes, and any sense that members of a tribe represented any particular region was much diluted. In any case, tribal affiliation, in the Republic a matter of genuine significance as voting units in political assemblies, became a formality in the early empire. It was standard for a Roman citizen to include his tribe in his name on formal inscriptions, and provincials admitted to Roman citizenship were still all assigned to one tribe or another, but the rules for assigning one new citizen to a particular tribe and another to a different one are obscure, and in practice belonging to one particular tribe rather than another made no difference at all.[26]

DESPITE SOME surface similarities, the structure of Jewish society was very different from that of Rome. Jews, like Romans, believed that they had once been divided into tribes, and the symbolic notion of the twelve tribes still mattered to them despite their belief that ten of the twelve had been carried out of the land of Israel by the Assyrians in the eighth century BCE and had not returned. As Josephus puts it, "there are two tribes in Asia and Europe subject to the Romans, while until now there have been ten tribes beyond the Euphrates—countless myriads whose number cannot be ascertained."[27] According to Rabbi Akiva as cited in the Mishnah, "the ten tribes will not return again" to the land of Israel.[28] Others were more optimistic: according to the author of Acts, Paul spoke before the Jewish king Agrippa II about "the hope of the promise made to our fathers, to which promise our twelve tribes, intensely serving God, hope to come."[29] But these were pious wishes for an eschatological future. In the present, in Jerusalem in the first century CE, few referred to their own tribal origin. Paul himself was a rather surprising exception, describing himself as "an Israelite, of the seed of Abraham, of the tribe of Benjamin" and "of the race of Israel, of the tribe of Benjamin, a Hebrew of Hebrews"; the tribal affiliation was perhaps part of the generally archaic tone of these self-descriptions, intended to lend weight to his claim to Jewish respectability.[30]

The general decline in importance of tribes may well be in part a result of conversions to Judaism over the centuries. Unlike new Roman citizens, new Jews do not seem to have been assigned to any tribe, but the fact that (for instance) Herod the Great, descended from an Idumaean proselyte, belonged to no tribe did not make him less a Jew. Tribal affiliation mattered only for the members of the tribe of Levi, since, as we have seen, Levites and priests (a subgroup of the tribe, the descendants of Aaron) exercised, by right of birth, important duties in the Jerusalem Temple, and, in the case of the priests, enjoyed considerable concomitant privileges. On the other hand, there is nothing to suggest social solidarity between priests, let alone between priests and their fellow members of the tribe of Levi. On the contrary, Josephus describes how the servants of rich High Priests in his day "would go to the threshing floors and take by force the tithes of the priests . . . so it happened at that time that those of the priests who in olden days were maintained by the tithes now starved to death." Josephus, himself a priest (as he proudly informs his readers), remarks with disgust the innovation in the early 60s CE which allowed non-priestly Levites to dress like priests: "Those of the Levites—this is a tribe—who were singers of hymns urged the king to convene a council and get them permission to wear linen robes on equal terms with the priests . . . All this was contrary to the ancestral laws, and such transgression was bound to make us liable to punishment."[31]

Where Jewish society differed greatly from Roman in the early imperial period was in the role, or lack of role, of the extended family. It had not always been so. In biblical texts from Genesis onwards, the extended family, the *mishpaha*, had played a central role similar to that of the Roman *familia*, both in the sense that the family included not only those related by blood ties but also slaves and hired servants, and in the sense that all those who looked back to a common father figure felt a sense of solidarity with each other. The law in the biblical book of Leviticus envisaged that if a relative had been forced by penury to sell himself into slavery, "either his uncle, or his uncle's son, may redeem him, or any near kinsmen belonging to his family may redeem him." Jacob's family was described as including his sons, their little ones, their wives, his sons' sons, his daughters, and his sons' daughters, "all his offspring . . . sixty-six persons in all," not counting his sons' wives. The decline of such extended families as central units in Jewish society is well illustrated by changing attitudes to the law in Deuteronomy that, if a man died without children, his brother had a duty to "perpetuate a name in Israel" for his dead sibling by marrying his brother's widow (a process known as "Levirate marriage"). The rabbis cited in the Mishnah stated quite explicitly that this law was no longer appropriate in their day.[32]

There is thus not much trace, apart from the history of royal courts, of such extended families living as units in Jewish society in the first century CE, nor of cousins, apart from those of the Herodian family, acting together as a social unit. Herod relied on family members for political support, appointing his brother Pheroras and his uncle (and brother-in-law) Joseph to positions of authority, and linking members of his wider family by marriage to each other, but he behaved in this way not because it was standard among contemporary Jews but because he did not want to give power to outsiders who might have more natural authority with the Judaean population than he, as an Idumaean, could muster. In any case, as a despotic monarch and a Roman citizen, Herod could wield all the power of a Roman *paterfamilias*, but ordinary male Jews could not. The chilling account of treatment of rebellious sons as laid down in Deuteronomy amounts not to affirmation of parental power but to its restriction, since the affronted parents handed over punishment to the wider community:

> If a man has a stubborn and rebellious son, who will not obey the voice of his father or the voice of his mother, and although they chastise him, will not give heed to them, then shall his father and his mother take hold of him, and bring him out to the elders of his city at the gate of the place where he lives, and they shall say to the elders of his city, "This our son is stubborn and rebellious, he will not obey our voice; he is a glutton and a drunkard." And all the men of his city shall stone him to death with stones: so you shall purge the evil from among you; and all Israel shall hear, and fear.

Early rabbinic interpretation of this custom, as found in the Mishnah, makes clear that it was not in operation in their time. They restricted its application to teenage boys on the cusp of adulthood, "from the time that he can produce two hairs until he grows a beard (the lower one and not the upper one; howbeit the sages spoke in modest language), for it is written, 'If a man have a son';—a son and not a daughter." Despite the optimistic view expressed in the Mishnah that the law if it was applied would ultimately be of benefit to the son—"for the death of the ungodly is a benefit to them and a benefit to the world"—the rabbis cited in the Tosefta in the mid-third century CE believed that "a stubborn and rebellious son never was and never will be."[33]

The different approaches of Jews and Romans to sexual unions which might be construed as incest neatly reflect the different assumptions on which kinship relations in the two societies were based. One family relationship seemed too close for marriage to some in both Jerusalem and Rome while being permitted by others: both Jews and Romans forbade marriage between a man and his aunt, but were more ambivalent over whether a man could marry his niece. Such marriages were illegal at Rome until the emperor Claudius changed the rules to permit himself to marry his niece Agrippina, daughter of his brother Germanicus, whose popularity would bring him much-needed political support. Tacitus records the doubts of the nation: "marriage with a niece was unprecedented—indeed it was incestuous, and disregard of this might, it was feared, cause national disaster." Objections were overcome by a speech to the Senate by Lucius

Vitellius, who held the censorship alongside Claudius: "Marriages to the daughters of our brothers are new to us. Yet in other countries they are regular and lawful. Here also, unions between cousins, long unknown, have become frequent in course of time. Customs change as utility requires, and this innovation too will take root." This latter observation was perhaps Tacitean irony, since in Tacitus' own day, in 97 CE, the emperor Nerva had prohibited marriage to a niece. In Jewish society, by contrast, the issue of uncle-niece marriage revolved, characteristically, around interpretation of the Bible. The list of forbidden relationships laid out in Leviticus included that of a woman with her nephew, and the Dead Sea sectarians apparently deduced from this by analogy that a man should not marry his niece, who is his "near kin": "though the laws against incest are written for men, they also apply to women. When, therefore, a brother's daughter uncovers the nakedness of her father's brother, she is near kin [and therefore forbidden]." By contrast, the rabbis in the Tosefta insisted that it was not only legal for an uncle to marry his niece, but that "a man should not take a wife until the daughter of his sister has grown up."[34]

Even more than in Roman society, among Jews the main unit for domestic life was the nuclear family, which also often had an economic role: early rabbinic texts envisage that a man might set up his wife as a shopkeeper, or a couple might go together to the harvest or olive-picking or vintage; by contrast, they have nothing to say about relations between a woman and her mother-in-law or about property relations between a man and his father, although in Jewish law, unlike Roman, a man could own his property outright in his father's lifetime. The father in a nuclear family was responsible simply for the welfare of his wife and children: whatever his wife earned belonged to him, and, although rabbinic texts presuppose that women participated in public economic life such as selling goods in the market, the standard duties assumed for a wife were entirely domestic, "grinding flour and baking bread and washing clothes and cooking food and giving suck to her child and making ready his bed and working in wool"; women could indeed gain a certain financial independence, but only under male supervision.[35]

Evidence for the operation of family law in Jewish society in the early centuries CE has been much enhanced in recent years by the discovery and publication of numerous legal documents unearthed from caves in the Judaean desert: marriage contracts, wills, divorce documents and deeds of sale show real life in action among Jews in the province of Arabia in the first half of the second century CE, although it is hard to know to what extent custom among such Jews, whose communities were not in the centre of Jewish settlement, reflected Jewish life in the capital city of Jerusalem before the Temple was destroyed. There is a danger that our entire picture of how families worked in Jewish society may depend on the convoluted relationships revealed in the large cache of documents which belonged to a certain Babatha, who hid her most important papers in a leather bag and deposited them in a cave some time soon after August 132 CE, which is the date of the latest document in the bundle. Babatha had been twice married and widowed, and she was rich. Her papers reveal that she was able to own extensive property in her own right, but that she could only control her property through a male guardian, since she had no right to represent herself in court in person.[36] This last at least was probably true of all Jewish women.

In general, it appears both from these documents and from the legal rulings preserved in the rabbinic tradition that in much of their family law in the first centuries CE Jews followed more or less the same practices as their non-Jewish contemporaries, just stressing the biblical warrant for some of those practices in order for them to appear more Jewish. In Jewish society, as in Roman, marriage was a contract rather than a sacrament in the Christian sense, but it was marked by a process of betrothal known in the Mishnah as *kiddushin*, "consecration" of the bride to the groom, which could be achieved "by money or by writ or by intercourse"—that is, by the man ceremonially handing over a sum of money or a document of betrothal, or by the couple living together for the purpose of betrothal; according to the rabbinic rulings, these actions needed to be accompanied by a statement of purpose from the groom: "Be you betrothed to me with this silver dinar." The terms of the marriage contract were written down in a document agreed with the groom by the bride's father or other male guardian. The contract laid down most importantly the rights of the bride to maintenance in the event that she was widowed or divorced. Such contracts, embodying important safeguards for women on their transfer from parental to marital home, are unknown in the Bible but were evidently standard, at least among Jews in the land of Israel, by the late Second Temple period. A number of such documents have been found in the Judaean desert, including the cache preserved by Babatha. They exhibit some variety in terminology and also in the precise conditions laid down for the contract, but the general pattern, which exhibits much in common with contemporary Greek marriage contracts known from Egypt, is clear. In early rabbinic texts such marriage deeds are taken for granted and only the details disputed. The deed was known simply as a *ketubah*, "written document," as if this was the only sort of written text standard in Jewish society. The term was also used by transference to refer to the amount of money a wife might be guaranteed by the document on divorce: "The *ketubah* of a virgin is two hundred *denars*, and of a widow one *mina*."[37]

Prenuptial agreements with arrangements for terms on divorce were thus standard in Jewish marriages by this period, suggesting a general acceptance of the possibility of breakdown of marriage much as in contemporary Rome, but there is also much evidence, as in Rome, that the marriage bond was viewed as far more emotional than the dry legalities might suggest. The wedding itself involved processions, feasting and dancing—the Mishnah records the prohibition of such rejoicing by the rabbis in the war of 66–70: "During the war of Vespasian they forbade the crowns of the bridegrooms and the [wedding] drum." More significantly perhaps, both the prophets in the Bible and the rabbis used marriage as a symbol of perfect relationships, such as Israel and Torah, Israel and the Sabbath, and Israel and God: "I remember the devotions of your youth, your love as a bride, how you followed me in the wilderness."[38]

Thus divorce was not considered desirable, but it was recognized by Jews as possible, as sanctioned by the Torah, and, despite occasional denunciation of men for putting away "the wife of your youth, to whom you have been faithless, though she is your companion and your wife by covenant" (so wrote the prophet Malachi), as no reason for shame for either party.[39] The process differed from that in Rome in the general rule, rather crucial for wives, that divorce could only be effected at the behest of the husband. The procedure as outlined in Deuteronomy is simple: "When a man has taken a wife and marries her, and it comes to pass that she finds no favour in his eyes because he has found some indecency in her, and he writes for her a bill of divorce and puts it in her hand and sends her out of his house, and she departs out of his house, and if she goes and becomes another man's wife . . ."[40] According to the Gospel of Matthew, Joseph was minded to divorce Mary when she was found to be with child of the Holy Spirit: "Joseph, her husband, being a just man, and not willing to make her a public example, was minded to put her away quietly."[41] Discussion among the early rabbis centred only on the nature of the "indecency" in the wife which sufficed to justify divorce, with views ranging from trivial misdemeanours to serious sexual transgression: "The School of Shammai say: 'A man may not divorce his wife unless he has found unchastity in her' . . . And the School of Hillel say: 'Even if she spoiled a dish for him . . .' Rabbi Akiva says: 'Even if he found another fairer than her.' " Each view was supported, naturally enough, by a Bible text, read differently in each case to fit the interpretation.[42]

The Herodian princess Salome took the initiative in divorcing her husband, the Idumaean Costobar, but she was presumably following Roman rather than Jewish law, since she at least was a Roman citizen through her father: in the words of Josephus, she "had occasion to quarrel with Costobar and soon sent him a document dissolving their marriage, which was not in accordance with Jewish law. For it is the man who is permitted by us to do this, and not even a divorced woman may marry again on her own initiative unless her former husband consent."[43] It is possible that early rabbinic opposition to unilateral divorce by wives arose out of a concern that Jewish women who were Roman citizens might more generally take such advantage of the more liberal provisions of Roman law. On the other hand, some early rabbis envisaged the wider community compelling a husband to give his wife a bill of divorce in certain circumstances, at her request: "These are they that are compelled to put away their wives: he that is afflicted with boils, or that has a polypus, or that collects [dog's excrements], or that is a coppersmith or a tanner . . . It once happened in Sidon that a tanner died and had a brother who was a tanner. The Sages said: 'She may say, "Your brother I could endure; but you I cannot endure.' "[44]

Jewish mothers, like Roman women, were vulnerable to losing contact with their children on divorce, since the offspring of a marriage would stay with the father, but this drastic blow, and the alienating loss of self-esteem that must have been a natural corollary of return from the marital household to the paternal home left months or years earlier amid celebrations and rejoicing, might sometimes be avoided by the husband resorting to bigamy rather than divorce, an option not open to contemporary gentile Romans. Most notorious of Jewish polygamists in this period is Herod the Great, whose ten wives were clearly reckoned unusual, since they provoked the comment from Josephus that all had been "chosen for their

beauty and not for their family, since marrying many was permitted by
Jewish custom and the king enjoyed having many." Herod was not, however, alone, for, as Josephus writes elsewhere in less disapproving fashion,
"it is an ancestral custom of ours to have several wives at the same time."[45]
The rabbis in the Mishnah envisaged the problems when a man married to
four wives died: "the [claim of the] first wife comes before that of the second, that of the second before that of the third, and that of the third before
that of the fourth. . . ."[46] The Christian Justin Martyr fulminated in the
mid-second century CE to the Jew Trypho about "your blind teachers, who
even still now agree that each of you can have four or five wives."[47] To the
Christian such polygamy was shocking, and at least some Jews seem to have
agreed: the *Temple Scroll* found at Qumran laid down, among the statutes
incumbent on a king, that "he shall take a wife for himself from his father's
house, from his father's family. He shall not take another wife in addition
to her, for she alone shall be with him all the time of her life."[48] By contrast, one view cited in the Mishnah was that the rule laid down in
Deuteronomy that the king should not "multiply wives to himself" should
be interpreted to mean that he must restrict himself to just eighteen.[49] It
may reflect Greek, or even Roman, influence that the practice of polygamy
seems in fact to have been rather rare among Jews in Judaea. None of
Herod's male descendants is known to have been married to more than one
wife at a time, and all stories about early rabbis presuppose monogamy.
However, the rich widow Babatha, whose documents were found in the
Judaean desert, married a second husband, Judah, who already had a wife,
Miriam. The two women seem to have kept separate households: in a summons, dated 9 July 131 CE, to appear before the provincial governor,
Babatha accuses Miriam of seizing everything in Judah's house after his
death, to which Miriam replies that she had previously warned Babatha to
stay away from Judah's possessions.[50]

Among Jews, then, as among Romans, the nuclear family unit could be
quite complex, with stepparents, children from previous marriages, and
others all part of the household. Jews, like Romans, could expect to
employ slaves, except in the poorest families. All Jewish sources of this
period suggest that Jews took the ownership of slaves as entirely normal,
apart from the Essenes who, according to Philo, "condemn slave-owners as
unjust in that they offend against equality, but still more as ungodly, in that
they transgress the law of nature which, having given birth to all men

equally and nourished them like a mother, makes of them true brothers, not in name but in reality";[51] Josephus also remarks that the Essenes did not own slaves, "since they believe that [slave ownership] contributes to injustice."[52] The rabbinic texts, by contrast, envisage slaves as integrated into domestic life and discuss legal safeguards for their well-being. Tabi, slave of Rabban Gamaliel, was a household servant. To clinch an argument that the Passover offering can be roasted on a grill, Rabbi Zadok is cited in the Mishnah as noting that Rabban Gamaliel once told his slave Tabi to go and do just that. He lived in close proximity to his master. "If a man sleeps under a bed in the Sukkah [the booth used as a temporary dwelling on the festival of Tabernacles] he has not fulfilled his obligation . . . Tabi, the slave of Rabban Gamaliel, slept under the bed, and Rabban Gamaliel said to the elders, 'You have seen Tabi, my slave, that he is a learned scholar, and knows that slaves are exempt from [the law of] the Sukkah; and so he sleeps under the bed.' " Tabi, however, was exceptional. When he died, Rabban Gamaliel "accepted condolence because of him. They said to him, 'Master, did you not teach us that men may not accept condolence for slaves?' He replied, 'My slave Tabi was not like other slaves; he was a worthy man.' "[53]

Slaves thus formed part of the family, but, unlike in Roman households, there was not likely to be a gaggle of slave children, the offspring of the master and his maidservants. Sexual abuse of female slaves undoubtedly occurred, but such behaviour was generally treated as disgraceful. Despite the biblical prototypes of Abraham and Hagar, and many others, ordinary Jews by this date no longer openly had slave concubines alongside their wives. The Hasmonaean king Alexander Jannaeus in the early first century BCE, who, according to Josephus, "feasted with his concubines in a conspicuous place" while he ordered the crucifixion of eight hundred of his Jewish opponents, seems to have been following the custom of Hellenistic monarchs rather than Jewish practice. There is no evidence that ordinary Jews set up home with their female slaves as, in effect, common-law wives, as seems to have been quite common among poorer Romans.[54]

One complication common in Roman families seems to have been unknown among Jews, and that was adoption from another family. No such adoption laws are to be found in the Hebrew Bible, although, as elsewhere in the ancient Near East, a father might decide to "adopt" as a legitimate heir one of his own sons by a concubine. The precise relationship of

Naomi in the book of Ruth to Ruth's baby Obed looks rather like adoption—"Boaz took Ruth . . . and she bore a son . . . and Naomi took the
child, and laid him in her bosom, and became his nurse, and the women her
neighbours gave him a name, saying, 'There is a son born to Naomi.' And
they called his name Obed"—but since Obed was already her grandson by
the law of Levirate marriage, "son" may mean no more than that.[55] The
assertion in the book of Esther that Mordechai brought up his orphaned
cousin Esther and "took her for his own daughter" looks more like real
adoption, but it is noticeable that the Hebrew text consistently refers to
their relationship as cousins; if she had been adopted in the Roman sense,
she would have referred to Mordechai, rather than her real parent Abihail,
as her father.[56] In any case, adoption is unknown in late Second Temple and
rabbinic texts. A foundling might be fostered, but he or she could not take
on a new identity as a full member of the foster family. For Jews it
remained always crucial to retain the memory of actual parentage. In theory gentiles who converted to Judaism became radically new individuals
and severed all connection with their previous families, but this did not
prevent rabbinic sages, as reported in the Palestinian Talmud, from debating whether a gentile man married incestuously to his sister should divorce
her if he became a proselyte. His sister was still his sister, even if he had
been "born again."[57]

Within the nuclear family, education of children was primarily the
duty of the father, and the use of corporal punishment of children to incul-
cate teachings was taken for granted as much by Jews as by Romans. Rabbinic texts enjoin the father to give practical as well as ethical instruction:
"The sages said: 'By the law of the Torah a man is obligated to circumcise
his son, to redeem him [if he be a first-born], to teach him Torah, and to
teach him a trade, and to get him a wife.' Rabbi Akiva says: 'Also to teach
him how to swim.' " In the highly moralistic version of the story of the
revolt of the Maccabees to be found in the edifying philosophical work
known as 4 Maccabees, the mother of the seven sons about to be martyred
exhorts them to stand fast by reminding them of their father, who had
taught them the Law and the Prophets: "He read to you of Abel, killed by
Cain, of Isaac, offered as a burnt-offering, and of Joseph, in prison. He
spoke to you of the zealous Phineas, and taught you about Hananiah,
Azariah and Mishael in the fire"; she says nothing about the teachings she
herself had provided. Relations of mothers with daughters may have been

closer but they will often have been curtailed, as in Roman society, by the transfer of girls soon after puberty to the houses of their husbands.[58]

The nuclear family in Jewish society was thus controlled by the father as much as in Roman society, but in one area of life, religion, the role of Jewish women in the family was much more important than that of Roman *matronae*. Most of the religious activities in a Roman house were performed by men, but for Jews the process of keeping many of the laws in the Torah required, in essence, doing housework in a particular way, and, among Jews as among Romans, housework was women's work. Most obviously, the rules for the preparation of kosher food fell above all on the women in a household. What this would mean in practice would depend on the kind of Judaism espoused by the family (which, in turn, would make it hard for most women to attach themselves to groups different from their husbands). The wife of a *haver*, "fellow," who piously took upon himself only to eat food which could be guaranteed properly tithed and who would only eat in the state of purity usually reserved for priests eating sacred foodstuffs, would presumably have a harder time than the wife of a Sadducee who only took upon himself the written laws found in the Bible; but, even so, the task of turning the home into a locus of sanctity to a great extent rested with her. It is not accidental that the three transgressions for which, according to the Mishnah, women die in childbirth, involve the purity of the marriage bed, the preparation of food, and a failure to designate correctly within the house the sacred time of the Sabbath: "heedlessness of the laws of the menstruant, the dough-offering, and the lighting of the lamp." On the other hand, although the women lit the lamp which proclaimed the start of the festival on which all manner of work would cease, the rabbis assumed that it was her husband who told her to do so: "Three things must a man say within his house when darkness is falling on the eve of Sabbath: 'Have you tithed?', 'Have you prepared the *erub*?' and, 'Light the lamp.' "[59]

## FRIENDSHIPS, PATRONAGE AND COMMUNITY

NEITHER JEWS nor Romans in the first century CE had as strongly developed a sense of distinction between public and private life as we now take for granted, so these differences in the ordering of Jewish households might in principle come to be known to Romans, although it is hard to see why they should lead to hostility (and no evidence that they did so). More likely to arouse comment, admiring or disdainful, would be the way Jews helped each other even when they were not kin. But in fact Roman ties between friends could be just as binding as those of Jews, even if they were based on different principles.

Roman friendships could be marked quite formally, especially among the upper class, creating ties of obligation which could last a lifetime and beyond, to the next generation. Cicero's treatise *On Friendship* reveals a whole discourse about what it entailed and should entail: "We now have to determine in our discussion of friendship what are the limits and, so to speak, the boundary lines of affection . . . It is your duty on every occasion to consider carefully both what you will demand from a friend and what you will permit him to obtain when he makes a demand on you." The making and breaking of friendships were clear-cut. Romans knew precisely who they thought of as their friends. The signs of friendship were universally recognized—admission to the *salutatio*, the morning welcoming ritual in the house of a rich man; invitations to dine; a mention in a will, even if only for a small bequest. Hoping for bequests seems to have been a preoccupation among some in the circle of the younger Pliny in Rome, probably less because they needed the money than as recognition of their social links. If Latin literature in the early empire seems to put a remarkable degree of emphasis upon such tokens of esteem, it was partly because they pointed to relationships of greater social significance—the way to advancement in a career, the link to a successful marriage—but also because they were vulnerable to caprice when friendships were unequal. In practice, a friend was often either a patron or a client, to be helped or to be applied to as a source of help himself. The tact required in relationships between real equals, to avoid giving offence, was all the more exquisite.[60]

In contrast to the vocabulary of friendship required between friends themselves, in describing to third parties a friendship between unequals Romans did not hesitate to use the language of patronage, which the Greek observer Dionysius of Halicarnassus described in the time of Augustus as a distinctive feature of Roman life that went back to the time of Romulus, who "placed the plebeians as a trust in the hands of the patricians, by allowing every plebeian to choose for his patron any patrician whom he himself wished . . . [and] assigned friendly offices to both parties, thus making the connection between them a bond of kindness." It was, as

Dionysius noted, a practice much preferable to similar relationships among the Greeks, in which abuse or contempt for the poor led all too often to class warfare. Nonetheless, the unequal relationship could be demeaning for the client forced to wait to be noticed; humiliation may indeed sometimes have been intended as a way to emphasize his inferiority. Moralizing Romans like the younger Seneca complained about such boorish behaviour at a *salutatio*:

> How many are there who keep away their clients by staying asleep, or by self-indulgence, or by being rude? How many are there who rush off on a pretence of urgent business after torturing the client by a long wait? How many avoid going through an atrium packed with clients and escape through a concealed door, as if it were not ruder to deceive than to exclude? How many, still hung-over and half-asleep from last night's drinking, will yawn disdainfully at men who have interrupted their own sleep in order to wait upon his awakening, and will mumble a greeting through half-open lips, bestowing the right name only after it has been whispered to them?[61]

The younger Pliny notes with distaste the perpetration of similar snubs by an acquaintance who gave different food to his dinner guests depending on their status: "For he served the best dishes to himself and a few guests, but cheap and paltry portions to the others . . . There was one wine for himself and us, another for his lesser friends (for he has his friends graded), and a third kind for his and our freedmen." Pliny goes on to insist that he himself advocates equality at dinner: "I serve the same to everyone, for when I invite guests it is for a meal, not to be marked by class distinctions. I have brought them as equals to the same table, so I give them the same treatment in everything—even the freedmen, for on these occasions I regard them as my fellow diners, not freedmen."[62] Part of the delicacy involved in talking about patronage between free-born Romans derived from the need to distinguish their link from the formalized dutifulness of the freedman, who in practice might be more a part of his patron's household than of his own and might end up, if he remained in his patron's good books, buried in the family tomb.

Beyond such friendships between individuals, some Romans attached themselves to voluntary associations which might provide them with a social circle quite separate from family (though not necessarily in conflict with it). There were many different kinds of club, from the circle of intense worshippers of Mithras or Isis to the more mundane self-help group of poorer citizens who banded together to pay for each other's funeral. Many of these associations are known only from the detailed rules of conduct for members which, in characteristically Roman fashion, they often liked to display engraved on stone:

> It was decided unanimously that anyone who wished to join this club should pay an initiation fee of a hundred sesterces and an amphora of good wine. Then each month he should pay five asses. It was also decided that if any member has not paid his fair share for six months in a row, and then meets death, arrangements will not be made for his funeral, even if he has made a will. It was also decided that if any member of this club has paid his dues regularly and then dies, three hundred sesterces will be allotted from the club treasury for his funeral. From this amount fifty sesterces will be used to reimburse participants in the funeral procession. The fifty sesterces will be divided up at the site of the funeral pyre. However, participants must walk.

Many of these associations seem to have drawn their members from particular walks of life, and people with particular occupations clearly felt a sense of communal identity, as political graffiti for local elections in Pompeii illustrate: "All the goldsmiths ask you to elect Gaius Cuspius Pansa as aedile." In the late Republic associations had been frequently co-opted by politicians to foment unrest, and at one stage in the 50s BCE were banned in Rome altogether, but close state control by emperors from Augustus onwards was effective in preventing any recurrence.[63]

Much behaviour in Roman society was thus structured around friendships and clubs, which could be quite clearly distinguished from the commercial relations, with trader, banker, employer or employee, into which ordinary Romans expected to be drawn but for which they sought confirmation not in social convention but in the possibility of appeal to law. You were expected to help your friends or, conversely, if you did a favour for someone, like helping him in a court case, he became your friend (and to act against him in the future, should circumstances so dictate, would be uncomfortable). The letters of Cicero and of Pliny are replete with requests for patronage both for their own friends and for their friends' friends. Conversely, Romans recognized no social obligations to those with whom they had no social ties, even indirectly. Not that the giving of benefits to friends was therefore an uncomplicated issue of reciprocity: on the contrary, the younger Seneca wrote seven books *On Benefits* to unravel the complex issues of intention and attitude that could turn a gift into a bribe or nullify a favour by the condescension of the donor—although "there is no reason why the multitude of ingrates should make us more reluctant to be generous." But the more that the moralist insists that "the man who, when he gives, has any thought of repayment deserves to be deceived," the more it is clear that this was precisely the attitude of most Romans, for whom the primary purpose of generosity was reciprocity. To the rich and moderately well-off, the very poor were thus invisible. Charity, in the sense of giving to the needy as a virtue for its own sake, was not a concept that Romans understood. There were indeed beggars in Rome, who relied on arousing pity in their search for alms, but they had a hard time. When the poet Ovid violently attacked in verse a detractor who had mocked at the misfortunes that had sent him into exile in the last years of Augustus, he noted optimistically that fortunes can be reversed: "The man who once denied cheap food to the wretched is now himself fed from begged bread."[64]

IT WAS almost a cliché among Greek and Latin authors who wrote about Jews and Judaism that Jews stuck together in their synagogues, and that these synagogues were full of beggars, although why this should have been more true of Jews than of others they did not seek to enquire.

Doubtless, beggars in Jewish society also had a hard life, but at least the attitude of Jews to beggars depended not on pity or on the reciprocity of the relationship, as among Romans, but on divine command. Charity was a duty incumbent on all Jews, even if the recipient was previously not even an acquaintance. The Mishnah laid down rules about the minimum to be given to a person in need, and the degree of destitution which qualified an individual to accept the different kinds of poor-relief laid down in the Bible, from the grain left by harvesters in the field, either in the corners or as forgotten sheaves or as gleanings, to the communal meals and funds established to alleviate the worst effects of poverty: "A poor man that is journeying from place to place should be given not less than a loaf worth a *pondion* . . . If he spends the night he should be given what is needful to support him for the night. If he stays over the Sabbath he should be given food enough for three meals." There was neither need nor expectation that the recipient would be known to the donor in any such gift of charity, although it seems generally to have been assumed that the poor who bene-fited would be fellow Jews, a proviso highlighted by the exception stipu-lated in a ruling in the Tosefta: "A city in which Israel and gentiles are: the collectors of funds for the support of the poor . . . provide support for the poor of the gentiles along with the poor of Israel, for the sake of peace." Among the characteristic nuisances of Rome which Martial cited as a rea-son to leave the city for rural peace and quiet was the Jew "taught by his mother to beg." Juvenal also complained about Jewish beggars. Jews were hardly the only poverty-stricken community in Rome, but presumably begging as a means to seek a livelihood was more worthwhile within Jew-ish society, which treated charity to the poor as normal, than elsewhere in Rome.[65]

However, it should not be deduced that these more general duties to fellow Jews precluded altogether recognition by Jews of the special claims to be made on an individual by personal friends. The classic biblical story of friendship was that of David and Jonathan, when "the soul of Jonathan was knit to the soul of David, and Jonathan loved him as his own soul," to the extent that Jonathan was prepared to provoke the anger of his father Saul in order to protect his friend. Josephus' narrative of the intrigues which beset him during his command of the Jewish forces in Galilee at the start of the war against Rome in 66–7 CE frequently explains political deci-sions by himself and others of the Jewish ruling elite as a natural result of friendships. John of Gischala, Josephus' main rival in Galilee, hoped that the Pharisee Simon son of Gamaliel would persuade the national assembly in Jerusalem to depose Josephus from power and appoint him instead, because he "was John's old and intimate friend." Josephus, too, had friends on whom he could rely: details of plots being hatched against him in Jerusalem were sent to him in a letter from his father to whom the informa-tion had been leaked by Jesus son of Gamalas, "an intimate friend of mine." This description of political allegiances in terms of personal friendships comes close to the Roman system. In the admittedly fraught circumstances of the struggle for power between ambitious Jewish leaders in Jerusalem during the brief independence of the city in 66–70, those competing to win control achieved positions of authority not by virtue of constitutional right but through personal charisma and a network of political friends, rather like the informal power of a mafia boss.[66]

Jews as much as Romans could also forge commercial bonds, seeking legal redress rather than social pressure if the partner in the relationship failed to do what was expected. Thus, for instance, biblical law forbidding interest on loans was in practice circumvented by a variety of legal fictions, such as fixing the time limit for repayment and levying a "fine" when it was breached, so that sophisticated financial deals were possible between individuals who recognized no other social tie between them. But what Jews seem to have lacked were the pervasive patronage ties across divisions of class and status, unrelated either to commercial advantage or to the exercise of political power, which were so important in Rome. Patronage links did not, it seems, extend beyond the relationships of the most politically powerful, such as the members of the Herodian family, to their followers. Josephus was a rich landowner with estates near Jerusalem. If he had been in a similar position in Rome he would have felt himself beholden to a coterie of clients who in turn would have accompanied him in public when they could and generally bolstered his public image as a great man. Josephus records that some Jerusalem aristocrats did indeed gather retinues around them in the early 60s CE, but he decries such practices as intimidation. In a feud between a High Priest and his predecessor, "each collected a band of the most reckless sort and it frequently happened that after exchanging insults they went further and hurled stones." It does not seem that poorer Jews would gravitate, as in Rome, into the patronage of a rich co-religionist. There is not even evidence for the formal link between a freed slave and his or her former owner which in Rome was the paradigm of a patronage relationship enforced not just by custom but by law. The impoverished Jew looked not to an individual patron but to the charity of the community as a whole, and the freed slave became a full member of the community without residual ties to the site of their former enslavement.[67]

But if non-family ties to specific other Jews, as patrons, clients or friends, seem to have been weaker in Jewish than in Roman society, the prevalence of solidarity to voluntary associations seems to have been stronger. The groups which bonded together to hear the Torah being read and expounded at weekly services were self-regulated and self-funded. In the land of Israel the provision of a synagogue would be one of the responsibilities of local village administrators—or at least such was the assumption of the early rabbis cited in the Tosefta: "The townspeople [should] require one another to build a synagogue, and to buy a scroll of the Torah and prophets." In the diaspora, local Jews would have to band together to buy a suitable place and agree on administration. Each of the synagogues in the city of Rome formed a separate community led by its own officials, most of them now known only from the titles on tombstones found in the catacombs: "Here lies Annius, *gerusiarch* of the synagogue of the Augustesians. In peace his sleep." The inscriptions all date probably to the third century CE and later, but already in the early first century CE Augustus knew that Roman Jews "have houses of prayer and meet together in them, particularly on the sacred seventh days when they receive as a community a training in their ancestral philosophy." Voluntary associations of diaspora Jews were also to be found in Jerusalem, organized in much the same way as in diaspora cities despite the Jewishness of their surroundings. Among those who debated with the early Christian Stephen in Jerusalem were "certain of the synagogue, which is called 'of the *Libertinoi*,' " "freedmen." It is likely that these people preferred each other's company for the reading of the Torah if only because they were more comfortable hearing it in Greek. Those who called themselves "the Freedmen" were probably the descendants of Jews who had been taken as slaves to Rome by Pompey or after later wars and, on being freed, had returned to Jerusalem; if so, retention of a Latin name for their synagogue suggests a certain pride in their connection to the imperial city despite the servile status of their ancestors. Since there was no need for each synagogue community to own an impressive building, and in principle they could meet in private houses or even in the open, there were hundreds of such groups in first-century-CE Jerusalem. Some relied on the generosity of wealthy donors. The provision of such donations is explicitly attested in the one extant synagogue inscription (dated to the first century CE by the letter forms used) to survive from the ancient city: "Theodotus, [son] of Vettenus, priest and archisynagogue, son of an archisynagogue, grandson of an archisynagogue, built the synagogue for the reading of the Law and the teaching of the commandments, and the guest-house and the rooms and the water supplies for the lodging of strangers in need, which his fathers founded and the elders and Simonides." Who this Simonides was, no one now knows.[68]

Other Jewish voluntary associations brought together those who shared not just a language, like the Greek-speaking synagogue communities of Jerusalem, but specific and idiosyncratic ideas and emphases in the interpretation of the Torah. Of these, much the best known group was that of the Essenes, who were described in considerable detail by both Philo and Josephus. Philo, who called the group "Essaeans," a name he associated with the Greek word *hosiotes*, "piety," put forward the Essenes as examples of virtue in support of his argument "that every good man is free," and described their communal life at length:

> Fleeing the cities because of the ungodliness customary among town-dwellers, they live in villages; for they know that, as noxious air breeds epidemics there, so does the social life afflict the soul with incurable ills . . . Almost alone among all mankind, they live without goods and without property; and this by preference, and not as a result of a reverse of fortune . . . No house belongs to any one man; indeed, there is no house which does not belong to them all, for as well as living in communities, their homes are open to members of the sect arriving from elsewhere. Secondly, there is but one purse for them all, and a common expenditure.

Philo's description is of course idealized, not least to bring the Essenes into line with his own notions about piety—he asserts, for instance, that "instruction is given to them by means of symbols," the method he himself advocates—and he produces a rather different account of them in an apologetic treatise apparently intended for gentile readers, in which, for instance, he asserts that "Essaeans" in fact lived in towns, rather than fleeing them as hotbeds of moral diseases. But much in both Philo's accounts is found also in the apparently independent description provided by Josephus (at considerable length) in the second book of his *Jewish War*. Josephus shared Philo's admiration for the communal asceticism of the Essenes, but he also portrayed them as involved in the affairs of the wider Jewish world. A certain John the Essaean was given authority in the north and west of

Judaea when commands were allocated by the provisional government in Jerusalem in autumn 66 CE, near the beginning of the war against Rome.[69]

By contrast, some of the Dead Sea sectarians, with whom the Essenes have frequently, but probably wrongly, been conflated, viewed their community as the true Israel, to be preserved separate from the rest of the Jewish nation, who had gone astray. Of these sectarians, one group (which produced the so-called *Damascus Document*, a text combining moral exhortation with a systematic presentation of legal statutes, which was found in two manuscripts of the tenth to twelfth centuries in the Cairo Genizah and in a number of fragmentary copies among the Dead Sea scrolls) lived in towns within the wider society of Judaea, envisaged the marriage of its members, and was separated from other Jews not so much physically as by way of life and mental attitude. The more monastic enthusiasts who produced the *Community Rule*, known only from copies found at Qumran, organized themselves as a mirror of wider Jewish society as imagined in the Bible. Divided into priests and laity, they separated themselves further, at least notionally, into units of thousands, hundreds, fifties and tens: "The priests shall enter first, ranked one after another according to the perfection of their spirit; then the levites; and thirdly all the people one after another in their thousands, hundreds, fifties, and tens, that every Israelite may know his place in the community of God according to the everlasting design. No man shall move down from his place nor move up from his allotted position." These monastic sectarians called themselves "the men of holiness." They were to keep themselves "separate from the habitation of unjust men." Their virtuous lifestyle, directed by a just council, would atone for the wickedness of others:

> In the council of the community there shall be twelve men and three priests, perfectly versed in all that is revealed of the law, whose works shall be truth, righteousness, justice, loving-kindness and humility. They shall preserve the faith in the land with steadfastness and meekness and shall atone for sin by the practice of justice and by suffering the sorrows of affliction. They shall walk with all men according to the standard of truth and the rule of the time. When these are in Israel, the council of the community shall be established in truth . . . They shall be witnesses to the truth at the Judgement, and shall be the elect of

goodwill who shall atone for the land and pay to the wicked their reward.

Inevitably, life in such a community had to be strictly regulated:

> If he has spoken in anger against one of the priests inscribed in the book, he shall do penance for one year and shall be excluded for his soul's sake from the pure meal of the congregation. But if he has spoken unwittingly, he shall do penance for six months. Whoever has lied shall do penance for six months. Whoever has deliberately insulted his companion unjustly shall do penance for one year and shall be excluded. Whoever has deliberately deceived his companion by word or by deed shall do penance for six months. If he has failed to care for his companion, he shall do penance for three months. But if he has failed to care for the property of the community, thereby causing its loss, he shall restore it in full. And if he be unable to restore it, he shall do penance for sixty days . . . Whoever has interrupted his companion whilst speaking: ten days. Whoever has lain down to sleep during an assembly of the congregation: thirty days. And likewise, whoever has left, without reason, an assembly of the congregation as many as three times during the assembly, shall do penance for ten days . . . Whoever has muttered against the authority of the community shall be expelled and shall not return. But if he has murmured against his companion unjustly, he shall do penance for six months.[70]

There is no reason to suppose that such opting out of wider Jewish society was common, but attachment to a group of like-minded enthusiasts within the Jewish community may well have been. The communal lifestyle of early Jewish Christians was thus not exceptional in first-century Jerusalem: "And the multitude of those that believed were of one heart and of one soul: neither said any that any of the things which he possessed was his own; but they had all things common."[71]

# CHAPTER SIX

# PERSPECTIVES

## THE NATURE OF MAN

D ID JEWS and Romans just see the world differently? And, if they did, did such contrasting perspectives matter? Attitudes to birthdays may provide an enigmatic clue. Among the more domestic documents preserved among the incised wooden tablets found at Vindolanda on Hadrian's Wall was a letter, written *c.* 100 CE, from a Roman woman inviting a friend to a birthday party: "On the third day before the Ides of September, sister, for the day of the celebration of my birthday, I give you a warm invitation to make sure that you come to us, to make the day more enjoyable to me by your arrival." Romans took birthday celebrations seriously. They were occasions for gifts and banquets, but also for prayers, vows and offerings to the gods. From the time of Augustus there began a fashion for the composition of speeches and poems as birthday presents, like that of Propertius to his girlfriend: "I wondered what omen the Muses had sent me as they stood before my couch in the red sunlight of dawn. They sent me a token that 'twas the birthday of my mistress, and thrice with propitious sound they clapped their hands. May this day pass to its close without a cloud, may the winds be motionless in heaven, and may the threatening wave sink to calm on the dry shore."[1] Throughout the Roman empire the birthdays of emperors and members of the imperial family were celebrated by millions of their subjects. By contrast, Jews had no special ritual at all to mark the anniversary of births. The only birthday marked as such in the Hebrew Bible is that of Pharaoh in Egypt. The difference in practice does not seem to reflect different attitudes to the passing years. As already noted (in Chapter 4), Jews could make great play on the significance of events recurring at the same date on different years. The difference, on which ancient writers are not known to have remarked, may reflect rather different conceptions about the import of getting older, and making progress through the career of life.

THE EFFECT of different perspectives began already before birth. Most Roman women married young, soon after puberty, sometimes even before. Despite the use of contraception techniques—not all of them wholly ineffective—they could expect frequent pregnancies. The result, however, was rarely a large family. Mostly this resulted from a very high rate of infant mortality, but it may also in part have depended on conscious choices. Romans did not write much about birth control. The topic belonged, with sewage disposal, among the necessary but unpleasant aspects of life that people took for granted. The elder Pliny mentions contraception in his voluminous *Natural History* "only because some women are so fertile and have so many children that they need a respite." Not that the information he provides, culled from the writings of Caecilius, will have been very helpful: he writes of a "type of spider, called a hairy spider, which has an enormous head. If this is cut open, one finds inside, it is said, two small worms. If, before sunrise, these are tied on to women with a strip of deer hide, they will not conceive . . . This contraception retains its force for one year."[2] Abortion was treated in the medical literature as, in effect, late contraception. The poet Ovid berates his fictional lover Corinna for aborting her child for cosmetic reasons, but this was a work of erotic elegy, and it is unlikely that ancient abortions were undergone frivolously: "No lioness dares to destroy her unborn young, yet tender girls do—but not unpunished, for she who destroys her own children in her womb often dies herself. She herself dies, and is carried to the funeral pyre with hair unloosed, and everyone who sees her pyre shouts, 'She deserved it.' " Despite the strong likelihood of physical damage, there is little evidence that mothers, or indeed fathers, were psychologically disturbed by the practical measures advocated in the medical handbooks. The physician Soranus of Ephesus, who practised in Rome, and wrote in the time of Trajan and Hadrian a valuable treatise on gynaecology and obstetrics which is still extant, discussed the various possible methods in a quite matter-of-fact fashion: "A woman who intends to have an abortion must, for two or three days beforehand, take long baths and eat little food and use emollient pessaries and abstain from wine. You then need to open a vein and extract a good deal of blood." The Roman Stoic philosopher Musonius Rufus, who taught in Rome under Nero and the Flavians (except for the periods when he was banished by the regime), is said to have forbidden the induction of abortions, but his concern may have been more for the welfare of the state than for the welfare of either the foetus or the mother.[3]

Up to this point many in secular Western society would find the Roman attitude easy enough to recognize (if not always to approve). A (free) woman's body was her own; she had the right to choose. But the actions of Roman parents when the pregnancy came to term strike the modern observer as more alien. Like the embryo and the foetus, the treatment of the newborn infant, just emerged from the womb, was also left to the discretion of the parents. The point at which a child was accepted into Roman society was not its first breath but the ceremony in which its father, by lifting it up, formally acknowledged its legitimate existence. A baby not vouchsafed such recognition could be killed, left to die by exposure or sold as a slave. In all such cases the infant was treated as not fully human.

The fate of newborns not so acknowledged aroused distress which Romans felt more able to admit in public than the trauma of abortion. Ovid narrates the myth of the girl Iphis, disguised as a boy by her mother because, before she was born, her father told her pregnant mother that they did not have the money to pay for the upkeep of a girl: "if you should bear a girl—I say this with great reluctance; may I be pardoned for the impiety—if you should bear a girl, let her be killed." It is probable that active infanticide, by suffocation or some other method, was less common than exposure of the baby to die of neglect. At any rate, exposure was common enough to raise issues about the legal status of children found abandoned, as we have seen, and for fiction to capitalize on the romantic possibilities of an exposed child reared by others and reunited in adulthood with its family. This theme had been incorporated into the plots of Latin comedy in the middle Republic, and was still found in the later *Ethiopian Story* of Heliodorus, in which the heroine, Charicleia, was exposed by her mother, the Ethiopian queen, because she had been born white. Such stories suggest a certain ambivalence about the relative influences of nature and nurture. The abandoned infant of an aristocrat both was and was not a potential aristocrat. The pervasive sense of glory as a quality inherited from ancestors was here in conflict with the real practice of disowning unwanted off-spring, and the real practice of adoption of children from one family into another.[4] Notwithstanding such romantic fictions, the effect of exposure was presumably usually intended to be a moderately rapid death, although a healthy newborn might survive for quite some time in the open air in the warmer periods of the year, and the application of direct force would probably have been more merciful.

In contrast to Romans, Jews abhorred abortion, except in extreme circumstances, and in all cases infanticide. According to Josephus, "the Law orders all offspring to be brought up, and forbids women either to cause abortion or to destroy the foetus; a woman convicted of this is regarded as a child-killer, because she destroys a soul [*psyche*] and diminishes the race." Tacitus, less sympathetically, also notes that Jews "take thought to increase their numbers, for they regard it as a crime to kill an undesired child." This Jewish attitude was not wholly different from that of Musonius Rufus, but it was strange enough in the ancient world to have come to the notice of the Greek author Hecataeus of Abdera in the early third century BCE: "[Moses] required those who dwelt in the land to rear their children." Procreation was the first commandment in the Bible: "Be fruitful, and multiply," and there was a general assumption that, since man was made in the image of God, human life was sacred. The attitude expressed by Josephus in *Against Apion*, that to kill a foetus is to destroy a soul, marked a difference between Jews and Romans, even if real life often involved complications and compromises.[5]

The Jewish texts do not have much to say about contraception—unsurprisingly, in the light of the commandment to procreate—but they show awareness of various devices in use. The death of Onan after he "spilled his seed on the ground" while having intercourse with his wife was generally interpreted as a prohibition of coitus interruptus, but Hiyya, a rabbinic sage of the late second and early third century CE, is cited in the Babylonian Talmud as having envisaged the use of female contraception when the woman's health is an issue: "Judith, the wife of Rabbi Hiyya, having suffered . . . agonizing pains in childbirth, changed her clothes and appeared before Rabbi Hiyya. 'Is a woman,' she asked, 'commanded to propagate the race—[or does the law apply only to men]?' 'No,' he replied. And she went and drank a sterilizing potion." Nor were attitudes to abortion entirely clear-cut. The rabbis could envisage cases in which even very late abortion might be permitted, in contrast to the total ban asserted by Josephus in *Against Apion* and the strong line taken by many early Christians. In the Mishnah, the killing of a child already born is treated as murder, but abortion is not: a foetus only becomes a person when the "greater part of the head" emerges from the womb. From this rule emerged clear rules about the permissible use of abortion if the mother's life is in danger during pregnancy: "If a woman is in hard travail, they cut up the embryo while it is in the womb and bring it out member by member, since the life of the mother has priority over the life of the embryo; but if the greater part of it has already emerged, it may not be touched, since the claim of one life cannot override the claim of another life." Philo, on the other hand, seems to have treated the killing of a foetus once formed into human shape as murder:

> If a man comes to blows with a pregnant woman and strikes her on the belly and she miscarries . . . if the offspring is already shaped and all the limbs have their proper qualities and places in the system, he must die, for that which answers to this description is a human being, which he has destroyed in the laboratory of Nature who judges that the hour has not yet come for bringing it out into the light, like a statue lying in a studio requiring nothing more than to be conveyed outside and released from confinement.[6]

On the other hand all Jews, it seems, took for granted that killing the child once born was out of the question. There was nothing in the Bible that explicitly prohibited the most common method of dealing with unwanted children in the early Roman empire, which was exposure, but Philo made an impassioned effort to claim that exposure, as practised by gentiles, was implicitly forbidden by Moses:

> As to the charges of murder . . . of their own children in particular the clearest proofs of their truth is supplied by the parents. Some of them do the deed with their own hands; with monstrous cruelty and barbarity they stifle and throttle the first breath which the infants draw or throw them into the river or into the depths of the sea, after attaching some heavy substance to make them sink more quickly under its weight. Others take them to be exposed in some desert place, hoping,

they themselves say, that they may be saved, but leaving them in actual truth to suffer the most distressing fate . . . [In contrast] Moses implicitly and indirectly forbade the exposure of children, when he pronounced the sentence of death against those who cause the miscarriage of mothers in cases where the foetus is fully formed . . . When the child has been brought to the birth it is separated from the organism with which it was identified and being isolated and self-contained becomes a living animal, lacking none of the complements needed to make a human being. And therefore infanticide undoubtedly is murder, since the displeasure of the law is not concerned with ages but with a breach of faith to the race.

It is probably reasonable to assume in the light of such comments that Jews were less likely to abandon unwanted infants than other people, but the Mishnah may suggest that the practice was not wholly unknown, even if Jewish parents made the baby's survival more probable by leaving it somewhere where it was likely to be found, rather than exposing it in a "desert place." In a discussion of the parentage of Jews which might make it illegitimate for them to intermarry with other Jews, the Mishnah refers to a category of individual termed *asufi*, which is taken to mean "any that was picked up from the street and knows neither his father nor his mother." In other words, a foundling.[7]

The grief of parents who exposed their babies must have been assuaged in part by the hope that the infant might be picked up and saved to be a slave in another family, but to be a slave was itself considered by many Romans to be not fully human. The life of a slave was envisaged in Roman law as equivalent to that of an animal put to work by its owner, sometimes as a pet, or for display, more often simply for the benefit of its physical labour. When the novelist Apuleius imagined the life of his hero changed into an ass, with no control over his own person, he was describing what it was like to be a slave who could be beaten, raped or moved from one place to another whenever his master desired. As we have seen, a slave was property in the same sense that animals were property. The elder Cato advised the prudent landowner to dispose of worn-out oxen, poor cattle and sheep, and old and sickly slaves, as superfluous. It should not be his concern what might happen to these living beings once they were off his estate. Not that this general depersonification of slaves was altogether unchallenged in

Roman antiquity. Like the killing of infants, treatment of slaves as less than human inevitably evoked a certain unease, if only because, just as infants could grow, so slaves could "become" fully human on achieving their freedom, and even the grandest Roman might one day become a slave. In his mid-twenties Julius Caesar had been captured by pirates in the Aegean and kept by them for nearly forty days before his travelling companions succeeded in raising the fifty talents required for his ransom; if the money had not been forthcoming, he would have been sold as a slave. Aristotle's assertion that a slave is "by nature" servile was difficult to reconcile with such changes of status in their own society. Some eminent intellectuals, like the Stoic Epictetus, who numbered senators among his distinguished pupils, had once been slaves. Stoics in particular worried that degrading treatment of slaves demeaned their owners, since all men are equal citizens of the universe: "Some people say, 'They're just slaves.' But they are fellow human beings! 'They're just slaves.' But they live with us! 'They're just slaves.' In fact, they are our fellow slaves, if you stop to consider that fate has as much control over us as it has over them." So wrote Seneca, the immensely rich tutor and friend of the emperor Nero, whose own household depended on the work of many slaves. He could encourage them to be satisfied with their lot in life, as he was with his, as all Stoics at least tried to be. But the Stoic appeal to treat slaves as human was a reaction to a society which generally did not. Some Roman slaves wore collars with identification tags, such as "I have run away. Capture me. When you have returned me to my master, Zoninus, you will receive a reward." All slaves could expect appalling punishment if they tried to escape, from beating to crucifixion or being sold to fight as a gladiator, which meant almost certain death.[8]

Jews as much as Romans took slaves for granted primarily as domestic workers, but once in the ownership of a Jew a slave could expect much more humane treatment. Biblical law treated a slave as a chattel, fully owned by the master, to whom compensation was to be paid if the slave was injured by a third party, but the master's power to maltreat the slave was limited by the law. If a slave was permanently maimed as a result of a beating, the slave must be compensated with freedom: "if a man smite the eye of his male slave, or the eye of his female slave, that it perish; he shall let him go free for his eye's sake." If the slave died as a result of a beating by his or her owner, the owner was to be punished. Occasional comments in postbiblical Jewish literature suggest that many laws requiring humane treatment were in practice ignored, such as (perhaps) the rabbinic aphorism that "the more female slaves, the more lewdness," which may reflect an assumption that slaves could be sexually abused with impunity in Jewish society as in Roman. But underlying the Jewish attitude to slaves as humans was a principle which it is impossible to imagine in the social consciousness of Romans. The Bible urged that, in treating slaves well, and in particular in giving them their freedom, "you shall remember that you were a slave in the land of Egypt, and the Lord your God redeemed you; therefore I command you this today." The haggadah, the narration of the Exodus performed by all Jewish families before the Seder meal on the first night of Passover, already existed in roughly its present form by the time of the Mishnah in *c.* 200 CE. It begins with the personal reminder: "We were slaves in Egypt. . . ." The identification with past slavery must have made a greater impact in a household where domestic slaves themselves participated in the ritual and poured the four cups of wine to each of those present as they reclined on couches in celebration of their present freedom.[9]

It is less easy to see a clear distinction between Romans and Jews in their ideas about exactly what a human being is. Both were very confused, not least as a result of incomplete and incoherent adoption of Greek ideas about the soul (in Greek, *psyche*; in Latin, *anima*), which, among Romans, cohabited uneasily with notions inherited from earlier times, such as the Roman concept of the *genius*, the "self" which made a man what he was. Such confusion emerged in Rome most starkly in attitudes to the dead. Postmortem existence was not itself a major preoccupation of the Romans, in marked contrast to the Egyptians and, closer to home, the Etruscans, whose influence on Roman culture in other respects had been considerable in the archaic period of the city. Romans espoused quite radically varied ideas about what would happen to them when they died. Epicureans defiantly denied the possibility of any immortal soul or afterlife, as in the tombstone which declares NFFNSNC (*non fui, fui, non sum, non curo*, "I was not, I was, I am not, I care not"). Vergil writes movingly about the shadowy Stygian realm inhabited by "shades of the past, even as light winds, and most like a winged dream." There was widespread belief in ghosts, *lemures*, as frightening shades of the unburied departed, to be appeased at the festival of the Lemuria held each year on three days in May.[10]

It was generally assumed that only a few, exceptional, individuals might continue to exist after death as individualized divine beings worthy of cult.

Cicero provides a rationale for such a belief from within Stoic philosophy in the last book of his philosophical treatise *On the Republic*, which contains the *Dream of Scipio*, a vision vouchsafed to Scipio Aemilianus. In this dream, according to Cicero's imaginative text, Scipio's adoptive grandfather, the great Africanus, reassures him about the future, when "all those who have preserved, aided, or increased their fatherland have a fixed place prepared for them in the heavens, where they may enjoy eternal life in happiness." This was not pure theory: in the depths of his grief for his daughter Tullia, who died in 45 BCE in her mid-thirties, he planned to build a shrine to worship her as a goddess. He wrote to his friend Atticus about his intentions: "I want it to be a shrine, and that idea cannot be rooted out of my mind. I am anxious to avoid the appearance of a tomb, not so much because of the legal penalty as to achieve as much as possible 'apotheosis.' " (It may be significant that he dropped out of Latin into the Greek *apotheosis* to express the notion of deification.)[11] Among the wider Roman populace, for whom the complexities of Stoic philosophy were less important, the possibility of being recognized as a god after death was brought home forcefully soon afterwards with the formal deification in 42 BCE of the dead Julius Caesar. The way in which this event was reported suggests that it was reckoned no small matter, although it should be kept firmly in mind that Caesar was only one god among the many worshipped by Romans: for a polytheistic Roman to call an emperor a god was wholly different from a Christian, who denied the existence of any other gods, proclaiming the divinity of Jesus. Caesar's special status was ratified by celestial confirmation: "He was numbered among the gods, not only by formal decree, but also in the conviction of the vulgar. For at the first of the games which his heir Augustus gave in honour of his apotheosis, a comet shone for seven successive days, rising about the eleventh hour, and was believed to be the soul of Caesar, who had been taken to heaven." Such apotheosis was generally to be confined in ensuing generations to emperors and members of their family: it was beyond the hope and expectation of ordinary Romans, despite Cicero's earlier plans for his deceased daughter.[12]

Roman funerary rituals left space for all these varied ideas to cohabit, but only rather uneasily. In the late Republic the very poor were simply buried in huge open pits, but the rich were cremated, with their ashes placed in family tombs. By the early empire cremation had become standard, perhaps as a reflection of the increasing wealth of the population in general. Ensuring a decent funeral was felt to be of sufficient importance for many poorer Romans to pay an entrance fee and a monthly subscription to join a funeral club or mutual society to cover the expenses and make the arrangements. The urns containing the ashes were housed in niches in vaulted brick tombs like dovecotes. Funerals themselves were designed to separate the deceased as clearly as possible from the space of the living, especially that of his or her family. The final resting place must be outside the city "lest the sacred places of the city be polluted"; as a result, the roads leading out of Rome housed a series of cemeteries.[13] The cremation or burial, if properly carried out, was believed to permit the deceased to join the ranks of the *di manes*, the spirits of the dead. Graves had the standard formula inscribed *Dis Manibus Sacrum*, "sacred to the gods of the dead." In the imperial period, the name of the deceased was often added. There was a sense that the dead, after proper disposal, became part of a divine group, the *manes*, to whom the community as a whole offered worship on the last day of the Parentalia each February; the earlier days of the Parentalia, which lasted eight days altogether, were set aside for families to pray for their private dead, above all, parents. The concern whether to recognize as divine dead emperors, most entertainingly reflected in Seneca's *Apocolocyntosis*, "Pumpkinification," about the deification of Claudius, shows that those in the category of *di manes* were somehow seen as a lesser form of divinity than the apotheosized emperor. Epicureans must have found it quite hard to fit any of these widespread assumptions to their sceptical ideas, but perhaps no more so than the other general assumptions of their society about the role of religion.

Perhaps most revealing about attitudes to death, and the nature of the person whose self may or may not have died with the physical body, are the words used in consolation of the bereaved. Letters of condolence formed a literary genre of their own. The dialogue addressed by the younger Seneca to a certain Marcia who had lost a son tries every possible means of consolation, from flattery ("if I did not know, Marcia, that you were as far removed from womanish weakness of mind as from all other vices, and that your character was looked upon as a model of ancient virtue, I should not dare to assail your grief . . .") to claims that the dead are in a better place:

There is no need, therefore, for you to hurry to the tomb of your son; what lies there is his basest part and a part that in life was the source of much trouble—bones and ashes are no more part of him than were his clothes and the other protections of the body. He is complete—leaving nothing of himself behind, he has fled away and wholly departed from earth; for a little while he tarried above us while he was being purified and was ridding himself of all the blemishes and stains that still clung to him from his mortal existence, then soared aloft and sped away to join the souls of the blessed. A saintly band gave him welcome.

Such letters run the gamut of platitudes that can be produced to try to assuage grief, referring to the qualities of the deceased, the sorrow of all who knew him or her, the need to be strong. "There is no grief which the passage of time does not lessen and soften," as a friend wrote to Cicero after the death of his daughter. Seneca's consolation presupposed the Greek philosophical concept of the immortality of the soul which became sufficiently part of common Roman vocabulary in the late Republic to appear in verse epitaphs. But such epitaphs show no sign of a coherent picture of the nature of the soul's afterlife. They express wishes and speculation rather than doctrines.[14]

Incorporation of the Greek notion of the immortal soul was as partial and sporadic among Jews in the late Second Temple period as it was among their Roman contemporaries. In the Hebrew Bible, man was conceived as an animated body rather than an incarnated soul. According to the narrative in Genesis, "The Lord God formed man of dust from the ground and breathed into his nostrils the breath of life; and man became a living soul [nefesh]." Most of the authors of the biblical books seem to have envisaged the nefesh as the vital principle which gives life to the body without imagining it as something which could survive in separation from the flesh. For most biblical writers, an individual did not have a body. He or she was a body, animated by the life principle.[15]

Many Jews in the late Second Temple period continued to subscribe to this simple anthropology, and when the concept of an immortal soul was adopted it was often incoherent. Most impressively confused was the author of the Wisdom of Solomon, a text composed, probably in Greek, sometime between the mid-second century BCE and the early first century CE. The anonymous king in whose person the book is written, clearly intended as Solomon, describes how "as a child I was by nature well endowed, and I obtained by lot a good soul; or rather, being good, I entered an undefiled body." The author seems unable to decide whether his essence lay in the body (which was given a good soul) or the soul (which was given a fine, pure body). Philo adopted a more rigorous version of the Platonist doctrine of the soul as the only important part of an individual, which needed to be freed from the shackles of the body, and Josephus attributed to the Essenes a similar idea, in this case explicitly described as shared by "the sons of Greece":

> For it is a firm belief of theirs that the body is corruptible and its constituent matter impermanent, but that the soul is immortal and imperishable. Emanating from the finest ether, these souls become entangled, as it were, in the prison-house of the body, to which they are dragged down by a sort of physical spell; but when once they are released from the bonds of the flesh, then, as though liberated from long slavery, they rejoice and are borne aloft . . . Their aim was first to establish the doctrine of the immortality of the soul, and secondly to encourage virtue and to deflect from vice. Indeed, the good are made better in their lifetime by the hope of a reward after death, and the passions of the wicked are restrained by the fear that, even though they escape detection while alive, they will undergo eternal punishment after their decease. Such are the theological views of the Essenes concerning the soul, whereby they irresistibly attract all who have once tasted their wisdom.

Josephus may have coloured his account to some extent in order to appeal to his Greek and Roman readers, to whom he presented the Essenes as an example of practitioners of a praiseworthy Jewish philosophy, but there is no reason to reject altogether what he said about their doctrines. On the other hand, he wrote explicitly about these doctrines as espoused by a specific Jewish group, and it would be unjustified to deduce from his description that these ideas were in fact more widespread: the notion that a human is essentially carnal—a body animated by a spirit—was much more common among the rabbis.[16]

All Jews seem to have accepted the biblical assumption that physical life in this world is a supreme blessing. In Deuteronomy, Israel is described as given a choice between life and death, a blessing and a curse: "therefore choose life, that both you and your seed may live." The life of man was the result of God's plan. Man existed because the Lord God had formed him "out of dust of the ground, and breathed into his nostrils the breath of life." Life in this world is precious, and the hope that life in another, different world would compensate for disappointments in this world was not standard; in this respect, the doctrines espoused by some in the early Church marked an important break. In fact, there was as much disagreement among Jews as among Romans about what happened to people after they died. Belief in an afterlife was not obviously part of the world-view of any of the authors of the biblical books apart from the author of Daniel chapter 12 (composed probably in the second century BCE), which states that, at the end of days, "many of them that sleep in the dust of the earth shall awake, some to everlasting life, and some to shame and everlasting contempt." The Psalmist laments, more pessimistically, that "the dead praise not the Lord, neither any that go down into silence." The author of Ecclesiastes remarks that "he who is joined to all the living has hope, for a living dog is better than a dead lion."[17]

It is all the more remarkable that by the first century CE a belief in some sort of life after death had become widespread among Jews, at least in Judaea, despite lack of agreement even on the basic questions. According to the Acts of the Apostles, Pharisees and Sadducees argued acrimoniously on the subject, to the extent that Paul could break up a meeting of the High Priest's council simply by crying out, "Men and brethren, I am a Pharisee, a son of Pharisees: of the hope and resurrection of the dead I am being judged." The Gospels describe Jesus as disputing with the Sadducees on the same topic, a rare case of intellectual exchange with them, his arguments being portrayed far more often as with Pharisees:

The same day came to him the Sadducees, saying that there is no resurrection, and asked him, saying, "Teacher, Moses said, If a man die, having no children, his brother shall marry his wife, and raise up seed for his brother. Now there were with us seven brothers: and the first, when he had married a wife, deceased, and, having no issue, left his wife his brother. Similarly the second, and the third up to the seventh. And last of all the woman died also. Therefore in the resurrection whose wife shall she be of the seven? for they all had her." Jesus answered and said to them, "You are in error, not knowing the scriptures, nor the power of God. For in the resurrection they neither marry, nor are given in marriage, but are as the angels of God in heaven."

By the early third century CE the rabbis cited in the Mishnah and Tosefta insisted on the importance of belief in the afterlife, but the vehemence of their denunciation of heretics who denied the doctrine suggests that the issue was still debated: "All Israel have a share in the world to come . . . And these are they that have no share in the world to come: he that says that there is no resurrection of the dead [prescribed in the Torah]." Rabbis, and indeed Christians, contrived to derive the doctrine of resurrection from the Bible, but only by exceptionally ingenious interpretation.[18]

All testimonies agree that, in contrast to Sadducees, Pharisees preached the possibility of resurrection, but even Josephus, who claimed in his autobiography to have "gone through" the hard work of learning about Pharisaism and to have decided in his nineteenth year to "govern his public life following the school of the Pharisees," was contradictory about precisely what Pharisees thought resurrection would be like. Sometimes he implied that they believed "that souls have power to survive death and that there are rewards and punishments under the earth for those who have led lives of virtue or vice." At other times he described the Pharisaic doctrine as rather closer to the reincarnation of the soul: "Every soul, they maintain, is imperishable, but the soul of the good alone passes into another body, while the souls of the wicked suffer punishment." In both descriptions Josephus may have coloured the Pharisee view in order to appeal to his Greek and Roman gentile readers, to whom, at least in these passages, he presents the Pharisees, like the Essenes, as followers of a respectable philosophy. He drops into similar language about the soul as the essence of the individual in the high-flown rhetoric about the morality of suicide he puts into his own mouth in his *Jewish War*: "Know you not that they who depart this life in accordance with the law of nature and repay the loan which they received from God [only] when He who gave it is pleased to reclaim it, win eternal renown; that their houses and families are secure; that their souls, remaining spotless and obedient, are allotted the most holy place in heaven, whence, in the revolution of the ages, they return to find in chaste bodies a new habitation?"[19] Such rhetoric, composed in Rome in the 70s CE, was aimed at Roman readers all too familiar with contemporary discussions in justification or denigration of the spectacular suicides of Seneca, Thrasea Paetus and others of the Roman elite under Nero. The arguments put forward by Josephus against suicide in this passage are nicely balanced by the arguments in favour of taking one's own life he puts into the mouth of Eleazar son of Yair, leader of the Jews on Masada in 73 CE who, as we shall see in Chapter 12, killed each other to avoid falling into Roman hands. Erudite Roman readers will have enjoyed the rhetorical and literary juxtaposition of the two invented speeches. The arguments will have had much less of an impact on most Jews, who took for granted that suicide is simply wrong unless it is clearly undertaken to avoid a worse fate (as in the case of Saul after his defeat by the Philistines) or to achieve some other desirable aim, like the self-inflicted death of Samson which brought with it the destruction of many of the enemy. The rabbis permitted suicide only to avoid committing one of the three cardinal sins of murder, adultery or idolatry. In the short rabbinic treatise *Semachot*, compiled between the sixth and eleventh centuries but the earliest Jewish discussion of suicide outside the pages of Josephus, suicide is treated as murder, prohibited by an ingenious reading of the verse in Genesis: "For your own life blood, I will require a reckoning." It seems significant, in contrast to Roman glorification of the noble suicide whose decision to die is taken rationally and calmly, that the rabbis of the Talmud do not seem to have considered such an attitude possible. In later Jewish law it is generally assumed that those who commit suicide must by definition be of unsound mind. Life is assumed to be a supreme good for all, even if, as Josephus asserts, in emphasizing Jewish reverence for their writings, it was "an instinct with every Jew, from the day of his birth . . . if necessary, gladly to die on their behalf." The historian's distinction between such principled martyrdom, which was evidently expected to impress his Greek and Roman readers, and unjustified suicide, which smacked of vainglory, reflected the contemporary debate in Rome, about the value of "noble death."[20]

Most of the Jews who, like Josephus, thought or wrote in Greek, picked up vocabulary about the *psyche,* soul, as the essence of each individual, but for many Jews, the Greek terminology was little more than a fashionable gloss, rather like the use of psychological and other jargon in common discourse today. Thus even Josephus, when he wrote about resurrection in *Against Apion*, the apologetic for Judaism in which he explicitly contrasted the excellence of Jewish doctrines with the inadequacies of Greek, proved quite capable of describing the future life without recourse to the concept of an immortal soul:

> For those, on the other hand, who live in accordance with our laws the prize is not silver or gold, no crown of wild olive or of parsley with any such public mark of distinction, but each individual, relying on the witness of his own conscience and the law giver's prophecy, confirmed by the sure testimony of God, is firmly persuaded that to those who observe the laws and, if they must needs die for them, willingly meet death, God has granted a renewed existence and in the revolution of the ages the gift of a better life.

As we have seen, the early rabbis affirmed dogmatically that the resurrection of the dead would be in bodily form. The Palestinian recension of the standard Jewish daily prayer, the *amidah*, found in a document discovered in Cairo and dated to the late first millennium CE, addresses God as "mighty, humbling the proud . . . thou livest for ever and raisest the dead . . . thou providest for the living and makest the dead alive. . . ." The body of a dead person was to be treated with the greatest respect. To bury a corpse was a great religious duty: one of the conspicuous acts of piety by the eponymous hero of the book of Tobit had been to bury those who were killed by the king. Burial of a hanged man should take place on the day of death to avoid defiling the land. Corpses contaminated all who touched them or entered into the building or tent where they lay, but, despite this, the duty to bury the dead, particularly close relatives, was more important than the avoidance of pollution: even a priest should incur corpse-pollution to attend the funeral of "his nearest of kin: for his mother, and for his father, and for his son, and for his daughter, and for his brother, and for his virgin sister. . . ."[21]

The integrity of the body was preserved among all Jews by disposing of corpses through careful burial. The Roman Tacitus asserted that Jews "bury the body rather than burn it, thus following the Egyptians' custom," but in fact Jews behaved like Egyptians only in the way that both peoples "bestow the same care on the dead," which meant that, for both peoples, the Roman custom of cremation was anathema. The preference for inhumation was not because of simple conservatism in Jewish society, for the practical methods of disposal used in burial varied considerably. Most Jews were buried in communal rock-cut tombs, with the bodies laid out in coffins on ledges which branched out from central chambers, but some, including those buried at Qumran by the Dead Sea, were buried in single graves marked by heaps of stones placed on the surface. It is possible that these different ways of burial reflected different notions of the role of the individual in society, such as different evaluations of the importance of family ties, but such speculation can hardly be proven. Nor can there be any certain explanation for the adoption in the mid-first century BCE by many Jews in the areas of Jerusalem and Jericho of the practice of ossilegium, the collection of the bones of the deceased after the flesh had rotted away so that they could be carefully deposited in a small casket. Many hundreds of such ossuaries, mostly made of stone but in a few cases of pottery, have been found in the Jerusalem region. Those which have been found in tombs can be dated to the short period from the beginning of Herodian rule to the destruction of the Temple. Scholars have made valiant efforts to provide some religious or other ideological explanation, but without success. The literary sources preserved by the rabbis show awareness of the custom but offer no rationale. Such use of ossuaries was known in some other places, notably western Asia Minor, but not in any other contemporary culture with which Judaean Jews are likely to have made close contact. It has been suggested, quite plausibly, that use of ossuaries reflected a desire by richer Judaeans to mark more clearly the individual within a family crypt, avoiding the anonymity of previous practice, but the best explanation (hard though it may be to accept for those convinced that there ought to be a more serious reason for such an important change) is the same as that offered for the Roman shift from cremation to inhumation in the second century CE—that is, simply fashion. In a society where the rich were impressed by Roman customs, the use of an ossuary was as close as Judaean Jews could get to the Roman use of urns to hold the ashes of the dead. If such an explanation is correct, it emphasizes all the more strongly the Jewish taboo against cremation. It was all right to behave like a Roman—but not if it involved the destruction of the body by burning.[22]

## COSMOLOGIES

JEWS AND ROMANS were thus not likely to disagree strongly in their understanding of what it is to be human, but their views were much more divergent when they assessed the place of man in the cosmos. For Jews, the creation myth in Genesis played a central role. The world had been created by a single divine being who retained a constant watch on everything and intervened occasionally in accordance with a plan only partly comprehensible to humans. All Jews were expected to hear the story of the creation once a year when the annual cycle of readings from the Torah reverted to the beginning of the book of Genesis. According to the Mishnah, when the priests and Levites of one of the twenty-four "courses" that took turns to serve in the Temple went up to Jerusalem, "Israelites that are of that course come together to their cities and read the story of creation." The story was discussed and elaborated, as by the author of the book of *Jubilees* in the second century BCE:

> For on the first day he created the heavens, which are above, and the earth, and the waters and every spirit which ministers before him: the angels of the presence, and the angels of holiness, and the angels of the spirit of fire, and the angels of the spirit of the winds, and the angels of the spirit of the clouds and darkness and snow and hail and frost, and the angels of resoundings[?] and thunders and lightnings, and the angels of the spirits of cold and heat and winter and spring and harvest and summer, and all of the spirits of his creatures which are in the heavens and on earth.

Josephus began his account in twenty books of the "ancient history and political constitution" of the Jews with "in the beginning God founded the heaven and the earth." In this, so he wrote, he was following the exemplary wisdom of "our lawgiver Moses," who, when he framed his laws, led the thoughts of his fellow citizens "up to God and the construction of the world, persuading them that, of all God's works upon earth, we men are the fairest. . . ." Earlier in the first century CE Josephus' predecessor Philo placed at the beginning of his systematic presentation of Mosaic legislation, the *Exposition*, a treatise specifically dedicated to the creation of the world. According to Philo, Moses implied that the "cosmos is in harmony with the Law and the Law with the cosmos, and that the man who observes the law is constituted thereby a *cosmopolites* ("citizen of the world"), regulating his doings by the purpose and will of Nature." The philosopher condemned those who, "having the cosmos in admiration

rather than the Maker of the cosmos, pronounce it to be without beginning and everlasting, while with impious falsehood they postulate in God
great inactivity; whereas we ought on the contrary to be astonished at his
powers as Maker and Father, and not to assign to the cosmos a dispropor-
tionate majesty."[23]

By contrast to Josephus, Livy's history of Rome "from the founding of
the city," completed in one hundred and forty-two books near the start of
the same century, ignored cosmology altogether and launched straight
into the myths of Aeneas and the founding of Rome itself. The account
of the creation of the cosmos was to be found not in a work of history or
moral philosophy, but in the *Metamorphoses* of Ovid, finished just before he
was banished into exile on the Black Sea in 8 CE. The *Metamorphoses* weaves
together a long series of mythical stories culled by Ovid from Greek writings, from Homer and Hesiod down to more recent times:

> Before the sea was, and the lands, and the sky that hangs over all, the
> face of nature showed alike in her whole round, which state have men
> called chaos: a rough, unordered mass of things, nothing at all save
> lifeless bulk and warring seeds of ill-matched elements heaped in
> one . . . God—and kindlier nature—composed this strife; for he rent
> asunder land from sky, and sea from land and separated the ethereal
> heavens from the dense atmosphere. When thus he had released these
> elements and freed them from the blind heap of things, he set them
> each in its own place and bound them fast in harmony . . . A living
> creature of finer stuff than these, more capable of lofty thought, one
> who could have dominion over all the rest, was lacking yet. Then man
> was born: whether the god who made all else, designing a more perfect
> world, made man of his own divine substance, or whether the new
> earth, but lately drawn away from heavenly ether, retained still some
> elements of its kindred sky—that earth which the son of Iapetus mixed
> with fresh, running water, and moulded into the form of the all-
> controlling gods. And, though all other animals are prone, and fix their
> gaze upon the earth, he gave to man an uplifted face and bade him stand
> erect and turn his eyes to heaven. So, then, the earth, which had but
> lately been a rough and formless thing, was changed and clothed itself
> with forms of men before unknown.

Ovid's great achievement was to combine disparate myths into a single narrative linked by the loose rubric of "miraculous changes" brought about by the gods.

Some elements of the story told by Ovid resemble the Genesis account, but the differences matter more. Ovid is unclear about the identity of the creator who brought about the cosmos: "a god and a better nature" or "whoever he was of the gods." Philosophers like Cicero accepted the argument put forward by the Stoics that the regularities of the heavens proved the operation of a creative mind; the denial by Epicureans of the standard belief that the universe is ordered, and their claim that it was created out of a meaningless set of atoms, was a deliberate rejection of the common view. But what the common view lacked, and what was found in abundance among Jews, was the strong belief that the divine force which had created the world had done so for a purpose, and that this divine force continued to care for and intervene in its creation.[24]

The divine realm in the imagination of Romans was a society of competition, alliances, strife and friendships—in other words, a realm of relationships much like those of humans. When the gods intervened in the natural world, it was often a result, not of concern for people, animals or other inhabitants of the earth, but of quarrels and scheming among themselves. In the creation myths inherited by Romans from the Greeks, the early history of the world was envisaged as a scene of strife between the original gods, the monstrously powerful Titans, overthrown by the gods of Olympus, who themselves came under attack by the Giants. Strife continued between the gods on Olympus, as family quarrels set Hera against Zeus (in the Roman version, Juno against Jupiter) because of his amorous adventures, or the lame Hephaistos, identified by Romans with Vulcan, against Ares (Mars), the lover of his wife Aphrodite (Venus). The forces which created and now influence the cosmos act in conflicting ways beyond our comprehension.

Romans thought about the gods much as the scientifically illiterate nowadays think about germs, microbes and viruses. We do not all know exactly what such entities are, and we cannot see, touch, hear or smell them at all, but we believe that they surround us in their millions and that they have the power radically to affect both us and the world about us. Some gods were "known" and could be named and expected to intervene

in the world specifically or mainly within certain spheres: the divinity
Robigus or Robigo, whose festival of the Robigalia was celebrated by
Romans on 25 April, was described by some Latin writers as a divinity
worshipped for the purpose of averting blight from young cornfields,
although his (or her) other characteristics were apparently obscure. Since
the cosmos contained an indefinitely large population of gods, most
divinities were unknown to humans—hence invocations to a divine figure
"*sive deus, sive dea*" ("be it god or goddess"), and the Roman state prayers
which list a series of divinities but still end, cautiously, with "and all the
other gods." Romans thought of these supernatural beings as belonging in
a number of different categories: *deus* (a god who had always been immortal), *divus* (a god who had once lived as a human), nymph or spirit. Some
were more powerful than others, some (like nymphs) generally benevolent
to humans, others less so. Some, like the divinities inherent in abstract
qualities such as Iustitia (Justice) or Fides (good faith), had no real personality or stories about their characters.

Both cult and myth portrayed Jupiter as ruler within a hierarchy of
immortals, but his rule was not absolute, nor the hierarchy entirely secure.
The Olympian gods were reckoned generally more powerful than other
supernatural beings, but relationships might vary. Thus Roman worship of
Fortuna in various forms was common, and at Praeneste (modern Palestrina) she was considered to be, in her character of Fortuna Primigenia
("Primordial Fortune"), the mother of Jupiter and Juno, but in general
both she and her Greek equivalent Tyche were only vaguely incorporated
into the Olympian myths, if at all. The attack by Josephus on Greek religion applied equally strongly to Romans—and, as among Greeks, there
were Roman intellectuals who disapproved, as much as the Jew Josephus,
of common pagan conceptions:

> Who, in fact, is there among the admired sages of Greece who has not
> censured their most famous poets and their most trusted legislators for
> sowing in the minds of the masses the first seeds of such notions about
> the gods? They represent them to be as numerous as they choose, born
> of one another and engendered in all manner of ways. They assign
> them different localities and habits, like animal species, some living
> underground, others in the sea, the oldest of all being chained in Tar-
> tarus. Those to whom they have allotted heaven have set over them one

who is nominally Father, but in reality a tyrant and despot; with the result that his wife and brother and the daughter, whom he begot from his own head, conspire against him, to arrest and imprison him, just as he himself had treated his own father. Justly do these tales merit the severe censure which they receive from their intellectual leaders.

For Romans the *existence* of the gods was accepted by almost everyone as true but tales *about* the gods were freely described as the inventions of the poets. It is indeed rather hard to imagine Jupiter approving or encouraging the wide dissemination of the stories about his sexual misdemeanours; these were not stories designed to increase reverence for the gods. Romans did not often ask themselves the function of their myths—it is hard, within a society, to stand back sufficiently from fundamental beliefs and attitudes in order to raise such issues—but a plausible explanation may be that the myths helped to make sense of the world as it was, or seemed to them: a mass of competing, contradictory forces, lacking any overall structure or purpose, in which cataclysmic change by earthquake, storm or death might strike at any time for reasons unknown and unknowable to humans, but a product of the struggles of the gods.[25]

It is not easy to live with such a shifting, uncertain cosmology, and many Romans sought evidence of greater stability in the universe from the regular movements of the stars and planets. It was common for individuals to have their horoscopes cast, in order to discern what the future might bring, on the basis of the positions of the sun, moon, planets and fixed stars at the time of their birth or conception. The underlying concept which gave credence to such practices was a belief, most coherently expressed by Stoics, that a "universal sympathy" connects all parts of the cosmos, so that a link between events in the heavens and those on earth is not difficult to understand: for the great astronomer Ptolemy in Alexandria in the second century CE, astrology was simply the application in the world of knowledge about the heavens: "Of the means of prediction through astronomy . . . two are the most important and valid . . . we apprehend the aspects of the movements of sun, moon and stars in relation to each other and to the earth, as they occur from time to time; [and] . . . by means of the natural character of these aspects themselves, we investigate the changes which they bring about in that which they surround." In Rome in the last years of Augustus and early years of Tiberius, the Stoic poet Marcus Manilius composed the *Astronomica* in five books to teach the value of astrology. Manilius, about whom nothing is known outside his somewhat tortuous work, was evidently steeped in Greek as well as Latin literature, but his rather peculiar use of the Latin language was probably more the result of his rebarbative subject than any unfamiliarity: "By the magic of song to draw down from heaven god-given skills and fate's confidants, the stars, which by the operation of divine reasoning diversify the chequered fortunes of mankind; and to be the first to stir with these new strains the nodding leaf-capped woods of Helicon, as I bring strange lore untold by any before me: this is my aim." The scepticism of some about the value of astrological predictions was based less on the theory than on the "incompetence" of those popular astrologers whose predictions proved wrong.[26]

Since astrology was a technical art relating one part of the cosmos to another and it did not require any specific form of worship, or indeed any specific beliefs about how the celestial bodies had come into being, it was just as possible an art for Jews as for Roman polytheists, and Jews were just as likely as Romans to pick up from Babylonia, and from Alexandria in the Hellenistic age, the necessary techniques as well as the ideas which underlay them. In fact, however, astrology does not seem to have been practised by Jews before Hellenistic times. The few passages in the Hebrew Bible which refer to astrology seem to treat it as a Babylonian custom only. It is thus all the more remarkable that the Egyptian Jewish writer Artapanus claimed in the second century BCE that Abraham had once taught astrological methods to the Egyptian pharaoh Pharethothes. Astrological ideas are found in a number of the more esoteric Jewish writings from the late Second Temple period, most notably in some of the Dead Sea scrolls, among which was a Hebrew text written in a simple cipher around the end of the first century BCE, describing in astrological terms the features and destiny of some individual and the configuration of the stars at the time of his birth: "His spirit consists of six [parts] in the House of Light and three in the House of Darkness. And this is the birth-time in which he was born: in the foot of the Bull . . ." The influence of the heavenly planets on life on earth is taken for granted in much rabbinic literature of the fourth and fifth centuries CE: "There is not a herb which has not a planet [*mazal*] in heaven which strikes it and says, 'Grow!' " (so *Genesis Rabbah*, redacted in Palestine) and "Not the day's planet, but the constellation of the hour has influence" (so the Babylonian Talmud).[27]

At the same time some Jews expressed reservations about the value of astrological predictions on the grounds that any attribution of influence to the stars and planets might seem to undermine acknowledgement of the universal power of the one God: "There is no *mazal* for Israel." The futility of astrological predictions was one of the earliest discoveries of Abraham, according to the book of *Jubilees*:

> And in the sixth week, in the fifth year of it, Abram sat up during the night on the first of the seventh month, so that he might observe the stars from evening until morning in order to discover what the nature of the year would be with respect to rain. And he was sitting alone and making observations; and a word came into his heart, and he said, "All the signs of the stars and the signs of the moon and the sun are in the hand of the Lord. Why am I seeking? If he so wills, he will make it rain morning and evening, and if he so wills he will not send [it] down; and all things are in his hand."

The design of the blue, scarlet and purple tapestry which hung in the Jerusalem Temple, depicting "a panorama of the heavens except for the signs of the Zodiac," was probably calculated to avoid encouraging any belief in the power of the stars over human life, although (according to Josephus) the works of art placed just outside the Holy of Holies included the seven lamps of the lampstand, representing the planets, and the twelve loaves of the shewbread on the table, representing "the circle of the Zodiac and the year": placing these heavenly signs at the centre of God's Temple demonstrated that "all things are of God and for God." Insistence on the universal significance of the symbolism of the depictions on the sacred objects in the Temple seems to have been a common Jewish theme, although the details of the allegory varied.[28]

All Jews (apart perhaps from Sadducees) assumed that God cares for and looks after his creation. Josephus in one passage interestingly turned on its head the standard argument that the regularity of the heavens proved that they were the work of a creative mind: according to him, Abraham was

> the first boldly to declare that God, the creator of the universe, is one . . . This he inferred from the changes to which land and sea are subject, from the course of sun and moon, and from all the celestial

phenomena. For, he argued, were these bodies endowed with power, they would have provided for their own good order, but, since they lacked this last, it was manifest that even those services in which they cooperate for our greater benefit they render not in virtue of their own authority, but through the might of their commanding sovereign, to whom alone it is right to render our homage and thanksgiving.

The universe created by the one God contained not just the natural, sensible world and the celestial phenomena but also numerous supernatural beings. The account of creation in Genesis concentrated on the relation of God to man as the two most important figures in the cosmological drama, but by the first century BCE Jews, as much as pagan polytheists, envisaged a divine realm whose denizens might have an impact on their lives in unexpected ways. Jews only worshipped one God, but it is an error to think of them as pure monotheists in this period. They often wrote about God as if he was a single divine force, but this was a practice widely shared by pagan polytheists, particularly Stoics, who could and did refer to "god" in the singular even as they participated in the worship of multiple divinities. A strict adherence to monotheism—the belief that the world is affected by only one supernatural being—is hard to maintain, although in later periods some Jews, under the influence of Islam, were to attempt to do so. In the early centuries CE some Jews, such as Philo, came close to describing God as possessed of two natures, a tendency which allowed preservation of the concept of the divine as perfect and unsullied while also allowing for divine intervention in human affairs; such language (as in the depiction of *Sophia*, Wisdom, in the Wisdom of Solomon, preserved in the Apocrypha) also enabled Jews to envisage the feminine aspects of divinity alongside the masculine. If pushed about the conflict between these ideas and the unity of God, such Jews would probably have defended such expressions as metaphorical. More concrete, and more widespread, was the interpretation of their world by Jews as the product of interventions not only by the God of Israel (however he be described) but also by other supernatural beings, variously described as angels or demons.[29]

Angels appear as messengers of God already in the Hebrew Bible— ordering Abraham to refrain, at the last moment, from sacrificing his only son, Isaac; feeding Elijah in the desert; protecting the faithful in all their ways. They can appear in human form, but they can also appear and disappear at will. In the imagery of Jacob's ladder, angels are envisaged as commuting between heaven and earth, but other texts envisage them as a celestial host, along with the winged cherubim, on whom God flies through the heavens, and the six-winged seraphim, which stand beside the throne of God in heaven and sing his praises. By the first century BCE many Jews imagined the hosts of angels in much greater detail. According to Acts, Sadducees did not believe in angels or spirits; but, even if this report is correct (and it is hard to reconcile with Sadducee acceptance of the authority of the Bible), it would make them exceptions in a world where the interventions of angels and spirits were taken for granted. In the book of *Enoch*, as in other writings of this period, angels came to be regarded as the controlling spirits of the celestial bodies and the winds and of the seasons, and of abstract notions such as peace and healing. Angels were pictured as a hierarchy, headed by a small group of archangels, designated by specific names—in *Enoch*, Michael, Raphael, Gabriel and Phanuel. Other angels also had names: Essene neophytes took an oath "carefully to preserve . . . the names of the angels," and many angelic names, often of obscure origin, are preserved in the Talmuds and in Jewish magical literature.

Angels came to be conceived as messengers not only from God to man but also from man to God: when the angel of the Lord revealed himself to Tobit and his son Tobias, he described himself as "Raphael, one of the seven holy angels, who present the prayers of the saints, and who go in and out before the glory of the Holy One." The author of 2 *Baruch* imagined the angelic host held in check close to the throne of God, ready to take action on command like an obedient army. The Dead Sea sectarians seem to have had a particular interest in imagining the angelic realm. Some have even argued that the sectarians believed that they themselves were both human and angelic, or even both human and divine. This view is hard to substantiate, but it is certainly not impossible, since the assumption that at least one Jew, Moses, had been "named god" of Israel, and that he had been quasi-divine or become immortal is found in a number of early Jewish writings: Artapanus asserts that Moses was "deemed worthy of honour equal to the gods," and Philo, presumably inspired by the marvellous circumstances associated with Moses' death as described in Deuteronomy, writes of him that "the time came when he had to make his pilgrimage from earth to heaven, and leave this mortal life for immortality"; Josephus, presumably aware of this tradition, and keen to restate Moses' humanity, asserts that Moses "has written of himself in the sacred books that he died, for fear that they should dare to say that, because of his surpassing virtue, he had returned to the deity."

Eight manuscripts survive from Cave 4 at Qumran, along with small fragments from Cave 11 and a large fragment from Masada, of the *Songs of the Sabbath Sacrifice*, the angelic praises of God assigned to the Sabbaths for the first quarter of the solar year:

> The [cheru]bim prostrate themselves before Him and bless. As they rise, a whispered voice of gods [is heard], and there is a roar of praise. When they drop their wings, there is a [whispere]d voice of gods. They bless the image of the throne-chariot above the vault of the cherubim, [and] they praise [the majes]ty of the luminous firmament beneath His seat of glory. When the wheels advance, angels of holiness come and go. From between His glorious wheels, there is as it were a fiery vision of most holy spirits. Around them is the appearance of rivulets of fire in the likeness of electrum.

One angel in particular, Melchizedek, who is identified with the archangel Michael, is portrayed as presiding over the final judgement: "[And it will be proclaimed at] the end of days concerning the captives as [He said, 'To proclaim liberty to the captives.' Its interpretation is that He] will assign them to the inheritance of Melchizedek; f[or He will cast] their [lot] amid the po[rtions of Melchize]dek, who will return them there and will proclaim to them liberty, forgiving them [the wrong-doings] of all their iniquities."[30]

Not all these celestial beings are by nature kindly to humanity. There are references to specific malign figures in the Hebrew Bible, such as Lilith, and in the Septuagint translation of the Bible the Hebrew *shedim* was rendered into Greek as *daimonia*, "demons." Such demons came to be thought of as a distinct order of malign spirits at war with the forces of God. The idea emerges most clearly in the Greek manuscripts of the *Testaments of the Twelve Patriarchs*, but this may not reflect precisely the world-view of the author of the original Jewish text of the *Testaments*, since the Greek version shows signs of considerable rewriting by its later Christian editor. Similar ideas emerge within the Dead Sea scrolls in the sectarian literature itself, as in the *Community Rule*: "All the children of righteousness are ruled by the Prince of Light and walk in the ways of light, but all the children of injustice are ruled by the Angel of Darkness and walk in the ways of darkness. The Angel of Darkness leads all the children of righteousness astray, and until his end, all their sin, iniquities, wickedness, and all their unlawful deeds are caused by his dominion in accordance with the mysteries of God." Both the Dead Sea sectarians and other Jews sometimes described these forces of darkness as led by a specific being of particular malevolence, in the scrolls generally Melkiresha or Belial, "the worthless one," and, in the book of *Jubilees*, Mastema. *Jubilees* indeed provides a creation myth to explain Mastema's power as granted to him by God in the time of Noah, when Noah prayed that the polluted demons, which began to lead astray the children of his sons, be locked away.

> And the chief of the spirits, Mastema, came and said, "O Lord, Creator, let some of them remain before me, and let them obey my voice. And let them do everything which I tell them, for if some are not left for me, I will not be able to exercise the authority of my will among the children of men because they are [destined] for corruption and to be led astray before my judgement because the evil of the sons of men is great." And he said, "Let a tenth of them remain before him, but let nine parts go down into the place of punishment."

The world is thus full of demons, only a few of them specifically identified, like Asmodeus, the evil spirit who strangled the seven husbands of Sara, the daughter of Raguel, according to the book of Tobit.[31]

Demonic possession is not in fact widely attested in extant Jewish texts as an explanation of illness, but Josephus, in praising the wisdom of Solomon, described an exorcism he had himself witnessed:

> God granted him [Solomon] knowledge of the art used against demons for the benefit and healing of men. He also composed incantations by which illnesses are relieved, and left behind forms of exorcisms with which those possessed by demons drive them out, never to return. And this kind of treatment is of very great power among us to this day, for I have seen a certain Eleazar, a countryman of mine, in the presence of Vespasian, his sons, tribunes and a number of other soldiers, free those possessed by these demons, and this was the manner of the cure: he put

to the nose of the possessed man a ring which had under its seal one of the roots prescribed by Solomon, and then, as the man smelled it, drew out the demon through his nostrils, and, when the man at once fell down, adjured the demon never to come back into him, speaking Solomon's name and reciting the incantations which Solomon had composed. Then, wishing to convince the bystanders and prove to them that he had this power, Eleazar placed a cup or foot-basin full of water a little way off and commanded the demon, as it went out of the man, to overturn it and make known to the spectators that he had left the man. And when this was done, the understanding and wisdom of Solomon were clearly revealed.

Similar exorcisms are attributed in early Christian literature both to Jesus and to the apostles. The procedure is taken so much for granted by the author of Acts that the only issue raised in the exorcisms described was the authority of the exorcist, which may be insufficient to deal with the demon: "Then certain of the wandering Jews, exorcists, took upon them to call over them which had evil spirits the name of the Lord Jesus, saying, 'I adjure you by Jesus whom Paul proclaims.' And there were seven sons of one Sceva, a Jew, and chief priest, who did so. And the evil spirit answered and said, 'Jesus I know, and Paul I know; but who are you?' "[32]

A modified dualism thus pervades much of Jewish understanding of the world in this period, but it is a qualified dualism. The word *satan*, to mean "accuser," appears a number of times in the Hebrew Bible, and the "satan" is responsible for the testing of Job, but Satan starts to appear regularly as a personal name of a demon only in the late Second Temple period, and even then the name is used less often than Belial, Mastema and others. In the Babylonian Talmud, Satan is sometimes just the evil inclination which infects humanity, although the notion that the ram's horn is sounded at the New Year to confuse Satan suggests a more concrete concept of a demonic power. No other Jewish texts give Satan the prominence which he is accorded in the New Testament, where he is mentioned by name thirty-five times. In all the Jewish texts it is made clear, wherever the origins of Satan are discussed (which is not often), that he, like the other demons, is the creation of God, and that, ultimately, his fight against God will end in defeat and subjection: he will be chained by God's holy spirit and cast into a consuming fire.[33]

This assumption that one benevolent power will always ultimately prevail is what most distinguishes the Jewish perspective on the cosmos from the Romans. Hence for Jews the natural world was inherently excellent because God has a permanent and direct responsibility for it. On the sixth day of the creation, "God saw everything that he had made, and, behold, it was very good." After the flood in the time of Noah, God had made a covenant with the world: "While the earth remains, seed-time and harvest, and cold and heat, and summer and winter, and day and night shall not cease." In the words of the Psalmist, "the heavens declare the glory of God, and the firmament proclaims his handiwork." The role of the creator as artisan of the world was important also for Cicero and Seneca, as it had been for Plato, but for most pagan Romans the wonders of nature provided evidence not of an overall design but of the activities of individual deities, such as Volcanus; worshipped at Rome from early in the history of the city, he was the god of destructive, devouring fire, whose presence, as Strabo noted in the time of Augustus, was particularly felt near the brooding presence of Mount Vesuvius, which was to erupt so disastrously in 79 CE.[34] On the other hand, although explanations in terms of intervention by a specific divinity could be given for any natural phenomenon, Romans, unlike Jews, sometimes also sought alternative scientific explanations which might exclude direct divine action. In the second century CE the illustrious medical writer Galen, discussing the nature of eyelashes, explicitly and correctly contrasted his own opinion (which he shared with "Plato and the other Greeks who follow the right method in natural science") with "the position taken by Moses," that God can, and does, do the impossible: "for the latter it seems enough to say that God simply willed the arrangement of matter and it was presently arranged in due order; for he believes everything to be possible with God, even should he wish to make a bull or a horse out of ashes. We however do not hold this; we say that certain things are impossible by nature and that God does not even attempt such things at all but that he chooses the best out of the possibilities of becoming." The whole of the sixth book of Seneca's *Natural Questions* was devoted to scientific speculation about the causes of earth tremors, prompted by an earthquake which had struck Pompeii and the rest of Campania in 62 CE, some seventeen years before the eruption of Vesuvius that was to destroy the city and much of the surrounding region. Seneca's basic conclusion was the need for resignation in the face of disaster, and the inevitability of death.

We are in error if we believe that any part of the world is exempt and safe from this danger [of an earthquake]. All regions lie under the same laws: nature has not created anything in such a way that it is immobile . . . It will be profitable also to keep in mind that gods cause none of these things and that neither heaven nor earth is overturned by the wrath of divinities. These phenomena have causes of their own; they do not rage on command but are disturbed by certain defects, just as our bodies are.[35]

Neither Romans nor Jews had much interest in the aesthetic qualities of natural landscapes, beyond awe at the size of mountains and the force of rushing rivers. The Roman taste for bucolic poetry, such as Vergil's *Eclogues* (composed in the late 40s BCE) and the seven pastorals written by Calpurnius Siculus in the time of Nero, reveals a nostalgia within the urban elite for a world in a managed countryside of natural simplicity. In practical terms in Rome, this appreciation of tamed nature was manifested in a passion for formal gardens, whether near the centre of a city, like the famed gardens of Maecenas on the Esquiline in the city itself, or as organized "natural" space in the grounds of a villa in the countryside, as in Hadrian's villa in Tivoli. "Natural" features such as streams, hills and caves were reshaped or created, with much use of water and shade to create a pleasant ambience. Topiary, flower planting, carefully sited sculptures and other stimuli to the senses were all part of a leisured, urban appreciation of the delights of an imagined rural life. This aesthetic appreciation of the delights of managed nature was ultimately derived by Romans, through the influence of Hellenistic practices, from the great ritual and royal gardens of the ancient Near East, so it is notable that similar tastes do not seem to have developed to the same extent within Jewish culture, which was equally (or more) open to the same influences. Jews speculated on the primordial garden of Eden, but only as a place of extraordinary fertility. Josephus knew, from the account by the Babylonian historian Berossos, about the hanging gardens of Babylon, constructed by Nebuchadrezzar from "lofty stone terraces, in which he closely reproduced mountain scenery, completing the resemblance by planting them with all manner of trees . . . because his wife, having been brought up in Media, had a passion for mountain surroundings," but Jews seem to have made no attempt to emulate such horticultural feats. The lawns, groves, carefully laid-out walks and abundant use of water for streams, ponds and fountains in Herod's palace show that he had picked up the Roman taste for ornamental gardens and could afford to indulge it even in the restricted space, and with the restricted water supply, of Jerusalem, but the garden of Gethsemane, where Jesus was arrested, was a kitchen garden or an orchard. For Jews, delight in nature was generally limited to appreciation of the useful: the ploughed field, the dressed vine or the carefully tended fig tree.[36]

But the greatest difference between Jewish and Roman attitudes to nature derives from the Jewish view that God cares deeply for the health of the land of Israel. Romans were as aware as Jews of the need for agricultural land to be allowed periodically to rest if it was to remain productive, and detailed practical discussions of fallowing and rotation of crops, and the relation of such practices to yield, are to be found in Roman agrarian writers. But such Roman practices have little ideologically in common with the concept of the sabbatical year in the land of Israel as espoused by Jews. Every seventh year "the land must keep a Sabbath to the Lord . . . for the land is Mine; for you are strangers and sojourners with me." Whatever practical reasons there may originally have been for this Jewish custom, by the first century CE Jews believed that its justification was religious and that the land of Israel, divinely owned, has the right to rest just as does the people of Israel. That Jews observed the sabbatical year was known to Julius Caesar, who, as we have seen, exempted them from tax in those years for this reason, although in later years Tacitus, uncharitably, attributed the practice not to piety but to sloth.[37]

Nor do Jews seem to have been sentimental about the animal world. According to Genesis, animals had been provided for humans to use. Such use had to be compassionate: a series of stories and rulings in the Hebrew Bible restrict cruelty to animals, most dramatically when Balaam's ass complained with justification at being beaten: "What have I done to you, that you have beaten me those three times? . . . Am I not your ass, upon which you have ridden all your life long to this day?" According to one view, expressed in the Babylonian Talmud, some actions generally forbidden on the Sabbath are permitted when their purpose is to relieve the pain of animals: "Rab Judah said in Rab's name: 'If an animal falls into a dyke, one brings pillows and bedding and places them under it, and if it ascends it ascends.' " However, most of the domestic animals about which Jewish legal or ethical literature makes mention are beasts of burden or animals reared for food. Jews do not seem to have had any strong conception of animals as pets or companions. Cats were treated as wild (in contrast to their status as sacred animals in contemporary Egyptian society) and dogs as sheepdogs and guard dogs only; an interesting possible exception is the dog which, according to the book of Tobit, accompanied the hero Tobias to the land of Media and back, perhaps to protect him on his travels. The biblical requirement to let the mother bird go before taking her young from the nest, "that you may prolong your days," may treat the feelings of the parent bird anthropomorphically, but it more probably reflects a less sentimental, but more fundamental, concept that the divine treatment of humans accords with treatment of animals by humans.[38]

Roman attitudes to animals seem to have been both more cruel and more sentimental. There was an intense philosophical debate about whether animals have reason and (therefore) need to be justly treated. The conclusion reached by Aristotle and followed in the Roman world by Epicureans and Stoics was negative, and Romans took great pleasure from witnessing the pain and death of animals of all kinds. For the leisured classes, country sports, such as the hunting of boars, stags, foxes and hares, were popular, and the very rich, like the emperor Hadrian, engaged in big game hunting for lions and bears. Ordinary Romans could not afford to participate in such activities, but they could watch the splendid wild-beast fights in the amphitheatres, in which large numbers of exotic animals were killed. Cicero recorded one occasion in 55 BCE when the cries of agony from the elephants being stabbed to death with spears aroused a certain sympathy from the spectators, "and a feeling that there was a kind of fellowship between that huge beast and the human race," but such compassion was very rare—if it had been more common, the aristocrats who courted popularity by spending huge sums arranging these public exhibitions of slaughter would have saved themselves the expense. The only Jew in the late Second Temple period known to have shared this Roman passion for hunting was Herod the Great. Herod was "always foremost in the chase, in which he distinguished himself above all by his skill in horsemanship. On one occasion he brought down forty wild beasts in one day: for the country breeds boars and, even more, stags and wild asses." Josephus' reference to boars and asses makes abundantly clear, if it was needed, that this aspect of Herod's persona was not intended to highlight his Jewish side. The two great hunters in the Hebrew Bible were Nimrod and Esau, both treated in

Jewish tradition as non-Jews. The hunting envisaged in the Mishnah was not the aristocratic sport in which Herod indulged but the more mundane procedure of trapping animals with nets for food: since, in order to be fit to be eaten by Jews, the animal would have to be ritually slaughtered, the hunting of animals with bows and spears in the Roman style would be useless for that purpose.[39]

Roman delight in hunting and watching the spectacular deaths of wild beasts proved compatible with an appreciation of tame animals as companions. Romans, like Jews, kept dogs to guard property, but they also kept dogs for hunting and as pets for which, according to the epitaphs some composed, they could harbour real affection: "Drenched with tears have I borne you, our little puppy . . . Now, Patricus [?], you will not any more give me a thousand kisses nor will you be able to lie happy on my neck . . ." The younger Seneca and the elder Pliny both assumed that readers of their writings would be acquainted with cats living as part of a household. People kept monkeys, snakes and many kinds of bird, particularly those which could be taught to talk. The elder Pliny records that "Claudius Caesar's consort Agrippina had a thrush which mimicked what people said, which was unprecedented. At the time when I was recording these cases, the young princes [Britannicus and Nero] had a starling and also nightingales that were actually trained to talk Greek and Latin, and moreover practised diligently and spoke new phrases every day, in still longer sentences." Catullus writes of the deep emotion exhibited by his Lesbia for her sparrow. The care of such tame animals was the perfect example of nature brought under the control of man.[40]

## MORALITIES

PERHAPS THE MOST striking contrast between Jewish and Roman views of the world lay in their understanding of the roots of morality. Some thoughtful Romans found ways to justify their conservative moral instincts from the teachings of the Hellenistic philosophical schools, which rarely prescribed specific patterns of behaviour but which encouraged ethical attitudes to ordinary life, reinforcing standard prejudices by different means. Thus Epicureans, despite an undeserved reputation for encouraging hedonism, based on Epicurus' dictum that "pleasure is the beginning and end of living happily," could in practice adopt a quite ascetic lifestyle:

since seeking pleasure is itself painful, the best to be hoped for is the avoidance of pain or freedom from disturbance. Logically such a philosophy should have encouraged avoidance of public life, as Epicurus had indeed advocated, but some Epicureans compromised their beliefs enough to stand for office: Josephus writes of a senator in the time of Gaius that "he had gone through nearly all the magistracies, but in other respects was an Epicurean and therefore was one who practised a life free from business." It may be that the need for such compromise by those elite Romans who sought public recognition was a prime cause of the decline in popularity of Epicureanism in the early empire. In the late Republic the poet Lucretius had made a powerful plea for Epicurean doctrines in his great Latin poem *On the Nature of Things*, and his slightly older contemporary Philodemus, originally from Gadara in Syria (just south of the south-east corner of the Sea of Galilee), had popularized Epicurean ideas among young Roman aristocrats in the circle of Lucius Calpurnius Piso Caesoninus, the consul of 58 BCE. Philodemus' philosophical writings were recovered in the eighteenth century on about a thousand papyrus scrolls that were found, charred but legible, in the library of a villa in Herculaneum, probably once owned by Piso, which was destroyed in the eruption of Vesuvius in 79 CE. Perhaps such doctrines of disengagement appealed particularly to the troubled generation of aristocrats who reached manhood in the turmoil of the last years of the Republic, when moral certainties in political life were so elusive. At any rate, professions of Epicurean morality are harder to find in the ensuing centuries.[41]

Much more common in the first century CE, among those who professed a philosophical allegiance of any kind, was Stoicism, a school which, as we saw in Chapter 2, had originated in Athens at the same time as Epicureanism. Stoic teachings had been brought to Rome by a series of Greek philosophers from the mid-second century BCE. As a result, most surviving Stoic literature is a product of the first two centuries CE and most of it was written by philosophers with a close connection to Rome, notably the younger Seneca and, a century later, the emperor Marcus Aurelius. The teachings of Gaius Musonius Rufus, a rich gentleman originally from Volsinii (modern Orvieto, in Etruria), who flourished in the 60s and 70s CE, and of his pupil Epictetus, an ex-slave from Phrygia who had once belonged to Nero's freedman Epaphroditus, are known only through records kept by their students. Many of the discourses of Epictetus were published by one particularly distinguished student, the historian and senator Arrian, who had fallen under his spell. The moral stature of both teachers was magnified by the sufferings they had incurred as a result of their devotion to philosophy, since both were required to endure exile from Rome. Epictetus proved a magnet for enthusiasts when he withdrew from Rome to Nicopolis on the Adriatic following the expulsion of philosophers from Rome by Domitian. The essence of the Stoic view of ethics was the assertion that virtue, moral perfection, belongs in a class of its own; that to be virtuous is to be happy; and that only what is morally perfect can be truly good. All other apparent "goods," such as wealth and pleasures, are not really good, because they can be used for bad purposes. Knowing what is always morally right requires wisdom, so the virtuous man must be wise. Most things normally considered either good or bad are in fact morally indifferent, and do not really impinge either on the virtue of the wise man or on his happiness. On the other hand, some morally indifferent characteristics (health and wealth) were preferable to others (illness and poverty), so the pursuit of the preferable was philosophically justified, provided that this was recognized as ultimately of little importance compared to the pursuit of the morally good. Such doctrine was perfectly suited to comfort a man like Seneca, the ambitious and immensely wealthy tutor and adviser of the emperor who yet knew, all too clearly, how such fortunes might crumble:

> Place me in the most sumptuous home, where gold and silver are in common use: I shall not think well of myself on account of that; they may be in my house, but they are not in me. Remove me to the Sublician Bridge and set me among the destitute: I shall not despise myself because I am seated among those who stretch out their hand for alms. If a man does not lack the power to die, what does he care if he lacks a piece of bread? But what follows from this? I still prefer that splendid home to the Bridge . . .[42]

The philosophical contradictions inherent in a life devoted to self-advancement, the pursuit of glory, wealth and power, while preaching the unimportance of such values, were thrown into stark relief by the rather more clear-cut and uncompromising ethics of Cynics, like Seneca's friend Demetrius, exiled from Rome, first by Nero and then, after his temporary return, by Vespasian, for speaking his mind. Cynics preached that life should be "lived according to nature," which, for those who carried out the doctrine wholeheartedly, involved a total disdain for all social norms, and a disregard for material possessions beyond the bare minimum. All social, sexual and racial distractions were worthless, as were power, authority, art and intellectual speculation. Unsurprisingly, those who tried to live according to such beliefs were sometimes treated by the authorities as dangerous anarchists, but attitudes were ambivalent. Cynic diatribes against conventional behaviour had a profound influence on many who did not consider themselves to be Cynics, such as the younger Seneca himself or Plutarch, and Cynic ideas surface frequently in Roman satire. Many who lived a Cynic lifestyle, like the itinerant Peregrinus whose career and spectacular suicide at the Olympic games were mocked by Lucian, saw themselves, and were seen by others, as outside normal society.[43]

In all this discussion of ethics and restraint of passions and pleasures, religion played little part. It was not that the gods were believed to be uninterested in what humans did—only Epicureans thought that, and they were often unfairly characterized as atheists as a result. Nor was there any lack of commitment to worship of the gods. On the contrary, religious practices were woven into the fabric of the life of every Roman. The gods in general were assumed to approve of good behaviour and to be angry at immorality. But it was all very vague, not least because the gods had not laid down any very specific rules for human behaviour, and there was a curious disjunction between religious practices and moral discourse. No one preached a sermon or read an improving text when Romans visited shrines and altars to make or watch sacrifices and bring offerings. Not all Romans were happy about this state of affairs. A certain Valerius Maximus, who composed during the reign of Tiberius a sententious handbook of illustrative examples of "memorable deeds and sayings," puts forward rather emotionally the view that religious issues affect all aspects of life. The actions he advocates for emulation are approved because they share characteristics with the gods, especially the divinities who were essentially deified abstractions such as *Amicitia*, Friendship; and the actions he deprecates had been punished by the gods over the centuries. Epictetus, who held the Stoic view that there is a divine force which shapes and constitutes all things, including man, had to impress upon his students the connection between this abstract notion and the cultic actions they performed every day:

Why do you not know whence you have come? When you eat will you not remember who you are that is eating and whom you are nourishing? When you indulge in intercourse with a woman, who is doing that? When you mix in company, when you take exercise, when you engage in conversation? Do you not know that you are nourishing God, exercising God? You carry God around with you, miserable creature, and do not know it. Do you think I mean some god outside you, a god made of silver or gold? It is within yourself that you carry him, and do not perceive that you are defiling him with your unclean thoughts and filthy actions. In the presence of an image of God you would not dare to do any of those things you now do, but in the presence of God himself within you, who watches and hears all, are you not ashamed to be thinking and doing such things as these, insensible of your own nature and earning the wrath of God?

The passion driving Epictetus' discourse arose precisely from the fact that such a concept of the divine was not obvious to those he addressed, for whom, as for all ordinary Romans, the point of worship was less the reinforcement of human morality than a simple desire to give to the gods their due.[44]

By contrast, the God of Israel had laid down for Jews exactly how they should live: relations between man and man as well as between man and God. As Josephus expresses the special nature of the Torah in his apologetic treatise *Against Apion*, the very nature of Moses' legislation is "far more useful than any other; for he did not make piety a part of virtue, but the various virtues—I mean justice, temperance, fortitude and mutual harmony in all things between the members of the community—parts of piety. Piety governs all our actions and occupations and speech; none of these things did our lawgiver leave unexamined or indeterminate." As far back as the fourth century BCE the philosopher Theophrastus, a disciple of Aristotle, had praised the Jews as "philosophers by race." Thus in the eyes of others Judaism was sometimes viewed as a philosophy, a way of life on a par with Stoicism, Epicureanism or Cynicism, as much as a form of piety, but for Jews the good life consisted in doing what God required, and to discover what that meant in practice it was, in principle, only necessary to know what was written in sacred scripture and how it should correctly be interpreted. In practice, of course, interpretation varied widely, hence the emergence of philosophical groupings within the philosophy of Judaism—Pharisees, Sadducees, Essenes and others. Many of the teachings of these Jewish philosophies bear some relation to those of contemporary Greeks and Romans. Josephus refers to the Pharisees as "a sect having points of resemblance to that which the Greeks call the Stoic school," and the Essenes as "a group which follows a way of life taught to the Greeks by Pythagoras." He never quite calls Sadducees "Epicureans," but he does assert of Sadducees that "they place God outside doing or seeing anything bad" and that "they totally do away with fate," saying that men have complete free will, notions very close to the doctrines of the Epicureans who, as he writes elsewhere (but, in this case, with explicit disapproval), "exclude providence from life and do not believe that God governs its affairs."[45]

There is no particular reason to doubt that the moral issues disputed by the Hellenistic philosophical schools were also discussed by Jews in Jerusalem. After all, the Epicurean Philodemus, whose teachings were so influential in late-Republican Rome, came originally from Gadara just across the lake from Galilee, and the great Alexandrian Jewish philosopher Philo, praised by Josephus for his philosophical expertise, interpreted the Torah entirely through the lens of Platonic and Stoic thought. But Philo's writings also make abundantly clear how Jewish ethics differed from those of Greeks and Romans, because everything in the voluminous corpus of his surviving writings is based on the text of the Bible, and specifically the Pentateuch. Jewish morality was based on divine instructions, the word of God.[46]

As Josephus stresses, no Jew could profess ignorance of what God required for moral behaviour, because the institution of the synagogue existed to ensure their instruction:

> For ignorance he [Moses] left no pretext. He appointed the law to be the most excellent and necessary form of instruction, ordaining, not that it should be heard once for all or twice or often, but that every week [Jews] should desert their other occupations and assemble to listen to the law and to obtain a thorough and accurate knowledge of it . . . Should anyone of our nation be questioned about the laws, he would repeat them all more readily than his own name. The result, then, of our thorough grounding in the laws from the first dawn of intelligence is

that we have them, as it were, engraven on our souls. A transgressor is a rarity; evasion of punishment by excuses an impossibility.

Josephus exaggerates of course, but the essence of his claim about the unique nature of Jews' relationship to their law was true enough. The synagogue as an institution for mass moral education was indeed unique in the Roman world, not least because the closest parallels, the philosophical schools, generally confined their clientele to the intellectual elite. For Jews in the land of Israel as much as the diaspora, the local synagogue was the main place to which they went for religious edification. It was not a holy place, and worship in the form of sacrifices (as in the Jerusalem Temple) could not be performed there, but it did provide an opportunity for communal prayer and, above all, for teaching. What encouraged Jews to "philosophize on the seventh days the ancestral philosophy, dedicating that time to the acquiring of knowledge and study about nature" in "schools of prudence and courage and temperance and justice and also of piety, holiness and every virtue by which duties to God and men are discerned and rightly performed" (as Philo writes), was not an abstract interest in the philosophical underpinnings of life, nor, as in Roman philosophical schools, the pursuit of the nature of happiness or virtue for its own sake, but a very real need to know what behaviour was required of them by God if they were properly to fulfil their side of the covenant agreed by God and Israel on Mount Sinai.[47]

Religion was the justification for every aspect of Jewish morality, but most Jews believed that moral behaviour was the result of a partnership between God and men. The Essenes, according to Josephus, attributed everything to the will of God, while the Sadducees "do away with fate altogether." But the stance of the Pharisees, shared also by later rabbis as well as by Stoics, seems to have been more common: they "attribute everything to Fate and to God; they hold that to act rightly or otherwise rests, indeed, for the most part with men, but that in each action Fate cooperates." In a wisdom saying attributed by the Mishnah to Rabbi Akiva, the paradox is stated even more bluntly: "All is foreseen, and [yet] free will is given." For Jews, the expulsion of Adam and Eve from Eden had marked the transition of humankind from childhood innocence to adult responsibility. Most Jews in this period seem to have lacked any notion of original sin and a fall from grace such as was to be developed in early Christianity.

On the contrary, the covenant between God and Israel ensured that God would show mercy to his erring people like an indulgent husband to a faithless wife, as portrayed by the suffering prophet Hosea: "Then said the Lord to me, 'Go again, love a woman beloved of a paramour and an adulteress, according to the love of the Lord toward the children of Israel, though they turn to other gods.' " As in a marriage, Israel was bound to keep her side of the covenant, but she could expect forgiveness when she sinned—indeed, forgiveness was guaranteed to the truly penitent. But it must be true penitence:

> The sin offering and the unconditional guilt offering effect atonement. Death and the Day of Atonement effect atonement if they are with repentance. Repentance effects atonement for lesser transgressions against both positive and negative commands; and for greater transgressions it suspends judgement until the Day of Atonement comes and effects atonement. If a man says, "I will sin and repent, and sin [again] and repent," he will be given no chance to repent. "I will sin and the Day of Atonement will effect atonement," then the Day of Atonement effects no atonement. For transgressions that are between man and God, the Day of Atonement effects atonement, but for transgressions that are between a man and his fellow, the Day of Atonement effects atonement only if he has appeased his fellow.[48]

The whole of this moral framework of guilt, repentance and divine forgiveness was alien to the Roman moral discourse of honour and shame.

# CHAPTER SEVEN

# LIFESTYLES

S O LONG AS neither side tried to impose their views on the other, the contrast between Jewish and Roman perspectives on the world was unlikely to create friction, but more difficult to ignore was the way that people lived every day. Small divergences in dress or cuisine can sometimes mark a major divide between communities. How different were the lifestyles of the inhabitants of Jerusalem and Rome?

It would be too crude to characterize the contrast between Jews and Romans as a comparison between libertarianism and puritanism, but neither would the caricature be wholly wide of the mark, even at the basic level of the way that they treated their bodies and bodily functions, and especially in attitudes to nudity, male and female.

In Greek cities in the classical period fit young male citizens had been idealized as the defenders of the state, and gymnasiums were instituted as places of exercise to prepare them for military service, but the professionalization of the Roman army in the early empire allowed most Roman men to avoid such exertions. As a result, body images for men could evolve in quite different ways. Both literary texts and portrait conventions sometimes harked back to an ideal of the peasant farmer's tough body in archaic times—hence the stern features of the emperor Nerva—but weather-beaten features and strong muscle could also easily be taken as evidence of rustic or servile occupation, and some emperors opted instead for a softer image. Nero presented himself as a plump epicure, smooth-skinned and hairless, the unashamed product of pampered leisure, although trying to maintain a youthful look might be construed as dangerous evidence of pathic homosexual leanings, and such rumours did indeed circulate about

Nero. Among those who favoured the pampered look in imitation of the effete luxury believed to have been normal in the courts of the Ptolemies in Alexandria, there was no shame in being overweight. As in eighteenth-century Britain, corpulence could be flaunted as a sign of social prestige, or at least of wealth.[1]

Romans were unselfconscious about male nudity, displayed most conspicuously at the communal baths, a form of recreation which attracted all sections of society. It was possible to honour an emperor by depicting him nude in heroic pose, although some emperors, notably Commodus at the end of the second century CE, seem to have encouraged depictions of their unclothed form more than others (in his case, he wanted to be seen as Hercules). Surviving wall paintings, mosaics and statues from Pompeii reveal a society unabashed in the portrayal of phalluses and sexual intercourse: anyone entering the home of one wealthy family was confronted by a statue of a youth whose erect phallus operated as a fountain. There is no way to be certain how Roman women reacted to this overt celebration of male sexuality, but they showed sexual interest in male gladiators, whose athletic, muscled bodies attracted their admiration. Roman images of ideal female bodies are known only from a male perspective: statues of nude women generally depict them as young and slim, that is, as nubile. Notions of feminine beauty seem to have been adopted wholesale from the Hellenistic world, along with conventions in its depiction, such as the absence of body hair—in the third century CE a tombstone of a freedwoman from Perugia, in praising her (perhaps not wholly seriously) for her perfect appearance, noted that, "beautiful with her kindly body, she bore her limbs smooth; everywhere she had a hair, it was sought out." Erotic wall paintings in Pompeii give an idea of the ideal female form in the sexual imaginations of men. If women themselves would have preferred to become more muscled, there is no evidence for it. What is clear is that many Roman women were as unabashed in displaying themselves naked as men. It was possible to go to women-only baths, but mixed establishments, in which men and women stripped together, became increasingly common from the early first century CE. As the Christian author Clement of Alexandria complains in the late second century: "The baths are open for men and women; there they strip for lust."[2]

All in all, the Roman attitude to the body was exceptionally relaxed. There were indeed sexual activities which might be deemed to demean one or other of the participants, but nothing was wholly ruled out. Romans did have very clear notions of sexual boundaries, but these were boundaries that could be transgressed, particularly for sexual pleasure (as by Nero, who was alleged both to have castrated a boy and tried to "transfigure him into a woman's nature" in order to marry him "with all the usual ceremonies," and to have himself taken the woman's role in a second "marriage" with one of his freedmen), even if such behaviour elicited disapproval from the more conservative: accusations of acting like a woman were part of the common currency of invective among the male Roman elite, and Seneca complained that in his day women were suffering from hair loss and gout, "male diseases," because they behaved like men, staying up too late, drinking too much, wrestling with men and taking an active role in sexual intercourse. Such intercourse was at least normally indulged in private. Other natural functions took place quite publicly. Bath houses commonly housed latrines—benches with holes over drains—for customers to use. Large urinal pots stood at the street corners; their contents were used in textile production. Romans show no trace of any notion that excrement, urine, menstrual blood, semen or any other bodily effluent might in any way pollute.[3]

The attitudes of Jews to their bodies could not have been more different. The concept of pollution was much discussed already in the Pentateuch. There and in some other parts of the Hebrew Bible, purity was considered important primarily as a requirement for those, especially priests, entering the sanctuary for worship, a concept found also in the sacred laws of many Greek temples in the classical period. But by late Second Temple times the laws of purity and their significance had been much elaborated by those Jews who came to see physical purity as a powerful metaphor for spiritual purity. In the first century CE purity was an issue of major significance for Jews of many different backgrounds and religious persuasions.[4]

Among the main potential sources of pollution were the emission of some bodily fluids (semen or menstrual blood) or, as we have seen, contact with a human corpse, which was the most severe source of impurity. The significance of suffering pollution varied both from case to case and in the eyes of different Jews. In the biblical purity system it is generally assumed that there is nothing wrong or worrying about being impure. Such a state is both natural and unavoidable. Its only consequence is temporary exclusion from the sanctuary until appropriate purification has been undergone. However, in some postbiblical texts pollution was sometimes treated as intrinsically undesirable and avoidance of pollution as a moral act. It is hard to distinguish clearly in all such cases between metaphorical and practical uses of pollution language. References to purity and pollution permeate the sectarian texts found among the Dead Sea scrolls. Early rabbinic texts incorporate a complex and coherent purity system evolved in discussion and debate about minutiae whose details can be traced from one generation to the next over nearly two centuries. According to Josephus, emphasis on this aspect of Judaism was a particular characteristic of the Essenes: "They consider oil defiling, and anyone who accidentally comes in contact with it scours his person, for they make a point of keeping a dry skin and of always being dressed in white . . ." As we have seen in Chapter 4, they even treated excrement as a form of ritual pollution, unlike other Jews.[5]

The laws governing restrictions on food are enunciated in the Bible in contexts quite separate from the laws about bodily emissions and corpse pollution, but they enshrine the same view of the body as a fragile vessel to be preserved free of taint. The prohibited foodstuffs listed in Leviticus include camels, horses, pigs, eagles, owls, mice, lizards, snails and moles. There has been much scholarly discussion of the underlying rationale of these specific prohibitions, and the categories into which they are placed by the biblical authors: animals that are not cloven-footed or do not chew the cud, fish without fins and scales, most fowls "that creep, going on all four." Whatever the rationale of such taboos, there can be no doubt of their power, nor of their tendency, as a result, to expand far beyond the restrictions envisioned in the Bible.

At some point in the Second Temple period the often repeated biblical prohibition on seething a kid in its mother's milk was extended by many Jews to require avoidance of any mixture of meat with dairy products, with a few exceptions. The Mishnah says: "No flesh may be cooked in milk excepting the flesh of fish and locusts . . . It might be inferred that a bird, which is forbidden under the law of carrion, is forbidden to be seethed in milk, but the Bible says, 'In its mother's milk,' so a bird is excluded since it has no mother's milk." But, whatever doubts there may have been in the early third century, later rabbis were to rule clearly that mixtures of the flesh of fowls with milk were also forbidden.

The Mishnah refers to further prohibited foods: "These things of the gentiles are forbidden . . . milk which a gentile milked when no Israelite watched him; their bread and their oil . . . stewed or pickled vegetables into which it is their custom to put wine or vinegar; minced fish, or brine containing no fish." The prohibition of gentile olive oil is particularly significant because it was unrelated either to any biblical text or to any known pagan custom, and yet it seems to have been a taboo widely observed. According to Josephus, the Hellenistic king Seleucus Nicator gave a special privilege to the Jews in his kingdom "that those Jews who were unwilling to use foreign oil should receive a fixed sum of money from the gymnasiarchs to pay for their own kind of oil; and when in the present war [66–70] the people of Antioch proposed to revoke this privilege, Mucianus, who was then governor of Syria, maintained it." Josephus' attribution of this privilege to Seleucus Nicator, who ruled from 312 to 281 BCE, is suspect, because the historian liked to claim the earliest possible origin of all Jewish privileges, and in fact a later Hellenistic king may have been responsible; but it is clear at the least that Jewish objections to "foreign" oil were common in the Syrian diaspora by the mid-first century CE. Indeed, knowledge of the taboo provided an opportunity for John of Gischala to make a fortune for himself:

> With the avowed object of protecting all the Jews of Syria from the use of oil not supplied by their own countrymen, he sought and obtained permission to deliver it to them at the frontier. He then bought up that commodity, paying Tyrian coin of the value of four Attic drachms for four amphorae, and proceeded to sell half an amphora at the same price. As Galilee is a special home of the olive and the crop had been plentiful, John, enjoying a monopoly, by sending large quantities to districts in want of it, amassed an immense sum of money.

Perhaps the most remarkable feature of this particular taboo is the fact that it came to an end in the early third century CE. According to the passage in the Mishnah cited above, "Rabbi [Judah haNasi] and his court permitted the oil." The Mishnah provides reasons neither for the original taboo nor for its abrogation, and the rabbinic discussions in the following generations, recorded in the two Talmuds, express bafflement. The prohibition on using gentile oil had serious consequences, since oil was widely used for soap and lighting as well as for food, but it seems to have originated not in a religious ordinance but in shared instincts. Jews defined who they were partly by the way that they treated their bodies.[6]

Thus, although in the course of the Roman imperial period Jews were to develop a taste for baths in the Roman style, more important than such bathing for pleasure, and indeed for cleanliness, was bathing for purity. The surface of the body had to be cleansed of pollution. The Bible required those who were impure to immerse themselves in "living waters," a phrase that was taken by rabbis in the time of the Mishnah to mean either a river or sea or a bathing installation whose water supply came at least in part from rainwater. These same rabbinic texts reveal some debate about the precise size and design required for such purification to be deemed valid. The discovery of many stepped pools in Jerusalem close to the Temple, in Qumran, in Masada, and in many other sites where Jews lived in the first century CE, suggests that the rabbis were attempting, as often, to lay down rules for existing practices, determining to their own satisfaction and that of their followers when customary behaviour should be endorsed and when not. How much ritual washing was customary among diaspora Jews is more difficult to pin down, and may well have varied even more. According to the *Letter of Aristeas*, the pious Jews who produced the Septuagint "following the custom of all the Jews, washed their hands in the sea in the course of their prayers to God . . . as witness that they have done no evil, for all activity takes place by means of the hands." Such an explanation would make sense to gentile pagans: Pilate is said to have washed his hands to demonstrate his innocence of the death of Jesus.[7]

The Mishnah contains a story of a discussion between the great rabbinic sage Rabban Gamaliel, who lived in the late first century CE, and a gentile philosopher Proklos after they met accidentally in the baths of Aphrodite in Akko. In the baths both were naked, but before Gamaliel answered the philosopher's question he insisted that they went outside, presumably clothed, for "one does not make answer in the bath." Jews were self-conscious about nudity in a way that differentiated them strikingly from both Greeks and Romans. This kind of modesty (or prudery) was a characteristic common to much of the Near East, where in extant sculptures both males and females were typically portrayed wearing clothing. A number of rabbis are praised in the Talmuds for never having even looked at their own circumcised penises; it is a curious fact that male Jews assumed that the physical characteristic which most marked them out as Jews, circumcision, should be hidden from public view once the public performance of the operation on the baby boy was complete. On the other hand, the early rabbis had plenty to say about sex in the sense of the physical differences between men and women, because it was important to determine the sex of any Jewish individual in order to know which set of religious duties he or she should carry out. Hence detailed discussions about the nature and status of eunuchs, androgynes and persons of dubious sex: "The androgyne is in some things like to men and in some things like to women, and in some things like both to men and to women, and in some things like neither to men nor to women . . ."[8]

Provided that the purity of the body was protected, what the body was like does not seem to have been a matter of great concern to Jews. The defenders of Jerusalem in 70 CE presumably included some impressive-looking youths, for Josephus reports that in the disposal of prisoners after the fall of Jerusalem the "tallest and most handsome of the youth" were reserved for the triumphal procession in Rome, and he makes reference to other fighters of impressive strength, but there is no evidence that Jews believed in physical exercise for its own sake. Among the cultural traits adopted from the Hellenistic world, the gymnasium seems to have been assiduously avoided by Judaean Jews after it had become a symbol of alien culture in the propaganda surrounding the revolt of the Maccabees. In early rabbinic texts the ideal male is depicted as subservient to God, reliant on divine help for success and prepared to suffer martyrdom rather than fight like a warrior. Whether this passive male figure was a standard ideal in non-rabbinic Jewish circles is less clear, since it can hardly have been the image projected by the military commander Shimon bar Kosiba, whose tough qualities as the leader of the Judaean revolt of 132–5 made him a hero to many. In the three descriptions of individual physiques to which spiritual characteristics are attributed in the physiognomical fragments found among the Dead Sea scrolls, thick fingers, hairy thighs, fat cheeks, short toes and uneven teeth are associated with the "House of Darkness" (the forces of evil); black glowing eyes, gentle voice, long thin fingers, toes in alignment, smooth thighs and medium stature are associated with the "House of Light" (the forces of good).[9]

On Jewish notions of the perfect female body the sources are almost silent. The Mishnah presupposes that a woman's hair and breasts may be sexually alluring to men: when a suspected adulteress underwent the rite laid down in the book of Numbers to establish or refute her guilt, "a priest lays hold on her garments . . . so that he lays bare her bosom. And he loosens her hair. R. Judah says: 'If her bosom was comely, he did not lay it bare; if her hair was comely, he did not loosen it.' " How comeliness was defined, whether it was thought better for a woman to be fat or thin, and whether it would be thought a good thing for her to develop a muscular body, are quite unknown. The interest of the extant sources lies entirely in her function as marriage partner and bearer of children, and as the regular source, through menstruation, of a pollution which she had a religious duty to control in such a way that others did not become impure through contact with it.[10]

These contrasting attitudes to their bodies underlie the very different approach of Jews and Romans to the enjoyment of life. Among the primary pleasures in any culture are eating, drinking, sex and shopping (or, at least, expenditure on self-gratification and display), but cultures differ in the way these are experienced and the social restrictions on such enjoyment. Due allowance must be made for the shades of opinion within both societies and shifts in fashion over time—the Roman elite in particular underwent occasional bouts of self-disgust and self-imposed moderation, so that it may be wrong to take as typical the lurid stories about the aristocracy which found their way into the narratives of Tacitus and Suetonius, and the culture of the Roman plebs, manifested in entertainments such as popular games and songs and transmitted orally or through traditional practices passed down the generations, can only occasionally be glimpsed in the evidence which survives. But there does seem to have been a general acceptance of ostentatious consumerism in Rome which cannot be paralleled in Jerusalem outside the households of the Herodian family.

Richer Romans enjoyed eating exotic foods: Marcus Gavius Apicius, a resident of Minturnae on the southern edge of the Latian plain to the south of Rome, created in the early first century CE a "science of the eating house" and became so celebrated that his name was attached to later collections of recipes, like the extant cookery book, On Cooking Matters, composed some three centuries or more after his death. Apicius' specialty, and a major concern of Roman cookery, was the invention of powerful sauces to disguise the taste of the primary ingredients—luxury foods, brought into Rome from a distance, can rarely have been eaten fresh. The popularity of haute cuisine emerges from the complaints of moralists and satirists about excesses. In a letter to his friend Septicius, who had failed to turn up to a dinner party when invited, the younger Pliny contrasts his, evidently modest, dinner with the luxury that Septicius has enjoyed elsewhere. Pliny has dined off lettuce, snails, eggs, barley soup, sweet wine mixed with snow to cool it, with olives, beets, cucumbers, onions, "and a thousand other items no less sumptuous." But, writes Pliny, "you preferred the oysters, sows' wombs, and sea urchins . . . at someone else's house." Pliny's own meal—mainly vegetables of different kinds—was presumably closer to what ordinary Romans could afford, although it may well be that those with a little money attempted sometimes to emulate the banquets of the very rich, albeit with cheaper ingredients and only on special occasions. At any rate the practice of disguising the taste of food was widespread. As we have seen, there is much archaeological evidence for extensive trade in fermented fish sauce, a preserved pickle somewhat like modern Worcestershire sauce, poured on all kinds of food. It is a peculiarity of Mediterranean culture that this condiment, whose use was very widespread throughout the Roman period, seems to have fallen out of production altogether in the Middle Ages.[11]

For parties, the most common beverage was wine, of which the Roman world produced many different kinds, whose qualities were appreciated and disputed by connoisseurs. The Roman *convivium* was a formal occasion for eating as well as drinking, an opportunity for a host to demonstrate his largesse to his friends, who reclined, men and women together, on benches arranged in a square, with places allotted according to rank. At such parties drunkenness was not formally the main aim, but by the late Republic Romans had taken up many of the practices of Greek symposia, in which aristocratic males drank together as a bonding exercise, and feasts could degenerate into alcoholic disorder. The extent of Roman concern about alcoholism, against which Lucretius, Seneca and the elder Pliny all wrote, is evidence of a real social problem. Accusations of over-indulgence were levelled at many prominent politicians, most notably, from this period, Mark Antony (who wrote a pamphlet in his defence, entitled "Concerning his Drunkenness"), and (among emperors) Tiberius, Claudius and Vitellius. Nor was this only a masculine vice. Stories were told of Julia, daughter of Augustus, as a notorious tippler, in contrast to her father, who was "by nature most sparing in his use of wine."[12]

For adult male Romans, sex was another branch of physical recreation, aided by the uninhibited attitudes to the body and its natural functions graphically illustrated in the erotic pictures displayed in the public mixed baths at Pompeii. Romans did indeed have taboos against sexual relations with particular fellow citizens (of either sex), which could variously be branded as incest, adultery or *stuprum*, "debauchery" or "violation," but so long as the sexual partner was a slave almost anything could be envisaged. Roman males showed no embarrassment about any forms of phallic penetration, nor indeed about masturbation. The general assumption was that a man could enjoy such pleasures as much as he liked provided that he did not infringe the dignity of a Roman woman married to someone else, or that of a son of a Roman citizen. Recourse to female prostitutes was so much taken for granted that their earnings were taxed by the state, which also legislated to ensure that investment in brothels was secure. Slave prostitutes were commodities, the property of the brothel owner, who was usually, but not always, male. Jottings about an innkeeper's bill inscribed on a hotel wall in Aesernia in central Italy illustrate the matter-of-fact attitude of ordinary Romans: "You have one *sextarius* of wine, one *as* worth of bread, two *asses* worth of relishes . . . a girl for eight *asses*." Most prostitutes were slaves, although it was not unknown for a free citizen to prostitute his daughter or even his wife. A prostitute was not expected to arouse any feelings of affection, and all the literary sources take for granted that she was to be despised. Legally, she was characterized as *infamis*, "of ill repute."[13]

Roman attitudes to male homosexuals were equally pragmatic, provided that the submissive partner was of low rank, preferably a slave, despite the general assumption that homosexual love was a Greek practice, not known in the more austere Rome of distant antiquity. Poets imitated from Greek originals the motif of the beautiful boy on the verge of manhood as the object of male erotic desire, and in some circles life imitated art, most notably in the very public liaison, noted above, of the emperor Nero with his slave and the passion of Hadrian for his lover Antinous, whose premature death was commemorated in the foundation of a city, Antinoopolis, in Egypt. It is not incidental that both these emperors were philhellenes. Roman texts often assume that the best boys came from the province of Asia (modern Turkey), which was associated in the Roman mind with luxury and effeminacy. Romans had no notion of such sexual acts as sinful. Shame was possible only for an adult male citizen thought to have been the submissive partner in a homosexual relationship. The troops of Julius Caesar mocked the sex life of their commander, alleged to have been the paramour of King Nicomedes of Bithynia: "All the Gauls did Caesar vanquish, Nicomedes vanquished him; Lo! now Caesar rides in triumph, victor over all the Gauls; Nicomedes does not triumph, who subdued the conqueror." Octavian, the future emperor Augustus, was also in his youth taunted with effeminacy by his political enemies, and his arch-opponent Mark Antony alleged that he had pandered himself to Caesar, his great-uncle, in order to be adopted by him. Lucius Antonius, Mark Antony's brother, scoffed that "after sacrificing his honour to Caesar he [Octavian] had given himself to Aulus Hirtius in Spain for three hundred thousand sesterces, and that he used to singe his legs with a nut heated till it glowed, to make the hair grow softer."[14]

Almost all the evidence for sex as recreation comes from the point of view of adult males. All the more remarkable therefore is the poetry of Sulpicia, daughter of a senior senator and famous jurist of the late Republic. The surviving six short elegies composed by her to record her love affair with a certain "Cerinthus" of her own aristocratic background were preserved among the poems of Tibullus. They display both passion and sexual independence: "At last has come a love which, Rumour, it would shame me more to hide than to disclose to anyone. Won over by my Muse's prayers, the Cytherean goddess has brought and placed him in my bosom. What Venus promised she has fulfilled . . . Let all hear that I, who am worthy, have been with him, who is worthy." The court gossip transmitted by Tacitus about the love affairs of female members of the imperial family suggests that these women sought sexual freedom parallel to their menfolk, but that their behaviour elicited not wry acceptance but scandal, and condemnation for adultery or fornication. When in 19 CE, under Tiberius, the Senate passed further stringent decrees against adultery, a woman called Vistilia, belonging to a family that had held the praetorship, was deported from Rome because she "had advertised her availability to the aediles, in accordance with the custom of our ancestors who believed that immoral women would be sufficiently punished by the declaration itself." It may be that Vistilia needed the money from prostitution, but this seems unlikely, given her aristocratic background. Suetonius explicitly interprets such behaviour as a product of the sexual proclivities of the women involved: "Notorious women had begun to declare publicly that they were prostitutes, to avoid the punishment of the laws by giving up the privileges and rank of matrons." It was (perhaps) worthwhile losing social dignity if it allowed sexual freedom. About lesbian relationships Romans had little to say. The philosopher Seneca wrote with strong dislike about strapping women and their use of dildoes to satisfy other women, but it is presumably a by-product of the private nature of female pleasures in the ancient world that no female same-sex relationship is known to have been paraded in the court gossip of the whole early imperial period.[15]

A pleasure for women that was less subjected to moralizing censure was expenditure on fashion: clothes, hairstyles, cosmetics, were in Rome a feminine preserve, but men generally had other ways to pamper themselves. Petronius, described by Tacitus as "arbiter of elegance" at the court of Nero, was a specialist in refined hedonism in eating, drinking and sex: "To the emperor, nothing was smart and delicate unless Petronius had given it his approval . . . ," but (so far as is known) experimenting with dress was not for him an issue. In general, male dress changed little: the unwieldy toga, a semicircular piece of cloth wrapped like a blanket and held by a pin at the shoulder, was standard uniform for public affairs, a simple tunic for relaxation, with a cloak for warmth, although the satirist Martial could imagine a precocious teenager being berated by his slave *paedagogus* for his "Tyrian" clothes (presumably of a purple colour) and for putting ointment on his hair. Men did not usually use perfume or make-up; only at the risk of accusations of effeminacy did they depilate their legs or apply face masks to keep the skin looking young (according to Suetonius, the emperor Otho, who ruled briefly in 69 CE, applied moist bread to his face every day in order to keep his skin smooth and soft). More respectable, and more common, was the standard method of ensuring cleanliness in the baths. An attendant applied olive oil to the skin and then scraped off the oil and dirt with a strigil, a thin metal instrument of which many specimens have been found in excavations all over the Roman world. But a visit to the baths was not simply to get clean, or fit—no one did lengths of the pool. Bathing was self-pampering, a luxury frankly enjoyed throughout Roman society. Under the principate, entry to the public baths was free, so everyone could go, although purchase of the oils, perfumes and refreshments that completed the bathing experience could be expensive.[16]

Women, too, might suffer disapproval if they showed excessive concern for perfumes, cosmetics or dress, but they had far greater latitude in such matters than men. Female clothing evolved almost as little as male, but hairstyles for rich and fashionable women became in the early empire an area of innovation and sometimes rather bizarre experimentation. The standard female hairstyle, with braids drawn into a knot behind, was replaced by elaborate structures of hair piled on top of the head in varied fashions which evolved sufficiently rapidly to constitute a reliable criterion for modern scholars analysing the date of production of ancient statues. Women also spent much effort on cosmetics and jewellery. Ovid even contrived to compose a didactic poem on "Cosmetics for the Female Face," a catalogue of recipes: "Learn now how, when sleep has let go your tender limbs, your face can shine bright and fair . . . Whoever shall treat her face with such a prescription will shine smoother than her own mirror."[17]

Moralists' complaints about the luxurious prodigality of wastrel aristocrats illustrate the numerous other pleasures fashionable among the rich, and especially those in their youth. Cicero accused the debt-ridden aristocrat Catiline of seeking support for revolution in 63 BCE from among those who had wasted their ancestral fortunes on sex, gluttony and gambling, although gambling was technically illegal in Rome except during the Saturnalia in December. But the most effective way to spend a fortune was on property. Horace lamented in the time of Augustus: "Soon regal residences will leave only a few acres for the plough." Huge sums were spent on villas and their gardens, although literary texts that praise such expenditure rather than express disapproval are not to be found before the late first century CE, when the poet Statius praises the decorative use of exotic marbles and, a little later, the younger Pliny describes with pride the appointments of his own villas: his Laurentine place by the sea, close enough to Rome to reach after a day's business, had a particularly fine dining room jutting out into the spray and suites of rooms carefully designed to make the best of summer weather but to be cosy in winter; his house in the Tuscan hills was designed to make the best of a spectacular view and catch the sun in its south-facing colonnade. The commissioning of architects and interior designers seems generally to have been an expression of male taste rather than female. The ultimate in such conspicuous expenditure was built by Nero in the centre of Rome following the great fire of 64, when

> he made a palace extending all the way from the Palatine to the Esquiline, which at first he called the House of Passage, but when it

was burned shortly after its completion and rebuilt, the Golden House . . . Its vestibule was large enough to contain a colossal statue of the emperor a hundred and twenty feet high and it was so extensive that it had a triple colonnade a mile long. There was a pond too, like a sea, surrounded with buildings to represent cities, besides tracts of country, varied by tilled fields, vineyards, pastures and woods, with great numbers of wild and domestic animals. In the rest of the house all parts were overlaid with gold and adorned with gems and mother-of-pearl. There were dining rooms with fretted ceilings of ivory, whose panels could turn and shower down flowers and were fitted with pipes for sprinkling the guests with perfumes.[18]

Even moderately rich Romans expended effort and money on painting and sculpture in the early imperial period. The centre of Rome was full of statues commemorating the great figures of Rome's past: the erection of such a statue was widely recognized as an honourable reward for public service. Sculptures were produced in a wide variety of materials, and the fact that most sculpture still extant is marble reflects mainly the ease with which cast metal can be melted down by later generations and used for other purposes, leaving behind as testimony to their former existence only the inscribed stone bases. Under Augustus, Roman artists developed a particular taste for reproducing from Greek originals restrained classical images of the human body, particularly the male nude, and narrative reliefs with figures in formal poses, like the dignified processions depicted on the walls of the Altar of Peace. Distinctively Roman, and in contrast to these idealized classicizing figures, was a concern for realistic, or apparently realistic, portraiture. The portraits of aristocratic Romans, both on busts (a popular form of art) and on coins, are sometimes, to the modern eye, extraordinarily ugly. Whether this reflected the simple representative truth or (less likely) changing ideas of beauty or an attempt to depict worldly wisdom, experience, or some other such quality, is uncertain.

Sculpture of this kind was found both in public and in private houses as architectural embellishment or for ownership, but most effort in the interior decoration of private houses was expended on mosaics and paintings. Floor mosaics in the early empire were most often simple geometric or floral designs in black and white, but luxury mosaics imitating the effects of painting in a style perfected in the Greek world in the third and second centuries BCE were occasionally to be found, sometimes to magnificent effect, like the outstanding Nile mosaic found at Praeneste (modern Palestrina). Mosaic was used on walls and vaults, with many fountains in first-century Rome and Pompeii decorated with shells, small stones and pieces of glass, using patterns related to wall painting. For the contemporary developments in Roman wall painting, the evidence from Pompeii and neighbouring Herculaneum, where the interiors of houses were preserved by layers of volcanic ash following the eruption of Vesuvius, enables much more to be known than would be possible from the fragments which survive from Rome itself. It is clear that painting directly onto the wall was preferred to portable works of art such as were popular in the Hellenistic world, and that Italian wall painting underwent a gradual development of styles in the century following the mid-first century BCE. The so-called Second Style at Pompeii in the late Republic favoured panels in which depictions of buildings in rich colours, especially red and black, give an illusion of solid architecture. Towards the end of the first century BCE taste veered towards more delicate, flatter pictures, with a greater focus on large central pictures of groups of figures set against a landscape, often depicted in miniaturist detail. Then, in the course of the first century CE, artists began again to seek to give a feeling of depth to the paintings, and the central pictures in each panel became smaller. Fashion in art clearly matured, for house owners paid to have pictures painted in the new styles over those in the old. Presumably an old painting grated on the eye much as wallpaper from other eras can sometimes look incongruous in a modern house.

Other pleasures were less expensive, at least for the individual consumer. For the erudite, there was the cerebral pleasure of hearing readings, not just of the classics, learned as a child, but of new literature. Public readings of new works were popular occasions in certain elite circles, although the younger Pliny records, with disapproval, a reading attended by the great general Iavolenus Priscus that went wrong: "Paulus was giving a public reading and began by saying 'Priscus, thou dost command—' at which Iavolenus Priscus, who was present as a great friend of Paulus, exclaimed 'Indeed I don't command!' You can imagine the laughter and witticisms which greeted this remark."[19] Rome under Augustus witnessed a remarkable literary efflorescence, most especially in poetry: Vergil's epic *Aeneid*, the gentle satires of Horace, escapist bucolic and clever didactic verse, the love elegies of Cornelius Gallus, Tibullus, Propertius and Ovid.

Appreciation of new literature was fashionable: poets, as recognized repos-
itories of inspired creativity, were fêted like novelists in the modern world.
The writings of the Augustan age were themselves rapidly conceived as
classic, for poets during the following century to emulate, outdo or sub-
vert. Thus there was a rash of epic poems, by Statius, Valerius Flaccus and
Silius Italicus, all trying in the Flavian period to produce a work worthy of
Vergil, and attempts by Persius under Nero, and by Martial and Juvenal at
the end of the first century and beginning of the second, to restore to the
genre of satire something of the satirical bite it had lost in the poems of
Horace. Such literary productivity owed much to the generosity of
patrons, especially emperors, and the open ambition of Augustan poets to
produce a Latin literature to rival that of Greece, but it owed even more to
the public recognition accorded such artistic creativity. Before he wrote
about emperors, the biographer Suetonius composed a set of lives entitled
*On Illustrious Men*. All were celebrated literary figures, arranged by category: grammarians and rhetoricians, poets, orators, historians, philosophers (although Suetonius, himself a man of letters, perhaps exaggerated
their importance).

No other high art achieved quite the social respect of literature. Music
was a necessary part of the education of high-class children, girls as well as
boys. Playing an instrument and singing competently were desirable
accomplishments for women. Music was a common accompaniment to
religious rituals and provided background entertainment at dinner parties.
Seneca records a large-scale orchestral concert: specifically comparing current to ancient custom, Seneca notes that "we have a larger number of
singers than there used to be spectators in the theatres of old. All the aisles
are filled with rows of singers; brass instruments surround the auditorium;
the stage resounds with flutes and instruments of every description; and
yet from the discordant sounds a harmony is produced." More common
were solo recitals on the pipe or lyre. A few musicians, like the Sardinian
Tigellius, who was believed to have much influence with Julius Caesar
towards the end of Caesar's life, became socially prominent and a friend of
Augustus, but most were content to perform as professionals, within one
or other of the musicians' guilds. Tigellius, the exception, is described by
Horace as a male prima donna: "All singers have this fault: if they are
begged to sing among friends they can never persuade themselves to do it;

if they are not asked they never leave off. That Sardinian Tigellius was of this sort."[20]

There is much evidence that amateur singing was a common feature of the everyday life of ordinary Romans of all classes, and that the same was true of dancing. Ancient dances were used in the religious ceremonies of the Salii and the Arval Brethren, but professional dancers, and especially the girls who provided entertainment at dinner parties, were generally slaves. The closest in Roman society to classical ballet dancers as exponents of high art were the pantomime artists, who represented mythological themes on stage simply through dance, with the support of a chorus and instrumental backing: the art was introduced to Rome from Greece in 22 BCE and rapidly became popular, and literary figures such as the poets Lucan and Statius wrote pantomime libretti, presumably for a chorus. Tragic subjects were preferred, and performances provided essentially a serious form of entertainment, but this did not prevent the younger Pliny expressing disapproval of the elderly Ummidia Quadratilla, who in her seventies owned a company of pantomime dancers "and enjoyed their performances with more enthusiasm than was proper for a woman of her social rank." Performances of more sober Latin tragedy, on the model set by the tragedians of classical Athens, had begun in Rome in the mid-third century BCE, and tragedies were still being written and performed for public religious festivals down to the first century CE; but they seem not to have been considered by later generations as great works of literature worthy of preservation. The poet Lucius Varius Rufus wrote a tragedy about Thyestes for the games held by Octavian in 29 BCE to celebrate his victory at the battle of Actium, and Ovid composed a tragedy about Medea, but it is probable that the tragedies of the younger Seneca, of which a number survive, were primarily intended to be recited or read rather than staged: there was no great audience for such wordy drama. By contrast, a description in Apuleius' *The Golden Ass* of a pantomime about the mythical choice of Venus by Paris suggests that depiction of myth could be a cover for displays of erotic dancing: "Then came a young man representing Paris as a Phrygian shepherd, gorgeously costumed in a cloak of foreign design which flowed down from his shoulders . . . Then Venus appeared, displaying her perfect beauty, naked, unclothed, except for a thin silk piece of material which shaded her remarkable pubic region so that the inquisitive wind amorously now blew aside the fringe . . . now lasciviously blew it back to press it clingingly against her to show clearly the delights of her members . . ."[21]

Less pretentious and even more exploitative of sexual innuendo was the mime, in which the actors and actresses spoke as well as danced. Mime companies performed standard scenarios of dramatic events, like the escape of an adulterer or the pursuit of tricksters. Some literary mime scripts were composed, although none survives, but the script for mimes was less important than the spectacle. In this respect they differed from the Latin comedies, many based originally on Greek prototypes, which were staged, and still occasionally composed, from the mid-second century BCE until the first century CE, or the improvised masked Atellan farces with their stock characters, such as Maccus, "the clown." Atellan farces were thought by the emperor significant enough for the author of one to be burned alive by the emperor Gaius in the middle of the arena of the amphitheatre for composing a humorous line of double meaning. The mimes were the main draw for mass audiences. The first permanent theatre in Rome was built only in 55 BCE, but it held ten thousand spectators, and more were soon built to the same design. In theatres of such size it must have been hard for all the audience to hear every word: the attraction lay in the realism of the representation on the stage and the emotions aroused among those watching.[22]

But the audiences for all such entertainments were dwarfed by the huge crowds at the amphitheatre and the circus. Gladiatorial games were staged only to mark special occasions, although some emperors, such as Gaius, could invent more such occasions if they wanted to please the populace by providing more performances. No permanent home was provided for them in Rome until the erection of a small amphitheatre by Statilius Taurus in the Campus Martius in 27 BCE, but a much larger wooden structure was erected there by Nero and, after that was burned down in the great fire of 64 CE, the vast stone Colosseum was built by Vespasian and Titus in the 70s. The attraction for the spectators was only in part the witnessing of bloodshed and death (although it was important for everyone to be able to witness the kill). Gladiators were highly trained, impressively fit, athletes, whose public displays of courage gave them a certain glamour. Thus, although many gladiators were condemned criminals or slaves, some free volunteers took up fighting as a profession, and both Augustus and Tiberius were impelled to prevent more aristocratic members of society from seeking glory in the arena; the emperors considered that their participation demeaned the dignity of the upper class as a whole. Adoption of the career was not wholly suicidal, since inscriptions attest to the honourable retirement enjoyed by some former gladiators—presumably, by definition, the best. The fate of exotic animals—lions, bears, elephants, panthers and many others—imported to Rome for display in wild beast hunts was more certain. At the inauguration of the Colosseum in 80, nine thousand animals died. The sense of danger could be increased by ensuring that some humans also died in the course of the proceedings, for which purpose criminals could be provided. Christian martyrdom narratives give a rare glimpse of the attitude of some victims, but the spectators can rarely have felt much empathy with those whose suffering they watched. As St. Augustine wrote much later, at the end of the fourth century, the sight of violence in action exercises a horrible fascination. He wrote of his friend Alypius who, originally reluctant to go to the games, tried when he got there to keep his eyes shut, but was finally tempted by the roars of the crowd to look—and then "he was charmed by the barbarity of the combat and he became drunk on bloody pleasure." In earlier centuries a dash of intellectual or aesthetic sophistication might occasionally be added in the form of re-enactments of stories ending in the expected violence. In the third century the Christian Tertullian recorded in disgust that he had seen one criminal being burned to death in the role of Hercules and another being castrated as Attis, the mythological consort of the goddess Cybele. In an epigram composed probably by the poet Martial in a collection commemorating the opening of the Colosseum by Titus, the magnificent spectacle is described of an "Orpheus," surrounded by a marvellous wood, every kind of wild beast, a flock of sheep and many birds—only to be torn apart "by an ungrateful bear," presumably to the delight of the audience. Such "fatal charades" evidently exercised a particular charm.[23]

Compared to all this the Roman passion for chariot racing seems to us rather innocent. The city boasted a number of huge circuits—the size necessary both to enable the competitors to race safely and to seat the many thousands of spectators. The Circus Maximus, right in the centre of the city between the Palatine and Aventine hills, was fitted with permanent seating by Julius Caesar and rebuilt in even more spectacular style by Trajan. Chariot teams were managed by factions distinguished by colours. Blue and green were the favourite teams in the early empire, although red

and white also competed, and Domitian at the end of the first century CE
tried to introduce a new "imperial" faction with purple and gold as its
colour. The enthusiasm shown by the emperor Gaius only carried to notorious extremes the passion of ordinary fans. As Suetonius recalls:

> He was so passionately devoted to the green faction that he constantly
> dined and spent the night in their stable . . . He used to send his soldiers
> on the day before the games and order silence in the neighbourhood, to
> prevent the horse Incitatus from being disturbed. Besides a stall of mar-
> ble, a manger of ivory, purple blankets and a collar of precious stones,
> he even gave this horse a house, a troop of slaves and furniture, for the
> more elegant entertainment of the guests invited in his name; and it is
> also said that he planned to make him consul.[24]

The excitement lay in the skill of the drivers and allegiance to faction:
gamblers in Rome staked their chances, not on the outcome of races, but
on the fall of dice.

To MANY, and probably to most, Jews in first-century-CE Jerusalem, many
of these pleasures to which contemporary Romans aspired were sinful or
disgusting, but at least a few Jews will have been less easy to shock. Herod
and many of his descendants through the first century visited Rome and
saw and participated in the hedonism of the imperial capital, and some of
the practices of the imperial court were replicated in their households at
home in Judaea. Josephus' narrative of the sexual intrigues and scandals in
Herod's own court and in that of Agrippa II, accused of incest with his sister, matches closely the atmosphere of the Julio-Claudian palace. The
birthday party of "Herod the Tetrarch," Herod Antipas, at which, according to the account in the Gospels, his stepdaughter's dance so pleased him
that he offered her whatever she wished and she asked for John the Baptist's
head on a charger, would have suited the macabre mentality of the most
despotic of the Caesars. But the very fact that this was a birthday party
takes Antipas' celebration out of the normal run of Jewish behaviour,
since, as we have seen, Jews generally did not celebrate their birthdays.

Jews did of course indulge in feasting, as Romans did, both as part of
religious rites and on family occasions, such as at the circumcision of a boy

eight days after birth. For some ritual meals there was a set menu, notably the barbecued lamb eaten on the first evening of the Passover festival, at least so long as the Temple still stood, and the eating of fish for the Sabbath evening meal was highly prized. But in other respects Jews do not seem to have developed a distinctive cuisine, except in the avoidance of specific foods which contravened the law as elaborated from the original lists in Leviticus. The detailed discussions preserved in rabbinic texts of the ingredients and manufacture of many foodstuffs reflect not so much the value of the act of eating as the importance attributed to avoiding transgression of these taboos. They also, incidentally, provide particularly good information about food preparation techniques, but they do not suggest any particular cultural fascination in late antiquity with eating as a means of establishing Jewish identity—the cultural phenomenon later known among assimilated Jews in the Hapsburg empire as *Fressfroemmigkeit*.

The liturgy of the Passover eve meal owed much to the format of the standard Roman dinner, with the participants all reclining on their left side, men and women at the same table, and the proceedings punctuated by the formal drinking of four glasses of wine. "Even the poorest in Israel must not eat unless he sits down to table, and they must not give them less than four cups of wine to drink, even if it is from the [Paupers'] Dish." Wine was also integral to other celebrations, on the Sabbath, at weddings and at circumcisions. Moderate consumption was deemed good for health. "Give strong drink to him who is perishing, and wine to those in bitter distress. Let him drink, and forget his poverty, and remember his misery no more." The Babylonian Talmud records a tradition that some rabbis wanted to prohibit altogether the drinking of wine after the destruction of the Temple, but that such a demonstration of mourning would have proved insupportable for ordinary people. Jews believed that wine brought joy, and that abstention by those who chose to mark their devotion to God by taking a vow of self-denial was a product of supererogatory piety. On the other hand, attitudes to excessive inebriation were ambivalent. Intoxication in worship in the Temple was prohibited already in the Pentateuch, and Josephus notes that "the law does not allow the birth of our children to be made occasions for festivity and an excuse for drinking to excess." Habitual drunkenness was one of the charges that might be brought by his parents against a rebellious son. Nonetheless, there was a positive injunction, according to the fourth-century Babylonian rabbi Rava cited in the

Talmud, to become so drunk on the festival of Purim that it became impossible to distinguish which of the leading characters of the story, Haman and Mordechai, was virtuous, and which the villain.[25]

The contrast with Roman notions of pleasure is more stark in attitudes to sex. Most Jews, apart from those like Philo influenced by Platonic philosophy, discussed marital sex as an enjoyable and desirable activity for both husband and wife; this was one area of life which sharply distinguished rabbinic Jews from Christians in later antiquity. But sex within marriage was the only sort they could envisage without qualms. For Josephus, "the law recognizes no sexual connections, except the natural union of man and wife, and that only for the procreation of children." Jewish men might commit adultery or have recourse to gentile prostitutes, but they assumed that all such behaviour was sinful. Both Josephus, in his paraphrase of biblical history, and the authors of the Targum, the Aramaic translation of the Bible, rendered the profession of Rahab, the heroine who saved the Jewish scouts sent by Joshua to spy out the land, as innkeeper rather than harlot. Where Jews differed even more from Romans in sexual mores was in a taboo against male masturbation and an abhorrence of male homosexuality. The prohibition against masturbation was based loosely on the biblical narrative of Onan, who "spilled" his seed "on the ground" to avoid making Tamar pregnant and thereby producing progeny for his dead brother Er, the general principle being that seed should not be wasted from its primary purpose of procreation. Male homosexual relations were condemned much more explicitly in the Pentateuch: "You shall not lie with mankind as with womankind: it is abomination," totally forbidden alongside bestiality. In Josephus' formulation: "Sexual relations of males to males [the law] abhors, and death is the punishment if anyone should attempt it." It is significant that the only reference by Josephus to homosexuality as a real issue among Jews involved a Roman. When Mark Antony saw a portrait of the young Hasmonaean prince Aristobulus III, he asked Herod for the boy to be sent to him in Egypt, but Herod declined: "He decided that it would not be safe for him to send Aristobulus, who was then most handsome—being just sixteen—and of a distinguished family, to Antony, who was more powerful than any Roman of his time, and was ready to use him for erotic pleasures and was able to indulge in undisguised pleasures because of his power." According to the Mishnah, one rabbi, worried about sexual temptation, taught that "an unmarried man may not herd cattle, nor may two unmarried men sleep under the same cloak." But, adds the Mishnah, "the sages permit it." It is probable that such leniency reflected a view, not that homosexuality did not matter, but that "Israelites are not suspected of pederasty or bestiality." Lesbian sex, not specifically outlawed in the Bible, unconnected to the prohibition of "wasting seed," and rarely mentioned, was treated as deplorable licentiousness but not as wicked on the level of male homosexuality or female prostitution.[26]

According to the Babylonian Talmud, it was a religious duty for all Jews, men as well as women, to wear special clothes on the Sabbath: "your Sabbath garments should not be like your weekday garments. . . ." In general, however, expenditure on personal appearance was assumed by Jews to be a characteristic of women rather than men. Jewish clothing, apart from the uniforms of the priests and Levites, seems generally to have been the same as that of others in the eastern Mediterranean. It would be wrong to imagine the Jewish *tallit* as an identity marker similar to the distinctively Roman toga; *tallit* in Hebrew means simply "cloak" and the use of such a garment as a dedicated prayer shawl did not begin until after late antiquity. The biblical prohibition on wearing garments manufactured from wool and linen, stated simply as a general law in Deuteronomy, was explained by Josephus as a way to preserve the unique status of the priesthood: such raiment "is reserved for the priests alone." That priests did indeed wear clothes made from such materials is confirmed in the Mishnah. When the Pharisees chose to "make broad their phylacteries and enlarge the borders of their garments," they did this in order "to be seen of men"; but such ostentation must have been unusual for it to be alleged that it attracted Jesus' criticism, and it is probably significant that no gentile pagan source betrays any knowledge of this distinctive Jewish custom. The Jewish figures in the frescoes from the synagogue at Dura-Europus have fringes on the corners of some of their cloaks, but if this reflected standard male Jewish practice, the fringes must generally have been discreet. Jewish men did not specially cover their heads. The dress of Jewish women also seems to have been much the same as that of gentile contemporaries; the Christian Tertullian remarked in Carthage at the end of the second century CE that Jewish women could be recognized as Jews by the fact that they wore veils in public, but it seems likely that such veils, common in the eastern Mediterranean, marked them out less as specifically Jewish than as simply oriental in the Roman West, where women were generally unveiled. According to the Mishnah it was regarded as immodest and shaming for a married woman to wear her hair loose. The Mishnah refers to types of jewellery that a woman should not carry on a Sabbath: "She may not go out . . . with forehead-band or head-bangles if they are not sewn, or with a hair-net . . . or a necklace or nose-rings . . ."[27]

Too much pride by males in their long hair was dangerously immoral, as the story of Absalom showed: he gloried in his hair, so he was hanged by it. A few male hairstyles were specially forbidden by the rabbis in the Tosefta on the grounds that they looked too gentile and therefore smacked of idolatry or magic: "What are matters which constitute 'the ways of the Amorites?' He who trims the front of his hair, and he who makes his locks grow long, and he who makes a baldness in front for a particular star . . ." But these restrictions are the exception that prove the rule, that Jews generally looked like non-Jews. Romans often noted that foreign peoples looked different from themselves, but (apart from male circumcision) they never noted this of the Jews. One passing remark by a Roman author does, however, suggest that some Romans thought Jews had a distinctive smell: the historian Ammianus Marcellinus recorded in the fourth century CE a comment of the philosopher emperor Marcus Aurelius in the second century CE about the Jews as malodorous. This was not a standard form of abuse of other people in the Roman world. It may even have some basis in a real difference. If modesty requires more clothing, in a hot climate old sweaty clothes may become smelly. If everyone smells equally, no one notices, and the issue of body odour (except of tanners) fails to surface in the Jewish texts.[28]

Could the Jews of Jerusalem imagine public entertainments like those enjoyed in Rome without travelling to the capital itself? Yes, without doubt, for, so Josephus writes, Herod built a theatre in Jerusalem, and a very large amphitheatre nearby, and celebrated quadrennial contests in honour of Augustus, with athletes, actors and musicians. There was also a hippodrome near the city, in which Herod mounted races both of horses and of chariots, and in the amphitheatre he staged fights between wild beasts and exhibited the public execution of condemned criminals by being torn apart by lions and other animals.[29] But such entertainments do not seem to have continued in Jerusalem after Herod died. In the inscriptions which record the achievements of great athletes and other competitors in the cities of the eastern Roman empire, including places such as Tyre and Sidon and Caesarea on the coast of Judaea, the Jerusalem games are not included. And whereas, as we have seen in Chapter 2, gladiatorial games were one Roman innovation that became popular very quickly in much of the Greek world in the early imperial period, they never became fashionable in the Jewish city. Josephus states explicitly that the theatre and amphitheatre built by Herod, and the athletic contests, were contrary to Jewish custom; that the native Jews believed it to be a "glaring impiety" to "throw men to wild beasts for the pleasure of other men as spectators"; and that they aroused much popular hostility, including indeed a conspiracy to kill the king for forcibly introducing practices "not in accord with custom, by which their way of life would be totally altered." It is possible that rabbinic dicta in opposition to Jews going to such spectacles in the third and fourth centuries CE presuppose that a proportion of the Jewish population in Palestine in later centuries did in time acquire a taste for them, but they had not done so yet in the first century. Nor should one imagine the theatre in Jerusalem being used for the production of Greek plays, let alone the mimes and pantomimes popular in Rome. Philo wrote that he went once to a performance in Alexandria of a play by Euripides—the audience got carried away when they heard the line "the name 'free' is worth everything"—but no one staged such dramas in his time in Jerusalem.[30]

Jerusalem Jews did have their own entertainments, but these seem to have been comparatively tame, although the impression from the surviving evidence that Jews thought and wrote only about religious themes may reflect primarily the transmission of this evidence through later religious traditions. Jews can be shown to have written a literature in Hebrew and Aramaic in a variety of genres—history, law, psalms and hymns, wisdom texts, Bible interpretation, apocalyptic visions, didactic stories like the books of Judith and Tobit—but none of these, except historiography, seems to owe its form to the Greek background which had such a decisive impact on the development of contemporary Latin literature, although Greek ideas may have occasionally had some effect on the ideas these texts expressed. On the other hand, some Jews did write in Greek for their fellow Jews, although how common this was in Jerusalem, rather than the diaspora, is debated. The author of 2 Maccabees wrote about the revolt against Antiochus Epiphanes in the dramatic and emotional style popular in contemporary Greek historiography, but he stated explicitly his reliance on a longer account composed by a certain Jason of Cyrene, whose name (if it is not a literary fiction) indicates his origins in the Jewish community of North Africa. Philo of Alexandria wrote works of serious philosophy and was at least known as a philosopher to the Jerusalem Jew Josephus, even if no Jew in first-century Jerusalem is attested as having developed either such philosophical expertise or, indeed, such philosophical interests. A stilted epic poem written in Greek before the mid-first century BCE by a certain Philo (not the philosopher), with the title "About Jerusalem," enthused about a fountain that it is dry in winter and full in summer, but this Philo could have written anywhere. The same is true of the Ezekiel whose rather fine version of the Exodus story was rendered in the form of an Aeschylean tragedy. If some, or many, Jerusalemites were bilingual or trilingual in Greek, Hebrew and Aramaic, as Josephus was, a Jerusalem audience too might have appreciated Ezekiel's efforts, but if Jews in Jerusalem attended public readings of epic poetry or public performances of tragic plays, even with such impeccably Jewish themes, there is no surviving evidence of it.[31]

Even more difficult to pin down is Jewish appreciation of comedy, or, indeed, a Jewish sense of humour. No Jewish literary text announces itself as humorous, and nothing like a public performance of comedy or mime is known. Mockery in biblical texts tends to be polemical, aimed especially at idolaters for the foolishness of their beliefs. Some have seen humour also in the pathetic efforts of the priests of Bel to pretend that their god ate their offerings, their deception revealed, according to the author of the Greek additions to the biblical book of Daniel, by the marks of their footsteps in the morning light. The overturning of expectations in the story of Susanna—the two old men lusting after the beautiful girl and coming to grief as a result of their own wicked schemes—may seem droll from a certain perspective. Polemical irony was the main ingredient of the disastrous joke played by a group of young Jews in Jerusalem in 66 CE when, according to Josephus, they mocked the Roman governor, who had been demanding payment of unpaid taxes, by handing round a begging bowl for his benefit; the ensuing retaliation by the governor was an important step in the preliminaries to the outbreak of war. There is little evidence of the self-deprecating wit characteristic of more recent Jewish humour, or of the robust, often obscene humour of the jests favoured in contemporary Rome (although learned discussions preserved in the Babylonian Talmud about the varying sizes of the phalluses of different rabbis may reflect a tradition of Jewish appreciation of the grotesque).[32]

By contrast, dance was appreciated as an art form both to indulge in and to watch, particularly on the festival of the water libation that took place in the Temple on the last days of the festival of Tabernacles: "Men of piety and good works used to dance before them with burning torches in their hands, singing songs and praises, and countless Levites [played] on harps, lyres, cymbals and trumpets and instruments of music, on the fifteen steps leading down from the Court of the Israelites to the Court of Women, corresponding to the fifteen songs of ascents in the Psalms; upon them the Levites used to stand with instruments of music and utter a song." Such ritual dancing, akin to the dances of the Salii and other priests in Roman society, had a long tradition, reflected in numerous biblical stories, like the dance of David before the Ark. The book of Judith describes a victory dance of the women when Holofernes is dead and the Assyrians have fled: "Then all the women of Israel ran together to see her, and blessed her, and made a dance among them for her; and she took branches in her hands and gave them to the women who were with her. And they were garlanded with olive, she and those with her, and she went before all the people in the dance, leading all the women." Girls would dance before the men on 15 Ab each year and hope to win a spouse: "The daughters of Jerusalem go forth and dance in the vineyards. And what did they used to say? 'Young man, lift up your eyes and see what you choose for yourself: set not your eyes on beauty, but set your eyes on family.' " But all of these practices differed greatly from Roman enjoyment of the art of skilled slave dancing girls after dinner, or the public performance of mime. The rabbis could imagine the erotic poetry of the Song of Songs being sung at or after dinner, so that Rabbi Akiva is said to have specifically objected, that "he who trills his voice in the chanting of the Song of Songs in the banquet halls and makes it like an ordinary song has no share in the world to come." But despite the story of the after-dinner dance which led to the execution of John the Baptist, the rabbis do not seem to have envisaged this particular form of lewdness as a problem in their society.[33]

Jewish culture was more oral than visual: when Jews referred to themselves in Hebrew as understanding a truth or a command, they would say that they had heard it; by contrast, in Latin, as in Greek and in English, the metaphor for comprehension is to "see" the truth. The aural metaphor, however, cannot have been overwhelming in the Jewish mentality, for Philo, writing in Greek, refers repeatedly to a false etymology of the name "Israel" as derived from the Hebrew *ish-ra'ah-el*, taken to mean "he who sees God." At any rate, Jews in Jerusalem certainly demonstrated an appreciation of visual aesthetics both in the Temple and in the interior decoration of their houses. Excavated houses from the time of the war against Rome in 66–70 are decorated with patterned mosaic floors and wall plaster painted in the Pompeian Second Style. These provincials imitated Italy as others did elsewhere in the empire, even if they were behind the times in the fashions they followed. The major difference, clearly deliberate, was that the paintings in Jerusalem were wholly devoid of images of humans and only rarely included images of animals. The architectural frames of the pictures painted direct onto the plaster, and the deep reds and blacks, are all in the Italian style, but the central interest in each picture in Roman as in Hellenistic art, the depiction of the interplay of living bodies, is wholly lacking. The taboo which precluded such depictions was by no means static or universal among Jews, since later in antiquity Jews in the land of Israel were to commission fine synagogue mosaics with detailed images of humans and animals, and in the mid-third century CE the Jews of Dura-Europus depicted in detail on the walls of their synagogue a series of biblical scenes. Even in the first century, when Herod completed his rebuilding of the Temple by erecting an image of an eagle over its entrance, he must have believed this to be permitted in Jewish law, since he had just spent years, and huge amounts of money, in ensuring that the building be seen by his subjects as both magnificent and kosher. However, the riots that greeted the eagle image suggest that other first-century Jews disagreed with Herod's interpretation. The "two sophists," as Josephus describes the ringleaders of the crowd who tried to tear the eagle down, evidently saw the image as an affront, presumably in light of the commandment in Exodus, "You shall not make for yourself any graven image, or any likeness of any thing that is in heaven above, or that is in the earth beneath, or that is in the water under the earth," although the symbolism of the eagle as an image of Rome may also have aggravated their anger. Later Jews were to interpret the commandment in Exodus in the light of the following verse ("You shall not bow down yourself to them [the images], nor serve them"), thus permitting images of all kinds providing that they are not worshipped, but most first-century Jews seem to have taken a hard line: the iconography on Jewish coins minted during the revolt against Rome reveals a willingness to depict objects such as palm branches, pomegranates and a chalice, but neither people nor animals. Jewish homes thus lacked the riot of statues, reliefs and other images that enlivened the houses of their Roman contemporaries, and the public spaces of Jerusalem had no commemorative statues to link the citizens to the historic figures of the past.[34]

A Roman coming to Jerusalem would thus find not just a pale imitation of the culture in the metropolis, such as he would experience in many towns in the western provinces of the empire, but a society whose entire lifestyle seemed bound up in its idiosyncratic religion. Public spectacle was centred round the Temple, rather than entertainments in theatre or circus. Intellectual debate took place between religious enthusiasts rather than orators and philosophers. And the rhythms of the city followed the Temple calendar, the whole populace hushed at rest each Saturday, the pilgrims greeted in their many thousands each spring and autumn.

Thus Romans accustomed to asceticism as a counter-cultural statement (as by Cynics) or as evidence of self-control (as by Stoics) noted as remarkable the observance of self-denial by Jews infused by religious devotion: in describing the emperor's frugal eating habits, Suetonius records that Augustus once wrote to his stepson, the future emperor Tiberius, "Not even a Jew, my dear Tiberius, keeps a fast so scrupulously on Sabbaths as I have kept my fast today." The practices of fasting and sexual abstinence followed in their own society by Pythagoreans, who avoided a long list of foodstuffs including both animal flesh and beans, were rarely adopted by ordinary Romans, who saw nothing moral or healthy in observance of such taboos. They would be taken aback by the crowds of nazirites in Jerusalem who dedicated themselves to avoid all grape products, including wine, for a specified period or (more rarely) for life, and to forswear cutting their hair during this time. The nazirite (from the Hebrew *nazir*, "one who abstains") was a man or woman who took a vow to consecrate him- or herself to God by accepting these prohibitions, which went beyond those observed by other Jews. The value of such self-dedication was assumed in the rules governing the behaviour of nazirites laid down already in the Pentateuch. In the Bible the archetypical nazirite was Samson. By the first century CE the rationale for such self-abnegation veered between a forward-looking vow and gratitude for past favours, and crowds of nazirites could be identified in the Temple—presumably, in the case of men, from their long hair. The proselyte Helena of Adiabene became a nazirite, as did the Herodian princess Berenice. Evidently commitment to what the Septuagint called "the great vow" was attractive as a form of conspicuous piety for women: when it came to eating and drinking, the opportunities for exemplary virtue were not gender-specific.

More extreme asceticism, in the form of fasting, was one of the characteristics of Jews most noticed by gentiles: Tacitus claims that the Jews "even now bear witness by frequent fasts to the long hunger with which they were once distressed," and Pompeius Trogus was one of many Romans who seem to have believed, wrongly, that the Sabbath was a fast day: "Moses . . . for all time consecrated the seventh day . . . for a fast day, because that day had ended at once their hunger and their wandering."[35] The great national fast to secure God's attention and confirm repentance for sin was on the Day of Atonement, but the Mishnah also describes periodic public fasts called in time of drought or other calamity: "If a city suffered from pestilence or if its houses fell, that city fasts and sounds the ram's horn, and the places around it fast but do not sound the ram's horn . . . The elders once went down from Jerusalem to their own towns and decreed a fast because in Ashkelon there appeared blight the extent of an oven's mouth. Moreover they decreed a fast because wolves devoured two children beyond the Jordan."[36]

# CHAPTER EIGHT

# GOVERNMENT

ALTHOUGH, as we saw in Chapter 5, Jews and Romans had different ideas about the ultimate authority on which their governments were based, that there should be states and governments of some kind was not generally questioned in either society. But how should governments operate and relate to individual citizens? When did the good of the community override the rights of the individual? And when was the use of force justified in imposing the will of the state?

In one crucial area of government, the extraction of tax to pay for the activities of the state, Jews and Romans were in general agreement, although in practice the impact of taxation in the first century CE on the inhabitants of Jerusalem was far greater than its impact on the inhabitants of Rome. In theory, the right of the authorities to extract tax in order to pay for communal facilities of all kinds was taken for granted in both societies. But in contrast to the land tax levied in Judaea by both Herod and Roman governors, direct taxation on property, which brought in the bulk of the income of the Roman state, was not levied at all under the emperors either in the city of Rome or in the rest of Italy. Romans considered such taxes on the property of citizens as suitable only for emergencies when state finances were in severe difficulties, and since the mid-second century BCE there had been sufficient income from Rome's overseas conquest for such emergencies to be very rare. In this respect, then, those who lived in Rome got off lightly, but Romans as much as Jerusalemites paid indirect taxes on sales, and they too found the price of goods raised by tolls levied on goods imported into the city.[1]

What did Romans and Jews expect their states to do with the money thus raised?

## JUSTICE

THE CONSTRUCTION of a coherent, clearly categorized structure of law was one of the great achievements of the Roman empire. The huge extant corpora of legal opinions in Justinian's *Digest*, and of judicial decisions by emperors in the Codes of Theodosius and Justinian, were compiled only in the fifth and sixth centuries CE, but the process of compilation had already been begun in the early Republic a millennium earlier. According to Roman tradition, the Twelve Tables, the earliest such collection, had been compiled by a commission of ten senior senators in the mid-fifth century BCE in order to write down as statutes the provisions of customary law and thus put an end to arbitrary decisions by magistrates. Regardless of the veracity of this tradition, by the late Republic the text of the Twelve Tables in archaic Latin was much cited, and commentaries on their provisions were composed by scholars: when Cicero was young, Roman boys were required to memorize their precise wording, such as "Persons shall mend roadways. If they do not keep them laid with stone, a person may drive his beasts where he wishes," or "If theft has been done by night, if the owner kill the thief, the thief shall be held lawfully killed," even though some of the clauses had ceased to apply for centuries and (as Cicero complained) "no one learns them nowadays." Other Roman works of legal literature took the form of discussion of difficult cases, real or imaginary, and commentaries on the edict issued by the urban praetor when he took office. The prolific and influential legal authors Marcus Antistius Labeo and Gaius Ateius Capito were both senators in the time of Augustus, but from the time of Claudius professional jurists had a greater impact on legal literature, and the classical period of Roman law, when jurists were at their most productive, was in the late second and early third centuries CE. This Roman law was perceived by Romans as man-made, a product of political decisions by assemblies and magistrates, of experience, in the form of case law, and of reasoning. The interests of jurists were practical and precise. Many were well versed in Greek philosophy, but the underlying questions, such as the nature of justice, which preoccupied Socrates, Plato or Aristotle, were not their concern. At no point did they claim divine authority for their views. Religious law for them consisted in the regulations made by magistrates to ensure that men avoided offending the gods, as the jurist Gaius made clear in the second century CE:

> The highest division of things is into two classes; for some are subject to divine law, some to human law. Within divine law, some things are sacred, some religious. Things sacred are those consecrated to the gods above; things religious are those left to the gods below [*manes*]. Nothing can be considered sacred unless it has been consecrated by the authority of the Roman people, which can result either through the passing of a law or through a decree of the Senate. On the other hand, things can become religious by our own act of will when we bury the dead in our own ground.[2]

The theoretical basis of most Jewish law was quite different, since the written Torah enshrined in the Pentateuch covered all aspects of life, religious and secular together, and was believed to have come direct from God to Moses. The Pentateuch dealt with law of all kinds—private and public, civil and criminal, issues of property ownership and questions surrounding ritual actions in the Temple—as did also the Mishnah, a collection of legal opinions redacted in about 200 CE on a series of issues arising mostly from interpretation of the laws in the Pentateuch, in which the opinions cited are those of a quite restricted cadre of jurists who shared allegiance to the movement which became rabbinic Judaism, or at least were believed by the compiler of the Mishnah to have belonged to this group. How standard their view of the law was among their Jewish contemporaries is disputed: much of the law found in the documents discovered in the caves in the Judaean desert, such as those which belonged to Babatha, whose affairs were discussed in Chapter 5, is similar to the law presupposed by the early rabbis, but not identical.

Common obeisance by Jews to the authority of the biblical text gives an impression of uniformity within differing systems of Jewish law which can be rather misleading. In fact, there are a number of laws presupposed in the Mishnah for which no basis is offered in the Bible itself. As the Mishnah states explicitly, mixing religious law and civil law, "[the rules about] release from vows hover in the air and have nothing to support them, and rules about the Sabbath . . . are as mountains hanging by a hair, for Scripture [thereon] is scanty and the rules many. . . ." Thus, for instance, no reference to marriage documents of any kind is to be found in the Pentateuch, so it is highly unlikely that this element of Jewish law derived from elaboration of Pentateuchal law. The Pharisees, who considered themselves to be the most accurate interpreters of the law, believed that in accepting ancestral custom they were fulfilling what the written law "really" said. By the third century CE rabbis were to codify a similar (but not identical) principle, with the assertion that the Torah was handed down from Mount Sinai in two forms, one written, one oral. According to this doctrine, ascribed (unreliably) in the Babylonian Talmud to Hillel and Shammai in the late first century BCE, the "Torah that is by mouth" was given by God to Moses at the same time as the written scriptures and then handed down from one generation to the next by trustworthy teachers.[3]

On occasion Jews were even prepared to admit quite freely that some of their laws were entirely man-made. It is hard to tell how much the Dead Sea sectarians believed that their own special regulations derived from the mind of the Teacher of Righteousness whom God had "raised . . . to guide them in the way of his heart," or the Master envisaged in the *Community Rule*, who "shall acquire all the wisdom that has been gained according to the ages," and "shall conceal the teaching of the Law in the midst of the men of injustice, but shall reproach [with] true knowledge and righteous judgement those who have chosen the way." More explicit were the early rabbis, who ascribed some, though not many, specific laws to the authoritative decrees of the sages. Most audacious of these was a decree about repayment of loans attributed to the great rabbinic sage Hillel, who lived around the beginning of the first century CE. Biblical law required all loans to be rendered null and void on the onset of each sabbatical year (that is, every seven years). "At the end of every seven years you shall grant a release. And this is the manner of the release: every creditor shall release what he has lent to his neighbour; he shall not exact it of his neighbour, his brother; because the Lord's release has been proclaimed." The danger that this might result in a drying up of loans as the sabbatical year approached was already envisaged in Deuteronomy: "Beware that there be not a base thought in your heart, saying, 'The seventh year, the year of release, is at hand'; and your eye be hostile to your poor brother, and you give him nothing, and he cry to the Lord against you, and it be sin in you." But evidently such injunctions did not always work, so, according to the Mishnah,

Hillel devised a legal procedure, the *prozbul*, by means of which the creditor could enforce repayment: "When he saw that the people refrained from giving loans one to another and transgressed what is written in the Law, 'Beware that there be not a base thought in your heart . . . ,' Hillel ordained the *prozbul*. This is the formula of the *prozbul*: 'I affirm to you, such-a-one and such-a-one, the judges in such-a-place, that, with regard to any debt due to me, I shall collect it whenever I will.' And the judges sign below, or the witnesses." In analysing the development of Jewish law it may be less important to determine whether Hillel really was responsible for this legal innovation (and it is quite likely that he was not), than to marvel at the later rabbis' insouciant attribution to the great sage of a measure that in its effect directly contradicted God's Torah.[4]

Both Jews and Romans have sometimes been accused of excessive legalism, a regard for legal minutiae for their own sake regardless of the demands of justice. The caricature is itself unjust—all societies have laws, and to accuse others of legalism may simply be abuse—but it reflects accurately the fascination shown by both Romans and Jews in the process of elucidating laws by close analysis of their wording. This interest might take an essentially scholarly form, jurists elaborating ever more complex scenarios in order to tax their legal ingenuity: the specialist Roman jurists belonged to a self-contained intellectual world in which the experts pitted themselves against the challenges of complex legal conundrums sometimes more than a little removed from reality. Some Jews, too, may have shared some of the intellectual enjoyment of attempting solutions to artificial legal puzzles; it is hard to understand the more nitpicking discussions in the Mishnah in any other way:

> Shreds of wool which the washerman pulls out belong to him; but those which the woolcomber pulls out belong to the householder. If the washerman pulled out three threads they belong to him, but if more than this they belong to the householder. If there were black [threads] among the white, and he took them all out, they belong to him. If the tailor had left over thread sufficient to sew with or a piece of cloth three fingerbreadths square, these belong to the householder.[5]

On the other hand, to denigrate the making of such detailed distinctions may miss their real practical significance: in a complex society economic relations can sometimes require very precise regulations of just this type. One hundred and forty wax tablets, generated by the family of the Sulpicii at Puteoli during the course of thirty-five years of financial dealings in the first century CE, were preserved in a villa at Murecine, a suburb of Pompeii. They reveal the use by quite ordinary Roman financiers of precise legal jargon as a means to enforce their rights, and many of the intricate problems thrashed out by Roman lawyers were potentially significant for the facilitation of commerce:

> A number of merchants had on board the same ship a variety of cargoes . . . A great storm arose and they had to jettison. The following questions arose: must all parties contribute to make up the loss, even those whose cargoes added no weight to the ship, such as gems or pearls? And what is the basis of apportionment? . . . And by what action is all this to be achieved? The answers were: all who had a [pecuniary] interest in the jettison taking place must contribute, because things thereby saved owe contribution; therefore the owner of the vessel is himself liable for a share. The sum of loss is to be apportioned *pro rata* to the values of the respective cargoes . . . The owners of the goods sacrificed will have an action on their contract of hire with the captain, i.e. the shipmaster.[6]

Nonetheless, the Bible sometimes rightly distinguishes law from justice, and the existence of complex rules was not enough to ensure that justice was done for individuals, either in Jerusalem or in Rome. In both societies access to justice was restricted by practical difficulties in enforcing rights in civil cases; by lack of protection against abuses by the state when the judiciary was identical to the executive; by obstacles blocking access by private individuals to the courts; by lack of a police force to discover and apprehend criminals except for those most dangerous to the state itself; and by the absence of any public system to ensure that court decisions in private civil cases were effectively enforced. None of these problems is wholly unknown in many societies now, but such issues were particularly acute for Romans and Jews in late antiquity.

Access to a court for a decision on a civil claim was perhaps more of a problem in the city of Rome than in Jerusalem. In Rome a claimant needed to persuade a magistrate—a praetor or aedile—of the nature of his complaint, and the magistrate, having defined the matters at stake, would then usually appoint one or two arbitrators to decide on the facts. Difficulty will have lain primarily in ensuring that the magistrate had time even for the beginning of the procedure, given the huge population of the city. To a great extent legal transactions in Rome required the physical presence of the parties or their representatives at a specified place, and the enunciation of specified words: written documents functioned to record transactions, but only as proof of what had been said. Stories from the provinces, where the magistrate in question was the governor, tell of the frustrating months of waiting for a hearing. It is likely that in Rome, too, the wealth and connections of particular claimants will have pushed their cases to the front of the queue. The system does not seem to have allowed for more local district courts. Doubtless many cases were settled by informal arbitration, with all the inherent dangers of later repudiation of the verdict by the losing side. It is probable that increasing use in the early empire of a different and simpler system, which involved a designated official investigating and carrying out the whole trial, was a partial response to this problem.

In Jerusalem, by contrast, none of the judges in a civil or criminal case had to be appointed by the state, so far as is known. The only requirement specified by early rabbis was that judges should be adult, male and Jewish. If that was a generally accepted view, access to a court should in theory have been easy. In practice, however, matters may have been complicated by the possibility of appeal to non-Jewish jurisdiction: nothing, apart from difficulty of access and possible social disapproval from fellow Jews, prevented a disgruntled litigant from ignoring the decision of a Jewish court and taking a case to the Roman governor. Precisely this seems to have been the intention in the province of Arabia in the early second century CE of the litigious Babatha, whose papers (as we have seen) were found in the Judaean desert. Despite the use of Jewish terms and formulae in the documents which regulated her private affairs, suggesting that she expected (for instance) her rights on divorce to be upheld by a Jewish court, when she sought redress against the guardians of her son by her first marriage (known in the documents consistently, if bizarrely, as "the orphan," because his father was dead even if his mother was not), she had recourse to the Roman governor: among her papers were found three copies of a Greek version, slightly amended, of the praetor's formula about guardianship as known from the *Institutes* written by the jurist Gaius.[7]

Access to a court of any kind can bring justice only if the judges can be trusted. All judicial systems must grapple with the dangers of bias and corruption. The solution adopted in classical Athens, where cases were tried before large juries, was to seek fairness in numbers, a notion that both Romans and Jews would recognize but Romans would rarely adopt in practice. In Republican Rome, appeals against alleged injustice by magistrates had been heard by the people in assembly or by jurors selected from a panel drawn from the richer echelons of Roman society, but by the early empire only few vestiges of this system continued to operate, in cases involving the exceptionally wealthy. Trials before popular assemblies ceased, and little is heard of the functioning of the "perpetual jury-courts" whose operation and selection had been major political issues in the time of Cicero. Disputes over inheritance of large estates were heard in the centumviral (literally, "hundred-man") courts before one hundred and eighty jurors, and criminal trials of senators and their relatives sometimes took place in the Senate itself, so that elite politicians were judged by their peers; but ordinary appeals by ordinary Romans went no longer to any popular court or mass jury but to the unreliable, and final, decision of the emperor. According to Cassius Dio, already in 30 BCE, before he was accorded the name Augustus, Octavian was given the right to hear appeals and, at his discretion, to exercise the prerogative of mercy. Hence the speech of Paul to the Roman governor Festus, as reported in Acts: "I stand at Caesar's judgement seat, where I ought to be judged . . . For if I be an offender, or have committed anything worthy of death, I do not refuse to die: but if there is nothing in these things of which these people accuse me, no one should gratify them by delivering me to them. I appeal to Caesar."[8]

By contrast, the Mishnah notes that "non-capital cases are decided by three and capital cases by three and twenty . . . ," and elsewhere envisages also an even larger court, comparing "the greater Sanhedrin . . . of one and seventy" to "the lesser of three and twenty." And, although it is unclear how much these comments relate to any real institution in first-century Jerusalem, or indeed at any other time or place in Jewish history, the terms of the rabbinic discussion presuppose the principle that the larger the number of jurors who hear a case, the more reliable the verdict will be: thus the early rabbinic sources envisage larger courts dealing with more serious issues, such as murder, and tackling the more tricky legal problems unresolved by the smaller courts, although they do not seem to have entertained the concept of an appeal against sentence by a lower court—in ordinary cases, the decision of a small local court of three or more judges would presumably be final. A similar assumption that more judges ensured better justice is found in the judicial procedures described by Josephus, in his account of his own career as revolutionary commander in Galilee in 66–7. He claims in the *Jewish War* that he "selected from the nation seventy persons of mature years and the greatest distinction, and appointed them as magistrates of the whole of Galilee, and seven individuals in each city as judges of petty disputes, with instructions to refer more important matters and capital cases to himself and the seventy," although in his autobiography, published some twenty-five or so years later, he suggests a rather more restricted advisory role for these seventy "magistrates," whom he describes as being already in authority in Galilee before his arrival: "I made them my friends and companions in travel, took them as assessors to cases which I tried, and obtained their approbation of the sentences which I pronounced; endeavouring not to fail in justice through precipitate action and in these matters to keep clear of all bribery." On the other hand, Josephus asserts in his *Antiquities* that the requirement that "seven men should rule in every city" had originally been laid down by Moses himself, and that someone who accidentally lost a deposit should "come before the seven judges and swear by God that nothing had been lost through his own intention and malice," which suggests—since the number seven for the quota of judges is not found anywhere in the Bible—that use of such larger tribunals was standard in his own day.[9]

Among the courts mentioned in the ancient sources, the composition and functions of the Jerusalem Sanhedrin of seventy-one judges is the most difficult to pin down in the history of judicial operations among Jews in antiquity. The institution is not found in the Hebrew Bible, and the fact that the name in Hebrew was derived from the Greek word *synhedrion*, "council," suggests that it originated in Jewish society some time after the fourth century BCE, when Judaean Jews first came under Greek influence. The rabbis envisaged a court composed of sages like themselves, presided over by a rabbinic *nasi*, "patriarch" or "prince." This picture runs counter to the description of the Sanhedrin to be found in the New Testament, where the presiding officer was assumed to be the High Priest, as after the arrest of Peter, when "the high priest came, and they that were with him, and called the Sanhedrin and all the council of the children of Israel, and sent to the prison to have them brought," and the Sanhedrin before which Paul was brought was envisaged as including in its membership both Pharisees and Sadducees. Josephus also assumed that the Sanhedrin could be convened by a High Priest—in 62 CE the High Priest Ananus son of Ananus "convened a Sanhedrin of judges and brought before it the brother of Jesus called the Christ, by name Jacob, and certain others"—but elsewhere he uses the term *synhedrion* to refer to the advisory council of Agrippa II and even of the Roman emperor Augustus. It may be that an advisory council was all that the term implied: for important decisions it was important for Jewish leaders, like Roman aristocrats, to take appropriate advice. Thus when the High Priest Caiaphas needed to decide what to do with Jesus, he was surrounded by "all the chief priests and the elders and the scribes," just as a Roman magistrate would surround himself with his trusted friends and in the same way as Josephus "obtained their approbation of the sentences which I pronounced" from his seventy assessors in Galilee. The Sanhedrin thus played a judicial role in first-century Jerusalem, but only as adjunct to the High Priest, about whose role as judge Josephus is explicit: "with his priestly colleagues, he [the High Priest] will sacrifice to God, safeguard the laws, adjudicate in cases of dispute, punish those convicted of crime. Any who disobey him will pay the penalty as for impiety towards God himself."[10]

In court procedure, the most striking difference between Jews and Romans lay in the treatment of witnesses. The testimony of any individual was valued in a Roman trial, including that of slaves, who could be subjected to torture to extract the truth, except against their master. Even this exception could be circumvented: in the trial of a certain Marcus Scribonius Libo Drusus, accused of treason in the early years of Tiberius' rule, the identification of his handwriting on an incriminating paper was done by his slaves. The only way to confirm that they were not misleading the court was to torture them. So the emperor ordered their sale to the state treasury. Torture was not standard, and was only used in criminal cases, but it might also be used on citizens suspected of conspiracy, like the freedwoman Epicharis, who escaped continued torture by Nero only by heroic suicide. By contrast, Jewish rules of evidence were very restrictive indeed. In practice, Herod used torture to investigate rumours of plots against him by his sons, and the brutality of his investigations sometimes led to the death of his victims, but no source suggests that torture was admissible in Jewish law. According to both the Bible and the Mishnah, only testimony from adult male Jews was acceptable, and, even in such cases, evidence from at least two witnesses was essential. The legal tradition placed strong moral pressure to testify on those in possession of knowledge relevant to a case: "if a soul sin, and hear the voice of swearing, and is a witness, whether he has seen or known—if he does not utter, then he shall bear his iniquity." Moral pressure could of course translate into social stigma, and refusal to testify must have been difficult. On the other hand, testimony must be based on direct knowledge and not on hearsay. Early rabbinic literature is strongly condemnatory of gossip (*leshon ha-ra'*, "evil tongue"), talebearing even when the information imparted is true, and asserts that a skin disease like leprosy is divine punishment for scandalmongering: " 'Remember what the Lord thy God did unto Miriam': what does this have to do with the matter under discussion? The connection here is intended to show you that plagues come only as a result of evil talk . . ." The attitude to gossip seems to have been very different in Roman court cases, in which allusions to every conceivable aspect of the character and previous history of a defendant could be invoked by the parties to a dispute. The use of unsubstantiated stories to blacken the reputation of an opponent was standard procedure in Roman public life, in court as much as in politics. There were no rules to forbid either the presentation in court of rumour as fact or the introduction of information irrelevant to the case in dispute, and experienced pleaders, like Cicero, often offered arguments which would be wholly inadmissible in a trial under most modern legal systems.[11]

The restriction that in most cases witness by women, children or slaves had to be ignored in a Jewish court, combined with the need for two adult male witnesses to agree for their testimony to be used, may often have made the Jewish criminal law unenforceable. Some scholars have indeed suggested that this result might have been deliberately fostered by the rabbis in times and places where they were prevented by non-Jewish authorities from putting Jewish criminal law into practice. In favour of such an interpretation is the notable relaxation of strict biblical law about single witnesses to be found in the sectarian *Damascus Document* of which numerous fragments were discovered among the Dead Sea scrolls:

Every sin which a man commits against the Law, and which his companion witnesses, he being alone, if it is a capital matter he shall report

it in his presence, with rebuke, to the Guardian [the highest official in
the sect]; and the Guardian shall personally record it, until he commits
it again before one man and he reports it to the Guardian once more.
Should he repeat it and be caught in the act before one man, his judgement shall be complete. And if there are two [witnesses], each testify-
ing to a different matter, the man shall be excluded from the pure Meal
provided that they are trustworthy and that each informs the Guardian
on the day that he saw him [offending]. In matters of property, they
shall accept two trustworthy witnesses and shall exclude from the pure
Meal on the word of one witness alone.

In some cases involving personal status, the early rabbis too envisaged
occasionally relying on the evidence even of a woman, even if she was the
sole witness: "If a woman and her husband went beyond the sea and there
was peace between him and her and peace in the world, and she came back
and said, 'My husband is dead,' she may marry again."[12]

Enforcing the court's decision in civil cases was left, both in Roman and
in Jewish society, to the legal victor, without any intervention by the state:
in essence, the upshot of legal procedures could be no more than to grant
permission to a private individual to use reasonable force to gain what was
rightfully his without incurring the wrath of the authorities. The enforcement of punishments following criminal convictions was much more systematic. In Roman society, the range of penalties inflicted depended not
only on the offence committed but also on the status of the guilty party.
Some of the most violent punishments were reserved for slaves. Imprisonment was not usually in itself seen as a punitive measure but simply as a
means to prevent absconding before trial. Little use was made of fines
payable to the state (as opposed to restitution to injured parties, as in the
punishment of provincial governors convicted of stealing from their erstwhile subjects), or of corporal punishment such as flogging (which was,
however, common in the enforcement of military discipline). The main
sanctions for more important citizens were loss of status, a powerful deter-
rent in a society where being a senator or *eques* mattered a great deal, or rel-
egation to some place outside Rome, or (more generally) exile. The more
humble were condemned to work in the mines or other public projects
requiring intense physical labour. The ultimate penalty for all classes was
execution, which could take various forms, from the brutal simplicity of

crucifixion, a standard mode for disposing of ordinary criminals, to the ceremonial casting of traitors from the Tarpeian rock, a cliff on the side of the Capitoline hill. Condemnation to fight as a gladiator was effectively a delayed death sentence. These very public deaths doubtless fulfilled a useful social function as deterrence against criminal behaviour. It was also important that for every crime the penalty should seem to be appropriate. What was considered appropriate was in many cases a matter primarily of tradition: for instance, in the Republic, the convicted murderer of a close relative was drowned in the sea, tied up in a sack with a dog, a cock, an ape and a viper. The state expected public approval for the use of such justified violence to protect society. The edicts, official letters and coins of the emperors proclaimed IUSTITIA, "Justice."[13]

Jews too recognized the desirability of punishment appropriate to the offence, and in principle accepted that the death penalty should be inflicted for crimes such as murder. The biblical injunction "an eye for an eye, a tooth for a tooth, a hand for a hand" was interpreted to mean that appropriate monetary compensation should be made for personal injury, or financial restitution in the case of damage to property. Josephus states that the law laid down by Moses required that "he that maims a man shall undergo the like, being deprived of that limb whereof he deprived the other, unless indeed the maimed man be willing to accept money; for the law empowers the victim himself to assess the damage that has befallen him and make this concession, unless he would show himself too severe." For the rabbis, the amount to be paid was to be fixed not (as for Josephus) by the victim but by a court. No such negotiation was possible for the punishment of deliberate homicide, for which the death penalty was required, as also, in biblical law, for a series of other offences, sexual and religious. Hence the types of death penalty envisaged in the Mishnah are nearly as varied as those in the Roman system: "Four kinds of death penalty were entrusted to a court: stoning, burning, beheading and strangling," although to what extent these punishments were actually inflicted in the late Second Temple period has been much debated, not least because of the explicit statement ascribed in the Gospel of John to "the Jews" in conversation with Pontius Pilate before the death of Jesus: when he told them to judge Jesus "according to your law," they stated "it is not lawful for us to put any man to death." The author of the Gospel glosses this assertion with the aside that thus "the saying of Jesus might be fulfilled, which he spoke, indicating by what death he should die." It is possible that the restriction on Jewish use of the death penalty applied only at the specific time of year when Jesus' trial took place, since it coincided with the pilgrim festival of the Passover. Or it may be argued, in the light of the history of the early Church, that an allegation that Jews were not permitted to put Jesus to death explained to gentile Christians why the death which Jesus had suffered was of a distinctively Roman type despite the traditions that the Roman governor had judged him guiltless, and that the charge of blasphemy on which he was condemned was of concern not to Romans but to Jews.[14]

It is in any case a reasonable assumption that both Hasmonaeans and Herodians used Jewish criminal law at least to some extent when they were in power in Jerusalem, not least because Josephus records popular opposition to a legal innovation by Herod designed to crack down on theft:

> In his administration of the state the king in an earnest effort to put a stop to the successive acts of injustice committed both in the city and in the country made a law in no way resembling earlier ones, and he enforced it himself. It provided that house-breakers should be sold (into slavery) and be deported from the kingdom—a punishment that not only weighed heavily upon those who suffered it but also involved a violation of the laws of the country. For to be enslaved to foreigners and to those who did not have the same manner of life (as the Jews) and to be compelled to do whatever such men might command was an offence against religion rather than a punishment of those who were caught, especially as the following kind of penalty was anciently observed. The laws ordered that a thief was to pay a fourfold fine, and, if he were unable to do so, he was to be sold, but in any case not to foreigners, nor was he to suffer lifelong slavery, for he was to be released after six years.

The implication of this passage is that in normal times in Jerusalem the courts tended to impose fines as legal penalties for theft, and both biblical and rabbinic law envisaged corporal punishment in the form of flogging for specified offences: "How many stripes do they inflict on him? Forty save one . . . They bind his two hands to a pillar on either side, and the minister of the assembly lays hold on his garments . . . And he that smites, smites with his one hand with all his might." There is no reason to believe that such judicial beatings were not imposed more or less in this way both in the periods when Jerusalem was an independent state and also, with the consent of the accused to accept the jurisdiction of the Jewish court, when supreme power in Jerusalem was in the hands of a Roman governor and in Jewish communities in the diaspora. Paul, eager to demonstrate his Jewishness, as well as his willingness to suffer for the sake of Christ, boasted that "of the Jews five times I received forty [stripes] save one."[15]

## WAR

BOTH ROMANS and Jews made war frequently in the first century BCE and the first century CE. Roman campaigns of imperial expansion were to continue at irregular intervals throughout the early empire, whenever an emperor felt the need of a great military achievement to consolidate his image, notably Claudius in Britain in 43 CE, Domitian in the 80s and Trajan in Dacia in the first decade of the second century and in northern Mesopotamia in the second decade. Even more frequent were wars to suppress rebellions within the frontiers. Jews fought wars of conquest under the late Hasmonaeans, and, as we have seen, an extended war of liberation in 66–70. Jews also served as mercenaries for the Ptolemies in the second and first centuries BCE, and both Babylonian and Idumaean Jews were professional soldiers in the pay of Herod. For both Jews and Romans, war was an inevitable part of life.

EVERY SPRING the priests of the Roman state threw open the gates of the temple of Janus to indicate the beginning of the campaigning season. The temple gates were usually shut again only when the onset of winter brought fighting to a standstill. In 28 BCE, and on two later occasions, Augustus ceremonially shut the gates in the middle of the year to symbolize the completion of a current campaign, but this signified only a temporary hiatus in what was, in essence, a permanent state of war. Indeed, the political system of Rome categorized the citizenry by their military potential, with rich cavalrymen (*equites*) at the top, the poorer (who were less able to arm themselves well) nearer the bottom, and women and children, who were excluded from fighting, also excluded from all formal influence over policy. From the beginning of Augustus' rule, after his victory over Mark

Antony at Actium, in practice the Roman army was as professional and permanent as that of the Ptolemies had been, but the ideology of Rome as a state dependent on its armed citizenry persisted in the history books of Augustus' contemporary Livy, and in Roman images of their ideal society.

Despite this underlying militarism, Romans in the Republic valued the implausible notion that all the wars they fought were defensive. Only thus was divine approval guaranteed. It may seem surprising that any Roman in the first century BCE could believe, or even half-believe, that they had conquered the entire Mediterranean world in defence of their city in central Italy, but the illusion that they fought only in defence was achieved by a formality which, although it might appear now a mere pretext, Romans seem to have taken very seriously. Religious law required the enemy to have unreasonably rejected Roman demands if the ensuing conflict was to be denoted just, as Cicero records: "As for war, equitable rules touching it are drawn up in the . . . law of the Roman people in the most sacred fashion; and from this it may be gathered that no war is just, unless it is entered upon after an official demand for satisfaction has been submitted or warning has been given and a formal declaration made." Cicero (or a later interpolator) added an improving story to illustrate:

> Popilius was general in command of a province. In his army Cato's son was serving on his first campaign. When Popilius decided to disband one of his legions, he discharged also young Cato, who was serving in that same legion. But when the young man out of love for the service stayed on in the field, his father wrote to Popilius to say that if he let him stay in the army, he should swear him into service with a new oath of allegiance, for in view of the voidance of his former oath he could not legally fight the foe. So extremely scrupulous was the observance of the laws in regard to the conduct of war.

However, the demands on enemies could, if required, be made as unreasonable as necessary to produce the desired hostile response, as when, for instance, Rome in 200 BCE requested that Philip V of Macedon should not make war on any Greek state or intervene in the possessions of the Ptolemies, and that he should submit to arbitration with respect to the injustices he had perpetrated against Attalus and Rhodes, on pain of war with Rome if he did not immediately accept such terms: Philip refused,

Rome declared war, and in 197 BCE Philip was decisively defeated at the battle of Cynoscephalae. Nonetheless, by the imperial period not even this charade seems to have been followed. The senatorial historian Tacitus puts into the mouth of the Celtic chieftain Calgacus, faced in the 80s CE by the Roman forces commanded in Britain by Tacitus' father-in-law and hero Agricola, the cynical observation that "the Romans are the only people who invade, with equal ardour, the wealth and the poverty of nations. To rob, to murder, and to ravage, the liars call 'empire.' When they have made the world a solitude, they call it peace." But not all Romans were as aware as the cynical Tacitus of the unsubtle subterfuges that had been employed in the spread of Roman power, and there are few traces of guilt about the indulgence in warfare which had led Romans so directly and successfully to the current prosperity of their city.[16]

One reason for insouciance about warfare and its terrible consequences may have been the ability of many inhabitants of Rome in the early empire to pass their entire lives without witnessing war directly. Triumphal processions gave them a sense of the most dramatic moments, carefully selected for maximum impact, but to the spectators, it was like watching a story, the bloodshed kept at a safe emotional distance, as in the depersonalized slaughter of gladiatorial fights. Hence mass enthusiasm for war in distant countries was combined with a reluctance to admit that the human cost fell on anyone who mattered. The battle scenes depicted on Trajan's column, erected in celebration of the Dacian war, showed moments of extreme violence in the subjugation of the enemy. Dehumanizing the enemy was the key to Roman military success, and Tacitus' effort in his biography of Agricola to conjure up the feelings of Rome's (and Agricola's) opponents, and express them with a rhetoric of patriotism, honour and liberty put into the mouth of Calgacus, was as unusual and subversive as much of the rest of his histories:

> When I consider the motives that have roused us to this war; when I reflect on the necessity that now demands our firmest vigour, I expect everything great and noble from that union of sentiment that pervades us all. From this day I date the liberty of all Britain. For you are all here together, still untouched by slavery. Beyond this spot there is no land where liberty can find a refuge . . . We have not so much as seen the melancholy regions of slavery, our eyes have been unpolluted by the

sight of tyranny . . . In a private family the slave who is last bought in
provokes the ridicule even of his fellow slaves; and in this general
world-wide servitude, we, the most recent and worth least, are marked
out for destruction.

Such empathy with the conquered was rare, or at least rarely expressed. No
one in Rome preached pacifism.[17]

The Roman army which achieved these conquests was famously disciplined, with a clear structure of command. The legionaries, all Roman citizens, were highly trained foot-soldiers, all provided with the same
equipment and organized into small groups of eighty men, *centuriae*, each
under the command of a centurion. The centuries were grouped into
cohorts (usually six centuries to a cohort), and ten cohorts made up a
legion, each usually commanded (from the time of Augustus) by a
legionary legate of senatorial rank. Each legion was supported by auxiliary
forces of non-citizens, also organized into cohorts and used both as
infantry and for other military purposes, such as cavalry. An ethos of service, obedience and loyalty flourished in units in which, in the imperial
period, colleagues might spend their whole lives together, from birth "in
the camp" to retirement in a colony of veterans after legionary service of
twenty or more years. The result was impressive military efficiency at the
level of the cohort and the legion, although there was less competence in
the strategic operations of the legions as a whole: it may be significant that
Romans talked of "the legions" or "the armies" (in the plural) rather than
"the army." In wartime the Roman forces stationed round the empire's
frontiers were too fragmented for efficient cooperation. Communications
were slow and local commanders were frequently left to their own devices.
Hence the tally of defeated troops in the early empire is long. Most notorious was the loss of three legions by Publius Quinctilius Varus in the Teuto-
burger forest in 9 CE, which is said to have brought Augustus close to
despair. The contemporary historian Velleius Paterculus could only lament
the disaster in which "an army unexcelled in bravery, the first of Roman
armies in discipline, in energy, and in experience in the field, through the
negligence of its general, the perfidy of the enemy, and the unkindness of
fortune was surrounded . . . Hemmed in by forests and marshes and
ambushes, it was exterminated almost to a man." These Roman soldiers
could rely for victories on no novel infantry tactics such as the Macedonian

phalanx which had enabled Alexander the Great to conquer the Near East in the fourth century BCE, but they excelled in siege warfare and especially the use of the *testudo,* "tortoise shell," in which

> the heavy-armed troops who use the oblong, curved and cylindrical shields are drawn up around the outside, making a rectangular figure; and, facing outward and holding their arms at the ready, they enclose the rest. The others, who have flat shields, form a compact body in the centre and raise their shields over their own heads and the heads of all the others, so that nothing but shields can be seen in every part of the phalanx alike, and all the men by the density of the formation are under shelter from missiles.

This formation "is so marvellously strong that men can walk upon it, and whenever they come to a narrow ravine, even horses and vehicles can be driven over it." In open battle the rather rigid methods used by the heavily armed legionary infantry often had to be supplemented by the more fluid fighting techniques of auxiliary troops, who operated not just as light infantry but as cavalry or archers, or camel riders.[18]

In practice the course of battles might be decided less by firepower or military skill than by psychology, as in the Roman victory at the battle of Zama in 202 BCE, according to the account composed, probably mostly from his imagination, by Livy in the time of Augustus: "The Punic battle-line had been stripped of its cavalry when the infantry clashed, now no longer matched either in their hopes or in their strength. In addition there were what seem small things to mention, but at the same time were highly important in the battle: a harmony in the shouting of the Romans, which consequently was greater in volume and more terrifying; on the other side discordant voices, as was natural from many nations with a confusion of tongues." In a long fight it was physically impossible to keep actively engaging the enemy without exhaustion. Victory came only when the enemy were persuaded, by displays of force, that they could not win. In any ancient battle, the moment when one side turned to flee was decisive. Soldiers were poorly protected from the rear and could rarely reform once in retreat. Psychology also helped the Romans to win wars even when they lost battles: they treated defeats in battle as temporary reverses and refused to give up, and they ensured that their enemies knew the awful violence they would suffer when Rome was eventually victorious. No matter the scale of the Roman disaster, reinforcements would always come eventually, even if it took years. Even the remarkable career of Arminius, war-chief of the Cherusci, who successfully defeated Varus in 9 CE, showed the inexorability of Rome. His victory led to the abandonment of all the land annexed by Augustus between the Elbe and the Rhine, but he himself was subjected to a series of attacks by Roman and pro-Roman forces. In 16 CE he was defeated and wounded and, after a series of intrigues, he died in 19 at the hands of his own kin. Even the change in Roman strategy in the region was disguised by the institutionalization of two Roman armies and two provinces, one of Upper Germany and one of Lower Germany, each in fact with a base on the western bank of the Rhine: for the Roman public, "Germania" was under Roman rule, even though much of the Germany Augustus had once conquered or hoped to conquer in fact remained free. The Romans treated defeated enemies with a ruthlessness unusual in the ancient world. In marked contrast to the ancient Greeks, who subscribed, at least in theory, to gentler rules for the conduct of war, Roman soldiers expected to indulge in extreme violence in the sack of cities at the close of a siege. They treated a period of looting, rape and indiscriminate slaughter of civilians as a natural reward for soldiers as recompense for their efforts. It is unsurprising that many of their opponents preferred to make terms and surrender rather than risk facing such savagery.[19]

Not that all Romans wholly lacked scruples about warfare. Cicero asserts that: "the only reason to go to war is that we may live in peace unharmed; and when the victory is won, we should spare those who have not been bloodthirsty and barbarous in their warfare," and he urged that "as to destroying and plundering cities, let me say that great care should be taken that nothing be done in reckless cruelty or wantonness," although such scruples did not prevent Cicero himself from glorying in his victory over brigands on the Amanus mountain range during his governorship of Cilicia (in modern Turkey) in 51–50 BCE, for which he earned a public supplication in Rome and hoped, unsuccessfully, for a triumph. With rather more integrity, the Stoic philosopher Gaius Musonius Rufus risked his personal safety by preaching peace to the Flavian army before the battle of Cremona on 24 October 69 CE: "he mixed among the soldiers, and, reasoning much concerning good and evil, began a dissertation on the blessings of peace, and the calamities of war. Many were moved to ridicule by his words, more were bored; and there were some who would have jostled him and trampled on him, if he had not listened to the warnings of the quieter individuals and the threats of others and given up his ill-timed maxims of wisdom." Musonius Rufus would have had little chance of success with such arguments even in a purely philosophical milieu. His fellow Stoic Dio Chrysostom argued later in the first century CE that morality dictated the fulfilment of duty, which could include fighting for your country. The Stoic emperor Marcus Aurelius composed his *Meditations* while on campaign. The role of philosophy for such Romans was not to provide a moral basis for warfare but to put war into a wider perspective. For the true philosopher, only the interior self really mattered, and it was an error to become too concerned by the horrors of the world around.[20]

Jews as much as Romans viewed war as a natural condition but, unlike Romans, they sometimes expressed a hope that this might change. Deuteronomy lays down rules for conscription, and for the conduct of troops during conflicts, which presuppose total war. All adult male Israelites, with only a few exceptions, are to fight. The enemy in cities "very far from you" are to be offered a choice of total subjection or the violent consequences: "When the Lord your God has delivered it into your hands, you shall put all its males to the sword, but the women, and the little ones, and the cattle, and all that is in the city, even all the spoil, shall you take to yourself, and you shall enjoy the spoil of your enemies." As for the cities in the land of Israel, "which the Lord your God gives you for an inheritance, you shall save alive nothing that breathes; but you shall utterly destroy them." Hence the treatment of the kingdom of Ai by Joshua more than a thousand years before Jews and Romans came into contact, in the conquest of the land as described in the biblical book of Joshua:

When Israel had made an end of slaying all the inhabitants of Ai in the open wilderness where they chased them, and when all of them to the very last had fallen by the edge of the sword, all Israel returned to Ai, and smote it with the edge of the sword. And all who fell that day, both men and women, were twelve thousand, all the people of Ai. For Joshua did not draw back his hand, with which he stretched out the spear, until he had utterly destroyed all the inhabitants of Ai. Only the

cattle and the spoil of that city Israel took as their booty, according to
the word of the Lord which he commanded Joshua. And Joshua burned
Ai, and made it for ever a heap of ruins, as it is to this day.

Cicero, who approved of the razing "to the ground" of Carthage and
Numantia in 146 and 133 BCE, would have been at home in the savage world
in which Ai and its inhabitants were said to have been destroyed. In stark
contrast, the biblical prophets Isaiah, Micah and Joel all looked forward
with longing to a time when there would be no more war at all.

> And it shall come to pass in the latter days that the mountain of the
> Lord's house shall be established as the highest of the mountains, and
> shall be exalted above the hills; and all nations shall flow to it. And
> many peoples shall come and say: "Come let us go up to the mountain
> of the Lord, to the house of the God of Jacob; that he may teach us his
> ways, and that we may walk in his paths." For out of Zion shall go forth
> the law, and the word of the Lord from Jerusalem. And he shall judge
> between the nations, and shall decide for many peoples; and they shall
> beat their swords into ploughshares, and their spears into pruning
> hooks: nation shall not lift up sword against nation, neither shall they
> learn war any more.

This notion of permanent peace, *shalom*, and an end to war, espoused by
Isaiah was quite different from the Roman notion of *pax*, which constituted little more than a pause to take stock between victorious and glorious
campaigns.[21]

Jews in the first two centuries CE were heir to both these biblical traditions. Early rabbis, intent on divining the real meaning of the Bible, distinguished "religious" wars and "mandatory" wars in defence of the Holy
Land from "permitted" wars for increase of territory, requiring, in line
with Deuteronomy, that no surrender terms be offered to an enemy in
mandatory wars. If God requires his people to conquer and kill, it is not for
them to argue: "Rabbi Judah said . . . 'In a mandatory war all go forth,
even the bridegroom out of his chamber and the bride out of her
bridechamber.' " The biblical story of the fate of Saul, who was deprived
by God of his kingdom in Israel for sparing alive Agag, the king of the
Amalekites, against express divine command, as mediated by the prophet

Samuel, to "destroy all that they have, and spare them not, but slay both man and woman, infant and suckling, ox and sheep, camel and ass," functioned as a sufficiently clear lesson. On the other hand, the sacred obligation on Jews in all generations to annihilate the Amalekites and "blot out the remembrance of Amalek from under heaven," as the injunction was expressed in Deuteronomy, was softened by Josephus, following the version in Exodus, into a prediction by Moses that in fact the Amalekites would be exterminated by an unspecified agent, presumably God. Rabbinic wisdom sayings, attributed to sages such as Hillel, urged generally that Jews should seek peace: "Be of the disciples of Aaron, loving peace and pursuing peace, loving mankind and bringing them close to the Torah," though this is as likely to refer to the cessation of domestic strife as to avoidance of warfare.[22]

It seems unlikely from their reported behaviour that any Jews in late antiquity thought of any of the conflicts in which they were involved as "mandatory" wars such as are described in Deuteronomy, although it is evident that they believed they fought with religious authority. Judas Maccabee, in his struggle to free the Temple from idolatry in the 160s BCE, is said to have destroyed and plundered the hostile city of Ephron with a ruthlessness equal to Roman practice: "He destroyed every male with the edge of the sword." Judas' call to arms is described in biblically heroic fashion in 1 Maccabees:

> Then was the congregation gathered together, that they might be ready for battle, and that they might pray, and ask mercy and compassion . . . Then they fasted that day, and put on sackcloth, and put ashes upon their heads, and tore their garments, and spread out the book of the law, wherein the heathen had sought to paint the likeness of their images. They brought also the priests' garments, and the firstfruits, and the tithes: and they stirred up the nazirites, who had fulfilled their days. Then cried they with a loud voice towards heaven . . . But as for such as were building houses, or had betrothed wives, or were planting vineyards, or were timid, those he commanded that they should return, every man to his own house, in accordance with the law.

The use of Temple images on the coins of the rebels in Jerusalem in 66–70 suggests strongly that these Jews also believed, at the least, that they were fighting with divine approval, but there is no hint in either Jewish or gentile sources of the ruthless treatment of the gentile enemy in the land of Israel that was prescribed in Deuteronomy for mandatory wars. On the contrary, according to Cassius Dio the Jews in Jerusalem even welcomed deserters from the Roman side in the course of the siege of the city. Reference to holy war seems to have been confined to imaginative accounts of the final eschatological battles at the end of days, as envisaged in the *War Scroll* from Qumran: "All these shall pursue the enemy to destroy him in an everlasting destruction in the battle of God. The priests shall sound for them the trumpets of pursuit, and they shall deploy against all the enemy in a pursuit to destruction; and the cavalry shall thrust them back on the flanks of the battle until they are utterly destroyed." In general, however, warfare as described in the *War Scroll* was not very realistic. It was more like a ritual dance, led by the priests: "And as the slain men fall, the priests shall trumpet from afar; they shall not approach the slain lest they be defiled with unclean blood. For they are holy, and they shall not profane the anointing of their priesthood with the blood of nations of vanity."[23]

When Jews fought what later rabbis called "permitted" wars, they seem to have considered themselves more bound by rules of war than Romans did. Josephus, in his summary of the laws of the Jews in *Against Apion*, chose to include the claim that Moses required Jews to be "considerate even to those who have been adjudged enemies. He does not allow us to burn up their country or to cut down their fruit trees, and forbids even the spoiling of fallen combatants; he has taken measures to prevent outrage to prisoners of war, especially women . . . [He] bade us even in an enemy's country to spare and not to kill the beasts employed in labour. Thus, in every particular, he had an eye to mercy." Some of this description was taken from Deuteronomy, but selectively, and some—no burning of enemy territory; no spoiling of dead bodies; sparing beasts of burden—was either traditional or (less likely) invented by Josephus. What is curious is Josephus' evident belief that such an emphasis on the mercy shown by Jews in warfare would appeal to his Roman readers, since he was quite able to write for the same readers in his *Jewish War*, without obvious disapproval, about the standard violent behaviour of Roman generals in the Jewish world, including, conspicuously, in the treatment by Vespasian in 67 of captured rebels in Tarichaeae, a town on the shore of the Sea of Galilee:

After the battle Vespasian took his seat on his tribunal at Tarichaeae, and, separating the native population from the crowd of immigrants who had evidently given the signal for hostilities, consulted with his commanders whether the lives of the latter also should be spared. All unanimously declared that their liberation would be pernicious; once let loose, these expatriated men would never keep quiet, and would, moreover, be capable of forcing into revolt those with whom they sought refuge. Vespasian recognized that they were undeserving of being saved and that they would only abuse their liberty to the detriment of their liberators, but he asked himself how he could make away with them: if he killed them on the spot, he suspected that he would bitterly alienate the residents, who would not tolerate the massacre in their city of all these refugees who had sued for mercy; on the other hand, he could not bring himself to let them go, and then, after pledging his word, to fall upon them.

But Josephus records that Vespasian was persuaded to overcome his scruples:

> Vespasian accordingly granted them an amnesty in equivocal terms, but permitted them to quit the city by only one route, that leading to Tiberias. Prompt to believe what they earnestly desired, the wretches set out in complete confidence, carrying their effects without any disguise, in the prescribed direction. The Romans, meanwhile, lined the whole road to Tiberias, to prevent any deviation from it, and on their arrival shut them into that town. Vespasian followed in due course and had them all removed to the stadium. He then gave orders for the execution of the old and unserviceable, to the number of twelve hundred; from the youths he selected six thousand of the most robust and sent them to Nero at the isthmus. The rest of the multitude, numbering thirty thousand four hundred, he sold, excepting those of whom he made a present to Agrippa, namely the former subjects of his realm; these Vespasian permitted him to deal with at his discretion, and the king in his turn sold them.[24]

Josephus was not alone in stressing the mercy enjoined on Jews by the Torah. Philo also had emphasized this aspect of the Torah to the greatest

extent possible without actually directly contradicting the laws laid down
in Deuteronomy. He wrote of the "general commands he [the lawgiver]
addresses to the whole nation in common, advising them how to behave
not only to friends and allies but also to those who renounce their
alliance." Since the rules which follow mention all those laws about warfare not included in Deuteronomy in the category of mandatory laws
required by God for the purification of the Holy Land, it seems that Philo,
unlike the early rabbis, and even more unlike the Romans, did not even
entertain the possibility that the Torah might permit wars of conquest.
According to Philo, the treatment of such rebels must always follow the
path of reason:

> The Jewish nation is ready for agreement and friendship with all who
> are like-minded whose intentions are peaceful, yet is not of the con-
> temptible kind which surrenders through cowardice to wrongful
> aggression. When it takes up arms it distinguishes between those whose
> life is one of hostility and the reverse. For to breathe slaughter against
> all, even those who have done very little or nothing amiss, shows what
> I should call a savage and brutal soul, and the same may be said of
> counting women, whose life is naturally peaceful and domestic, to be
> accessories to men who have brought about the war.

Philo elsewhere praises extravagantly the pacifism of the Essenes: "In vain
would one look among them for makers of arrows, or javelins, or swords,
or helmets, or armour, or shields; in short, for makers of arms, or military
machines, or any instrument of war, or even of peaceful objects which
might be turned to evil purposes."[25] This aspect of the Essenes was not
mentioned by other Greek and Latin writers, nor indeed by Philo in his
other account of the group, and it may well be attributable to his desire to
idealize his picture of them, but the production of the ideal by a Jewish
author writing about Jews of ideal piety in the middle of the first century
CE is itself significant. It is evident that some Jews liked to think of themselves as less indiscriminately militaristic than most contemporary
Romans. Whether in practice there was any difference in behaviour when
the opportunity for war arose is of course another matter. But at least in
the case of Jews ethical considerations about the welfare of the enemy

could sometimes be raised as a pertinent moral issue, however difficult in practice it might be to enforce such scruples in the heat of conflict. The suggestion that Jews were not belligerent would have sounded bizarre to Romans by 70 CE, after the suppression of a bloody Jewish revolt, but in the time of Philo these unhappy events lay in the future.

# CHAPTER NINE

# POLITICS

## STATUS

B Y WHOM should government be run? How much did Romans and Jews agree on the qualities required of their political leaders? Just as Romans generally lacked doubts about the morality of imperialist wars, so successful leadership in war against a perceived national enemy was the surest route to political prestige in Roman society. The heroes of the distant past were soldiers, distinguished for their courage, whose exploits fill the pages of the history of early Rome composed by Livy in the time of Augustus, like the mythical story of the young Roman noble Gaius Mucius, whose willingness to die to free Rome was narrated through his stirring speech when brought captive before the Etruscan enemy in 508 BCE: "I am a Roman citizen . . . I am your enemy, and as an enemy I would have slain you; I can die as resolutely as I could kill: both to do and to endure valiantly is the Roman way." The wily politician Cicero, fiercely opposed to the ambitions of Julius Caesar which were to overthrow the constitution of the Republic, could yet appeal in the Senate to general admiration for Caesar's conquest of Gaul, "for he [Caesar] believed not only that it was necessary to wage war against those who he saw were already in arms against the Roman people, but also that all Gaul must be subjected to our sway, and so he has fought with the fiercest peoples, in gigantic battles against the Germans and Helvetians, with the greatest success. He has terrified, confined and subdued the rest, and accustomed them to submit to the rule of the Roman people." Augustus' *Res Gestae*, published after his death, lists his military achievements not just by regions and peoples conquered but by numbers of victories acclaimed. Even the least militarily inclined of emperors, like Claudius, might feel himself impelled to present an image of himself as warrior in the conquest of Britain in order to justify his tenure of power.[1]

By contrast, the attitude of the Jews to their national warrior heroes was ambivalent. The biblical narrative provided many instances of military prowess: Saul, David, Jonathan. David's rise to fame and his struggle with Saul were encapsulated in the song of the women as they returned from battle against the Philistines: "Saul has slain his thousands, and David his ten thousands." According to the story, the phrase became a commonplace at the time and Saul feared for his kingdom: "They have ascribed to David ten thousands, and to me they have ascribed thousands: and what more can he have but the rule?" Jews thus believed that there had once been a Jewish society ruled by a warrior elite. But by the early Roman period this was no longer the case. Most of the surviving literature from the late Second Temple period has little to say about contemporary military leaders, and not much comment on the great biblical warriors as fighters. Josephus, in his rewriting of biblical history in his *Antiquities*, stresses the courage and military prowess of ancient Jewish heroes, from Moses, conqueror of Ethiopia, to Joshua and David, but his emphasis may have been stimulated less by general Jewish traditions than by the requirements of Greek historiography, in which politics and war always took pride of place, and by the apologetic need to present Jews as disciplined fighters: Josephus reports that the Greek orator Apollonius Molon, who came from Asia Minor in the first century BCE, had attacked the Jews, "in one place . . . reproaching us as cowards, whereas elsewhere, on the contrary, he accuses us of temerity and reckless madness." The rabbinic tradition put less emphasis on the prowess of the warrior and more on the power of divine intervention as a response to piety. Great feats of valour could be achieved only through God's help. The festival of Hanukkah, whose origins were discussed in Chapter 1, was celebrated in rabbinic tradition not for the achievements of the warrior Judas Maccabee but as the occasion of divine intervention for the rededication of the Temple: the pure oil, sufficient to keep the candelabrum in the Temple alight only for one day, lasted miraculously for eight. The rabbis were almost wholly silent about the leaders of the armies of the Jewish state in 66–70, including the eventual commander-in-chief, Simon son of Gioras. About Simon's military career, the rabbis, who knew about the war against the Romans as a whole, must certainly have known something. For the Roman historian Cassius Dio, in the early third century, "Bargioras," as he called him, was the Jews' leader: "and he was the only one to be executed in connection with the triumphal celebration." For Josephus, although he was writing about a political opponent, Simon was a vicious and bloodthirsty tyrant, but he was impressive for his physical strength and daring. By contrast, Simon figured not at all in rabbinic memory.[2]

Rabbinic views of war may of course have been jaundiced by the defeat suffered by the Jews in 70, but even before then, if the surviving fragments are a good guide, the biblical stories that Jews chose to retell in this period were not the narratives of battle and heroism which they could have found in abundance in the sacred texts. In the detailed depiction of conflict provided by the *War Scroll* found at Qumran, the human participants are mere numbers and formations. The only hero is the divine warrior, God:

> For the battle is yours! Their bodies are crushed by the might of your hand and there is no man to bury them. You did deliver Goliath of Gath, the mighty warrior, into the hands of David your servant, because in place of the sword and in place of the spear he put his trust in your great name; for yours is the battle. Many times, by your great name, did he triumph over the Philistines. Many times have you also delivered us by the hand of our kings through your loving-kindness, and not in accordance with our works, by which we have done evil, nor according to our rebellious deeds. For the battle is yours and the power is from you! It is not ours. Our strength and the power of our hands accomplish no mighty deed except by your power and by the might of your great valour.[3]

Jews did not ascribe glamour to war, as Romans did.

IN MANY RESPECTS both Roman society and Jewish society were open, providing opportunities for the ambitious from any background, but in both cultures there were areas of life where ancestry alone mattered, and some others for which, by common consent, good ancestry was not essential but could be important. Where they differed was in their understanding of what sort of ancestry was worth boasting about.

> Whenever someone from the ranks of the illustrious dies, as a part of his funeral procession out of the city he is carried into the forum to the so-

called *rostra*. Usually his body is conspicuous in an upright pose; more rarely, he is lying down. When all the people are standing round, a grown-up son, if the deceased has left one and if he happens to be present, or, if not, some other relative mounts the *rostra* and speaks about the virtues and lifetime achievements of the deceased . . . After they have buried him and performed the customary rites, a wax image of the deceased is placed in a very conspicuous spot in the house, in a wooden shrine. This image is a mask made strikingly similar to the facial features and expression of the deceased. The family puts these images on display on the occasion of public sacrifices, decorating them with great care. When any illustrious family member dies, the family takes them to the funeral, putting them on men who seem to be most similar in height and size to the original . . . When the speaker who delivers the oration for the man to be buried has finished his speech about him, he then mentions the achievements and accomplishments of each of those other men whose masks are present, beginning with the most ancient.

Politicians in Rome were expected to extol the glory of their forefathers whenever it reflected well on them. Polybius in this passage was writing about the funerary customs of the upper class in the mid-second century BCE, but reverence for noble ancestry persisted into the imperial period, as in Tacitus' account of the appeal to Tiberius by Marcus Hortensius Hortalus, a young noble who, as a grandson of the famous orator Quintus Hortensius, had been persuaded by a grant from Augustus to marry and have children, to prevent the extinction of his famous family: "I married, because the emperor told me to. Behold the stock and offspring of so many consuls, so many dictators! I say this in no competitive spirit but to arouse your compassion. Under your glorious rule, Caesar, they will win whatever honours you choose to give. Meanwhile I beg you to save from destitution the great-grandsons of Quintus Hortensius, the fosterlings of the deified Augustus." The speech will have been Tacitus' invention, but not the occasion or the sentiment, and in fact Tiberius made a grant of two hundred thousand sesterces to each of Hortalus' male children. Significant is the assumption by Hortalus, and Tacitus, that the merits of a great-grandfather should ensure the financial well-being of boys as yet too young to have achieved anything for themselves.[4]

The most impressive formal family status in Rome was that of patrician. In the earliest centuries of Rome's history as a city, the patricians had provided the governing aristocracy who ruled over the rest of the Roman population, the plebeians. During most of the Republican period, patrician status was defined by descent alone, but from the time of Julius Caesar onwards, and under the emperors, the status might also be conferred on favoured individuals as a privilege. By this time, however, the status meant little, since by the end of the Republic, the distinction between patricians and plebeians had lost almost all political and social significance: rich plebeians had long exercised political power as magistrates, and plebeian and patrician families had long intermarried. In formal terms, the small number of patricians still left had only a few privileges, such as the right of some of them to be part of the company of Salii, who processed through Rome in March and October, performing elaborate ritual dances at specified places on the route, beating their shields with staves and singing a special song in unintelligible Saturnian verse in honour of Mars. But the status still brought prestige: it was his patrician origin that encouraged Galba to seize power as emperor in the coup in 68 CE which brought down Nero and ended finally the long domination of the Roman state by the descendants of Julius Caesar.

Less formal than the patriciate was the label of *nobilitas* applied by common consent in the early empire to descendants of those who had been consul either in the Republic or in the triumviral period which had preceded the decisive victory of Octavian at Actium in 31 BCE. The families of *nobiles*, "known men," had dominated the top magistracies of the state for centuries to the time of Cicero, not because such birth was a necessary qualification for these posts but simply as a matter of custom. The snobbery inherent in such attitudes continued to have an effect on the politics of the early empire, despite the transfer of power into the hands of one man. Emperors who wished to show their respect for the Senate and its traditions tended to contrive that descendants of such prestigious families were favoured when it came to the election of the first pair of consuls for each year, in whose name the year's date was recorded for posterity throughout the Roman world.

The prejudice that political status could and should be inherited emerged even more blatantly in the transfer of power from one emperor to the next. When Julius Caesar died in 44 BCE his great-nephew Octavian, the future emperor Augustus, made great play of his relationship to the murdered dictator, calling himself "Caesar" even before the right to bear the name as Julius' adopted son was formally bestowed upon him by the Senate, and encouraging the issue of coins which proclaimed him DIVI FILIUS, "son of a god." The role of hereditary factors in the succession to Augustus himself on his death in 14 CE was complicated by the fact that the new emperor, Tiberius, his adopted son, was in any case by far the most important politician in Rome by that date, not least by virtue of his military feats. But on Tiberius' own death in 37 there was nothing to be said for the young and vicious Gaius apart from the popularity once accorded to his natural father Germanicus, whose death in 19 CE had caused such widespread grief, and the fact that Tiberius had adopted him as his son. Gaius' relationship to both fathers, natural and adoptive, was essentially a private matter, but in practice both were treated by the Roman public as legitimation of the transfer of supreme power. By 37 the empire was, in effect, though never formally, a hereditary monarchy, until the power of the dynasty which had begun with Julius Caesar was broken by the uprisings of 68.[5]

The importance of ancestry could not be more vividly exemplified, but Rome was not in the end a caste-based society. Those, like Cicero, born into the "wrong" family could assert vehemently their superiority based on their qualities as "new men": "I have not the same privileges as men of noble birth, who sit still and see the honours our nation bestows land at their feet; the present conditions of political life oblige me to behave far otherwise . . . We are aware with what jealousy, with what dislike, the merit and energy of new men are regarded by certain of the nobles . . ." Some could even acquire a new, fictitious, identity, like the rich ex-slaves given the right by the emperor to wear a gold ring as a mark of their (pretended) free birth. An ancestral line insufficiently distinguished by famous forebears could be much enhanced by the adoption of a god or goddess at the top of the family tree, as the Julii claimed Venus to have been founder of their line. In an unusual act of reverse legalistic mendacity (rather like renouncing a hereditary peerage in order to stay in the House of Commons), the patrician Publius Clodius Pulcher had himself adopted into a plebeian *gens* in 59 BCE in order to facilitate his election to the post of plebeian tribune, which was closed to those of patrician birth and had proved in the preceding decades an effective platform for those with exceptional political ambitions.[6]

By contrast, Josephus' self-description in his autobiography neatly encapsulates the two very different lineages that brought high status in Jewish society. He could boast an impressive ancestry both priestly and royal:

My family is not insignificant, tracing its descent far back to priestly ancestors. Different societies base their claim to good birth on various grounds; with us a connection with the priesthood is the hallmark of an illustrious line. Not only, however, were my ancestors priests, but they belonged to the first of the twenty-four courses—a peculiar distinction—and to the most eminent of its constituent clans. Moreover, on my mother's side I am of royal family; for the posterity of Asamonaeus, from whom she sprang, for a very considerable period were kings, as well as High Priests, of our nation . . . With such a pedigree, which I cite as I find it recorded in the public registers, I can take leave of the would-be detractors of my family.[7]

The Jewish priesthood was a quasi-caste, defined by descent from Aaron through the male line. Priests, *kohanim*, were a sub-group from within the tribe of Levi; other Levites had lesser privileges. Hence the importance of archival proof of the family tree in the continuous records preserved in the public registers, although priests were not restricted to other priestly families in their choice of marriage partner, and many non-priests might thus have priest relations. To the male priests were reserved the most important functions in the Temple in Jerusalem, above all the performance of sacrifices and other offerings in the special court next to the Holy of Holies which was reserved for their use. The knowledge that priests came, or could come on those occasions they served in the Temple, so much closer to the Holy of Holies than other Israelites gave them a special aura. It must have helped that in the land of Israel many people would know which men were priests and which not, not because they wore special clothing outside the Temple but because they were recipients of tithes. A proportion of all agricultural produce was payable by non-priests to priests. It did not matter which priest was selected for the gift, so in the nature of things most Israelites will have handed over their tithes to the priests in their neighbourhood, although more powerful priests, like Josephus when he was rebel commander in Galilee in 66 CE, might be offered more than their fair share. In protesting his integrity, Josephus notes that "I even declined to accept from those who brought them the tithes which were due to me as a priest." By contrast, the colleagues sent with him from Jerusalem had wanted to return home right at the beginning of their mission, "having amassed a large sum of money from the tithes which they accepted as their priestly due."[8]

Restrictions on permissible marriage partners for male priests ensured care in the preservation of records of the lineage also of non-priests, as Josephus also boasts:

> Not only did our ancestors in the first instance set over this business men of the highest character, devoted to the service of God, but they took precautions to ensure that the priests' lineage should be kept unadulterated and pure. A member of the priestly order must, to beget a family, marry a woman of his own race, without regard to her wealth or other distinctions; but he must investigate her pedigree, obtaining the genealogy from the archives and producing witnesses. And we practise this not only in Judaea itself, but wherever there is a Jewish community, there too a strict account is kept by the priests of their marriages; I allude to the Jews in Egypt and Babylon and other parts of the world in which any of the priestly order are living in dispersion. A statement is drawn up by them and sent to Jerusalem, showing the names of the bride and her father and more remote ancestors, together with the names of the witnesses.[9]

Priests were forbidden to marry any woman, such as a divorcee, whose offspring might just possibly prove not to be his and thus might sully the purity of priestly descent. A naive reading of the list of permitted marriages found in the Mishnah might suggest that Jewish society was entirely based on caste restrictions of this kind: "Ten genealogies went from Babylon: the priestly, Levitic, and the Israelitish; the impaired priestly; the proselyte, freedman, bastard and *nathin* [Temple servant] . . . The priestly, Levitic and Israelitish may intermarry . . . the proselyte, freedman, bastard, *nathin* . . . may all intermarry."[10] However, many of the "genealogies" to which the Mishnah referred were fairly theoretical, deduced from interpretation of the Bible. Thus the *nathin* would be a descendant of the Gibeonites whom Joshua was said to have made into Temple slaves far back in antiquity. The only categorizations of Jews by birth to appear regularly in all the Jewish evidence, including the Dead Sea scrolls, were the priests, Levites, proselytes and "Israel," that is, ordinary Jews. The Levites were defined simply as those members of the tribe of Levi who were not descendants of Aaron, whose limited task of caring for the Temple and singing psalms sometimes led to tension with the priests.

The prevailing sentiment that what mattered was to belong to the "right" family had political consequences in competition for the position of High Priest. There seems to have been no formal restriction in eligibility for the High Priesthood beyond the requirement that the person appointed must come from unimpeachable priestly origins—thus Herod appointed as High Priest in 37 BCE a certain Ananel from Babylonia, described by Josephus in one place as "of a high priestly family" but elsewhere as deliberately selected because he came from an "undistinguished" background. In theory, it seems, any priest could become High Priest, but during the early Second Temple period the custom had arisen of appointing to this most prestigious position only those who could claim descent from Zadok, who had been the High Priest in the time of Solomon and whose line had been treated by Ezekiel as alone fit to "offer the fat and the blood" before God. The reluctance of the first of the Maccabees, Judas, to arrogate the High Priesthood to himself after the purification of the Temple in 164 BCE following its desecration by Antiochus Epiphanes (see Chapter 1), seems to have been connected to his recognition of the popular view that he did not deserve appointment to the position because he was not of Zadokite stock, and the opposition to the later Hasmonaeans by the sectarians who wrote the Dead Sea scrolls was based on their view that these Hasmonaeans were invalid High Priests, unlike their own priestly leaders, who sometimes called themselves specifically "sons of Zadok." By the first century CE the Zadokite line had probably become more mythical than actual, but the general notion that High Priestly ancestry brought social prestige continued, albeit for new families. Thus Josephus complained that the appointment of the rustic Phannias by the Zealots in 67 or 68 "abrogated the claims of those families from which the High Priests had been designated in turn," and the questioning of Peter and John was carried out, according to Acts, by (among others) "Annas the high priest, and Caiaphas, and John, and Alexander, and as many as were of high priestly stock." It is clear from Josephus' detailed narrative of the political struggles in Jerusalem before 66 CE that relationship to any High Priest, past or present, was an instant guarantee of considerable social status.[11]

Royal origins, such as Josephus boasted, were naturally rare, and it may be doubted whether his ability to trace his family tree back two and a half centuries, to the time of the Hasmonaean High Priest Jonathan, could be emulated by many Jews. Nor, indeed, is it likely that he could have filled in the gaps in his family tree where his ancestors were less distinguished— even the names that he does give are chronologically confused. But it does seem clear that asserting royal Hasmonaean ancestry could be expected to gain respect in first-century Jerusalem. The same seems to have been true of those who could claim a relationship to the Herodian royal family— hence, according to Josephus, the successful if criminal careers of two brothers, Costobar and Saul, who "were of royal lineage and found favour because of their kinship with Agrippa" and took a leading role in urban violence in Jerusalem in the early 60s CE. Most prestigious of all, but difficult to prove, would be descent from the royal line which had been sanctioned by God, that of David. It seems impossible that anyone could then provide the sort of documentary evidence for Davidic ancestry that Josephus claimed for his, but it is clear that claims of such ancestry were made: the Church historian Eusebius, who obtained his information from the second-century Christian author Hegesippus, probably a native of Palestine and, according to Eusebius, a converted Jew, reports that "Vespasian, after the capture of Jerusalem, ordered a search to be made for all who were of the family of David, that there might be left among the Jews no one of the royal family." Hegesippus' story may well be a Christian legend, since no other source refers to the "great persecution of the Jews" which he states arose as a result, and the same author refers to searches for descendants of David "from the royal tribe of the Jews" also under both Domitian and Trajan. More certain is the ascription, most probably indeed by invention, of Davidic ancestry to individuals seen as exceptional for other reasons. In the early third century CE, if not earlier, the family of Rabbi Judah haNasi, compiler of the Mishnah, was alleged to be descended from King David. And, of course, in the first century the same was claimed of Jesus, "the son of David, the son of Abraham," although the genealogies supplied for Jesus in the Gospels of Matthew and Luke are very different. For Luke, the lineage was not incidental to the story of Jesus, because it explained the special circumstances of the nativity: "And Joseph also went up from Galilee, out of the city of Nazareth, into Judaea, to the city of David, which is called Bethlehem, because he was of the house and lineage of David." The conflict between ascription of Davidic origins to Jesus, inherited through Joseph, Mary's husband, and the story of the virgin birth does not seem to have troubled Luke (unlike some other early Christians), even though both Luke and Matthew specifically note that Joseph was not really Jesus' father. Jesus' Davidic ancestry was stressed also by Paul and by the author of Revelation. Matthew stresses that Joseph accepted Mary as his wife, but any notion that this could constitute adoption of a child not his own seems to have been alien to Jewish custom, as we have seen.[12]

ROMANS COULD NOT imagine entrusting political authority to anyone who was not rich. It was impossible to be a senator without being worth a sizeable fortune. Prestige from wealth was reinforced by ostentatious munificence for the benefit of the wider community, like the trust fund for a town in Italy, set up by his daughter Procula in the mid-first century CE in memory of a certain Titus Helvius Basila, son of Titus, "aedile, praetor, proconsul, legate of Caesar Augustus, who bequeathed to the people of Atina four hundred thousand sesterces, so that out of the income their children are to be given grain until they reach maturity, and thereafter one thousand sesterces each." In the city of Rome during the Republic, and in the municipalities of Italy and the provinces still in the imperial period, the rich competed in currying favour from the populace by conspicuous expenditure on spectacles such as gladiatorial games or on buildings for public use or on other acts of very public philanthropy. Hundreds of surviving inscriptions record such gifts, which were both offered voluntarily and at the same time were expected, as the younger Pliny intimated in a congratulatory letter to his friend Maximus about a gladiatorial show he had put on

for our people of Verona, who have long shown their affection and admiration for you and have given you many honours. Verona was also the home town of the excellent wife you loved so dearly, whose memory you owe some public building or show, and this kind of spectacle is particularly suitable for a funeral tribute. Moreover, the request came from so many people that a refusal would have been judged obstinate rather than resolute on your part. You have also done admirably in giving the show so readily and on such a lavish scale, for a great soul is seen even through actions of this kind. I am sorry the African panthers you had bought in such large quantities did not turn up on the appointed day, but you deserve the credit although the weather prevented their arriving in time; it was not your fault that you could not exhibit them.

In the city of Rome itself, under the rule and patronage of emperors all grand donations to the public good were naturally made by the emperors themselves, whose wealth far outstripped all others. The provision of bread and circuses, derided by the satirist Juvenal as the only things which interested the city mob, was not just bribery to achieve political quiescence (although it also served that function). The display of wealth also confirmed fitness to rule.[13]

For wealth as prerequisite of status, it did not matter much how the wealth had been acquired. Roman senators in the Republic entertained inhibitions about admitting to over-involvement in commerce, but this was primarily because some commercial activities, in particular the collection of taxes for the state, might produce a conflict of interest with the senator's role as politician seeking the best policy for Roman society as a whole. In the early empire there is in fact much evidence of senators maximizing their income by setting up potteries and brick kilns and taking up shares in shipping companies. In a society that could appreciate so openly the value of public uses of private wealth, philosophical objections to excessive interest in the accumulation of material possessions should not be taken too seriously. The younger Seneca wrote that "the wise man cannot suffer loss, because he keeps all within himself and trusts nothing to fortune. He has goods which are secure because he finds contentment in virtue, which does not depend on chance events and can therefore be neither enlarged nor diminished." Seneca may well have been sincere, but he was also one of the richest men in the Roman empire of his day.[14]

It should not be inferred that possession of wealth by itself conferred prestige in Roman society. Wealth was a necessary but not a sufficient condition, as is all too clear from the disparaging portrayal in Petronius' *Satyricon* of the nouveau-riche ex-slave Trimalchio, who "does not even know how much he has, he is so wealthy." Trimalchio's own description of his rise to wealth after he built (and lost) a series of ships laden with cargo was intended both to amuse and to disgust the reader: "What the gods want, quickly happens. In one trip, I made a clear ten million. I bought back all the estates which had belonged to my former owner. I built a house. I bought slaves and cattle. Whatever I touched grew like a honeycomb. Once

I began to own more than the whole of my own country, I quit. I retired from active work and began to lend money to freedmen."[15] The tradition that antique Romans had once lived simple peasant lives led to some inevitable inconsistency about the value of displaying conspicuous wealth. Julius Caesar tried through state action to check extravagance in meals and buildings, as did Augustus, although Tiberius declined to intervene on the grounds that prohibiting such indulgence was futile.[16]

Among Jews, by contrast, the possession and expenditure of wealth were almost irrelevant to social status. In the sixteenth book of his *Antiquities*, Josephus describes the magnificent benefactions conferred by Herod on the cities of Syria and Greece, and the lavish generosity with which he celebrated his building projects within his own kingdom of Judaea. Some people, writes Josephus, think that such generosity must have been at war with Herod's evil tendency to extort wealth from his subjects, but he (Josephus) thinks that the two tendencies belong together: "These excesses he committed because of his wish to be uniquely honoured." In other words, Herod expected his gifts to bring him renown: "I can cite what was done by him in honour of Caesar and Agrippa and his other friends: for the very same attentions which he showed to his superiors he expected to have shown to himself by his subjects, and what he believed to be the most excellent gift that he could give another he showed a desire to obtain similarly for himself." But, unfortunately for Herod, the Jewish people from whom he sought honour were unimpressed, as Josephus states explicitly:

> As it happens, the Jewish nation is by law opposed to all such things and is accustomed to admire righteousness rather than glory. It was therefore not in his [Herod's] good graces, because it found it impossible to flatter the king's ambition with statues or temples or such tokens. And this seems to me to have been the reason for Herod's bad treatment of his own people and his counsellors, and of his beneficence towards foreigners and those who were unattached to him.

The public display of wealth on behalf of the community did not in itself bring social status in Judaean society.[17]

One effect of this strikingly different attitude was that rich people could be more private in the enjoyment of their wealth in Jerusalem than in Rome. The existence of some very wealthy families in first-century

Judaea is confirmed by the excavation of luxurious houses close to the Temple site, but such people had no incentive, beyond the moral imperative of giving charity to the poor, to spend their wealth on the public. Money expended on public buildings, including the Temple itself, came not from rich Judaeans seeking public recognition but either from the public purse or from Herodian rulers (which sometimes came to much the same thing) or, in a few cases, from diaspora Jews motivated by piety rather than a desire to gain prestige in Jerusalem. Thus, according to the Mishnah, important gifts to the Temple were made by the proselyte royal family of Adiabene: "King Monobaz made of gold all the handles for the vessels used on the Day of Atonement. His mother Helena set a golden candlestick over the door of the Sanctuary. She also made a golden tablet on which was written the paragraph of the Suspected Adulteress." Similarly, the bronze gates given by a certain Nicanor had come from Alexandria and had been transported by a miracle:

> When Nicanor was bringing them from Alexandria of Egypt, a gale rose in the sea and threatened to drown them. They took one of them and threw it into the sea, and they wanted to throw in the other but Nicanor would not let them. He said to them, "If you throw in the second one, throw me in with it." He was distressed all the way to the wharf at Yafo [Joppe]. Once they reached the wharf at Yafo, the other door popped up from underneath the boat. And there are those who say one of the beasts of the sea swallowed it, and when Nicanor came to the wharf at Yafo, it brought it up and tossed it onto land.

Because of the miracles associated with his gates, Nicanor's name "was kept in honour," but his expenditure did not make him a powerful figure in Jerusalem society.[18]

Jews, unlike Romans, could ascribe high social status and authority to those without wealth. According to Josephus, the teachings of the Sadducees appealed only to those who were well off, but he does not suggest that those rich Sadducees controlled religious life in Judaea. On the contrary, "the Sadducees have the confidence of the wealthy alone but no following among the populace, while the Pharisees have the support of the masses" and are "extremely influential among the townsfolk; and all prayers and sacred rites of divine worship are performed according to their exposition." Some priests were immensely rich but others were so very poor that, when they were deprived by the violence of slaves sent by the High Priests from collecting the tithes due to them at the threshing floors, they "starved to death," but such poverty would not debar them from their priestly duties in the Temple and the prestige it conferred upon them. It would be hard to argue from the value assigned by Josephus to the asceticism of his teacher Bannus or John the Baptist, or to the simple lifestyle adopted by Essenes and Pharisees, that Jews ascribed a positive value to poverty itself. An ascetic lifestyle is impressive only when it is adopted by those with the economic means not to have chosen it. But the influence wielded by some ascetics, such as John the Baptist, does at least show that being rich was not essential for social prestige in first-century Jerusalem.[19]

BOTH ROMANS and Jews assumed that those who are older should in general be accorded both deference and authority, and in this respect the differences between the two societies were less than in their attitudes to wealth. The assembly of middle-aged and old men which constituted the bulk of the Roman Senate in the early empire was reinforced by regular recruits in their twenties, but the Latin term *senatus* means "a council of elders." For politicians, the honour paid to increasing age was a concomitant of the notion of a career, the passage of a successful individual through the "course of honours," the *cursus honorum*, for the main stages of which eligibility was, at least since the early second century BCE, in principle dependent on having passed a certain minimum age. Thus from the time of Sulla in 81 BCE a quaestor had to be at least twenty-nine, a praetor thirty-nine, and a consul forty-two. In the late Republic these age limits were frequently breached by ambitious politicians, including the emperor Augustus himself in his early career, who through force of personality, influence of friends or family or threat of violence achieved these positions before the legal minimum, and in the early empire flouting the rules was standard for the emperor's favourite close relatives, but the privilege they enjoyed was effective only because the standard age restrictions were so generally accepted for others.

Such reverence for elders is in marked contrast to the emphasis on youth in other cultures, where greying hair is seen as detrimental in a search for political authority. In Greek cities in the Hellenistic period and early Roman empire, young men were treated as an important group in society, with their own association, the ephebate, to represent them to their fellow citizens: ephebes underwent a cultural education somewhat on the lines of a privileged university student today, and inscriptions record the efforts of city authorities to keep them under control while recognizing their role. There was no directly parallel institution in Rome, but the need to avoid disaffection among more aristocratic teenagers and channel their ambitions towards the new regime led Augustus to give to the *iuvenes*, "youth," of Rome, boys of equestrian rank aged between fourteen and seventeen, a novel form of public recognition. These select young men paraded in the great festivals and held their own special games, the younger boys competing in the public "Troy Game," while the older teenagers participated in more serious athletics and sat in sections of the theatres specially designated for the young. All of this constituted recognition of a kind, and Augustus may have been uneasily aware that his own violent rise to power had begun when he was a teenager, but the function of recognition was to encourage patience: by setting up such institutions, the state implicitly recognized the right of these young men to positions of status—but only in due course, when they were old enough.

By contrast, there seems to have been no retirement age for those in positions of power. Old men (and women) were not always held in awe for their wisdom; the bald, dribbling, toothless, senile, irritable, loquacious bore was a standard figure for mockery by satirists, a fact which elicited some thoughtful literary reflections on ageing by some such as Cicero. Nonetheless, emperors ruled until their death: the first emperor to vacate his position, in the vain hope of ensuring an orderly succession, was Diocletian in 305 CE. Vacancies in the prestigious state priesthoods filled by senators arose only when a priest died. Senators could and did attend the Senate at an advanced age unless they became too frail. Precisely because of their seniority their views carried authority: in the Senate those called upon to speak were the members whose tenure of the consulate had been longest ago. The prestige of the very old was enhanced by their rarity. Probably in the second century CE, someone—the work is preserved under the name of Lucian, but he was not its author—composed in Italy a whole treatise in the Greek language on the topic of the long-lived. The dry list consists mostly of individuals from Greek myth and history, with a brief mention of the more exotic "philosophical" lifestyles of religious experts in Egypt, India, "among the Assyrians and Arabs," and in other barbarian places. The author has little to say about Rome beyond the advanced ages reached by the antique kings of the city: Numa Pompilius and Servius Tullius lived beyond eighty; Tarquin, exiled to Cumae, lived beyond ninety. Further information about Rome and Italy is promised in another work, which does not survive, although the author does relate the sad death of Asander, "whom the divine Augustus named king of Bosphorus after being ethnarch": still unbeaten in battle on horseback and on foot at the age of about ninety, when he saw his people passing over to a rival, he renounced all food and starved himself to death at the age of ninety-three.[20]

Age markers were less clear among the Jews than in Roman society, but a passage inserted after the original redaction of the text into some manuscripts of the Mishnah has a thoughtful analysis of the stages of life:

At five years old [one is fit] for Scripture, at ten years for Mishnah, at thirteen for [the fulfilling of] the commandments, at fifteen for Talmud, at eighteen for the bride-chamber, at twenty for pursuing [a calling], at thirty for strength, at forty for discernment, at fifty for counsel, at sixty to be an elder, at seventy for grey hairs, at eighty for special strength, at ninety for bowed back, and at a hundred a man is as one that has died and passed away and ceased from the world.

Early rabbinic law distinguished the dependent boy from the responsible adult, but this change in status was not celebrated by any ceremony: the Bar Mitzvah ritual, in which a boy affirmed his new status as a responsible adult at the age of thirteen and a day by reading in public from the Torah, was not introduced into Jewish liturgy until the Middle Ages. There was no category for teenagers and young men to correspond to the Roman concept of *iuvenes,* nor any equivalent to the Roman rite of passage at the first shaving of the beard (if only because Jews did not go clean-shaven). There is little evidence of any minimum age for status and authority once a boy had become a man although, according to the Bible, there were minimum ages for service by the Levites in the Temple, given variously as twenty, twenty-five or thirty. It is uncertain whether there was also a minimum age for the High Priest. Josephus notes that when Herod won power in Jerusalem in 37 BCE he passed over for the High Priesthood the Hasmonaean prince Aristobulus III, who was then sixteen, "because he was a mere lad" although his youth cannot have disbarred him automatically, since Josephus writes that Aristobulus' mother was so "disturbed and aggrieved by the indignity offered her son" that she invoked the aid of Cleopatra in Egypt to ask Mark Antony to obtain the post for him and he was appointed the next year at the age of seventeen. Youth, it seems, was no bar to authority. Josephus writes with pride of his own reputation in his teenage years when "while still a mere boy, about fourteen years old, I won universal applause for my love of letters, insomuch that the chief priests and the leading men of the city used constantly to come to me for precise information on some particular in our ordinances." A similar story of precocity was told of Jesus at the age of twelve, when his parents left him behind by mistake in Jerusalem after celebrating the Passover there, and "it came to pass that after three days they found him in the Temple, sitting in the midst of the teachers, both hearing them, and asking them questions. And all that heard him were astonished at his understanding and answers."[21]

Nonetheless, the Bible, not least the Pentateuch, took for granted the authority of "the elders," those who sit in the gates and act as judges. "With the aged is wisdom, and in length of days understanding," as Job remarked to his friends. As often, the difficulty is to separate the moralizing ideal from the standard reality. Philo noted among the virtues of the Essene communities the fact that "the aged . . . are surrounded with respect and care: they are like parents whose children lend them a helping hand in their old age with perfect generosity and surround them with a thousand attentions," although the elderly patriarch lacked anything like the Roman *patria potestas* to give him institutionalized legal authority over the lives and property of his descendants. However, Jews, unlike Romans, envisaged fixed retirement ages from prestigious positions. The biblical book of Numbers laid down a maximum age for the Levites who served in the Temple: "From the age of fifty years they shall withdraw from the work of the service, and shall serve no more, but shall minister to their brethren in the tent of the meeting, to keep the charge, and shall do no service." In the *Damascus Document* found among the Dead Sea scrolls, not only was a retirement age stipulated for judges, but its rationale, the danger of senility, was made explicit: "No man over the age of sixty shall hold office as Judge of the Congregation," for "because man sinned his days have been shortened, and in the heat of His anger against the inhabitants of the earth God ordained that their understanding should depart even before their days are completed." In practice, Jewish priests must also have retired perforce from their work in the Temple, since the infirmity of old age would make it impossible for them to carry out the physically demanding tasks which involved, above all, animal slaughter—unlike Roman state priests, who could devolve the hard work to specially trained slaves. On the other hand, there does not seem to have been a mandatory retirement age for High Priests. Josephus notes that it is unlawful to deprive anyone of this office once he has assumed it (although he also immediately notes some cases when this has been done). The barbaric treatment of Hyrcanus II by his nephew Antigonus, who (as we have seen) cut off his ears, thus taking care that the High Priesthood should never come to him another time (because he was now mutilated, and "the law requires that this office should belong only to those who are sound of body"), only made sense if Hyrcanus, who by then was over sixty, could nonetheless have hoped for reinstatement.[22]

KNOWLEDGE IS POWER, but the views of professors do not carry weight in all societies. Scholarship and philosophy were acceptable attributes among members of the political elite in Rome, but they were neither necessary accoutrements nor particularly helpful in establishing a politician's authority. Both were products of the leisure time to which the rich professed to aspire, but they could also be done equally well, if not better, by professionals, including ex-slaves, further down the social scale. The future emperor Claudius had turned to intellectual pursuits precisely because he was excluded from politics by Augustus and Tiberius, writing about Carthage and the Etruscans and protected by his reputation for inoffensive antiquarian pedantry from the dangerous scheming of his predecessors in the imperial court. The only aspect of educational accomplishment generally acknowledged as prestigious for Roman politicians was the art of rhetoric. During the late Republic, when public life was conducted in an open arena before fellow politicians and a wider citizen audience, oratorical ability had provided an important route to political success, particularly for those deprived by lack of opportunity or talent of the rewards of military prowess, but political debate in the imperial period was less visible, with many decisions taken behind the doors of the emperor's palace. A belief that rhetorical expertise was desirable for their public lives remained part of the senators' self-image, but in practice display speeches were now generally confined either to praise of the emperor or to battles in the civil courts, only very occasionally enlivened by the criminal trial of a politician for extortion or some other misdemeanour. The learning of scholars, philosophers and orators further down the social scale might bring renown but could not guarantee status and authority any more than the reputations of modern celebrities.

By contrast, a reputation for learning carried more prestige among Jews, if only because all Jews lived by a written text which required interpretation. Parchment and papyrus copies of the Bible were precious objects, hence the deposition of many scriptural texts for safe-keeping in the great storage jars hidden in the caves above the site of Qumran, and Josephus' boast that he received a gift of sacred books after the destruction of Jerusalem through the kindness of Titus, a favour he recorded along with the release of fellow countrymen from captivity and crucifixion.[23] Those who could write, read and explain texts of such significance were bound to be accorded respect. Thus, according to the Gospels, among the prestigious Jewish groups with whom Jesus came into contact, and sometimes conflict, in Galilee and Judaea were the scribes "who love to go around in long robes, and salutations in the marketplaces, and the chief seats in the synagogues, and the first seats at feasts; who eat up the property of widows, and for a pretence make long prayers."[24] It is something of a puzzle that scribes do not similarly appear as a social group in other ancient texts written in or about late Second Temple society; they are not, for example, an identifiable group in the writings of Philo or in Josephus, for whom a "village scribe" is a lowly royal official and "sacred scribes" (*hierogrammateis*) interpreters of omens. Since the prime function of a scribe is, by definition, to write, the use of the term in the Gospels may be best understood as a reference to those who wrote out scrolls of the Law. Among Jews who reverenced every word of that Law, and had no printed Bible with which to check the accuracy of the text read out to them in synagogues, great trust had to be given to the scholar who had copied the text and to the scholar—not, of course, necessarily the same person—who read it aloud. The significance of this latter function in establishing the meaning of the words was much increased by the lack of vowels and punctuation in the words as written on the scroll. As the extant ancient translations into Greek and Aramaic testify, there was much room for idiosyncratic interpretation. It is perhaps odd that testimony to the important public role of readers of the Torah scrolls is not found alongside the references to the significance of scribes. Philo, in praising Jews' knowledge of their laws, writes that "some priest who is present or one of the elders reads the holy laws to them and expounds them point by point." Elsewhere he ascribes this teaching role in the synagogue to "one of the most experienced."[25] In the Gospel of Luke, Jesus is portrayed as teaching in this fashion in the Nazareth synagogues when, "as his custom was, he went into the synagogue on the Sabbath day, and stood up to read. And there was delivered to him the book of the prophet Isaiah."[26] It seems obvious that pious Jews would recognize the authority of those they trusted to interpret correctly the complex laws by which, they believed, God had required them to live their lives.

In principle one might expect even greater status to be accorded to those individuals who did not just interpret divine law but who enjoyed direct communication with the divine realm. Both Jews and Romans took for granted that the gods can sometimes speak to or through humans, and that this had occurred in the past, but they were reluctant to rely in their own day on the leadership of those who claimed such divine inspiration. Thus Romans believed that the gods communicate with men through oracles, but that this did not imply that there was anything special about the oracular seer. The Sibylline prophetess at Cumae, in Campania south of Rome, was said by Vergil to have made her ecstatic utterances under the inspiration of Apollo, and coins minted at Cumae commemorate the Sibyl of the city, but nothing is known about the women themselves who performed this role. Each was simply the mouthpiece of the god. Augurs and other interpreters of divine signs on behalf of the Roman state were at most religious technicians, entrusted with the application of traditional methods of divination. There was nothing religiously special about the many priests who presided over the communal sacrifices to the gods. They represented men to the gods, not the gods to men.

For Jews, that God could speak directly to men was obvious, since the Torah had been vouchsafed in this way to Moses, who alone had conversed with God "face to face." God had spoken to prophets in ancient times. Even the role of Jewish priests differed from that of Roman priests as a result: where Romans saw their tasks as the continuation of human traditions in providing to the gods the offerings that earlier priests believed the gods to desire, Jewish priests believed themselves to be interpreting the rules and regulations which God himself had stipulated through Moses.

However, first-century Jews believed that the direct divine communication once vouchsafed to the prophets of old had come to an end by their day. The author of 1 Maccabees refers to the difficulties created by the lack of prophets to teach Israel how to act: when Judas Maccabee cleansed the defiled sanctuary in Jerusalem after defeating the forces of Antiochus Epiphanes, he "laid up the [defiled] stones in the mountain of the Temple in a convenient place, until there should come a prophet to show what should be done with them." His brother Simon was appointed by the Jews "their leader and High Priest for ever, until there should arise a faithful prophet." But to some extent such assertions can be treated as little more than nostalgia, for Josephus could still imagine God speaking directly to some special individuals in more recent times. The Hasmonaean ruler John Hyrcanus, son of Simon Maccabee, "was the only man to unite in his person three of the highest privileges: the supreme command of the nation, the High Priesthood, and the gift of prophecy. For so closely was he in touch with the Deity, that he was never ignorant of the future. Thus he foresaw and predicted that his two elder sons would not remain at the head of affairs . . ." Josephus seems to have assigned to John's time the last use of the oracle of the Urim and Thummim, the devices on the High Priest's breastplate which revealed, by means now unknown, the divine will. This oracle, writes Josephus, "ceased to shine two hundred years before I composed this work because of God's displeasure at the transgression of the laws." According to the Mishnah, the Urim and Thummim had ceased rather earlier, "when the first prophets died."[27]

Josephus seems then to have assumed that prophets of his own day did not quite reach the standard of those whose inspired sayings were preserved in the Bible. Nonetheless, he was certain that God sent messages to privileged men, since he believed himself to be one such. When he was havering whether to surrender to the Romans rather than commit suicide alongside his companions in Jotapata in 67 CE, "suddenly there came back into his mind those nightly dreams, in which God had foretold to him the impending fate of the Jews and the destinies of the Roman sovereigns. He was an interpreter of dreams and skilled in divining the meaning of ambiguous utterances of the Deity; a priest himself and of priestly descent, he was not ignorant of the prophecies in the sacred books." It seems that God's will was revealed both directly in dreams and indirectly through study of Scripture, but in either case Josephus emerged as a trustworthy prophet, as was demonstrated after his surrender, when, so he claimed, he forecast accurately to Vespasian and Titus their future glory as emperors. The centrality of this episode in Josephus' life makes it all the more significant that he never described himself as "prophet," and that his expertise in foretelling the future through contact with the divine did not feature in his self-presentation in his autobiography. There do seem to have been individuals who gathered followers in first-century Judaea by presenting themselves as prophets, but Josephus criticizes them as false prophets, and as "impostors and deceivers"; such a man was the Egyptian "who declared that he was a prophet and advised the masses of the common people to go out with him to the mountain called the Mount of Olives, which lies opposite the city at a distance of five furlongs, for he asserted that he wished to demonstrate from there that at his command Jerusalem's walls would fall down, through which he promised to provide them an entrance into the city." The Egyptian was attacked by the Romans and defeated, and he disappeared.[28]

It thus seems that in the first century CE an ordinary Jew who claimed to have heard voices or seen visions could not expect automatically to be treated as a recipient of divine inspiration. Scepticism was comparable, perhaps, to that of most modern Christians and Jews: it is axiomatic that revelation is possible and has been known in the past, but it is not to be expected that it will actually occur to ordinary people now. Such general scepticism may explain the trend by authors of apocalyptic writings in the Second Temple period to present the accounts of these visions in the person of an ancient biblical figure such as Enoch, Baruch or Ezra, unless the apocalypticist felt himself to be the ancient sage reincarnated (as is possible). If such visions were believed to have come to men of old, they were more likely to be treated with the reverence for which the authors of the apocalypticist texts undoubtedly hoped.[29]

# POWER

IN ROME, political status derived primarily from wealth, noble ancestry, age and (above all) military glory. In Jerusalem, what mattered was lineage (priestly or royal), learning in the law and (occasionally) a claim to divine inspiration. But in many societies the focus of power is to be found less within formal institutions or among those accorded public status and respect than among those who can capitalize on informal access, insider knowledge and contacts to influence events, and the same was true in first-century Rome and Jerusalem. The exercise of power in the shadows is necessarily harder to reveal than the public face of government, but what can be reported are the rumours, often hostile and not infrequently titillating, which circulated especially among those excluded from the inner circles of influence. It is rarely possible to verify the truth of such rumours even in the contemporary world, let alone across the span of two millennia, but the rumours themselves are historical facts which reveal much about the way that Romans and Jews believed themselves to be governed.

IN PRINCIPLE, authority in Rome was shared between the rich male aristocrats who were elected by the people to the magistracies of the city and who sat in the Senate, which acted as an advisory body to the consuls and the other executives of the state, but in practice all power in imperial Rome derived ultimately from the emperor as autocrat. Despite the theoretical restraints of constitutional and legal safeguards and the danger of moral disapprobation, an emperor could do more or less exactly what he wanted—and, it seems, many of them did exactly that. Thus Augustus was notorious for the seduction of the wives of fellow senators: according to his biographer Suetonius, "Mark Antony accused him . . . of taking the wife of an ex-consul from her husband's dining room before his very eyes into a bed-chamber, and bringing her back to the table with her hair in disorder and her ears glowing," behaviour that Augustus' friends were said to have excused "as committed not from passion but from policy, the more readily to keep track of his adversaries' designs through their women." Tiberius, bored by the burdens of government, retired for the last twelve years of his life to seclusion on the island of Capri. Gaius was believed to have lived incestuously with all three of his sisters and to have so revelled in his absolute power that "at one of his more sumptuous banquets he suddenly burst into a fit of laughter, and when the consuls, who were reclining next to him, politely enquired at what he was laughing, he replied: 'What, except that at my one nod each of the two of you could have your throat cut on the spot?' " The historians and biographers who relate such anecdotes, in each case naturally only after the emperor's demise, do so with a mixture of fascination, horror and disgust at such manifestations of unchecked power. The autocrat could do whatever he wished unless and until he was unseated by a coup, which would lead inexorably to the loss of his life along with his power.[30]

Such a coup could never have been effected by the great mass of the emperor's subjects who lived in the provinces. Not even the most successful provincial uprising, like that of Arminius in Germany in 9 CE, could deprive the emperor of his power—the autocrat could always ensure that someone else shouldered the blame. Nor did the institutions in Roman society from which the emperor derived his legal and moral authority, the people and the Senate, have the means to engineer his removal. The will of the people, expressed through the enactment of laws, could do little more than recognize the reality of imperial power. Thus in January 70 CE, after Vespasian had already defeated his rivals in civil war, the people declared not only that "he shall have the right and power, just as the deified Augustus and Tiberius Julius Caesar Augustus and Tiberius Claudius Caesar Augustus Germanicus had, to transact and do whatever things divine, human, public and private he deems to serve the advantage and the majesty of the state," but also that "whatever was done, executed, decreed or ordered before the enactment of this law by the emperor Caesar Vespasian Augustus, or by anyone at his order or command, shall be as fully binding and valid as if they had been done by order of the people or plebs." In other words, the bronze tablet simply recorded that the Senate and people had accepted a fait accompli. The popular will was sometimes evident in less formal public arenas, such as the circus or other public entertainments where a crowd might give voice to discontent, secure in the knowledge that the emperor was unlikely to punish so many, but few issues of policy could engender sufficient unanimity for mass demonstrations to be effective— and no spontaneous uprisings of the Roman populace in fact occurred. To counteract the greater danger of hostility from senators, sensible emperors took great care to present an image of themselves to their fellow aristocrats as first among equals in the Senate: as Augustus expressed it in his posthumous *Res Gestae*, "I took precedence over all in rank, but I possessed no more power than the others who were my colleagues in each magistracy." The image of the emperor as "just" another senator served a useful purpose in preserving the *amour-propre* of ordinary senators and hence a healthy supply of rich Romans prepared to dedicate themselves to a senatorial career and the command of armies which could win glory for the emperor. But the Senate as a body had almost no power and, in fact, almost nothing to

do. What in the Republic had been the engine room of Roman government became under the emperors a sterile debating chamber. Decisions on
important issues were taken elsewhere, by the emperor and his advisers. It
would be a grave mistake to envisage the relationship of Senate to emperor
as analogous to that of a United States president to Congress. In theory,
senators could speak in the house against an imperial decision or seek to
arraign the emperor before a court as they could other magistrates. In practice, no one would be so stupid: not just the careers and fortunes of all senators, but their lives, could be forfeit at the emperor's whim.[31]

The basis of this overwhelming power wielded by the emperor was his
control of the armies. Some emperors, including Augustus, came to the
purple through military victories over their political opponents, but even
those other emperors whose rule had started in more peaceful circumstances could still rely on the latent threat of force. Usually, the threat sufficed. Augustus had retained a standing army of enormous size in order to
ensure that any potential rival would start from a military disadvantage—
or, preferably, not start at all. The emperor had at his disposal in the early
first century CE about a quarter of a million soldiers stationed around the
empire. Only a small proportion was required for fighting against external
enemies of the state. Dispersal of forces facilitated rapid responses to low-
level hostilities on the empire's frontiers but—and this was probably more
important for the emperor's peace of mind—it also discouraged conspiracies between army commanders, who would find it difficult to coordinate
opposition to the emperor across such wide distances. When the governor
of Dalmatia, Lucius Arruntius Furius Camillus Scribonianus, rebelled
against Claudius in 42 CE with the backing of the two legions he commanded, his attempt to win power for himself foundered as soon as it
became clear that other provincial commanders were not prepared to
throw their lot in with him. Two legions had no chance when faced by the
prospect of opposition from the rest of the army. Scribonianus' troops
deserted him and "his rebellion was put down within five days, since the
legions which had changed their allegiance were turned from their purpose
by superstitious fear; for when the order was given to march to their new
commander, by some providential chance the eagles could not be adorned
nor the standards pulled up and moved." Even if the legionary commanders might be prepared to risk all, lured by the prize to be won from victory, their troops were likely to be more cautious.[32]

Such reasons for caution applied rather less to the small force of elite troops stationed on the outskirts of Rome, since, if they turned disloyal to the emperor while he was in the city, they could act before he had time to summon the rest of his armies to his aid. The nine praetorian cohorts, nearly five and a half thousand heavily armed soldiers, were permanently encamped from the time of Augustus on the edge of Rome. Their official role was to protect the headquarters, the *praetorium*, of the emperor, since his constitutional position, by virtue of which he commanded armies, was that of a general on campaign, with the special privilege that he could conduct those campaigns, by use of subordinates, from the comfort of Rome. The praetorians were the only major military presence in Rome, far outclassing the much lighter armed *vigiles*, watchmen, who operated more like a police force and fire brigade. The power of the praetorians came from their physical proximity to the autocrat. As Gaius discovered on 24 January 41 CE, trapped in a narrow exit from the arena for the Palatine games, his personal German bodyguard was useless once the praetorians struck.[33]

Most powerful of all the praetorians was their prefect, to whose command the soldiers owed allegiance in addition to their oath of loyalty to the emperor as commander-in-chief. The emperor needed to put full confidence in the man selected for this crucial role. It was not easy. To avoid praetorian prefects seeking supreme power for themselves, two were generally appointed at any one time in the hope that, as with the shared power of the consuls in the Republic, the influence of one might be checked by the other. For the same reason praetorian prefects were selected from those of equestrian rather than senatorial rank, and the honours voted to them were carefully graded on the one hand to keep them loyal, on the other to keep ambition under control.

The dangers faced by emperors from a praetorian prefect of dubious loyalty first became evident through the career of Lucius Aelius Seianus ("Sejanus") under Tiberius. Sejanus was made joint prefect with his father Lucius Seius Strabo at the beginning of Tiberius' rule in 14 CE, but when Strabo was appointed prefect of Egypt, he was placed in sole command. A man with influential connections in the Senate—his mother's brother had been consul in 10 CE—he capitalized on the emperor's age and increasing reluctance to be drawn into political intrigue in order to concentrate power into his own hands. In 30 CE the historian Velleius Paterculus described him in extravagant terms, as "one who claims no honours for himself and so acquires all honours, whose estimate of himself is always below the estimate of others, calm in expression and in his life, though his mind is sleeplessly alert. In the value set upon the character of this man, the judgement of the whole state has long vied with that of the emperor"; but just the following year, after he had been elected consul in recognition of his merits, he was dragged to his death from the Senate House in Rome, having been denounced, through an intermediary, by Tiberius, who was ensconced, old and unarmed, on Capri. Tiberius' problems in procuring the demise of his subordinate had been largely practical. The only fully armed troops in the vicinity of Capri were praetorians, and he could not know if they would side with him or Sejanus if he required them to decide. Sejanus made regular visits to Capri as part of his duties. As prefect he was expected to wear a sword in the emperor's presence. To dispatch Tiberius, dressed in his toga or tunic, would take only moments at a private audience, and Sejanus might reasonably calculate that the praetorians would find the choice easier once the emperor was dead. Their livelihoods, with pay levels well in excess of those earned by ordinary legionaries and a comfortable existence away from the privations of the frontiers for most of their careers, depended on there being an emperor to protect, but it did not much matter which emperor it was, provided that he paid them their due, and they could as easily have promoted the consul Sejanus in 31 as they were to push forward the elderly Claudius ten years later.[34]

The crux of Sejanus' power, physical proximity to the emperor, was shared by others whose lack of formal status left them more in the shadows except when they were caught up in conspiracies. Many in the imperial household—the emperor's barber, butler, valet, and all his other personal attendants—had the ability to do him harm. For the same reasons, they had considerable power, for all that they were slaves or ex-slaves, to do good for other people by dropping a word into the emperor's ear at the right time. Hence the reports of the immense influence of Narcissus, Pallas and other freedmen under Claudius and Nero. Their influence was resented because it was overt, but "good" emperors necessarily relied just as much as "bad" on the services and advice of their freedman secretaries, who wrote their letters, managed their accounts and organized their personal diaries. So Augustus, who left at his death "a summary of the condition of the whole empire: how many soldiers there were in active service in all parts of it, how much money there was in the public treasury and in the imperial treasuries, and what revenues were in arrears," also added, according to Suetonius, "the names of the freedmen and slaves from whom the details could be demanded." The only difference between Augustus and some of his successors was that Augustus was careful to emphasize the social gulf between high-status Romans and these low-status, but powerful, servants. His will, drawn up in two notebooks in the year before his death, had been written "in part in his own hand and in part in that of his freedmen Polybius and Hilarion." These two ex-slaves must have wielded immense influence, but nothing whatever is known about them: like civil servants, they were kept out of the limelight.[35]

The power of some of the women in the imperial family could be advertised rather more publicly than that of freedmen, once the general taboo against formal recognition of female power had been effectively broken by Augustus' treatment of his wife Livia, who as early as 35 BCE received, along with her sister-in-law Octavia, the sacrosanctity of a tribune of the people and freedom of financial action, so that she entered the male political world in her own right: she recorded in her own name, not that of Augustus, her role in rebuilding appropriate shrines such as the temple of Fortuna Muliebris ("Fortune of women"), which stood four miles from Rome on the Via Latina. Livia's public prominence was exceptional for a woman in the early empire, although there was a partial parallel in the power flaunted by her great-granddaughter, Julia Agrippina, niece and wife of the emperor Claudius and mother of Nero. Nonetheless, even if they might receive public recognition, women could not hold magistracies or command armies, and any control they could exercise over policy was necessarily through men; and in this respect the wives and daughters of emperors benefited as a matter of course from the opportunities provided by access to the autocrat.

In a society unabashed at the overt role of patronage, there was no embarrassment in approaching the emperor through his wife, as Josephus did when, as we have seen in Chapter 2, he visited Rome to try to help his Jerusalem friends who had been sent to Rome in bonds by Felix, governor of Judaea, "on a slight and trifling charge": Josephus made friends with a Jewish actor, Aliturus, and "through him I was introduced to Poppaea, Caesar's consort, and took the earliest opportunity of soliciting her aid to secure the liberation of the priests." Poppaea's influence depended entirely on her ability to allure the autocratic Nero. She had become mistress to

Nero in the late 50s CE while she was married to the future emperor Otho, who, out of prudence or sympathy for his immoral tastes (so Tacitus alleged), abandoned her to the emperor. Her influence was sufficient, it was alleged, for her to have encouraged Nero to free himself from stifling maternal influence by the drastic means of murdering his mother, Agrippina, in March 59. Soon Otho conveniently divorced her. Nero was persuaded to divorce his wife Claudia Octavia, daughter of the emperor Claudius, on the pretext that she was sterile, and Poppaea became the emperor's wife. Power thus acquired was dangerous for its possessor. In 63 Poppaea produced a daughter for Nero, but the baby died after a few months. As evidence of imperial favour Poppaea was given the name Augusta—a title for which Livia, earlier in the century, had been required to wait until the death of her husband Augustus in 14 CE. But Nero was not a comfortable person with whom to be at close quarters. In 65, when Poppaea was pregnant again, her husband kicked her "in a chance fit of anger." Tacitus notes that some writers record that she was poisoned, "but this sounds malevolent rather than truthful, and I do not believe it—for Nero wanted children and love for his wife was an addiction." Certainly he treated her well after death. "Her body was not cremated in the Roman fashion, but was stuffed with spices and embalmed in the manner of foreign royalty." She was buried in the mausoleum of Augustus.[36]

Equivalent to the emperor in Rome as the source of all real power in Jerusalem was the single individual to whom the province was entrusted by the Roman state: from 37 to 4 BCE, Herod the Great; from 4 BCE to 6 CE, his son Archelaus; from 6 to 41, and from 44 to 66, the Roman governor; from 41 to 44, Herod's grandson, Agrippa I. In his description of political events in Jerusalem before the great revolt which broke out against Rome in early summer 66 CE, Josephus had frequent recourse to periphrases in describing the Jews who wielded, or tried to wield, power in the city. Decisions and actions were taken by "the principal citizens," "the leading citizens," "those in authority," "the powerful," "the rulers," "the notables," or others described by similar phrases. Quite who was meant by these descriptions emerges from his narrative only when specific individuals or particular groups, such as the entourage of a High Priest, are named. The concentration of influence in Jerusalem, as in Rome, was located not in institutions or status but among those who could gain access to the ultimate source of brute power—in 66, the Roman governor, who commanded troops and, if really pressed, could summon to his aid the legions from Syria. In the province of Judaea the governors listened above all to the scions of the Herodian family and to the relatives of those appointed— either by Herodians or by governors themselves—to the High Priesthood; but, beyond that, there was also a penumbra of rich Jews, both priestly and lay, who were trusted by the Roman authorities simply because they belonged to a type of wealthy landowner that Romans recognized as a natural aristocracy. It was to such people, the "magistrates and councillors" or "the magistrates with the powerful," that Rome could turn for the collection of imperial taxes in Jerusalem and the rest of the country. For Rome to delegate power to the local rich was standard practice in provincial administration: the rich had the most to gain from settled prosperity, and the most to lose from disorder.[37]

A ruling class thus defined had no correlation in Jewish categories of status nor in local institutions. A role for formal institutions as the loci of political decisions, like the assembly and Senate in Republican Rome, is rarely attested in first-century Jerusalem. Under the rule of Herod, a popular assembly was convened by the king in 12 BCE to present to the people his three sons as heirs to his throne, but such an assembly was not a forum for debate. As in contemporary Rome, the Jerusalem crowd was a blunt political instrument. The fate of the last Hasmonaean High Priest, the young Aristobulus III, was sealed when a public demonstration in 35 BCE revealed widespread regret at his exclusion from political power and, "on the occasion of a festival, when the lad approached the altar, clad in the priestly vestments, the multitude with one accord burst into tears. He was, consequently, sent by night to Jericho, and there, in accordance with instructions [from Herod], plunged into a swimming bath . . . and drowned." It is clear from such stories that the populace was not conceived as wielding formal political powers: it could only protest and cajole. Similarly the ruling class under Roman rule, unless it resorted to calling on the use of force by the governor, had to rely on persuasion to control the passions of the city crowd: when in *c.* 52 CE the Jewish masses took up arms against the Samaritans in intercommunal violence begun after the murder of a Galilean pilgrim,

> those in authority tried to mollify them and reduce the disorder, and
> offered to induce Cumanus [the Roman governor] to punish the mur-

derers. The masses, however, paid no heed to them, but, taking up arms . . . fired and sacked certain villages of the Samaritans. When the affair came to Cumanus' ears, he . . . marched out against the Jews and, in an encounter, slew many, but took more alive. Thereupon those who were by honour and birth the leaders of the inhabitants of Jerusalem, when they saw to what depth of calamity they had come, changed their robes for sackcloth and defiled their heads with ashes and went to all lengths entreating the rebels.

There was probably rather greater formality about the proceedings of the Sanhedrin, but it would be a mistake to imagine it as a legally constituted body with the sense of collective responsibility so apparent in the references to itself made by the Roman Senate, or as a parliament divided into competing parties. So far as is known, there were no elections to its membership. In the end, the Sanhedrin's power to achieve its goals depended entirely on the authority of its president, whether High Priest or king, and that, in turn, depended on the extent of his influence with the local representatives of Rome.[38]

Well integrated into the network of "the powerful" in Jerusalem were members of the Herodian family. For some Herodians, of course, this power was formally delegated to them by Rome as king, ethnarch or tetrarch, or as custodian of the Temple, but even those Herodians who held no official position could still wield much power in the city. As in Rome, the ambiguous nature of this informal power was most noticeable when it was wielded by women. Thus Berenice, sister of Agrippa II and daughter of Agrippa I, tried hard and very publicly to stave off the rebellion of 66 when provocation by the governor Florus was at its height and the city was in uproar. Josephus may have exaggerated her importance in order to flatter, but not her general role, when she "constantly sent her cavalry-commanders and body-guards to Florus to implore him to put a stop to the carnage, but he, regarding neither the number of the slain nor the exalted rank of his suppliant, but only the profit accruing from the plunder, turned a deaf ear to her prayers . . . and she would come barefoot before the tribunal and make supplication to Florus, without any respect being shown to her, and even at the peril of her life." In this case, of course, the princess's intervention failed, but it is significant that she believed herself entitled to intervene, although a fully accurate picture of her influence and motivation in such stressful times is elusive because all the extant evidence about her life was written down during or after her notorious love affair with the future emperor Titus, and evaluation of her colourful earlier career was inevitably affected by knowledge of this later liaison. Josephus' frankness will have been inhibited even more, at least in the 70s CE when he was writing his *Jewish War*, by the need to rely on the patronage in Rome of Agrippa II, although by the time that Josephus wrote the last book of his *Antiquities*, in the early 90s, he was sufficiently independent of the royal brother and sister to feel free to mention the rumour that the two of them had an incestuous relationship. It is possible that by this date Agrippa was dead, or at any rate out of favour. In the 90s, or the years following, the satirist Juvenal could allude in passing to the scandal, describing "a diamond of great renown, made precious by the finger of Berenice. It was given as a present long ago by the barbarian Agrippa to his incestuous sister, in that country where kings celebrate festal Sabbaths with bare feet, and where a long-established clemency suffers pigs to attain old age." Nonetheless it is clear that in Jerusalem in the 60s, long before she could yet dream of her life in Rome as Titus' mistress, Berenice had been a powerful figure on the local stage. Her great wealth and her connections inevitably gave her power within Jewish society. Josephus mentions in passing in his autobiography the crucial intervention she made to her brother Agrippa to save the life of his future secretary, Justus of Tiberias, when Justus was convicted of leading raids at the beginning of the war in 66 against gentile cities on the borders of Galilee.[39]

The position of Berenice's brother Agrippa II in Jerusalem during these same years was more officially recognized by Rome, but in practice his ability to control the volatile politics of Jerusalem was similarly dependent on a combination of royal prestige, massive wealth, patronage and influence in the imperial court. As king of lands north and east of Judaea, he had access to troops, but his soldiers were normally stationed not in Jerusalem but in his sovereign territories (by the mid-50s comprising much of Galilee and parts of Transjordan as well as land east of the Sea of Galilee). This anomalous arrangement, by which a king with territory some considerable distance away was expected to take responsibility for the care of the Temple and its operations, seems to have been a novel idea of Herod of Chalcis in reaction to the furore provoked by the governor Cuspius Fadus, whose period of rule in 44–6, following the death of Agrippa I, was marred by his insistence that the ritual clothes of the High Priest should be left in the custody of the Romans rather than the priests themselves. A delegation of Jews to Rome succeeded in persuading the emperor to reverse Fadus' directive, and Claudius evidently felt that delegating all such issues to Herod of Chalcis would be a sensible devolution of responsibility while ensuring that the Jewish shrine was managed with greater sensitivity than Fadus had achieved. This contrived and unique solution to a long-running problem—since Fadus was not the first governor to upset the Jews by the way he administered the affairs of the Temple—was sufficiently successful in the few remaining years in which Herod of Chalcis was alive for the experiment to be continued, at least from 50, with Herod's nephew Agrippa II. Thus in the 50s and 60s Agrippa had the duty and prerogative delegated by Rome to ensure that the Temple was properly and peacefully managed.

Agrippa exercised control most obviously through appointment of the High Priest of his choice. This right he used frequently from the late 50s, perhaps as a way of discouraging any individual High Priest from becoming too powerful through the prestige of the post. A High Priest could in principle be appointed for life, but Agrippa installed six different men, each apparently from a different priestly family, between 59 and 66. Unsurprisingly, the relationship between king and leading priests was often fraught, most dramatically when Agrippa's attempt quite literally to oversee proceedings in the Temple was thwarted by the erection of a blocking wall. There was equal potential for tension between Agrippa and the Roman governor, although the king seems to have got on well enough with the procurator Festus, with whom relations may have been particularly close: according to the Acts of the Apostles, Festus allowed the king to question Paul even after his formal trial by the governor was complete and judgement—that he should be sent to Caesar—pronounced. It is hard to know whether Agrippa's comment to Festus at the end of the hearing, that "this man might have been set at liberty if he had not appealed to Caesar," constituted a private remark or a formal legal decision. If the latter, it might look dangerously possible for the king to undermine the governor's authority. But it may be that Festus' willingness to permit a hearing of Paul by Agrippa (and by Berenice, who was present "with great pomp" but is not portrayed as speaking during the proceedings, or as being addressed by Paul) was an exceptional act of friendliness in response to the politeness of the king and queen, who had come specially to Caesarea to greet Festus at the beginning of his period of office.[40]

It is significant that this hearing by the governor took place in Caesarea on the Mediterranean coast, since that was his headquarters and the place where the majority of his troops were stationed. The governor, and indeed the Roman state as a whole, had a much lower profile in the city of Jerusalem, which he visited only occasionally, at times of potential tension, such as the pilgrim festivals. The single cohort of between six and twelve hundred auxiliary troops stationed permanently in the Antonia fortress next to the Temple was commanded by a quite lowly military official, described in Acts as the "tribune of the cohort," whose task was to keep an eye out for trouble in the Temple court and to intervene before it got worse, as he did when "all Jerusalem was in an uproar" about Paul:

> As they went about to kill him, news came to the tribune of the cohort . . . who immediately took soldiers and centurions, and ran down to them; and when they saw the tribune and the soldiers, they stopped beating Paul. Then the tribune came near, and took him, and commanded him to be bound with two chains; and demanded who he was, and what he had done. And some cried one thing, some another, among the crowd: and when he could not know the certainty for the tumult, he commanded him to be taken to the barracks.

When the governor himself went to Jerusalem, he probably stayed in Herod's former palace in the west of the city, near what is now the Jaffa Gate, an impressive building and a well-fortified citadel in which he presumably quartered the troops brought with him from Caesarea for the duration of his visit. The inhabitants of Jerusalem were thus left in no doubt about the grandeur of their governor, but he was a distant figure most of the time. Even when he was in Jerusalem his residence was sited on the edge of the city, next to the city wall, at a distance, albeit only ten minutes' walk, from the Temple compound. By contrast, the much smaller, less pretentious, palace of Agrippa II was in the city's centre, overlooking the Tyropoeon valley and, of course, the Temple site. It must have felt sometimes as if the city had two masters, particularly when Agrippa was present and the governor was not.[41]

In any case, governors will have been uneasily aware that the political clout in Rome of some members of the Herodian family was considerably greater than theirs. In the first year of his reign, in 54, Nero placed the government of Armenia Minor into the hands of Aristobulus, son of the deceased Herod of Chalcis, for no known reason apart from his royal ancestry. By contrast, all governors of Judaea were of comparatively lowly Roman status—none was a senator, and Felix, governor from *c.* 52 to 60, was an ex-slave. Few governors will have been as close to the emperor as Agrippa II seems to have been. Educated probably at Rome, he was certainly in the imperial capital as a young man when his father, Agrippa I, died in 44, and was much favoured by Claudius, who wanted to appoint him immediately to his father's kingdom but was dissuaded on the grounds of Agrippa's youth. His relations with Nero were perhaps less close, as there is no explicit evidence that the two of them became friends and companions as Agrippa I and Gaius had done in the last days of Tiberius' rule. Nero was probably too young, aged only twelve when marked out for greatness in 49 by the marriage of his mother Julia Agrippina to the aged Claudius, to need a mentor ten years older. Nonetheless, Nero's warmth towards Agrippa was indicated by the grant to him of new territory when the young prince became emperor in 54, and Agrippa reciprocated by renaming his capital city "Neronias" in 62. Agrippa's coins bore Nero's name and image, and the king styled himself "philo-Caesar." It is possible that Agrippa and Nero were in fact closer than Josephus cared to recall by the 70s when he began writing his history. By then Nero was vilified as a monster, and cataloguing his vices had become hackneyed. All those politicians who had prospered under his regime might prefer reticence about this aspect of their past. Agrippa, as son of a Jewish king, had high status in the eyes of the Jews of Jerusalem, but his power ultimately derived entirely from the emperor in Rome. It will have been no surprise that, when revolt eventually erupted in 66 and his efforts at mediation had clearly failed, Agrippa abandoned both city and Temple, attaching himself and his soldiers to the army of Cestius Gallus, governor of Syria, as he marched south to recapture Jerusalem on behalf of the emperor.[42]

## CHAPTER TEN

# ROMANS AND JEWS

R OMAN COMMENTS about Jews were rarely hostile before the outbreak of war in 66. Far more common were amusement, indifference, acceptance, admiration and emulation. To enumerate the surviving Roman comments is in fact not all that difficult, since fragments survive from only some thirty or so Latin authors, and most of them make mention of Jews and Judaism only in passing. They include poets (Lucretius, Vergil, Tibullus, Horace, Ovid, Persius, Lucan), historians (Livy, Curtius Rufus), scholarly polymaths (Varro, the elder Pliny), the orator Cicero, the satirist Petronius. The characteristics of Jews they chose to mention varied enormously. The grammarian Erotian, who wrote the most famous Hippocratic lexicon composed in antiquity, notes the Jewish abhorrence of eating pigs when discussing the origin of the "Sacred Disease": "Some say that . . . this disease is god-sent, and being of divine origin it is said to be sacred. Others suppose that superstition is implied. They say that one should inquire to which type the sick man belongs, in order that if he is a Jew we should refrain from giving him pig's flesh, and if he is an Egyptian we should refrain from giving him the flesh of sheep or goats." Columella, an expert writer on agriculture, notes in a discussion of fertility and exceptional growth in nature and among humans that "recently we ourselves might have seen, among the exhibits of the procession at the games at the Circus, a man of the Jewish race who was of greater stature than the tallest German."[1]

Such material is far too disparate for a simple collation of all these comments to provide a complete picture of Roman attitudes to Jews and Judaism: different literary genres and different literary contexts elicited different sorts of comment. Some Latin writers seem blindly to have followed an earlier Greek literary tradition about the nature of Judaism which had been shaped by the anti-Jewish animus of Greeks in Egypt and by the propaganda of the Seleucid state in the time of Antiochus Epiphanes in the second century BCE, when the conversion of the Jerusalem Temple to pagan cult had provoked the revolt of the Maccabees. Some of these early Latin fragments have survived only through preservation by later authors whose own views about Jews were coloured by events in their own time or—like St. Augustine, through whose quotation comments by Varro and by Seneca are known—formed by a Christian agenda. Of the attitudes attested, the most frequent are amusement at the celebration of the Sabbath, circumcised genitalia and strange food taboos. Horace in the time of Augustus laughed at Jewish credulity: "let the Jew Apella believe it, not I." Persius, in the early years of Nero, mocked the observance of the Sabbath as an example of superstition like the beliefs of Phrygians and Egyptians: "But when the day of Herod comes round, when the lamps wreathed with violets and ranged round the greasy window-sills have spat forth their thick clouds of smoke, when the floppy tunnies' tails are curled round the dishes of red ware, and the white jars are swollen out with wine, you silently twitch your lips, turning pale at the Sabbath of the circumcised." Petronius, whose *Satyricon* is full of bawdy sexual references, had more to say about circumcision: when the hero Encolpius and his friends are on the run someone suggests painting themselves black to disguise themselves as Ethopian slaves, but another of his companions responds that this will be as useful as boring their ears to imitate Arabians, chalking their faces to look like Gauls—or circumcising themselves "so that we may seem Jews." As we saw in Chapter 7, Pompeius Trogus, whose account in Latin of the history of the Near East and Greece and especially the Hellenistic states before their fall to Rome was composed in the time of Augustus, but is now known primarily from an epitome in the third century CE, repeated the canard common at the time, that the Sabbath was a day of fasting: "Moses, having reached Damascus, his ancestral home, took possession of Mount Sinai, on his arrival at which, after having suffered together with his followers from a seven days' fast in the deserts of Arabia, he, for all time, consecrated the seventh day, which used to be called Sabbath by the custom of the nation, for a fast-day." Seneca censured the Sabbath as unprofitable (*inutile*): "by introducing one day of rest in every seven, they lose in idleness almost a seventh of their life, and by failing to act in times of urgency they often suffer loss." Of Jewish food taboos, much the funniest was deemed to be the avoidance of pork. Philo, describing the travails of his embassy to the emperor Gaius in 40, notes with exasperation the amusement that could be generated even by just mentioning the fact: "[The emperor] put to us this very great and solemn question, 'Why do you abstain from pig-flesh?' The question was greeted by another outburst of laughter from some of our opponents . . ."[2]

Roman attitudes to Jews were undoubtedly affected by the presence of a large number of Jews within the capital city itself. The community, well established before 61 BCE, when they were already sending gold to the Temple, was much swelled by the import of war captives by Pompey and Sosius after their captures of Jerusalem. In the normal way at Rome, such slaves were mostly in due course manumitted and became part of the free Roman populace. Eight thousand Jews in Rome lobbied Augustus in 4 BCE when deputations came to the emperor from Judaea after the death of Herod. By the mid-first century CE Jews were to be found in many different parts of the city, though with a concentration of settlement in the impoverished area of Trastevere. By 66 CE some of these Jews would have had ancestors who had become Roman citizens four or more generations earlier. Non-Jews were certainly aware of the Jews of the city as an identifiable and organized community, but they could also expect to come across individual Jews in the course of ordinary life—in the markets, in the baths, or in the crowds at public events. Jews did not have a distinct skin colour or facial type, nor did they wear unusual dress, but they did stick together, to be close to the synagogues where they congregated to hear the Torah read, and everyone knew that they had taboos about what they would eat, and that their males were circumcised.

Given the varied ethnic origins of so many people in Rome, and Roman tolerance of such a variety of religious practices, was there any reason for such Jews to feel less integrated into the life of the city than any other minorities? The Roman state seems to have treated the synagogues in the city much like other voluntary associations, to be controlled and occasionally suppressed, but generally tolerated, according to a document cited by Josephus: "Gaius Caesar . . . by edict forbade religious societies to assemble in the city, but these people alone he did not forbid to do so or collect contributions of money or to hold common meals."[3]

But if Jews were not seen as offensive aliens or a turbulent danger to law and order in the city, why were they (or, at least, some of them) periodically expelled in the first half of the first century CE? Expulsions took place both under Tiberius, in 19 CE, and under Claudius, probably in 49. Three aspects of the expulsions are the key to understanding why they took place. First, only a portion of Jews were expelled on each occasion, and, in each case, within a few years the Jewish community in the city was again visibly present and capable of influencing events: Jews were pushed out in 19, but they were present again during the late 20s (when they were in the city to suffer, so Philo alleges, the slanders of Tiberius' confidant and praetorian prefect, Sejanus); and in 41 they were so numerous that the new emperor Claudius "ordered them, while continuing their ancestral mode of life, not to hold meetings." Second, expulsion in 19 CE was not of Jews alone but also of those who practised Egyptian rites (a fact emphasized in all three main accounts, by Tacitus, Suetonius and Josephus). Third, and most important, was the coincidence of the expulsions of 19 with the crisis in the state following the traumatic death of Tiberius' heir Germanicus. The expulsion of practitioners of foreign rites at a time when magic was believed to have brought about the sickness and death of the favourite of the Roman people was a symbolic statement of the purification of the city: "A senatorial edict directed that four thousand descendants of enfranchised slaves, tainted with that superstition and suitable in point of age, were to be shipped to Sardinia and there employed in suppressing brigandage, and if they died because of the pestilential climate, it would be a cheap loss. The rest should leave Italy, unless they had renounced their profane rites by a certain day." So writes Tacitus. The briefer account by Suetonius makes clearer that those compelled into military service were Jews: "Those of the Jews who were of military age he assigned to provinces of less healthy climate, ostensibly to serve in the army, the others of the same race or who followed similar pursuits he banished from the city, on pain of slavery for life if they did not obey." Josephus, who (unlike Tacitus and Suetonius) alleged that the expulsion of the Jews followed a specific scandal, the embezzlement by four Jewish scoundrels of moneys donated to the Jerusalem Temple by a high-ranking proselyte called Fulvia, added that "a good many" of these conscripts were punished because they "refused to serve for fear of breaking the ancestral law."[4]

A second expulsion took place in the time of Claudius. Suetonius' brief notice states only that "since Jews constantly made disturbances at the instigation of Chrestus, he [Claudius] expelled them from Rome." The same event is mentioned in passing in Acts: Paul found in Corinth "a certain Jew named Aquila, born in Pontus, lately come from Italy, with his wife Priscilla, because Claudius had commanded all Jews to depart from Rome." Who Chrestus was, and why he was causing disturbances, is unknown. Identification with Jesus Christ, often suggested by scholars in the past, is possible but not likely, since "Chrestus" is to be preferred as the more difficult manuscript reading and, in any case, the name Chrestus was common in this period. Claudius (as reported by Josephus) had gone out of his way at the start of his rule to insist that "the Jews throughout the whole cosmos under our sway should . . . observe the customs of their fathers without let or hindrance," but he had gone on to enjoin the Jews "to avail themselves of this kindness in a more reasonable spirit, and not to set at naught the superstitions held by other peoples, but to keep their own laws." The emperor was evidently keen above all to keep order. In the passage in which Cassius Dio reported the prohibition on Jewish gatherings in 41 CE, the historian went on to record the dissolution of clubs and unruly taverns. Jews were welcome to practise their ancestral customs in Rome, but only provided that they did so discreetly.[5]

It is also not impossible that the expulsion of 49 had a symbolic role similar to that of 19. This was the year that the emperor, notorious for his pedantic antiquarianism, reinstated a raft of ancient Roman religious practices: the formal extension of the religious boundary of the city, the *pomerium*; celebration of the *salutis augurium*, a long-forgotten ritual which signalled the peace of the state; expiatory sacrifices in the grove of Diana to win back divine favour by means which dated back to the time of the Roman kings. A symbolic expulsion of Jews would fit nicely.[6] That the exile was indeed symbolic seems confirmed by the evidence for a sizeable Jewish community in the city in the time of Nero. According to Acts, Paul met local Jews as he awaited trial in Rome; they are portrayed as a settled community. Already in his own letter to "all that be in Rome, beloved of God, called to be saints," a letter written probably in Corinth in the mid-fifties, Paul assumed Priscilla and Aquila to be back in Rome. As we have seen (in Chapter 2), in the court of Nero there was an actor Aliturus, "Jewish as to race," who was a special favourite of the emperor and helped Josephus in his mission to secure freedom for some friends from Jerusalem who had been taken in chains to Rome in the early 60s.[7]

But though Jews might be tolerated, admiration for Jewish customs is less often attested in the Latin writers of the later Republic and early empire. There is no evidence of admiration of the qualities singled out as characteristic of other "barbarians," like the Germans or Dacians: there is nothing about Jews as noble savages or fine warriors. Perhaps Romans knew too much about Jews for such simplifications. But Jews did have some ideas of which thinking Romans could approve: according to St. Augustine, the learned scholar Varro (116–27 BCE), who devoted sixteen of the forty-one books of his *Human and Divine Antiquities* to a systematic exposition of Roman religion, identified the God of the Jews with Jupiter, "thinking that it makes no difference by which name he is called, so long as the same thing is understood." According to Varro, "the ancient Romans worshipped the gods without an image. And if this usage had continued to our own day our worship of the gods would be more devout." And, so Augustine notes, in support of his opinion Varro adduced, among other things, "the testimony of the Jewish race."[8]

Varro's contemporary Cicero was much less complimentary about Jews in two of his extant speeches. Such speeches provide ambiguous evidence about normal attitudes: on the one hand, an orator felt entitled to slant the presentation of facts as best suited his case; on the other, appeals to prejudice are only worth attempting if they are likely to strike a chord with the audience. Cicero inserted into a speech to the Senate, delivered in 56 BCE on the allocation of provinces to the consuls of 55, an attack on his political enemy Aulus Gabinius, who had been consul in 58 when Cicero was sent into exile. Cicero accused Gabinius of having ruined the Roman revenue farmers, who made a fortune by collecting taxes in many parts of the empire. Gabinius, as governor of Syria, had handed over responsibility for tax collection to local authorities in the province, as a result of which, said Cicero, "the revenue-farmers have already been almost crushed and ruined . . . by [his] avarice, arrogance and cruelty." As Cicero portrayed it, Gabinius had handed over the revenue-farmers "as slaves to Jews and Syrians, nations born to slavery." The point of the speech was that the Syrians and Jews had just been conquered by Rome, and allowing them, as recent enemies, to collect their own taxes was gravely damaging to the rich men in Rome accustomed to rake in huge profits by acting as middlemen between provincials and the Roman state. It is not irrelevant that many of these rich Romans were close friends of Cicero himself—and of many other members of the Senate. Nor is it irrelevant for the impact of the caricature that in the past few years there had been a flood of Syrian and Jewish slaves on the Roman market, many of them Jews brought by Pompey as prisoners of war after the conquest of Jerusalem in 63.[9]

Cicero's much stronger verbal assault on Jews and Judaism was found in a speech delivered in 59 in defence of a political ally, Lucius Valerius Flaccus, who was on trial for corruption during his term as governor of the province of Asia. Flaccus' guilt was notorious, but Cicero owed him support in return for his assistance as urban praetor in 63, when Cicero, as consul, had urgently needed help against the conspiracy of Catiline. The prosecution, led by another senator on behalf of the cities of the province, alleged that among Flaccus' misdeeds in Asia had been the theft of gold collected by the local Jews to send to Jerusalem. The confiscation itself was not denied, so Cicero's defence of his client had to rest on the assertion that Flaccus' actions had been legal and on emotions stirred up by casting aspersions on the Jews, asserting that the jury was being intimidated by the Jewish crowd outside the court. "To resist this barbarian superstition was an act of firmness, to defy the crowd of Jews, when sometimes in our assemblies they were hot with passion, for the welfare of the state was an act of the greatest seriousness . . . Even while Jerusalem was standing and the Jews were at peace, the practice of those sacred rites of theirs was inconsistent with the splendour of our empire, the dignity of our name, the customs of our ancestors." Cicero could not seem to state more clearly the incompatibility of Judaism with Roman life. It was a serious problem for the defence that Cicero's friend Pompey had conquered Jerusalem for Rome only four years previously, but that he had "touched nothing from that shrine." The only reason, said Cicero, was Pompey's wise caution, to avoid himself being accused of stealing. "I do not believe that the illustrious general was hindered by the religion of the Jews and his enemies, but by his sense of honour." Pompey does indeed seem to have felt strongly against the common practice of governors despoiling provinces for their own financial gain, and he had pushed strongly for the trial of Flaccus for that reason, but this was a feeble explanation of the respect that (in general, despite having entered the Holy of Holies) he showed to the Jerusalem

Temple, which he had captured precisely in order to install Rome's ally Hyrcanus as High Priest. It is a depressing reflection of the politicization of Roman justice in the late Republic that, despite Flaccus' manifest guilt, Cicero persuaded the senatorial and equestrian jurors to acquit him.[10]

More difficult to locate in its proper context is the rhetoric of Seneca in the time of Nero. When speaking of the Jews, he says: "Meanwhile the customs of this most wicked race have gained such influence that they are now received throughout all the world. The vanquished have given laws to their victors." The quotation, from Seneca's treatise *On Superstition*, was, like the citation of Varro, preserved by Augustine, in this case in his great theological treatise, *City of God*. Augustine cannot be trusted to have preserved accurately the whole context of the text he cited, but it is unlikely (though possible) that he (or his source, if he used an earlier compilation of excerpts) changed Seneca's actual words. According to Augustine, Seneca had censured the sacred institutions of the Jews "among other superstitions of the civil theology." It was in this context that he complained that the Sabbath leads to inexpedient loss of time, adding, however, that at least the Jews "are aware of the origin and meaning of their rites. The greater part of the people go through a ritual not knowing why they do so." Augustine does not explain whether the spread of Jewish practices lamented by Seneca referred to full conversion to Judaism or (more widespread and thus a more plausible target) the observance of customs like the Sabbath, which might more justifiably be described, with exaggeration of course, as having been "received throughout all the world." In any case, regret at the popularity of Jewish customs does not explain Seneca's description of Jews as a "most wicked race," *sceleratissima gens*. Why Seneca wrote about the Jews with such antagonism cannot now be ascertained with certainty, and most historians (probably wisely) are content to leave the puzzle unsolved. Neither this phrase nor any description of equivalent hostility is found in any other extant Latin literature about the Jews from before 66 CE. If it is correct to date the composition of *On Superstition* to near the end of Seneca's life, in 65, it may be relevant that his last years coincided with the time of the great fire in Rome in 64 for which Christians were punished as scapegoats. Seneca may have treated all Jews as guilty, by association, of the crimes of which Christians were accused, or he may have reflected a more general mood in Rome at this time of crisis that the "atheism" shared by Jews with Christians brought the state into danger. Perhaps the context of his description of Jews as a "most wicked race" was what mattered most: in a treatise for Romans on superstition, Jews would provide much the best known example of a notable "superstition," that no God should be worshipped apart from their own.[11]

It is in fact rather hard to see any reason why Jews should have experienced particular hostility from Romans before the rebellion broke out in 66. Jews were odd in some respects, but through their adoption of many of the cultural traits of Hellenism they resembled cultures quite familiar to Romans. Greek was a shared language, both in the eastern Mediterranean (where, as the language of Roman administration, it was also spoken at least by the upper-class Jews of Jerusalem) and in the city of Rome (where it was the preferred language of the Jewish community throughout the early imperial period rather than Hebrew or Aramaic). It has been well remarked that Jews seem to have retained a sense of a distinctive communal identity longer than the many other foreigners at Rome who melted into the wider urban population within one or two generations of arrival, but if Jews were lazy, would not eat pig, or mutilated the sexual organs of their sons, these practices had no effect on their neighbours. Jews might be ridiculous, intriguing, mysterious or contemptible, but they were certainly not dangerous to the safety and prosperity of Rome.[12]

All this evidence for general toleration of Jewish ancestral customs has skirted around the most remarkable, and least disputable, element of that toleration, which was the exemption of Jewish Romans from the normal rule that decent citizens must pray to the gods of their society. Romans knew that Jews, uniquely among the inhabitants of the empire, refused to worship any god apart from the jealous God worshipped in the Jerusalem Temple. Romans treated such behaviour as bizarre but not reprehensible. Unlike gentile Christians, who had abandoned the cults revered by their ancestors and thus risked the displeasure of their traditional gods, Jews, it was believed, had never believed it right to make offerings to any god other than their own. The special privilege of the Jews in this respect, and its importance to them, became clear when (as we saw in Chapter 2) it came under attack in the time of Gaius. Philo reports how, in the midst of the bitter dispute in 40 CE between Jews and Greeks from Alexandria, the leader of the Greek faction, the scholarly Apion, "scurrilously reviled the Jews, asserting, among other things, that they neglected to pay the honours due to the emperor. For while all the subject peoples in the Roman empire had dedicated altars and temples to Gaius and had given him the same attentions in other respects as they did the gods, these people alone scorned to honour him with statues and to swear by his name." As we have seen, a crisis was caused throughout the Jewish world by Gaius' resulting attempt to get the governor of Syria, Petronius, to set up a statue in the Jerusalem Temple. Many thousands of Jews met Petronius at Ptolemais with petitions not to make them transgress and violate their ancestral code: "Slay us first before you carry out these resolutions. For it is not possible for us to survive and to behold actions that are forbidden us by the decision both of our lawgiver and of our forefathers." No later emperor was to attempt to compel Jews to worship other gods, although a renegade Jew in Syrian Antioch tried, in the fevered atmosphere after the outbreak of war in Jerusalem in 66, to demonstrate proof of his conversion and of his detestation of Jewish customs by sacrificing after the manner of the Greeks, and "ordered that the rest [of the Jews] should be compelled to do the same." But even in these circumstances of strong emotion, the Roman legate Gnaius Collega brought order, and an end to persecution of the Jews. Once again it was made clear that it was no part of normal Roman policy to compel Jews to break their inherited customs.[13]

Tolerance of Jewish idiosyncrasies did not amount to positive enthusiasm for Judaism: it was possible to be permissive while despising Jewish practices or finding them ludicrous. However, Josephus reports that observance of the Sabbath as a day of rest had spread in his day to every city, along with other Jewish observances: "The masses have long since shown a keen desire for our religious piety, and there is not one city, Greek or barbarian, not a single nation, to which our custom of abstaining from work on the seventh day has not spread, and where the fasts and the lighting of lamps and many of our prohibitions in the matter of food are not observed." Josephus was of course writing after 70 CE, but his explicit reference to the long-term nature of Jewish influence on gentiles may be taken to show that the phenomenon he observed pre-dated the outbreak of the revolt. On the other hand, one cannot know if non-Jews adopted Jewish behaviour because it was Jewish or despite the fact that it was Jewish. The younger Seneca recalled that his vegetarianism had been suspect in the eyes of his father because some foreign rites were being promoted at that time: the clampdown on "foreign rites" to which Seneca referred was almost certainly the expulsion of Jews and adherents of the Egyptian gods in 19, but it is clear from his testimony that Seneca did not wish his own behaviour to be taken as a sign of his self-identification with either of those groups.[14]

How many such full converts to Judaism were to be found in Rome before 66 CE is wholly unknown, since Seneca's jibe (preserved by Augustine), that "the vanquished have given laws to their victors," may refer only to such spread of individual Jewish practices, but it is likely that some proselytes were to be found in a city of such a size, with a noticeable population of native Jews, since proselytes were certainly found in contemporary Alexandria. More common was recognition of the Jewish God as worthy of worship (even if there was no standard place for this divinity within the portfolio of cults patronized by an ordinary pagan). The power of the divinity worshipped in Jerusalem was evident from the glory of the Temple as it had been refurbished by Herod.

Among all the aspects of Judaism which pagan Romans found odd, much the least bizarre was the centrality in Jewish cult accorded to sacrifices, libations and the burning of incense, and the special sanctity ascribed to the part of the building which housed the divinity. All this was familiar enough from other cities. The Jerusalem Temple was particularly impressive only because its devotees uniquely concentrated all their resources in one place instead of dedicating shrines in the places where they lived. Up to 66 CE Romans generally treated the Jerusalem Temple with exceptional tact, not least because it was to the emperor's advantage to have the Jewish God as ally and protector. Josephus records the gifts given to the Temple by the emperor Augustus and his wife Livia; the hecatomb, a burnt offering of one hundred oxen, sacrificed there at the expense of Augustus' friend Marcus Vipsanius Agrippa during his visit in 15 BCE; the payments made by the state to ensure that the goodwill of the Jewish God would be directed towards the Roman emperor. Josephus says that the cost was borne by the Jews. But Philo writes that it was to be borne by Rome, that Augustus "ordered that for all time continuous sacrifices of whole burnt offerings should be carried out every day at his own expense as a tribute to the most high God."[15]

# PART THREE

# CONFLICT

# CHAPTER ELEVEN

# THE ROAD TO DESTRUCTION

## 37 BCE—70 CE

### JUDAEA

S O WHY *did* the Roman control of Jerusalem established by force of arms in 37 BCE end in the destruction of the city just over a century later? Clearly, as we have seen in Part II, the disaster was not inevitable. Nor was violence continuous: a long-lived Jerusalemite could have passed the whole period from 6 to 66 CE without ever witnessing the horrors of war.

Herod's iron repression of dissent from 37 to his death in 4 BCE prevented any need for Roman intervention in Judaea, but when he died the country descended into chaos for some months. Publius Quinctilius Varus, governor of Syria and later in his career commander of the three legions lost in Germany in 9 CE, marched south from Antioch to restore order. The causes of the disturbances he found were various, but not, or at any rate not all, anti-Roman. The Judaean populace had been left in a state of heightened tension when Herod died: one of his last acts had been to order that the teachers who had incited the people to tear down the image of an eagle, which he had installed above the Temple gate, should be burned alive as punishment for insurrection.[1] Intrigue between his sons in his last days, and even as the old king lay dying, had robbed the country of the most competent members of his family, in particular his two sons by the Hasmonaean Mariamme (both executed in 7 BCE) and an older son (by a different wife), the scheming Antipater, killed unceremoniously by Herod's bodyguards just days before Herod's own death.[2] Herod's third and final will, drawn up on his deathbed, named his son Archelaus as successor to the throne, but Archelaus had to seek ratification from Augustus for his father's wishes, and, when he arrived in Rome for this purpose, he found himself opposed by other members of his family—notably Herod Antipas, who had been appointed to the succession in the second will, only revoked at the last moment. In the absence as yet of an approved heir to Herod, the emperor's financial agent in Syria, a certain Sabinus, went to Judaea to take charge of the king's extensive properties. As a financial official, this man had no formal governmental role, but public and private ownership were not easily distinguished in the case of a king, and Sabinus was sucked into the atmosphere of violence, confident that he would overcome the rebels with the aid of a legion left in Jerusalem by Varus to keep order and of "a large number of his own slaves whom he had armed." The result was intense fighting during the pilgrim festival of Tabernacles in the early autumn, much of it in and around the Temple, to which Sabinus' men finally set fire. The Romans got possession of the Temple treasury, where the sacred funds were kept, "and a great part of these were stolen by the soldiers, while Sabinus openly took four hundred talents for himself," or so Josephus alleges.[3]

Such fighting, perhaps particularly because of the desecration of the Temple, and the lack of a legitimate central authority, encouraged outbreaks of violence all over the country. Soldiers who had been loyal to Herod could not decide whether to side with the Romans or the Jews. In Jerusalem, most of the royal troops joined the rebels but three thousand of Herod's pagan soldiers from Sebaste threw in their lot with Sabinus. Two thousand veterans rose in arms in Judaea, "either in hope of personal gain or out of hatred of the Jews," forcing the troops under Herod's cousin Achiab to retreat to the hills. In Galilee, Judas, son of the brigand Ezekias who had been captured and killed by Herod back in the 40s BCE, gathered a force which captured the royal palace in Sepphoris and seized all the weapons stored there. "He became an object of terror to all men by plundering those he came across in his desire for great possessions and his ambition for royal honour." The royal palace in Jericho was plundered by the local followers of a certain Simon, "a slave of King Herod but a handsome man, prominent in size and physical strength," and a period of looting followed until they were destroyed, in a long and great battle, by a combination of Roman and royal forces. Simon's head was cut off. Yet another group burned down one of Herod's palaces on the river Jordan. Rather longer lasting was the uprising led by a certain Athronges, a man distinguished neither for the position of his ancestors nor by the excellence of his character, nor for any abundance of means but merely a shepherd completely unknown to everybody although he was remarkable for his great stature and feats of strength . . . This man kept his power for a long while, for he had the title of king and nothing to prevent him from doing as he wished. He and his brothers also applied themselves vigorously to slaughtering the Romans and the king's men, towards both of whom they acted with a similar hatred, towards the latter because of the arrogance that they had shown during the reign of Herod, and towards the Romans because of the injuries that they were held to have inflicted at the present time.

Josephus' judgement on all these disturbances is concise: "And so Judaea was filled with brigandage. Anyone might make himself king as the head of a band of rebels whom he fell in with, and then would press on to the destruction of the community, causing trouble to few Romans, and then only to a small degree, but bringing the greatest slaughter upon their own people." When Varus learned from Sabinus what was happening, and particularly about the legion being besieged in Jerusalem, he marched rapidly from Antioch with his two other legions to restore order. On the way south a detachment of troops captured Sepphoris, reduced its inhabitants to slavery, and burned down the city, and Varus ordered the destruction of the town of Emmaus, "in revenge for those who had been killed there," the inhabitants having already abandoned their homes. Prudently, in the light of such ruthlessness, the Jews who had been besieging Sabinus in Jerusalem scattered at the approach of the army, and the locals left in the city claimed (successfully) to have been on the Roman side all along, "saying that the populace had come together because of the festival and that they had been involved in the war not of their own will but through the recklessness of the newcomers, for they had been under siege along with the Romans rather than having the desire to besiege them." Varus' final actions in Judaea before he returned to Antioch show that both he and the emperor appreciated the complex internal power struggles behind many of these disturbances, and (most crucially) the fact that many of those involved had not been motivated by hostility to Rome, since he "pardoned the great majority of those guilty of revolting but sent to Caesar any who had been their leaders. Caesar let most of them go and punished only those relatives of Herod who had joined them in fighting, because they had shown contempt for justice in fighting against their own side."[4]

After the initial assault on the Temple by Sabinus, the city of Jerusalem survived these upheavals with less trauma than might have been expected. There was no mass bloodletting as in 63 and 37 BCE, and no massed ranks of captives taken into slavery. The only violent episode from this year Tacitus deemed worthy of recall in his brief summary of Jewish–Roman relations before 66 CE was the uprising of the ex-slave Simon in Transjordan, who "assumed the name of king without waiting for Caesar's decision. He, however, was put to death by Quinctilius Varus, governor of Syria, and the sons of Herod ruled over a nation restrained and divided into three." Tacitus has nothing at all to say about events in Jerusalem, although when his older contemporary Josephus enumerates in *Against Apion* the invasions of Judaea which required the priests to compile fresh records of priestly lineages from the archives and to disallow priestly marriages with captive women, his list includes—along with the sieges by Antiochus Epiphanes and Pompey, and the war of 66–70 ("in our own times")—the invasion by Quinctilius Varus, suggesting that, compared to the chaotic conditions in 4 BCE until Archelaus finally returned from Rome with a mandate from Augustus to rule, the next seventy years to 66 were to be a long period of stability and peace.[5]

Roman governors did march from Syria to Judaea on a number of occasions within these seventy years, but they came not to suppress insurrection but as a precautionary measure, to forestall opposition to Roman actions which Rome feared might be inflammatory. Thus in 6 CE, when Archelaus was deposed from his rule in Judaea at the request of some of his subjects, and replaced by a Roman governor, it was rational for Publius Sulpicius Quirinius, governor of Syria, to expect the Jews to feel hostility both towards the end, after centuries, to rule in Jerusalem by a Jew (whether as king or High Priest or with some other title) and (more seriously) towards the imposition of a Roman census and Roman land taxes. Exactions of tribute were said to have provoked an uprising in Dalmatia in 10 BCE, and the Dalmatian Bato, who raised rebellion in Illyricum in 6 CE itself, explained to Tiberius when he eventually surrendered in 9 CE that he too had been stung into action in opposition to taxation: his people had revolted because the Romans sent to guard their flocks were "not dogs nor shepherds, but wolves." It would be unsurprising if similar hostility was encountered in Judaea. Josephus in fact states explicitly that the Jews at first took hard the news about the registration of property, and that opposition was only stifled by the persuasion of the High Priest Joazar, son of Boethus. The brief flurry of resistance to taxation, led by a certain Judas who came from outside Judaea, was presumably suppressed by force, although no evidence survives of the extent of the military campaign required. According to Gamaliel, as quoted in Acts, "Judas the Galilean rose up in the days of the census and drew many people after him, but he also perished, and all who obeyed him were dispersed." The first census bulked sufficiently large in the folk memory of Judaea to form the background to the birth narrative of Jesus found in the Gospel of Luke: "And it came to pass in those days that there went out a decree from Caesar Augustus that all the world was to be registered . . . And all went to be registered, every one to his own city." Evidently the census marked significant change—but not, apparently, violence on a scale to register with Roman historians as did contemporary uprisings in other parts of the empire.[6]

The reason for a show of force in 40 CE was even more clear-cut when Gaius had decided that his *amour-propre* required that his statue be placed for worship in the Jerusalem Temple. As we have seen, he instructed Publius Petronius, governor of Syria, to take two legions to Jerusalem to carry out his wishes. Petronius knew that so sacrilegious an action would be bound to evoke Jewish horror and that it would risk instigating an uprising. He wrote first to the emperor to urge him to delay, at least until the harvest had been gathered in, and then, persuaded of the seriousness of the matter by the pleas of a deputation of Jews, including the brother of Agrippa I, returned to Antioch with his mission abandoned, as Josephus records:

> The multitude cried out that they were ready to endure everything for the law. Petronius, having checked their clamour, said, "Will you then go to war with Caesar?" The Jews replied that they offered sacrifice twice daily for Caesar and the Roman people, but that if he wished to set up these statues, he must first sacrifice the entire Jewish nation; and that they presented themselves, their wives and their children, ready for the slaughter. These words filled Petronius with astonishment and pity at the spectacle of the incomparable devotion of this people to their religion and their unflinching resignation to death. So for the time he

dismissed them, nothing being decided. During the ensuing days he held crowded private conferences with the powerful, and public meetings with the people; at these he had recourse alternatively to entreaty, to advice, most often, however, to threats, holding over their heads the might of the Romans, the fury of Gaius, and the necessity which circumstances imposed upon himself. As, however, none of these efforts would induce them to yield, and as he saw that the country was in danger of remaining unsown—for it was seed-time and the people had spent fifty days idly waiting upon him—he finally called them together and said: "It is better that I should take the risk. Either, God aiding me, I shall prevail with Caesar and have the satisfaction of saving myself as well as you, or, if his indignation is roused, I am ready on behalf of the lives of so many to surrender my own." With that he dismissed the multitude, who rained blessings on his head.

Fortunately for Petronius, in due course Gaius was murdered before the governor suffered the inevitable fate for such wilful disobedience. Tacitus writes succinctly that "when Caligula ordered the Jews to set up his statue in their temple, they chose rather to resort to arms, but the emperor's death put an end to their uprising," but neither Philo, who was a contemporary of the episode, nor Josephus mentions any actual fighting, and their accounts are probably more accurate. But the same desperation which, according to Josephus, prepared the Jews for mass martyrdom could as easily have turned to mass violence.[7]

The mass protests against Gaius' plans were clearly motivated by religious zeal, but it is also clear that the tensions aroused in 40, as in 6 CE, were exceptional, and provoked less by movements, philosophies or pressures within Jewish society than by administrative decisions emanating from the government in Rome. Josephus is concerned in his two narratives of the political history of Jerusalem from 6 to 66 to enumerate and deplore all the incidents of violence that might be seen as having led to the conflagration that eventually overtook his native city. When one considers the length of time, sixty years, the list he provides is not extensive, and the small number of troops sufficient to suppress occasional disturbances shows them to have been of little significance. Quite how unimportant the incidents reported by Josephus were emerges clearly from a comparison of his version of events in Judaea in the reign of Tiberius with that given by the senatorial historian Tacitus. In Josephus' account, the long rule of Pontius Pilate as governor of Judaea, from 26 to 36, evoked a series of disturbances quelled only with force. The cause in each case was Pilate's lack of tact and his stubborn unwillingness to listen to complaints even on quite trivial issues—according to Philo, Pilate's contemporary, Agrippa I, described him in a letter sent to Gaius in 40 as "vindictive, with a furious temper." Josephus writes about demonstrations against Pilate when he used money sacred to the Temple to pay for an aqueduct to improve the water supply to Jerusalem, and further unrest at his introduction of military standards, bearing the image of the emperor, into the holy city. Appreciating the religious sensitivities behind Jewish objections to such action required a degree of empathy with his subjects that Pilate seems to have been unwilling to show, preferring the threat or use of violence. The crowd which besieged his tribunal in Jerusalem to complain about the use of sacred moneys for secular purposes was dispersed by soldiers "armed but disguised in civilian dress, with orders not to use their swords, but to beat any rioters with cudgels . . . Large numbers of the Jews perished, some from the blows which they received, others trodden to death by their companions in the ensuing flight. Cowed by the fate of the victims, the multitude was reduced to silence." It is easy enough to imagine how such an episode could take its place in Jewish folk memory of suffering under the Romans, and it seems fairly certain that Josephus' narratives came from the Jewish side rather than from any official Roman report. By contrast, the comment of the Roman Tacitus on all such minor incidents was characteristically terse. In contrast to the fighting with Quinctilius Varus in 4 BCE and the uprising against Gaius' megalomaniac plans for his statue in 40 CE, *sub Tiberio quies*, "under Tiberius [that is, from 14 to 37 CE], all was quiet."[8]

In Tacitus' account, the condition of public affairs in Judaea declined after Gaius' death because of the low social origins of the governors, Roman *equites* or freedmen: "one of the latter, Antonius Felix, practised every kind of cruelty and lust, wielding the power of a king with all the instincts of a slave." Such comments may reflect little more than social snobbery. Josephus too tells rather more stories about problems in the province in the period from 44 to 66 CE than in the earlier part of the century, perhaps reflecting only the lack of good information available to him about events which had occurred before his birth in 37, compared to his firsthand witness to the problems of Jerusalem from the 40s to the destruction of the city. It is all the more striking that much of the unrest and violence in Judaea recorded by Josephus in the reigns of Claudius and Nero was not really anti-Roman. The dispute between the Temple authorities and the procurator Cuspius Fadus in 44, over who should retain control of the vestments of the High Priest, became sufficiently bitter to require the governor of Syria to visit Jerusalem to mediate, but the issue was never likely to be violent, and it was eventually settled, after a Jewish embassy went to Rome, by decision of the emperor. More bloody was the suppression by the same procurator of an "impostor" or "sorcerer" called Theudas, who gathered a large crowd of followers and persuaded them to take up their possessions and follow him down to the river Jordan. According to Josephus, "he stated that he was a prophet and that at his command the river would be parted and would provide them easy passage." Such claims sound fairly harmless, and whether he intended any action against Rome is unknown—since his followers seem to have been unarmed, success in that direction would have required divine intervention. In any case, Fadus did not wait to find out. He sent a squadron of cavalry. Many of Theudas' followers were captured, many others killed. Theudas' head was cut off and brought to Jerusalem. Hence the dismissive words of Gamaliel as reported in Acts: "For before these days rose up Theudas, boasting himself to be somebody; to whom a number of men, about four hundred, joined themselves; he was slain, and all who obeyed him were scattered and brought to nothing."[9]

Bloodshed in the years following seems always to have been the result of quite specific incidents. During the festival of Passover in the late 40s or early 50s a Roman soldier bared himself, turned his backside to the assembled pilgrims and let out a noise like a fart, according to Josephus' account in his *Jewish War*; in the parallel narrative in the *Antiquities*, the insult was to display his genitals. (The accounts are of course not incompatible. Perhaps this was a cultural misunderstanding and Romans felt able blithely to joke about nudity and bodily functions in a way that Jews found disgusting.) In any case, the result was uproar, and when the governor, Ventidius Cumanus, brought in troops to quieten the mob, the rioters panicked and thousands—Josephus writes "twenty thousand"—died in the stampede through the narrow streets. It is as well to recognize in such incidents not the behaviour of an occupying force in fear of imminent revolt, but rather a governor uncertain when best to act tough, when to concede, in order to ensure efficient policing. Similarly heavy-handed and ill-judged was Cumanus' reaction to an isolated act of brigandage, when (in *c.* 50) some Jewish bandits attacked "a certain Stephen, a slave of Caesar" on the public road leading up to Bethhoron, twelve miles or so north-west of Jerusalem, and robbed him of his baggage. Cumanus responded by sending troops around the neighbouring villages with orders to bring the inhabitants to him in chains, reprimanding them for not having pursued and arrested the robbers. This is the account that Josephus gives in his *Jewish War*; according to the *Antiquities*, Cumanus "dispatched soldiers with orders to plunder the neighbouring villages and to bring before him their most eminent men in chains so that he might exact vengeance for their effrontery," which suggests an assumption of their complicity in the crime. Perhaps the rumours which reached Jerusalem, where Josephus was living in his early teens, were confused. In any case, the collective punishment misfired badly.

> One of the soldiers, who had found a copy of the laws of Moses that was kept in one of the villages, fetched it out where all could see and tore it in two while he uttered blasphemies and railed violently. The Jews, on learning of this, collected in large numbers, went down to Caesarea, where Cumanus happened to be, and besought him to avenge not them but God, whose laws had been subjected to outrage. For, they said, they could not endure to live, since their ancestral code was thus wantonly insulted.

Cumanus' response to the delegation showed that Roman government was working, albeit imperfectly. Cumanus had evidently not sanctioned the soldier's sacrilegious behaviour. After consulting with his friends, he had the man led to execution through the ranks of his accusers, and beheaded. On this occasion the anger of the Jews was thus effectively defused.[10]

The final downfall of Cumanus came about in *c.* 52 through a riot caused neither by Roman tactlessness to their Jewish subjects nor by Jewish rebelliousness against Rome but as a by-product of traditional hostility between Jews and Samaritans when, as we saw in Chapter 9, some Jews from Galilee were ambushed in Samaria on the way to Jerusalem. Cumanus' response to the outrage was slow—the Jews alleged bribery by the Samaritans—and a mob from Jerusalem took violent revenge on the Samaritan villages where the incident had occurred, provoking in turn a

Roman clampdown. The whole mess was sorted out once again by the governor of Syria, to whom both Jews and Samaritans sent embassies to complain, and Cumanus lost his job. It was presumably this last element in the story—the fall from grace of an imperial bureaucrat—which brought the affair to the attention of the senatorial historian Tacitus. At any rate, this was the aspect on which he concentrated in his brief and probably muddled notice about events in Judaea during the latter years of Claudius' rule.[11]

The unimpressive quality of the governors sent by Rome to Judaea was reflected by Tacitus also in his denigratory comments, already cited, about Cumanus' successor, the ex-slave Felix, and Josephus states explicitly that under Felix's rule, c. 52–60, Judaean society began to disintegrate. "The impostors and brigands, banding together, incited many to revolt, exhorting them to freedom, and threatening death to those who obeyed the domination of the Romans and saying they would forcibly suppress those who willingly accepted slavery." This general description by Josephus seems to imply the beginnings of rebellion against Rome, but it is strikingly unconfirmed by the two detailed narratives he wrote about events in Judaea during these years, which he witnessed firsthand as a teenager and in his early twenties. Those narratives, in the *Jewish War* and the *Antiquities*, portray a society not so much on the brink of insurrection as riven by internal dissensions and banditry.

Thus Josephus notes that Felix began his rule by clearing out brigandage from the countryside, but also notes that banditry was a long-standing problem in the hill regions: the brigand leader, Eleazar, who was captured and sent to Rome with many of his associates, had ravaged the country for twenty years, and "an incalculable number of ordinary people convicted of complicity" were punished. There was nothing particularly unusual either about the problem here faced, or Felix's solution: banditry was endemic in the less accessible regions of the empire, frequently with the tacit support of the local rural population, and its suppression was a standard task for all governors. More unusual was the emergence of "a new species of bandit," specific to Jerusalem, the so-called *sicarii*,

> who committed murders in broad daylight in the heart of the city. The festivals were their special seasons, when they would mingle with the crowd, carrying short daggers concealed under their clothing, with which they stabbed their enemies. Then, when they fell, the murderers

joined in the cries of indignation and, through their plausible behaviour, were never discovered . . . The panic created was more alarming than the calamity itself, everyone, as on the battlefield, hourly expecting death. Men kept watch at a distance on enemies and would not trust even their friends when they approached.

Josephus' vivid description suggests terrorism within Jewish society rather than revolt against Rome, and indeed he specifically states in the *Antiquities* that people suspected that the first victim of the sicarii, the former High Priest Jonathan son of Ananus, had been killed at the instigation of the Roman governor himself. At the same time, "there arose another body of villains, with purer hands but more impious intentions." These "deceivers and impostors" pretended to be inspired while bringing about "revolution and changes," persuading the multitude to go crazy, leading them out into the desert on the grounds that there God would show them "signs of liberty"; so Josephus writes in the *Jewish War*, although in *Antiquities* the impostors are said to have promised "unmistakable marvels and signs that would occur according to God's foresight," without any indication of the content of this divine revelation. It is not at all clear that such rather unworldly behaviour was a threat to Roman rule, any more than that of Theudas some decades earlier, but Felix, like his predecessor as governor, did not wait to find out. He treated such acts as preliminaries to insurrection and destroyed their perpetrators with a military force.[12]

Of only one such "pseudo-prophet" did Josephus assert a specifically anti-Roman agenda, the Egyptian who, as we have seen, led a crowd by a roundabout route from the desert to the Mount of Olives, where "he prepared to force an entrance into Jerusalem and, after overpowering the Roman garrison, to set himself up as tyrant of the people, employing those who poured in with him as his bodyguard." In the parallel account in *Antiquities*, Josephus alleges that this prophet claimed that forcing an entrance would be unnecessary, because at his command Jerusalem's walls would fall down. In one account Josephus ascribes thirty thousand followers to this inspired leader, stating that "most of his force" was killed or taken prisoner in the ensuing battle with Felix's infantry, although the Egyptian himself escaped; in the parallel narrative, casualties were given as four hundred dead and two hundred prisoners. The numbers involved were evidently considerable in either case, so it is particularly significant that Josephus explicitly asserts that, far from the Egyptian enjoying mass support, "all the people" joined Felix in the armed defence of the city against this outsider. It seems that when, as Josephus states, the "brigands" incited the people to war with Rome, most of the people refused to comply. The uprising and defeat of this unnamed Egyptian Jew was sufficiently notorious in the history of Judaea in that decade for Paul to be mistaken for him by the captain of the guard which took him captive in Jerusalem. By contrast, the charlatan said to have played a similar trick in the time of Festus, successor (60–62 CE) to Felix as governor, is not only unnamed in Josephus' sole account (in the *Antiquities*), but goes completely unnoticed in Josephus' narrative of the lead-up to revolt in his *Jewish War*. In his earlier history Josephus evidently did not feel that the story of another group of misguided Jews, killed by Roman forces in the wilderness to which they were led by their leader, who promised them "salvation and rest from evils if they chose to follow him," significant enough to deserve mention.[13]

This catalogue of sporadic incidents should not suggest that Jerusalem in these years was really a haven of peace, only that the tensions about which Josephus complains in general turn out from his detailed narrative to have been largely internal to Jewish society rather than symptoms of widespread resentment of Roman rule. The actions of brigands in looting the houses of the wealthy and murdering their owners were part of the class warfare which Josephus sums up in his account of the causes of the Jewish war towards the end of his narrative of the conflict, when "no deed of iniquity was left unperpetrated . . . those in power oppressing the masses, and the masses eager to destroy the powerful. These were bent on tyranny, those on violence and plundering the property of the wealthy," but the causes of such class resentment lay less in Roman rule than in the inequitable distribution of resources within what was an essentially prosperous society. The wealth attracted into Jerusalem from all over the Jewish world made the rich richer, but, for many of the poor, rising levels of land prices helped create new burdens of debt, and it was not accidental that one of the first actions of the rebels against Rome in 66 CE was to burn down the debt archives in the hope of encouraging debtors to join their number. If attacks on rich Judaeans sometimes looked like attacks on Roman rule, this was because, as has been seen, the local leaders through whom Rome ruled the province were wealthy. It was of course in the interests of the rich to portray themselves as victims of anti-Roman sentiment in the hope of stimulating a more vigorous protection of their interests by the Roman governor and his forces. But in fact the local ruling class was itself responsible, quite separately from the disruption by brigands or religious fanatics, for much of the disorder in Judaean society during the years leading up to revolt in 66, not because they disliked Roman rule (from which they benefited) but because the weakness of successive Roman governors gave an opportunity for factions within the elite supported by Rome to struggle between themselves for power. As we saw in the Prologue, the declaration of an independent Jewish state in 66 did not dampen such strife within Jewish society but gave it more scope, so that for most of the time until spring 70 the Jewish rebels were largely preoccupied in fighting not Romans but each other.[14]

If Josephus (and indeed Tacitus) are to be believed, underlying the incompetence of Roman governors was their venality. Josephus' condemnation of Albinus, governor from 62 to 64, is damning:

> There was no form of villainy which he omitted to practise. Not only did he, in his official capacity, steal and plunder private property and burden the whole nation with extraordinary taxes, but he accepted ransoms from their relatives on behalf of those who had been imprisoned for robbery by the local councils or by former procurators; and the only persons left in gaol as malefactors were those who failed to pay the price. Now, too, the audacity of the revolutionary party in Jerusalem was stimulated; the influential men among their number secured from Albinus, by means of bribes, immunity for their seditious practices; while of the populace all who were dissatisfied with peace joined hands with the governor's accomplices. Each ruffian, with his own band of followers grouped around him, towered above his company like a brigand chief or tyrant, employing his bodyguard to plunder peaceable citizens.

Josephus' verdict on Albinus' successor, Gessius Florus, the last governor of Judaea, under whom revolt broke out, is even more vitriolic: "The crimes of Albinus were, for the most part, perpetrated in secret and with dissimulation; Gessius, on the contrary, ostentatiously paraded his outrages upon the nation . . . To make gain out of individuals seemed beneath him: he stripped whole cities, ruined entire populations, and almost went the length of proclaiming throughout the country that all were at liberty to practise brigandage, on condition that he received his share of the spoils." Such polemic, composed by a historian unashamedly partisan in his dismay at the unhappy fate which had eventually befallen his home city, was not of course exactly objective, and these former governors were easy Roman scapegoats by the time Josephus was writing, since none of them, apart from the apostate Jew Tiberius Julius Alexander, is known to have enjoyed a successful political career after 70. But the difficulties inherent in controlling the greed of provincial governors in the imperial period, when such governors were appointed by the emperor, were considerable, and the scope for enrichment well recognized. It was a remarkable achievement, considered worth noting in the biography of Agricola by his son-in-law Tacitus, that the former had managed to serve as quaestor in the province of Asia without enriching himself in the process, even though "the wealth of the province made it easy prey to the unscrupulous."[15]

Right up to the outbreak of insurrection in 66, the Jerusalem populace reacted to such poor Roman government in precisely the ways that the imperial system expected and encouraged, by sending deputations to the governors themselves or, when that proved ineffective, either to the governor of Syria or (in extreme cases) to the emperor himself. Problems arose less from Jewish hostility to the system than from the obstacles faced by the complainants in trying to get their voices heard and from the poor quality of some of the decisions taken both in Syria and in Rome. Josephus traced in some detail the long and bitter dispute between Jews and gentiles in the city of Caesarea which by the 50s was claimed by Jews as theirs, because it had been founded by the Jewish king Herod, but also by the local "Syrian" gentiles as theirs, because it had been the site of a gentile settlement before Herod and because Herod's erection of statues and temples showed that he had intended his new foundation to be pagan. Intercommunal violence in the city was temporarily crushed by the military force at the disposal of the governor Felix, and to resolve the issue embassies were sent from both sides to Nero in Rome, but when Nero favoured the arguments of the gentile inhabitants, the Jews were not satisfied and Josephus reports the allegation of corruption: "The leader of the Syrians in Caesarea, by offering a large bribe, prevailed on Beryllus, who was Nero's tutor and who had been appointed imperial secretary for Greek correspondence, to request a letter from Nero annulling the grant of equal civic rights to the Jews. Beryllus exhorted the emperor and succeeded in getting his authorization for the letter. This letter provided the basis that led to the subsequent misfortunes that befell our nation." In other cases, difficulties in ensuring safe communication, and the danger that a complaint might leak back to the governor to the detriment of the complainant before any chance of redress, led to passivity even under gross maladministration, so that in Jerusalem in 66, as the situation deteriorated, "so long as Cestius Gallus remained in Syria discharging his provincial duties, none dared even to send a deputation to him to complain about Florus." Not that access to a forum for complaint made much difference in this case. When Cestius Gallus did visit Jerusalem on Passover, "a crowd of not less than three millions [!] implored him to have compassion on the nation and loudly denounced Florus as the ruin of the country," but Florus was standing next to Cestius, scoffing at their words, and Cestius must have been aware that the Judaean governor, who had acquired his post through the influence of his wife, Cleopatra, on Nero's beloved wife Poppaea, might have friends in high places in Rome. At any rate, all that he did, before returning to Antioch, was to promise that he would ensure more moderate behaviour from Florus in the future—which meant that, in practice, he did nothing.[16]

The travails of Judaea up to 66 do not suggest a society on the brink of rebellion for sixty years. The only specific Jewish action described by any ancient writer as clearly hostile to Roman rule in general, and not just opposed to some specific act or acts of the current Roman administration, was the abortive uprising led by "the Egyptian" in the time of Felix, and on that occasion, according to Josephus, "all the people" joined the Roman governor in its suppression. Any argument based on what the ancient narratives do not describe is vulnerable to the possibility that other stories of hostility to Rome may simply have been lost—after all, Josephus referred on a number of occasions to a general collapse of society in these years, without specifying exactly what he meant, and there might easily be minor incidents rapidly forgotten—but strongly in favour of judging Josephus' record of Jewish dissent as more or less complete is the motivation of his histories, and especially his *Jewish War*. Josephus' declared intention was to explain the outbreak and course of the war from 66 to 70, and for that purpose he ran through the causes of tension between the two parties to the conflict in the sixty years before the war started, in the same way that Thucydides, the historian on whom he modelled his presentation of his subject, had provided a narrative of the fifty years before the outbreak of the Peloponnesian war. Far from omitting causes of conflict, he might be expected to make as much as he could of all the cases he could conceivably cite. When he could provide instead only general authorial prognostications of doom (such as "from that moment particularly, sickness fell upon our city, and everything went steadily from bad to worse"), without indicating how the events described (in this case, power struggles within the ruling class) led to revolt from Rome, his vagueness and reticence may be taken as evidence that there was no real connection to be made, and that the reason he could not describe any more blatantly revolutionary behaviour to support his picture of a decline into war was that no such revolutionary behaviour occurred.[17]

In fact, once Josephus' historiographical purpose is recognized, what is striking is how little specific evidence he could cite of Jewish hostility to Rome before 66. Writing with hindsight, he can be assumed to have picked out all those incidents which might throw light on the eventual cataclysm. In all historiography events unimportant in their day loom large because of their later significance. Josephus' depiction, in the second book of his *Jewish War*, of a society heading inexorably to its doom contrasts tellingly with his description, in the sixth book of the same work, of the treatment meted out to an inoffensive prophet named Jesus son of Ananias four years before the war. This Jesus, "a rude peasant," took to crying out regularly in the Temple a disturbing message: "A voice from the east; a voice from the west; a voice from the four winds; a voice against the bridegroom and the bride; a voice against all the people." He was arrested by some of the notable citizens and beaten, but that failed to stop his ill-omened words. The Roman governor Albinus also had him beaten, but only elicited between each stroke the cry "Woe to Jerusalem." Since he declined to say who he was, where he had come from and why he was uttering these imprecations, the governor decided he was mad and let him go. He was to have a long career, uttering his woes for seven years and five months until he was finally killed by a ballista ball during the siege of the city in 70, "having seen his prophecy fulfilled." But at the beginning of the story, at the festival of Tabernacles in the autumn of 62, such prophecy was alarming precisely because it was implausible. At this time, writes Josephus, Jerusalem, four years before the war, "was especially in a state of peace and prosperity." It seems evident that deciding whether a society is on the brink of collapse is often a matter of perspective—and much easier to judge after the event than before. In modern society a celebrated or particularly heinous crime will often release an avalanche of newspaper stories about similar cases in previous years, without such cases having any impact on the attitudes or mood of the public in the intervening period.[18]

It is particularly remarkable that Josephus' detailed narratives of these sixty years make so little mention of any consistent anti-Roman ideology at the heart of all the variegated disturbances he describes, since in his account in *Antiquities* of the uprising led by Judas at the time of the Roman census in 6 CE he had alleged precisely that the "Fourth Philosophy" begun by Judas and his accomplice Saddok was responsible for the collapse of Jewish society and the eventual destruction of the Temple since

> they sowed the seed from which sprang strife between factions and the slaughter of fellow citizens. Some were slain in civil strife, for these men madly had recourse to butchery of each other and of themselves from a longing not to be outdone by their opponents; others were slain by the enemy in war. Then came famine, reserved to exhibit the last degree of shamelessness, followed by the storming and razing of cities until at last the very Temple of God was ravaged by the enemy's fire through this revolt. Here is a lesson that an innovation and reform in ancestral traditions weighs heavily in the scale in leading to the destruction of the congregation of the people.

A second, briefer, account in the *Antiquities* links Judas in 6 CE even more specifically with the rebellion under Gessius Florus sixty years later:

> As for the fourth of the philosophies, Judas the Galilean set himself up as leader of it. This school agrees in all other respects with the opinions of the Pharisees, except that they have a passion for liberty that is almost unconquerable, since they are convinced that God alone is their leader and master . . . The folly that ensued began to afflict the nation after Gessius Florus, who was governor, had by his overbearing and lawless actions provoked a desperate rebellion against the Romans.

It is all the more striking that, in all the following detailed narrative up to 66 CE, no group or individual in Judaea is ever again said by Josephus to have been prompted by the teachings of this philosophy which, unlike the Pharisees, Sadducees and Essenes, Josephus leaves unnamed. Since Josephus so strongly disapproved of the Fourth Philosophy, and since he deplored all the incidents of anti-Roman violence which preceded the revolt in 66 both in his *Antiquities* and in his *Jewish War*, it seems likely that he would have blamed the Fourth Philosophy for any incident in which it was implicated—and that, since he did not do so, this was because the Fourth Philosophy was not in fact so implicated.

Josephus' silence in this regard can be contrasted to his comments on the varied fates of Judas' descendants. He mentions that Simon and Jacob, Judas' sons, were executed by crucifixion in the mid-40s CE and that in 66, after the outbreak of revolt, "a certain Menahem, son of Judas called the Galilean, that most ingenious sophist who once upon a time under Quirinius had upbraided Jews because they submitted to Romans after [having as master] God," broke into Herod's armoury on Masada, a massive fortress on the edge of the Dead Sea, and tried unsuccessfully to take over command of the rebel forces in Jerusalem. But Josephus writes nothing about the ideology of Simon and Jacob, or indeed why they had deserved to be put to death, and Menahem, portrayed as behaving in Jerusalem "like a king," is depicted, probably deliberately, as an adherent of a philosophy directly antithetical to the libertarianism of his ancestor: "believing himself without a rival in the conduct of affairs he became an insufferable tyrant" and, as a result, the original instigators of the revolt against Rome rose against him. "They remarked to each other that, after revolting from the Romans for love of liberty, they ought not to sacrifice this liberty to a Jewish hangman and to put up with a master [note the terminology] who, even if he were to abstain from violence, was anyhow far below themselves." It seems likely that Judas did indeed teach some novel ideas in 6 CE, but it is very improbable that such ideas were widespread in Judaea in the years immediately before 66, let alone that they were responsible for the most serious acts of opposition to Rome.[19]

Similar arguments apply to the role, or lack of it, of messianic fervour in the disturbances during these sixty years. Josephus was aware of the promises of the "messianic oracle." Indeed, in a catalogue of portents, prophecies and oracles which preceded the war, he ends by asserting that "what more than all else incited them to the war was an ambiguous oracle, likewise found in their sacred scriptures, to the effect that at that time one from their country would become ruler of the world. This they under-stood to mean someone of their own race, and many of their wise men went astray in their interpretation of it." One would therefore expect to find Josephus describing at least some of the leaders of disruptive movements in Judaea before 66 as such would-be messiahs. But in fact, although he abuses them as "pseudo-prophets," "charlatans," "impostors" and "deceivers," he never ascribes to any of them the delusion that he would become ruler of the world. It is probable that the political force imputed to the oracle by Josephus reflected the important use of the Flavian interpretation of its meaning as referring to Vespasian: the identical account of the oracle's real significance as evidence of divine approbation of Vespasian's imperial ambitions is to be found also in the accounts of Tacitus and Suetonius. By contrast, Josephus does give specific examples in recent history of Jews acting—foolishly, of course—in the light of a more general eschatological hope. As the Temple was burning in 70 CE, "women and children and a mixed crowd up to six thousand" took refuge in the outer court, owing their destruction there to "a false prophet who had on that day proclaimed to the people in the city that God commanded them to go up to the Temple court to receive there the signs of their deliverance." Such searching for signs from God was exactly what other "impostors" had urged earlier in the century. Perhaps not all sign prophets preached the imminent arrival of the last days, but it does seem likely that advocacy of such radical reliance on divine intervention presupposed a radical change in the political environment which, even if not strictly eschatological, was at least otherworldly. But whether such hopes necessarily posed a threat to Rome was of course a different issue. As some early Christians urged, it was quite possible to hope that one day there would be a new heaven and a new earth while staying loyal to the emperor and the Roman state.[20]

In favour of remaining loyal to Rome was the generally light hand of Roman rule before 66. Judaea was emphatically not a police state. According to Josephus, Nero was so unconcerned about Jerusalem a year before the revolt broke out that Cestius Gallus took a census of the number of Passover pilgrims in order to persuade him of the city's strength. The governors sent from Italy were of low status precisely because there was no perceived need for a strong military presence. The Roman state maintained a standing army of about a quarter of a million men, but, of these, just a small number of auxiliary cohorts, only one resident in Jerusalem, sufficed for the whole province, around three thousand troops in all. Above all, and most surprisingly in terms of normal Roman government, Jews were permitted to congregate in Jerusalem in vast numbers three times a year at the pilgrim festivals, with the only security precaution the repositioning of a few troops from Caesarea to Jerusalem for the duration. And, although some governors, such as Pontius Pilate, offended Jewish religious sensibilities, they did all make some attempt to be tactful. Thus, uniquely in Judaea, the local bronze coinage minted by the Roman governors reflected local sensitivities, avoiding depiction of any human form, as had also the coins produced by Herod the Great. Human images were so ubiquitous on coins of this period elsewhere in the empire that their absence from local Judaean coins must certainly have been the result of deliberate policy.* Such scruples are all the more remarkable given the widespread use in the province of Roman silver *denarii* minted elsewhere. Hence the question asked by Jesus of the "Pharisees and Herodians" who, according to the Gospel of Mark, tried to catch him out by asking whether it is lawful to give tribute to Caesar or not. Jesus' response, as recorded in the Gospel, was to ask them to bring him a *denarius* for him to see. "And they brought it. And he said to them, 'Whose is this image and inscription?' And they said to him, 'Caesar's.' "[21]

Out of respect for Jewish customs, Jews were also exempted from appearing before a Roman magistrate on a Sabbath, and (though perhaps only on specific occasions) they might be exempted from conscription into Roman military service. Josephus preserves a somewhat garbled series of letters sent by Roman magistrates to the cities of Asia and to other Greek cities insisting that Jews should be granted such privileges. The dossier was undoubtedly selective in the Roman decrees it chose to preserve—indeed, Josephus is quite open about his reasons for including it in his history: "It seems to me necessary to make public all the honours given our nation and the alliances made with them by the Romans and their emperors, in order that the other nations may not fail to recognize that the kings of both Asia and of Europe have held us in esteem and have admired our bravery and

---

* Even in the Temple there were images of a humanlike figure on the coins: because of their reliably high silver content, Tyrian silver shekels were the coin preferred by the Temple authorities for receipt of offerings and other payments. It is a bizarre fact that the shekels approved for this sacred Jewish purpose depicted the Tyrian god Melkart, identified with the Greek god Heracles.

loyalty . . . Against the decrees of the Romans nothing can be said, for they are kept in the public places of the cities and are still to be found engraved on bronze tablets in the Capitol." It is likely that the rather eclectic corpus which Josephus then proceeds to cite had been gathered together by some other Jew before him, probably in aid of a court case pleading for Jewish rights before a Roman judge. But the privileges seem to have been genuine enough, and special treatment accorded to minority communities of diaspora Jews was a fortiori likely to be granted also to the Jews in their homeland.[22]

## DIASPORA

IN THE DIASPORA also, most Jews lived under Roman rule before 66 CE, without apparently feeling themselves at odds with the Roman state. On the contrary, in some parts of the diaspora, such as Asia Minor, Jews relied on intervention by Rome to uphold their rights as members of a minority group in a gentile society, as can be seen from the dossier cited by Josephus. There is no evidence that the Jews of Asia, who constituted a large population in total, suffered at the hands of any Roman governor after the rapacity of Flaccus, who stole gold intended for Jerusalem in the 60s BCE. The Jewish communities of this region seem to have flourished in peace down to late antiquity. The only diaspora community known to have suffered from a persistent threat to its welfare was that of Alexandria in Egypt, and the special reasons for the tribulations of the Jews in that city will be discussed shortly. Elsewhere Jews came to an accommodation with their neighbours and might be grateful for the imperial peace that helped to preserve the status quo, which it was in their interest to defend. But what of course they could not control was the politics of the homeland—and the possibility that events in Judaea might have an impact on Roman policy towards Jews in far distant lands.[23]

Not that diaspora Jews were always simply victims of decisions taken by their brethren in Jerusalem, since they seem to have taken a close interest in Judaean politics, and just occasionally they even intervened. Soon after the death of Herod in 4 BCE and the disposal of his territory by Augustus to three of the king's surviving sons, a young man appeared in Crete claiming to the Jews there that he was Alexander, one of Herod's sons by the Hasmonaean princess Mariamme. This Alexander had in fact been put to death, along with his brother Aristobulus (father of Agrippa I), in 7 BCE, convicted by his father Herod on a charge of treason, but the pretender who usurped his name traded on his alleged Hasmonaean and Herodian ancestry and became a celebrity. Josephus writes cynically that the Jews of Crete gave him much money, and the Jews of Melos even more, "because of their belief that he was of the royal family and their hope that he would recover his father's throne and reward his benefactors." The young man travelled in style to Italy, escorted by enthusiastic supporters, picking up further backing from the Jewish communities of Puteoli and Rome, where "the whole Jewish population went out to meet him . . . giving him a joyful welcome because of their racial tie with his mother [Mariamme] whenever he went through the narrow streets riding in a litter. And he had all the trappings of a king, which were provided at their own expense by his private sponsors. Great crowds thronged about him, shouting their good wishes." In due course this "Alexander" was summoned to Augustus, whose questioning on the whereabouts of Aristobulus ("left on the island of Cyprus out of fear of what might happen at sea," according to "Alexander") eventually elicited the youth's true identity as a Jew brought up in the city of Sidon in Phoenicia by a Roman freedman. The impostor's attempt to benefit from his remarkable physical resemblance to Alexander was betrayed by his excessive physical toughness, "in contrast to the softness of the real Alexander's body, resulting from luxury and noble birth." The youth was condemned to the galleys. The close involvement in this affair of the Jews from the city of Rome may be partly explained by the long period, from 27 to 10 BCE, that the real Alexander had spent in the city when sent there by his father for his education, but the other diaspora Jews who supported him can have known little more than his purported name and lineage. It seems likely that news about political intrigues in Jerusalem gained general currency in these distant communities, and that, even though diaspora Jews could rarely affect what happened in Judaea, they seized what opportunities they had.[24]

Conversely, the visit by Agrippa I to Alexandria in August 38 CE was a spark for rioting against the local Jews by the Greeks, appalled by the pomp and circumstance of the Jewish king, even though, according to the apologetic account by his contemporary Philo, he had tried his best to enter the city unobtrusively. The situation in Alexandria rapidly escalated, first to the stigmatization of the Jews of the city as foreign aliens and then to a pogrom, with the confinement of the Jews to one quarter of the city, which became in effect a ghetto, and the plunder of their houses and workshops. But, although Agrippa's arrival was the catalyst for this disaster and Philo could claim that the violence came out of the blue, his visit was not really its main cause. The origins of intercommunal tension lay in the earlier history of the city and were only loosely related to Roman rule.

Founded in the fourth century BCE by Alexander the Great, Alexandria had by 31 BCE grown into the greatest city of the Mediterranean world, the capital of the Ptolemaic state, the site of the royal palace and the centre of a huge administrative bureaucracy which controlled all Egypt and beyond. The city was a magnet for settlers, including Jews, who had been granted the right to live in Alexandria by Alexander the Great himself, according to Josephus—a claim to be treated with much suspicion, although there certainly was a large Jewish community in residence by the late third century BCE, a hundred years after the city's foundation. The special status of Alexandria which had led to its phenomenal growth came to an abrupt end in 30 BCE on the death of Cleopatra. With the demise of the Ptolemaic dynasty the city was no longer the capital of a rich and independent kingdom. The city's magistrates, not even permitted to form a municipal council like those standard in other Greek cities under Roman suzerainty, in effect administered a city which was, much more blatantly than Jerusalem, under foreign occupation: in the time of Augustus, a legion and the fleet were stationed in Alexandria itself, and by 23 CE two legions and three auxiliary units were permanently stationed just on the edge of the city, in the Roman camp at Nicopolis. Dispute over the status of the Jewish community in the city allowed the resulting disaffection of the resident Greeks to erupt without them directly confronting their Roman masters. The Romans tried to sort out Jewish civic rights, but to no one's satisfaction. Under Augustus the Jews had a separate state within the state, with their own courts and their own political leader, the ethnarch (literally, "nation-ruler"), while in terms of liability to poll tax, from which Greeks were excused, they were placed by the Romans on the same level as native Egyptians. By the 30s CE the evidence for a recognized Jewish ethnarch has evaporated, and in the intercommunal struggles documented by Philo the Jews are portrayed as demanding *isopoliteia*, "equal citizenship," which could mean either equal collective rights (recognition by the state of legal decisions by Jewish courts) or equal individual rights (the right to participate in the affairs of the city as a full citizen), or, quite possibly, both. The Greeks accused the Jews of trying to obtain privileges to which they were not entitled. Rivalry became intemperate. Both sides blamed the Roman authorities for favouring the other. In a corpus of literary works known only from a number of papyri, the Greek magistrates who opposed Jewish demands were celebrated as martyrs at the hands of the wicked Romans in much the same tone as Philo denigrates the tyranny of the prefect Flaccus during the rule of Gaius. According to Josephus' undoubtedly partial account, Claudius on his accession restored the Jews of the city to their former privileges, since the new emperor desired that "none of their rights should be lost to the Jews on account of the madness of Gaius," but this favour was not unequivocal. His decree ended with an exasperated order: "I enjoin upon both parties to take the greatest precaution to prevent any disturbance arising after the posting of my edict."[25]

The serious disturbances which afflicted the Jews of Alexandria, the only such conflicts attested in the diaspora before 66 CE, were probably thus a product of conditions specific to that city, and there is no reason to suppose similar tensions in other places. In a tough letter, of which a copy survives on papyrus, sent to the Jews and Greeks of Alexandria in 41, the emperor Claudius had shown himself aware of the danger that might be posed by scattered Jewish communities if they were to unite against the established order in the city, forbidding the Jews there "to bring in or welcome Jews who come in from Syria or Egypt, which will force me to conceive greater suspicions. If they do, I shall take all possible proceedings against them, on the grounds that they stir up a common plague for the whole world." But such cooperation in support of fellow inhabitants of the diaspora was rare. One looks in vain for any expression in this period of a fear that Jews might act as a fifth column within the empire. In the speech ascribed by Josephus to Agrippa II on the outbreak of revolt in 66 CE (see Chapter 2), he warned that diaspora Jews within the empire would suffer if war broke out in Jerusalem, but he did not even suggest that such Jews might join in the war on the side of the rebels, though perhaps this omission had a tinge of apologetic: it was not in Josephus' interest to allow even the thought that diaspora Jews might fight Rome, and the possibility of aid from kinsmen beyond the Euphrates, in Parthian territory, alleged by Josephus, in his introductory comments to his account of the war as a whole, to have been a hope of the Jews, is raised by Agrippa in the speech only to be discounted. In general, diaspora Jews were only to come into serious tension with the Roman state when something went drastically wrong in the homeland, such as Gaius' plan to desecrate the Jerusalem Temple by erecting his statue within it. Certainly, for some diaspora Jews, when full-scale revolt broke out in Jerusalem in 66 it proved impossible not to be affected.[26]

## WAR, 66–70 CE

THE ERUPTION of war in Jerusalem in the late spring of 66 was precipitated precisely by the Captain of the Temple, a young priest named Eleazar son of Ananias, who persuaded his fellow priests to stop offering those sacrifices traditionally made to the Jewish God on behalf of the Roman emperor. It was a statement of war by members of the ruling elite on whom the Roman administration could normally rely. They had lost confidence in the governor, Gessius Florus, and in the ability of higher Roman authorities, including the emperor in Rome, to deal satisfactorily with their complaints. A series of incidents, none particularly serious in itself, had escalated into national violence through the inability or unwillingness of the governor to take matters in hand. In Caesarea, the long-running dispute between local Jews and local gentiles came to a head when some gentile youths provoked Jewish riots by sacrificing a cockerel in the alleyway outside a synagogue, and the Jews of the city eventually abandoned the city en masse. When Florus failed to punish the gentile ringleaders of this outrage in Caesarea—a result of bribery, so Josephus alleges—his next appearance in Jerusalem, to collect back taxes, was confronted by a hostile crowd. An exercise in political theatre, in which a group of Jewish youths pretended to collect pennies for the indigent governor, backfired badly when Roman troops were let loose on the crowd. Florus demanded that the "chief priests, nobles and most eminent citizens" hand over the culprits for punishment, but they declined, "imploring pardon for the individuals who had spoken disrespectfully." The mutual trust between the local elite and the governor was broken. In fury, Florus set his troops on the rampage in the upper market in the south-west of the city, with orders to pillage and loot. Josephus writes that "the total number of that day's victims, including women and children, for even infancy received no quarter, amounted to about three thousand six hundred." But what really upset the historian and signified the collapse of Roman rule by consensus was the rank of some of those who died, "for Florus ventured that day to do what none had ever done before, namely, to scourge before his tribunal and nail to the cross men of equestrian rank, men who, if Jews by birth, were at least invested with that Roman dignity."[27]

Hence, in despair at ever controlling the excesses of Florus, Eleazar son of Ananias and his colleagues among the younger aristocratic priests began the revolt. Without the benefit of diaries or letters written at the time, it is impossible to know precisely what they wanted to achieve or what they expected to happen as a result of their actions. Doubtless different participants had different hopes, private sentiments differed from public proclamations, hopes changed from day to day. Josephus, present in the inner court of the Temple when the fateful decision was taken, was involved in the revolt from the start, but, writing only after its disastrous end and his own change of side, he claims that he had always seen his role as a mediator, trying to bring the uprising to a swift and honourable end with a minimum of destruction. In hindsight such would indeed have been a prudent course, and, as we have seen, it was urged publicly at the time, according to Josephus, by Agrippa II and Berenice. The crucial difference lay in their actions. Once war was inevitable, Agrippa and some other rich Jerusalemites left the city to join the Roman side, whereas Josephus stayed and in October 66 joined the revolutionary government as general in command of the defence of Galilee.[28]

Whatever the rebels really hoped for, it is easier to establish what they might reasonably have expected to achieve, given the nature of Roman imperial government and previous Roman interest, or lack of it, in Judaea. It was out of the question that the Romans would not react at all, any more than the state had allowed affairs in Judaea to drift in 4 BCE after Herod died, but it was not wildly over-optimistic to dream of a return to some form of Jewish independence under much looser Roman suzerainty. In 4 BCE Varus, as governor of Syria, had allowed the Jews to send a deputation of fifty envoys to Augustus to request autonomy for the nation—by which they must have meant primarily freedom from Herodian rule. But since then Judaea had known glory under a popular Jewish king, Agrippa I, and it was only twenty-two years since his reign had been ended by his premature death. The paucity of Roman troops stationed in Jerusalem suggests that Rome was not too concerned what went on in this unimportant territory, provided that Roman interests were not actually harmed. Nero was to proclaim the freedom of Greece either later in this same year or in 67, an act of propaganda with no substantive effect on the government of the province. For Judaea similarly to change its status by a stroke of the pen was not impossible, difficult though it is now to imagine in the light of what actually occurred. And indeed the Romans in 66 might well have been concerned simply to save face in Jerusalem rather than instigate more drastic upheaval. The emperor had been distracted by the conspiracy of a magnificent and popular but politically inept aristocrat named Gaius Calpurnius Piso in the previous year, and he had reacted by killing a great number of his erstwhile supporters as his suspicions became paranoid. Following precedents on previous occasions when there had been minor problems in Judaea, the governor of Syria, Cestius Gallus, marched south to restore order. King Agrippa, who joined him, could reasonably hope that he would soon be back in his role as guardian of the Temple, trying to select High Priests more effective in controlling the population and at the same time more amenable to wayward Roman governors than the present Temple authorities. The declaration of war had been the cessation of loyal sacrifices in the Jerusalem sanctuary. It would make sense if the immediate Roman aim was to ensure that such sacrifices started again.[29]

What caused such a drastic change in the following four years? The crucial element which raised the level of Roman suppression of unrest in Jerusalem from a police action to a full-scale military operation, involving thousands of troops, was, as we saw in the Prologue, the failure of Cestius Gallus to restore order in the summer of 66 CE, and, above all, the huge loss of men and equipment during his withdrawal from Jerusalem. Such damage to the prestige of the state required retaliation, and the use of collective punishments to deter opposition in the provinces was a standard Roman procedure. The infliction of punishment would require a major military operation, but its seriousness should not be exaggerated. The sixty thousand troops allocated to Vespasian for the task of teaching the Jews a lesson were significantly more than had been deployed for the invasion of Britain in 43 CE, and it is tempting in retrospect to see the huge size of his forces as evidence that the rebellion of the Jews was seen as a major threat to Roman hegemony, but a different explanation is more plausible: Vespasian was given command of this number of troops simply because they were available in the region and otherwise unemployed after campaigns against Armenia and Parthia by the greatest of Nero's generals, Gnaeus Domitius

Corbulo, had ended. Three legions had been transferred in succession from the Balkans in the late 50s to increase Rome's military strength in Syria for these campaigns, and they now lacked any military role. Nero did not intend using them for another expansionary campaign which would end either in defeat, and a loss of prestige, or (equally undesirable) in victory and the elevation of a new general to become a potential threat. As Corbulo himself had discovered early in Nero's reign, without something to do, the legions in Syria went soft and lost morale. Participation in a punitive expedition to Judaea would be good for the troops.

That the Roman assault on Jerusalem four years later was far more intense than a mere punitive expedition might have been explained by the extent of Jewish opposition once the revolt had started and an independent Jewish state was established in Jerusalem, but in fact the Jewish state was characterized less by organized hostility to Rome than by internecine struggles for power. A group of bandit sicarii tried to usurp leadership of the city but, when defeated, took themselves off to Herod's fortress on the rocky outcrop of Masada by the Dead Sea, where they took no further part in the war until Jerusalem had been captured. Lacklustre defence of territory outside Jerusalem pushed thousands of refugees into the capital city, where they vied for influence, with Galileans under John of Gischala pitted against Zealots from the villages of northern Judaea, and both opposed to the Idumaeans from the south, led by Simon son of Gioras. Between the retreat of Cestius Gallus and the start of the siege of Jerusalem in spring 70, Rome faced no resistance of any consequence—certainly not enough to warrant the destruction of the Temple in retaliation.

A change in Roman policy might also have been warranted if the declaration of an independent state in Jerusalem had evoked a mass uprising by the Jews in the rest of the Roman empire, but that strikingly failed to occur, although Cassius Dio states in his brief account of the siege of the city that "the Jews [in Jerusalem included] many from the place itself and many of those who professed the same customs, not only from the Roman empire but also from beyond the Euphrates." Despite Dio's assertion, the only diaspora Jews explicitly named by Josephus among the defenders of the city were from Adiabene in Mesopotamia—they included sons and kinsmen of their king Izates, who (as we saw in Chapter 4) had converted to Judaism some decades earlier. If other Jews came, from Asia Minor, Syria or Egypt, or indeed from Rome, Josephus kept silent about them, in contrast to his numerous references to groups and individuals from within the homeland. Perhaps Dio meant only to refer to Jews from the regions immediately adjacent to Judaea, such as Transjordan and Galilee. It is possible that Josephus was trying to disguise from his Roman readers the extent to which diaspora Jews had been involved in revolt, but it is more likely that most diaspora Jews distanced themselves from a quarrel which was not theirs. It will be recalled that the universal Jewish revulsion at Gaius' intended sacrilege in the Temple in 40 had led Philo temporarily to forget the parochial concerns of the Jews of Alexandria and Agrippa I to risk both his fortune and his life by confronting the tyrant emperor. The comparative passivity of diaspora Jews in 66–70 was in marked contrast, and suggests that they did not think that the future of the Temple cult itself was under threat.[30]

Not that declining to participate in the fighting in Judaea necessarily saved diaspora Jews from being dragged unwillingly into the fallout of the conflict in the homeland. Even before Cestius Gallus had been defeated in August 66, the Jews who lived as minorities in gentile cities close to the borders of the land of Israel found themselves dangerously vulnerable. In volatile Alexandria in the spring of 66, a riot began "now that disorder had become general among others," when Greeks holding a public meeting noted that many Jews had infiltrated the assembly in the amphitheatre.[31] Three of the Jews were burned alive, and the Jewish community rioted in revenge. Only deployment against the Jews of the two legions stationed on the city outskirts restored order. The ferocity of the Roman response may partly be explained by the need of the governor of Egypt, Tiberius Julius Alexander, himself an Alexandrian Jew, to demonstrate at this time of crisis that he was prepared to act firmly against his own people.

Even in places where Jews had enjoyed good relations with their fellow citizens in previous years, the conflagration in Jerusalem inevitably raised questions of loyalty. Neighbours who had coexisted in peace for years polarized according to their political affiliations. Pogroms threatened in many places close to Judaea and even as far away as Antioch in Syria. The reactions of the gentile civil authorities varied, some controlling, some abetting the violence, as Josephus records:

The inhabitants of Ascalon slew two thousand five hundred, those of Ptolemais two thousand, besides putting multitudes in irons. The Tyrians dispatched a considerable number, but imprisoned the majority in chains; similarly the people of Hippos and Gadara made away with the more daring of their enemies and kept the timid folk in custody; and so with the remaining cities of Syria, the action of each being governed by their feelings of hatred or fear of their Jewish neighbours. Only Antioch, Sidon and Apamea spared the residents and refused either to kill or to imprison a single Jew; perhaps, with their own vast populations, the cities disdained the possibility of Jewish risings, but what mainly influenced them, in my opinion, was their pity for men who showed no revolutionary intentions. The people of Gerasa not only abstained from maltreating the Jews who remained with them, but escorted to the frontiers any who chose to emigrate.[32]

In his autobiography, Josephus states that "the inhabitants of the surrounding cities of Syria proceeded to lay hands on and kill, with their wives and children, the Jewish residents among them, without the slightest ground of complaint; for they had neither entertained any idea of revolt from Rome nor harboured any enmity or designs against the Syrians." The protestation, though quite possibly true, was disingenuous, for in his *Jewish War* he reveals that the Jews living in the areas closer to Jerusalem had fallen victim to provocation of their gentile neighbours by the Jerusalem revolutionaries, who had sent detachments to pillage their land and villages. The hatred shown by these Jewish rebels to the local gentile population had in turn been sparked off by the massacre of the Jews in Caesarea, where "the Caesareans massacred the Jews who lived among them, so that within one hour more than twenty thousand were slaughtered and Caesarea was completely emptied of Jews, for those who fled were arrested by Florus and taken in chains to the dockyards." But the enmity had still deeper roots. It was local gentiles who had served as auxiliary troops in the Roman units which had acted so brutally in Jerusalem in the preceding months leading up to the outbreak of war. Gentile soldiers in a squadron of cavalry and five infantry cohorts recruited from Caesarea and Sebaste had expressed unseemly joy in 44 when Agrippa I, whom they considered too favourable to the Jews, died prematurely:

They hurled insults, too foul to be mentioned, at the deceased; and all who were then on military service—and they were a considerable

*The slaughter of Dacians by Roman troops, depicted on Trajan's column in Rome. The barbarian enemy was often dehumanized in imperial art.*

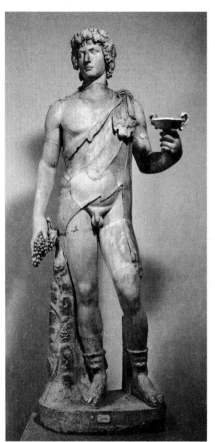 

(above left) *The sculpture of Antinous, the beloved of the emperor Hadrian, portrays him nude, in Greek style, and with the accoutrements of the god Bacchus: Antinous was deified by Hadrian after he drowned in the Nile in October 130* CE. *(above right) A wall painting from the household shrine of the House of the Centennial in Pompeii, depicting Bacchus, adorned with grapes and accompanied by a panther, next to a mountain, which probably represents Mount Vesuvius. The painting, with its many natural features, is dated to the 70s* CE.

*Symbols of the revolt of 66–70 CE. The silver shekel (above) minted by the rebels in 68 CE shows on the obverse a vessel used in the Temple; the reverse has a stem with three pomegranates. The captions, written in archaic Hebrew lettering, read "YEAR 3. SHEKEL OF ISRAEL" and "JERUSALEM THE HOLY." The relief (below) from the Arch of Titus, erected in or soon after 81 CE, depicts the triumphal procession in which the Temple utensils were carried through the streets of Rome.*

(above) *Bronze sestertius minted in Rome in 71 CE, with images celebrating the defeat of the Jews. On the obverse, the rugged features of Vespasian, with the inscription "Imperator Caesar Vespasian Augustus, high priest, with tribunician power, father of the nation, consul for the third time"; on the reverse, a date-palm tree and a mourning Jewess seated beneath it, with the inscription "JUDAEA CAPTA; by recommendation of the Senate." (below) An aerial view of Masada, showing Herod's palace on the northern tip of the rock. The Roman siege ramp is to the right of the picture. The Dead Sea is to the left.*

*(top left) The façade of the Jerusalem Temple depicted on a tetradrachm minted by the Jewish rebels in Judaea in 132 CE. (top right) Bronze coin of Aelia Capitolina, showing Romulus and Remus being suckled by a wolf; the design marks the city as a Roman enclave and the caption names it, in Latin, as COLONIA AELIA CAPITOLINA. (bottom) An oil lamp, from the Israel Museum, depicting the wild boar, the symbol of the Tenth Legion.*

*(above) The destruction of the temple of Dagon depicted in a mural from the synagogue at Dura Europus (mid-third century). (below) A Jewish sarcophagus from Rome, probably from the last quarter of the third century. Where a sarcophagus of this type would usually have a portrait of the deceased, in the roundel held by the two central winged victories over the three putti treading grapes in a basin, the sculptor has depicted instead a menorah.*

*The sun as a god, depicted as SOL INVICTUS, "Unconquered Sun," on coins of the pagan emperor Victorinus (who ruled briefly in a part of the western empire from 269 to 271 CE) (above left) and of the Christian emperor Constantine (above right), and in the center of a mosaic (below) showing the signs of the Zodiac on the floor of the synagogue at Hammat Tiberias in Galilee (fourth century).*

*Cuirassed bronze statue of Hadrian, found in 1975 at Tel Shalem, near the River Jordan, south of ancient Scythopolis. The portrait of the emperor is one of the finest bronze imperial portraits to survive from antiquity. The relation of the head to the torso, on which nude warriors are depicted in combat, has been disputed.*

number—went off to their homes, and seizing the images of the king's daughters [Berenice and Drusilla] carried them with one accord to the brothels, where they set them up on the roofs and offered them every possible sort of insult, doing things too indecent to be reported. Moreover, they reclined in the public places and celebrated feasts for all the people, wearing garlands and using scented unguents; they poured libations to Charon [ferryman of the dead], and exchanged toasts in celebration of the king's death.

Josephus asserts explicitly that these military units, composed of men from Caesarea and Sebaste who had shown such disrespect to the dead Agrippa, proved twenty-two years later "to be the source of the greatest disasters to the Jews by sowing the seeds of war in Florus' time."[33]

In the months following the defeat of Cestius Gallus in the summer of 66 the rebels in Jerusalem were too intent on establishing and defending their new-found freedom, and in fighting among themselves, to be able to embroil diaspora Jews farther in their fight. Jews living at a distance from the new state might hope to be left in peace. But such quietism did not protect the Jews of Antioch, where affairs in Jerusalem were presumably much discussed because, as the capital of the province of Syria and the largest city of the empire after Rome and Alexandria, this was the place from which Cestius Gallus and his troops had set out, and where Vespasian was mustering his army for the renewed assault. The Jews of the city had been left in peace in the spring of 66, but on Vespasian's arrival in the late autumn a certain Antiochus, himself a Jew and indeed the son of the chief magistrate of the local Jewish community, denounced his father and his fellow Jews as traitors intent on burning the city down. Fear of a Jewish fifth column was further stoked when Antiochus produced some Jews from foreign cities and accused them as accomplices in the plot. The implication that being Jewish was incompatible with being a loyal citizen of Antioch was explicit when Antiochus introduced a sacrifice test to establish which Jews supported the city: those who refused to sacrifice to the pagan gods were killed. As a renegade Jew, Antiochus clearly knew where to aim his blows, and his next step was to prohibit resting on the Sabbath. According to Josephus, Roman troops were enlisted to ensure that Jews on the Sabbath "did exactly as the other days," though quite how this was achieved is obscure. For a short time the observance of the Sabbath was abolished not only in

Antioch but "also in the other cities equally." Josephus does not specify which cities and where, nor how the persecution came to an end, but it is clear that Antiochus was still very much in evidence, and creating dangers for his former co-religionists, after the war was over. The travails into which innocent diaspora Jews were thus drawn by the turmoil in the mother city renders all the more striking their apparent reluctance to commit themselves to the defence of Jerusalem. At some level, presumably, they saw the distant war as none of their business. They lived a Jewish life happily enough as minority communities under Roman rule and protection. Perhaps they hoped that in due course Roman rule would be reestablished in Judaea, the rebel leaders punished, and a new pro-Roman High Priest installed in the Temple. Certainly, they had no reason to believe that the war which broke out in 66 would effectively result in a clash of civilizations and change the face of Judaism for ever.[34]

NONE OF these Jews, whether in the diaspora or in Jerusalem, could have possibly known about the change in the world political order in 68 CE which changed altogether the significance in terms of Roman politics of the Judaean campaign. The brutal realities of the exercise of power in the Roman world became dramatically clear when Nero died violently during the long year of struggle from mid-68 to December 69, during which five emperors—Nero, Galba, Otho, Vitellius, Vespasian—ruled in turn, and thousands of Romans were killed, a return to mass civil violence to a degree unknown in Roman society in the hundred years since Octavian had established autocracy through the crushing defeat of Mark Antony at Actium in 31 BCE.

That we can narrate these events of January 69 onwards in detail is due primarily to the writings of Tacitus, whose account of them survives in the first five books of his *Histories*, which originally took the story from 69 to the death of Domitian in 96. Tacitus describes the work on which he is entering as "a period rich in disasters, terrible with battles, torn by civil struggles, horrible even in peace." He is not, as he confesses, an unbiased witness: "I had no acquaintance with Galba, Otho or Vitellius, through either kindness or injury at their hands. [But] I cannot deny that my political career owed its beginning to Vespasian; that Titus advanced it; and that Domitian carried it further; but those who profess inviolable fidelity to truth must write of no man with affection or with hatred." The shock of renewed civil bloodshed was immense. It was not on the scale of the slaughter in the decade and more before Actium, but it involved far more of the Roman people than the elite intrigues and trials surrounding imperial politics for the first half of the first century CE. Tacitus wrote that "after the battle of Actium . . . the interests of peace required that all power should be concentrated in the hands of one man." The principle remained generally acknowledged, but the struggles to decide which man should be supreme were as potentially destabilizing as the last gasp of the Republic had been.[35]

The start of insurrection in 68 in fact showed the imperial system of divide and rule in effective operation. Gaius Iulius Vindex, governor of Gallia Lugdunensis and a local Gallic aristocrat, threw off his allegiance to Nero in January 68, proclaiming (according to the coins he minted) the "salvation of the human race," "Jupiter Liberator" and "Rome restored." A man of minor significance on the wider stage of Roman politics, Vindex attempted to garner support by writing to other governors, some of whom inevitably leaked the conspiracy to the emperor. All governors and army commanders were instantly pushed into the unenviable position that hesitation to condemn the uprising would lead to loss of imperial favour and almost certain death. In an episode now shrouded in uncertainty, the commander of the armies of the upper Rhine, Verginius Rufus, marched into central Gaul and met Vindex and his troops at Vesontio in late May. Since Vindex came to Vesontio with far fewer troops than Verginius Rufus, and since those troops were much less well equipped and trained, it is probable that he believed Rufus willing to join him in the rebellion against Nero. If so, his hopes were destroyed by the loyalty of Rufus' troops to Nero, or perhaps their dislike of Vindex's soldiers. In any case, the two armies fought, Vindex's forces were roundly defeated, and Vindex committed suicide. What Rufus thought at the time cannot now be discovered, but his epitaph, following his peaceful end in honoured old age thirty years later, constituted a masterly rewriting of history: "Here lies Rufus, who once, after Vindex had been defeated, liberated the imperial power, not for himself, but for his country." The whole episode, played out on a battlefield far from Italy, had left Nero unscathed.[36]

More effective in the transfer of power were contemporaneous events in Spain. The governor of Tarraconensis, Servius Sulpicius Galba, was in his early seventies, came from an ancient patrician family with a history of distinguished political service to the state in the Republic, had been consul thirty-five years before, and had been awarded triumphal insignia for his military achievements earlier in his impressive career. It is possible that Vindex approached him as a potential rival to Nero, but Vindex's failure and death obscured any such link in the later traditions about those years. What is certain is that Galba contrived to have himself proclaimed by his troops as representative of the Senate and people of Rome. His coins bore legends such as "Liberty of the Roman People." Other governors and commanders in Spain, including crucially Marcus Salvius Otho, legate of Lusitania, and Titus Vinius Rufinus, commander of the only Spanish legion, decided to support the insurrection; their backing provided sufficient impetus to eradicate local opposition. Control of Spain still did not obviously convey control of the wider empire: the legend on Galba's coins which asserted "Concord of the Spains and Gauls" revealed that such concord could by no means be taken for granted. In any case, it was a long way from Spain to Rome, and Nero sent a general to northern Italy to raise an army to ward off the expected invasion. It was still quite possible for Nero to hold on and wait for Galba's coalition of the ambitious and disaffected to crumble. But Nero did not hold on. His decision to capitulate may have had less to do with Galba than with a contemporaneous revolt by Clodius Macer, commander of the Third Legion, which was based in Africa and could thus cut off supplies of grain to the city of Rome—Macer seems to have operated independently of Galba, since it was to be by Galba's order that he was eventually executed in October of this same year. In any case it must have seemed to Nero that his authority had collapsed, and that his generals were rebelling on all sides without fear of retaliation by their colleagues. He planned to flee to Egypt, at which point the praetorian guard deserted him on the grounds that he was deserting Rome, and the Senate, taking its cue from the praetorians as it had done on the death of Gaius twenty-seven years before, proclaimed him a public enemy. Suetonius describes his end:

> Phaon [his freedman] urged him to hide for a time in a pit, from which sand had been dug, but he declared that he would not go underground while still alive . . . At last, while his companions one and all urged him to save himself as soon as possible from the indignities that threatened

him, he bade them dig a grave in his presence, proportioned to the size of his own person, collect any bits of marble that could be found, and at the same time bring water and wood for presently disposing of his body. As each of these things was done, he wept and said again and again: "What an artist I am as I perish!" . . . And now the horsemen were approaching who had orders to take him off alive. When he heard them, he . . . drove a dagger into his throat, aided by Epaphroditus, his secretary. He was half-dead when a centurion rushed in, and as he placed a cloak to the wound, pretending that he had come to aid him, Nero merely gasped: "Too late!" and "This is fidelity!" With these words he was gone, with eyes so set and starting from the sockets that all who saw him shuddered with horror.[37]

All Galba needed to do was to proceed to Rome in state and accept the homage of his subjects. After the excesses of the previous regime, it might seem easy enough to achieve popularity and security. In practice, however, frugality was castigated as meanness and the exercise of patronage that delighted the fortunate made enemies of those who were overlooked. It took time for a usurper to acquire the aura of inviolability which had protected even Gaius and Nero at their most bizarre, but Galba was not to be vouchsafed the time he needed: Nero died in early June 68; Galba was killed on 15 January 69. Galba's undoing was his advanced age. It was obvious, since he was in his early seventies, that power must quite soon pass to a successor. He had no son, so there was considerable pressure on him to adopt an heir. On the other hand, adoption of an appropriate successor could itself be dangerous, since it might encourage the ambitious to cultivate the prospective emperor rather than the incumbent. Galba's solution was to present to the Senate on 10 January 69 a young man of no political achievements or even ambitions. Lucius Calpurnius Piso Frugi Licinianus was an obscure scion of an originally illustrious family. In his early thirties, he had spent the last years of Nero's rule in exile, and he seems to have enjoyed almost no popularity with the wider population of Rome. The reaction of Galba's most energetic lieutenant, Otho, who had marched with him from Spain, was swift. If he was not to be designated heir, he would take power for himself. The praetorian cohorts were disgruntled in any case by Galba's failure to pay to them the bribe promised by their commander in June the previous year as reward for betraying Nero. On 15 January Otho went with Galba to sacrifice at the temple of Apollo, only to slip away from the imperial entourage and be taken by twenty-three soldiers to the praetorians' camp, where he was greeted warmly. Suetonius again provides a lurid account of the last moments of the aged emperor, hopelessly at the mercy of hostile troops as he went through the Forum, where

> the horsemen who had been ordered to slay him, spurring their horses through the streets and dispersing the crowd of civilians, caught sight of him from a distance and halted for a moment. Then they rushed upon him again and butchered him, abandoned by his followers. Some say that at the beginning of the disturbance he cried out, "What mean you, fellow soldiers? I am yours and you are mine," and that he even promised them money. But the more general account is that he offered them his neck without resistance, urging them to act and strike, since it was their will.[38]

Otho thus came to power through open and vicious bloodshed on the streets of Rome, but at least in his coup the bloodshed was limited in extent. Piso died on the same day as Galba, as did a number of other associates, but the violence by which the change in regime had been effected caused little disruption to the rest of the city, let alone the wider empire. Otho justified his murderous ambition by stressing his own ties with Nero, whom Galba had supplanted, restoring Nero's statues which had been torn down, and stressing the friendship Nero had shown him during the earlier and better years of his rule. In Rome, the tactic seems to have worked among all those groups which mattered—the Senate, the people and (above all) the praetorians. But Otho, who had been confined by Nero to Lusitania as governor from 58 until Galba's conspiracy, had enjoyed no opportunity to win a military reputation, had never been consul, and had no great following among other provincial commanders and armies. The threat to his power thus came not from within his own entourage but from Germany, where the illustrious Aulus Vitellius, a generation his senior and consul more than twenty years previously, was commander of the army on the lower Rhine and was persuaded by his troops to seek supreme power for himself—and, of course, less directly, to ensure thereby that they would profit from his victory.

Neither Vitellius nor his followers seem to have been particularly disenchanted with Otho. Their disaffection (or ambition) had been already apparent on 1 January 69, when the legions at Mainz refused to swear loyalty to Galba, but the changed regime at Rome seems to have made no difference to their aims. The German armies crossed the Alps at extraordinary speed, aided by weather milder than normal for February and early March, in order to march on Rome before Otho should be reinforced by troops from other provinces, particularly from the Balkans. Otho marched north to the Po valley and chose to meet Vitellius' troops in battle at Cremona on 14 April. Only few reinforcements had as yet arrived, and he was greatly outnumbered, but this was itself a reason to confront the rebels immediately, since by taking his troops north Otho had left all the rest of Italy, including the city of Rome itself, vulnerable to attack if some of Vitellius' forces were to leave his main army and march on Rome. In any case, Otho did not delay. Battle was joined and, after heavy loss of life, decisively lost. Tacitus' approval of Otho's bravery in his suicide is expressed in an affecting speech to his supporters attributed to him by the historian:

> To expose such courageous and brave men as you to further dangers, I reckon too great a price for my life. The greater the hope you offer me, if it were my wish to live, so much the more glorious will be my death . . . Others may hold the power longer than I; none shall give it up more bravely. Would you have me suffer so many of Rome's young men, such noble armies, to be again cut down and lost to the state? Let me carry with me the thought of your willingness to die for me; but you must live.

The precise words of the speech are of course Tacitus', not Otho's, and the favourable picture of Otho's last days owes much to the vilification of Vitellius by Tacitus' sources, for whom Vitellius, as the opponent of Vespasian, was a figure for denigration. In fact, there was little that Otho could have done once the battle was lost and the road to Rome lay open to his enemies; to hope for salvation from the Balkan legions, when and if they arrived, would have been hopelessly optimistic. The Senate, apprised of the news, compliantly bestowed imperial power on Vitellius on 19 April and sent a delegation north to Pavia, where it met the new autocrat in mid-May. Soon he was accepting the title "Augustus" by popular demand.[39]

The process through which Vitellius in turn yielded his power and his life to Titus Flavius Vespasianus, the last emperor of 69, was similar to his own coup in most respects—a fact rather embarrassing in antiquity to Flavian historians such as Josephus and (retrospectively) Tacitus. Vespasian had been appointed in 66 by Nero to command the Roman forces against the rebellious Jews partly because of his political insignificance. The son of a tax farmer, he was in his late fifties and had enjoyed a worthy but not a brilliant career. He had been granted no special favours by Tiberius or Gaius as he made his laborious way up the senatorial ladder in his twenties. He made a breakthrough of a kind as a legionary commander during the conquest of Britain by Claudius in 43, and in 51, aged forty-two, he reached the consulship. In the early 60s he was governor of Africa, a post that brought prestige but no power, since it involved command of no legions. Nero by October 66 was paranoid about conspiracies. The plot centred round Gaius Calpurnius Piso had been foiled the previous year, but not before the considerable extent of disaffection within the political class had been revealed, leading to suspicions of others who had probably not been involved. Among those whom Nero compelled to commit suicide was Corbulo, the most successful general of his time, who had won remarkable victories against Armenia and Parthia in the late 50s and early 60s. Under imperial disfavour Corbulo took his own life in October 66, just after the failure of Cestius Gallus' fateful expedition to Jerusalem. Nero could not brook the elevation of another successful general who might be a threat to his own security. Instead, he preferred to entrust the control of three legions for the Judaean war to Vespasian precisely because he was a competent mediocrity. That such a man might become emperor, without breeding or contacts among the aristocracy, was unimaginable. Suetonius summarizes succinctly: "Since to put down this rebellion [of the Jews] required a considerable army with a leader of no little enterprise, yet one to whom so great power could be entrusted without risk, he [Vespasian] was chosen for the task, both as a man of tried energy and as one in no wise to be feared, because of the obscurity of his family and name."[40]

According to Suetonius, this obscure senator decided to seek supreme power for himself, while Otho and Vitellius were striving for power, because he was spurred on by portents. "When he was dining, an ox that was ploughing shook off its yoke, burst into the dining-room, and after scattering the servants, fell at the very feet of Vespasian as he reclined at table, and bowed its neck as if suddenly tired out." Local oracles in Judaea usefully confirmed divine approval of his ambition: "When he consulted the oracle of the god of Carmel in Judaea, the lots were highly encouraging, promising that whatever he planned or wished, however great it might be, would come to pass. And one of his noble captives, Josephus, declared most confidently as he was being put in chains that he would soon be released by the same man, who would then, however, be emperor." But Suetonius combines this account, of divine blessing for ambition fulfilled, with a more prosaic version in which Vespasian was the pawn of the Danubian and eastern legions, eager for the rewards of victory in civil war, much as Vitellius had been manoeuvred by the legions on the Rhine:

> They took it into their heads to select and appoint an emperor, saying that they were just as good as the Spanish army which had appointed Galba, or the praetorian guard which had elected Otho, or the German army which had chosen Vitellius. Accordingly the names of all the consular governors who were serving anywhere were taken up, and since objection was made to the rest for one reason or another, while some members of the Third Legion, which had been transferred from Syria to Moesia just before the death of Nero, highly commended Vespasian, they unanimously agreed on him and forthwith inscribed his name on all their banners . . . When their action became known, Tiberius Alexander, prefect of Egypt, was the first to compel his legions to take the oath for Vespasian on the Kalends of July, the day which was afterwards celebrated as that of his accession; then the army in Judaea swore allegiance to him personally on the fifth day before the Ides of July.

In fact, the timing of these "spontaneous" declarations of enthusiasm for Vespasian, and the support expressed by Gaius Licinius Mucianus, governor of Syria and previously on poor terms with Vespasian, allows little doubt that the bid for power was carefully planned. It is an interesting question whether a conspiracy fully formed by early July would have been aimed at the removal of Otho if he had still been in power. As it was, Vespasian's supporters could portray themselves as intent on revenge: "The enterprise was greatly forwarded by the circulation of a copy of a letter of the late emperor Otho to Vespasian, whether genuine or forged, urging him with the utmost earnestness to vengeance and expressing the hope that he would come to the aid of his country."[41]

The original plan seems to have been for Mucianus to advance on Italy from Syria while Vespasian went to Alexandria in Egypt and, if necessary, interrupted the flow of grain to Rome in order to make Vitellius unpopular among the citizens (a risky strategy). Vespasian did indeed go to Alexandria, leaving the Judaean campaign in the highly competent hands of his son Titus, but Mucianus was anticipated in Italy by the Danubian legions under the legionary general Antonius Primus, who declared loyalty to Vespasian and, in the late afternoon of 24 October, destroyed Vitellius' forces in the same place, Cremona, where Vitellius had defeated Otho in April. Cremona itself was sacked. It was said that fifty thousand died in the battle and that the fire in Cremona lasted for four days. Primus pressed on to Rome and entered the city on 21 December. Vitellius, unlike Otho, had tried to delay the inevitable, with horrible results:

> The foremost of the army had now forced their way in, and since no one opposed them, were ransacking everything in the usual way. They dragged Vitellius from his hiding-place and when they asked him his name (for they did not know him) and if he knew where Vitellius was, he attempted to escape them by a lie. Being soon recognized, he did not cease to beg that he be confined for a time, even in the prison, alleging that he had something to say of importance to the safety of Vespasian. But they bound his arms behind his back, put a noose about his neck, and dragged him with rent garments and half-naked to the Forum. All along the Sacred Way he was greeted with mockery and abuse, his head held back by the hair, as is common with criminals, and even the point of a sword placed under his chin, so that he could not look down but must let his face be seen. Some pelted him with dung and ordure, others called him incendiary and glutton, and some of the mob even taunted him with his bodily defects . . . At last on the Stairs of Wailing he was tortured to pieces with exquisite refinement and then dispatched and dragged off with a hook to the Tiber.

The Senate, of course, immediately conferred all the necessary powers on Vespasian as the new emperor—although he dated the start of his rule not to their legal blessing but from 1 July, when the troops had first acclaimed him.[42]

Vespasian found it convenient to disown the barbarous violence of Antonius Primus, claiming that he had acted without authority. Primus, after a brief period of glory in control of Rome, was quietly sidelined into obscurity, living on for at least twenty-five years in retirement in his home town of Tolosa (Toulouse). Vespasian could portray his own actions as free of the taint of bloodshed and his elevation to power as the result simply of his popularity with the soldiers and the people, although in terms of real politics such a claim was blatantly untrue. Victory could only have been won by military means. But a different justification for the regime's seizure of power was needed to render the *coup d'état* palatable to a Roman populace which, as we have seen, had clear ideas of what gave status to political leaders. The new emperor chose to base his claim to the purple on his military services to the Roman state through the defeat of the Jews.

The death of Nero, the demise of the Julio-Claudian dynasty, the struggle for power by Galba, Otho and Vitellius, and, above all, the bid for the purple by Vespasian were all completely unexpected. Suddenly in July 69 the commander of Roman forces against Jerusalem was no longer an obscure senator of mediocre talent and minimal prestige in the court of the emperor. Now he was, or hoped to be, emperor himself. Vespasian's bid, and his need to advertise a victory over foreigners to give it legitimacy, explain the energy with which the attack on Jerusalem was suddenly prosecuted. Vespasian had won power in Rome from a distance. He had stayed in Alexandria, far away from the shedding of Roman blood through which his supporters, especially Antonius Primus at Cremona in October 69, won him power. Such civil bloodletting was not an auspicious start to a new reign. Vespasian's image urgently needed the gloss of foreign conquest— the surest foundation of authority for a Roman politician—for him to be portrayed in the capital as warrior hero and saviour of the state. Vespasian delayed his own journey to Rome until the summer of 70, in the meantime instructing his son Titus, left behind in Judaea, to win the war as rapidly and comprehensively as possible, regardless of the cost.[43]

At the heart of Titus' eventual victory was thus the ruthlessness of his assault, which paid little heed either to the damage caused to the city or to the losses on his own side. By the fall of Jerusalem huge numbers of Roman soldiers were dead and many more wounded. Precisely how heavy the

Roman casualties were, we cannot now tell: it was not in the interest of Titus, or Josephus, to advertise the figures, and governments are often reticent about the number of dead on their own side when they wish to emphasize a glorious victory. In a glittering parade held in the centre of his former camp at the conclusion of the siege, Titus handed out gold and silver insignia to those who had been distinguished for valour during the war, but so far as is known from Josephus' account, he made no mention of those who had made the supreme sacrifice, despite the uplifting rhetoric about "the immortality reserved for those who fall in the frenzy of battle" which, according to Josephus, he had used when encouraging his troops to assault the walls at peril of their lives.[44] The number of casualties was a direct result of haste. Titus was under pressure to capture Jerusalem quickly. The pressure was not military but political. A free Jerusalem would be no greater threat to Roman imperial power in 71 than in 70. Reports from deserters confirmed that starving out the defenders was proving successful. It was only necessary to wait. But Titus had his eye less on Jerusalem than on Rome, and the need to proclaim to the population of the imperial city that his father, the new emperor, acclaimed by his own soldiers just over a year ago in July 69 but otherwise with no claim whatever to the purple, was not a thuggish nonentity propelled to power by the slaughter of Roman citizens in civil conflict but a hero of the Roman state who had won victory in Judaea. Vespasian had been in Alexandria in Egypt since the early autumn of 69. In July 70 he set off for Rome to be greeted by his subjects in the capital city, where he arrived in late September or early October. When he left Alexandria Jerusalem was still under siege. He relied on Titus to complete the task at speed.

The final assault, which began as we have seen in the early summer of 70, left much of the city in ruins. Much was destroyed by fire, accidental or deliberate, during the fighting, and more was devastated by looting after resistance had ended. But Josephus writes specifically that, even at the height of the siege, Titus had not intended this destruction to include the Temple. At a council of his generals Titus declared that "he would not wreak vengeance on inanimate objects instead of men, nor under any circumstances burn down so magnificent a work; for the loss would affect the Romans, inasmuch as it would be an ornament to the empire if it stood."[45]

Some have doubted the truth of Josephus' claim, especially since the fourth-century Christian historian Sulpicius Severus relays a precisely opposing view, apparently derived from a lost passage of Tacitus' *Histories*, that

> Titus summoned his council, and before taking action consulted it whether he should overthrow a sanctuary of such workmanship, since it seemed to many that a sacred building, one more remarkable than any other human work, should not be destroyed. For if preserved it would testify to the moderation of the Romans, while if demolished it would be a perpetual sign of cruelty. On the other hand, others, and Titus himself, expressed their opinion that the Temple should be destroyed without delay, in order that the religion of the Jews and Christians should be more completely exterminated.

Josephus certainly might have wanted to pretend that the Temple's destruction was accidental, even if it was untrue. But there are powerful reasons to accept his version of events. He was writing within ten years of the council of war on which he was reporting. He had been in Jerusalem at the time of the siege, and had been close enough to the headquarters to know what orders emerged from the emperor's council, even if he did not know precisely who had expressed which opinion. His readers included Titus himself, and it would have been unwise to write something about the general which was patently false, since Josephus relied on imperial patronage. Such considerations apply particularly strongly to an assertion about his leadership which Titus can hardly have welcomed: the great general will not have been happy with the implication of Josephus' narrative, that his desire to save the Temple had been foiled by his inability to impose proper discipline on his troops. Josephus' assertion looks odd in the light of Titus' celebration of the Temple's demise once it had burned down, but that gives reason to believe the assertion, not to dismiss it.[46]

According to Josephus, the eventual conflagration came about by accident:

> At this moment, one of the soldiers, awaiting no orders and with no horror of so dread a deed, but moved by some supernatural impulse, snatched a brand from the burning timber and, hoisted up by one of his comrades, flung the fiery missile through a low golden door, which gave access on the north side to the chambers surrounding the sanctu-

ary. As the flame shot up, a cry, as poignant as the tragedy, arose from
the Jews, who flocked to the rescue, lost to all thought of self-
preservation, all husbanding of strength, now that the object of all their
past vigilance was vanishing. Titus was resting in his tent after the
engagement, when a messenger rushed in with the tidings. Starting up
just as he was, he ran to the Temple to arrest the conflagration; behind
him followed his whole staff of generals, while in their train came the
excited legionaries, and there was all the hubbub and confusion attend-
ing the disorderly movement of so large a force. Caesar, both by voice
and hand, signalled to the combatants to extinguish the fire; but they
neither heard his shouts, drowned in the louder din which filled their
ears, nor heeded his beckoning hand, distracted as they were by the
fight or their fury. The impetuosity of the legionaries, when they
joined the fray, neither exhortation nor threat could restrain; passion
was for all the only leader. Crushed together about the entrances, many
were trampled down by their companions; many, stumbling on the still
hot and smouldering ruins of the porticoes, suffered the fate of the vanquished. As they drew nearer to the sanctuary they pretended not even
to hear Caesar's orders and shouted to those in front of them to throw
in the firebrands. The insurgents, for their part, were now powerless to
help; and on all sides was carnage and flight. Most of the slain were
civilians, weak and unarmed people, each butchered where he was
caught. Around the altar a pile of corpses was accumulating; down the
steps of the sanctuary flowed a stream of blood, and the bodies of the
victims killed above went sliding to the bottom.

According to Josephus, even at this stage Titus believed that the structure
of the Temple might be saved. He rushed about, trying, by personal
appeals, to persuade the soldiers to extinguish the fire. But they did not
obey:

> Their respect for Caesar and their fear of the officer who was endeav-
> ouring to check them were overpowered by their rage, their hatred of
> the Jews, and a lust for battle more unruly still. Most of them were fur-
> ther stimulated by the hope of plunder, believing that the interior was
> full of money and actually seeing that all the surroundings were made
> of gold. However, the end was precipitated by one of those who had

entered the building, and who, when Caesar rushed out to restrain the troops, thrust a firebrand, in the darkness, into the hinges of the gate. At once a flame shot up from the interior, Caesar and his generals withdrew, and there was none left to prevent those outside from kindling a blaze. Thus, against Caesar's wishes, was the Temple set on fire.[47]

Once the deed was done, Titus had no choice but to celebrate. To proclaim to the Roman people that the destruction had come about through incompetence would be to allow the new regime to begin not with a famous victory over a dangerous enemy but with sacrilege on a grand scale. Perhaps Titus' attitude had been more ambivalent than Josephus suggests and there had been more than one council of war, likely enough in such fraught circumstances, and on a different occasion Titus had shown himself willing enough to countenance the Temple's demise, as Sulpicius Severus reported. It was not an easy decision, and both historians record that divergent opinions were expressed.

At any rate, with the Temple in ruins, Titus set about depicting the religion of the Jews as not worthy to exist, and the Temple's destruction as an act of piety to the gods of the Roman world. The sophist Philostratus, who wrote in the early third century, reflected this theology in an incident recorded in his life of the pagan sage Apollonius of Tyana, a contemporary of Titus, writing that "after Titus had taken Jerusalem, and when everything was filled with corpses, the neighbouring peoples offered him a crown; but he disclaimed any such honour to himself, saying that it was not he himself that had accomplished this exploit, but that he had merely given his arms to God, who had so shown his anger." The outcome of the war seems to have been very different from that intended by the Romans in 66. A campaign that had begun in order to ensure that Jews should offer regular sacrifices to their God in Jerusalem for the well-being of the emperor had ended by making any such offering impossible. The destruction of Jerusalem in 70 was the product of no long-term policy on either side. It had come about through a combination of accidents, most of them unrelated in origin to the conflict: the death of Nero, leading to Vespasian's bid for power in Rome and Titus' quest for the propaganda coup of a rapid conquest of Jerusalem, and the devastating effect in the summer heat of a firebrand thrown by a soldier into the Temple of God.[48]

# CHAPTER TWELVE

# REACTIONS

## 70–312 CE

## CONFLICT, 70–135 CE

NEITHER ITS ANTIQUITY, nor its deep wealth, nor its people spread over the whole habitable world, nor yet the great glory of its religious rites, were sufficient to prevent its ruin." So Josephus laments the destruction of the Temple. It would be hard to overestimate the impact of this cataclysmic event on all Jews, wherever they lived. In practical terms those most affected were the inhabitants of Jerusalem, and especially the priests who had served in the sanctuary, but the religious significance of what had happened was equally great for diaspora Jews who had never had an opportunity to visit the Temple while it stood. In the last century of its existence the Temple had been at its most magnificent, a symbol of God's glory and protective care for Israel. If God, ruler of the universe, had allowed his Temple to be destroyed, the explanation must lie in the sins of the Jews. There could not be clearer evidence of the withdrawal of divine favour. In retrospect, it was obvious that God had announced his intention not just in private dreams to the prophet Josephus but by public portents, when "a star, resembling a sword, stood over the city, and a comet which continued for a year," or "at the ninth hour of the night, so brilliant a light shone round the altar and the sanctuary that it seemed to be broad daylight; and this continued for half an hour," or "a cow that had been brought by someone for sacrifice gave birth to a lamb in the midst of the court of the Temple," or "the eastern gate of the inner court . . . was observed at the sixth hour of the night to have opened of its own accord," or "before sunset throughout all parts of the country chariots were seen in the air and armed battalions hurtling through the clouds and encompassing the cities," or "at the feast which is called Pentecost, the priests on entering the inner court of the Temple by night . . . reported that they were conscious, first of a commotion and a din, and after that of a voice as of a host, 'We are departing hence.' " Tacitus, too, knew about the most dramatic of these divine signs: "Contending hosts were seen meeting in the skies, arms flashed and suddenly the Temple was illuminated with fire from the clouds. Of a sudden the doors of the shrine opened and a superhuman voice cried: 'The gods are departing.' At the same moment the mighty stir of their going was heard."[1]

In the fortress of Masada down by the Dead Sea one Jew, a certain Joseph son of Nakson, was still behaving in 71 as if all was not lost. The divorce document he wrote for his wife Miriam was dated to "the first of Marheshvan, year six." The period that had begun so bravely in 66 could no longer be described as the era of the liberation of Israel, but perhaps hope lingered for the future of the nation as Joseph set his wife free "to become the wife of any Jewish man you wish." But for most Jews, misery, despair and gloom were the natural reactions. It would take time, a long time, for any Jew to find any positive lesson from the disaster.

> O Lord, my Lord . . . from all the cities that have been built you have consecrated Zion for yourself . . . and from all the multitude of people you have gotten for yourself one people; and on this people, whom you have loved, you have bestowed the Law which is approved by all. And now, O Lord, why have you delivered up the one to the many, and dishonoured the one root beyond the others, and scattered your only one among the multitude? And why have those who opposed your promises trodden down on those who believed your covenants? If you really hate your people, they should have been punished at your own hands.

The comfort offered, probably in the 80s, by the author of *4 Ezra* to himself and his fellow Jews in response to this lament was eschatological. In contrast to present miseries, in a new age all will be well: "And it shall be that whoever survives after all that I have foretold to you shall be saved and shall see my salvation and the end of my world."[2]

The only Jewish author whose writings composed between 70 and 100 survive extensively was Josephus. He wrote mainly, of course, about events before 70, but he also had something to say about the immediate aftermath of the war, and his apologetic treatise *Against Apion* reflected his views in the 90s. In none of these works does Josephus give any hint that a new and different Judaism had arisen from the ashes of the old, nor that such change could or should occur. In his frequent references to the varieties of Judaism which had flourished before 70—especially the Pharisees, Sadducees and Essenes—nothing suggests that these "philosophies" had ceased to attract Jews just because the Temple was in ruins. Most strikingly, when he comes to describe the Jewish religion as a whole in *Against Apion*, it is the Temple that he emphasizes: "One Temple of one God, for like is dear to like, common to all, of God common to all. Him the priests constantly worship, under the leadership of him who for the time is head of the line. He with his fellow priests will sacrifice to God." The use of the present and future tenses in referring to a sanctuary that had been destroyed a quarter of a century before was surely deliberate. Josephus was a Jerusalem priest and thus had a special interest in the Jerusalem sanctuary, but it is unlikely that his attitude was wholly different from that of Jews who were less personally concerned. The book of Deuteronomy in the Torah stated clearly enough that Jews suffered when they failed to keep the law as they should. The same Torah stated unequivocally that God required sacrifices in the sanctuary where he had chosen to be worshipped. If the Lord of the universe had temporarily made this impossible, it must be as punishment for sin. Pharisees would feel guilty at having failed to be good enough Pharisees, Essenes for their failings as Essenes, Sadducees for not fulfilling the laws as the Sadducaic philosophy required. All three schools of Judaism could continue without difficulty without the Temple cult—it would be possible to be a Pharisee, Sadducee or Essene even today, although to be an Essene one would need fellow Jews prepared to enter into a dedicated community—and each could provide a quite coherent, if depressing, explanation of the disaster on Deuteronomic lines. There was no need to seek for a novel theology. In any case, theological and philosophical reflection about a disaster of this magnitude can take many years. Only some decades after 1945 did Jewish theologians seriously begin to seek new theodicies to explain the Holocaust in twentieth-century Europe. Some Jews in 70, like some Holocaust survivors, will have lost their faith in a powerful, caring God. Others will have seen all the more reason to commit themselves to their earlier faith, just as after 1945 adherents of the different shades of Jewry—secular, religious, socialists, Zionists—affirmed that fuller commitment to their creed would have saved the communities that had perished.[3]

In due course a new Judaism was to emerge that preached forms of worship that might, at least partially, take the place of Temple sacrifices. Later rabbinic tradition portrayed the rabbinic sages at Yavneh (Jamnia), a small town on the Judaean coastal plain, as devising under the leadership of Yohanan ben Zakkai a new Judaism in which good deeds and prayer would take the place, at least in terms of theological efficacy, of the Temple cult. That such a new Judaism was eventually advocated by the rabbis in late antiquity, by the fourth century CE, is well attested; but that it was devised immediately following the destruction is deeply implausible. The changes attributed to Yohanan in the Mishnah are modest, and mostly concerned with liturgy: "Before time the palm branch was carried seven days in the Temple [on the feast of Tabernacles] but in the [rest of] the country for one day only. After the Temple was destroyed, Rabban Yohanan ben Zakkai ordained that in the country it should be carried seven days in memory of the Temple." In fact, the detailed prescriptions for the sacrifices to be found in the Mishnah, redacted around 200 CE, presuppose that even at that date rabbis expected, or at least hoped, that the Temple could and would be rebuilt. The hope was entirely reasonable. Jerusalem had lost one Temple in 587 BCE only to see it restored. The more Josephus pointed out the parallels between the two destructions, which had taken place in both cases on the same day of the month of Ab (in late July), the more plausible was a parallel rebuilding. The efforts need not have been onerous. The sacrificial cult did not require a building as magnificent as Herod's famous edifice. A small building for the Holy of Holies, an altar, and markers to delineate the perimeters of sacred ground, would suffice, provided that they were all in the correct place in Jerusalem. The most onerous task would be to clear the site of rubble. There were plenty of priests of good pedigree still alive able to fulfil their functions—of whom not the least well known was Josephus himself. The detailed instructions for the procedures of the Temple cult found in the Mishnah and in Josephus' histories show that people still knew what to do. At least according to later rabbinic tradition, there was still a supply of the ashes of the red heifer which alone could purify the severely defiled and ensure that the Temple cult was carried on in an appropriate state free from pollution. There is not a shred of evidence that any ordinary Jew at this time thought of the cessation of sacrifices as desirable. On the contrary, all Jews were waiting impatiently for God to be worshipped properly again, "speedily, in our days."[4]

In the context of normal practice in the Roman empire, the Jews' hopes should not have been idle. Temples burned down through accident quite frequently in the ancient world. Romans took for granted that the obvious response was to rebuild. The great temple of Jupiter Capitolinus in Rome was burned down during the civil strife between Vespasian's supporters and those of Vitellius in 69; the moving of the Terminus stone, the religious ceremony which marked the first step towards the temple's restoration, took place on 21 June 70. But the Roman state was not to allow the Jerusalem Temple to be rebuilt in the same way, a refusal which may reasonably be seen as a major cause of the sixty-five years of conflict to come. It is worthwhile emphasizing the enormity of this refusal in the context of ancient religious practice, and the extent to which it revealed a special prejudice against the Jews. Not just in their own eyes but also in the eyes of Romans, Jews were unable to bring offerings to their ancestral god in the fashion standard throughout the Roman world.

## VICTORY OVER JUDAISM

JOSEPHUS' extraordinarily vivid eyewitness account of the Flavian triumphal procession in June 71 is the fullest extant ancient description of any Roman triumph:

> Previous notice having been given of the day on which the pageant of victory would take place, not a soul among that countless host in the city was left at home: all issued forth and occupied every position where it was possible to stand, leaving only room for the necessary passage of those upon whom they were to gaze. The military, while night still reigned, had all marched out in companies and divisions, under their commanders, and been drawn up, not round the doors of the upper palace, but near the temple of Isis; for there the victorious generals reposed that night. At the break of dawn, Vespasian and Titus issued forth, crowned with laurel and clad in the traditional purple robes, and proceeded to the Octavian walks; for here the senate and the chief magistrates and those of equestrian rank were awaiting their coming. A tri-

bunal had been erected in front of the porticoes, with chairs of ivory placed for them upon it; to these they mounted and took their seats. Instantly acclamations rose from the troops, all bearing ample testimony to their valour: the princes were unarmed, in silk robes and crowned with bays. Vespasian, having acknowledged their acclamations, which they wished to prolong, made the signal for silence; then amidst profound and universal stillness he rose and, covering most of his head with his mantle, recited the customary prayers, Titus also praying in like manner.

After a celebratory breakfast, Vespasian and Titus put on their triumphal robes, sacrificed to the gods and sent off the procession.

It is impossible adequately to describe the multitude of those spectacles and their magnificence under every conceivable aspect, whether in works of art or diversity of riches or natural rarities; for almost all the objects which men who have ever been blessed by fortune have acquired one by one—the wonderful and precious productions of various nations—by their collective exhibition on that day displayed the majesty of the Roman empire. Silver and gold and ivory in masses, wrought into all manner of forms, might be seen, not as if carried in procession, but flowing, so to speak, like a river . . . But nothing in the procession excited so much astonishment as the structure of the moving stages; indeed, their massiveness afforded ground for alarm and misgiving as to their stability, many of them being three or four storeys high, while the magnificence of the fabric was a source at once of delight and amazement. For many were enveloped in tapestries interwoven with gold, and all had a framework of gold and wrought ivory. The war was shown by numerous representations, in separate sections, affording a very vivid picture of its episodes. Here was to be seen a prosperous country devastated, there whole battalions of the enemy slaughtered; here a party in flight, there others led into captivity; walls of surpassing compass demolished by engines, strong fortresses overpowered, cities with well-manned defences completely mastered and an army pouring within the ramparts, an area all deluged with blood, the hands of those incapable of resistance raised in supplication, temples set on fire, houses pulled down over their owners' heads, and after general desolation and woe, rivers flowing, not over a cultivated land, nor supplying drink to man and beast, but across a country still on every side in flames. For to such sufferings were the Jews destined when they plunged into the war; and the art and magnificent workmanship of these structures now portrayed the incidents to those who had not witnessed them, as though they were happening before their eyes. On each of the stages was stationed the general of one of the captured cities in the attitude in which he was taken. A number of ships also followed.

Josephus notes the extraordinary quantity of booty on display:

The spoils in general were borne in promiscuous heaps; but conspicuous above all stood out those captured in the Temple at Jerusalem. These consisted of a golden table, many talents in weight, and a lamp stand, likewise made of gold, but constructed on a different pattern from those which we use in ordinary life. Affixed to a pedestal was a central shaft, from which there extended slender branches, arranged trident-fashion, a wrought lamp being attached to the extremity of each branch; of these there were seven, indicating the honour paid to that number among the Jews. After these, and last of all the spoils, was carried a copy of the Jewish Law. Then followed a large party carrying images of victory, all made of ivory and gold. Behind them drove Vespasian, followed by Titus; while Domitian rode beside them, in magnificent apparel and mounted on a steed that was itself a sight. The triumphal procession ended at the temple of Jupiter Capitolinus, on reaching which they halted; for it was a time-honoured custom to wait there until the execution of the enemy's general was announced. This was Simon, son of Gioras, who had just figured in the pageant among the prisoners, and then, with a halter thrown over him and scourged meanwhile by his conductors, had been haled to the spot abutting on the Forum, where Roman law requires that malefactors condemned to death should be executed. After the announcement that Simon was no more and the shouts of universal applause which greeted it, the princes began the sacrifices, which having been duly offered with the customary prayers, they withdrew to the palace. Some they entertained at a feast at their own table: for all the rest provision had already been made for banquets in their several homes. For the city of Rome kept festival that day for her victory in the campaign against her enemies, for the termination of her civil dissensions, and for her dawning hopes of felicity.

Josephus may have touched up this highly coloured narrative in later editions to give a more prominent role to Domitian after Titus died in 81, but there is no reason to doubt that the text which survives represents fairly closely what he wrote just ten years or so after the fall of the Temple. In the light of his heartfelt comments elsewhere in his histories about the disaster which had befallen the Jews, the description of the ceremony is remarkable for its consistently Roman viewpoint. The triumph was to set the tone of the dynasty until its demise on the death of Domitian a quarter of a century later, and the relations of Rome to the Jews for the rest of antiquity.[5]

It must have been very soon after Titus became aware that the Jerusalem Temple could not be saved from the flames that he also realized that its destruction must be presented to the Roman world not as a disastrous accident but as a great achievement and a cause for Roman celebration. The logic of his campaign, seeking a rapid victory regardless of his losses in order to reap the propaganda benefit, required its culmination to be portrayed as glorious. It was not standard Roman practice to glory in the destruction of enemy temples. On the contrary, the ritual of *evocatio*, through which a Roman general offered to the patron deity of the enemy a better form of worship in Rome if the deity consented to cross to the Roman side, seems still to have been practised by Roman generals in Asia Minor in the wars of the first century BCE. The ritual presupposed that war was waged against human communities, not against their gods. Foreign gods had long been incorporated into the pantheon of deities worshipped in Rome. If in 205 BCE the cult of Cybele and in 218 CE the worship of the sacred black stone of Elagabal could both be incorporated into the religious rites of the Roman elite, the same could have been done in 70 CE for the God of Jerusalem. But that was emphatically not the stance of Vespasian and Titus, as the triumphal procession showed all too starkly. The most prominent objects exhibited among the spoils were the golden candelabrum, incense shovels and other paraphernalia of the Jerusalem Temple. These, perhaps, were selected for their ostentatious magnificence, to delight the spectators, but there was no mistaking the symbolic significance of the last of all the spoils of victory: "a copy of the Jewish Law," that is, a scroll of the Torah. There could not be a clearer demonstration that the

conquest was being celebrated not just over Judaea but over Judaism. No
one in Rome could have been unaware of the likely Jewish reaction. It was
after all only thirty years since Jews from many different parts of the
Roman world had joined in protest at the much less serious desecration of
the Temple envisaged by Gaius when he wanted his statue inserted in its
precincts. It is unlikely, too, that Vespasian and Titus were insensitive to
more subtle indications of the new status of Jewish religious susceptibilities: one of the insignia of the Tenth Legion (known as "Fretensis," or "of
the strait"), now stationed permanently on the site of Jerusalem, was the
wild boar, whose image is still to be found on many of the artefacts they
produced. Of all aspects of Judaism, one of those best known to ordinary
Romans was their abhorrence of pigs.[6]

That this war on Judaism was not to be only a temporary feature of Flavian propaganda is clear from the building projects into which it was incorporated. One of the first to be completed was the magnificent Temple of
Peace, erected to the south-east of the Forum Romanum and dedicated in
75. Trumping the Altar of Peace set up by Augustus after the cessation of
the civil wars of his day, Vespasian, who also in 71 closed the temple of
Janus to symbolize the attainment of peace through Roman arms, celebrated the end of bloodshed in the same ambiguous fashion, avoiding reference to the slaughter of Roman by Roman and to the part played by his
own partisans, and instead embellishing the new shrine with masterpieces
of painting and sculpture culled from all over the inhabited world, including the gold vessels from the Jerusalem Temple. Josephus reports, but does
not explain, that the Torah scroll ("their law") and the purple hangings of
the Temple sanctuary Vespasian kept safeguarded in the imperial palace.
Over the fifteen years or so following the conquest of Judaea the centre of
the city of Rome was remodelled to reflect the victory, with two triumphal arches dominating the traditional route of all triumphal processions. The relief sculpture showing the table of shewbread, incense cups,
trumpets and candelabrum, is still visible on the arch of Titus above the
Forum at the top of the Sacred Way (the arch was restored in 1824); the
Colosseum, the great Flavian amphitheatre completed in 80, was built on
the proceeds of sale of booty. Numerous coins, issued both in Rome and in
Judaea, proclaimed JUDAEA CAPTA, with an image of a bound female captive beneath a date-palm tree. Not that all this propaganda stressed the religious defeat of the Jews: the inscription which adorned the arch erected in

early 81 by the Senate and People at the south-east end of the Circus Maximus, one of the largest arenas ever created for watching sporting events and able to seat about a hundred and fifty thousand spectators, honoured Titus with the untrue flattery that "with the instruction and advice of his father he subdued the race of the Jews and destroyed the city of Jerusalem which had either been attacked in vain by all leaders, kings and people before him or had not been attempted at all." But wholly religious were the impact and symbolism of the new tax imposed by Vespasian on all Jews, wherever they lived. Josephus' report in the *Jewish War*, thus written before 81, is brief: "On all Jews, wheresoever they be, he placed a tax, ordering each to pay two drachmas every year to the Capitol as before they contributed to the Temple at Jerusalem." Cassius Dio, in the early third century, recorded that "from that time forth [i.e. the destruction of Jerusalem] it was ordered that the Jews who continued to observe their ancestral customs should pay an annual tribute of two drachmas to Jupiter Capitolinus." The tax was thus portrayed both as a substitute for the voluntary contributions previously made by adult male Jews for the maintenance of the regular communal sacrifices in Jerusalem, and as a payment, not to the Roman state in general, but specifically for the rebuilding of the temple of Jupiter on the Capitol which had accidentally burned down in 69. Not only were Jews to be denied the right to rebuild their own shrine, they were to be required instead to pay for the upkeep of the main pagan cult of Rome. The extraction of this new and unprecedented tax seems to have begun immediately. Already in 70 enthusiastic bureaucrats in Egypt were extracting back tax for the previous year. Women and children were compelled to pay as well as men. And, as Josephus explicitly notes, the Jews of the diaspora wheresoever they be, including those of Rome, were caught up in the collective punishment of their nation for the failed uprising in Jerusalem.[7]

IN JUDAEA itself after the fall of Jerusalem, Titus and his successors in command extinguished, with extraordinary thoroughness, all possible resistance. The captives from the city suffered terrible fates: Josephus records that the old and feeble were slaughtered indiscriminately by the rampaging soldiers, those younger than seventeen sold into slavery, fit adult males sent to work in the quarries or mines in Egypt or presented to the provinces "for destruction in the theatres by sword and wild beasts." Thousands died of starvation or ill-treatment while in holding camps inside the Temple compound. Josephus claims that "the total number of prisoners taken throughout the entire war amounted to ninety-seven thousand, and of those who perished during the siege, from first to last, to one million one hundred thousand." He clearly expected his readers to be incredulous at the numbers, since he proceeds to give reasons for their plausibility. In fact he may have taken the figures from Roman military records. In his autobiography he describes his own invidious role, as a friend (of sorts) of Titus, in using his influence to rescue his friends and relatives from the masses doomed to punishment:

> I made petition for my brother and fifty friends, and my request was granted. Again, by permission of Titus, I entered the Temple, where a great multitude of captive women and children had been imprisoned, and liberated all the friends and acquaintances whom I recognized, in number about a hundred and ninety . . . Once more, when I . . . saw many prisoners who had been crucified, and recognized three of my acquaintances among them, I was cut to the heart and came and told Titus with tears what I had seen. He gave orders immediately that they should be taken down and receive the most careful treatment. Two of them died in the physicians' hands; the third survived.[8]

Such ruthlessness provided good reason for Jews in the rest of Judaea to surrender all other strongholds without a fight, but a show of force was still needed. The Jewish garrison of the fortress of Herodium, near Bethlehem, surrendered to Lucilius Bassus, who had been sent out as the new governor of Judaea evidently with a brief to pacify the rest of the countryside. The fortress of Machaerus, east of the Dead Sea, "it was absolutely necessary to eradicate, lest its strength should induce many to revolt," and Bassus concentrated against it all his military force, including the Tenth Legion, beginning the massive earthworks necessary for the siege, but, in the event, a full-scale siege proved unnecessary: in return for the life of a captured youth, and permission for themselves to depart unharmed, they surrendered the fortress to the Romans.

The capture by Bassus' successor, Flavius Silva, of Herod's fortress palace on the rock of Masada, to the west of the Dead Sea, was to take longer. It will be recalled that the site had been occupied since 66 by sicarii, who took refuge there after failing to gain control in Jerusalem at the start of the revolt. Its natural defences, as described by Josephus, made it very hard to capture: it was "a rock of no slight circumference and high from end to end, abruptly terminated on every side by deep ravines, the precipices rising sheer from an invisible base and being inaccessible to the foot of any living creature, save in two places where the rock permits of no easy ascent." Herod had built for his own protection an impressive palace on the summit and stored there masses of corn, wine, oil, pulses and dates, all remarkably well preserved in 66, even after the passage of nearly a century, because of the dry climate. Huge cisterns efficiently preserved rainwater from sparse winter downpours. There was also a large supply of weapons and of iron, brass and lead, all hoarded by the king many decades before but left for the sicarii now to put to use against the Roman forces.

Josephus records how Flavius Silva encircled the fortress with a wall and encamped close by in order to prevent any escape by the besieged. For the Roman forces the isolation of the site created supply difficulties, for water as well as food, but there were plenty of Jewish slaves to provide the necessary manpower for transport. Silva set to work to throw up an embankment on the west side as a platform for siege engines, and a huge battering ram was used to break down the stone wall on that side of the defences. The sicarii threw up at speed a second wall inside the first, using huge wooden beams packed with earth, but that wall succumbed when set on fire—an uncertain weapon for the Romans to use, since at first a north wind directed the flames towards their own siege engines, until the wind veered "as if from divine providence" (so writes Josephus), and the wall was consumed. The fortress now lay wide open to attack, but before the final assault could take place the defenders were dead, killed by each other to avoid falling into Roman hands.[9]

This long description of the siege by Josephus has given Masada iconic status, although without Josephus' narrative the whole episode would be known only from the archaeological evidence, especially the siege ramp and the traces of Roman camps erected around the base of the rock on which the fortress was built; the elder Pliny, who mentions Masada as "a fortress on a rock, itself not far from the Dead Sea," was writing between 70 and 79 but makes no mention of any military campaign at the site.[10]

Josephus failed to note what is in some ways the most peculiar aspect of

the Roman operations at Masada, and the most obvious explanation of the
reticence about them in Roman sources: why the Romans bothered at all
to spend such time, resources and effort in the capture of a rock in the
wilderness of the Judaean desert. What was at stake was nothing more (or
less) than a desire for total victory: "Flavius Silva . . . seeing the whole
country now subdued in the war, but one fortress alone still rebelling,
brought together all the forces in the regions and marched against it." Presumably, in the eyes of the Romans it was economically desirable after 70
to ensure that no bandits based in Masada attacked the lucrative balsam
groves at En Gedi, since these were state property, but that only partly
explains the huge expenditure of time and resources on the capture of the
isolated rock fortress. Large numbers of troops camped out for months in
inhospitable terrain, gradually building the siege ramp which eventually,
inexorably, would bring the defenders to defeat. Roman determination
that this war was to be concluded without compromise could not have
been more clearly illustrated. The highly effective rhetoric of the philosophical platitudes on the justification for suicide which Josephus in his history puts into the mouth of Eleazar, the leader of the defenders, fails to
mention the most obvious rationale for seeking death at the hands of
friends rather than surrender to Rome. The real alternatives were not
either a quick death from a slit throat or enslavement, as Eleazar was made
to claim, enhancing the apparent heroism of those who made the former
choice. If Eleazar and his colleagues fell into Roman hands they could
expect to suffer death by crucifixion or some other method inflicted with
exceptional cruelty. Instead, on the first day of Passover in April 74 nine
hundred and sixty of them, including women and children, died at the
hands of each other: ten were chosen to kill the rest, then one of the ten
killed the nine others, and finally he committed suicide. The palace was set
on fire. According to Josephus, just two women and five children escaped
alive to tell the Romans what had happened.[11]

The thoroughness of the Roman victory in Masada and throughout the
country left a political vacuum in Judaea. Despite the death and devastation, there were still many Jews left living in the region of Jerusalem, but
the old ruling elite, led by the families of the High Priests, through which
Rome had once ruled, simply vanished from sight. Josephus, who had once
belonged to that elite, was relieved of his landholdings in Jerusalem:
"When Titus had quelled the disturbances in Judaea, conjecturing that the

field which I held in Jerusalem would be unprofitable to me because of the Roman garrison which was about to be settled there, he gave me another tract of ground on the plain [presumably near the Mediterranean coast]." Already in 70, before he set sail for Rome and his triumph, Titus was assuming that there would no longer be a ruling class of Jewish landowners in the city.[12]

Who else, then, could now mediate between the cowed Jews and their Roman masters? If Titus sought a single, powerful Jewish individual with a strong tradition of loyalty to Rome, the obvious choice was Agrippa II, who, at least according to Josephus, had tried so hard to keep Jerusalem at peace in the months before the war and had then, once it was too late to avoid conflict, committed both his troops and his expertise to speed a Roman victory. Agrippa's personal links with the new imperial regime were exceptionally close. Vespasian had stayed for a while in Agrippa's palace in Caesarea Philippi by the source of the river Jordan in 67 to rest his army after the campaign in Galilee, and (although Josephus does not say so) the king was presumably there again in the autumn of 70, when Titus visited him and "remained for a considerable time, exhibiting all kinds of spectacles. Here many of the prisoners perished, some being thrown to wild beasts, others compelled in opposing masses to engage one another in combat." The victors were recuperating in appropriate fashion now that the fighting was over. It would have been easy for Vespasian and Titus to claim to be following precedent if Agrippa, like his father, became king of Judaea. The possibility had indeed been mooted over a quarter of a century earlier by Claudius. The reason why it did not happen in 70 may lie as much in the wishes and desires of Agrippa as those of the Roman administration. To take over a kingdom in ruins was hardly enticing—indeed, people recalled that Agrippa's great-grandfather Herod had bribed the Roman general Sosius to call off his troops from looting Jerusalem in 37 BCE for precisely that reason. And Agrippa may well have had plans for a political career on a larger stage. The friendship of his sister Berenice with Titus was a source of gossip and scandal in Rome throughout the 70s, when, as Cassius Dio later recorded, "Berenice was at the very height of her power and consequently came to Rome along with her brother Agrippa. The latter was given the rank of praetor, while she dwelt in the palace, cohabiting with Titus. She expected to marry him and was already behaving in every respect as if she were his wife." It was not unreasonable of Agrippa to hope to win, through his connections with the imperial family, a position of influence and power in Rome such as his father had once, briefly, wielded in the courts of Gaius and Claudius.[13]

Since the Roman state did not give authority in Judaea after 70 either to the former ruling class or to Agrippa, it was not to be expected that any other Jewish leaders would be deemed appropriate for the task. Later Jewish tradition assumed that the role of rabbis such as Yohanan ben Zakkai as religious leaders inevitably led to their recognition by Rome as political spokesmen for the Jews, but the Romans were hardly likely now to give secular authority to a religious leader in Judaea when they did not follow such a practice anywhere else in their empire. The only special and different aspect of Roman attitudes to Judaism compared to other provincial religions was the destruction of the Jerusalem Temple, a reason for Rome to avoid giving any power to Jewish religious leaders rather than to encourage such a policy.[14]

In fact, it seems that Vespasian and Titus chose to rule Judaea not through Jewish intermediaries of any kind but by direct Roman control. Jerusalem after 70, in marked contrast to the general freedom from Roman interference enjoyed by the Jewish population before the war, became an occupied city. The Tenth Legion was "entrusted with its custody" and permanently garrisoned on or near the site, able to respond immediately to any potential trouble. Some land in the surrounding countryside, including fields belonging to Josephus, seems to have been assigned to the legion. In 72 or 73 a new and distinctively pagan town was founded in Samaria, near the sites of Shechem and Mount Gerizim, presumably to control the Samaritans after their abortive revolt in 67. The town, given the unimaginative name "New City" (*Flavia Neapolis*, hence Nablus), was to flourish over the coming centuries, and between 244 and 249 was granted the status of a Roman colony. Already in the immediate aftermath of 70 a new Roman colony was founded in Caesarea Maritima, which had long been the centre of Roman administration of the province. Now it was repopulated, in place of the former Jewish residents, with retired Roman soldiers. Thus Latin was used for private inscriptions in Caesarea in the late first century CE as well as for public proclamations in the city: Caesarea became a Latin-speaking island in an Aramaic- and Greek-speaking world. Eight hundred other veterans were assigned a place to live at a site thirty stades from Jerusalem, in a settlement probably to be identified (despite the difference in the alleged distance from Jerusalem) with the Emmaus mentioned in the Gospel of Luke. These former soldiers were available for military operations when called upon in a crisis. The pattern of foundation of veteran colonies in the provinces in the Julio-Claudian period suggests that they were expected to play an important role in enhancing the security of the region. Judaea was now under military rule, and Jerusalem lay at the centre of the militarized zone.[15]

Jews in the Mediterranean diaspora had tried to avoid engagement with the dangerous politics of Jerusalem while the war continued, but they found this option closed to them after 70. The universal imposition of the special tax on Jews throughout the empire affected the eirenic communities in Asia Minor and Greece as much as the militants in the homeland. The Jews of the city of Rome must have felt their dual loyalties under intolerable strain as the sacred relics of the Temple they revered were carried in mocking triumph through the streets of their adopted city, their pride at being Roman in direct conflict with the propaganda of the new imperial regime which, through the tax, suggested their responsibility for the costly and dangerous war in distant Jerusalem.[16]

For some diaspora Jews living closer to Judaea the dilemma was made even more acute in the immediate aftermath of the war by the need to respond to refugees from it who sought their help against Rome. Josephus reports that the Jews of Alexandria did their best to keep their distance when

certain of the faction of the sicarii who had succeeded in fleeing to that country . . . sought to induce many of their hosts to assert their independence, to look upon the Romans as no better than themselves and to esteem God alone as their lord . . . The leaders of the council of elders . . . convened a general assembly of the Jews and exposed the madness of the sicarii, proving them to have been responsible for all their troubles . . . They advised the assembly to beware of the ruin with which they were menaced by these men and, by delivering them up, to make their peace with the Romans. Realizing the gravity of the danger, the people complied with this advice, and rushed furiously upon the sicarii to seize them. Six hundred of them were caught on the spot; and all who escaped into Egypt and the Egyptian Thebes were before long arrested and brought back.

Such demonstration of their loyalty to Rome was not, however, altogether successful. The emperor, "suspicious of the interminable tendency of the Jews to revolution," took precautionary steps to avoid an uprising of Jews in Egypt like that in Jerusalem and closed down the Jewish temple at Leontopolis in the delta. In Cyrene (modern Libya), the refugee sicarii were led by a weaver called Jonathan, who seems to have captured the imagination of some of the poorer local Jews by taking them out into the desert and promising "signs and apparitions," much as various pseudo-prophets had done in Judaea earlier in the century. The unarmed crowd was easily enough suppressed by the troops sent by the Roman governor of the province, Catullus, but Jonathan's impact was much increased by his allegation to Catullus that he had been instructed in his actions by "the wealthiest of the Jews," giving the governor an opportunity to kill all three thousand well-to-do Jews and confiscate their property to the imperial exchequer. Josephus alleges that the charges were entirely fraudulent, and that Catullus was motivated by a desire that "he too might seem to have won a Jewish war." But Josephus' reliability in this particular part of his narrative is suspect, since, among the others of "the most respectable of the Jews in Alexandria and Rome" charged with sedition by Jonathan and his accomplices, was Josephus himself. In his autobiography Josephus reports that the accusation, which specified that he had provided Jonathan with weapons and money, came before the emperor Vespasian himself in Rome, but that the emperor dismissed the allegation as fabricated. In the *Jewish War* the intercession of Titus on behalf of the accused was said to have been decisive. The whole episode had clearly been traumatic. If even a Jew like Josephus, whose interests were so closely bound up with those of the new emperor, could be plausibly accused of plotting sedition, no Jew was safe from suspicion. It is significant that the governor Catullus, who according to Josephus had corruptly put to death thousands of respectable Jews of Cyrene, suffered nothing worse than a reprimand.[17]

All Jews in the Roman empire might now feel under threat. In Antioch the resident Jews were accused in 70 by their gentile neighbours of incendiarism when a fire burned down part of the centre of the city. They were rescued from a pogrom only by the firm action of the Roman authorities on the spot. It emerged on investigation that the fire had been started by debtors seeking to destroy the evidence of what they owed by setting fire to the marketplace and public records. In Antioch, as in Rome, the constant fear that a backlash against Jews would be directed at them must have been intensified by the presence in the city of large numbers of captives from Judaea sold in the slave market. When Titus visited the city after the fall of Jerusalem he was met by massed crowds demanding that the local Jews be expelled, to which he replied (all too accurately), that this was impossible because "their own country to which, as Jews, they ought to be expelled, has been destroyed, and no other place would receive them." A further request that at least the privileges of the Jews of Antioch, inscribed on bronze tablets, should be revoked, was similarly turned down. Josephus tells the story of these events in order to demonstrate the good will of Titus, but the story also reveals the vulnerability of these Jews to local hostility, expressed both by mass meetings and by the official council of the city.[18]

About the vulnerability of Jews in the city of Rome Josephus is less explicit. Perhaps it seemed unwise to remind his Roman readers of his own problems of dual loyalty. But the tensions which had emerged so chillingly in Antioch in 70 will have been at least as bad in the capital city. Just a hint of the anger can be glimpsed in Josephus' brief reference to his own tribulations once he had been installed in a lodging in the house in Rome which Vespasian had occupied before he became emperor. "My privileged position [as beneficiary of Vespasian's kindness] exacted envy and brought danger . . . Numerous accusations against me were fabricated by persons who envied me my good fortune." In the time of Domitian, the emperor showed his favour to Josephus by punishing the Jews who accused him— Josephus does not say of what, but he does add that among these enemies was his son's tutor, about whom he reveals only that he was a slave and a eunuch. Clearly, one should not imagine Josephus or any other Jew managing to live in peaceful comfort in the prickly atmosphere of Flavian Rome. For a government seeking to justify the seizure and retention of power by claiming to have defeated a dangerous enemy, it might seem a positive advantage that representatives of the defeated enemy were identifiable not just on the distant frontiers of the empire but spread throughout the civilized world, including the capital city itself, able through their subjection to testify to the achievements of the new emperor. In the late fourth century CE St. Augustine was to argue on similar lines that Jews should be allowed to remain in their mistaken faith within Christendom, but in a state of misery, to testify to the truth of the Church.[19]

## "IMPIOUS JEWS"

VESPASIAN AND TITUS had treated Jews as enemies of the state and Judaism as a religion no longer worthy of a Temple after 70, for propaganda reasons specific to their rule, but one might have thought that everything should have changed for the Jews once those emperors were dead. The hostility towards Egypt in the propaganda of Augustus after the battle of Actium did not continue under his successors, and even the most bitter of enemies can in time come to an accommodation, particularly if they can remember a period when they were once at peace. But not in this case. Vespasian died in 79 and Titus, still quite young, in 81, but there was no diminution in public hostility towards the Jews. Most blatant was the continuing refusal of the new emperor, Domitian, to contemplate the rebuilding of the Jerusalem Temple. Later theological apologeticism, even enthusiasm, for worship without sacrifices, and simply the passing of time, have deadened the responses of modern historians to this ban. In antiquity, it was outrageous. All over the empire there were myriads of shrines and altars to myriads of gods. There was nothing peculiar in Roman eyes about the sacrificial service in the Jerusalem Temple except the lack of a cult image. As the pagan emperor Julian was to expostulate in the mid-fourth century CE in his tirade *Against the Galileans* (as he called Christians), "the Jews agree with the gentiles except that they believe in only one God . . . since all the rest we have more or less in common with them—temples, sanctuaries, altars, purifications and certain precepts. For as to these we differ from one another either not at all or in trivial matters." Everyone else in the empire was free to continue to worship in the ways hallowed by their ancestors. It would be understandable if the Romans took greater care than they had before 66 to prevent the crowds at the great pilgrim festivals in Jerusalem getting out of hand, but that precaution would hardly require the Temple site to be left altogether in ruins. Treatment so harsh and unusual must have another explanation.[20]

It seems most likely that after 81, just as much as in 70, the explanation lay in the need of the emperor to manipulate his public image in order to ensure support for his regime; indeed, this may have been the prime cause of the maltreatment of the Jews down to the defeat of Bar Kokhba in 135. It was as much in the interest of Domitian to portray the Jews and Judaism as marginal as it had suited Vespasian and Titus, and, apart from a brief interlude in 96 on the accession of Nerva, glorification of the destruction of the Jerusalem Temple remained integral to the public persona of each emperor in the following decades. Such glorification may have led, more or less directly, to the Jewish frustration which erupted in violent uprisings in 115 and 132. If this was the case, the result for Jews and Judaism was to be catastrophic, but the cause will have had less to do with the Jews themselves than with politics at the centre of imperial power in Rome.

When Jerusalem was razed in August 70, Domitian was less than nineteen years old, so his public career had (unsurprisingly) been negligible when, a year earlier, his father in distant Judaea was acclaimed as emperor by his troops. Unlike his much older brother Titus, who won military glory as commander of one of the three legions in the Judaean campaign, Domitian had remained in Rome throughout the changes of regime following the death of Nero. The bid for power by his father engendered both danger and opportunity. When troops loyal to Vitellius captured the prefect of the city, Vespasian's brother, Flavius Sabinus, on the Capitol, Domitian escaped dressed as a devotee of Isis and stayed in hiding until the Vitellian party was defeated, although Flavius Sabinus was hacked to death by the mob. When Domitian later became emperor, he commemorated his avoidance of the same fate by dedicating a great temple to Jupiter the Guardian, with his own effigy in the lap of the god. When the Flavian army arrived in Rome in the last days of 69, fresh from victory in the battle of Cremona, Domitian was immediately saluted as an important scion of the new imperial family and on 9 January 70 he presided over a meeting of the Senate. Real power in Rome, until the arrival of Vespasian from Alexandria, was vested with Vespasian's close ally Mucianus, who was supported by the large army he had brought from Syria, but the teenaged Domitian was allowed, for a few months, to enjoy the limelight, until Vespasian and Titus returned to the capital and overshadowed him. The later traditions composed after Domitian's death were universally hostile to his memory because the dynasty which replaced him needed to portray him as a tyrant, and, according to that tradition, Domitian was treated with disdain by his father and brother. But Vespasian could hardly have made clearer the importance of his younger son in his dynastic plans than by including him in the triumph in 71 which celebrated the victory over Judaea. Vespasian had good political reasons for such generosity. His bid for power had received backing from other senators like Mucianus in good part because, in Titus, he had a son suitable to succeed him as emperor, so that the state might avoid the danger of a succession crisis such as had proven the downfall of Galba. But Titus himself had produced no son, so only by signalling the worthiness of Domitian to rule could Vespasian ensure that the regime would be seen as stable for the years ahead.

The honours for the young prince had to be carefully calibrated: his imperial role would not be taken up, Vespasian might reasonably hope, for many years, since Titus was still in the prime of life, so Domitian had to be encouraged, but not too much. Where Titus was elevated in July 71 to share tribunician power with his father and was appointed as censor, Domitian was honoured in a markedly more restrained fashion, although he too held repeated consulships and became, along with Titus, *princeps iuventutis*, "leader of the young men." It would not be helpful if he came to be seen as rival to Titus rather than prospective successor. Above all, he was to be given no opportunity to demonstrate his own military capacity. In contrast to the stories, faithfully relayed by Josephus, of the impressive personal bravery of Titus in the war against the Jews, Domitian's supporters could point to no such achievement. Suetonius records that the restriction chafed. Domitian in 70 "began an unnecessary expedition against Gaul and the Germanies . . . merely so that he might make himself equal to his brother in power and rank," but his father's friends dissuaded him, and "when Vologaesus, king of the Parthians, had asked for auxiliaries against the Alani and for one of Vespasian's sons as their leader, Domitian used every effort to have himself sent rather than Titus, and because the affair came to nothing, he tried by gifts and promises to induce other eastern kings to make the same request," but without success. Throughout his reign Vespasian denied military glory to his younger son, and the manipulation of the young prince's image seems to have been successful. When Vespasian died in 79 the succession of Titus as sole ruler was seamless, and Titus could show his confidence in his brother in 80 by appointing him ordinary consul for the year. When Titus died prematurely on 13 September 81 Domitian in turn moved smoothly into power as the new emperor.[21]

In the course of the next eleven years, Domitian went on campaign four times—to Germany in 83, to the Danube in 85 and in 92, and to the Rhine and Danube in 89. He contrived twenty-three imperial salutations and at least two triumphs, taking the title "Germanicus" in 83 for his victory over the Chatti, and setting up a plethora of triumphal arches. His need for military prestige to justify his rule could not have been more starkly demonstrated, but in 81 these campaigns still lay in the future. When he came to power Domitian had no victories to his personal credit apart from his spurious participation, riding on a white horse, in the triumph over Judaea. Thus it is less surprising than it might seem that the Jewish war continued to loom large, more than ten years after its end, during the early years of Domitian's reign. The Arch of Titus, unique among extant Roman triumphal arches in representing a triumphal procession, was finally dedicated not by Titus but by Domitian, and Domitian was still in 85 issuing coins with the caption JUDAEA CAPTA. According to his biographer Suetonius, writing in the 120s, in Domitian's time the treasury for Judaean affairs, which collected the special Jewish tax, operated "very fiercely," illustrated by a personal reminiscence of an evidently horrific incident which may strike the modern reader as similar to the behaviour of more recent totalitarian states enforcing a policy of racial discrimination: "I recall being present in my youth when the person of a man ninety years old was examined before the procurator and a very crowded court, to see whether he was circumcised." The story suggests that Jews in Rome who reacted to the hostility pervading their society by denying their Jewishness were not allowed to escape detection and branding as members of this alien group.[22]

Towards the end of Domitian's reign the emperor became increasingly tyrannical and, partly as a result, justifiably paranoid, executing at least twelve former consuls on charges of dissent or alleged conspiracy. Most prominent of these, Flavius Clemens, the consul of 95, grandson of Domitian's uncle Flavius Sabinus and husband of Domitian's niece Domitilla, was convicted of atheism because like "many others," he was "drifting into Jewish ways," according to Cassius Dio in the early third century. Some historians have taken the fate of Flavius Clemens as evidence that some upper-class Romans found attachment to Judaism attractive during these years, but the idea is implausible when the destruction of the Temple of the Jewish God had so dramatically put in question his power. In a polytheistic system which judged divine approval by material success, abject political defeat was evidence of religious failure. The Temple, with its awe-inspiring rituals which had encouraged Marcus Vipsanius Agrippa to make extravagant obeisance to the Jewish God in the time of Augustus, was now in ruins. It was hardly likely that Flavius Clemens would be attracted to the peculiar customs of a people so reviled or the cultivation of a God so transparently powerless. A better explanation of the charge reported by Cassius Dio may be that an accusation of "drifting into Jewish ways" had become a general term of opprobrium for enemies of the imperial regime or, perhaps, that defiant adoption of a "Jewish" lifestyle had become for members of the Roman elite a symbolic way to demonstrate republican independence of spirit, like the ostentatious Stoic virtues of other senatorial "martyrs" celebrated by Tacitus and the younger Pliny. If the latter was the case, the failure of Tacitus and Pliny to express sympathy with, or even mention, such "Judaizers" among the elite will have been the result of self-censorship, for, by the time they were writing under the rule of Trajan, Jews, Judaism and Judaizers were all once more in disfavour.[23]

Before hostility to Jews and Judaism returned in Trajan's time, there was a brief hiatus of tolerance after the murder of Domitian on 18 September 96 in a coup by a small group of those closest to him, including the praetorian prefects and, it was alleged, his own wife. The plan was put into operation by humble minions of the palace staff. Domitian had been a conscientious emperor, adopting a stance of moral uprightness and ensuring competent administration of the provinces, but he was fatally arrogant and unwilling to hide his absolute power as more tactful emperors had done since the time of Augustus. As a result he was so hated by the Roman elite that, when he died, his memory was damned by the Senate, so that his statues and votive shields were torn down and a decree was passed that his inscriptions should everywhere be erased: "all memory of him should be obliterated." Accordingly, his successor, the elderly aristocrat Marcus Cocceius Nerva, immediately set out to rule in a way that contrasted to the previous reign of terror. His coins advertised "salvation," "equity," "public freedom." Those on trial for treason were released. No one was tactless enough to mention it, but Nerva had done quite well through Domitian's favour, having enjoyed the special privilege of holding the ordinary consulship with him in 90—all the more reason strenuously to distance himself now from his predecessor. Nerva's legitimacy depended on denigration of Domitian's rule.[24]

Among the policies of the state Nerva chose to change right from the start of his reign was the treatment of the Jews. He himself had played no part in the campaign of 66–70, and had nothing political to gain from continued vilification of Jews and Judaism. The slogan inscribed on a series of bronze coins, issued in Rome by the new regime in mid-autumn and in December 96, with a third issue in the first half of 97, proclaimed a fresh start. The coins were adorned with an image of a palm tree, a type commonly found on Roman currency in or referring to Judaea. The inscription proclaimed FISCI IUDAICI CALUMNIA SUBLATA, a Latin phrase too compressed for its precise meaning now to be transparent, although, like advertising slogans nowadays, its import was doubtless clear enough at the time. The most probable translation is: "The malicious accusation [brought by] the treasury for Jewish affairs has been removed." Such a slogan makes best sense if the reform advertised by Nerva was an end to the collection of a tax, the two-*denarii* tax imposed since 70 on every Jew as punishment for the rebellion in Judaea more than twenty-five years before, which constituted by its very existence a malicious slur on the loyalty to Rome of the whole Jewish people. The repeated issues of the slogan on low-denomination coins calculated to get into the hands of many of his subjects suggest an important change of policy which Nerva expected his subjects to greet with enthusiasm.[25]

Distribution of Nerva's coins advertising his reform seems to have been limited to the city of Rome, where manipulation of the emperor's image for the security of his regime was most urgent, but it will not have taken long for Jews elsewhere in the empire to become aware of this effect of the regime change and their new freedom from the demeaning tax. It is easy enough to imagine their reaction to this dramatic improvement in their fortunes. After a quarter of a century of being pilloried as enemies of the state, Jews had suffered enough. It was time for the Temple to be restored. Priests like Josephus, who had served in the Temple when young, were ready and willing to play their parts again. It is probable that Josephus' treatise *Against Apion*, which so eloquently describes the essence of Judaism in unitary terms—one God, one Law, one Temple, one High Priest—was completed during this interlude of restored tolerance towards Jews and Judaism. Hence the confident bravado of his final encomium of his people:

I would therefore boldly maintain that we have introduced to the rest of the world a very large number of very beautiful ideas. What greater beauty than inviolable piety? What higher justice than obedience to the laws? What more beneficial than to be in harmony with one another, to be a prey neither to disunion in adversity, nor to arrogance and faction in prosperity; in war to despise death, in peace to devote oneself to crafts or agriculture; and to be convinced that everything in the whole universe is under the eye and direction of God?

The same spirit of optimism is reflected in the description of Nerva in the coded list of emperors which prefaces the fifth book of the *Sibylline Oracles*, composed by a Jew early in Hadrian's reign: of all the emperors, Nerva alone is described in glowing terms—in contrast to "cursed" Domitian, Nerva was "a mortal of reverend bearing." These Jewish hopes for the rebuilding of the Temple are reflected with markedly less enthusiasm in the polemic of the strongly anti-Jewish Christian author of the *Epistle of Barnabas*, whose composition has been dated by some to the time of Nerva for precisely this reason: " 'See, those who have destroyed this temple will themselves build it.' This is happening. For because they waged war, it was destroyed by their enemies. And now [they and] the servants of their enemies will [themselves] rebuild it."[26]

The Jews could not know how brief the interlude of hope was to be. The series of coins proclaiming the abolition of the tax came to an end in the middle of 97. In theory, of course, this might have been the result of chance. Nerva may have felt that he had already sufficiently advertised his enlightened new policy—the minting pattern was the same as that which proclaimed ANNONA AUGUST.: "the grain supply [ensured by Nerva] Augustus." Later coin issues might have been minted but left no trace, although that is unlikely. But the most plausible explanation is a reversal of imperial policy in November 97 caused by Nerva's adoption of Marcus Ulpius Traianus, destined to become, in January 98, the emperor Trajan.[27]

Before his adoption, Trajan seems to have had little contact with the elderly emperor, and selection of an heir was a necessity imposed on the childless Nerva by his political weakness. Nerva had been chosen to rule by the Senate because of his high birth, and the loyalty of the soldiers could not be guaranteed: on Domitian's death they "were greatly grieved and at once attempted to refer to him as divine, while they were prepared also to avenge him, if they had not lacked leaders." The chaos of civil war in 69 was still frighteningly fresh in the memories of the older generation, including Nerva himself, whose coins asserted optimistically CONCORDIA EXERCITUUM, "the agreement of the armies," with images of clasped hands. A year after Nerva's accession, in the autumn of 97, the praetorian guard and its commander mutinied, demanding the execution of Domitian's murderers. Nerva resisted the demand, but in vain. He looked frighteningly vulnerable, like Galba in the days before Otho's coup in January 69. His solution was to select as a successor and heir a general who would be sufficiently plausible to appeal to the armies but not so popular that he would try to oust Nerva himself. Marcus Ulpius Traianus was general in command of the three legions of Upper Germany. Aged forty-four, he had control of large numbers of troops close to Rome and he had demonstrated his capacity for loyalty by marching the legion he commanded in Spain to help Domitian suppress the revolt of Saturninus in 89. He was not related by blood to any former emperor; there was thus a fair chance that he would be content to wait for Nerva to die naturally and that he would proceed peacefully to the glorious future which now beckoned. As the younger Pliny noted in his panegyric of Trajan three years later, Nerva had "sought counsel not only of men but also of the gods," thus avoiding the disaster which had accompanied Galba's adoption of Piso in 69, which "not only failed to check an outbreak of rebellion but actually began it." The availability of so perfect a candidate was probably not the result of chance. Trajan's career before 97 had not included the military experience standard for a legionary command of such importance. A senatorial conspiracy to block the ambitions of Domitian's most prestigious general, Cornelius Nigrinus, governor of Syria, has been plausibly surmised. The senators in question were handsomely rewarded with consulships in the early years of Trajan's reign.[28]

But the choice of an heir so beneficial both to Nerva's rule and to the avoidance of civil strife in Rome entailed a return to the glorification of the Judaean campaign which had characterized the Flavian dynasty. Trajan's natural father, the elder Marcus Ulpius Traianus, came from the obscure municipality of Italica (modern Santiponce, near Seville) in Spain. The first of his family to enter the Roman Senate, he owed his eventual prominence entirely to his services to Rome in the war against the Jews, in which he commanded the Tenth Legion, the Fretensis, from 67 to 69. Traianus' link to the Flavian campaign could hardly have been closer. Of the two other legions deployed against the rebels in Jerusalem, one had been commanded by Titus. The close relationship between the two generals, and Traianus' tact in dealing with Vespasian, emerged in the course of the siege of a town in Galilee called Iapha in mid-67. Traianus had already more or less captured the place, with huge losses ("twelve thousand") on the Jewish side, but

> judging that the city was bereft of combatants or that any who still remained within would be paralysed by fear, he decided to reserve for his general the capture of the place. He accordingly dispatched messengers to Vespasian, requesting him to send his son Titus to complete the victory. The general, conjecturing that some work still remained to be done, sent with his son reinforcements consisting of five hundred cavalry and a thousand infantry. Titus rapidly marched to the city, drew up his troops for battle, posting Traianus on the left wing, and, himself taking command of the right, led them to the assault . . . For six hours the contest was maintained; the more efficient combatants were at length exterminated, and the rest of the population was then massacred in the open or in their houses, young and old alike. For no males were spared, except infants; these, along with the women, the Romans sold as slaves. The slain, whether in the city or in the previous action, amounted in all to fifteen thousand; the captives numbered two thousand one hundred and thirty.

If Josephus paid special attention to the narrative of this engagement, it may be because at the time he was writing, in the mid-70s, Traianus was at the height of his impressive career under Flavian patronage. He could not, of course, have guessed the glorious future which awaited Traianus' son.[29]

Traianus would have been one of the generals who urged Vespasian to march against Jerusalem in 68, since he was still in command of the Tenth Legion in 69, when he was involved in constructing a road from Caesarea to Scythopolis: he put up a milestone in the name of Vespasian some time in the second half of this year. Why he was no longer in post in Judaea in 70 and had been replaced by a new general is unknown. His fellow general, the commander of the Fifth Legion, Sextus Vettulenus Cerealis, served from 67 until the completion of the siege and even remained in Jerusalem after Titus' departure in 70 as commander of the garrison troops (as we have seen, Traianus' old unit, the Tenth Legion). Perhaps Traianus was ill or otherwise incapacitated. In any case, his loyalty to the new Flavian regime was not in doubt, for he was granted a consulship, probably in 70, and patrician rank, and from 73 to 77 or 78 he was an energetic governor of Syria, receiving triumphal ornaments for his success against the Parthians. It seems very likely from these marks of high favour that Traianus' support was vital in Vespasian's successful bid for imperial power in mid-69. The "spontaneous" proclamation of Vespasian as emperor in July by his troops in Judaea had been the result of gatherings of his officers as well as the junior ranks. Of the three legionary commanders, Titus was obviously an interested party, but the willingness of Cerealis and Traianus to risk their lives for Vespasian could not at all be taken for granted, and deserved reward when it proved successful. It is curious that Tacitus, composing the narrative of the civil war in his *Histories* during the first decade of Trajan's reign, does not mention Traianus by name in his account of the vital role played by Vespasian's officers and friends in strengthening Vespasian's resolve, but Traianus' contribution may have been largely passive, allowing himself to be carried along by the ambitions of his troops and his commander-in-chief, and, for Tacitus, the complex relationship between Vespasian and his main supporter and erstwhile rival, Mucianus, governor of Syria, allowed the portrayal of more dramatic tensions.[30]

It is not certain whether Traianus was still alive when Trajan was adopted by Nerva in November 97. If he was, he would have been very old. More certain is Trajan's emphasis on his natural father's achievements as justification of his own elevation to the principate. Unlike previously adopted emperors, Trajan did not upon adoption transfer to Nerva's *gens*, preferring to retain his Ulpian lineage—hence the name of the Basilica Ulpia in Trajan's forum in Rome. The frequent references to the elder Traianus in the carefully crafted panegyric of the emperor delivered by the younger Pliny in 100 must reflect the image that Trajan wished to project: "Posterity may find it hard to believe that one whose father was a patrician and of consular rank and won a triumph, who was himself in command of a mighty army of brave soldiers devoted to their general" would wait meekly for his obedience to Nerva's orders to enable him to become emperor rather than seize power for himself. Trajan had been too modest to decline a third consulship as urged by the Senate: "Can a third consulship really be promotion for the son of a consular father granted a triumph? Is it not rather his due, his proper reward, if only as a member

of a distinguished family?" Near the end of the speech, Pliny apostro-
phizes first the deceased "divine Nerva"—"what happiness you must feel
today, on beholding him whom you judged the best candidate for your
choice proving that he is best"—and then "father Traianus": "for you too,
though not raised to the stars, must surely occupy the nearest place [and]
must know such delight when you see [from heaven?] your son who was
tribune and soldier under you now risen to be supreme commander and
emperor, when you enter into friendly rivalry with his adopter so as to
determine where the greater glory must be assigned—to his begetter or to
the one who made him his choice." In evoking military glory Trajan could
more easily boast about his real than his adoptive father, since Nerva had
achieved little of his own to impress. Nor could Trajan claim victories of
his own, since he had as yet done little—the frantic campaigning which
marked his rule may illustrate his need to establish, like the emperor
Claudius before him, a military reputation to justify his hold on power.
The glorification of Traianus, already conspicuous in these early years of
Trajan's rule, was to increase rather than diminish with the passage of time,
as Trajan turned his close relatives, including his wife, sister, niece and even
great-nieces into a new royal family celebrated on coins and sculptures. In
112 Trajan sealed the significance of his natural father to the new regime by
his deification.[31]

Thus it was in the interest of Trajan that the Flavian view of the Jewish
war as a great triumph for Rome, and of the Jews as the natural enemies of
the Roman state, should be quietly resumed: this was one alleged aberra-
tion of Domitian which it had been unwise of Nerva to repudiate. Certainly, if the collection of the Jewish tax at Edfu had indeed stopped in the
reign of Nerva, it had recommenced within months of Trajan taking
power. Nerva succumbed to fever on 27 January 98. On 28 June of the
same year a Jew named Dosarion son of Iesous was given a receipt for nine
drachmai two obols "in respect of the Jewish tax for the 1st year of our lord
Trajan."[32]

The tax receipts from Edfu can reveal no more than the bald fact that
Jews continued to pay this poll tax in the years following. What they
thought about Rome after their hopes had been raised by Nerva, only to be
so crushed so soon, can only be imagined. They could hardly appreciate
the nuances of the new emperor's public image. For them, the dashing of
expectations after so brief a glimpse of future felicity, or at least normality,

without Jews anywhere having acted against Rome, must have seemed arbitrary, monstrous and tyrannical. What could they do? So far as is known, all that the Jews did at first was to wait and hope, and grow more despairing with the passing years. None of the extant Jewish writings preserved by either Christians or rabbinic Jews can be shown to have been written while Trajan was emperor, so Jewish sentiment can only be surmised from the violence of the uprising when it came, in 115 or 116. There is no particular reason to suppose that Jews stopped writing in the first decade of the second century CE, or seeking for a theological explanation of their uniquely demeaning state of subjection; that what they wrote does not now survive is the result only of the hazards of preservation. The earliest extant rabbinic compilations were put together a whole century later, providing only scanty testimony to the disputes among rabbinic sages in this period. And Christians, who had up to *c.* 100 CE used and copied religious writings in Greek by non-Christian Jews, from around this date ceased to treat with reverence texts composed by non-Christians, now that the Church had expanded sufficiently to produce its own literature.

There is no particular reason to suppose that Trajan took any further action against the Jews after the tax had been reinstated, and the principle thus implicitly confirmed that the Jerusalem Temple would not be rebuilt—it will be recalled that the tax had been instituted as a means to transfer to Jupiter in Rome funds which would once have been paid for the upkeep of the Temple of the Jewish God. Trajan was fully engaged in establishing a great military reputation for himself, both in order to ensure the support of his "excellent and most loyal fellow soldiers" and to celebrate his achievements in public monuments in Rome, most blatantly the honorific column, dedicated in 113 as part of his new forum, on the frieze of which the emperor's victorious campaigns were depicted in impressive, if stylized, detail. The invasion of Dacia beyond the Danube ended eventually, after two wars, in the creation of a new Roman province in 106. On 22 March of the same year the old kingdom of the Nabataeans was turned into a new province of Arabia, without apparent opposition, although the governor of Syria was given triumphal ornaments for the achievement. The new military road built from the Red Sea to Damascus may well have been connected to plans for further expansion to the east. In 114 Trajan picked a quarrel with the Parthians over control of Armenia and in 115 he attacked Parthia itself through Mesopotamia. Coins proclaimed that "Armenia and

Mesopotamia have been brought into the power of the Roman people." Cassius Dio, commenting caustically on these campaigns a century later, asserts that Trajan's conquests to the east were prompted by a desire for glory. He was almost certainly right.[33]

Throughout these events the Jews, already a conquered people, seem to have been ignored. When their resentment and fury finally broke out with ferocious violence in different parts of the eastern Mediterranean, the uprising caught the Romans by surprise. Cassius Dio describes it thus:

> The Jews in the region of Cyrene had put a certain Andreas at their head, and were destroying both the Romans and the Greeks. They would eat the flesh of their victims, make belts for themselves of their entrails, anoint themselves with their blood and wear their skins for clothing; many they sawed in two, from the head downwards; others they gave to wild beasts, and still others they forced to fight as gladiators. In all two hundred and twenty thousand persons perished. In Egypt, too, they perpetrated many similar outrages, and in Cyprus under the leadership of a certain Artemion. There, also, two hundred and forty thousand perished.

A century after Dio, Eusebius of Caesarea provided a Christian interpretation of the same disastrous conflicts, linking the uprisings in the Mediterranean diaspora also to the despair of the Jews of Mesopotamia, who might with some justice view with horror the extension of Roman power to include the lands where they had lived under tolerant Parthian rule for centuries:

> While the teaching of our Saviour and the Church were flourishing daily and moving on to further progress the tragedy of the Jews was reaching the climax of successive woes. In the course of the eighteenth year of the reign of the emperor a movement of Jews again broke out and destroyed a great multitude of them. For both in Alexandria and in the rest of Egypt and especially in Cyrene, as though they had been seized by some terrible spirit of rebellion, they rushed into sedition against their Greek fellow inhabitants, and increasing the scope of the rebellion in the following year started not a small war while Lupus was governor of all Egypt. In the first engagement they happened to over-

come the Greeks, who fled to Alexandria and captured and killed the Jews in the city, but though thus losing the help of these Jews, the Jews of Cyrene continued to plunder the country of Egypt and to ravage the districts in it under their leader Lucuas. The emperor sent against them Marcius Turbo with both land and sea forces, and even cavalry. He waged war vigorously against them in many battles for a considerable time and killed many thousands of Jews, not only those of Cyrene but also those of Egypt who had rallied to Lucuas, their king. The emperor suspected that the Jews in Mesopotamia would also attack the inhabitants and ordered Lusius Quietus to clean them out of the province. He organized a force and slaughtered a great multitude of the Jews there, for which success he was appointed by the emperor governor of Judaea.[34]

By no means everything in these brief but highly coloured narratives is to be trusted. Atrocity stories of cannibalism are a regular feature of the depiction of savage enemies. The appalling casualty figures may well be exaggerated. But comments by contemporaries confirm the extreme violence. In a papyrus letter found in Egypt, an unknown correspondent reports dramatically (in Greek) that "the one hope and expectation that was left was the push of the massed villagers from our district against the impious Jews; but now the opposite has happened . . . our forces fought and were beaten and many of them were killed."[35] On 28 November in (probably) 117, an official named Apollonius applied to the prefect of Egypt for leave of sixty days, complaining that "because of the attack of the impious Jews, practically everything I possess in the villages of the Hermopolite nome and in the metropolis needs my attention."[36] A number of Egyptian papyri deal with the confiscation and reallocation of Jewish property after the revolt had ended, and with issues which arose in dealing with property destroyed in the uprising. The contemporary historian Appian, himself from Alexandria, records a lucky escape which confirmed the Arabian power of divination:

When I was fleeing from the Jews during the war which was being waged in Egypt and I was passing through Arabia Petraea in the direction of the river, where a boat had been waiting in order to carry me over to Pelusium, an Arab served me as guide at night. When I believed us to be near the boat a crow croaked, just about day-break, and the troubled man said: "We have gone astray." And when the crow croaked again, he said: "We have gone much astray." Then I became disturbed and looked for some wayfarer. I saw none, since it was early morning and the country was in a state of war. When the Arab heard the crow a third time, he said rejoicing: "We have gone astray to our advantage and we have gained the road." I only laughed, thinking we would gain the wrong path again, and despaired of myself as we were surrounded everywhere by enemies, and it was not possible for me to turn back because of those behind from whom I was fleeing. However, being at a loss, I followed and gave myself up to the augury. Being in such a state, unexpectedly I perceived another river very near to Pelusium and a trireme sailing to Pelusium. I embarked and was saved, while the boat which awaited me at the other river was captured by the Jews. So much I had good luck and marvelled at the augury.[37]

Such personal experience lends credence to Appian's chilling note, in passing, that Pompey's tomb near Alexandria had been devastated by the Jews "while the Roman emperor Trajan was destroying utterly the Jewish race in Egypt." Another contemporary, the historian Arrian, who wrote an account of Parthian history which concentrated on the campaigns of Trajan in the East, seems to have been referring to the Jews when he recorded that "Trajan was determined above all, if it were possible, to destroy the nation utterly, but if not, at least to crush it and stop its presumptuous wickedness." Inscriptions from Cyrenaica (modern Libya), using the Latin term *tumultus* ("disturbance") to refer to the uprising, record that Hadrian "ordered the Caesareum [the temple of the imperial cult] which had been destroyed in the Jewish disturbance to be rebuilt for the city of the Cyreneans," and the restoration of a basilica, the temple of Zeus, baths and public roads which had been damaged enough to need major repairs. The disturbances were evidently directed not just against the Roman state but also against neighbouring gentiles—including, in Egypt, the native Egyptians as well as the Greeks whose hostility in Alexandria had been so long-standing. A papyrus records the celebration in 199 of an annual festival established by the Greek inhabitants of the Egyptian town of Oxyrhynchus to commemorate the suppression of the revolt some eighty-two years earlier. Cassius Dio explicitly refers to the consequences of the rebellion in his own day, a hundred years after it had ended: because of the huge death toll caused by the Jews in Cyprus, "no Jew may set foot on this island, but if one of them is driven upon its shores by a storm he is put to death."[38]

The exceptional violence of the uprising and the devastating effects of its suppression are not in doubt, but neither Cassius Dio nor Eusebius in their brief narratives gives an explanation of its outbreak, although they agree, despite discrepancies in the detailed chronology and sequence of events, in assigning the rebellion to the last years of Trajan, during his Parthian campaign. It is left to modern historians to explain an uprising unprecedented not just in its savagery but in its geographic spread. Large numbers of Jews lived in Parthian territory, so the coincidence of the outbreak with Trajan's Parthian campaign is unlikely to be accidental, whether the rebellious Jews sought to free those in Mesopotamia from the Roman yoke Trajan was imposing, or to take advantage of the deployment of Roman forces in the frontier campaign to rebel within the empire. Some have suggested that the diaspora uprisings were coordinated with a strategic aim of attacking the Roman state at a moment of weakness, others that vague eschatological leanings were exploited by messianic leaders—in Cyrene, Andreas or Lucuas; in Cyprus, Artemion—hoping by violence to inaugurate a new and better age. A more mundane explanation would be a gradual escalation of violence, with unintended consequences, fuelled by Roman over-reaction to Jewish unrest. As Trajan extended his military capabilities to their limit in the search for conquest, he will have known that the Jews within the empire were potentially friendly to Parthia because they maintained contact with their co-religionists in Parthian territory—after all, Jews from Adiabene had joined in the defence of Jerusalem in 70, so it was reasonable for Romans to suspect the possibility of reciprocity.

All such explanations are possible and certainly none can be disproved, but all rest on the primary assumption that Jews in the Roman empire hated Roman rule. For that hate, taken for granted by Dio and Eusebius and by contemporary observers, the history of the past forty-five years was to blame, and especially the frustration of hopes that had been raised, all too briefly, by Nerva. In contrast to the Parthians, who had allowed the Jews in their empire to worship as they liked without interference, the Romans had burned down the Temple and gloried in its demise. Every year, when the tax collectors called, Jews were reminded that this heinous act had present consequences and that Rome continued its war against Judaism by refusing to allow Jews the freedom, permitted to all ordinary subjects of the emperor, to rebuild their destroyed sanctuary. During the disturbances the temples of Apollo, Zeus, Demeter, Artemis and Isis in the city of Cyrene were all destroyed or damaged. The evidence for this destruction, all either archaeological or epigraphic, cannot reveal whether it resulted from deliberate action by the Jewish rebels against pagan cult centres as well as against their gentile neighbours, or simply as an unintended consequence of conflict. But it would be unsurprising if Jewish frustration at Roman attacks on Judaism manifested itself in a war against the religion of the oppressive state.[39]

Judaea was affected by these upheavals only indirectly. Alongside their co-religionists in Rome, Asia Minor and Greece, the Jews of the homeland seem to have remained quiescent despite the bloodshed, although their non-participation should not be taken to indicate lack of sympathy, but only a reluctance to risk all in what proved to be a hopeless cause. Indeed the reluctance of these other communities to be involved itself argues against the notion that the uprising was coordinated rather than a spontaneous outburst of rage, but the passivity of the Jews in Judaea did not free them from Roman suspicion. Eusebius records that Lusius Quietus, the Moorish chieftain who had cleared out the Jews of Mesopotamia with great savagery, was appointed governor of Judaea by the emperor in 117. Quietus commanded an independent cavalry unit of Moors which had fought with distinction alongside regular Roman forces both in Trajan's Dacian campaign and in the invasion of Parthia and, as a reward for his services, was enrolled in the Senate, becoming consul probably in the same year that he went to Judaea. An ex-consul with a fine military record could expect to command at least two legions, and a milestone from Galilee confirms that a second permanent legion was stationed in the province at least from early in Hadrian's reign and probably while Trajan was still alive. As far as the Romans were concerned, disaffection among Jews in one part of the empire necessarily threw under suspicion those in another, as they had shown consistently ever since Vespasian adopted his policy of hostility to Judaism in 70.[40]

Precisely when the last traces of the diaspora revolt flickered out is uncertain, and violence may well have continued in some places during the first months of Hadrian's rule. But the circumstances of Hadrian's accession, following the death of Trajan while he was with his troops in Cilicia during the Mesopotamia campaign on 8 August 117, discouraged the new emperor from adopting any clear policy towards the Jews until his own position was secure, which took considerable time. Aelius Hadrianus was a cousin of Trajan and his ward, but his adoption as Trajan's son and heir was announced only the day after the emperor had died. There was a plausible rumour that the succession had been stage-managed by Plotina, Trajan's wife, who championed Hadrian's interests and contrived the support of the army. Hadrian was faced by a distinct lack of enthusiasm among his fellow senators. In order to concentrate on ridding himself of political opposition in Rome and among the elite, he relinquished Trajan's hard-won new provinces of Mesopotamia and Armenia. Among the powerful and influential senators to be dismissed from their posts was Trajan's favourite, Lusius Quietus; in 118 he was executed, along with three other ex-consuls, on a charge of conspiracy. Hadrian evidently set his own political security above the need for a strong military commander in the Jewish homeland. He had no opportunity in such an atmosphere to draw up comprehensive plans to deal with the Jews. In any case some of the Jewish rebels, where not already violently suppressed, may have been pacified by the unexpected withdrawal of Roman forces from Mesopotamia—to the Jews of that region, at least, the Roman retreat may well have looked like vindication of the uprising, since they can have known little about the nuances of political intrigue at the heart of imperial rule which seem in fact to have been responsible for the reversal of Roman policy.

The solution to the Jewish problem would have to wait. In the year after Trajan's death Hadrian was confronted by provincial disturbances as far apart as Britain and Mauretania, where an uprising was probably inspired by support for Lusius Quietus after his abrupt dismissal from his command in Judaea. By the time Hadrian arrived in Rome on 9 July 118 he was keen to promote an image of settled normality. A posthumous triumph was held to celebrate Trajan's victories over Parthia, despite the abandonment of the territory he had conquered. There were lavish gladiatorial games and generous gifts to the plebs of the city and bankrupt senators. In the face of much hostility from his fellow senators, Hadrian sought to consolidate his power, establishing a distinctive atmosphere in his court through the patronage of Greek culture. He prided himself on his own expertise in Greek rhetoric as well as other arts, including architecture, poetry and music. The new regime was celebrated by the inauguration, probably on 21 April 121, of a huge new temple near the Colosseum dedicated to Venus and the goddess Roma. The largest temple ever built in the city, and designed by Hadrian himself, the building evoked the image of Rome as eternal and divine. This was the first time that the goddess Roma, long worshipped in the Greek world, had received the honour of a cult in the city of Rome itself.[41]

Once his position in Rome was consolidated, Hadrian set out, as other emperors had done, for the provinces, but with different aims in mind. Further conquests were to be eschewed. Instead, Hadrian set out to reorganize the government of the empire, adopting the name Hadrianus Augustus as indication of his ambitions to impose his personality on the Roman world as decisively as Augustus had once done. There followed a series of financial, military, administrative and legal changes on a scale that had not been seen for a century and a half. The new policy of security within fixed frontiers was advertised in some places in concrete form. A continuous palisade was erected in Upper Germany and Raetia, forming the first artificial frontier to be erected to limit the exercise of Roman power. From 122 a great wall, running for eighty Roman miles and far more elaborate than anything elsewhere, was built "to separate Romans and barbarians" on the northern edge of the province of Britannia. Hadrian himself went in person to each province, strengthening military discipline but also advertising his beneficence by the foundation of new cities and other similarly magnificent gestures. His contributions to Athens, favoured especially as the fount of Greek culture, were so extensive that a great arch was erected on which inscriptions proclaimed on one side "This is the city of Solon," on the other, "This is the city of Hadrian." The arrival of the emperor in each province was commemorated by the issue of a coin series depicting the province in idealized form, with the legend ADVENTUS AUGUSTI, "the emperor's visit." The demonstration of such a personal interest in the detailed administration of each part of the empire was entirely novel, as the issue of the distinctive ADVENTUS coins seems to acknowledge.[42]

In 128 Hadrian set off on his final tour, going to Africa and Mauretania, then Greece and, the following year, Asia Minor and Syria, where he spent the winter in Antioch. A bilingual honorific inscription from Palmyra in the Syrian desert records the services provided by a local man called Males for looking after Hadrian's troops when he visited that city. A triumphal arch was dedicated in 130 by the city of Gerasa (Jerash) in Trans-jordan, now in the province of Arabia. Finally, on the way south to Egypt, Hadrian came to Judaea. The (by now) standard coins were issued to cele-brate the emperor's presence, recording ADVENTUS AUG IUDAEAE. Frag-ments of a large Latin inscription from Tel Shalem, close to Scythopolis, suggest that the legion installed at the nearby camp set up an impressive arch to commemorate his visit. A massive cuirassed bronze statue of Hadrian, accidentally unearthed in the same area, was also probably manufactured as part of the celebrations of the emperor's arrival. There was every reason, given his record in other provinces, for the inhabitants of Judaea to expect the visit to have momentous results. So, indeed, it did—but not those that Hadrian intended.[43]

The main types of ADVENTUS coins for Judaea show Hadrian facing a female image representing Judaea. She holds a cup or some similar object in her left hand. The coins depict next to her two children, each holding a palm, the standard symbol on Roman coins as an attribute of Judaea. Minted in Rome, these coins, like others in the ADVENTUS series, portray the emperor in the act of sacrificing a bull at an altar. Judaea is to become a normal part of the pagan world. The Judaea that Hadrian had in mind was not to be Jewish at all: "At Jerusalem, he [Hadrian] founded a city in place of the one which had been razed to the ground, naming it Aelia Capitolina, and on the site of the temple of the god he raised a new temple to Jupiter." So, succinctly, Cassius Dio as condensed by Xiphilinus. Hadrian's reformed province was to have at its heart not a rebuilt Jewish Temple but a Roman colony, named "Aelia" in recognition of his own family and himself and "Capitolina" in honour of Jupiter Capitolinus, whose cult was to be of central importance in the new city. The creation of a pagan city on the site most sacred to the Jews seems an act so provocative that some scholars have been tempted to explain it not as a cause of the ensuing revolt but as a response to it, following the remarks of Eusebius that work on building the new city was carried out after the revolt had ended; but finds of coins pro-duced by the new colony in hoards alongside coins produced by the rebels strongly suggest that the sequence of events as given by Dio is correct: "This [the foundation of Aelia Capitolina] brought on a war of no slight importance."[44]

Hadrian was presumably happy with his reform of Judaea, for he did not stay long. By the summer he was in Egypt, where he was distracted by personal tragedy: he had fallen totally in love with a young Bithynian boy named Antinous, and the boy's death by drowning in October 130 was devastating. The foundation of a new city, Antinoopolis, to commemorate his beloved, and declaring him a god, provided small consolation. Hadrian went to Lycia, and by the winter of 131 was again in Athens, where he seems to have been happiest, setting up the Panhellenion, an organization of Greek cities which celebrated the culture of the Greeks and their loyalty to Rome, and especially to the Panhellenion's founder, Hadrian himself. Hadrian's consistent philhellenism, which led him to promote Greek cultural traits even when, as in his extravagant love affair with Antinous, it rather embarrassed fellow Romans, might encourage the view that his mission in Judaea was, like Antiochus Epiphanes' three hundred years before, to bring the Jews to Greek culture. At Athens, Hadrian had revived a project, the completion of the great temple to Olympian Zeus, which Antiochus Epiphanes had intended but not achieved. The author in the late fourth century CE of the biography of Hadrian preserved in the so-called *Augustan History* asserts that "the Jews began the war because they were forbidden to mutilate the genitals," and there is considerable evidence that Hadrian did indeed ban circumcision of males throughout the empire as inimical to what he considered civilized behaviour, just as castration had been banned by Domitian in the previous century. However, it is quite clear from the account in Cassius Dio that Aelia Capitolina was not to be a haven for Hellenized Jews who had accepted Greek culture. The war broke out because "the Jews deemed it intolerable that foreign races should be settled in their city and foreign religious rites planted there." Aelia Capitolina was not to be refounded as a Greek city in which Jews might settle and be "civilized," but as a Roman colony, inhabited by gentiles, from which Jews were to be excluded.[45]

The most obvious explanation of Hadrian's decisive action is that it was intended as the definitive solution to the problems which had led to the appalling uprising of diaspora Jews in 115–17. Hadrian seems to have liked to deal with one province at a time and then to sort it out once and for all, most grandiosely in the erection of the frontier wall in Britain. By planting a Roman colony on the site where the Jewish Temple had once stood, he made it crystal clear that the Temple was not to be rebuilt. Leaving the site of Jerusalem empty for sixty years had proven an invitation to the Jews to agitate for a return to their former glories. To expect Rome to disband a

Roman colony would be so obviously ridiculous that agitation would evaporate.

It is unlikely that Jews will have understood the reasons for the delay in inflicting this punishment thirteen years after 117. After 70 Roman retaliation had been instant and vicious. Now, by contrast, the years passed by and those Jews who had not suffered directly in the Trajanic revolt were no more ground down by the state than they had been before. The mixed emotions, of fury and despair at the bloody suppression of the rebellion and denial of the right of Jews to worship in their ancestral fashion, and relief and hope at the possibility of imminent felicity under the new emperor, are evident in the coded prophecies preserved in the fifth book of the *Sibylline Oracles*. Certainty about the identity, religious orientation and place of origin of the authors of these pseudonymous oracles, and the time and unity of their composition, is elusive, but the author's continuing grief at the destruction of the Jerusalem Temple emerges clearly:

> The desired house has long ago been extinguished by you, when I saw the second house cast headlong, soaked in fire by an impious hand, the ever-flourishing, watchful shrine of God made by holy people and hoped by their soul and body to be always imperishable . . . But now a certain insignificant and impious king has gone up, cast it down, and left it in ruins with a great horde and illustrious men. He himself perished at immortal hands [?] when he left the land, and no such sign has yet been performed among men that others should think it right to sack a great city.

The assertion that Titus had died "at immortal hands" parallels the later rabbinic traditions about his awful sufferings as punishment for his sacrilege; that he died through divine intervention may have proved tenable because he did at least die comparatively early, albeit a natural death. The Sibyl denounces Rome with exceptional bitterness: "You will be among evil mortals, suffering evils, but you will remain utterly desolate for all ages yet . . . With you are found adulteries and illicit intercourse with boys. Effeminate and unjust, evil city, ill-fated above all. Alas, city of the Latin land, unclean in all things, maenad, rejoicing in vipers, as a widow you will sit by the banks, and the river Tiber will weep for you, its consort." The book opens with a survey of the "woeful history of the Latins," in which the author condemns, among others, Nero, "a strange snake," Vespasian, "a certain great destroyer of pious men," and Trajan, "a Celtic mountain-walker, who, rushing to an eastern war, will not avoid an unseemly fate, but will die; foreign dust will cover him, a corpse." All the more striking are the author's favourable judgements on Nerva, and, especially, on Hadrian, "a silver-headed man, who will have the name of a sea [the Adriatic]. He will also be a most excellent man and he will consider everything." Such praise so lavishly poured by the author on Hadrian would be impossible for a Jew after 130. This passage provides, indeed, the main clue to the date of the composition of the text.[46]

In 130 this "most excellent" emperor turned the site of Jerusalem into a miniature Rome, devoted to Roman religious rites and settled by gentiles, probably by Italians. Among the deities later worshipped in the colony were Bacchus, Sarapis, Astarte and the Dioscuri, all of whom are represented on the city's coinage, but the main cult was that of Jupiter Capitolinus. The symbolic transfer of the Jews' annual tribute from the Temple of the Jewish God to the temple of Jupiter Capitolinus in Rome had now gone one stage further. Now in Jerusalem, too, Jupiter Capitolinus was to dominate the new, Roman, city, ideologically, if not physically, displacing once and for all the cult of the Jews. Thus was the suppression of the revolt under Trajan linked to the foundation of Aelia Capitolina and, in turn, to the outbreak of a further terrible war in 132. The ancient writers explain none of these disasters, so modern historians must try to do so in the light of normal Roman imperial practice and the known idiosyncrasies of Hadrian. What happened next was described succinctly but coherently by Cassius Dio:

> [The foundation of Aelia] brought on a war of no slight importance nor of brief duration . . . So long, indeed, as Hadrian was close by in Egypt and again in Syria, they remained quiet, save in so far as they purposely made of poor quality such weapons as they were called upon to furnish, in order that the Romans might reject them and that they themselves might thus have the use of them; but when he went farther away, they openly revolted. To be sure, they did not dare try conclusions with the Romans in the open field, but they occupied the advantageous positions in the country and strengthened them with mines and walls, in order that they might have places of refuge whenever they should be hard

pressed, and might meet together unobserved underground; and they pierced these subterranean passages from above at intervals to let in air and light. At first the Romans took no account of them. Soon, however, all Judaea had been stirred up, and the Jews everywhere were showing signs of disturbance, were gathering together, and giving evidence of great hostility to the Romans, partly by secret and partly by overt acts; many outside nations, too, were joining them through eagerness for gain, and the whole earth, one might almost say, was being stirred up over the matter. Then, indeed, Hadrian sent against them his best generals. First of these was Julius Severus, who was dispatched from Britain, where he was governor, against the Jews. Severus did not venture to attack his opponents in the open at any one point, in view of their numbers and their desperation, but by intercepting small groups, thanks to the number of his soldiers and his under-officers, and by depriving them of food and shutting them up, he was able, rather slowly, to be sure, but with comparatively little danger, to crush, exhaust and exterminate them.[47]

All the other evidence for the revolt of 132–5 is less coherent than this story told by Cassius Dio, but it tends to confirm the general accuracy of his narrative. The rabbis commented mostly on the character of the Jewish leader of the revolt, Shimon bar Kosiba, on the siege of Bethar (about seven miles south-west of Jerusalem) which brought the uprising to an end, and on the persecution which ensued; their stories accreted more and more legendary elements over time, but, unlike the diaspora rebellion, this war was securely entrenched in the rabbinic historical consciousness, along with the great revolt of 66–70. On the non-Jewish side of the conflict, the contemporary historian Appian notes, in discussing Pompey's destruction of Jerusalem in 63 BCE, that it was afterwards rebuilt, but that "Vespasian destroyed it again, and Hadrian did the same in our time." Appian notes also that, as a result of these rebellions, "the poll tax imposed upon all Jews is heavier than that imposed upon the surrounding peoples." Thirty years after the war the orator and teacher Fronto tried to console the philosophical emperor Marcus Aurelius for Roman losses in a different campaign, against the Parthians, by reminding him "what a number of soldiers were killed by the Jews under the rule of your grandfather Hadrian." Revealing of the ideology of the rebels are the images and slogans on the abundant and varied coinage they produced, and fragments of military documents and letters written by the insurgents which have been found in increasing quantities over the past half-century in Judaean desert caves. Revealing of their tactics are the excavations of many underground hiding complexes, with narrow tunnels leading to larger storage chambers and cisterns, which seem to confirm Cassius Dio's reference to their use of "places of refuge . . . underground" and "subterranean passages."[48]

War broke out eventually in 132 after lengthy and organized preparation. The rebels must have been well aware of how the Romans would react: the bloody conflict under Trajan had ended only fifteen years before. A new Jewish government had to be created in secrecy and the population primed to accept its authority under war conditions. In contrast to the internal political struggles leading up to revolt in 66, the Jews in 132 were operating in almost a political vacuum, although some rabbinic sources presuppose, perhaps rightly, that rabbinic support was offered to the rebel leadership by at least one leading rabbinic sage, Akiva. In any case the minting of an impressive series of coins in the first year of the war suggests a new state firmly governed; coins of course served an important purpose in paying for military necessities for the war, but for an underground state without other means to disseminate its messages, the wide distribution of coinage also provided an excellent medium for that purpose. This impression of organized efficiency is confirmed by the tone of surviving documents issued by the rebel administration, from a series of rent agreements for what had previously been imperial property in En Gedi and was now assumed to be the property of the Jewish state, to peremptory orders to military subordinates: "Shimon bar Kosiba to Yehonatan and to Masabala . . . let all men from Tekoa and other places who are with you, be sent to me without delay. And if you shall not send them, let it be known to you, that you will be punished." In the event these Jewish fighters were to maintain their independence for some three and a half years, inflicting heavy losses on the Roman force sent to suppress them, until in 135 they were finally overwhelmed.[49]

Historians have debated the size of the force sent by Hadrian to crush the Jews, but it is probable that it was very large. Hadrian took command in person, at least for a time, and his personal involvement drew in the best military minds of the age. The celebrated architect Apollodorus of Damascus sent him designs for new siege engines, although evidently at some distance from the field of battle. Gaius Iulius Severus, "first" of Hadrian's "best generals" according to Cassius Dio, was supported in the campaign by the governor of Syria and the governor of Arabia. Hadrian's imperial persona since he came to power had been far less militaristic than that of his predecessor—perforce, perhaps, because he had found it politically necessary to abandon Trajan's conquests in the East—but precisely the lack of military commitments elsewhere would have made it easier for him to concentrate all his efforts on the total crushing of the Jewish rebels. The geographical spread of the uprising faced by Hadrian is not clear. Judaea was certainly the main arena of the conflict, but Galilee may also have been caught up in the fighting, although the discovery of rebel coinage in Galilean underground complexes may reflect only the plight of refugees from Judaea after the war. The demise in the Judaean desert of one group of fugitives became gruesomely apparent when their skeletons, along with some of the precious documents they had taken with them for safekeeping, were found in the cave where they had died. The documents themselves show that some of these victims originated in the province of Arabia to the east, suggesting that Jews from outside Judaea were drawn into the uprising either as voluntary participants or through suspicion from gentile neighbours such as had caused the pogroms of 66. Cassius Dio states explicitly that not only "all Judaea had been stirred up," but "the Jews everywhere were showing signs of disturbance, were gathering together, and giving evidence of great hostility to the Romans," which suggests strongly that diaspora Jews were voluntarily involved, although due allowance must be made for rhetorical exaggeration: "Many outside nations, too, were joining them through eagerness for gain, and the whole earth, one might almost say, was being stirred up over the matter."[50]

The shape and weight of the coins issued by the rebel government, and the types and slogans chosen, suggest a direct ideological link to the Jewish state which had collapsed in 70. The new state, like the old, was named "Israel," once again a significant choice because it was a name never used by the Roman state to refer to the Jews. Many of the same slogans ("freedom," "redemption," "Jerusalem") and the same images (palm trees, *lulavim*) were found on the new coins, although the coins started a new era with the new leadership, and there were some other changes which are quite striking in contrast to the earlier types: thus, for instance, the coins make no reference to Zion (only Israel and Jerusalem). Even more than the coins of 66–70, the issues of 132–5 are remarkable for the extraordinary variety of types chosen, which include many images of buildings, some of them probably idealized versions of part of the destroyed Temple in Jerusalem. The slogan "For the freedom of Jerusalem," found on undated coins probably to be assigned to Year Three of the rebellion, was presumably programmatic, since there is no evidence, apart from Appian's claim that Hadrian destroyed the city, that Jewish forces ever gained control of Jerusalem, which was, after all, the headquarters of the Tenth Legion. Certainly the rebels of 132–5 lacked the protection of the city walls which had given security for so long to their predecessors in 66–70: the defences of Jerusalem had been razed to the ground by Titus.[51]

Both Jewish and Christian sources are eloquent on the qualities of the rebel leader, Shimon bar Kosiba, known in the Christian sources, and occasionally by the rabbis, as Bar Kokhba, "son of the star," presumably his preferred designation, but usually in the rabbinic sources as Bar Koziba, "son of the lie," emphasizing his claim to messianic status and the ruthless dedication which, according to one legend, led him to test the courage of his soldiers by requiring each of them to cut off a finger. Some of the coins carry simply his name SHIMON. Others have the legend SHIMON NASI YISRAEL, "Simon, prince of Israel." According to the Palestinian Talmud, "when Rabbi Akiva saw Bar Koziba, he cried out, 'This is King Messiah.' Thereupon Rabbi Yohanan son of Torta said to him, 'Akiva, grass will grow out of your cheek-bones and the Son of David will still not have come.' " The vitriolic judgement of other rabbinic sages, that Shimon was "son of the lie," is amply explained by the abject failure of a messianic leader whose uprising had promised so much.[52]

The bloodshed in this last war was as awful as anything that had gone before. Cassius Dio notes that

> very few of them [the Jews] in fact survived. Fifty of their most important outposts and nine hundred and eighty-five of their most famous villages were razed to the ground. Five hundred and eighty thousand men were slain in the various raids and battles, and the number of those that perished by famine, disease and fire was past finding out. Thus nearly the whole of Judaea was made desolate . . . Many Romans, moreover, perished in this war. Therefore Hadrian, in writing to the Senate, did not employ the opening phrase commonly used by the

emperors, "If you and your children are in health, it is well; I and the legions are in health."

Neither the Roman legions nor the Jews were "in health." After seventy years of tension and conflict, Jews could never again realistically hope to live in the Roman empire with the same freedom as other minorities to practise their ancestral customs and worship their God in their own land.[53]

## "MALODOROUS JEWS"

THE PUBLIC presentation of Rome's victory over the Jews in 135 was different from the celebrations in 70. Neither the war itself nor its outcome, with such heavy casualties on the Roman as well as the Jewish side, fitted well with Hadrian's persona as proponent of peace and culture. He liked to be seen as omniscient, civilized, organized, poetic and romantic, and his achievements as the encouragement of architecture and art across the empire. He wished his subjects in Rome to admire his wisdom and foresight, not his conquest of distant lands. He stressed, of course, the military competence which was an essential requisite for the emperor, and he was not averse to being portrayed on many statues, particularly in the Greek East, as a cuirassed warrior, but, as he showed by the dispositions made during his provincial tours, under his rule military might was to be used for peace and security, not to win glorious campaigns. The necessity of fighting a war against the Jews cannot have been welcome. There was not, then, to be a triumphal procession or any glorification of the victory. Hadrian did not present himself as conqueror of Judaea as Vespasian and Titus had done, nor did he trumpet his achievements as Trajan had done after this campaigns in Dacia and Parthia. The iconography of the regime made no reference at all to the Jews. No coins celebrated the successful end of the campaign. It was a war that should not have happened.

The intensity of the conflict and the involvement both of the emperor in person and of so many troops made it politic to glory in Roman heroism even if not much could be said about the outcome of the war, much as modern states maintain war memorials to the dead of wars they would prefer to forget. Hadrian himself accepted acclamation as *imperator* by his troops, so that *imperator II* was inserted into his official title. His motivation for accepting the honour was probably the need to encourage military

morale after a bruising encounter. The service of numerous ordinary soldiers was appropriately recognized by the presentation of military decora-
tions, and triumphal ornaments were bestowed not just on Iulius Severus,
who had taken primary responsibility for the campaign, but also on
Haterius Nepos, governor of Arabia, and Publicius Marcellus, governor of
Syria. If Roman soldiers were to continue to risk their lives for the
emperor, public acknowledgement of their efforts was prudent, but it did
not amount to glorification of the war.

Roman burial of memories of the conflict had an impact on the Jews
even more disastrous than the triumphalism of 70. It was to be as if the Jews
had never been in Jerusalem. In his apologetic address to Antoninus Pius
and his sons, the Christian Justin, "the son of Priscus and grandson of Bac-
chius, natives of Flavia Neapolis [Nablus] in Palestine," informed the
emperor, a decade or so after the defeat of Bar Kokhba, that the desolation
of the land of the Jews had been known to Isaiah, whose prophecy, as para-
phrased by Justin, had foretold that "the house of our sanctuary has
become a curse, and the glory which our fathers blessed is burned up with
fire, and all its glorious things are laid waste." Justin added for the
emperor's benefit that "concerning its desolation, and that no one should
be permitted to inhabit it, there was the following prophecy by Isaiah
[again, paraphrased]: 'Their land is desolate, their enemies consume it
before them, and none of them shall dwell therein.' And that it is guarded
by you lest any one dwell in it, and that death is decreed against any Jew
apprehended entering it, you know very well." When addressing, in a different treatise, the Jew Trypho, the same Christian writer blames Jews'
observance of the law of circumcision for their exile. "For the circumcision according to the flesh, which is from Abraham, was given for a sign,
that you may be separated from other nations, and from us, and that you
alone may suffer that which you now justly suffer; and that your lands may
be desolate and your cities burned with fire, and that strangers may eat
your fruit in your presence, and that no one of you may go up to
Jerusalem." Writing in the early fourth century CE, Eusebius quotes a certain Ariston of Pella who had recorded that "Hadrian commanded that by
a legal decree and ordinances the whole nation should be absolutely prevented from entering thenceforth even the district around Jerusalem, so
that not even from a distance could it see its ancestral soil." "Thus," notes
Eusebius, "when the city came to be bereft of the nation of the Jews, and

its ancient inhabitants had completely perished, it was colonized by foreigners." The name of Jerusalem had already ceased to exist officially in 130. Now the name of the whole province was changed to Syria Palaestina, resurrecting an ancient Greek designation of the region, which referred not to the Jews but to their ancient enemies, the Philistines.[54]

Such a response to rebellion was unique in Roman history, both before and after 135. For a province to change its name for administrative purposes was not unusual, but not, as in Judaea, as punishment of the natives for their uprising. Despite revolts in Pannonia, Germany and Britain, the Romans continued to call each province after the name of its native people. Only the *Iudaei* ceased to have a homeland because of what they had done. Nor was transfer of populations a standard Roman procedure. Under Augustus, some of the inhabitants of the Spanish highlands were compelled to move down into the coastal plains as a precaution against insurrection, and more generally the Celtic peoples of northern Europe who had sought security in hill-top forts were moved after Roman conquest into urban centres on lower ground less easily fortified against Rome by the disaffected; but these precautionary measures were quite different from the mass punishment to which the Jews of Judaea were subjected. In the eyes of Rome and at the behest of Hadrian, the Jews had ceased to exist as a nation in their own land.

To what extent the hostility of the state was reflected in the attitude of ordinary Romans towards the Jews can be surmised only from occasional hints in the extant literature, and from plausibility. Violent terminology occasionally surfaces. Under Domitian, the great authority on rhetoric Quintilian wrote of Jews as a baleful nation (*perniciosa gens*). For Tacitus in the reign of Trajan, most Jewish customs are base, abominable and depraved, so that "the Jews regard as profane all that we hold sacred, while they permit all that we abhor"; to Florus, a younger contemporary, Jews were an "impious nation." In the distant city of Oenoanda in what is now Turkey, the Epicurean philosopher Diogenes had inscribed, probably during the reign of Hadrian, in large letters for the benefit of his fellow citizens advice to seek contentment by not behaving credulously like the Jews: "A clear indication of the complete inability of the gods to prevent wrongdoings is provided by the nations of the Jews and Egyptians, who, while being the most superstitious of all peoples, are the vilest of all peoples." Whether such hostile attitudes became standard in the city of Rome or elsewhere in the empire after 135 cannot now be determined, but they are unlikely to have evaporated quickly.[55]

Nothing in the comparatively settled elite politics of Rome over the next hundred years encouraged succeeding emperors to dispense with the policy so clearly established in 135. Just as Hadrian's legitimacy as ruler of the Roman world derived from his alleged adoption by Trajan, so every emperor down to 193 owed his position to adoption by Hadrian or his adopted successors. By the mid-second century CE the prestige of imperial adoption was so fully accepted that an emperor's choice could not safely be set aside even when it might seem to everyone in authority potentially disastrous for the empire. When Hadrian's successor Antoninus Pius died in March 161, the new emperor Marcus Aurelius insisted that the Senate confer the rank of Augustus on his adoptive brother Lucius, implying an equal share of power, despite his lack of political and military experience or competence, and despite Marcus Aurelius' own popularity. The only justification was the fulfilment of Hadrian's wishes as expressed just before his death twenty-three years earlier. Even when the strict line of adoptive succession, continuous since 96, came to an end with the murder of the deranged Commodus in 193, the desire to justify current rule by appeal to the past did not vanish. Commodus was succeeded by a series of generals, each seeking supreme power for himself, much as had occurred in 68 on the death of Nero. Septimius Severus, who emerged as sole victor only in February 197, came from Africa and was of Punic descent. He had no connection to the regime of Commodus, except as a competent senator; he had become emperor because in 193 he was governor of Upper Pannonia and won the support of the legions stationed on the Rhine and Danube, and because in the ensuing wars against rival claimants the crucial battles went his way. But even in the midst of such blatant realpolitik, image mattered, and in 195 Severus proclaimed himself a son of Marcus Aurelius and thus brother of Commodus; for this relationship to bring the prestige desired, Commodus' memory, which had been enthusiastically condemned by the Senate following his assassination, was restored, and he was declared to be a god. Severus' son, the future emperor nicknamed Caracalla, was given the name "Marcus Aurelius Antoninus." By such means, artificially but effectively, the political heritage of Hadrian was carried through into the Severan dynasty, which was to last, in somewhat indirect form, to the death of Severus Alexander in 235. Thus, for a hundred years after the defeat of Bar Kokhba, there was no incentive for any Roman ruler to challenge the ethos of the empire created by Hadrian. The marginalization of the Jews was to remain in force.

Continuation of the policy of hostility to the Jews is less easy to demonstrate from the surviving evidence than its original imposition. The coins issued by the colony of Aelia Capitolina show that it flourished as a pagan city on the site where Jerusalem had once been. The earliest coin types show the emperors as founders of the colony, ploughing its boundaries, the she-wolf with the twins Romulus and Remus, the legionary standards, the temple of Jupiter Capitolinus and the Capitoline Triad. Three coin types from the time of Marcus Aurelius depict Rome as a goddess, armed and seated, with her left arm resting on a spear and in the palm of her extended right hand the figure of a winged victory. Later coins, in the third century, exhibit less distinctively Roman traits, with images most often of the goddess Astarte and the god Sarapis, but they are still defiantly pagan. The Tenth Legion, whose camp continued to occupy the southwestern hill of Jerusalem, near what is now the Jaffa Gate, advertised its presence on ceramic roof tiles, bricks and pipes, each stamped LEG X FRE (sometimes just LXF) and often bearing the legion's insignia of a galley and a wild boar. The wide distribution of roof tiles produced by the legion shows that they were used extensively for purely civilian purposes, and it is reasonable to assume that the soldiers were well integrated into the life of the colony. The main centre of the civilian colony seems to have been sited to the north of the legionary camp, in what is now the northern quarter of the Old City, where the modern street plan still follows in part its rectangular layout. The arched gate leading onto the main colonnaded north–south street is still visible below the Damascus Gate built by Suleiman the Magnificent in the mid-sixteenth century. This and other arched gates, such as the so-called Ecce Homo arch on the Via Dolorosa, fulfilled a propaganda rather than defensive function. Impressive arches of this sort were a common feature of cities in the Roman Near East in the second and third centuries CE. Aelia Capitolina does not seem to have been walled. The inhabitants could be confident that, despite all that their city represented to the Jews, they would be secure. In *c.* 201 CE a memorial medallion was struck in Aelia Capitolina bearing the heads of the emperor Septimius

# Aelia Capitolina

N
W   E
S

Triumphal Gate
Column Square
Temple of Aesclepius
Pools
Colonnaded street
Cardo
Triumphal Arch
Pool
City limit
Basilica
The rock of the Antonia
High-level aqueduct
Temple of Venus-Aphrodite
Gate
Temenos
Secondary (eastern) Cardo
Pool
Forum
Temple Mount
Decumanus
"David's Tower"
Ophel
Camp of the Tenth Legion
Low-level aqueduct
City of David
Ruins of the Lower City
Siloam Pool
Line of city wall of Second Temple period (not in use)

0   100   200   300
yards

The location of the Temple of Jupiter is disputed.

Severus and his wife Julia Domna on one side and the figures of their sons, Geta and Caracalla, on the other, apparently to commemorate a visit to the colony by the emperor. This public affirmation of the status of Aelia Capitolina by Septimius Severus was echoed by permission to add the names *Pia* and *Felix* ("Pious" and "Happy") as soubriquets to the name of the city. There is no sign of any doubt in the Roman state about the wisdom of the policy inaugurated by Hadrian. The gradual move of the Tenth Legion to a new base at Aela on the Red Sea in the second half of the third century CE did not reflect any shift in attitude to Aelia Capitolina by emperors but the strategic unimportance of the site now that the Jews were no longer a threat to the peace of the empire.[56]

Without a Jewish state during the one hundred and seventy-five years between Bar Kokhba's defeat and the accession to power in 312 CE of the first Christian emperor, Constantine, Jews feature only rarely in the historical narratives composed by Romans. The fourth-century pagan historian Ammianus Marcellinus notes in passing, during his discussion of a quip attributed to the emperor Julian in the mid-fourth century, that Julian believed his own witticism to be related to one uttered two centuries earlier by Marcus Aurelius: "as he was passing through Palestine on his way to Egypt, being often disgusted with the malodorous and disorderly Jews, [Marcus] is reported to have cried with sorrow: 'O Marcomanni, O Quadi, O Sarmatians, at last I have found a people more unruly than you.' " The author of the strange emperor biographies included in the *Augustan History*, probably a pagan writing in the 390s, writes that Antoninus Pius "through legates and governors, crushed the Germans and the Dacians and many other tribes, and also the Jews, who were rebelling," and that the Senate decreed to Caracalla (at the age of twelve!) a triumph over Judaea, *Iudaicus triumphus*, because of the successes achieved by Severus in Syria. Writing at the same time, in the late fourth century, the Christian Jerome noted in his *Chronicle* for the year 197 CE that "a Jewish and Samaritan war broke out," which could refer either to a revolt by both peoples against Rome or to a war between the two groups. But there is a striking lack of contemporary literary, archaeological, epigraphic or any other sort of evidence from the second and third centuries to support these stories, composed in the fourth century, about conflict two hundred years earlier. It is just possible that this apparent contemporary silence is the result of chance, and that these conflicts did indeed take place in one way or another, but

more probably these stories show only that, even in later generations and
even when they were at peace, Jews retained their reputation as rebels and
as a disruptive element in the empire.[57]

It would be unsurprising, of course, if Roman hostility to Jews diminished gradually as memories of the violence between 70 and 135 faded; but
no emperor did anything at all about the main complaint of the Jews
against Rome, that the state prevented them from worshipping God in
their Temple. The Jews' desire for the rebuilding of the sanctuary, so evident in Josephus' description of Jewish worship in *Against Apion*, written at
the end of the first century, was not in any way diminished by the early
third century, for a large proportion of the Mishnah, redacted at just this
time, concerned the rituals to be performed in a restored Jerusalem sanctuary: of the six divisions, one, on "Hallowed Things," was entirely devoted
to the topic, and references to the Temple cult permeate the other five divisions also. Severus Alexander could hardly have been unaware of what the
Jews wanted. He himself came on the maternal line from a family which
had for generations dominated as priests the worship of the sun-god of
Emesa, modern Homs, on the Syrian Orontes. His cousin and predecessor
as emperor, nicknamed Elagabalus, after the sun-god himself, had not only
promoted this cult in his home city but had brought his ancestral forms of
worship to Rome. Compared to such innovation, to permit the restoration
of the famed Temple of the Jews might have seemed uncontroversial, if
prejudice against the Jewish cult had not been so deeply entrenched in
Roman minds by this time.

That this failure to rebuild the Jewish shrine was the result of Roman
policy, and not of any insuperable physical or other problem, became clear
in 361, over two centuries after Bar Kokhba had been defeated, when the
Roman state inaugurated precisely such a rebuilding. The emperor Julian,
an apostate to paganism from Christianity, ordered the reconstruction of
the Jewish Temple not so much to please the Jews as in order to spite his
erstwhile Christian co-religionists: he knew that Christians believed that
the destruction of the Temple was a sign of the veracity of their version of
the religious tradition they shared with Jews, and that if the Temple was
restored it would undermine this argument. In any case, Julian believed
that encouraging traditional worship through sacrifices was in itself a good
thing. Julian's contemporary and admirer, Ammianus Marcellinus, records
with approval the commencement of the "great work" which Julian

planned "to extend the memory of his reign," and the practical difficulties faced in its execution. Julian, writes Ammianus,

> planned at vast cost to restore the once splendid temple at Jerusalem, which after many mortal combats during the siege by Vespasian and later by Titus, had only with difficulty been stormed. He had entrusted the speedy performance of this work to Alypius of Antioch, who had once been vice-prefect of Britain. But, though this Alypius pushed the work on with vigour, aided by the governor of the province, terrifying balls of flame kept bursting forth near the foundations of the temple, and made the place inaccessible to the workmen, some of whom were burned to death; and since in this way the element persistently repelled them, the enterprise halted.

What obstructed rapid rebuilding was evidently not the presence on the site of other buildings or any such problem, but natural phenomena, perhaps earthquakes. The contemporary Christian writer, the bishop Gregory of Nazianzus, who had been at school with Julian, claimed that the sacrilegious attempt to foil the divine will had been subverted by a miracle. Such Christian considerations will have carried no weight for the pagan emperors before Constantine. If they did not try to rebuild the Jewish Temple, it was not through fear of divine retribution, or the practical difficulties of the site, but out of a continuing belief that the Jewish cult was dangerous in the Roman world.[58]

## WICKED EDOM

MANY, perhaps most, of those Jews who survived in the new province of Syria Palaestina must have reacted to the defeat of Bar Kokhba by ceasing to think of themselves as Jews. The rabbinic texts of the third century ce and later contain recollections of a period during or immediately after the revolt when displaying any outward sign of Judaism could be fatal and some Jews even underwent an operation to reverse the mark of circumcision; the rabbis laid down a general rule for ordinary Jews that, because of the overwhelming preciousness of life, in such times of persecution any part of the Torah can be contravened to save one's life except the cardinal sins of idolatry, killing another person, and adultery or incest.[59] The archaeological and epigraphic remains from the land of Israel for the two centuries after 135 contain little that is clearly related to Judaism. Public buildings lacked any of the Jewish iconography which was to become standard on the mosaic floors of Palestinian synagogues in the late fourth to sixth centuries, when a repertoire of Jewish images (the ram's horn, palm branch, and especially the candelabrum from the Temple) was ubiquitous. Since the Roman state had always accepted without quibble the validity of apostasy from Judaism, as Tiberius Julius Alexander had demonstrated by the success of his public career in the first century, it might seem sensible for Jews to respond to Roman hostility to their religion by choosing to abandon it, particularly since their God seemed to have abandoned them. This may indeed be the best way to understand the assertion in Christian writers, such as Justin Martyr in the mid-second century, that Jews were forbidden after Bar Kokhba to live in their homeland. It would not have benefited the settlers in Aelia Capitolina to find the lands they were allotted in the new colony deprived of a local workforce. Doubtless they could employ slave labour to some extent, particularly when slave prices were low in the aftermath of the war, but much farm work must have been done by descendants of the original Jewish inhabitants who had given up Jewish customs and elected to merge into the wider gentile population of the region.[60]

At least some of those Jews who remained faithful to their ancestral religion developed a deep loathing for the Roman state because the Romans prevented them from worshipping God as laid down in the Torah. How general such loathing was is unknown. Hostility to the state was not of course an attitude that it would be prudent to express in public display of any kind, so the evidence is confined to the surviving Jewish literary texts from this period, of which the vast majority were produced by and for rabbinic sages. Whether many other Jews shared the rabbinic viewpoint can only be guessed, but that some rabbis came to see Rome as wicked and malevolent, and "good" Romans as the exception, is clear. The rabbis, as recorded both in legal texts like the Mishnah and in more discursive works of Bible interpretation, saw Rome as an instrument of war, and Rome was frequently equated by them with the hereditary enemy of Israel, Edom, which had been identified already in the biblical book of Genesis with the descendants of Esau, brother of Jacob, so that relations between Israelite and Edomite had the bitterness of fraternal hatred.[61] They elaborated traditions about pious martyrs in the revolt of 132–5, and especially about

Rabbi Akiva, who, arrested because "the wicked kingdom made a decree that people should not be occupied with Torah, and anyone who occupies himself with Torah will be stabbed with a sword," was said to have died smiling because martyrdom allowed him to fulfil the injunction in Deuteronomy to "love the Lord, your God, with all your soul."[62] The rabbis' hope for the final defeat of the evil empire of Rome was rooted for the rabbis not just in general speculation about the end times but in the more specific expectation of a cycle of four empires to precede the last days and the belief that the fourth of these empires was Rome. The cycle of empires had been described in the biblical book of Daniel and was applied to the future of Rome already by Josephus in his *Antiquities*, but the rabbis, composing an esoteric literature in Hebrew and Aramaic for Jewish readers, could afford to be less circumspect than Josephus, who felt constrained to be tactful for his Roman audience.[63]

The rabbis demonstrated no great knowledge of the intricacies of Roman politics—indeed, it would be impossible to write even the most schematic coherent account of the political and military history of the Roman world if it was necessary to rely on the rabbinic texts alone. They made comparatively frequent reference only to a few specific emperors: Vespasian, Titus, Trajan, Hadrian, Diocletian. Allusions to other political events, including the intensive campaigns by third-century Roman emperors in the Near East over territory in Syria and Mesopotamia where large numbers of Jews lived, campaigns in which emperors themselves were often personally involved, are sparse and often elliptical, and are comprehensible only in the light of non-rabbinic evidence. "Antoninus" was used as a generic name for a good emperor prepared to talk to, and take lessons from, rabbinic sages. Other emperors lacked a distinct personality in the rabbinic imagination, apart from Titus, the archetype of evil, about whom a whole folklore grew up, with enthusiastic speculation about the tortures he experienced before he died:

> This was the wicked Titus who blasphemed and insulted Heaven. What did he do? He took a harlot by the hand and entered the Holy of Holies and spread out a scroll of the Law and committed a sin on it . . . Titus further took the curtain and shaped it like a basket and brought all the vessels of the Sanctuary and put them in it, and then put them on board ship to go and triumph with them in his city . . . A gale sprang up at sea

which threatened to wreck him. He said: "Apparently the power of the God of these people is only over water. When Pharaoh came He drowned him in water, when Sisera came He drowned him in water. He is also trying to drown me in water. If he is really mighty, let him come up on the dry land and fight with me." A voice went forth from heaven saying: "Sinner, son of sinner, descendant of Esau the sinner, I have a tiny creature in my world called a gnat. Go up on the dry land and make war with it." When he landed the gnat came and entered his nose, and it knocked against his brain for seven years. One day, as he was passing a blacksmith's, it heard the noise of the hammer and stopped. He said: "I see there is a remedy." So every day they brought a blacksmith who hammered before him. If he was a non-Jew they gave him four *zuz*, if he was a Jew they said, "It is enough that you see the suffering of your enemy . . ." When he died he said: "Burn me and scatter my ashes over the seven seas so that the God of the Jews should not find me and bring me to trial."

It is interesting to see the Roman practice of cremation, still standard in the first century CE, interpreted in a Jewish text as a means to avoid punishment by God.[64]

Hostility to the Roman state did not preclude the rabbis in Palestine between the second and fifth centuries CE adopting many of the cultural traits of the Roman world, but acculturation did not necessarily imply accommodation, either for them or for the non-rabbinic Jews who were their contemporaries, about most of whom knowledge can only be derived from inscriptions and archaeology. No one was likely to express hostility to the state on a recognizable permanent monument, and if some Jews vented their rage in graffiti none has been recognized. But it may be worth noting that, in the privacy of the interior of the Dura-Europus synagogue, built by the Euphrates in the mid-third century CE, the artist felt free to display on the wall frescoes the violent destruction of a pagan shrine, albeit as illustration of the dramatic biblical scene in the book of Samuel, when the Philistines took the ark of the Lord into the house of Dagon "and set it by Dagon":

And when the people of Ashdod arose early the next day, behold, Dagon was fallen face downward on the ground before the ark of the

Lord. And they took Dagon and put him back in his place. But when they rose early on the next morning, behold, Dagon had fallen face downward on the ground before the ark of the Lord and the head of Dagon and both his hands were lying cut off upon the threshold; only the trunk of Dagon was left to him. This is why the priests of Dagon and all who enter into Dagon's house do not tread on the threshold of Dagon in Ashdod to this day. But the hand of the Lord was heavy upon the people of Ashdod, and he terrified and afflicted them with tumours, both Ashdod and its territory. And when the men of Ashdod saw how things were, they said, "The ark of the God of Israel must not remain with us; for his hand is heavy upon us and upon Dagon our god."

The same artist at Dura framed the main panel of his painting of the west wall of the prayer room around a depiction of the Temple in Jerusalem, which dominated the Torah niche in the centre of the fresco and was surrounded by other reminders of the Jerusalem cult, including a huge depiction of the Temple menorah. The Temple was as important to the Jews of Dura and the rest of the diaspora as it was to the Jews of Palestine. They had not forgotten what the wicked kingdom of Edom had done.[65]

## ROMANS OF THE JEWISH FAITH?

IN 197 CE, a dedicatory inscription in Greek was set up in Kasyoun in Upper Galilee "for the safety of our lords, emperors, Caesars, Lucius Septimius Severus Eusebes Pertinax Augustus and Marcus Aurelius [Anton]-inus . . . [and G]eta, his sons . . . [by] vow [prayer?] of Jews." Whether the inscription was set up in a synagogue or on a pagan site is uncertain, as is any connection with any specific event in imperial history, but the stone testifies to enthusiasm in public for the Severan dynasty by at least some Jews in the Galilee region in the late second century. The terminology may reflect no more than cautious obeisance, but it may reflect Jewish hopes, as a century earlier in 96, that the new regime, which had come to power after four years of intermittent civil war, would return the Jews to the status they had enjoyed before 70, at least with regard to the practice of their religion. Certainly fourth-century sources record the Severan dynasty, which ruled in the early third century, as more favourably disposed towards the Jews than their Antonine predecessors. Thus Jerome (*c.* 347–420) reports that some of the "Hebrews" in his day understood the passage in the biblical book of Daniel, "When they fall, they shall receive a little help. And many shall join themselves to them with flattery," to refer to the emperors Severus and Antoninus (Caracalla), "who loved the Jews very much" (although others took the text as a reference to the emperor Julian). The biographer in the *Augustan History* of the emperor Severus Alexander, who ruled from 222 to 235, portrayed this emperor as particularly friendly: he "kept the privileges for the Jews" and "used often to exclaim what he had heard from someone, either a Jew or a Christian, and always hung on to, and he also had it announced by a herald whenever he was disciplining anyone: 'What you do not wish to be done to you, do not do to another.' " How seriously to take such a story in the *Augustan History* is hard to judge. To some extent these frivolous and unreliable biographies seem to have been composed to amuse, and the author evidently found Jews and Jewish customs funny, but some confirmation of a more friendly attitude to Jews in Severan times may also be read in a law cited in the *Digest*, the great compilation of jurists' opinions compiled in the mid-sixth century CE at the behest of the Byzantine emperor Justinian, in which the opinion of the prolific lawyer Ulpian was recorded, that "the Divine Severus and Antoninus permitted those that follow the Jewish *superstitio* to acquire honours, but also imposed upon them duties such as should not harm their *superstitio*."[66]

A change in Roman attitudes may also explain rabbinic traditions about the high status in Palestine in the early third century CE of Judah haNasi, "Judah the Patriarch," the compiler of the Mishnah. According to later rabbinic tradition, Judah haNasi was an immensely wealthy aristocrat who was also a rabbinic sage: "from the time of Moses until Rabbi [Judah] we have not found Torah and greatness in one place."[67] Hence the historical significance of the rash of stories in rabbinic texts about a close relationship between Judah haNasi and a Roman emperor called "Antoninus," culminating in the implausible tradition that Antoninus converted to Judaism. The stories themselves belong to the same genre of moralizing folk tales as other rabbinic narratives about gentiles (governors, philosophers, "matrons") being instructed in the truth by rabbinic sages.

Antoninus made a candelabrum for the synagogue. Rabbi [Judah haNasi] heard about it and said, "Blessed be God, who moved him to make a candelabrum for the synagogue." Rabbi Samuel son of Rabbi Isaac, "Why did Rabbi say, 'Blessed be God'? Should he not say, 'Blessed be our God'? If he said, 'Blessed be God,' it indicates that Antoninus never in fact converted to Judaism. If he said, 'Blessed be our God,' it indicates that Antoninus in fact converted to Judaism." There are some things that indicate that Antoninus was converted, and there are some things that indicate that Antoninus was not converted.

In all these tales the culmination is the demonstration of his superior wisdom by the rabbi, who often brings the discussion to an end by citation of an appropriate biblical proof text. In most cases there is no reason to imagine any real historical dialogue as having given rise to the rabbinic story. But since the traditions about "Antoninus" and Judah haNasi are not generally paralleled for other sages and emperors, it is likely, at the least, that Judah haNasi did indeed have a closer relationship to the Roman government than his predecessors and successors in the rabbinic community, a relationship characteristically expressed in terms of patronage and gifts: "Antoninus gave Rabbi two thousand fine fields [in the area of Yabluna in the northern Golan] as a tenancy." To which emperor the name "Antoninus" in the rabbinic texts refers is unknown, but if Judah haNasi flourished in the early third century it is reasonable to link these traditions to an improvement in the attitude of some rabbis towards the Roman state in the Severan period and perhaps to accommodation by at least some Jews to Roman rule.[68]

On the other hand there is no evidence that rabbis ever thought of themselves, at this or any date, as "Romans of the Jewish faith" even when, in legal terms, they were fully entitled to do so. Rabbinic sources never refer to the single greatest innovation of the Severan dynasty which, in theory, might in one stroke have ended the Jews' perception of themselves as a persecuted minority in a hostile empire, when, in 212, the emperor Caracalla by edict bestowed Roman citizenship on all the inhabitants of the Roman world, including Jews. In a formal sense, the Mishnah, and later rabbinic texts such as the Palestinian Talmud, can be described as products of Roman literature, and Judah haNasi could have used a Roman name, but in fact there is no hint in the Mishnah, or indeed in any of the Palestinian rabbinic texts, that any of these Jews identified themselves as Roman. Rome, for third-century Palestinian Jews, was a foreign power which had subdued Israel. It would not, it seems, have occurred to Judah haNasi to think of himself as Roman in the same way as "Antoninus" was, even though the Roman identity of Caracalla, whose father was of Punic origin from North Africa and whose mother came from Emesa in Syria, was no less genealogically fictive than was that of Judah haNasi (and, indeed, the Roman identity of almost all Romans in his day).[69]

Far from integrating Palestinian Jews into the Roman world, the effect of a more benign imperial regime in the third century CE seems to have been a licence to some Jews to manage their own affairs in self-imposed isolation from the heavy hand of the state, as the Christian Origen (c. 185–c. 254) describes: "Now that the Romans rule and the Jews pay the two drachmas to them, we, who have had experience of it, know how much power the *ethnarch* ["ruler of the people"] has among them and that he differs in little from a king of the nation. Trials are held according to the law, and some are condemned to death. And though there is not full permission for this, still it is not done without the knowledge of the ruler." Origen, who was living in Caesarea Maritima on the coast, appealed to local knowledge about the condition of Jews in contemporary Palestine: "We found out about this to our certainty when we spent much time in the country of that people [the Jews]."[70]

The power of the ethnarch to put people to death as described by Origen was informal, derived from his local prestige among Jews rather than from authority delegated to him by Rome. "Ethnarch" does not seem to have been an official Roman title, but was used by Origen as a Greek equivalent of the Hebrew title *nasi*, "patriarch," accorded to Judah haNasi and his descendants during the rest of the third century and on to the early fifth. The third-century *nasi* as described in rabbinic texts was a local leader who declared fast days, instituted and annulled bans, sent judges to serve communities, controlled the calendar, and, with his court, issued decrees about religious obligations such as the laws of sabbath, purity, tithing and the sabbatical year, but he was not described as involved in the standard tasks of a local authority that was delegated power by the Roman government, such as the collection of taxes on behalf of Rome. Rabbinic stories about the use of Gothic bodyguards by the patriarch Judah Nesiah, grandson of Judah haNasi, show him as more like a mafia boss or powerful patron than an appointee of the Roman state.[71]

In contrast to the self-isolation of the Jews of Palestine, one might imagine that to identify themselves with the Roman state would have come more naturally to Jews in the city of Rome itself. Those Jews in Rome in the third century CE, whose ancestors had first settled in the city and had become Roman citizens as long ago as the first century BCE, might reasonably have felt themselves to be Roman as well as Jewish, regardless of the current attitude of the state to the observance of their religion. It is not easy now to discover how they balanced these two aspects of their identity; arguments about how they described themselves can become dangerously circular. Thus the use of a full Roman name is rare in the (mostly funerary) extant inscriptions from Rome identified by scholars as Jewish, being found in fewer than ten out of six hundred or so, so that it might appear that, when it came to commemoration after death, Roman Jews preferred to stress their Jewish rather than their Roman status; but since the inscriptions of or about Jews are often identified in the first place by their Jewish name, the epitaph of a Jew who used a purely Roman name (like that of Tiberius Julius Alexander) and did not use Jewish iconography would not be identified now as Jewish even if the individual in question had in fact been a pious Jew.[72]

In late-first-century Rome, at least one Jew who was a Roman citizen, Flavius Josephus, seems never to have portrayed himself in his writings as Roman, despite his ability as a historian to describe the Judaean campaign and Titus' triumph from the Roman side.[73] But the same was not obviously true two centuries or so later of a certain Cresces Sinicerius, whose epitaph, inscribed in Latin on a plaque of coarse-grained grey-blue marble in the catacombs below the Villa Torlonia, records that "Cresces Sinicerius, Jewish proselyte, lived 35 years, took his sleep. His mother [had] made for her dearest son what he should have [had] made for me." A convert to Judaism, Cresces had begun life as a Roman citizen and had only later become a Jew. He was entitled to think of himself, if anyone was, as a Roman of the Jewish faith rather than a Jewish outsider in Roman society. It is probably significant that this inscription is in Latin, unlike the great majority of Jewish epitaphs from Rome, which, as in the rest of the Mediterranean diaspora, were in Greek. The mother of Cresces Sinicerius expressed her mourning in terminology common on pagan tombstones (including the addition of the date: "*VIII K[a]l[endas] Ian[uarias]*," 25 December), but of course she, unlike her son, may not have converted to Judaism.[74]

The number of such proselytes in the city of Rome in the second and third centuries CE is impossible to gauge since the surviving Jewish inscriptions from Rome record only a tiny fraction of the community, and there is no reason to assume that the relatives of all converts chose to include on their epitaphs the information that they had not always been Jewish. The practice is indeed rather odd, and could also be dangerous in the light of the periodic effort by the state to ban such conversions: the jurist Modestinus, discussing the rights of masters over their slaves, notes that "by a rescript of the divine Pius [Antoninus Pius]" Jews are permitted to circumcise only their own sons, and that "if anyone shall perform this act on one who is not of the same religion, he shall suffer the punishment of a castrator." The unreliable *Augustan History* states baldly that Septimius Severus "forbade under heavy penalty [anyone] to become Jewish." A text contained in the codification of Roman attitudes to circumcision included in the *Sententiae*, attributed to the early-third-century jurist Paul but composed in the late third century, also lays the blame on the proselyte as well as on the Jews responsible for the conversion: "Roman citizens, who suffer that they themselves or their slaves be circumcised in accordance with the Jewish rite, are exiled perpetually to an island and their property confiscated; the doctors suffer capital punishment. If Jews shall circumcise purchased slaves of another nation, they shall either be banished or suffer capital punishment." It is all the more striking that the relatives of Cresces Sinicerius and others were prepared to state so openly that they were indeed converts to Judaism.[75] Whatever the attitude of the state, ordinary Roman attitudes to proselytes fluctuated. In the early second century CE Tacitus asserted that new converts to Judaism were immediately taught "to disown their fatherland." By contrast Cassius Dio, writing a century later under the milder regime of the Severans, exhibited no such overt hostility to proselytes: "I do not know how this title ['Jews'] came to be given to them, but it applies also to all the rest of mankind, although of alien race, who affect their customs. This class exists even among the Romans, and though often repressed has increased to a very great extent and has won its way to the right of freedom in its beliefs."[76]

By the late third century CE there were still many Jews, both native and proselyte, in the Roman world. Many lived in the diaspora, but a good proportion still inhabited the land of Israel where, excluded from Jerusalem, they congregated primarily in Galilee and in the cities of the

Mediterranean coast. To what extent those Jews not part of the rabbinic movement still thought of themselves as Jews since the disaster of 135 cannot be known, but it would be surprising if most of them lost all sense of their Jewish culture since, as Dio noted, the Romans allowed them to believe what they liked about the nature of the world.[77]

Jews could observe their dietary laws as their customs allowed. They could circumcise their sons and congregate to hear the Torah read. No one compelled them to break the rules of resting on the Sabbath or to participate against their conscience in the worship of other gods. But they were still deprived of the main focus of their religious piety. As Dio and all Romans knew, the Jews had once worshipped their God with sacrifices in an "extremely large and beautiful temple," which continued to lie in ruins.[78]

# CHAPTER THIRTEEN

# THE GROWTH OF THE CHURCH

S ET AGAINST this history of conflict, repression and hostility, it is a remarkable fact that one movement which began in Jerusalem in the first century CE came by the fourth century to govern the world-view of those who held power in Rome. Among the most important reasons for the growth and spread of Christianity during these years, one must be that after 70, and even more after 135, Christians presented themselves to the gentile world as unconnected to the Jews, whose alienation from mainstream Roman society had been sealed by the destruction of the Temple in Jerusalem. The very earliest Christians, like Jesus himself, were all Jews, but by the early fourth century, when Constantine became the first Roman emperor to portray himself as a devotee of Christ, the links between Christianity and Judaism had been deliberately obscured by Christians themselves. Most Christians in the second and third centuries avoided calling themselves Jews, and, far from hoping for the rebuilding of the Temple, they revelled in its demise, which they portrayed as confirmation of the prophecies which Jesus had spoken in his lifetime. And this distancing of Christians from Jews was evidently accepted by the Roman state, for, although (as we shall see) Christians were at times persecuted by officials of the state, they were punished not for being Jews but for being "atheists"— that is, for not worshipping the other gods. Since, as we have seen, exemption from such worship was a continuing, and special, privilege of Jews on the grounds that Jews had never participated in other cults, it is clear that those officials who punished Christians did not see them as any sort of Jew.

Much of the extraordinary success of Christianity in the Roman empire, and hence the creation of Christian Europe and many aspects of our world today, must be attributed directly to Constantine's personal commitment in 312. In 300, Christians were only a small minority in the empire, and Constantine's conversion was a shock to them and to pagans alike. Nonetheless, there were certainly many more Christians in 300 than in 30 CE. It is worth asking why.

Jesus lived and died in Galilee and Judaea in the first half of the first century CE. That this fact is one of the few which can be asserted with any certainty about the founding figure of the Christian Church is the result not of a paucity of ancient stories about Jesus but of contradictions between the multifarious tales which abounded among his followers in the two centuries after his death, as they tried to extract religious meaning from his life and teachings. The story of a remarkable individual put to death in Jerusalem but retaining great power after resurrection was elaborated and altered by the pious over succeeding generations. Finding the historical truth is not easy.

The stories now found in the New Testament Gospels coexisted with many others. The Gospel of Mark tells how Jesus was baptized by John the Baptist in the river Jordan and then attracted crowds as a preacher, healer and exorcist in Galilee and Judaea until he was handed over by the High Priestly leaders in Jerusalem to the Roman governor Pontius Pilate for trial and crucifixion. According to this Gospel, that Jesus was more than an ordinary human was revealed during his lifetime only to a chosen few, when he appeared transfigured in glory to his disciples Peter, James and John, but became more widely apparent when it became known that he was resurrected after death. The Gospels of Matthew and Luke agree with Mark in many respects but expand the narrative, including (among other things) stories about Jesus' birth and childhood. By contrast, the Gospel of John, which concentrates more on Jesus' activity in Judaea, evidently derives from a separate tradition. Mark portrays Jesus as struggling against temptations, overcoming evil, whereas in John's account he emerges as barely affected by human weakness. But early Christians knew other versions too, not all easily compatible with the kind and loving image which dominated the later images of Jesus. A certain "Thomas the Israelite," who narrated the "mighty childhood deeds of our Lord Jesus Christ" in (probably) the second century, portrays Jesus as a frighteningly powerful, if petulant, child prodigy: "When this boy Jesus was five years old . . . he went through the village, and a child ran and knocked his shoulder. Jesus was angered and said to him, 'You shall not go further on your way,' and immediately he fell down and died."[1]

That Jesus had been a teacher was widely acknowledged, but what he had actually said was much debated. The Gospels of Matthew and Luke contain many sayings attributed to Jesus which are not to be found in Mark, and it is generally supposed that Matthew and Luke obtained their material from an earlier source which has since disappeared. Most of the sayings thus recorded are parables and aphorisms, to which appeal could be (and was) made by early Christians in support of their practices. Not all the alleged sayings thus preserved can be easily reconciled into a coherent theology. So, for instance, it might surprise a reader familiar with the teachings of Jesus preserved in the canonical Gospels to learn from a Coptic papyrus of the mid-fourth century, which preserves a translation of an originally Greek document of the mid-second century and was discovered in Nag Hammadi in Egypt in 1945–6, that, according to "the secret words which the living Jesus spoke and Didymus Judas Thomas wrote down," Jesus taught that "every woman who makes herself male will enter the kingdom of heaven."[2]

As some of the followers of Jesus came rapidly to emphasize the otherworldliness of Jesus as Christ, and as Son of God, even Jesus' humanity was sometimes in doubt. In the mid-second century Justin Martyr was able to preach that Jesus was both fully human and had always been Lord and God: since Jesus was "ever-existent Reason, pre-existent with the Father, begotten before all creation," he had been born "through" rather than "from" a virgin. But Justin himself referred often to the "mystery" of God, and not all Christians could combine such contradictory concepts with Justin's sophistication. It might be easier to think of Jesus as never having been a real man. One of Justin's contemporaries put into the mouth of Jesus the assertion that "I have suffered none of the things which they will say of me . . . You hear that I suffered, yet I suffered not . . . that blood flowed from me, yet it did not flow." Precisely such discrepancies about the nature of Jesus, and the significance of his life for contemporary Christians, led by the mid-second century to the selection by some Christians of just four Gospels as authoritative: the creation of what became the New Testament canon was required to exclude the unreliable and the dangerous, so that the faithful should not be led astray.[3]

For anyone now to build a narrative of Jesus' life out of evidence so patently composed for non-historical purposes seemed so difficult for much of the twentieth century that the search for the historical Jesus was by many scholars deemed hopeless. Such despair was premature. That Jesus lived in Judaea and was executed by Pontius Pilate was known both to the Jewish historian Josephus at the end of the first century and to the pagan Roman historian Tacitus in the early second century. The modern notion that the whole biography of Jesus to be found in the various Gospels was pure invention is deeply implausible—not least because a story of this type about the career of a Galilean peasant was neither characteristic of religious literature of the time nor obviously helpful in spreading to the wider world the central Christian message that Jesus was also Christ and Lord. But beyond the near-certainty that Jesus lived and died, the only hypotheses that can be asserted about Jesus' life with real confidence are those based on the parts of the Christian traditions about Jesus which Christians preserved despite the difficulties they faced in fitting them in to their own self-image and theology as the Church burgeoned.[4]

Such a minimalist procedure naturally provides only a skeleton of the historical truth, but the skeleton is moderately firm. Thus, for instance, it is highly likely that Jesus came from Galilee since such origins had to be explained away by those, like the author of Luke's Gospel, who wished to link him to the Davidic city of Bethlehem in Judaea. It can also be firmly stated that Jesus was in some way connected to the missionary preacher John the Baptist, since the relationship between the two men was a matter of embarrassed dispute among early Christians. It is similarly almost beyond doubt that Jesus was a Jew who (unlike many of his later followers) preached only to other Jews, with little contact with a gentile world until his death, and that this death, by means of the ignominious and horrible punishment of crucifixion, was carried out in Jerusalem by order of the Roman governor, a fact exceptionally problematic for those early Christians who tried to portray themselves as no threat to the Roman state.[5]

According to the Gospels, in the days immediately preceding his trial and crucifixion in Jerusalem, Jesus attracted great crowds of enthusiastic Jews, but almost all deserted him once he was in the custody of Pontius Pilate. After Jesus' death his followers remained a small group, initially scattered to Galilee and elsewhere but in due course forming a community in Jerusalem. What led these Jews to affirm their faith in Jesus must have been mostly memories of his ethical teachings while he was alive and the

eschatological fervour which had accompanied his preaching of the kingdom of heaven. As Jews they will have been impressed also by claims that
Jesus' life had been foretold by the prophets and by the notion that he was
the Messiah, the anointed of God for whom, as we have seen (in Chapter
4), many Jews yearned, however uncertain they might be about his nature.

How many Jerusalem Jews were persuaded into the nascent Christian
community by such arguments is harder to ascertain. The author of Acts,
probably the same gentile Christian who composed the Gospel of Luke in
the second half of the first century, describes the leader of the apostles,
Peter, and the other disciples of Jesus gaining three thousand souls on one
day soon after Jesus had been crucified, but it seems unlikely that the total
number of Christians in the city was very large by the time revolt broke
out in 66, since they seem to have played no role at all in the upheavals
either before or during the war. To most Jews the message preached by
Jesus' followers, Peter, James and the others, must have seemed as maverick
as those of all the other idiosyncratic movements within Judaism. Hence
the comparison, put into the mouth of the Pharisee Gamaliel in Acts,
between the apostles and earlier Jewish leaders, such as Theudas and Judas
the Galilean, who had threatened to bring disorder. In the account in Acts,
Gamaliel argues from this comparison that the apostles should be left in
peace: "Refrain from these men, and let them alone. For if this counsel or
this work be of men, it will come to naught. But if it be of God, you cannot overthrow it, lest you be found fighting against God." But Gamaliel
was not portrayed as sufficiently tempted by such arguments to become a
Christian himself. About the Jewish Christians in Galilee after Jesus' death
almost nothing is known.[6]

Adoption of Christian teachings was much more rapid, it seems, among
the gentiles, outside the land of Israel, primarily, in the early years,
through the efforts of Paul. Paul was, as we have seen, both a Jew and,
according to Acts, a Roman citizen. Shortly after the crucifixion of Jesus,
he came into contact with some of the followers of the new movement and
persecuted them in Jerusalem, but on the way to Damascus as an agent of
the High Priest to arrest converts there, he was himself converted on the
road by a vision of the risen Jesus and devoted the rest of his life to his work
as "apostle of the gentiles." Acts provides a detailed, if doubtless idealized,
account of his missionary journeys with companions to the coastal cities of
the Mediterranean world, such as Antioch, Ephesus and Corinth. Quite

early on, before Paul's arrival there, the Christian message had also reached Rome. According to Acts, Paul tried first to bring his message to the Jews in each place, and it was only when that failed that he turned to the local gentiles, but in his own letters he makes no reference to such past failures, addressing himself only to the gentile Christian communities he founded. Paul evidently felt under compulsion to preach—"Woe is unto me, if I preach not the Gospel"—in part because he espoused an eschatological theory that gentiles must be "won" to Christ primarily on the grounds that only once this was done would God bring about the salvation of Israel, but the main impact of his heroic missionary efforts lay in the conversion to Christ of the gentiles themselves.[7]

This sense of mission set Christians apart from other religious groups, including Jews, in the early Roman empire. The notion that it is desirable for existing enthusiasts to encourage outsiders to worship the god to whom they are devoted was not obvious in the ancient world. Adherents of particular cults did not generally judge the power of their divinity by the number of congregants prepared to bring offerings or attend festivals. On the contrary, it was common for pagans to take pride in the local nature of their religious lives, establishing a special relationship between themselves and the god of a family or place, without wishing, let alone expecting, others to join in worshipping the same god. Christians in the first generation were different, espousing a proselytizing mission which was a shocking novelty in the ancient world. Only familiarity makes us fail to appreciate the extraordinary ambition of Paul, who seems to have invented the notion of a systematic conversion of the whole world, area by geographical area. Paul portrayed his own calling as divinely vouchsafed at a time when the end of the world was imminently expected by him and his companions.[8]

Paul wrote that "not all can be apostles," and there is no evidence that, for a long time after the first generation of eschatological fervour, ordinary Christians felt impelled to follow his example in devoting themselves to the conversion of unbelievers. The pagan Celsus was even able to assert in *c.* 180, probably in Alexandria, that "if all men wished to be Christians, the Christians would no longer want them," although the response, in the third century, by Origen to this accusation by Celsus reveals the extent to which, despite the diminution of intensive missionizing on the model of Paul, it remained important to Christians like him to assert their desire to convert as many unbelievers as they could: "That the statement [by Celsus] is a lie is clear from this, that Christians do not neglect, as far as in them lies, to take measures to disseminate their doctrine throughout the whole world. Some of them, accordingly, have made it their business to go round not only cities but even villages and farms to make others also pious towards God." By the second century, Christian ideas were generally spread through contacts with relatives, or at work or in the marketplace, or by the travels of believers as merchants, or through literary texts: when a certain Speratus was martyred in Scillieum in North Africa in 180, he told his judge, the governor Saturninus, that what he carried in his satchel were "books and the letters of Paul, an upright man." Few converts can have been brought over by a direct vision of Christ like that vouchsafed to Paul, on which he based his status as an apostle. More common was witness of miracles, particularly healing in the name of Jesus. The evidence from martyrdoms that some were prepared to die for their beliefs attracted curiosity and some conversions.[9]

It is evident that the argument from fulfilled prophecy was used to persuade gentiles as well as Jews, despite the need to tell gentiles, unaware of the contents of the Jewish Bible, the nature of the prophecies which had now come to pass. The Syrian Tatian, who became a Christian in Rome in the mid-second century, was converted by reading the Septuagint, the Greek version of the Hebrew Bible; it is interesting that, by this date, what he read encouraged him to become a Christian rather than a Jew. In the letters of Paul, as "apostle to the gentiles" writing to communities of gentile Christians, what was most stressed was the crucifixion, resurrection and lordship of Christ. In many ways this is surprising, since there was so little consensus among early Christians about the precise relationship between Jesus as man and God. The development of the concept of the Trinity, which was adumbrated in the Gospels but only gradually evolved during the second and third centuries, proved so complex that it continued to arouse fierce controversy for centuries afterwards. It is remarkable that a religion so imprecise about the nature of the divinity to be worshipped attracted adherents at all—a prominent feature of other cults in the Roman world, such as devotion to Isis, was citation in detail of the specific virtues and nature of the god honoured.

Lack of clarity on this crucial issue encouraged the efflorescence in the early centuries of many idiosyncratic strands of Christianity, many of them imbued to some extent with the mystical dualism found, most influentially, in the teachings of the Gnostic Valentinus, a native of Egypt who came to Rome in *c.* 136 and preached a complicated myth about the origins of this hostile visible world in the fall of one of the "aeons," Sophia or "Wisdom," from the spiritual world; the imprisonment of a divine element within the visible world at the mercy of the Demiurge (identified with the God of the Old Testament); and the potential for redemption through another "aeon," Christ, who united with the human Jesus to bring saving knowledge, *gnosis*, to those who are spiritual (that is, Valentinus' followers) and a lower form of salvation to other Christians. It is tempting to dismiss such doctrines as nothing to do with real Christianity, but it would be anachronistic to do so. Tertullian recorded that Valentinus had had hopes of being elected bishop of Rome because of his intelligence and eloquence. The Church in the second century embraced a huge amount of theological innovation so that almost the only characteristic shared by all who called themselves Christian was some belief about Christ. But at the same time Christians had a strong feeling of belonging to a single community of belief and practice, and the most striking innovation of all in terms of ancient religious history was the gradual defining of Christianity in the last years of the second century by the systematic exclusion of ideas not deemed acceptable to the mainstream. When Irenaeus (*c.* 130–*c.* 200), leader of the Christians in Lyons, composed his major work, *Against the Heresies*, denigrating and denouncing all the new ideas which he believed incompatible with the four canonized Gospels, the letters of Paul, and the authority of the bishops derived from the original apostles, he began a process of clarification which greatly strengthened the Church as an institution but pushed not just those like Valentinus, but also many other innovative thinkers, outside the Christian community.

It is not known whether such theological disputes about the nature of God and the universe were an attraction to potential converts. It is not impossible: in the history of conversion to other religions, it is not unusual for challenges of language and thought, and the heat of polemic, to be a positive lure to the outsider convinced that those who argue with such passion must have right on their side. But the lack of clarity in Christian thought on these topics contrasts strikingly to the one distinctive and coherent concept, found in all strands of Christianity, which is known to have been deeply attractive. In contrast to the uncertainty, agnosticism or denial of many Roman pagans and some Jews, all Christians asserted with total confidence their belief in a life after death and the restriction of that life to those saved through Christ. The philosophical Christian Justin Martyr in the mid-second century describes the faithful in his *Second Apology* as "those who have been persuaded that the unjust and intemperate shall be punished in eternal fire, but that the virtuous and those who lived like Christ shall dwell with God in a state that is free from suffering—we mean, those who have become Christians."[10]

The total number of Christians would have grown through such conversions only if the newcomers stayed within the fold. That some apostatized is certain: the younger Pliny mentions in his letter to Trajan in 110 that some reported to him as Christians denied the charge, "saying that they had indeed been Christians, but had stopped, some three years before, some more years before, a few even twenty years before." In his satirical account of the death of the Cynic philosopher Peregrinus, who publicly immolated himself at the Olympic games in 165, Lucian describes Peregrinus' time as a leading Christian, maintained by Christian communities, until "because he committed some offence even against them—for he was seen, I fancy, eating some of their forbidden foods—they no longer accepted him." Christian sources naturally reveal little about such defectors.[11]

Encouraging defection was the danger of suffering at the hands of others for being a Christian—we have already seen that such attacks could sometimes lead even to death. The motivation of persecutors differed and cannot always now be discovered: most evidence comes from the Christian side, and there was no reason for the martyrs to seek to understand the mentality of those who attacked them. Persecution of Christians by Jews was a phenomenon confined to the first generations, in the first century CE. Since, as we have seen, first-century Jews tolerated great theological variety, hostility to Christians was more often sparked by social and political issues than by Christian theological claims, which were more likely to provoke derision than violence from those Jews who chose not to accept them. So, for example, the diaspora Jews who hounded Paul out of their cities in Asia and Greece were concerned that he might threaten their precarious relationship with the gentile civic authorities by his self-presentation as a Jew when he preached to local gentiles that they should give up their pagan worship.

Persecution by pagans (whether urban mobs, civic leaders, or represen-tatives of the Roman state) was not generally for what Christians did but for what they did not do—that is, for failure to worship the pagan gods. In contrast to the prohibition by the state on Jews worshipping their God in the Jerusalem Temple, gentile Christians were not punished for praying to Christ—they were free to meet together and worship as and when they desired—but for failing to support society by bringing sacrifices to the altars of the other gods as their (implicitly gentile) ancestors had done. When Pliny, as we have seen, put Christians on trial in Bithynia and Pontus by the Black Sea, all they had to do to escape punishment for the past was to make a sacrifice now to the gods.[12]

But encouraging solidarity with fellow Christians were many good social reasons for converts to stay loyal once they had joined a Christian community. Prime among these was the separation from family, friends and neighbours which might often accompany rejection of the pagan ritu-als which formed an integral part of ordinary social life. No Christian text from this period suggests it was easy to convert to Christianity—the mod-ern notion that becoming Christian involved fewer "encumbrances" than becoming Jewish, because males did not have to be circumcised, ignores the far more drastic nature of this self-isolation from existing relationships. The life enjoined by Jesus on his apostles, according to the Gospel of Matthew, was not an easy one: "Think not that I am come to send peace on earth: I come not to send peace, but a sword. For I am come to set a man at variance against his father, and the daughter against her mother . . . He that loves father or mother more than me is not worthy of me."[13] But more positively, the new Christian, once he or she had severed ties with the past, could be guaranteed a secure home in a new, supportive community of brothers and sisters in Christ. Local churches do not seem often to have functioned like the Jewish Christians in Jerusalem, who, according to Acts, "had all things in common" like their Essene contemporaries and the Dead Sea sectarians, but they do generally seem to have taken care of widows, orphans and the destitute, and to have allowed equal religious prestige, though not equal authority, to those of low social standing, including slaves.[14] It must also have helped the morale of converts that on baptism they became full members of their new Christian society without any per-ceived taint from their previous lives—there was no Christian equivalent to the status of proselyte among Jews as member of the community but of a distinct separate category. Furthermore, a convert to Christ could hope for religious perfection almost from the moment he or she became a Christian. The great heroes of early Christians were martyrs, and to be killed for the sake of Christ took neither status nor time nor education nor any special quality other than courage and the opportunity to declare "I am a Christian" when Christians were on trial. Hence an incident before the urban prefect Urbicus in Rome around 160 recorded by Justin Martyr:

> Ptolemaeus confessed, since he loved the truth and was no cheat or liar at heart, that he was a Christian . . . Urbicus ordering him to be led to execution, a certain Lucius, who was himself also a Christian, seeing how unreasonable the sentence was, said to Urbicus: "What is the reason for punishing this man, who is convicted neither as an adulterer nor a fornicator nor a murderer nor a thief nor a robber nor of committing any crime whatever, but confesses to being called by the name Christian? Your judgement, Urbicus, is not worthy of the emperor Pius nor the philosopher, the emperor's son, nor the sacred Senate." Without any other answer he said to Lucius: "You too seem to me to be such a one." When Lucius said: "Absolutely," he commanded that he too be led away.

Such opportunities for martyrdom did not arise for all—or, probably, except in the times of organized state persecution under Decius and Diocletian, for many—but special devotion of a different kind, to voluntary chastity, was easier to achieve and gave, in particular, an honoured role for some women, the forerunners of nuns. It was a major attraction of Christianity for those of low social standing that, although Christians were not concerned to overthrow existing social structures, any Christian, even a slave-girl, could achieve esteem among her fellow Christians by intense devotion to her faith, particularly if it ended in her death.[15]

Of course, both martyrdom and chastity will have tended to reduce rather than increase the number of Christians, but such demonstration of piety was for most Christians an ideal to encourage faith rather than a norm to live by, and other aspects of Christian ideology positively encouraged an increase in the Christian population disproportionately greater than their pagan neighbours. As the *Epistle to Diognetus*, a letter written by an unknown Christian to an otherwise unknown enquirer in the second or third century, explains, Christians "marry like the rest of the world and they breed children" but, like Jews, they abhorred infanticide and abortion: "They do not cast their offspring adrift." Combined with the practice of charity to support the poor, such attitudes will have encouraged larger families to survive, so that, already by the reign of Hadrian, most Christians were probably born into the faith rather than converts, and by the time of Constantine's conversion many Christians could look back to ancestors who had been committed to the faith for generations.[16]

For the spread of Christian ideas across the Mediterranean world the long periods of peace, stability and prosperity in the Roman empire during the first three centuries were ideal. Merchants could travel freely. So too could correspondence and books, keeping Christians in touch with each other over huge distances. Greek and Latin could be used to communicate religious ideas. The concentration of Christians less on rituals or buildings than on a philosophical approach to life, specifically a moral commitment with a strong belief in an afterlife, made their faith much easier to transport than other cults, such as the worship of Mithras, which required the construction of sanctuaries to a specific design and the offering of sacrifices. Early Christians not only managed without animal sacrifices to their God; unlike Jews in the early centuries, they even came up with arguments against such sacrifices in principle, and the Eucharist, "thanksgiving," involved only the consumption of bread and wine, with reference to the sacrifice of the Lamb relegated to the realm of metaphor. By the end of the third century Christians were only a small minority in most places where they were found, but they were exceptionally well organized and aware of their solidarity as a community, and they were to be found almost everywhere in the empire.

How much did any of these Christians believe that the life to which they committed themselves had anything to do with Jews and Judaism? At the beginning they were all Jews, and after the crucifixion of Jesus in Jerusalem in *c.* 30 some of his disciples continued to preach in his name to other Jews in the holy city, where, according to Acts, the nascent Christian community met "daily with one accord in the Temple." The disputes which surface in the earliest Christian documents, the letters of Paul, about whether non-Jews who came to faith in Jesus should take on Jewish practices such as the circumcision of males, provide evidence that at least some Christians in the first generation assumed that they were preaching not a

new religion but simply a new kind of Judaism. The puzzled response
attributed in Acts to the apostle Peter when faced by a divine revelation
sent to tell him to eat non-kosher food only makes sense if the author of
Acts believed him to have been an observant Jew until he

> saw heaven opened, and a certain object descending like a great sheet
> knit at the four corners, and let down to the earth, wherein were all
> manner of four-footed beasts of the earth and creeping things, and
> fowls of the air. And there came a voice to him, "Rise, Peter; kill, and
> eat." But Peter said, "Not so Lord; for I have never eaten any thing that
> is common or unclean." And the voice spoke unto him again the second
> time, "What God has cleansed, that you should not call common."

Even Paul, who called himself the "apostle to the gentiles," was happy to
portray himself sometimes as a Jew: "Unto the Jews I became as a Jew, that
I might gain the Jews." The author of Acts portrays Paul as participating in
the services in the Jerusalem Temple along with four nazirites who needed
to make special offerings, precisely in order to demonstrate that he himself
continued to behave as a Jew and that he expected other Jews to do the
same. James the brother of Jesus was sufficiently prominent a figure in
Jerusalem in *c.* 62 to attract attention, ire and finally condemnation from
the High Priest Ananus son of Ananus, who accused him and others of
having transgressed the law, and delivered them up to be stoned. Josephus,
who records this event in the context of the dissension within Jerusalem in
the years preceding the outbreak of revolt in 66, condemns Ananus as "rash
in his temper and unusually daring," noting with disapproval that he was
"savage in judgement" because he was a Sadducee, and that "those of the
inhabitants of the city who were considered the most fair-minded and who
were strict in observance of the laws" were offended at his conduct. Four
years later Ananus was to become Josephus' ally and commander-in-chief
in the war against Rome, and, as we saw in the Prologue, he merited a
eulogy when he died in 68 at the hands of the Zealots, so the historian's
evident disgust at the treatment of James is remarkable. A few years before
the martyrdom of James in Jerusalem, probably in *c.* 58, Paul's letter to the
Christians of Rome assumed that there were Jewish believers in the community there also, since he was keen to improve their relations with the
gentile Christians of the city. Both in Jerusalem and in Rome, there was

clearly disagreement among early Christians about how Jewish a gentile believer in Christ should become, but no one in the Christian community before 70 seems to have seen any problem in a Jew who had joined the assembly of the faithful continuing to think of himself or herself as Jewish as well as a follower of the new movement.[17]

Such tolerance was to become much more rare after the destruction of the Temple. Historians both of early Christianity and of Judaism in late antiquity agree that at some point in the first four centuries CE the ways of the two religions parted. There is much less agreement about the date when this parting occurred and the extent of continued debate, rivalry and mutual influence between Jews and Christians after the separation. All depends on perspective. Viewed from the standpoint of Jews and Christians in the twenty-first century, the historical trajectories which mattered in late antiquity are those which were to create two distinct religious systems in due course, but the beginnings of those trajectories may have been almost unnoticed by those who followed them. Some Jews might have thought that some fellow Jews who believed in Christian doctrines were still Jews, while others, less tolerant, did not. The early Christian traditions that Jewish Christians were persecuted by their fellow Jews and expelled from synagogues are not reflected in the rabbinic sources, which is not to say that they are not true: the rabbis in fact had very little to say about Christians of any kind, treating Christians born as Jews within the general category of heresy and those born as gentiles simply as idolaters. Conversely, when ancient Christians described fellow believers as Jews or Judaizers they might be referring either to the ethnic origins of such Christians or to their continued practice of Jewish customs such as the circumcision of males, or simply to more scrupulous attention to the Old Testament than other Christians believed appropriate.[18]

Distinctions obvious at the time to the writers and readers of the Christian texts of the first three centuries are often obscure to us now. The simple fact that Christians in the second and third centuries sometimes attacked other Christians as Jews and Judaizers need not necessarily imply that there continued to be Christians in these years who saw themselves also as Jews, since these opponents in polemical texts may sometimes be deliberately men of straw, or a cover term of hostility towards Christians whose theological differences from the mainstream in fact owed little or nothing to allegiance to Judaism. Justin Martyr in the mid-second century asserted, in contrast to some less pluralist Christians, that "if some, through weak-mindedness, wish to observe such institutions as were given by Moses . . . yet choose to live with the Christians and the faithful . . . not persuading them either to be circumcised like themselves, or to keep the Sabbath, or to observe any other such ceremonies, then I hold that we ought to join ourselves to such, and associate with them in all things as born from the same womb and as our brothers," but such Jewish Christians were unusual by his time. Frequently in his own *Dialogue with Trypho the Jew*, from which this last quotation comes, Christianity is defined as the antithesis to Judaism.[19]

The process by which "the Jews" came to be portrayed as the archetypal enemies of Christians had its roots in ideas expressed already in *c.* 50, in the earliest extant Christian text, the first letter to the Thessalonians, in which Paul decries the wickedness of the Jews in violent terms: "[they] both killed the Lord Jesus, and their own prophets, and have persecuted us; and they please not God, and are contrary to all men." But Paul, it will be recalled, could also be "as a Jew to Jews" when it seemed to him appropriate. The divide was much sharper after 70. In the Gospel of Matthew, composed probably in the last quarter of the first century, there is a careful distinction between "their" synagogue and the Church. In the first Christian account of a martyrdom presented within a separate literary work, the narrative of the death of Polycarp, bishop of Smyrna, in *c.* 155, the Jews play an important symbolical role. Polycarp's execution for atheism was at the hands of the Roman governor and at the instigation of the local pagans during a public pagan festival, but this did not prevent the author of the *Martyrdom of Polycarp* (according to the text itself, composed within a year of the events, for the edification of Christians elsewhere) from referring rhetorically to the Jews as enthusiastic bystanders: when Polycarp was condemned to be burned, the crowds gathered firewood from the workshops and baths, "with the Jews assisting at this particularly enthusiastically, as is their custom." Whatever the truth or otherwise of Jewish participation in the events surrounding Polycarp's awful death, it is clear from the martyrdom account itself that the Jews of Smyrna did not actually bring it about, but also that they were believed by the author and his readers to be so instinctively opposed to Christians that it was something they would have wished to do. In a poetic homily on Easter composed a few years after Polycarp's martyrdom, Melito, bishop of Sardis, blamed "lawless Israel" for the crucifixion of their God. "It is he that has been murdered. And where has he been murdered? In the middle of Jerusalem. By whom? By Israel . . . O lawless Israel, what is this unprecedented crime you committed, thrusting your Lord among unprecedented sufferings, your Sovereign, who formed you, who made you, who honoured you, who called you 'Israel'? . . . For him whom the gentiles worshipped and uncircumcised men admired and foreigners glorified, over whom even Pilate washed his hands, you killed him at the great feast."[20]

Melito attacked "Israel" as god-killers, but other Christians in his time portrayed the Church as "the True Israel." In his *Dialogue with Trypho the Jew*, Justin Martyr asserts that "the true, spiritual, Israel, and descendants of Judah, and Jacob, and Isaac, and Abraham . . . are we who have been led to God through this crucified Christ." "We," the Christians who are the new Israel, are contrasted by Justin in the *Dialogue* with "you," the Jews. The idea that gentile Christians are the "Israel of God" was floated as early as the early 50s by Paul in his letter to the Galatians, but the explicit claim to the name in contrast to Jews is first found here in this treatise by Justin, a literary account of what was probably a real dialogue some time in the mid-second century, which took place, according to the text, in Ephesus in Asia Minor. "Israel" was by this date a name of particular significance to Jews: as we have seen, it had been the preferred self-designation of the independent Jewish state both in 66–70 and in 132–5, when it was the name emblazoned on their coins and borne by Shimon bar Kosiba, "prince of Israel."[21]

There were manifold reasons for this usurpation of Israel's identity by Christians. The prime issue was the role of Scripture in Christian thought and worship. Christians knew that the "Old Testament," the collection of sacred texts which provided, in the guise of prophecies realized in the life of Jesus, the foundation of their faith, belonged first to the Jews. Texts of the holy writings were to be found in synagogues, where they were regularly read in public and discussed. Most available copies of the texts in the second century will have been the work of Jewish scribes. Most interpretation of the (vast majority of) scriptural passages for which Christians had as yet found no specifically Christological reference depended on the long traditions of Jewish exegesis. Christians even relied for the text itself on a Greek version of the biblical books, the Septuagint, which they well knew to have been the work of Jews. Both Jews and pagans thought of the Jewish scriptures as the authoritative charter for the ancestral customs of the Jews, which justified and explained their insistence on peculiar Jewish observances such as the Sabbath, circumcision and food laws. The sharing of these texts was one characteristic which united Jews and Christians and differentiated them from pagans, but—and herein lay the problem for all Christians who did not think of themselves also as Jews—because Paul and others had taught already in the first generation after Jesus had been crucified that for gentiles who came to Christ it showed a lack of faith also to keep the Jewish law, most gentile Christians wanted to reject precisely the practical injunctions in the scriptures which made the lives of Jews in the ancient world distinctive.

At least one Christian in the second century, a certain Marcion, asserted firmly that true Christians should follow the logic of Paul's rejection of the Jewish law for gentiles, and rid themselves of the Jewish scriptures altogether. Marcion preached that the Demiurge, the creator of the world and the God of the Jews, was wicked, despotic and cruel; that the whole Old Testament, the product of the law of the Demiurge, should be rejected; and that the Saviour God of the Christians was an entirely different divinity. The Christian Gospel, he claimed, was entirely a Gospel of love, and the God of love, revealed by Jesus, had come to overthrow the Demiurge worshipped by the Jews. Marcion, originally from the Black Sea region, spread his doctrines particularly among the Christians of Rome, where his ideas became very influential. In his own estimation his insights had been fully appreciated before his time only by Paul. Other Christian writers, he reckoned, had been too infected by Judaism. Marcion's theology as a solution to the problem of scriptures shared with Jews was extreme, but he did deal with a real problem which faced all Christians. Treatment of the Old Testament texts in extant Christian writings from the early second century varied greatly. It was not easy both to affirm the supreme value of these writings and to deny their current validity, particularly when confronted by contemporary Jews who claimed that they continued to treat the texts as manuals for living (although many Jews, too, naturally subjected the texts to idiosyncratic interpretation of their own, as has been seen).

The perceived threat, and probably the widespread attraction, of Marcion's wholesale rejection of the Jewish roots of Christianity was reflected in the need felt in the late second century by fellow Christians from all parts of the Roman world (Corinth, Lyons, Antioch, Carthage, Edessa,

Alexandria and Rome) to mount attacks on his doctrine. But ultimately more significant for the development of Christians' relationship with Jews was the elaboration of responses to Marcionism. For most Christians it was unthinkable to reject the Old Testament, precisely because it contained the prophetic passages whose fulfilment in Christ they had preached from the first generation. Instead they read the Bible allegorically to refer to the Church, a procedure not dissimilar to the exegetical methods of the Dead Sea sectarians, Philo and the rabbis, in referring biblical narratives to contemporary Jewish society, and already used by Paul in his letter to the Galatians: "For it is written, that Abraham had two sons, the one by a bondmaid, the other by the free woman. But he who was of the bond-woman was born after the flesh; but he of the free woman was born through the promise. Which things are an allegory . . ."[22]

The usurpation of the name "Israel" by Christians like Justin Martyr in the mid-second century, alongside the consistent denigration of the name "Jew," helped Christians to present themselves to the wider Roman world, for whom the name of the Jews evoked hostility and fear after the devastation caused by the rebels of 66–70, 115–17 and 132–5. Justin Martyr himself composed an "address and petition" on behalf of Christians "to the emperor Titus Aelius Adrianus Antoninus Pius Augustus Caesar, and to his son Verissimus the philosopher, [and to Lucius the philosopher, the natural son of Caesar, and the adopted son of Pius, a lover of learning], and to the sacred Senate, and to the whole people of the Romans." The *Apology*, composed in Rome, was one of a number of pleas in defence of Christianity similarly directed to emperors in the mid- to late second century. Whether emperors ever read these texts is unknown; it is not impossible that, in practice, such apologeticism served mainly to succour the faithful. Nonetheless, these apologies all presented arguments in defence of Christianity which would have been comprehensible to Romans—and which aligned Christians firmly on the Roman side in the depiction of hostility between Romans and Jews.[23] In practice, Christians had an opportunity at least once a year to distance themselves from Jews in the eyes of the Roman state, since Christians did not register to pay the special Jewish tax which had been imposed by Rome in 70 CE, unless they wished to define themselves as Jewish as well as Christian. As the Christian Tertullian implied, writing in Carthage around the end of the second century, by not paying such a levy Christians laid themselves open to prosecution for publicly boycotting pagan cults, in contrast to Jews, who enjoyed *vectigalis libertas*, "freedom that brings in revenue [to the state]," and thus could meet openly on the Sabbath to read the Bible. It seems clear that, despite any dangers to themselves in distinguishing themselves from Jews in the presentation of their religion to Romans, Christians in the second century were determined to make such distinctions as clearly as possible, thereby avoiding the hostility towards Jews which had become engrained in Rome after the great revolts under Trajan and Hadrian. For those Christians who also wished to emphasize the roots in antiquity of their creed, and therefore to present to Romans the national history in the Old Testament as in some way Christian before Christ, it was exceptionally effective to designate themselves by the name "Israel," which, as we have seen, was not a name apparently ever used by pagan Romans to refer to Jews.[24]

The importance to Christians of presenting themselves in the most favourable light possible to Roman gentiles has not always been accorded the attention it deserves in the parting of the ways between Judaism and Christianity. Persuading Romans to accept the new faith was an integral part of the Christian message already in the time of Paul, both for missionary purposes, to encourage gentile converts, and for apologetic reasons, to defend against hostility those already committed to Christ. It was not an easy task, particularly when the figurehead of the whole movement had been publicly crucified by the Roman state (albeit, so Christians asserted, on a false charge and only under pressure from the local Jewish authorities) and followers in later years had been cruelly put to death by the state: Peter, who was crucified in Rome head downwards according to Origen in the third century and Eusebius in the fourth, and Paul, who is said to have been beheaded, and others. Some Christians, like the author of the book of Revelation, composed probably at the very end of the first century CE, simply condemned Rome as evil, much as the rabbis did. Rome was portrayed as the wicked whore of Babylon, "the Mother of harlots and abominations of the earth" in whose impending downfall and the triumph of the Church the author revelled; but his attitude of open hostility to Rome is highly unusual in extant early Christian literature. Plenty of Christian writers expressed disgust at particular aspects of the Roman world, notably sexual libertarianism, bloodthirsty entertainments such as wild beast fights and gladiatorial games, and, above all, idolatry. Tatian, a Syrian Christian writing probably in Rome in the mid-second century, in his *Ora-*

*tion to the Greeks* attacked with vituperation acting, dancing, mime, theatre, philosophy and rhetoric as well as gladiatorial shows, with special disgust for sexual perversions: "Pederasty is held criminal by barbarians, but considered privileged by Romans, and they try to gather together herds of boys like herds of grazing horses." But whereas the rabbis always inveighed against these practices as characteristic of a neighbouring society from which good Jews should keep their distance, many Christians seem to have thought about them as the sins of a society with which they identified and which they wished to reform from within. As Melito of Sardis asserts in his *Apology* addressed to the emperor Marcus Aurelius, "our philosophy [Christianity] first flourished among barbarians, but having come to flower among your peoples at the time of the great reign of Augustus your ancestor, it became particularly for your empire an auspicious benefit. Since then the might of the Romans has increased to be great and splendid." Already in the first century, the author of the Gospel of Luke and of Acts portrayed to his fellow Christians both Jesus and Paul as at home in the Roman world and innocent of any actions contrary to Roman interests. Hence the repeated protestations of Pilate as recorded by Luke, that "I find no fault in this man . . . I have found no cause of death in him," even though it was Pilate who eventually "gave sentence that it should be as they [the Jewish leaders] required." Paul was acquitted of wrongdoing, according to the author of Acts, by a series of just Roman governors before finally being sent to Rome. The message was that the teachings of the Christians were politically harmless, as Paul urges to Festus in Jerusalem: "Neither against the law of the Jews, neither against the Temple, nor yet against Caesar, have I offended anything at all."[25]

The need for such protestations that Christians should be accepted in Roman society was prompted in part by the accusations of some pagans that Christians were not only outsiders but positively dangerous. The alleged secrecy of Christian communities gave rise to accusations of immoral behaviour, as the African Christian Minucius Felix recorded in the second or third century: "Why do they make great efforts to hide and conceal whatever it is that they worship, when honourable deeds always rejoice in being made public, while crimes are secret? Why do they have no altars, no temples, no recognized images? Why do they never talk openly, never congregate freely, unless what they worship and conceal is either criminal or shameful?" Since Christians sometimes attacked each other for similar behaviour, it is not wholly impossible that there was something real behind the polemic, and that the desire of mainstream Christians to distance themselves from those, particularly in Gnostic groups, they dubbed heretics was motivated in part by the need to be able to claim with a clear conscience to the outside world that genuine Christians would never commit such immoral acts. Jews had been subject to similar attacks, but it is striking that their mode of defence, at least as reflected in Josephus' *Against Apion*, had been different from that of Christians: Josephus counters the charge that Jews "refuse admission to persons with other preconceived ideas about God, and [decline] to associate with those who have chosen to adopt a different mode of life" by stating that this habit is common to all people, whereas the unknown author of the *Epistle to Diognetus* explicitly denies that Christians live apart in separate cities of their own, speak any special dialect or practise any eccentric way of life. Many Christians wished to be seen by Romans as part of the Roman world and dedicated to the flourishing of the society they shared with pagans. They were part of a counter-culture only in the limited sense that, if forced to choose, they put divine authority above that of the emperor—which created no problem so long as there was no conflict between the two: as Jesus was reported to have said, "Render to Caesar, what is Caesar's, to God, what is God's." Christian apologists on the one hand denied with outrage the wicked behaviour alleged by their detractors, while claiming that their prayers for the state could be efficacious in a way that no pagan prayer could ever be. When the troops of Marcus Aurelius were saved by a sudden rainstorm from drought and defeat during his campaign on the Danube in 172, contemporary Christians attributed the miracle to the prayers of Christians among his soldiers. Some twenty or more years later, Tertullian claimed that this miracle was specifically mentioned by Marcus Aurelius, "most venerable of emperors," in his letters. Doubtless the letters were Christian forgeries: Tertullian was still a boy at the time of the events. The story grew in the telling, and when it was narrated by Eusebius, over a century later, there were further details, including that "lightning drove the enemy to flight and destruction." What matters is less the detail of the story than the underlying assumption, that Christians were, and should be, dedicated to the security and prosperity of the empire despite the occasional attempts by representatives of the state to subject them to persecution.[26]

Christian hopes for the conversion of the Roman empire were not diminished by such persecution. Tertullian addresses those in authority in the empire—described ironically as the "good governors," who are "most just"—to persuade them not to follow the demands of the mob "panting for Christian blood." The theme of Christian apologies was that persecutions arose through the actions of "evil men trying to stir up trouble against us," and that the Roman state, if it followed its own tenets of justice, would suppress such wickedness. So Melito of Sardis, in his *Apology* addressed to Marcus Aurelius after "new decrees throughout Asia" threatened persecution, claims that "shameless informers and lovers of other people's property . . . pillage us openly . . . [although] we have done nothing wrong . . . If this is done as your command, let it be assumed that it is well done . . . but, if it be not from you that there comes this counsel and this new decree, which would be improper even against barbarian enemies, we beseech you all the more not to neglect us when we are subjected to this mass brigandage." As reported by Eusebius, martyrdoms of Christians at Lyons in 177 were pressed upon the Roman governor by local pagans who saw the Christians in their city as dangerous outsiders. It was possible and reasonable for Christians to hope that the state, far from instigating persecution, would suppress it, even if sometimes they hoped in vain.[27]

In fact, most attacks on Christians were indeed locally inspired, and large-scale persecution of Christians by the Roman state was rare. In each case there was a specific reason for the state to take public action against Christians, although not necessarily as a result of anything in particular done by Christians themselves—in this respect the state behaved towards Christians much as it did towards the Jews of the city of Rome when they suffered periodic expulsions under the Julio-Claudian emperors. Thus the first great persecution of Christians broke out in Rome in 64 after a fire had devastated Rome. Despite the expenditure of vast sums for rebuilding and improving security in the future, and a series of religious ceremonies to appease the gods, Nero found himself still unpopular, with rumours that the fire had been started deliberately. According to Tacitus, writing half a century later, "to suppress this rumour, Nero fabricated scapegoats—and punished with every refinement the notoriously depraved Christians (as they were popularly called) . . . Their deaths were made farcical. Dressed in wild animals' skins, they were torn to pieces by dogs, or crucified, or made into torches to be ignited after dark as substitutes for daylight. Nero provided his gardens for the spectacle, and exhibited a display in the circus, mingling with the crowd—or standing in a chariot, dressed as a chariot-eer." Interestingly, Tacitus' contemporary Suetonius gave as cause of this awful persecution not the alleged incendiarism of the Christians, which he ignored, but their trouble-making beliefs, which put them into the same category as perpetrators of other abuses suppressed by Nero: "Punishment was inflicted on the Christians, a class of men of a new and mischievous superstition. He [also] put an end to the jests of the chariot drivers [accused of cheating and robbing for their amusement] . . . The pantomime actors and their supporters were banished from the city." It is not, of course, impossible that Nero's government combined different charges against the Christians. It was easier to blame Christians for the disaster if they were thought to be inherently troublesome, regardless of their guilt or inno-cence in this specific case.[28]

That after this persecution by Nero there was to be no central initiative by the emperors themselves against the Christians for nearly two hundred years may help to explain the optimism of the Christian apologists in aligning themselves with the state, although when the attack came, its impact was all the more horrific. In 249 the emperor Decius decreed that steps be taken to ensure that everyone in the empire (apart, presumably, from Jews) be shown to have sacrificed to the gods on behalf of the welfare of the state. His motivation was probably less hostility to Christians than a desire to unite the empire through a single cultic act at a time of military crisis precipitated by invasions across the Danube, but the impact on Chris-tians of his policy was immediate. Discovery in Egypt of certificates to confirm that an individual had sacrificed as required reveal how thoroughly the policy was carried out, at least in that province. In the city of Rome, the bishop Fabian who led the Christian community was killed, while many other Christians gave in under the pressure. The resulting schism, between the lapsed and those who, through courage or good fortune, had been able to hold firm, was almost as serious a threat to the Church as the persecution itself. Decius died in 251, and his religious campaign ended, but his successor Valerian in 257 resurrected a policy of attacks on Chris-tian clergy and property, forbidding Christians to meet. On the capture of Valerian by the Persians in 260, the new emperor Gallienus proclaimed an end to all religious persecution, and Christians were left in peace for more than forty years until Diocletian in 303 ordered the demolition of churches and the burning of Christian books. Like Decius, Diocletian was probably prompted by a desire to reinforce imperial unity: his reforms during his long rule from 284 to 306 constituted an attempt at a systematic reorganization of the empire on a par with the interventionist policies of Hadrian nearly two centuries earlier. It may be that an attack on Christians commended itself precisely because they were spread throughout the empire, and state action against them as "atheists," and thus for the goodwill of the other gods, would be witnessed by Diocletian's subjects all over the Roman world. In any case, his edict certainly provoked widespread unrest, which in turn promoted further edicts and many martyrdoms, with peace restored only by the ascent to power of Constantine through military victory on 28 October 312, and an edict of toleration for all religions proclaimed the following year in Milan.[29]

Christians were thus subjected only to brief outbursts of organized, empire-wide persecution by the state, but these episodes inflicted deep trauma. Christians developed a tradition that they were constantly at risk from Rome throughout the three hundred years before Constantine. It was indeed the case throughout this period that when and if a Christian was accused by provincials it was a Roman magistrate who put him or her to death. Stories of the martyrdom of early Christians reveal remarkable courage in the face of torture and death, supported by a strong confidence in the eventual promise of salvation in a future life. Roman officials simply did not understand the depth of their faith and commitment. In the contemporary account of the death of Polycarp, aged eighty-six, in Smyrna, the proconsul of Asia is portrayed as trying hard to save the aged bishop, urging him to "have respect for [his] age," but in the end it was the proconsul who ordered the execution, "sending his own herald to announce three times in the middle of the arena: 'Polycarp has confessed that he is a Christian.'" Correspondence of the younger Pliny with Trajan earlier in the second century about how to treat those accused of being Christians reveals an assumption that simply being a Christian and refusing to worship the pagan gods could be sufficient to merit death. Pliny wrote that "for the moment this is the line I have taken with all persons brought before me on the charge of being Christians. I have asked them in person if they are Christians, and if they admit it, I repeat the question a second and third time, with a warning of the punishment awaiting them. If they persist, I order them to be led away for execution; for, whatever the nature of their admission, I am convinced that their stubbornness and unshakeable obstinacy ought not to go unpunished." Trajan replied that Pliny had acted rightly, "for it is impossible to lay down a general rule to a fixed formula. These people must not be hunted out. If they are brought before you and the charge against them is proved, they must be punished, but in the case of anyone who denies that he is a Christian, and makes it clear that he is not by offering prayers to our gods, he is to be pardoned as a result of his repentance however suspect his past conduct may be." If "these people must not be hunted out," the safety of Christians depended not on the policy of the Roman state but on their relations to their pagan neighbours, whose hostility, if aroused, could be fatal.[30]

In practice, most Christians lived quite peacefully for the first three centuries of the Church, but accounts of martyrdoms served as powerful confirmation of the validity of Christian faith. From the second century onwards, martyrology became a distinctive Christian literary genre. It was uplifting to read about the devotion of those prepared to die horribly for their faith. Eusebius in the fourth century knew of "trophies" of the apostles Paul and Peter which commemorated their martyrdoms in Rome. The original monument to Peter seems to have been an unpretentious structure built around 170 and found below the apse of the church of St. Peter built in the fourth century by Constantine. A more substantial memorial to Peter and Paul was erected on the Appian Way south of Rome in the mid-third century and was a focus for private prayers scratched as graffiti on its walls. By this time celebrations at the burial sites of local martyrs in Christian cemeteries had become so important for Roman Christians that their commemoration was firmly fixed into the liturgical calendar. The memorable image coined by Tertullian in the late second century was an accurate historical analysis: "we increase in number whenever we are mown down . . . the blood of Christians is seed."[31]

For a Roman governor like the younger Pliny in the early second century, the Christians whom he put on trial were defined by their worship of Christ, in whose honour "they chant verses alternately among themselves . . . as if to a god." Nothing in his description of the "great many individuals of every age and class, both men and women," from both towns and countryside, who had been "infected through contact with this wretched cult," suggested that they had anything whatever to do with Jews. The same was true of Pliny's contemporary Tacitus, who did indeed note that the founder of this "deadly superstition" had been executed in

Tiberius' reign by Pontius Pilate in Judaea, and that after Christ's death the "mischief" had continued in Judaea, but vaguely attributed the popularity of Christianity in Rome to the disgraceful predilections of the inhabitants of the city, "where all things horrible or shameful in the world collect and find a vogue." Evidently, by the time Trajan was emperor no pagan Roman would think of Christianity as a type of Judaism, not least because the insistence that Christians must make sacrifices to "our gods," taken for granted by both Pliny and Trajan, had never been imposed by Roman officials on Jews: the sacrifice test imposed briefly on the Jews of Antioch in 66 had been applied by the Greek city authorities, not the Roman governor. The religious logic behind the punishment of Christians was precisely that they should return to their ancestral pagan rites, as Pliny claimed was happening in his province as a result of his actions: "There is no doubt that people have begun to throng the temples which had been almost entirely deserted for a long time. The sacred rites which had been allowed to lapse are being performed again, and flesh of sacrificial victims is on sale everywhere, though up till recently scarcely anyone could be found to buy it." By contrast, Jews in Pliny's time will all, in principle, have been known to the Roman state, since they were all required to pay the annual Jewish poll tax, and none of them will have been required to sacrifice to pagan gods. Pliny's contemporary Suetonius specifically describes the Christians in the time of Nero as given to a *new* superstition.[32]

In fact, in marked contrast to the agonizing in extant Christian sources about the relationship between the new faith and Judaism, extant pagan Roman sources are consistent in referring to the members of the Church as "Christians," a name which itself suggests a Roman perspective on the new movement. "The disciples were called 'Christians' first in Antioch": so writes the author of Acts in his reconstruction of the early history of the Church, referring to the time spent in the city by Paul and Barnabas near the very beginning of their missionary journeys, in about 40. The comment presupposed both that the name was not an obvious one to use, and that it was more common when Acts was composed in the late first century than it was in the years to which the narrative referred. "Christian" was not a self-designation used by Paul in his extant letters—he preferred to refer to his fellow believers as "the saints" or "brethren" or by other periphrases—and in the other books in the New Testament the terms used are "disciples," "believers" and other words which functioned more as descriptions than as proper names. In the only two other uses of the name "Christian" in the New Testament writings, it is put, either explicitly or implicitly, into the mouth of a non-believer: according to Acts, when Paul defends himself before Agrippa II and Berenice in Caesarea, Agrippa remarks, in admiration, "Paul, almost you persuade me to be a Christian"; in the first letter of Peter, composed almost certainly after 70, the author encourages his readers "if [any man suffer] as a Christian, let him not be ashamed, but let him glorify God on his behalf."[33]

It is likely, then, that *Christianos* was a term used for the followers of the new movement originally by outsiders, and, since the word is a Latinism, those outsiders were probably Roman. (Such a Latinism was not impossible for Greek speakers, but a Greek name to mean "the party of *Christos*" would usually be expected to end in *-eios,* not *-ianos.*) If Acts is right to date the first use of the word "Christian" to Antioch in *c.* 40, it will have been the Roman officials there who invented the term, rather than the local populace, or Jews, or Christians themselves. The implication of the name in Latin was that Christians were the party of Christ. Tacitus, in his account of the fire in Rome in 64, states explicitly that this was the name in common use for members of the Church already in Nero's time. For Pliny, and later pagan writers, the name was standard. It is all the more striking that by the early second century Ignatius, bishop of Antioch, had adopted the term to refer to himself and his flock. In his letter to the community in Ephesus, he expresses his hope to "share the lot of the Ephesian Christians," and to the Magnesians, he writes quite specifically that "it is fitting not only to be called Christians, but also to be [Christians]." He even uses an abstract word, *Christianismos,* derived from *Christianos,* to describe the new faith. Around the same date, the author of the *Didache,* a manual containing both ethical and ritual instructions for Christian communities, also termed an itinerant brother who "comes in the name of the Lord" as a *Christianos,* provided that he is genuine and behaving appropriately: "if he does not want to behave like this, he is a *Christemporos* [a "Christmonger"]," to be avoided. In martyr acts which purport to be transcripts of trials before Roman authorities in the second century, the martyrs accept the name willingly: "Rusticus said: 'Finally, are you then a Christian?' Justin said: 'Yes, I am a Christian.'" When it came to witnessing to their faith at times of greatest stress and danger, what these martyrs urged to their Roman audience was the lordship and divinity of Christ. A certain Sanctus, martyred at Lyons in 177, withstood tortures "with such constancy that he would not even tell his own name, nor race, nor city of origin, nor whether he was slave or free, but to all the questions replied in Latin: 'I am a Christian.' " What defined the religion of Christians was simply the God to whom they owed allegiance. According to both the pagan and the Christian accounts, neither Roman nor Christian at these times of trial ever made any mention of the link between Christianity and the Jews.[34]

Thus it was to the lordship of Christ rather than the God of the Jews that the Roman emperor Constantine in 312 declared his allegiance. Constantine's espousal of Christ as his protector seems to have stemmed from motivations similar to those of Roman leaders earlier in imperial history. As Venus had been the patron deity of Julius Caesar and Mars of Augustus, and as Aurelian, who ruled from autumn 270 to early 275, attempted to establish the worship of the Unconquered Sun at the centre of Roman state religion, with himself as the god's vicegerent, Constantine believed that he had come to power through the support of Christ, and that his rule would therefore be best maintained by devotion to Christian worship. What distinguished Constantine's devotion to his chosen divinity from that of his predecessors to theirs was the demanding nature of Christian worship, including especially the antipathy of Christians to the worship of other gods.

Constantine had much need of such divine support. His father, Constantius I, had been a soldier of Illyrian stock who was appointed as Caesar in 293 when the emperor Diocletian tried to institute a system of collegiate government for the empire, with two senior members ("Augusti") and two junior ("Caesars"). By the time of his death in York on 25 July 306, Constantius was the senior Augustus. Constantius' troops proclaimed his son Constantine as a new Augustus, but this was not acceptable to the other members of the tetrarchy, and for the next six years Constantine tried to establish his right to power in the fashion standard in imperial politics, by dynastic marriages and by war. In 312 he invaded Italy to unseat Maxentius, son of the former Augustus Maximian, who (like Constantine) had struck out for himself. In a battle near Verona Maxentius' forces were defeated and his prefect killed. Despite being heavily outnumbered, Constantine marched on Rome and met the army under Maxentius' personal command just outside the city, at Saxa Rubra. What happened next was famously described soon after the event by the Christian apologist Lactantius:

Constantine was advised in his sleep to mark the heavenly sign of God on the shields and then engage in battle. He did as he was commanded and by means of a slanted letter X with the top of its head bent round, he marked Christ on the shields. Armed with this sign, the army took up its weapons. The enemy came to meet them . . . the lines clashed . . . the fighting became fiercer, and the hand of God was over the battle-line. The army of Maxentius was seized with terror, and he himself fled in haste to the bridge, which had been broken down; and, pressed by the mass of fugitives, he was hurtled into the Tiber.[35]

By the end of his life, Constantine was to claim that in the battle itself he had seen a miraculous image of a cross above the sun, with the words, "Be victorious in this."[36] The event seems to have gained in significance with the passage of time, but there is no reason to doubt that Constantine's troops went into battle with Christian signs on their shields, nor that a great victory ensued. Maxentius was drowned near the modern Ponte Milvio. It was to take time for the full implications of Constantine's new religious allegiance to become clear, and he was not himself baptized until shortly before his death on 22 May 337, but from the beginning he tried to unite the Church to the secular state as closely as possible, and his success may be gauged from the fact that in the eastern Church he was in due course to be named the Thirteenth Apostle and venerated as a saint. His devotion to Christ was to be imitated by his sons and successors for generations and would lead directly to the Christian Europe of the Middle Ages. As so often in the Roman world, the personal decision of an emperor, himself primarily concerned to create and maintain his image as a military leader blessed with divine favour, had a momentous effect on the ideology of all of Roman society.

That Christianity became the dominant religion in the Roman world by the late fourth century would have been impossible without this very personal commitment by Constantine and his successors, but it is important to recognize how "Roman" the mainstream Church had already become before Constantine became its patron, despite the concurrent Christian attitude to the state as the source of persecution. Even the administrative structure used by Christians mirrored the provinces and cities of the secular organization of the empire, with government by bishops based in the major urban communities and councils of bishops convened usually at the behest of the bishop of one of the largest communities, such as Alexandria, Antioch, Carthage or Rome: reference to bishops (in Greek, *episkopoi*, literally "overseers") as leaders of the new Christian communities founded in the cities of Asia Minor in the first generation is already found in the New Testament. Although the distinction between those accorded this title and those called "presbyters" may not always have been clear in the first century, by the middle of the second century all the leading centres of Christianity were led by bishops, each of whom exercised quasi-monarchical authority over his flock. By the late third century the central role of Jerusalem in the Christian hierarchy had all but vanished along with the link to contemporary Jews. In the first century, before 70 it was to Jerusalem, according to Acts, that Paul went to gain permission for his mission to the gentiles at the first Church council, but by the early 250s the Christian presence in Jerusalem, now of course the Roman colony of Aelia Capitolina, was slight: since 135 all Christians in the city were of gentile origin, and the link with the family of Jesus, and with James, "the Lord's brother," had been broken. By contrast, by the mid-third century the community in Rome was large. Eusebius reported that under the bishop Cornelius there were, according to Cornelius himself, forty-six presbyters in the city, seven deacons, seven sub-deacons, forty-two acolytes, fifty-two exorcists, readers and doorkeepers, and over one thousand five hundred widows and persons in distress, "a great multitude . . . a number who by God's providence were rich and increasing, with an immense and countless laity." Cornelius, and Eusebius, evidently gave these figures (around the time of the Decian persecution) because they were large in the Christian context. They seem to imply a total Christian community in Rome at least in the tens of thousands (and confirmation that, except in times of organized state persecution, Christian congregations were generally left alone).[37]

But even much earlier, when the Christian community in Rome was still small in Christian terms, the very fact that it was at the heart of the empire had given it an importance beyond its size. It was here that the two great apostles Peter and Paul were buried. Clement, bishop of Rome in the late first century, had intervened when there was a conflict among the Christians in Corinth. Irenaeus, bishop of Lyons in the late second century, referred his readers to "the greatest, most ancient and well-known church, founded and established by the most glorious apostles, Peter and Paul, in

Rome." Irenaeus went further than praise, suggesting that "with this church, on account of her more powerful principality, it is necessary that every church should agree." The stage was already set in the third century for Rome and its bishop to take over the leadership of the Church as a whole, particularly in the western empire, in the fourth century. The gradual emergence of the Roman papacy in its full form was ultimately dependent on the changed attitude of the state after Constantine's vision and his victory by the Ponte Milvio, but long before Constantine the origins of Christianity in a community of Jews in Jerusalem had ceased to be of much significance in the faith of most of those who lived and died for Christ.[38]

Thus, when the conversion of Constantine to Christianity brought values from first-century Jerusalem to fourth-century Rome, the history of Christian self-presentation over the preceding centuries prevented the emperor from recognizing his new religious allegiance as in any respect Jewish. On the contrary, the state pronouncements of the Christian emperor were even more profoundly hostile to Judaism than those of his pagan predecessors, as can be seen in the vituperative tone of a law promulgated by Constantine on 18 October in, probably, the year 329: "Emperor Constantine Augustus to Evagrius, praetorian prefect. We wish the Jews, their leaders and their patriarchs to be informed, that if anyone—once this law has been given—dare attack by stoning or by other kind of fury one escaping from their deadly sect and raising his eyes to God's cult, which as we have learned is being done now, he shall be delivered immediately to the flames and burned with all his accomplices." Similar hostility to the Jews and Judaism was expressed by the emperor in other pronouncements, like the letter he sent to all the churches in the empire on 19 June 325 about the date of Easter: "Let there be nothing in common between you and the detestable mob of the Jews . . . What could those people calculate correctly, when after that murder of the Lord, after that parricide, they have taken leave of their senses, and are moved, not by any rational principle, but by uncontrolled impulse, wherever their internal frenzy may lead them?"

Constantine evidently saw such anti-Judaism as part of his expression of his new-found faith, to which he ostentatiously devoted himself. Huge sums were spent on building new churches, which were to house a distinctive form of worship without sacrifices. The emperor threw himself into trying to settle doctrinal disputes within the Christian community, in the explicit belief that Christian unity was essential for the well-being of the state. Privileges, wealth and access to the imperial court were showered upon the Christian clergy. Above all, a new rhetoric of Christian piety, high-flown and often vague, became standard in court parlance, even in the promulgation of law. Constantine portrayed his reign as an ideological revolution, a decisive break from the crude pagan past to a bright Christian future. Vituperation against Jews was part of this discourse, an element of Christian rhetoric that had developed over the period of self-definition in relation to Judaism in the first two centuries of the Church.[39]

How far had the Christianity adopted by Constantine strayed from its Jewish roots? Christians like him did not follow most of the customs which made Jews distinctive in the eyes of their fellow citizens, such as the Sabbath, circumcision and dietary laws. They talked less about physical purity as a metaphor for sanctity and more about sexual asceticism. They saw marriage as an unbreakable bond rather than a contract between man and wife. They revered the same Bible as the Jews but reinterpreted it in the light of a New Testament that did away with the plain meaning of the shared text. And (crucially) they saw no value in animal sacrifices, had no desire to worship God in any temple, and so had no interest in the rebuilding of the Temple of Jerusalem.

On the other hand Christians like Constantine preserved the Jewish notion of history as a divinely ordained progression from creation to final judgement. Like Jews, they placed high value on sacred time (leading to intense debates about, as we have seen, the correct date to celebrate Easter each year). They believed, like Jews, that God had laid down how humans should live well, and they shared the Jewish notions of sin, guilt, confession, repentance and divine forgiveness for those who strayed. Members of Christian communities supported each other as Jews did in their synagogues, with similar opposition to infanticide and similar emphasis on charity and the duty to care for widows and orphans. Like Jews they were puritanical about indulgence in sex outside marriage and prudish about nudity. And, as we have seen, Christians, like Jews, adamantly refused to participate in the worship of gods other than their own.

The successful imposition of such alien ideals on traditional Roman society, even by the most forceful of emperors, was necessarily difficult. Theatrical performances, dance, gladiatorial games, wild beast shows, all continued in the fourth century, popular despite the disgust expressed by some Christians, much as they had flourished in the early empire despite the disapproval of some thoughtful pagans like the younger Pliny. But Christianity under Constantine did bring some changes to Rome. Thus, for instance, in recognition of the belief that man is made in the image of God, Constantine wrote on 3 March 316 to Eumelius, governor of Africa, that "if any person should be condemned to the arena or to the mines, in accordance with the nature of the crime in which he has been detected, let him not be branded on his face, since the penalty of condemnation can be branded by one mark on his hands and on his calves, so that the face, which has been made in the likeness of celestial beauty, may not be disfigured." While the history of the Jews was decried as the travails of a "detestable mob," the history of Israel and of the Hebrews became also the history of Rome: in Eusebius' account, in his *Ecclesiastical History*, of the defeat and death of Maxentius at the Ponte Milvio, the model for Constantine's victory was taken not from ancient Rome but from Moses: "As . . . in the days of Moses himself and the ancient and godly race of the Hebrews, 'Pharaoh's chariots and his host has he cast into the sea, his chosen horsemen, even captains, they were sunk in the Red Sea, the deep covered them'; in the same way also Maxentius and the armed soldiers and guards around him 'went down into the depths like a stone' . . . He himself, that most wicked of men, and then also the shield-bearers around him, as the divine oracles foretell, sank as lead in the mighty waters."[40]

Constantine spoke the Jewish language of monolatry and of disgust at the veneration of idols even if he refrained from the use of force to ensure that the temples closed, explaining that "the customs of the temples and the agency of darkness" would have been removed altogether "were it not that the violent rebelliousness of injurious error is so obstinately fixed in the minds of some, to the detriment of the common weal." In his panegyrical biography after Constantine's death, Eusebius praised the impact of the emperor on the distribution, through Church institutions, of charity to the very poor, "in one place bestowing estates, and elsewhere grain allowances to feed poor men, orphan children, and women in distress. Then with great concern he also provided huge quantities of clothing for the naked and unclad." Attitudes to sex became markedly more puritanical, at least in public: in an imperial court dominated by Christian moralizing, not least on the lips of the emperor himself, it became impossible to imagine a writer seeking advancement by composing verse like Ovid's descriptions of the art of love or novels like Petronius' *Satyricon* or Apuleius' *Golden Ass*—sex was no longer amusing or entertaining in a society where, from 326, the emperor forbade any married man to have a concubine in his house, and nurses who encouraged girls to elope were to be horribly put to death: "the mouth and throat of those who offered nefarious incitements shall be closed by ingestion of molten lead." Familiar to Jews would have been the weekly abstention of all townspeople from work, including legal business, enforced by Constantine in a law promulgated in 321 and evidently in operation as far away as Oxyrhynchus in Egypt in 325: a papyrus preserves a report, dated to 2 October 325, of legal proceedings over ownership of some buildings or building land, the day's business ending with the decision of the judge that "since some part of the coming sacred Lord's Day has supervened, the case will be deferred till after the Lord's Day." Constantine permitted farm labour on his day of rest, so to that extent it differed from the Jewish Sabbath on which agricultural work was specifically prohibited, and the day selected was not Saturday but "the Lord's Day," Sunday, but the Jewish rhythm of the seven-day week was now firmly established in Roman life.[41]

In a speech delivered in Jerusalem in 336 to celebrate the thirtieth anniversary of Constantine as emperor of Rome, the Christian Eusebius used rhetoric that would have struck a chord with the Jew Josephus two and a half centuries earlier. Josephus had praised the one-ness of Judaism: God is one, Jews have only one belief about God, "we have but one Temple for the one God, for 'like is always dear to like.' " Eusebius' argument to praise the Christian monarch was similar:

Invested as he is with an image of the heavenly sovereignty, he directs his gaze above, and frames his earthly government according to the pattern of that original, gaining strength in its imitation of the monarchy of God. And this conformity is granted by the universal King to man alone of the creatures on this earth: for he only is the author of royal power, who decrees that all should be subject to the rule of one . . . There is one King; and his word and royal law is one: a Law not expressed in words and syllables, not written or engraved on tablets, and therefore subject to the ravages of time; but the living and

self-subsisting Word, who himself is God, and who administers his
Father's kingdom on behalf of all who are under him and subject to his
power.

One God, one Word, one ruler.[42]

Constantine's preparation of his final resting place when he died in 337
shows that he wished to be remembered by future generations as consort-
ing, as Jesus had done, with the pious Galilean Jews who had accompanied
Jesus to Jerusalem three hundred years before. "He erected twelve reposi-
tories like sacred monuments in honour and memory of the company of
the Apostles, and put his own coffin in the middle with those of the Apostles ranged six on either side . . . in the belief that their memorial would
become for him a beneficial aid to his soul." Nothing, it might seem, could
better illustrate the migration of the values of Jerusalem to the heart of
Rome—except that neither Constantine nor his Christian subjects
thought of the Holy Apostles as Jewish, and this Roman emperor erected
his monumental tomb-shrine not in the ancient Rome where Augustus lay
in his mausoleum, but in a new Rome, the city of Constantinople freshly
built on the site of Byzantium.[43]

# CHAPTER FOURTEEN

# A NEW ROME AND
# A NEW JERUSALEM

## URBS VENERABILIS AND ALTERA ROMA

I N THE SECOND half of the fourth century the pagan historian Ammianus Marcellinus saw Rome as a city past her prime: "Declining into
old age, and often owing victory to its name alone, it [Rome] has come to
a quieter period of life. Thus the venerable city, after humbling the proud
necks of savage nations, and making laws, the everlasting foundations and
moorings of liberty, like a thrifty parent, wise and wealthy, has entrusted
the management of her inheritance to the Caesars, as to her children."
The process of decline from centre of power to venerated symbol was
already well advanced when Constantine entered the city as conqueror on
28 October 312. Already for decades, most emperors had chosen to rule
from elsewhere in order to be closer to the frontier armies on whose support their power depended. Emperors preferred to live in the East, at Antioch or Thessalonica, or at Sirmium in the Balkans, or at Trier or Milan,
gracing the city of Rome with only brief symbolic visits.[1]

Rome nonetheless remained a city much larger than others in the
empire. The population still relied on huge supplies of oil, wine, grain and
timber imported into Ostia by ship from Africa, southern Italy, Sicily,
Provence and Spain and brought up the river Tiber to the city wharves.
The great aqueducts were kept in good repair. So too were the roads leading to all parts of Rome's dominions: the Via Appia going south to Naples,
the Via Flaminia tracing its way to the northern Adriatic and the Danube,
and the rest of the highway network which had accompanied and enabled
the acquisition of empire. The Senate continued to meet and legitimize
imperial acts, though patently only as a formality. The city's monuments—

statues, arches, forums, commemorative columns—were reminders of what had been achieved. The great senatorial families, some of whom had acquired vast wealth, still saw the city as the pre-eminent place to display their influence. The impressive new defensive city walls erected by Aurelian and Probus in the 270s, and raised to double their original height in 309–12, encompassed a vast area, not all of it built up. There had been new building under Diocletian, notably a vast new baths complex and a rebuilt Senate house, the Curia, which had been destroyed by a fire; and between 306 and 312 Maxentius had overseen an extensive building programme, rebuilding Hadrian's temple of Venus and Rome, burned down by accident in 306, and constructing a huge new basilica in the Forum. So Rome was by no means in decay, but it lacked the excitement and importance it had had in the age of Augustus. In the absence of the emperor and imperial patronage, it was for much of the time a prisoner of its own past, surrounded by nostalgic reminders of the time when the debates of senators and the clamour of the urban mob in the Forum could shape the future of the whole Mediterranean world.

In the physical appearance of this ancient city the presence of Christianity was almost invisible. "House churches," as the name suggests, looked just like other houses from the outside, blending in with the tenements, workshops and other buildings in the residential areas, and excluded from the public spaces on the Palatine and in the various forums. In this respect, at least, the change under Constantine was to be dramatic, although not, probably, as overwhelming as he desired: he was perhaps constrained in his early years by the need to win over to his side by public munificence an urban populace which had warmed to his rival Maxentius, not least because Maxentius was the last of Rome's rulers to make his residence in the capital. Constantine's intention to turn Rome into a Christian city so far as he could was signalled soon after his victory in 312 by the decision to build a large basilica for the use of the bishop of Rome on the Caelian hill, just inside the Aurelian walls, some way to the east of the ancient monumental centre of the city around the Capitol. The building was deliberately huge and magnificent, but it was hidden from the view of most Romans, and the site seems to have been available for building only because it belonged to Constantine's wife, Fausta. The gift to the Church was by the emperor, not the state, and the new basilica, among mansions and gardens rather than temples and forums, was discreetly tucked away at the edge of the city.

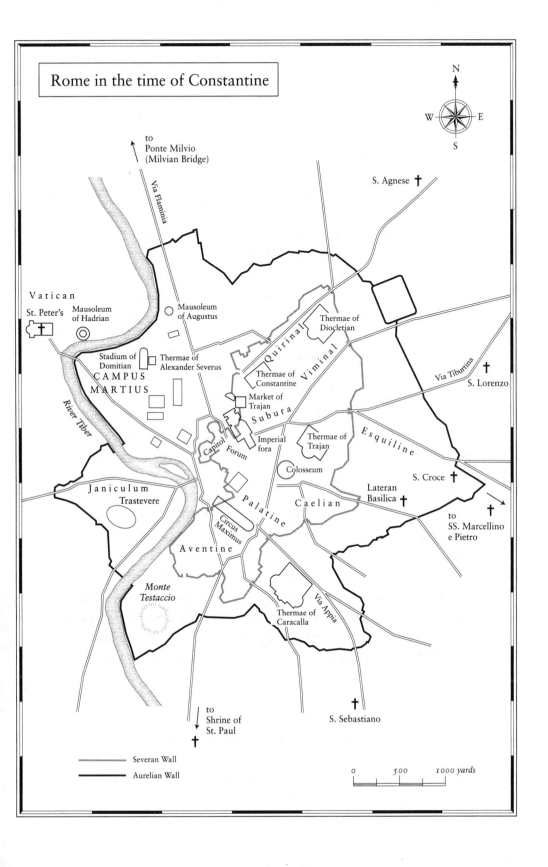

Rome in the time of Constantine

N
W E
S

to
Ponte Milvio
(Milvian Bridge)

S. Agnese ✝

Via Flaminia

Vatican
St. Peter's  Mausoleum
of Hadrian   ○ Mausoleum
of Augustus

Thermae of
Diocletian

Quirinal

Viminal

Via Tiburtina ✝
S. Lorenzo

Stadium of
Domitian   Thermae of
Alexander Severus
CAMPUS
MARTIUS

Thermae of
Constantine

Market of
Trajan

Subura

River Tiber

Imperial
fora

Thermae of
Trajan

Esquiline

Capitol Forum

S. Croce ✝

Colosseum

Lateran
Basilica ✝

Janiculum
Trastevere

Palatine

Caelian

✝
to
SS. Marcellino
e Pietro

Circus
Maximus

Aventine

Monte
Testaccio

Via Appia

Thermae of
Caracalla

to
Shrine of
St. Paul
✝

S. Sebastiano ✝

———— Severan Wall
———— Aurelian Wall

0      500      1000 yards

Even more discreet was the only other great church built by Constantine within the walls. To the north-east of the Lateran, the church of S. Croce in Gerusalemme was founded, probably in the 320s, within an existing palace hall. Viewed from outside, the church looked like just one of the buildings in the complex used by the imperial family, its special Christian character essentially private to the emperor and his Christian friends.[2]

That the reticence of Constantine's building within the city walls was to some extent imposed on him rather than voluntary is suggested by the contrast with his Christianizing of the landscape of the surrounding countryside, where there was less competition with pagan temples. The burial sites of martyrs had long been venerated by local Christians, albeit in modest ways. Now magnificent basilicas, mostly on imperial property, were built near catacombs, to serve as burial grounds for the faithful, as centres for pilgrimage on the martyrs' anniversaries, and as a clear, public statement of imperial favour for a faith once persecuted. The vast church of St. Sebastian, built over the cult centre of the apostles on the Appian Way, was crowded with graves on the floor and along its walls; another basilica, even larger, stood by the Via Tiburtina next to the tomb of St. Laurence; a third, attached to the tombs of the martyrs Marcellinus and Peter, was augmented by a mausoleum, still extant, in which Constantine's mother Helena was laid to rest. Most impressive of all was St. Peter's, erected despite the physical difficulties on the sloping shoulder of the Vatican hill, enclosing the existing necropolis, in which, although the Christian tombs were only a minority among the pagan graves, the architects took great care to maintain access to the cemetery where the bones of St. Peter were supposed to lie. The shrine of the martyr was made the focus of the basilica, the upper part of the memorial to the saint remaining above the large artificial terrace which overlay the necropolis and formed the floor of the church. As in the other buildings erected by Constantine in Rome for the glory of the Christian God, St. Peter's impressed by its vast size, grand interior and lavish furnishing in gold and silver. The exterior, though visible from afar, was simple and unadorned.

Through such imaginative projects Constantine amply demonstrated his own religious commitment and made more than sufficient provision for the needs of the local Christian community. St. Peter's can rarely have been filled even on days of special pilgrimage to pray at the martyr's tomb. But Constantine also demonstrated inadvertently that what he could bring about outside the city walls, with imperial largesse lavished on imperial property directly under his control, was less feasible in the monumental centre of the ancient city on land belonging to the state, where major public building might risk arousing hostility by the demolition of existing public structures. Here Constantine built like emperors before him, and in particular like his rival Maxentius, completing the great new basilica for secular commercial use which had been begun under Maxentius in the Forum but was now to bear Constantine's name and house his colossal statue. On the Quirinal he built new baths almost as large as those erected before him by Caracalla and Diocletian. But, apart from the "saving sign" (of the Cross? or the Chi-Rho symbol of Christianity?) to be seen represented in the hand of Constantine's statue, there was nothing remotely Christian about these public edifices in the public heart of the city. To the great senatorial families of Rome, proud of their long custody of the worship of Rome's gods on behalf of the state, the Christian allegiance of the emperor was a private quirk which could not be allowed to detract from his crucial traditional role as *pontifex maximus*, "chief priest" of the pagan cults, a role which Constantine therefore retained to the end of his life despite his dislike of the worship a *pontifex* was expected to promote. The resistance of the senators was made starkly apparent by the ambiguous inscription on the triumphal arch next to the Colosseum dedicated in 315 by the Senate and people of Rome in recognition of his victory, "to the Emperor Caesar Flavius Constantine, Maximus, Pius, Felix, Augustus . . . because, by the prompting of the divinity, by the greatness of his mind, he, with his army, at one moment by a just victory avenged the state both on the tyrant and on all his party." The arch, decorated with reliefs taken from monuments mostly of the second century CE, proclaimed that the emperor had won at the Milvian bridge *instinctu divinitatis*, "by the prompting of the [or "a"] divinity." The sculptures bore no Christian symbols at all: the gods of Constantine were portrayed as the Sun and Victory. Building had already begun on the Lateran basilica, and Constantine was already issuing laws filled with Christian rhetoric, so the ambiguity of the wording on the inscription hardly came about through ignorance of the emperor's new religious allegiance. The senators knew what Constantine preferred, and most declined to acquiesce. By the mid-320s, after his conquest of the eastern part of the empire following the decisive battle of Adrianople on 3 July 324, Constantine seems to have decided not to press on with the further

Christianization of the old Rome, and sought to build instead a new Rome at Byzantium, to be a more Christian capital of a more actively Christian empire.[3]


"THE CITY which had up to then been called Byzantium [Constantine] developed, surrounding it with great defensive walls and decorating it with diverse monuments. Having put it on an equal level with Rome, the ruling city, and having changed its name to Constantinople, he prescribed by a law that it should be called 'Second Rome.' " The details in this report by the Church historian Socrates, writing a century after Constantine, are probably confused, and earlier evidence to corroborate his assertion that Constantine himself prescribed by law that his new city be called a "Second Rome" is not wholly convincing, but in 324 Alexander, the bishop of Constantinople, was already being addressed by the bishops meeting in a synod at Antioch as "bishop of the new Rome," and in 325 or 326 the poet Optatianus Porphyrius, in a poem addressed to Constantine, referred to "the nobility of the Pontus" as *altera Roma*, "another Rome." Thus, whether Constantine himself gave the title of "New Rome" to the city which took his own name is disputed, but that it was conceived by him as in some sense a Second Rome there is no doubt. The city became the emperor's main residence from its dedication on 11 May 330 until he died in 337. The new city was made attractive to new inhabitants by the distribution of free grain, and honoured by being granted the right to a senate of its own. The focus of the city was the imperial palace, with the hippodrome adjacent, and the statue of the emperor on top of a column in the new oval forum.[4]

The city was thus above all a monument to Constantine himself, and as such it was a place where he could present himself openly, defiantly, as devoted to the Christian God, as Eusebius ecstatically reports:

> In honouring with exceptional distinction the city which bears his name, he embellished it with very many places of worship, very large martyr-shrines, and splendid houses, some standing before the city and others in it. By these he at the same time honoured the tombs of the martyrs and consecrated the city to the martyrs' God. Being full of the breath of God's wisdom, which he reckoned a city bearing his own

name should display, he saw fit to purge it of all idol-worship, so that nowhere in it appeared those images of the supposed gods which are worshipped in temples, nor altars foul with bloody slaughter, nor sacrifice offered as holocaust in fire, nor feasts of demons, nor any of the other customs of the superstitious. You would see at the fountains set in the middle of squares the emblems of the Good Shepherd, evident signs to those who start from the divine oracles, and Daniel with his lions shaped in bronze and glinting with gold leaf. So great was the divine passion which had seized the Emperor's soul that in the royal quarters of the imperial palace itself, on the most eminent building of all, at the very middle of the gilded coffer adjoining the roof, in the centre of a very large wide panel, had been fixed the emblem of the saving Passion made up of a variety of precious stones and set in much gold. This appears to have been made by the Godbeloved as a protection for his Empire.

Eusebius exaggerates the suppression of paganism in the city—at least some of the pagan temples of old Byzantium were left untouched, and some two centuries later the pagan Greek historian Zosimus even claimed (perhaps not wholly reliably) that two new temples were built during Constantine's rule, to Rhea and to the Fortune of Rome. But the emperor's determination to ensure the Christian character of his new Rome emerges clearly in a letter he wrote to Eusebius requesting multiple copies of the Bible for the use of the new church congregations because

in the City which bears our name by the sustaining providence of the Saviour God a great mass of people has attached itself to the most holy Church, so that with everything there enjoying great growth it is particularly fitting that more churches should be established . . . The preparation of the written volumes with utmost speed shall be the task of your Diligence. You are entitled by the authority of this our letter to the use of two public vehicles for transportation. The fine copies may thus most readily be transported to us for inspection; one of the deacons of your own congregation will presumably carry out this task, and when he reaches us he will experience our generosity. God preserve you, dear brother.

The success of Constantine's policy can be seen in the rhetoric used by the author of the biography of the fifth-century stylite saint Daniel, and by other Christians in later centuries: through the accumulation of Christian relics, Constantinople came to be known not only as a second Rome but also as a second Jerusalem.[5]


THE REACTIONS to Constantine's enthusiasm for Christianity to be found among the Jews living in this new Rome may well have differed from those to be found among the Jews in Italy. Jews had long been settled in the coastal cities of Asia Minor and the Black Sea region, and it was from Adramyttium, not so many miles away to the south-west of Byzantium, that the Roman governor Flaccus had stolen the funds collected by the Jews of Asia in 62–61 BCE, in the time of Cicero. Byzantium was a small place in the third century CE, but in 318 CE Jews had a synagogue there also, in the area of the copper market, well before the city was taken over by the grandiose plans of Constantine. How these local Jews reacted to the transformation of their surroundings in the 320s and 330s can readily be guessed. Like other inhabitants they must have admired the great works of art, looted from other places, with which Constantine adorned the streets of his New Rome, and they may well have felt a certain local patriotism, but the anti-Jewish rhetoric of the emperor, whose palace now loomed over their homes and whose presence dominated the city, must have left them uneasy—even though it was not until 422 that their synagogue was converted into a church.[6]

The position of the Jews in old Rome was rather different, precisely because Constantine had not sought to establish his faith in the city with the zeal he was prepared to show in the eastern part of his empire. The edict issued in Milan in 313 by Constantine and Licinius had quite specifically offered freedom of worship to everyone in the empire.

> We thought that, in accordance with salutary and most correct reasoning, we ought to establish our purpose that no man whatever should be refused complete toleration, who has given up his mind either to the observances of the Christians, or to the religion which he felt most fitting to himself . . . that every man have a free opportunity in the prac-

tice of whatever worship he has chosen. This we have done to ensure that no cult or religion may seem to have been diminished by us.

The pagan senators of Rome took this policy at face value, as has been seen, and continued to devote themselves to the ancient cults of the city. Why should not the same be true also of the Jews? The Jewish community in fourth-century Rome was far larger than that in contemporary Byzantium and had picked up some of the cultural traits of wider Roman society. Jews commissioned stone sarcophagi from fashionable local workshops, requiring only the insertion of specifically Jewish iconography, such as an elaborately carved menorah rendered in relief on a tondo, and beautiful gold glasses, in which Jewish objects, such as the menorah, ethrog and lulav, are represented in gold leaf which has been sealed between two layers of glass. A letter in Latin preserved in fragmentary form in an early-ninth-century manuscript in Cologne under the heading "Here begins the Letter of Anna to Seneca about pride and idols" may have been composed by a Roman Jew in this period and reminds us of the likelihood that Roman Jews, like Greek Jews in late antiquity, produced a literature of their own in Latin which was not preserved either by rabbis or by Christians and thus is now lost to us.[7]

This acculturated community, still sufficiently aware of its separate identity within the Roman population to bury its dead in special catacombs, might reasonably see the declaration of toleration by the newly arrived emperor in 313 as the end of discrimination. Constantine's predecessor Galerius had proffered to the Roman people two years earlier a logical reason for ending persecution of Christians which might equally well apply to Jews: since Christians had "in very great numbers held to their determination, and we saw that these same people neither gave worship and due reverence to the gods, nor [because it was forbidden] worshipped the god of the Christians," Galerius pardoned them, allowed them to "establish their meeting-places," and asserted that "it will be their duty to pray to their god for our safety, and that of the state, and their own, that the state may endure on every side unharmed, and they may be able to live free of care in their habitations." The religious logic was the same as Philo and Josephus had asserted for the loyal sacrifices to the Jewish God on behalf of the Roman emperor in the first century CE: Jews might not worship the emperors as gods, but their prayers to their own God for the emperor's well-being were uniquely efficacious. Jews had not forgotten their Temple and frequently depicted it, and the sacrifices which took place there, on the mosaic floors of the synagogues they built from the fourth to the sixth centuries. If there was to be real freedom of worship as Constantine and Licinius promised, surely now the Jewish Temple should be restored in Jerusalem.[8]

Such hopes among Roman Jews, and their dashing during the following decades of Constantine's rule, in which quite different plans emerged for Jerusalem, can be surmised even if they cannot be documented from the meagre archaeological and epigraphic remains from which the history of this community has to be reconstructed. Jews and Christians in the city may have had little contact in the century before the edict of Milan. Christian sources have little to say about the Jews of Rome in their accounts of the vicissitudes of the local Church. It would not be surprising if many Jews were unaware of the theological imperative which rendered a rebuilt Temple in Jerusalem anathema to many Christians precisely because Jesus was believed to have predicted its destruction. It would take time for Jews to realize the significance for them of the emperor's adoption of his new faith. In the meantime, the city of Rome was to remain for much of the fourth century a society of genuine religious pluralism. In a book presented to a senator in 354, the pagan festivals in honour of Venus, Quirinus, Ceres, Flora, Sarapis and various divine emperors were recorded in a traditional Roman calendar alongside a Christian calendar of the martyrs of Rome.[9]

At least one Roman Jew seems to have been affected by this tolerant atmosphere sufficiently to propose the compatibility of Jewish law with the law of Rome. In this extraordinary Latin treatise, entitled the *Collatio Legum Mosaicarum et Romanarum*, the author, who was probably writing in the late fourth century, lists biblical texts from chapters 20 to 22 of Exodus, roughly according to the order of the second half of the Ten Commandments, following each text by excerpts from Roman jurists and imperial constitutions. The ostensible purpose of the *Collatio* was to demonstrate the excellence of the "divine law" which "Moses, the priest of God" had laid down, and the (alleged) remarkable congruity between the biblical and the Roman laws quoted. Such congruity is explained in one passage by the priority of Moses: "know, jurists, that Moses earlier decided this." The author lays special stress on the sanctity of the "divine scripture" he cites, but his own versions of particular passages are free and compressed, suggesting that he had in mind a readership familiar with the Bible, perhaps in a different language, either Hebrew or Greek—in other words, fellow Jews. Despite his evocation of Roman jurists, no expert in Roman law was likely to be much impressed by such implausible claims of identity between the law of Moses and that of Rome as "Moses says: 'If a fire breaks out and finds thorns and catches hold of threshing floors or ears of corn or a field, he who lit the fire will make restitution of its valuation.' Paulus [a Roman jurist of the early third century CE], in the fifth book of his *Sentences* under the title *About Incendiaries* [writes]: 'Whoever has set fire to a cottage or farm for the sake of enmity: the more humble are condemned to the mine or to public works, the more honourable are relegated to an island.' " By contrast Roman Jews might have been genuinely impressed by the collection of Roman legal materials from a variety of sources and the apologetic assertion that this learned compilation somehow affirmed the validity of the Torah in a Roman world. If author and intended readers were indeed Jews, the *Collatio* stands alone among extant ancient Jewish writings from the fourth century CE as an attempt by a Jew to persuade other Jews in the empire that their Roman identity did not conflict with their Judaism, or their Judaism with their Romanness—a real, if brief, attempt at accommodation before the Christian empire once again relegated Jews to the margins. The signs of the intolerance to come could be seen during Constantine's reign less in the pluralist atmosphere of Rome than in the dramatic changes imposed by Constantine on the homeland of the Jews and especially on Jerusalem.[10]

## A NEW JERUSALEM

"NEW JERUSALEM was built as the very Testimony to the Saviour, facing the famous Jerusalem of old, which after the bloody murder of the Lord had been overthrown in utter devastation, and paid the penalty of its wicked inhabitants. Opposite this then the Emperor erected the victory of the Saviour over death with rich and abundant munificence, this being perhaps that fresh new Jerusalem proclaimed in prophetic oracles, about which long speeches recite innumerable praises as they utter words of divine inspiration." So Eusebius in 337 described Constantine's building of the church of the Holy Sepulchre in Jerusalem. Through his wealth and piety, Jerusalem was to become again under imperial patronage a great religious centre, a magnet for pilgrims, but, as the rhetoric made clear, emphatically not for the wicked Jews whose Temple had been destroyed because of "the bloody murder of the Lord."[11]

Before the city's transformation by Constantine, the ancient status of Jerusalem was, for ordinary Romans, at most a distant memory. "Aelia," the name of the Roman colony which had replaced the Jews' sacred city, was so firmly entrenched that it continued in official use even under Christian emperors, with the significant omission of the second part of the original name—"Capitolina," which denoted the dedication of the colony to Jupiter Capitolinus, was felt no longer appropriate. Even the Church historian Eusebius used the name "Aelia" along with "Jerusalem" indiscriminately in his gazetteer of biblical sites in Palestine, the *Onomasticon*. In another work, the *Martyrs of Palestine*, he described a dramatic scene on 16 February 310, just before Constantine's conversion, when the pagan Roman governor of Palestine, Firmilianus, interrogating in Caesarea Eusebius' revered Christian teacher Pamphilus, was quite baffled by the martyr's insistence that "Jerusalem was his fatherland, meaning, indeed that Jerusalem of which it was said by Paul: 'But the Jerusalem that is above is free, which is our mother,' and 'You have come to Mount Sion, and to the city of the living God, the heavenly Jerusalem' . . . The judge . . . was puzzled and shook with impatience, thinking that the Christians had certainly established a city somewhere at enmity and hostile to the Romans; and he was much occupied in discovering it, and enquiring into the said country in the East." The spiritual geography of the Christian martyr made no sense to the Roman magistrate, just a few years before the new Christian Jerusalem was to arise. In fact, Aelia, at the date of Pamphilus' martyrdom, had ceased to be of much importance in the administrative, economic and military life of the province. With the departure of the Tenth Legion from the colony over the course of the third century, the influx of wealth from the central state, in the form of military pay, had dried up. Aelia was well connected by military roads to Caesarea and other garrison towns, such as the secondary legionary base at Legio in the Jezreel valley, but the colony was isolated in the Judaean mountains and lay on no major trade routes. With no special natural resources, even intensive exploitation of the surrounding countryside could bring only meagre rewards. There is no reason to doubt that Aelia enjoyed the standard facilities of any city in the Roman East, such as public baths and a theatre, but, deprived of the oxygen of a large military presence or crowds of religious enthusiasts, it was sinking into obscurity.[12]

But for Christians, of course, the site of this obscure colony was significant because of what had happened there long ago. Back in the mid-second century CE, Melito of Sardis, author of the virulent depiction of the Jews as deicides in his poem on Easter, travelled "to the east," where he "learned accurately the books of the Old Testament" in "the place where [these things] were preached and done." Melito was the first known of a stream of pilgrims to the Holy Land, who came "for the purpose of prayer and investigation of the places." In the case of Alexander, bishop of a community in Cappadocia in the time of Caracalla, the visit to Jerusalem proved permanent, since "the people there gave him the most cordial welcome, and suffered him not to return home again, in accordance with another revelation which was seen by them also at night," and "with the common consent of the bishops who were administering the churches round about . . . compelled him of necessity to remain." In due course, during the Decian persecution, Alexander "appeared once more for Christ's sake at Caesarea before the governor's courts, and for the second time distinguished himself by the confession he made; he underwent the trial of imprisonment, crowned with the venerable hoary locks of ripe old age. And . . . after the splendid and manifest testimony that he gave in the governor's courts, he fell asleep in prison." But, although other Christians too were attracted to Jerusalem by its scriptural history, the Christian community there remained small in the second and third centuries, overshadowed by the much more powerful congregation in the provincial capital Caesarea, where the biblical scholar Origen was based in the mid-third century, and where Eusebius himself lived in the early fourth, becoming bishop soon after the edict of toleration in 313. There is little evidence that any Christians before Constantine thought the sites in Jerusalem, made famous (to them) by their biblical associations, were themselves to be venerated as holy. On the contrary, the new Jerusalem to which Christians like the martyr Pamphilus looked was not of this world. The new Jerusalem belonged to the last days envisaged many centuries before by the prophet Ezekiel and applied to the Church by the seer in the book of Revelation when he wrote of

that great city, the holy Jerusalem, descending out of heaven from God,
having the glory of God: and her light was like unto a stone most precious, even like a jasper stone, clear as crystal . . . And I did not see a
temple therein: for the Lord God Almighty and the Lamb are the temple of it. And the city had no need of the sun, neither of the moon, to
shine in it: for the glory of God did lighten it, and the Lamb is its light.
And the nations shall walk in the light of it: and the kings of the earth
bring their glory to it.

In the second half of the second century one prophetic Christian, Mon-
tanus, whose teachings were later to be condemned as heresy but who in
206 had won the allegiance of, among many others, Tertullian, had even
claimed that the heavenly Jerusalem would soon descend in his homeland,
in Pepuza in Phrygia. Such influence as the Christians of Aelia, the site of
the real Jerusalem of old, exerted in the third and early fourth centuries
over Christians in the wider region derived more from their role in com-
bating heresies and in providing heroic martyrs, such as bishop Alexander,
for admiration and emulation, than from the mystique of their sacred
sites.[13]

The plan of Constantine to create a new Christian Jerusalem thus upset
the long-established structures of power among the Christians of Palestine, who looked primarily to the bishop of Caesarea for guidance.
Already at the Church council in Nicaea in 325, just a year after Constantine's conquest of the East, the assembled bishops agreed that "since custom and ancient tradition has held firm, that the bishop of Aelia should be
honoured, let him have the honour due to him in accordance with such
tradition, saving to the metropolis [i.e. Caesarea] the honour which
belongs to it." It is hard to know how much this ruling reflected the personal predilections of the emperor who presided at the council, how much
the influence of the prominent bishop of Jerusalem, Macarius. Eusebius,
our main informant about the council, was not disinterested in the matter,
since, as bishop of Caesarea, he had much to lose; but it was Eusebius who
recorded, in his biography of Constantine, the direct role taken by the
emperor to enhance the status of Christian Jerusalem by clearing away
pagan shrines and identifying places of Christian significance, particularly
the Holy Sepulchre, since

he decided that he ought to make universally famous and revered the most blessed site in Jerusalem of the Saviour's resurrection . . . the cave of the Saviour that some godless and wicked people had planned to make invisible to mankind, thinking in their stupidity that they could in this way hide the truth. Indeed with a great expenditure of effort they brought earth from somewhere outside and covered up the whole place, then levelled it, paved it, and so hid the divine cave somewhere down beneath a great quantity of soil. Then as though they had every-thing finished, above the ground they constructed a terrible and truly genuine tomb, one for souls, for dead idols, and built a gloomy sanctu-ary to the impure demon of Aphrodite; then they offered foul sacrifices there upon defiled and polluted altars . . . At a word of command those contrivances of fraud were demolished from top to bottom, and the houses of error were dismantled and destroyed along with their idols and demons . . . As stage by stage the underground site was exposed, at last against all expectation the revered and all hallowed Testimony of the Saviour's resurrection was itself revealed, and the cave, the holy of holies, took on the appearance of a representation of the Saviour's return to life.

Once the underground site of the resurrection had thus been revealed, "against all expectation," Constantine undertook the building of the greatest of all martyr churches, the Holy Sepulchre, right in the centre of the colony. The church was described by Eusebius, soon after its dedica-tion, in admiring detail:

As the principal item he first of all decked out the sacred cave. It was a tomb full of agelong memory, comprising the trophies of the great Saviour's defeat of death, a tomb of divine presence, where once an angel, radiant with light, proclaimed to all the good news of the rebirth demonstrated by the Saviour . . . On the side opposite the cave, which looked towards the rising sun, was connected the royal temple, an extraordinary structure raised to an immense height and very extensive in length and breadth. Its interior was covered with slabs of varied mar-ble, and the external aspect of the walls, gleaming with hewn stone fit-ted closely together at each joint, produced a supreme object of beauty by no means inferior to marble. Right up at the top the material which encased the outside of the roofs was lead, a sure protection against stormy rain; while the interior of the structure was fitted with carved coffers and like a vast sea spread out by a series of joints binding to each other through the whole royal house, and being beautified throughout with brilliant gold made the whole shrine glitter with beams of light . . . This then was the shrine which the Emperor raised as a manifest testimony of the Saviour's resurrection, embellishing the whole with rich imperial decoration. He adorned it with untold beauties in innumerable dedications of gold and silver and precious stones set in various materials. In view of their size, number and variety, to describe in detail the skilled craftsmanship which went into their manufacture would be beyond the scope of the present work.[14]

This magnificent remodelling of the centre of Aelia to provide a Christian focus for the city was intended less for the benefit of local inhabitants (as in Rome) than for pilgrims from around the Christian world. Constantine himself never visited the Holy Land after his schemes had been put into action, although his mother-in-law Eutropia did, and so, famously, did his own mother Helena, founding one church, the Eleona basilica on the Mount of Olives, and another, at the site of the nativity, in Bethlehem; in the course of the fourth century there arose a tradition that she had also discovered the wood of the original Cross on Golgotha, although the story, unknown to Eusebius, must have been a pious fabrication after Constantine's death. In contrast to his cautious approach in Rome, the emperor seems to have taken no account at all of the sensibilities of local pagans in Aelia as he demolished the temple "to the impure demon of Aphrodite" to make way for the Holy Sepulchre, or the pagan shrine at Mamre near Hebron to permit a new church there. Some, perhaps most, of the inhabitants of Aelia may have continued in their pagan beliefs and practices long after Constantine had died, but disgruntled pagan provincials posed no threat. Far more important, in Constantine's eyes, were the elite from across the empire whom he hoped to win over to his new faith. The churches of the Holy Land, with buildings smaller than the vast edifices built by Constantine in Rome, but large areas of open space, were designed for the reception of pilgrims in large numbers. Colonnades provided shelter in the great open courtyard of the Holy Sepulchre as the visitors gazed in awe at the newly discovered tomb, beautified with columns and other embellishments. On the side of the courtyard which faced the tomb was the Golgotha basilica, faced all over with gleaming marble, the place for liturgy, ritual and communal prayer. Since the whole complex seems to have sheltered behind impressive precinct walls, the locals uncommitted to the faith could only glimpse the pilgrims on their way to pray, and hope to earn something from this new source of income from religious tourism, but conversion must have attracted many: Constantine did not just ignore the susceptibilities of the pagans of Aelia, he positively attacked them through the destruction of the "hideous burden" of their idols and the suppression of their cults. The decision to build the great Christian basilica in the monumental centre of Aelia, in the northern part of the forum erected under Hadrian, may owe less to local traditions about the site of Christ's tomb than to Constantine's desire to demonstrate that this city was to be both Roman and Christian. It is an attractive hypothesis that the dedication of the Holy Sepulchre was fixed for September because the Ides of that month, 13 September, was the day for the ancient Roman festivals in honour of Jupiter Optimus Maximus, whose tutelage of the colony, long symbolized by the name "Capitolina," had now been supplanted by that of Christ.[15]

It is less certain that the emperor was concerned to put the Jews in their place, since they had long been formally excluded from the city's territories in any case. The theology of Eusebius, for whom the glory of the new Jerusalem shone all the brighter because of the visible devastation of the old, was expounded at length in his various writings and had a long history in earlier Christian thought, but there is no evidence that such sophisticated notions were shared by Constantine, whose grasp of biblical materials, beyond the very basic, was shaky. On the other hand, Constantine also had no cause to favour the Jews in his Christian city. The Temple site was still left in ruins in 333, when it was visited by a pilgrim from Bordeaux: it was dominated by two great statues which the pious pilgrim took to represent the emperor Hadrian. In the mid-third century Origen, who probably also visited the site, thought that although one of these statues was of Hadrian, the other was of Gaius or Titus. In fact it was probably a representation of Hadrian's successor, Antoninus Pius, since a statue plinth with his name survives, incorporated upside down above the lintel of the Double Gate in the south wall of the Harem esh Sharif, built when the site became an Islamic shrine in the seventh century or after. It is significant, as evidence of Christian ideology, that the Christian Jerome, writing in nearby Bethlehem at the end of the fourth century, believed that the image was in fact a statue of Jupiter, the god whose worship had supplanted the God of the Jews, only to be supplanted in turn by Christ.[16]

Constantine was too preoccupied with pagans to attack Jews in Jerusalem, but such peace was not to last. At the end of the fifth century, or the beginning of the sixth, the pagan Zosimus, describing the exile from Constantinople in 395 of the wife and daughter of the murdered praetorian prefect Rufinus, wrote that they were allowed "to sail away to Jerusalem, which in olden times had been a habitation of Jews but from the reign of Constantine onwards was honoured with buildings by Christians." The passage is an unusual example of a pagan adopting a viewpoint which had become increasingly common among Jerusalem Christians in the fourth century, and especially in the writings of Cyril, who was bishop from about 347 to 386, that to create a truly Christian Jerusalem required confrontation with deeply rooted local Jewish myth and symbolism and its replacement by those of the Church. In the time of Constantine, when the struggle which interested the emperor was not with the Jews but with paganism, Jews around the Holy City seem, for the most part, to have been left in peace, but the seeds of future conflict were all too well embedded in shared traditions about sites mentioned in the Bible. Once funds from the emperor and other wealthy Romans were available for the erection of monuments at places designated as holy to Christians, such sharing became increasingly difficult to sustain, as is clear from the enthralled description of Jerusalem and its environs which was composed by the Bordeaux pilgrim in 333, soon after the beginning of Constantine's building projects. His (or her) extraordinary document is memorable for the presentation, to a Latin readership at the other end of the Mediterranean, of Jerusalem as the centre of their spiritual world. The "itinerary from Bordeaux to Jerusalem and from Heraclea through Aulona, and through the city of Rome to Milan" was written mostly in the form of a list of towns along Roman roads, noting the distance between them, with occasional touristic asides interspersed: "here lies king Hannibal" or "from here was Apollonius the magician." But when the description reaches Palestine, it changes into a sacred landscape evocative of scriptural stories. The reader is invited into the landscape by frequent use of second person singular verbs in the

# Jerusalem in the time of Constantine

N
W · E
S

Cemetery

Cemetery

Pool of Bethesda

Gate    Pool

Pool

Church of the
Holy Sepulchre

The rock of
the Antonia

to Mount
of Olives
church

High-level aqueduct

Pool of the
Patriarch

Forum

Decumanus

Temple
Mount

(ruins)

"David's
Tower"

Cardo – colonnaded street

Secondary (eastern) Cardo

Ophel

Mount
Zion

City of
David

Low-level aqueduct

"David's
Tomb"

Street

Gate

Gate(?)

0    100   200   300

yards

present tense: "you can see where David had his palace . . . as you leave there and pass through the wall of Sion . . ." For both writer and reader, the Holy Land was now clearly different from all the rest of the empire.

The tone of the pilgrim's report reaches a new pitch of piety as Jerusalem is reached:

> In Jerusalem beside the Temple are two large pools, one to the right and the other to the left, built by Solomon . . . There is also a crypt there where Solomon used to torture demons, and there is the corner of a very lofty tower, which was where the Lord climbed and said to him who tempted him, and the Lord said to him: "You shalt not tempt the Lord your God, but him only shall you serve." And there also is the great corner-stone of which it was said, "The stone which the builders rejected has become the head of the corner." And below the pinnacle of this tower are very many chambers where Solomon had his palace. There too is the chamber in which he sat and wrote Wisdom, and it is roofed with a single stone . . . And in the sanctuary itself, where the Temple was which Solomon built, on the marble in front of the altar you would say the blood of Zacharias had only been shed there today. All around you can see the marks of the hobnails of the soldiers who killed him, as plainly as if they had been pressed into wax . . . Inside Sion, within the wall, you can see where David had his palace. Seven synagogues were there, but only one is left—the rest have been "ploughed and sown" as was said by the prophet Isaiah . . . Near by, about a stone's throw away, are two memorial tombs of remarkable beauty. In one of them, formed from a single rock, the prophet Isaiah was laid, and in the other lies Hezekiah, king of the Jews . . . Four miles from Jerusalem, on the right of the highway to Bethlehem, is the tomb in which was laid Jacob's wife Rachel. Two miles further on, on the left, is Bethlehem, where the Lord Jesus Christ was born; there a basilica has been built by command of Constantine. Not far away is the tomb of Ezekiel, Asaph, Job, Jesse, David and Solomon. Their names are written in Hebrew characters low down on the wall as you go down into the crypt.[17]

The only reference by the Bordeaux pilgrim to contemporary Jews in Jerusalem is the brief mention of their annual mourning ritual at the Temple site: the pilgrim notes that, not far from the statues of Hadrian was "a pierced stone which the Jews come and anoint each year. They mourn and groan and tear their garments, and then depart." Occasional hints in rabbinic texts compiled in the fourth century and later suggest that, despite the prohibition by Hadrian on Jewish settlement in the city, in practice Jews had been visiting the site of the Temple in small numbers at least since the early third century CE: "Rabbi Jonathan was going up to worship in Jerusalem, when he . . . was seen by a Samaritan. He asked him, 'Where are you going to?' He said: 'To worship in Jerusalem.' " To which the Samaritan is said to have responded, "Is it not better to pray at this blessed mountain than at that dung hill?" Later rabbis preserved a tradition that a group of pupils of Rabbi Meir founded a small "holy community" in Jerusalem in the Severan period, although there is no reference to any Jewish settlement in the city by the time of Constantine. Eutychius, patriarch of Alexandria in the tenth century, asserted that Constantine prohibited the Jews from living in Jerusalem or passing within it, but, if this was not simply a confusion with the edict of Hadrian, it represented no more than a reaffirmation of existing law, perhaps strengthened by the enthusiasm of the local bishopric. Evidently the Jews who came to mourn at the Temple site, presumably on the fast of 9 Ab, were perceived neither by pagans nor by Christians as a threat.[18]

In the time of Constantine Jews might not have been seen as a threat to Christianity in the new Jerusalem, but they, as much as pagans, could be converted to the true faith, as is evident from the efforts in these years by a certain Joseph, originally a Jew from the court of the Jewish patriarch in Tiberias, to bring the Jews of Galilee to Christianity. The story of Joseph was told by Epiphanius, bishop of Salamis, in his huge and unreliable *Refutation of All the Heresies*, composed in the second half of the fourth century. Epiphanius was himself a native of Palestine and had met Joseph when the latter was an old man of seventy years or more. According to Joseph's own account, as mediated through Epiphanius, he had been introduced to Christian ideas through reading Christian books kept in the archives of the Jewish patriarch in Tiberias, and had converted to Christianity while on a mission to the Jews of Cilicia on behalf of the patriarch. Shunned and attacked by the Jews there, he underwent baptism and was welcomed at the court of Constantine and honoured with the title *comes*, "Count," returning to Galilee to build churches under imperial protection in the cities and villages of the Jews where no one had ever been secure enough to put up churches, since there were no pagans, Samaritans, or Christians in their midst . . . Joseph, taking the letters and the authority accompanying his rank, went to Tiberias, having also letters authorizing his expenditures from imperial funds. He had himself been granted the honour of receiving supplies from the emperor. Thus he began to build in Tiberias . . . Now he needed quicklime and other material. So he ordered that many kilns be built outside the city . . . But the dreadful Jews, bold to try anything, did not refrain from their habitual tricks of magic. These noble Jews made every effort to restrain the fire with magic and strange arts, but they did not reach their goal . . . When those assigned to put the fuel on the fire reported to Joseph what had happened, he was stung, and, burning with zeal for the Lord, he ran outside the city, and, ordering water to be brought in a vessel . . . took the flask in the sight of everyone (a crowd of Jews had gathered at the sight, eager to see what would happen and what Joseph would try to do), and signing the cross upon it with his own finger, he called upon the name of Jesus in a loud voice: "In the name of Jesus the Nazoraean, whom the fathers of me and of all these bystanders crucified, may power come to be in this water to render void all sorcery and magic which these people have practised, and to activate the power of the fire in order to finish the house of the Lord." And he takes the water in his hand and sprinkles each [kiln] with the water. And the spells were broken, and the fire blazed forth in the sight of all. The crowds present, shouting, "There is one God, who helps the Christians!," departed. Those men [the Jews] continued to treat Joseph badly, but finally he built some part of the shrine in Tiberias and, having completed a small church, left.

The fact that these efforts to build churches with the patronage of Constantine took place precisely in the part of the land of Israel in which the rabbinic academies were to be found, and the alleged relationship of Joseph himself to the patriarchs (named by Epiphanius as Hillel and his son Judah, "from the family of that first Gamaliel who lived at the time of the Saviour"), make all the more striking the lack of attested rabbinic reaction to this extraordinary change in imperial interest in their country. It seems almost inconceivable that the rabbis had nothing to say about the uprooting of pagan shrines which had existed for centuries in the land, or about the dire punishments threatened by Constantine in 329 for Jews who, "as we have learned is being done now," dared to attack apostates from Judaism "by stoning or by other kind of fury." The silence of the rabbis about such changes was more probably the product of solipsism than deliberate ignoring. That conversions of Jews to Christianity did indeed occur is evident not just from the career of Joseph but from Constantine's repetition on 21 October 335 of the burden of the law issued almost exactly six years earlier, and apparently not sufficiently effective: "if one of the Jews shall unlock for himself the door of eternal life, shall bind himself to the holy cults and choose to be Christian, he shall not suffer ought of harassment or molestation in the hands of the Jews. For if anyone of the Jews shall consider that a Jew who became Christian should be attacked and injured, we want the instigator of such contumely to be subjected to avenging punishments commensurate with the nature of the crime committed."[19]

Not all Jews in the land of Israel in the time of Constantine had anything to do with the intense circles of scholars who produced rabbinic literature, and other Jews, like the pagans (and perhaps the Jews) in the city of Rome, may have taken Constantine's edict of toleration at face value as an opportunity to accommodate their religion within a pluralist world. Certainly the fourth and fifth centuries saw an increasing production of artefacts and buildings within the land which displayed a distinctively Jewish iconography alongside appropriation of characteristics of the culture of wider society. Perhaps the most startling example of such accommodation was the display of images of the sun god Helios in depictions of the signs of the zodiac on the mosaic floors in late-Roman synagogues. It is not impossible that such images were intended by those who commissioned them to represent the Jewish God, since centuries earlier Josephus had described the Essenes as "offering certain prayers" to the sun before sunrise, "as though entreating him to rise" and as "covering their excrement [with a spade] to avoid offending the rays of the deity," and early rabbis sometimes conceived of God in terms both anthropomorphic and fiery, noting that, because God is fire, it is impossible to go up to the heavens to join him.[20] But regardless of the intentions of those who paid for or made these images in late-Roman synagogues, the mosaic pictures are hard to divorce from the ubiquitous image of the sun god in the non-Jewish world of the time. Sol Invictus ("the Unconquered Sun," in Latin) and Helios ("Sun," in

Greek) were frequently depicted in imperial religious propaganda in the third and fourth centuries in forms close to those found in the synagogue mosaics. That the sun became the symbol of monotheism among pagans in the fourth century is attested most coherently in the *Hymn to King Helios* composed by the pagan emperor Julian in the 360s. The worship of the sun was closely connected to the widespread cult of Theos Hypsistos, "the Highest God," whose adherents lacked (like Jews) any iconography of the deity but worshipped sun and fire. The essence of the divinity was encapsulated in an oracle of Apollo of which a copy was engraved in an inscription at Oenoanda in Asia Minor: "Born of itself, untaught, without a mother, unshakeable, not contained in a name, known by many names, dwelling in fire, this is god . . . Aether is god who sees all, on whom you should gaze and pray at dawn, looking towards the sunrise." Constantine's continued depiction of the sun god on his coins after his conversion to Christianity is best understood as his identification of the Sun with the Highest God worshipped by Christians. When the emperor Julian planned to rebuild the Jewish Temple in Jerusalem in 361, he described it, according to the report of John the Lydian two centuries later, as the shrine of Theos Hypsistos. Since, in his letter to the emperor Gaius quoted by Philo, Agrippa I had used the term *Hypsistos*, "the Highest," to denote the Jewish God, as had Josephus when quoting a decree by Augustus in favour of the Jews, the Jews in fourth-century Palestine who used the image of Helios to grace their synagogue floors may have been demonstrating their confident conviction that the God to whom both pagans and Christians paid greatest observance was the God of Israel.[21]

All that remained to be done was for Jews to be allowed to worship their God in the way he had laid down, through sacrifices and libations in a rebuilt Temple in Jerusalem. Constantine had put an end to pagan practices in the city. The shrines of Jupiter and Aphrodite were destroyed or empty. Whatever was going on in the new church of the Holy Sepulchre did not involve sacrifices to idols, and, in any case, Jews more aware of imperial rhetoric might see it as a shrine to the God of the Jews erected by those whom rabbis referred to in this period as gentile "fearers of heaven": in fourth-century Aphrodisias, in Asia Minor, an inscription records honour paid by the local Jewish community to a large number of such *theosebeis*, "god-reverers," who appear to have contributed to a Jewish communal fund. The Temple site itself remained in ruins, ripe for redevelopment.

Memories of how to organize the cult in accordance with the divine will had been codified in the Mishnah in considerable detail. Plenty of priests could be identified and called into service: attestation of local knowledge about the priestly courses in Palestinian synagogue inscriptions of the fifth and sixth centuries is more likely to reflect continuity since 70 CE than a reinvention of tradition. The epitaph of a Jew buried in Zo'ar, on the southern edge of the Dead Sea in the province of Arabia, in 358/9, dates his death to "year 290 after the *hurban*, destruction." The passage of nearly three hundred years had not removed the sense of loss.[22]

If any Jews did react with such optimism to the conversion of Constantine and the Christianization of Jerusalem, they were gravely deceived. Over the following decades of the fourth century, the leaders of the Jerusalem Church bolstered their position within the Christian world not least by virulent hostility to Jews and Judaism. When on 7 May 351 a cross, "flashing and sparkling with brilliant light," was seen in the sky above Jerusalem, the bishop of Jerusalem, Cyril, informed the emperor, Constantine's son Constantius, that the sign signified that the Son of Man was coming to judge the enemies of the Church, and that these enemies were the Jews:

> During these holy days of the holy Paschal season, at around the third hour, a gigantic luminous cross was seen in the sky above holy Golgotha, extending as far as the holy Mount of Olives; not seen by one or two only, but clearly visible to the whole population of the city; nor, as might be expected, quickly vanishing like an illusion, but suspended for several hours above the earth before the general gaze and by its dazzling splendours conquering the sun's rays . . . Immediately the whole population, overcome with joy mingled with fear of the heavenly vision, ran to the holy church: young and old, men and women of every age, even to the maidens closeted in their homes, local and foreign Christians, as well as visiting pagans—all with one accord, and as with a single voice, extolling Christ Jesus our Lord, the Only-begotten Son of God, the worker of wonders . . . In this miracle, your most God-beloved Majesty, testimonies of the Prophets and the holy words of Christ contained in the Gospels find now their fulfilment—though they will be more amply fulfilled hereafter. For in the Gospel according to Matthew, the Saviour, imparting the knowledge of future events to

his blessed Apostles, and through them to later generations of Christians, declared plainly beforehand: "And then will appear the sign of the Son of Man in the heaven." When you take in your hands, as you are accustomed, the sacred book of the Gospels, you will find written there the predictions of this prodigy. I urge you above all men, my Lord, to peruse this prophecy with the more anxious attention on account of the whole context of the passage, for the predictions of our Saviour demand the most reverent study if we are to escape injury in the hands of the opposing Power.

And what would the emperor discover when, as Cyril urged, he perused the context of the text to which the bishop drew his attention? A verse in the Gospel of Matthew deals with the final judgement—"And then shall all the tribes of the earth mourn, and they shall see the Son of Man coming in the clouds of heaven with power and great glory"—and in his catechetical lecture on this subject, Cyril made clear his view that those who, according to Matthew's prophecy, would mourn when a sign of the Son of Man appeared in heaven would be the Jews:

> A sign of a luminous cross precedes the King, showing Him who was formerly crucified; in order that the Jews, who before had pierced Him and plotted [against Him], on seeing it, will mourn tribe by tribe, saying, "This is He who was struck with blows, this is He whose face they spat upon, this is He whom they fastened with bonds; this is He whom of old they crucified and held in derision. Where shall we flee from the face of your wrath?" They will ask, but, surrounded by the angelic hosts, they will not be able to escape anywhere. The sign of the Cross brings fear to the enemy.[23]

For the great Christian scholar Jerome, writing half a century after Cyril, it was imperative that any Jews who came to Jerusalem should do so only to mourn the Temple destroyed for their sins. Jerome, who came to know a number of Jews in the process of producing in Bethlehem his new Latin version of the Hebrew Bible, nonetheless describes with some relish the lamentations of the Jews in Jerusalem on 9 Ab, the anniversary of the destruction of the city in 70 CE as in 586 BCE:

Right up to the present day the treacherous inhabitants, having killed the servants and finally the Son of God, are prohibited to enter Jerusalem except to lament, and they pay a price to be allowed to weep over the ruin of their state. Thus those who once bought the blood of Christ buy now their own fears, and not even their grief is free. On the day when Jerusalem was captured and destroyed by the Romans you may see a mournful populace arrive, a confluence of decrepit females and old men "covered with rags and years," demonstrating in their bodies and their condition the wrath of the Lord. The congregation is a crowd of wretches, but as the yoke of the Lord glitters, and His resurrection shines, and from the Mount of Olives the standard of His cross gleams, the populace keening over the ruins of their Temple is pitiable, yet not suitable to be pitied. So you have tears streaming down cheeks and arms blue from bruises and hair in disarray, and a soldier demands a fee for allowing them to weep more. And would anyone, when he saw these things, be in doubt about the day of tribulation and straitness . . . ?[24]

Earlier in the fourth century, in Constantine's time, a full appreciation of the theological underpinning of this Christian animus against the Jews and against their longing for a restored Temple was perhaps beyond most Jews in Palestine, or, indeed, anyone who was not, or at least had not been at some time, a Christian. The plan of the pagan emperor Julian to rebuild the Jerusalem Temple was that of a former Christian who knew what would hurt most his erstwhile co-religionists. If Julian's attempt in 361–3 had come to fruition, the marginalization of the Jews in the Roman world which had begun in 70 CE, nearly three hundred years before, would have come to an end. But Julian died and was succeeded by Christian rulers, the rebuilding was abandoned, the site of the Temple was left in ruins, and Jews throughout the empire had to learn to live within an increasingly Christian society, their status as outsiders in the Mediterranean world fixed for many centuries to come.

Jerusalem became for the Jews a city to mourn and idealize. "A man may plaster his house, but he should leave a small area unfinished in remembrance of Jerusalem. A man may prepare what is needed for a meal, but he should leave out an item of the menu in remembrance of Jerusalem.

A woman may put on all her ornaments but should leave out some small thing, in remembrance of Jerusalem." The rabbinic sages speculated on the glorious Jerusalem to come, when the Holy one will build Jerusalem out of sapphire stone, "and these stones will shine like the sun, and the worshippers of stars will come and look upon the glory of Israel." Jews scattered all over the world continued to face towards Jerusalem in their prayers. The Seder service on the eve of Passover ended with the hopeful prayer, "Next year in Jerusalem," and at the end of every recitation of the Amidah, the main statutory prayer in Jewish worship both public and private, spoken standing before God three times a day, a petition was added: "May it be your will that the Temple be rebuilt soon in our days." The tears of mourning concealed hope, and hope refused to die.[25]

# THE ORIGINS OF ANTISEMITISM

W HY THEN had the Roman world in the time of Constantine become so much more hostile to Jews and Judaism than it had been in the time of Jesus, three centuries earlier? Was there a seam of malevolence which had simply taken time to surface, a latent suspicion of Jews as strange which inevitably led to dislike and suppression? Was it the unruliness of the Jews that was to blame, or their aspirations for their nation and their God? Was it their prickly exclusiveness, or their acceptance of outsiders as proselytes? Was it just the fact that they were different, and that, although they adopted much of the culture around them, they did not adapt quite enough? Or had the hostility of Rome to the Jews arisen by accident, unintended by either side, propelled by events which the Jews were unable to influence and whose impact on their own concerns they could not have imagined?

Much has been written on the origins of antisemitism in classical antiquity. Hatred of the Jews has been traced by some to Egypt in the third century BCE, by others to the propaganda against the Jews produced by Antiochus Epiphanes in the second century BCE. Some have emphasized the resentment aroused in neighbouring Greek cities by the expansionist policies of the Hasmonaeans in Judaea, others the separateness of Jewish communities in the diaspora which made Jews distinctive and therefore vulnerable as scapegoats. There has been much discussion of the differences between theological roots of Christian anti-Judaism, based on the assertion that the Jewish covenant with God is rendered obsolete by the new covenant of Christ, and the less focused anti-Jewish comments to be found in pagan Greek and Latin authors. It is not my purpose to dispute the value of any of these discussions, which all have their merits, but to emphasize something which has not received the attention it deserves.[1]

I have tried to show that the Jewish world in which Jesus lived was under Roman rule but was not, and did not feel, oppressed by Rome. The power wielded by Pontius Pilate in Jerusalem did indeed rest ultimately on military might, and occasionally he, like other governors, deployed his troops with devastating and unsurprising insensitivity, but for the most part the agents of the Roman state were invisible, their presence felt only in the occasional demand for payment of taxes, the building of a few main roads, and a minimal police presence in the Antonia fortress and the palace of Herod.

The Jerusalem to which Jesus came at Passover in 30 CE was a glorious city, adorned with new gleaming buildings and awash with enthusiastic pilgrims from all over the Roman empire and beyond. The might of the God of the Jews was patent in the astonishing spectacle of the rebuilt Temple. Roman peace had been good for Jerusalem. The Jews prayed for the well-being of the emperor as they had prayed for other royal benefactors in earlier times, and as they still revered the Persian king Cyrus who had restored their ancestors from exile over five centuries before.

It is hard to appreciate the felicity of Judaea in those days only because later events have cast a pall of gloom over memory. Jesus was to be crucified by Pilate and some of his followers thrown to the lions by Roman governors. The magnificent Temple would be reduced to rubble. But at the time no one knew this. Herod had built a city to last. Jerusalem could hope to stand eternally alongside Rome. Jewish society was more open than it had ever been to new ideas. Jews felt free to argue about deep philosophical issues such as the limits of free will, and to debate the finer points of the way of life laid down by the Torah, discussing what it should mean in practice to rest on the Sabbath or conscientiously to pay the tithes due to the priests who served at the altar where sacrifices were performed on behalf of all. They did so secure in the knowledge that all was well in a world in which God was worshipped as he had prescribed. They remembered that they had once been in exile in Babylon and that they had once been ground down by the abomination of desolation with which Antiochus Epiphanes had desecrated God's holy place, but they knew that they themselves lived in better times, in which Roman power deterred assaults by neighbouring peoples and left Jews at liberty to worship as their fore-fathers had.

The Romans were well aware that Jews were different in many aspects of their lifestyle and outlook, but they were used to ruling over strange peoples and revelled in the variety of their subjects. The presence of a Jewish community in Rome gave them opportunities to discover rather more about this nation than others, although they did not always understand what they saw. They thought that Jewish taboos against worshipping other gods than their own or engraving human images on coins were bizarre, but that they could easily be accommodated. Appreciation of Jewish customs led occasionally to emulation, as in the popularity of the weekly Sabbath rest, and occasionally to full adoption, by proselytes, but more often to tolerant amusement. Jews were exotic in the eyes of Romans and the Roman state, and they were sometimes treated as despicable because they were a defeated nation, but they were not seen as dangerous or hostile.

Such tolerance came under stress when revolt broke out in Jerusalem in 66 CE, sparked not by Jewish revulsion against Roman imperialism as a whole but in reaction to maladministration by an individual low-grade governor. The initial Roman response was little more than a police action, a show of force, but it escalated in response to the disaster suffered by Cestius Gallus in his incompetent withdrawal after he had almost conquered the city. His loss of the equivalent of a complete legion at the hands of the inhabitants of an established province of the empire was without precedent and could not be kept quiet. Punitive action was required before other subjects of Rome tried to follow suit.

But the punitive action planned in 66 escalated much further in 70, into an intensive siege of Jerusalem and the eventual destruction of the city. The cause was less the strength of Jewish resistance than a series of *coups d'état* in Rome which culminated in the decision of Vespasian to seek supreme power for himself. The total defeat of the Jews was needed to provide him with the aura of a victorious general which might justify his rise to power. It was not the first or last time that a foreign war had been used to disguise embarrassing truths in domestic Roman politics, and such practices are not unknown in the modern world. But it was unusual for the enemy to be a people who had been within the Roman sphere for over a century, and it was even more unusual for the demonization of the defeated nation to have effects which lasted for centuries. The reasons, again, were political.

Once the Temple in Jerusalem had been destroyed by Roman troops, it was imperative for Vespasian and Titus to claim that what they had done was good for Rome. The centre of Rome was remodelled under the Flavians to reflect the glory of the war. The story of the victory in Judaea became part of the historical consciousness of ordinary Romans, so that poets could evoke it by oblique allusion, and Cassius Dio, a century and a half later, could still describe its course in detail. Once the Flavians had established their power on the back of the defeat of the Jews, it was not in the interest of most subsequent emperors to tamper with the image so carefully constructed, let alone to challenge it directly by allowing the Jews to rebuild their Temple. The exception was Nerva in 96, the only emperor concerned to distance himself from his Flavian predecessors. He did indeed institute change but, as we have seen in Chapter 12, it did not last.

Demonization of the Jews was made easier because, as we have seen in Chapter 10, they were a distinctive group in the city of Rome. In certain political conditions, when mainstream society is looking for a scapegoat, even minor peculiarities in lifestyle can be treated as a reason for hatred. In any case, the lists of those who paid the annual Jewish tax ensured that it was public knowledge who was a Jew. It was still known in the third century that this tax, which was still being collected each year, was a punishment for the revolt of 66–70 CE.[2]

I charted in Chapter 12 the growing despair of the Jews after 70 as their new status in the Roman world began to dawn on them, as also the violence that ensued in 115 and 132, and the even more violent Roman response. But in the long term the most significant development in the century after 70 was a by-product of the hostility of Rome to the Jews, the emergence of Christian antisemitism. Roman imperial power gradually disintegrated in the western Mediterranean and northern Europe from the beginning of the fifth century CE, and although the empire of New Rome, in Byzantium, continued far longer, it too fell in 1453 to the Ottoman Turks. But Rome's living legacy in Europe throughout the Middle Ages to our own times has been the institution and ideology of the Church, and in the eyes of some Christians, ever since the first generation, Judaism has been a religion that ought to have ceased to exist in the first century CE: the Old Testament had been wholly superseded by the New. It is of course important to stress that anti-Judaism based on such religious convictions does not necessarily lead to antisemitism, but it was not by accident that some Christians began in the second century to distance themselves from Jews with language of increasing vitriol at the same time that similar terminology was being used in the centre of imperial power at Rome.

The impetus to the parting of the ways between Judaism and Christianity had come less from the Jewish side than from the Christian. Ordinary Jews in the first century CE accepted that there were many odd Jewish groups who interpreted the Torah in idiosyncratic ways and, in some cases, attributed authority to teachers of their own without claiming biblical warrant, as the Dead Sea sectarians followed the Teacher of Righteousness and the rabbis the decrees of their sages. Jews were used to disagreeing about belief and practice without denying to their opponents a place within the nation of Israel. That the authorities in Jerusalem before 70 CE could also tolerate the doctrines of the earliest followers of Jesus is evident from the report in Acts that the first generation of Christians preached openly in the Temple, occasionally arousing suspicion and being instructed to stop, but mostly being left in peace, so that "daily in the Temple . . . they ceased not to teach and preach Jesus Christ."[3] When the Christians claimed that Jesus was the expected Messiah, in the eyes of non-Christian Jews they were simply mistaken. They could be pitied or mocked for their folly, but there was no need to expel them from the Jewish fold.

The impetus for Christians to distance themselves from Jews after 70 was much more clear-cut. By that date many, probably most, Christians lived outside Judaea, and most of them had not been born Jews. Many, probably most, of them had come under the influence of the doctrine, preached by Paul, that for gentile Christians to take onto themselves the Jewish law would be to show a lack of faith in Christ. Except in their wish to see themselves as descendants of Abraham and to claim the good parts of the ancient history of Israel as their own, they had no need to portray themselves as a variety of Judaism.

But, more crucially in the development of antisemitism, to gain credibility in the Roman world after 70 Christians needed not only to deny their own Jewishness but to attack Judaism altogether. It would have been quite possible for early Christians to have maintained a view of Judaism as another, older, relationship with God, as Paul had sometimes done, and as has become more common, too, among modern Christian theologians.

But if Christians were to defend their own good name and seek converts in
a Roman world in which, after 70, the name of the Jews excited opprobrium, it was easier to join in the attack and agree with the pagans that the
defeat of the Jews and the destruction of the Temple were to be celebrated
as the will of God. As we have seen (in Chapter 12), some Christians, like
Augustine, made the even stronger claim that the miserable state of the
Jews was testimony to the truth preached by the Church, and that it was
necessary to preserve Jews in subjection, rather than convert them to
Christianity, in order that observation of their parlous condition might
strengthen the faithful. For Christians, as for pagan Romans, it was
unthinkable for nearly two millennia, until 1948, to allow a Jewish state to
rise again.

Of course the antagonism to Judaism found in many Christian writings
of the second century was given a theological gloss. The Jews were those
who had rejected Christ and suffered accordingly; in a more extreme form,
the Jews were those who had killed him. The accusation is too familiar to
appreciate readily how bizarre it is. According to the Gospels themselves,
Jesus gained many Jewish followers in Jerusalem, as did his disciples after
the crucifixion. It was no more (or less) true that "the Jews rejected Christ"
than it was true that the other inhabitants of the Mediterranean world
rejected the missionaries who came to them: in all such places, some were
persuaded, some were not. Nor was it true that the Jews as a whole had
killed Jesus. His death was engineered by the High Priestly authorities in
the Temple, intent on avoiding disturbances in the volatile pilgrim season,
but it was impossible to know how many other Jews considered that it was
"right for one man to die for all the people." The Gospels record that the
crowd of Jews, asked by Pilate who should be released, asked for freedom
to be given to a robber called Barabbas rather than Jesus, but how large or
representative was the crowd? What is certain is that the order to execute
Jesus was given ultimately by Pontius Pilate as Roman governor but that,
when he washed his hands of responsibility, he succeeded in eventually
whitewashing for later Christians not just himself but the Roman imperial
regime as a whole.[4]

In any case, as during the second and third centuries Christian theological discourse took on a life of its own, attitudes towards the Jews hard-
ened. By the time of Constantine, Christians took for granted that Jews
were to be despised and shunned. The assumption was inherited by medi-

eval Christendom from the Christian Roman empire, and has by no means wholly faded away in the modern world.

CAN PREJUDICES so firmly rooted in the soil of antiquity ever be eradicated? Can Jews ever be treated in a Christian world as a nation like any other? So hoped the visionary philosopher Moses Hess (1812–75). Originally from an orthodox Jewish background in Bonn, Hess devoted himself in the 1840s and 1850s to the analysis and promotion of European politics and ethical socialism, becoming in the process an associate of Marx and Engels. But in 1862, after twenty years of estrangement, he felt drawn back to his Jewish heritage, prompted by his observation of the liberation of oppressed nationalities around Europe. Might not the solution for other peoples also be valid for the Jews? Might not a Jewish state, founded on the soil of Palestine for the first time since antiquity, bring the travails of the Jews to an end? For Hess, there was no better evidence that such dreams were possible than the emergence in Italy in 1857 of an independent secular state, freed, after a war of liberation, from the power of the Vatican: "The liberation of the Eternal City on the Tiber marks the emancipation of the Eternal City on Mount Moriah. Jerusalem's orphaned children will also be allowed to participate in the awakening from the hibernation of the Middle Ages with its evil dreams." Hence the name he gave to his visionary tract was *Rom und Jerusalem*.[5]

Nearly two thousand years after the Temple was destroyed, two hundred years after Hess's birth, and sixty years after the establishment of an independent Jewish state in Palestine, it is too early yet to say whether Hess's optimism was justified, and the legacy of prejudice created and entrenched as a result of the political ambitions of a series of Roman emperors after 70 CE finally expunged.

# NOTES

## ABBREVIATIONS

Abbreviations follow the conventions in S. Hornblower and A. Spawforth (eds.), *The Oxford Classical Dictionary*, 3rd edn. (Oxford, 1996); D. N. Freedman (ed.), *The Anchor Bible Dictionary* (New York, 1992), for biblical and apocryphal texts and for Jewish and Christian texts not in *OCD*; H. Danby, *The Mishnah* (Oxford, 1933), 806, for rabbinic texts; G. Vermes, *The Complete Dead Sea Scrolls in English* (Harmondsworth, 1997), for Dead Sea scrolls; E. Schürer, rev. G. Vermes *et al.*, *The History of the Jewish People in the Age of Jesus Christ*, 3 vols. (Edinburgh, 1973–87), vol. 3, pp. 812–13, for the works of Philo not in *OCD*.

## OTHER ABBREVIATIONS

| | |
|---|---|
| b. | *ben* ("son of") |
| *b.* | Babylonian Talmud |
| *CPJ* | V. A. Tcherikover *et al.*, *Corpus Papyrorum Judaicarum*, 3 vols. (Cambridge, Mass., 1957–64) |
| *DJD* | D. Barthélemy *et al.*, *Discoveries in the Judaean Desert*, 39 vols. (Oxford, 1956–2002) |
| *JIWE* | D. Noy, *Jewish Inscriptions of Western Europe*, 2 vols. (Cambridge, 1993–5) |
| *JJS* | *Journal of Jewish Studies* |
| *m.* | *Mishnah* |
| *P Yadin* | B. A. Levine *et al.*, *The Documents from the Bar Kokhba Period in the Cave of Letters*, 2 vols. (Jerusalem, 1989–2002) |
| R. | Rabbi |
| *RPC* | *Roman Provincial Coinage* |
| *t.* | *Tosefta* |
| *y.* | *Palestinian Talmud* |

## INTRODUCTION: THE MAIN WITNESS

1. On Josephus' career, see T. Rajak, *Josephus: The Historian and His Society* (London, 1983).
2. On Josephus' private sentiments: Joseph. *BJ* 1. 9; for scholarship on his writings, see L. H. Feldman, *Josephus and Modern Scholarship, 1937–80* (Berlin, 1984); idem, *Josephus: A Supplementary Bibliography* (New York and London, 1986); and the introductions to the new transla-

tions of Josephus' works published by Brill, S. Mason *et al.* (eds.), *Flavius Josephus, Translation and Commentary* (Leiden, 2000–).

### PROLOGUE: THE DESTRUCTION OF JERUSALEM, 66–70 CE

1. Joseph. *BJ* 2. 305–7.
2. Ibid. 2. 326–7.
3. Ibid. 2. 409.
4. Ibid. 2. 451–5.
5. Ibid. 2. 540.
6. Ibid. 2. 532.
7. Ibid. 2. 648–9.
8. Tac. *Hist.* 5. 10.
9. For the different coin types, see Y. Meshorer, *A Treasury of Jewish Coins from the Persian Period to Bar Kokhba* (Jerusalem and Nyack, NY, 2001).
10. M. Goodman, "Coinage and Identity: The Jewish Evidence," in C. Howgego, V. Heuchert and A. Burnett (eds.), *Coinage and Identity in the Roman Provinces* (Oxford, 2005), 163–6.
11. H. Eshel, "Documents of the First Jewish Revolt from the Judaean Desert," in A. M. Berlin and J. A. Overman (eds.), *The First Jewish Revolt: Archaeology, History and Ideology* (London and New York, 2002), 157–63.
12. Euseb. *Hist. eccl.* 3. 5. 2–3.
13. On Ananus: Joseph. *BJ* 4. 319.
14. Ibid. 4. 560–63.
15. Tac. *Hist.* 5. 12. The statement by Tacitus that John was known as Bargioras is confused. This was in fact the name of Simon, eventually commander-in-chief of the Jewish forces.
16. Joseph. *BJ* 7. 263–71.
17. Luke 19: 43.
18. Joseph. *BJ* 5. 427–30, 512–15, 567, 569–71; 6. 197.
19. Ibid. 6. 201–13. The story may well be apocryphal, since the eating of children was a standard motif in biblical descriptions of the horrors of siege (cf. Lev. 26: 29).
20. Joseph. *BJ* 5. 450–51.
21. Ibid. 5. 299.
22. Ibid. 5. 334.
23. Ibid. 5. 349–53.
24. Ibid. 5. 362, 375, 420, 422.
25. Ibid. 6. 54–5, 58–66.
26. Ibid. 6. 222–6, 228.
27. Ibid. 6. 271–6.
28. Ibid. 6. 316.
29. Ibid. 6. 322.
30. Ibid. 7. 1–3.

### CHAPTER ONE: A TALE OF TWO CITIES

1. Joseph. *AJ* 15. 310; Livy 40. 29.
2. Deut. 11: 14–15 (Heb.); Mic. 4: 4.
3. Joseph. *BJ* 3. 516–21.
4. Threefold division: Joseph. *BJ* 3. 35–58; on Palmyra, see I. Browning, *Palmyra* (London, 1979).

5. "Not a country with a sea coast": Joseph. *Ap.* 1. 60; on Babylonian Jews, see J. Neusner, *A History of the Jews in Babylonia,* vol. 1: *The Parthian Period* (London, rev. edn. 1969).

6. F. Millar, *The Roman Near East, 31 BC–AD 337* (Cambridge, Mass., and London, 1993).

7. Plin. *HN* 5. 15 (70).

8. Augustus, *RG* 19–20 (new temples); Suet. *Aug.* 28. 3; 29. 5.

9. On the gardens: Suet. *Iul.* 83. 2.

10. W. Scheidel, "Human Mobility in Roman Italy, 1: The Free Population," *JRS* 94 (2004), 1–26; N. Purcell, "Rome and Its Development Under Augustus and His Successors," *CAH* vol. 10 (Cambridge, 1996), 782–811.

11. Strabo, *Geog.* 5. 3. 2, 7–8.

12. Dion. Hal. *Ant. Rom.* 3. 67. 5.

13. Ov. *Pont.* 1. 29 (city life), 33–8.

14. Strabo, *Geog.* 5. 3. 8.

15. Ibid.

16. Plin. *HN* 3. 5. 67.

17. Vitr. *De arch.* 2. 8. 17.

18. Juv. 10. 81.

19. See in general J. Carcopino, *Daily Life in Ancient Rome,* trans. E. O. Lorimer (London, 1941).

20. Polyb. 26. 10 (=26.1 in W. R. Paton [ed.], *Polybius: The Histories,* vol. 5 [London, 1927], 480).

21. F. Millar, "The Background to the Maccabean Revolution," *JJS* 29 (1978), 1–21.

22. On the early Hasmonaeans, see J. Sievers, *The Hasmonaeans and Their Supporters: From Mattathias to the Death of John Hyrcanus I* (Atlanta, 1990); on the date of composition of 1 Maccabees, see S. Schwartz, "Israel and the Nations Roundabout: I Maccabees and the Hasmonean Expansion," *JJS* 42 (1991), 16–38.

23. *m. B.K.* 6. 6.

24. On Alexander Jannaeus, see E. Schürer, rev. G. Vermes *et al., The History of the Jewish People in the Age of Jesus Christ,* 3 vols. (Edinburgh, 1973–87), vol. 1, pp. 219–28.

25. See D. R. Schwartz, "Josephus on Hyrcanus II," in F. Parente and J. Sievers (eds.), *Josephus and the History of the Greco-Roman Period* (Leiden, 1994), 210–32.

26. Joseph. *AJ* 14. 77–8.

27. Ibid. 14. 403.

28. Palace: Joseph. *BJ* 5. 177–81; theatre and amphitheatre: *AJ* 15. 268, 272, 279; hippodrome: *AJ* 17. 255; *BJ* 2. 44; Memorial of Herod: *BJ* 5. 108, 507; in general, P. Richardson, *Herod: King of the Jews and Friend of the Romans* (Columbia, SC, 1996); D. W. Roller, *The Building Program of Herod the Great* (London, 1998).

29. *Let. Arist.* 83–4, 116; Polybius ap. Joseph. *AJ* 12. 136.

30. Joseph. *AJ* 15. 380–82, 384–5, 387.

31. Ibid. 15. 392, 394–6.

32. Ibid. 15. 412–13.

33. *m. Ab.* 5. 5.

34. Acts 2: 5, 9–11; on pilgrimage: M. Goodman, "The Pilgrimage Economy of Jerusalem in the Second Temple Period," in L. I. Levine (ed.), *Jerusalem: Its Sanctity and Centrality to Judaism, Christianity, and Islam* (New York, 1999), 69–76.

35. 18,000 unemployed: Joseph. *AJ* 20. 219–22; on Helena, *AJ* 20. 35, 49, 51, 101; on the monument: *AJ* 20. 95; *BJ* 5. 55; Paus. 8. 16. 4–5.

36. On population figures, see the salutary caution of B. McGing, "Population and Proselytism: How Many Jews Were There in the Ancient World?," in J. R. Barlett (ed), *Jews in the Hellenistic and Roman Cities* (London, 2002), 88–106.

37. Joseph. *BJ* 6. 420–25; Philo, *Spec. Leg.* 1. 69.

38. *m. Bikk.* 3. 3.

## CHAPTER TWO: ONE WORLD UNDER ROME

1. Joseph. *BJ* 2. 355–64, 370, 378; T. Rajak, "Friends, Romans, Subjects: Agrippa II's Speech in Josephus's *Jewish War,*" in L. Alexander (ed.), *Images of Empire* (Sheffield, 1991), 122–34.

2. Aelius Aristides, *To Rome,* with analysis by J. H. Oliver, "The Ruling Power," *TAPA* 43 (1953), 871–1003; S. L. Dyson, "Native Revolt Patterns in the Roman Empire," *ANRW* II.3 (1975), 138–75.

3. Arr. *Peripl. M. Eux.* 17. 2.

4. *BM Coins, Rom. Emp.* vol. 2, nos. 301–8.

5. Plin. *Ep.* 10. 74; see, in general, K. Hopkins, *Conquerors and Slaves* (Cambridge, 1978), chapter 5.

6. C. F. Noreña, "The Communication of the Emperor's Virtues," *JRS* 91 (2001), 146–68.

7. A. S. Hunt and C. C. Edgar, *Select Papyri,* 2 vols. (London, 1932–4), no. 211; text of Senate decree: W. Eck, A. Caballos and F. Fernández, *Das Senatus Consultum de Cn. Pisone Patre* (Munich, 1996).

8. On the false Neros, see G. W. Bowersock, "The Mechanics of Subversion in the Roman Provinces," in A. Giovannini (ed.), *Opposition et résistances à l'empire d'Auguste à Trajan* (Genoa, 1987), 291–320.

9. Smallwood, *Docs. . . . Gaius,* no. 43.

10. *FIRA,* vol. 1, no. 74, lines 8–10.

11. Joseph. *AJ* 14. 263–4.

12. See Chapter 12.

13. *P Yadin* no. 11.

14. Plin. *Ep.* 10. 27–8; Apul. *Met.* 9. 39; F. Millar, "The World of the Golden Ass," *JRS* 71 (1981), 63–75.

15. Acts 25: 10–12.

16. Philo, *In Flacc.* 97–101.

17. Plin. *Ep.* 3. 4; 10. 65 (foundlings).

18. Ibid. 10. 41–2; 10. 17b–18.

19. P. Garnsey and R. Saller, *The Roman Empire: Economy, Society and Culture* (London, 1987), chapter 2; J. E. Lendon, *Empire of Honour: The Art of Government in the Roman World* (Oxford, 1997).

20. Joseph. *Vit.* 13–16.

21. Acts 12: 1–19; D. R. Schwartz, *Agrippa I: The Last King of Judaea* (Tübingen, 1990).

22. *m. Sot.* 7. 8.

23. Joseph. *AJ* 18. 159.

24. Suet. *Calig.* 37. 1.

25. Joseph. *AJ* 18. 203–4; Tac. *Ann.* 6. 50 (rumoured suffocation by order of Macro); Joseph. *AJ* 18. 239.

26. Suet. *Calig.* 11, 37; Joseph. *AJ* 18. 256; J. P. V. D. Balsdon, *The Emperor Gaius (Caligula)* (Oxford, 1934).

27. Philo, *Spec. Leg.* 278–9, 290–91, 327.

28. Joseph. *AJ* 19. 1–273.

29. Cass. Dio 60. 8. 2–3; Suet. *Claud.* 25. 5; Joseph. *AJ* 19. 275.

30. Joseph. *AJ* 19. 341.

31. Acts 12: 23; *OGI* no. 419 (titles of Agrippa).

32. Citations from Pliny: Plin. *HN* 36. 9 (51) (trans. Eicholz) (marble); 33. 21 (66) (trans. Rackham) (gold); 36. 66 (193–5) (trans. Eicholz) (glass); 12. 32 (63–5) (trans. Rackham, adapted) (frankincense). On the ecology of the Mediterranean in general, see especially P. Hordern and N. Purcell, *The Corrupting Sea: A Study of Mediterranean History* (Oxford, 2000).

33. Dion. Hal. *Ant. Rom.* 20. 15. 1–2.
34. Strabo, *Geog.* 3. 2. 5 (144); 15. 1–2.
35. Plin. *HN* 35. 46 (160–61).
36. Ibid. 36. 1 (1–3).
37. Ibid. 13. 27 (89).
38. Strabo, *Geog.* 2. 2. 3.
39. Cass. Dio 55. 31.
40. Strabo, *Geog.* 4. 4. 3 (197).
41. Ibid. 5. 2. 12 (218).
42. Suet. *Dom.* 7. 2.
43. On the archaeological evidence for trade: K. Greene, *The Archaeology of the Roman Economy* (London, 1986); on the role of entrepreneurs, see P. Temin, "A Market Economy in the Early Roman Empire," *JRS* 91 (2001), 169–81; on the role of the state, L. Casson, "The Role of the State in Rome's Grain Trade," in J. H. D'Arms and E. C. Kopff (eds.), *The Seaborne Commerce of Ancient Rome* (Rome, 1980), 21–33.
44. S. Hong, J.-P. Candelone, C. C. Patterson and C. F. Boutron, "Greenland Ice Evidence of Hemispheric Lead Pollution Two Millennia Ago by Greek and Roman Civilizations," *Science* 265 (1994), 1841–3.
45. Vitr. *De arch.* 10. 2. 8–10. See in general A. Wilson, "Machines, Power and the Ancient Economy," *JRS* 92 (2002), 1–32.
46. Suet. *Vesp.* 18.
47. *ILS* no. 5863.
48. Plin. *HN* 18. 7 (35).
49. *FIRA* vol. 1, no. 103, lines 19–27.
50. *P Yadin* no. 16, lines 29–33.
51. Isoc. *Paneg.* 50.
52. H. I. Marrou, *History of Education in Antiquity* (London, 1956), 168.
53. A. I. Baumgarten, *The Phoenician History of Philo of Byblos* (Leiden, 1981).
54. Hor. *Epist.* 2. 1. 156–7.
55. A. E. Astin, *Cato the Censor* (Oxford, 1978); on Apollo: Livy 4. 25. 3; J. Gagé, *Apollon romain* (Paris, 1955).
56. Dan. 7–12; 1 Macc. 5. 6–9; Wis. 13. 10.
57. Joseph. *Ap.* 1. 6–7; Juv. 3. 58–61.
58. Eupolemus, frag. 1, and Artapanus, frag. 3, in C. R. Holladay, *Fragments from Hellenistic Jewish Authors,* 4 vols. (Chico, Calif., 1983–); Josephus on Plato: *Ap.* 2. 257; on Philo: *AJ* 18. 259; on Philo, see S. Sandmel, *Philo of Alexandria: An Introduction* (New York and Oxford, 1979).
59. A. Erskine, *Troy between Greece and Rome* (Oxford, 2001); 1 Macc. 12. 5–23 (citation from 12: 20–21); E. Rawson, *The Spartan Tradition in European Thought* (Oxford, 1969).
60. On the ancient construction of contrasts between Greek and Roman attitudes to knowledge, see e.g., S. Cuomo, *Ancient Mathematics* (London, 2002), 192–201; on the Maccabean revolt as a clash of cultures: Tac. *Hist.* 5. 8; 2 Macc. 2. 21 and 14. 38 (*ioudaismos*) and 4. 13 (*hellenismos*); M. Goodman, "Jewish Attitudes to Greek Culture in the Period of the Second Temple," in G. Abramson and T. Parfitt (eds.), *Jewish Education and Learning* (Reading, PA, 1994), 167–74.
61. 2 Macc. 4. 12–16; on Aristobulus: Joseph. *AJ* 12. 318; on Hasmonaean tombs: 1 Macc. 13. 25–30; on coins of Alexander Jannaeus: Y. Meshorer, *A Treasury of Jewish Coins from the Persian Period to Bar Kokhba* (Jerusalem and Nyack, NY, 2001), 37–41, 301–3.
62. For all these discussions, see Y. Shavit, *Athens in Jerusalem: Classical Antiquity and Hellenism in the Making of the Modern Secular Jew* (London, 1997).

63. Rom. 2: 9–10.

64. Joseph. *AJ* 18. 183; 20. 173–8; *BJ* 2. 266–8; 3. 409; M. Hengel, *Hellenism and Judaism*, 2 vols. (Philadelphia, 1974); idem, *The "Hellenization" of Judaea in the First Century after Christ* (Philadelphia, 1989).

65. L. I. Levine, *Judaism and Hellenism in Antiquity: Conflict or Confluence?* (Seattle, 1998); M. Goodman, "Epilogue," in J. J. Collins and G. E. Sterling (eds.), *Hellenism in the Land of Israel* (Notre Dame, Ind., 2001), 302–5; *m. Sot.* 9. 14; S. Lieberman, *Hellenism in Jewish Palestine*, 2nd edn. (New York, 1962); E. S. Gruen, *Heritage and Hellenism: The Reinvention of Jewish Tradition* (Berkeley and London, 1998).

66. L. Robert, *Les Gladiateurs dans l'Orient grec* (Paris, 1940).

67. On Nepos: H.-G. Pflaum, *Les Carrières procuratoriennes équestres sous le Haut-Empire romain*, 2 vols. (Paris, 1960–61), no. 95; Hamian archers: Smallwood, *Docs. . . . Nerva*, no. 323a; Virilis: *ILS* no. 2653; Tac. *Hist.* 2. 80.

68. Joseph. *AJ* 14. 226–7.

69. *Let. Arist.* 12–14 (captives taken to Egypt); Philo, *Spec. Leg.* 281–2.

70. *CPJ* nos. 14, 38, 43, 46, 48; Philo, *Spec. Leg.* 129 (seizure of merchandise); *In Flacc.* 56–7 (pillaging); Acts 18: 1–3 (Aquila); Joseph. *Ap.* 2. 44; *AJ* 12. 150; letter of Claudius: *CPJ* no. 153.

71. Tac. *Hist.* 5. 5; *Let. Arist.* 181; Gal. 2: 12 (Peter); *3 Macc.* 3.4; Diod. Sic. 34/35. 1. 2.

72. Herod Antipas: Luke 13: 32; Joseph. *AJ* 18. 113; Antiochus of Commagene: Joseph. *AJ* 20. 139; Drusilla and Felix: Joseph. *AJ* 20. 141–4; on Berenice, see Chapter 12.

73. Timothy: Acts 16: 1–3; on endogamy: Philo, *Spec. Leg.* 3. 29.

## CHAPTER THREE: DIVERSITY AND TOLERATION

1. App. *Mith.* 116–17.

2. Verg. *Aen.* 8. 722–3.

3. Strabo, *Geog.* 3. 4. 20.

4. Ibid. 11. 8. 4; Acts 18: 2; S. Mitchell, "In Search of the Pontic Community in Antiquity," in A. K. Bowman *et al.* (eds.), *Representations of Empire: Rome and the Mediterranean World* (Oxford, 2002), 35–64.

5. J. M. C. Toynbee, *The Hadrianic School* (Cambridge, 1934), 29, 55–6, 123–5.

6. R. R. R. Smith, "*Simulacra Gentium*: The *ethne* from the Sebasteion at Aphrodisias," *JRS* 78 (1988), 50–77; on Augustus' portico: Serv. *Ad Aen.* 8. 721.

7. Augustus, *RG* 26–7, 30–32.

8. Smith, "*Simulacra*"; Toynbee, *Hadrianic School*, 152–9.

9. Plin. *HN* 3. 5 (43); on *itineraria*, see O. A. W. Dilke, *Greek and Roman Maps* (London, 1985), 112–29; K. Brodersen, *Terra Cognita* (Hildesheim, 1995), 165–94; on ethnography and politics, see C. Nicolet, *Space, Geography and Politics in the Early Roman Empire* (Ann Arbor, 1991).

10. On the Celts, see Strabo, *Geog.* 4. 4. 2–6 (from Posidonius?), citation from 4. 4. 4; on Varro and Cicero, see A. Momigliano, *Alien Wisdom: The Limits of Hellenization* (Cambridge, 1975), 69–72.

11. Strabo, *Geog.* 17. 3. 24–5.

12. Ibid. 17. 3. 7 (trans. Jones); K. Clarke, *Between Geography and History: Hellenistic Conceptions of the Roman World* (Oxford, 1999).

13. Tac. *Germ.* (citations from 2; 4; 15; 18; 23–4; 26; 5. 3; 19. 2–3).

14. Ubii: Tac. *Germ.* 28–9; W. Eck, *Köln in römischer Zeit* (Cologne, 2004); Batavi: Tac. *Germ.* 29; Arminius: Tac. *Ann.* 2. 88; auxiliaries: A. K. Goldsworthy, *The Roman Army at War, 100 BC–AD 200* (Oxford, 1996), 68.

15. Phlegon, *Mir.* 9, 34–5.

16. Ibid. 13–14.

17. Plin. *HN* 7.3 (35) (hippocentaur), 10. 2 (5) (phoenix); Tac. *Ann.* 6. 28.

18. See Chapter 2, pp. 86–92.

19. Plin. *HN Praef.* 13, 17 (aims), 12. 54 (111–23) (balsam); 31. 18 (24) (sabbatical stream); on the elder Pliny's working methods: Plin. *Ep.* 3. 87; on the Joppe skeleton: Plin. *HN* 9. 4 (11).

20. Ibid. 30. 2 (11) (magic); 31. 44 (95) (fish sauce); 5. 15 (73) (Essenes).

21. Ibid. 37. 77 (203) (on Spain); on the origins of Latin authors, *CHCL,* vol. 2.

22. Strabo, *Geog.* 3. 2. 13 (Turdetania); S. Keay, "Recent Archaeological Work in Roman Iberia," *JRS* 93 (2003), 146–211.

23. R. Batty, "Mela's Phoenician Geography," *JRS* 90 (2000), 70.

24. Pomponius Mela, *De Chorographia* 2. 6 (96) (Tingentera), 1. 12 (66) (Tyre and Sidon), 1. 8 (41) ("our custom"), 2. 7 (105) ("Roman disaster").

25. Ibid. 2. 6 (86) (Spain); 2. 5 (83); 3. 6 (57) ("our authors"); 3. 6 (46) (Gades); 3. 10 (108) ("our strait"); Batty, "Mela's Phoenician Geography," 88; on the manuscript tradition of *De Chorographia,* A. Silberman, *Pomponius Mela: Chronographie* (Paris, 1988), pp. xliii–li.

26. *ILS* no. 8794, lines 25–6 (Nero's speech); Plut. *Prae. ger. reip.* 10 (805A).

27. Plut. *Quaest. Rom.* 6 (265B), 7 (265E), 10 (266C), 105 (289A); on Plutarch's career, see C. P. Jones, *Plutarch and Rome* (Oxford, 1971).

28. On Athenian laws, see J. H. Oliver, *The Civic Tradition and Roman Athens* (Baltimore, 1983), 103–4; on Polemo: Philostr. *VS* 535.

29. Plut. *Lyc.* 28.6 (on the character of Lycurgus); P. Cartledge and A. J. Spawforth, *Hellenistic and Roman Sparta: A Tale of Two Cities* (London, 1989), 190, 203–7.

30. Paus. 8. 52. 1; C. Habicht, *Pausanias' Guide to Ancient Greece* (Berkeley and London, 1985).

31. Philostr. *VS* 580 (Aristogeiton), 588–9 (Hypereides); on coins: *RPC,* 171 (Nysa), 144 (Pergamum).

32. On Arrian, see P. A. Stadter, *Arrian of Nicomedia* (Chapel Hill, NC, 1980); in general, G. Woolf, "Becoming Roman, Staying Greek," *PCPS* 40 (1994), 116–43.

33. Dio Chrys. *Or.* 7.

34. Paus. 10. 4. 1.

35. Smallwood, *Docs. . . . Gaius,* nos. 373 (a) and (b).

36. Augustus, *RG* 27; names: A. K. Bowman, *Egypt after the Pharaohs* (London, 1986), 124; Diod. Sic. 1. 271; N. Lewis, *Life in Egypt under Roman Rule* (Oxford, 1983), 69–70 (Kronion archive), 158 (census document), 44 (brother-sister marriage); imperial edict: *Cod. Iust.* 5. 4. 17.

37. A. S. Hunt and C. C. Edgar, *Select Papyri,* 2 vols. (London, 1932–4), vol. 2, no. 278.

38. Bowman, *Egypt,* 174–8.

39. *P Oxy.* 1029 (hieroglyph cutters).

40. Bowman, *Egypt,* 183 (Socnopaiou Nesos); P. W. van der Horst, *Chaeremon* (Leiden, 1984), frag. 10.

41. M. Lichtheim, *Ancient Egyptian Literature: A Book of Readings,* 3 vols. (Berkeley, 1973–80), vol. 3, p. 141 (Setne), pp. 184–209 (wisdom text [Papyrus Insinger]); S. West, "The Greek Version of the Legend of Tefnut," *JEg. Arch.* (1969), 161–83.

42. *P Oxy.* 2332 (*Oracle of the Potter*); *CPJ,* no. 156b, col. I, lines 17–18; no. 156c, col. II, lines 22–6; no. 156d, col. III, lines 9–12 (Isidorus).

43. Acts 14: 11 (Lystra); in general, R. MacMullen, "Provincial Languages in the Roman Empire," *AJPhil.* 87 (1966), 1–17; F. Millar, "Local Cultures in the Roman Empire: Libyan, Punic and Latin in Roman Africa," *JRS* 58 (1968), 126–34.

44. H. J. W. Drijvers (ed.), *The Book of the Laws of Countries: Dialogue on Fate of Bardaisan of Edessa* (Assen, 1965), 57.

45. Tac. *Agr.* 21.

46. Cass. Dio 57. 4. 6 (ed. Boissevain); I. M. Ferris, *Enemies of Rome: Barbarians Through Roman Eyes* (Stroud, 2000); B. Isaac, *The Invention of Racism in Classical Antiquity* (Princeton, 2004).
47. Ptol. *Tetr.* 2. 3. 65–6.
48. Suet. *Claud.* 25. 5; Plin. *HN* 30. 4 (13).
49. On Gordianus, see *L'année épigraphique* 1954, no. 138.
50. On Agrippa I, see above, pp. 76–85; on Philo, see above, p. 82.
51. On Tiberius Iulius Alexander: Tac. *Ann.* 15. 28; *Hist.* 1. 11; Juv. 1. 130–31; V. A. Burr, *Tiberius Julius Alexander* (Bonn, 1955).

## CHAPTER FOUR: IDENTITIES

1. Acts 22: 24–6, 28.
2. A. N. Sherwin-White, *Roman Citizenship,* 2nd edn. (Oxford, 1973).
3. Cic. *Arch.* 9 (19, 21).
4. Suet. *Aug.* 40. 3; A. M. Duff, *Freedmen in the Early Roman Empire* (Oxford, 1928); K. R. Bradley, *Slaves and Masters in the Roman Empire* (Oxford, 1984), chapter 3.
5. S. J. D. Cohen, *The Beginnings of Jewishness: Boundaries, Varieties, Uncertainties* (Berkeley and London, 1999).
6. Story of Adiabene conversions: Joseph. *AJ* 20. 17–96.
7. Ibid. 20. 18, 34–5, 38–42, 43–8.
8. M. Goodman, "Identity and Authority in Ancient Judaism," *Judaism* 39 (1990), 192–201.
9. Gen. 41: 50–52 (Asenath); *t. Kidd.* 4. 16; Acts 16: 1–3.
10. "Ambrosiaster," commentary on Galatians 2: 4–5 (*CSEL* 81. 3. 20–21). But see the sceptical discussion in Cohen, *Beginnings,* 360–77.
11. Joseph. *BJ* 2. 466–8.
12. There is a good introduction to much of this literature in G. W. E. Nickelsburg, *Jewish Literature between the Bible and the Mishnah,* 2nd edn. (Minneapolis, 2005).
13. Deut. 23: 13–15.
14. Joseph. *BJ* 2. 137, 148–9.
15. Philo, *Legum allegoriae* 3. 153.
16. *b. Yoma* 75b.
17. *b. Ket.* 5a.
18. On Samaritan identity: A. D. Crown (ed.), *The Samaritans* (Tübingen, 1989); temple in Heliopolis: *BJ* 7. 427–32; on self-description of Samaritans in relation to Jews: Joseph. *AJ* 9. 291.
19. Cic. *Rep.* 4. 20; see C. Nicolet, *Space, Geography and Politics in the Early Roman Empire* (Ann Arbor, 1991).
20. Tac. *Agr.* 10.
21. Augustus, *RG* 26.
22. Ov. *Fast.* 2. 683–4.
23. Jerusalem as navel: LXX Ezek 38: 12, cf. M. Tilly, *Jerusalem—Nabel der Welt* (Stuttgart, 2002); on levels of "centrality" in the world: *Tanhuma* (Buber), *Kedoshim* 10 (on Lev. 19: 23ff.); Pilate and the standards: Joseph. *AJ* 18: 55–9; gentiles in Temple: Acts 21: 28–9.
24. 1Q *ApGen* 21. 10–12.
25. *Sifre on Deuteronomy* 51 (ed. Horovitz-Finkelstein, pp. 117–18).
26. Lev. 18: 24, 28.
27. On Roman ethnography, see Chapter 3; on rabbinic caricatures, see S. Stern, *Jewish Identity in Early Rabbinic Writings* (Leiden, 1994), chapter 1; on Josephus' geography, see Y. Shahar, *Josephus Geographicus: The Classical Context of Geography in Josephus* (Tübingen, 2004), 269–70.

28. Deut. 17: 8; *Sifre on Deuteronomy* 152 (ed. Horovitz-Finkelstein, p. 206).

29. Table of the nations: Gen. 10: 32.

30. *Jub.* 8. 10–9. 15; 10. 27–35 (see J. M. Scott, *Geography in Early Judaism and Christianity: The Book of Jubilees* [Cambridge, 2002]).

31. Joseph. *AJ* 1. 128 (Chethimos), 129 (Noah), 121 (Greeks invent names).

32. *1 En.* 33. 1–3 (in M. A. Knibb [ed.], *The Ethiopic Book of Enoch* [Oxford, 1978], 123).

33. Suet. *Aug.* 7. 2.

34. Horatius: Cic. *Dom.* 54 (139); Livy 2. 86–8.

35. For numerous stories about the younger Cato, see Plut. *Cat. Min.*

36. Macrob. *Sat.* 1. 16. 2 (festivals).

37. Ibid. 1. 16. 16 (days wrong for war); 1. 16. 20 (defence permitted); Plut. *Luc.* 27. 7.

38. Joseph. *Ap.* 1. 209–11.

39. Plut. *De superst.* 8 (169B).

40. *m. Ber.* 1. 1.

41. On Pentecost and the *omer:* Lev. 23: 15; *m. Men.* 10.3 (on the dispute over dating with the "Boethusians").

42. Lev. 25: 10; Joseph. *AJ* 14. 202 (Julius Caesar); *DJD* vol. 2, no. 18; *m. Shebi., passim.*

43. Joseph. *AJ* 3. 280–86 (Jubilee).

44. C. R. Holladay, *Fragments from Hellenistic Jewish Authors,* vol. 1: *Historians* (Chico, Calif., 1983), with citation of Pseudo-Eupolemus on p. 174; Cleodemus in Joseph. *AJ* 1. 240–41; on the Christian motivation for preserving these texts, S. Inowlocki, *Eusebius and the Jewish Authors: His Citation Technique in an Apologetic Context* (Leiden, 2006).

45. *m. Ab.* 1. 1–12.

46. Joseph. *Ap.* 1. 41 (on historiography); *AJ* 18. 314–70 (Asinaeus and Anilaeus).

47. Joseph. *Ap.* 1. 37–9; Philo, *Migr.* 1–2; *QpHab* 9. 8–10; on names: T. Ilan, *Lexicon of Jewish Names in Late Antiquity,* vol. 1 (Tübingen, 2002), with M. H. Williams, in *ZPE* 140 (2002), 279–83 (on Moses), and S. Honigman, in *ZPE* 146 (2004), 279–97 (on Abraham).

48. Rabbinic discussion in *m. Ber.* 1. 2 (blue and white); for the claim that Jews had a distinctive notion of time, see S. Stern, *Time and Process in Ancient Judaism* (Oxford, 2003).

49. Verg. *G.* 3. 284; Sen. *Ep.* 1. 3; Joseph. *Ap.* 2. 279, 290.

50. *t. Sot.* 13. 3; Joseph. *AJ* 3. 218 (Urim and Thummim); *m. Sot.* 9. 12 (death of first prophets).

51. Nostalgia for Second Temple: *m. Sot.* 9. 12; sin brings disaster: *Pss. Sol.* 8. 8, 13–15, 19–20.

52. Lucr. 2. 77–9; Eccl. 1: 2–4.

53. Sen. *Ep.* 71. 15; Verg. *Ecl.* 4. 4–7, 21–2, 43–5 (trans. Fairclough, adapted); *aeterna urbs:* Tib. 2. 5. 23; Ov. *Fast.* 3. 72; for the coins: *BM Coins, Rom. Emp.* vol. 2, nos. 423–4; *RIC* vol. 2, p. 51, no. 309; H. Mattingly, *Roman Coins* (London, 1927), 160.

54. Joseph. *AJ* 10. 209, 277, 278, 280.

55. Dan. 2: 35.

56. Joseph. *AJ* 10. 210.

57. *m. Taan.* 4. 6; Joseph. *BJ* 6. 267–8.

58. *1QM* 9. 5–6.

59. *4 Ezra* 6. 22–8.

60. *Pss. Sol.* 11. 1–9.

61. On prayer text, E. Schürer, rev. G. Vermes *et al., The History of the Jewish People in the Age of Jesus Christ,* 3 vols. (Edinburgh, 1973–87), vol. 2, p. 457; *Jubilees* text: *Jub.* 23. 30–31.

62. Leviathan: *2 Bar.* 29. 4.

63. Philo, *Praem.* 85, 89–90; Isa. 11: 6–9.

64. *Pss. Sol.* 17. 21–2, 32.

65. *2 Bar.* 30. 1–2, 4.

66. *1QS* 9. 9–11.

67. J. Neusner, W. S. Green and E. Frerichs (eds.), *Judaisms and Their Messiahs at the Turn of the Christian Era* (Cambridge, 1987) ("Judaism without Messiah").
68. On Herod on the Temple: Joseph. *AJ* 17. 161–3.
69. Ibid. 1. 14.
70. *Pss. Sol.* 17. 34.
71. *2 Bar.* 72. 2–4, 6.
72. Isa. 2: 2–3.
73. On the new Jerusalem: 5Q 15; Ezek. 40–48.

### CHAPTER FIVE: COMMUNITIES

1. Hor. *Carm.* 3. 2. 13.
2. 2 Macc. 7. 1–3.
3. R. Mellor, *Thea Roma* (Göttingen, 1975), 201 (on cult in Rome itself); Sall. *Cat.* 10. 6.
4. Joseph. *BJ* 7. 259–60; 2. 264; 5. 19.
5. Augustus, *RG* 6; Cass. Dio 53. 17. 1–2.
6. Plin. *Pan.* 63. 2–8; Suet. *Calig.* 30. 2.
7. Joseph. *BJ* 4. 320; 1 Macc. 14: 28 (Simon); Joseph. *BJ* 1. 457–66; M. Goodman, *The Ruling Class of Judaea* (Cambridge, 1987), chapter 9.
8. Joseph. *Ap.* 2. 164–6.
9. 1 Sam. 8: 5, 7.
10. Joseph. *Ap.* 2. 185; *AJ* 20. 251; 4. 223.
11. Joseph. *AJ* 11. 111–12.
12. Hecataeus ap. Diod. Sic. 40. 3. 4–6.
13. Joseph. *BJ* 2. 118.
14. Ibid. 4. 154–7.
15. 1 Sam. 8: 5.
16. Philo, *Moses* 1. 148.
17. On this power struggle, see J. J. Price, *Jerusalem Under Siege: The Collapse of the Jewish State, 66–70 C.E.* (Leiden, 1992). For arguments that Jews are naturally disposed to monarchy, see D. Goodblatt, *The Monarchic Principle: Studies in Jewish Self-Government in Antiquity* (Tübingen, 1994).
18. See in general S. Treggiari, *Roman Marriage* (Oxford, 1991).
19. Sen. *Dial.* 12. 14. 3 (Seneca's mother); 6. 24. 1 (Marcia).
20. Mart. 4. 13. 9–10; Plin. *Ep.* 6. 33.
21. Plin. *Ep.* 10. 65–6; M. Corbier (ed.), *Adoption et fosterage* (Paris, 1999).
22. Sen. *De Ira* 2. 21. 1.
23. Sen. *Controv.* 1. 1. 1; E. Cantarella, "Fathers and Sons in Rome," *Classical World* 96 (2003), 281–98.
24. Plut. *Cat. Mai.* 20. 2.
25. Cic. *Off.* 1. 17 (55).
26. On the allocation of citizens to tribes in the late Republic, see L. R. Taylor, *Roman Voting Assemblies* (Ann Arbor, 1966), chapter 4; C. Nicolet, *The World of the Citizen in Republican Rome* (London, 1980), 226–34.
27. Joseph. *AJ* 11. 133.
28. *m. Sanh.* 10. 3.
29. Acts 26: 7.

30. Rom. 11: 1; Phil. 3: 5.

31. Joseph. *AJ* 20. 206–7, 216, 218.

32. Lev. 25: 49 (redeeming from slavery); Gen. 46: 5, 7, 26 (Jacob's family); Deut. 25: 5–10 (Levirate marriage); Matt. 22: 24–8; *m. Bekh.* 1. 7.

33. Deut. 21: 18–21; *m. Sanh.* 8. 1, 5; *t. Sanh.* 11. 6 ("never was and never will be").

34. Tac. *Ann.* 12. 5–6; Cass. Dio 68. 2. 4; Lev. 18: 12–13 (woman forbidden to her nephew); *CD* 5. 9–11; *t. Kidd.* 1. 4.

35. Family as economic unit: *m. Ket.* 9. 4 (shopkeeper); *m. Yeb.* 15. 2 (agriculture); *m. Ket.* 5. 5 (work of wife).

36. On Babatha, *P Yadin;* see in general M. L. Satlow, *Jewish Marriage in Antiquity* (Princeton, 2001).

37. B. S. Jackson, "How Jewish is Jewish Family Law?," *JJS* 55 (2004), 201–29; *m. Kidd.* 1. 1 (means of betrothal), 2. 1–2 (statements by groom); *m. Ket.* 1. 2 (amounts on divorce).

38. *m. Sot.* 9. 14 (bridal parties); Jer. 2: 2.

39. Mal. 2: 14.

40. Deut. 24: 1–2.

41. Matt. 1: 19.

42. *m. Gitt.* 9. 10 (grounds for divorce).

43. Joseph. *AJ* 15. 259.

44. On rabbis and divorce by women, see Jackson, "How Jewish . . ."; *m. Ket.* 7. 9–10 (grounds for compelling divorce).

45. Joseph. *BJ* 1. 477; *AJ* 17. 14.

46. *m. Ket.* 10. 5.

47. Justin, *Dial. Trypho* 134.

48. *TS* 57. 15–18.

49. Deut. 17: 17; *m. Sanh.* 2. 4.

50. *P Yadin* no. 26.

51. Philo, *Prob.* 79.

52. Joseph. *AJ* 18. 21.

53. On Tabi: *m. Pes.* 7. 2 (Passover offering); *m. Sukk.* 2. 1 (Sukkah); *m. Ber.* 2. 7 (condolence).

54. On slave women: Joseph. *AJ* 13. 380 (Alexander Jannaeus); on the sexual exploitation of maidservants, see T. Ilan, *Jewish Women in Greco-Roman Palestine* (Tübingen, 1995), 205–11.

55. Ruth 4: 13, 16–17.

56. Esther 2: 7, 15; 9: 29.

57. G. G. Porton, *The Stranger Within Your Gates: Converts and Conversion in Rabbinic Literature* (Chicago, 1994), 83.

58. *Mekilta de-Rabbi Ishmael Pisha* 18. 110–13 (Lauterbach); *4 Macc.* 18. 11–12; see S. J. D. Cohen (ed.), *The Jewish Family in Antiquity* (Atlanta, 1993).

59. *m. Shab.* 2. 6–7. The *erub* was a legal device to permit food to be carried from one house to another on the Sabbath when both opened onto a common courtyard.

60. Cic. *Amic.* 16 (56); 20 (76); Plin. *Ep.* 2. 20.

61. Dion. Hal. *Ant. Rom.* 2. 9. 2–3; Sen. *Dial.* 10. 14. 4.

62. Plin. *Ep.* 2. 6.

63. *FIRA* vol. 3, no. 35, lines 11–13 (Lanuvium, 136 CE); *CIL* vol. 4, no. 710 (goldsmiths).

64. Sen. *Ben.* 1. 1. 9, cf. M. Griffin, "De Beneficiis and Roman Society," *JRS* 93 (2003), 92–113; Ov. *Tr.* 5. 8. 5–6, 13–14.

65. *m. Peah* 8. 7 (minimum charity); *t. Gitt.* 3. 13; Mart. *Epigr.* 12. 57. 13.

66. 1 Sam. 18: 1; 20; Joseph. *Vit.* 192, 204; B. D. Shaw, "Tyrants, Bandits and Kings: Personal Power in Josephus," *JJS* 44 (1993), 176–204; Joseph. *AJ* 18. 328–9.

67. On prohibition of usury: Lev. 25: 36–7; fine for late repayment: *DJD* vol. 2, no. 18; hurling of stones: Joseph. *AJ* 20. 213.
68. *t. B.M.* 11. 23; *JIWE* 2, no. 96 (Annius); Philo, *Spec. Leg.* 156 (Augustus); Acts 6: 9; *CIJ* 1404 (Theodotus inscription).
69. Philo, *Prob.* 76–7, 85–6, 82; on John the Essaean: Joseph. *BJ* 2. 567.
70. On Essenes and the Dead Sea sectarians: M. Goodman, "A Note on the Qumran Sectarians, the Essenes and Josephus," *JJS* 46 (1995), 161–6; on the relationship of those who produced the *Community Rule* to those who produced the *Damascus Document,* see C. Hempel, *The Laws of the Damascus Document* (Leiden, 1998); citations from the *Community Rule: 1QS* 2. 19–23; 8. 13 (separation); 8. 1–10; 7. 2–18 (trans. Vermes).
71. Acts 4: 32.

## CHAPTER SIX: PERSPECTIVES

1. *Tabulae Vindolandenses* II. 291, lines 3–7; Prop. 3. 10. 1–6 (trans. Butler).
2. Plin. *HN* 29. 27 (85).
3. Ov. *Am.* 2. 14. 36–40; Sor. *Gyn.* 1. 20 (ed. Burguière, Gourevitch and Malinas, p. 64, lines 1–4).
4. Ov. *Met.* 9. 678–79; Heliod. *Aeth.* 4. 8.
5. Joseph. *Ap.* 2. 202; Tac. *Hist.* 5. 5; Hecataeus ap. Diod. Sic. 40. 3. 8; Gen. 1: 28.
6. Onan: Gen. 38: 9–10; *b. Yeb.* 65b; *m. Ohol.* 7. 6; Philo, *Spec. Leg.* 3. 108–9.
7. Philo, *Spec. Leg.* 3. 114–15, 117–18; *m. Kidd.* 4. 2.
8. On slavery and Apuleius, K. Bradley, "Animalizing the Slave: The Truth of Fiction," *JRS* 90 (2000), 110–25; Cato, *Agr.* 2. 7; Suet. *Iul.* 4. 1–2 (Caesar and the pirates); Sen. *Ep.* 47 (Stoic view); *ILS* 8731 (Zoninus).
9. Exod. 21: 26; *m. Ab.* 2. 7; Deut. 28: 57; on the haggadah, see B. M. Bokser, *The Origins of the Seder: The Passover Rite and Early Rabbinic Judaism* (Berkeley, 1984).
10. *ILS* no. 8164 (tombstone); Verg. *Aen.* 6. 702 (the image of Anchises which his son Aeneas tried to embrace); Ov. *Fast.* 5. 483–8 (Lemuria).
11. Cic. *Rep.* 6.13 (13); *Att.* 12. 36.
12. Suet. *Iul.* 88.
13. Paulus, *Sent.* 1. 21. 2.
14. Sen. *Dial.* 6. 1. 1; 25. 1 (trans. Basore); Cic. *Fam.* 4. 5. 6; R. Lattimore, *Themes in Greek and Latin Epitaphs* (Urbana, Ill., 1942).
15. Gen. 2: 7.
16. Wis. 8. 19–20; Joseph. *BJ* 2. 154–5, 156–8; on rabbinic attitudes, see D. Boyarin, *Carnal Israel: Reading Sex in Talmudic Culture* (Berkeley and London, 1993).
17. Deut. 30: 19; Gen. 2: 7; Dan. 12: 2; Ps. 115: 17; Eccl. 9: 4.
18. Acts 23: 6; Matt. 22: 23–30; *m. Sanh.* 10. 1 (the bracketed words are missing in some manuscripts).
19. On Pharisees: Joseph. *Vit.* 11–12; *AJ* 18. 14; *BJ* 2. 163; on suicide: Joseph. *BJ* 3. 374.
20. Gen. 9: 5; on martyrdom: Joseph. *Ap.* 1. 42; S. Weitzman, "Josephus on How to Survive Martyrdom," *JJS* 55 (2004), 230–45.
21. Joseph. *Ap.* 2. 217–18; on the Palestinian recension of the *amidah*, E. Schürer, rev. G. Vermes et al., *The History of the Jewish People in the Age of Jesus Christ*, 3 vols. (Edinburgh, 1973–87), vol. 2, pp. 459–62; on priests burying their kin: Lev. 21: 2–3.
22. Tac. *Hist.* 5. 5; S. Fine, "A Note on Ossuary Burial and the Resurrection of the Dead in First-Century Jerusalem," *JJS* 51 (2000), 69–76.
23. *m. Taan.* 4. 2–3; *Jub.* 2. 2; Joseph. *AJ* 1. 5, 27, 21; Philo, *Opif.* 3, 7.

24. Ov. *Met.* 1. 5–9, 21–5, 76–88 (trans. Miller, slightly adapted); Cic. *Nat. D.* 2. 15–16.

25. Joseph. *Ap.* 2. 239–42.

26. Ptol. *Tetr.* 1. 1; Manilius 1. 1–6 (trans. Goold).

27. Artapanus ap. Euseb. *Praep. evang.* 9. 18. 1; *4Q* 186 (frag. 1, col. 2, 11. 7–9); *Bereshit Rabbah* 10. 6 (ed. Albeck, p. 79); *b. Shab.* 156a.

28. *b. Shab.* 156a ("no *mazal*"); *Jub.* 12. 16–18; Joseph. *BJ* 5. 214, 217–18; on symbolism in general: Joseph. *AJ* 3. 179–87.

29. Joseph. *AJ* 1. 155–6; D. Boyarin on "binitarianism" in *Harv. Theol. Rev.* 94 (2001), 243–84; P. Schäfer, *Mirror of His Beauty: Feminine Images of God* (Princeton, 2002).

30. Angels in Bible: Gen. 22: 11 (Abraham); 1 Kgs. 19: 5 (Elijah); Ps. 91: 11 (protecting the faithful); Gen. 28: 12 (Jacob's ladder); 2 Sam. 22: 11 (cherubim); Isa. 6: 2–6 (seraphim); angels in late Second Temple times: Acts 23: 6–8; *1 En.* 40: 8–10; Joseph. *BJ* 2. 142 (Essenes); Tob. 12: 15 (ed. Hanhart); *2 Bar.* 51. 11 (angelic army); on Moses, see Philo, *Mos.* 1. 158 (Moses "named god"); Artapanus ap. Euseb. *Praep. evang.* 9. 27. 6; Philo, *Mos.* 2. 288; Joseph. *AJ* 4. 326; cf. W. A. Meeks, "Moses as God and King," in J. Neusner (ed.), *Religions in Antiquity* (Leiden, 1968), 354–71; on sectarians believing themselves both human and angelic or divine, see C. H. T. Fletcher-Louis, *All the Glory of Adam* (Leiden, 2002), with more cautious analysis in K. P. Sullivan, *Wrestling with Angels* (Leiden, 2004); *4Q* 405, frags. 20, col. 2, 11.7–10 (Songs of the Sabbath Sacrifice); *11Q* 13. 4–6 (Melchizedek).

31. Isa. 34: 14 (Lilith); *shedim:* Deut. 32: 17; Ps. 106: 37; *1QS* 3. 20–23; *Jub.* 10. 8–9.

32. Joseph. *AJ* 8. 45–9; Matt. 10: 1 (Jesus); Acts 16: 18 (Paul); 19: 13–15 (sons of Sceva).

33. Job 1: 7–8; *b. B.B.* 16a; *b. R.Sh.* 16b; *t. Levi* 18.12 (defeat of Belial); *t. Jud.* 25. 3 (cast into fire).

34. Gen. 1: 31; 8: 22 (after flood); Ps. 19: 2 (Hebrew); Strabo, *Geog.* 5. 4. 6.

35. R. Walzer, *Galen on Jews and Christians* (Oxford, 1949); cf. E. Segal, " 'The Few Contained the Many': Rabbinic Perspectives on the Miraculous and the Impossible," *JJS* 54 (2003), 273–82; Sen. *Q Nat.* 6. 1. 12; 6. 3. 1.

36. Joseph. *Ap.* 1. 141 (gardens of Babylon); on Herod's palace, see Chapter 1, p. 55.

37. K. D. White, *Roman Farming* (Ithaca, NY, 1970), chapter 4 (agrarian writers); sabbatical year: Lev. 25: 2, 23; Joseph. *AJ* 14. 202 (see above, p. 178); Tac. *Hist.* 5. 4.

38. Num. 22: 28, 30 (Balaam's ass); *b. Shab.* 128b; Tob. 6: 2; 11: 4 (on Jewish attitudes to cats and dogs, see J. Schwartz in *JJS* 52 (2001), 211–34; 55 (2004), 246–77); Deut. 22: 7 (taking birds from nests).

39. Cic. *Fam.* 7. 1. 3 (elephants); Joseph. *BJ* 1. 429.

40. *CIL* vol. 10. no. 659, lines 1–4; Plin. *HN* 10. 59 (120); Catull. 2–3 (for arguments against an obscene interpretation of "sparrow" in these poems, see D. F. S. Thompson, *Catullus* [Toronto, Buffalo and London, 1997], 202–3).

41. Joseph. *AJ* 19. 32; M. Gigante, *Philodemus in Italy: The Books from Herculaneum* (Ann Arbor, 1995).

42. F. H. Sandbach, *The Stoics,* 2nd edn. (Bristol, 1989); Sen. *Dial.* 7. 25. 1–2.

43. Lucian, *De mort. Peregr.*

44. H.-F. Mueller, *Roman Religion in Valerius Maximus* (London, 2002); Epictetus, *Diss.* 2. 8. 11–14.

45. Joseph. *Ap.* 2. 170–71 (Moses); Theophrastus, *De Pietate,* cited in Porph. *Abst.* 2. 26. 3; Joseph. *Vit.* 12 (Pharisees); *AJ* 15. 371 (Essenes); *BJ* 2. 164 (Sadducees and Epicureans).

46. On Philo's ethical teachings, see S. Sandmel, *Philo of Alexandria: An Introduction* (New York and Oxford, 1979).

47. Joseph. *Ap.* 2. 175, 178; Philo, *Mos.* 2. 216.

48. Joseph. *BJ* 2. 164 (Sadducees), 162–3 (Pharisees); *m. Ab.* 3. 15 (Albeck) (R. Akiva); on original sin: J. L. Kugel, *Traditions of the Bible* (Cambridge, Mass., 1998), 98; H. Reuling, *After Eden* (Utrecht, 2004); Hos. 3: 1; on penitence: *m. Yom.* 8. 8–9.

### CHAPTER SEVEN: LIFESTYLES

1. For portraits: S. Walker, *Greek and Roman Portraits* (London, 1995).
2. *CIL* vol. 6, no. 37965, lines 22–3 (see M. R. Lefkowitz and M. B. Fant, *Women's Life in Greece and Rome* [London, 1982], 137); Clement, *Paed.* 3.5 (32.2).
3. Suet. *Ner.* 28–9; Sen. *Ep.* 95. 20–21.
4. J. Klawans, *Impurity and Sin in Ancient Judaism* (New York and Oxford, 2000); idem, *Purity, Sacrifice and the Temple: Symbolism and Supersessionism in the Study of Ancient Judaism* (New York and Oxford, 2006); contrasting view in H. Maccoby, *Ritual and Morality: The Ritual Purity System and Its Place in Judaism* (Cambridge, 1999).
5. Joseph. *BJ* 2. 123, 149.
6. Biblical taboos: Lev. 11; Mishnah on fowl and milk: *m. Hull.* 8. 1. 3; Mishnah on other foodstuffs: *m. A. Zar.* 2. 6; oil: Joseph. *AJ* 12. 119–20; *BJ* 2. 591–2; discussion in M. Goodman, "Kosher Olive Oil in Antiquity," in idem, *Judaism in the Roman World: Collected Essays* (Leiden, 2007), 187–203.
7. *Let. Arist.* 305–6.
8. *m. A. Zar.* 3. 4 (baths in Akko); *t. Bikk.* 2. 3 (androgyne).
9. Joseph. *BJ* 6. 417; 4Q 186.
10. Num. 5: 11–31; *m. Sot.* 1. 5.
11. Plin. *Ep.* 1. 15.
12. Suet. *Aug.* 77.
13. Innkeeper's bill: *ILS* no. 7478.
14. Suet. *Iul.* 49. 4 (trans. Rolfe); *Aug.* 68.
15. Tib. 3. 13; on Vistilia: Tac. *Ann.* 2. 85; Suet. *Tib.* 35. 2.
16. Tac. *Ann.* 16. 18 (Petronius); Mart. *Epig.* 11. 39 ("Tyrian" clothes); Suet. *Otho* 12. 1.
17. Ov. *Medic.* 51–2, 67–8.
18. Sall. *Cat.* 14. 2 (accusation by Cicero); Hor. *Carm.* 2. 15. 1–2; Stat. *Silv.* 2. 2. 83–97; Plin. *Ep.* 2. 17; 5. 6; Suet. *Nero* 31. 1–2.
19. Plin. *Ep.* 6. 15.
20. Sen. *Ep.* 84. 10; on Tigellius: Cic. *Fam.* 7. 24 (on Tigellius' influence); Hor. *Sat.* 1. 3. 1–4.
21. N. Horsfall, *The Culture of the Roman Plebs* (London, 2003), 31–47; on Ummidia Quadratilla: Plin. *Ep.* 7. 24; Apul. *Met.* 10. 30, 31.
22. Suet. *Calig.* 27. 4.
23. August. *Conf.* 6. 8; Tert. *Apol.* 15. 5; Mart. *Spect.* 21; cf. K. M. Coleman, "Fatal Charades: Roman Executions Staged as Mythological Enactments," *JRS* 80 (1990), 44–73.
24. Suet. *Calig.* 55. 2–3.
25. Matt. 14: 1–11 (Herod the Tetrarch's party; on birthdays, see Chapter 6, p. 232); *m. Pes.* 10. 1 (wine for the poor at Passover eve); on drinking: *b. B.B.* 58b; Prov. 31: 6–7; *b. B.B.* 60b; Lev. 10: 8–11 (priests not to be intoxicated); Joseph. *Ap.* 2. 204; Deut. 21:20 (rebellious son); *b. Meg.* 7b (Purim).
26. On contrast to Christians: D. Boyarin, *Carnal Israel: Reading Sex in Talmudic Culture* (Berkeley and London, 1993); Joseph. *Ap.* 2. 199; Rahab: Josh. 2: 1; Joseph. *AJ* 5. 7; Gen. 38: 7–10 (Onan); Lev. 18: 22–3 (homosexuality and bestiality); Joseph. *Ap.* 2. 199 (homosexuality); *AJ* 15. 29 (Aristobulus); *m. Kidd.* 4.14; *b. Kidd.* 82A ("Israelites . . . not suspected"); on lesbianism: R. Biale, *Women and Jewish Law* (New York, 1984), 192–7.
27. Wool and linen: Deut. 22: 11; Joseph. *AJ* 4. 208; *m. Kil.* 9. 1 (worn by priests); Matt. 23: 5 (phylacteries); Tert. *De Corona* 4. 2 (veils); *m. Shab.* 6. 1 (jewellery).
28. *m. Sot.* 1. 8 (Absalom); hairstyles as idolatrous: *t. Shab.* 6. 1; on the smell: Amm. Marc. *Res Gestae* 22. 5. 5 (see Chapter 12).
29. Joseph. *AJ* 15. 268, 273–4.

30. Ibid. 15. 275–6, 280–91; 17. 255; for later centuries, Z. Weiss, "The Jews of Ancient Palestine and the Roman Games," *Zion* 66 (2001), 427–50 (in Hebrew); Philo in Alexandria: Philo, *Prob.* 141.

31. Joseph. *AJ* 18. 259–60 (Philo the philosopher); Euseb. *Praep. evang.* 9. 37. 1–3 (Philo the poet).

32. Joseph. *BJ* 2. 295; *b. BM* 83b; cf. Boyarin, *Carnal Israel,* 197–200.

33. *m. Sukk.* 5. 4; Jud. 15: 12–13; *m. Taan.* 4. 8 (15 Ab); *t. Sanh.* 12. 10 (Song of Songs).

34. Philo on "Israel": Philo, *Abr.* 57 and *passim;* Herod and eagle: Joseph. *AJ* 17. 149–54; biblical prohibition: Exod. 20: 4–5.

35. Suet. *Aug.* 76 (letter to Tiberius); on the nazirate, S. Chepey, *Nazirites in Late Second Temple Judaism* (Leiden, 2005); on fasting: Tac. *Hist.* 5. 4; Pompeius Trogus ap. Just. *Epit.* 36. 2. 14.

36. *m. Taan.* 3. 4, 6; on rabbinic attitudes, E. Diamond, *Holy Men and Hunger Artists: Fasting and Asceticism in Rabbinic Culture* (Oxford, 2004).

## CHAPTER EIGHT: GOVERNMENT

1. See D. W. Rathbone, "The Imperial Finances," *CAH* vol. 10 (Cambridge, 1996), 309–23.

2. Cic. *Leg.* 2. 23 (59); M. H. Crawford (ed.), *Roman Statutes* (London, 1996), no. 40, tables 7 and 8; Gai. *Inst.* 2. 2–6.

3. *m. Hag.* 1. 8; *b. Shab.* 31a (oral Torah).

4. *CD* 1. 11; *1QS* 9. 13, 17–18; on *prozbul:* Deut. 15: 1–2, 9; *m. Shebi.* 10. 3–4 (Hillel).

5. *m. B.K.* 10. 10.

6. L. Bove, *Documenti di operazioni finanzarie dall' archivio dei Sulpici* (Naples, 1984); *Dig.* 14. 2. 2. 2, cited by J. A. Crook, *Law and Life of Rome* (London, 1967), 224–5.

7. J. F. Gardner, *Being a Roman Citizen* (London and New York, 1993); G. P. Burton, "Proconsuls, Assizes and the Administration of Justice Under the Empire," *JRS* 65 (1975), 92–106; *P Yadin* nos. 28–30 (Greek version of text from Gai. *Inst.* 4. 47); see M. Goodman, *State and Society in Roman Galilee, AD 132–212,* 2nd edn. (London and Portland, Ore., 2000), chapter 10.

8. Cass. Dio 51. 19. 7 (emperor hears appeals); Acts 25: 10–11.

9. *m. Sanh.* 4. 1; 1. 6; Joseph. *BJ* 2. 570–71; *Vit.* 79; *AJ* 4. 214, 287.

10. On the Sanhedrin: M. Goodman, *The Ruling Class of Judaea* (Cambridge, 1987), 112–16; Acts 5: 21 (Peter), 23: 6 (Paul); Joseph. *AJ* 20. 200 ("Jacob," i.e. James); *AJ* 20. 216 (Agrippa II); *BJ* 2. 25 (Augustus); Mark 14: 53 (Caiaphas); Joseph. *Vit.* 79; *Ap.* 2. 194.

11. Tac. *Ann.* 2. 30 (slaves of Drusus); 15. 57 (Epicharis); Joseph. *AJ* 16. 245, 247 (Herod); Lev. 5: 1; *Sifre on Deuteronomy* 275 (ed. Horovitz-Finkelstein, p. 294) (on Miriam).

12. *CD* 9. 16–23; *m. Yeb.* 15. 1.

13. P. Garnsey, *Social Status and Legal Privilege in the Roman Empire* (Oxford, 1970); on *Iustitia* and other imperial virtues, F. Millar, *The Emperor in the Roman World (31 BC–AD 337)* (London, 1977), 516–17; C. F. Noreña, "The Communication of the Emperor's Virtues," *JRS* 91 (2001), 156–7.

14. Exod. 21: 24 ("eye for an eye"); Joseph. *AJ* 4. 280; *b. B.K.* 83b; *m. Sanh.* 7. 1; John 18: 31–2; P. Winter, *On the Trial of Jesus,* 2nd edn., rev. T. A. Burkill and G. Vermes (Berlin and New York, 1974); G. Vermes, *The Passion* (London, 2005).

15. Joseph. *AJ* 16. 1–3; *m. Makk.* 3. 10, 12–13 (procedures for flogging); 2 Cor. 11: 24.

16. Cic. *Off.* 1. 11 (36); Polyb. 16. 34. 3–4 (demands on Philip V); Tac. *Agr.* 30. 4–5.

17. Tac. *Agr.* 30. 1–2; 31. 2.

18. Vell. Pat. 2. 119. 1–2 (Varus); Cass. Dio 49. 30. 1–3 *(testudo);* D. B. Saddington, *The Development of the Roman Auxiliary Forces from Caesar to Vespasian* (Harare, 1982); *Brooklyn Museum Papyri* no. 24, in *JRS* 67 (1977), 51–2.

19. Livy 30. 34. 1 (Zama); Tac. *Ann.* 2. 88 (Arminius); A. Ziolkowski, "Urbs Direpta, or How the Romans Sacked Cities," in J. Rich and G. Shipley (eds.), *War and Society in the Roman World* (London and New York, 1993), 69–91.

20. Cic. *Off.* 1. 11 (35) (reasons for war), 24 (82) (cities); on Musonius: Tac. *Hist.* 3. 81.

21. Deut. 20: 1–17 (citations from 20: 13–16); Josh. 8: 24–8; Isa. 2: 2–4.

22. *m. Sot.* 8. 7 (R. Judah); 1 Sam. 15 (Saul); Deut. 25: 19; Exod. 17: 14 (Amalekite commandment); Joseph. *AJ* 3. 60; *m. Ab.* 1. 12 (Hillel).

23. On Judas Maccabee: 1 Macc. 5: 51 (Ephron); 3. 44, 47–50, 56 (call to arms); Cass. Dio 66. 5. 4 (welcome to deserters); *1QM* 9. 5–9.

24. Joseph. *Ap.* 2. 211–14; *BJ* 3. 532–41 (Tarichaeae).

25. Philo, *Spec. Leg.* 4. 219, with note by Colson in Loeb edn. *ad loc.;* 4. 224–5; on Essenes: Philo, *Prob.* 78.

## CHAPTER NINE: POLITICS

1. Livy 2. 12. 9; Cic. *Prov. cons.* 13 (32–3); Augustus, *RG* 4; on Claudius' self-representation, see Chapter 2, p. 71.

2. 1 Sam. 18: 7–8 (Saul and David); L. H. Feldman, *Josephus's Interpretation of the Bible* (Berkeley and London, 1998), 106–9; Joseph. *Ap.* 2. 148; on Simon bar Gioras: Cass. Dio 66. 7. 1; Joseph. *BJ* 4. 503–4.

3. *1QM* 11. 1–5.

4. Polyb. 6. 53. 1–2, 4–6; 54. 1; Tac. *Ann.* 2. 37–8.

5. C. H. V. Sutherland, *Roman Coins* (London, 1974), no. 166 (DIVI FILIUS in 40 BCE).

6. Cic. *2 Verr.* 5. 70–71 (180–81); on Clodius, E. S. Gruen, *The Last Generation of the Roman Republic* (Berkeley and Los Angeles, 1974).

7. Joseph. *Vit.* 1–2, 6.

8. Joseph. *Ap.* 2. 186–7; *Vit.* 80, 63.

9. Joseph. *Ap.* 1. 30–33.

10. *m. Kidd.* 4. 1.

11. Joseph. *AJ* 15. 22, 40 (Ananel); Ezek. 44: 15; on Phannias: Joseph. *BJ* 4. 148; *AJ* 20. 227; Acts 4: 6.

12. Joseph. *AJ* 20. 214 (Costobar and Saul); Hegesippus ap. Euseb. *Hist. eccl.* 3. 12 (Vespasian), 19–20 (Domitian), 32. 3–4 (Trajan); Matt. 1: 1; Luke 2: 4; 1: 34–5; Rom. 1: 3; Rev. 22: 16; Matt. 1: 24; on adoption, see Chapter 5.

13. *ILS* no. 977 (Atina); Plin. *Ep.* 6. 34; P. Veyne, *Bread and Circuses* (London, 1990).

14. Sen. *Constant.* 5. 4.

15. Petron. *Sat.* 37, 75–6.

16. Tiberius cited in Tac. *Ann.* 3. 53, 55.

17. Joseph. *AJ* 16. 156–9.

18. *m. Yom.* 3. 10 (Monobaz); *t. Kippurim* 2. 4 (Nicanor gate); *m. Yom.* 3. 10 (name of Nicanor).

19. Joseph. *AJ* 18. 15 (Pharisees and Sadducees); 20. 181 (poor priests).

20. Cic. *Sen.;* K. Cokayne, *Experiencing Old Age in Ancient Rome* (London, 2003); T. G. Parkin, *Old Age in the Roman World* (Baltimore, 2003); Lucian, *Macr.* 4, 8, 9, 29 (promised work), 17 (Asander).

21. *m. Ab.* 5. 21; minimum age limits for Levites: 1 Chr. 23: 24; Num. 8: 24; 4: 3; Aristobulus: Joseph. *AJ* 15. 34, 24, 51; Josephus as boy: Joseph. *Vit.* 9; Jesus: Luke 2: 46–7.

22. Elders: Deut. 19: 12; 21: 2; Job 12: 12; Philo, *Prob.* 87; Num. 8: 24–6; *CD* 10. 5–10, citing *Jub.* 23. 11; Joseph. *AJ* 15. 40–41 (High Priests); 14. 366 (Hyrcanus).

23. Joseph. *Vit.* 418.

24. Mark 12: 38–40.
25. Joseph. *BJ* 6. 291; C. Schams, *Jewish Scribes in the Second Temple Period* (Sheffield, 1998); Philo, *Hypoth.* ap. Euseb. *Praep. evang.* 8. 7. 13; Philo, *Spec. Leg.* 2. 62.
26. Luke 4: 16–17; cf. M. Goodman, "Texts, Scribes and Power in Roman Judaea," in A. K. Bowman and G. Woolf (eds.), *Literacy and Power in the Ancient World* (Cambridge, 1994), 99–108.
27. Deut. 34: 10 ("face to face"); 1 Macc. 4: 46; 14. 41; Joseph. *BJ* 1. 68–9 (John Hyrcanus); on Urim and Thummim: Joseph. *AJ* 3. 218; *m. Sot.* 9. 12.
28. Joseph. *BJ* 3. 351–2 (Josephus as prophet); *AJ* 20. 167, 169–72.
29. C. C. Rowland, *The Open Heaven: A Study of Apocalyptic in Judaism and Early Christianity* (London, 1982).
30. Suet. *Aug.* 69. 1; *Calig.* 24. 1 (incest); 32. 3 (consuls).
31. *FIRA* vol. 1, no. 15, lines 17–21, 29–33 (Vespasian); Augustus, *RG* 34; R. J. A. Talbert, *The Senate of Imperial Rome* (Princeton, 1984).
32. Suet. *Claud.* 13. 2.
33. On the praetorians in 41 CE, see Chapter 2; on the death of Gaius, Suet. *Calig.* 58.
34. Vell. Pat. 2. 127. 4–128. 1.
35. Suet. *Aug.* 101. 4.
36. N. Purcell, "Livia and the Womanhood of Rome," *PCPS* (1986), 78–105; Joseph. *Vit.* 13, 16; Tac. *Ann.* 16. 6 (Poppaea).
37. M. Goodman, *The Ruling Class of Judaea* (Cambridge, 1987), chapter 2.
38. Joseph. *BJ* 1. 457–66 (Herod's sons), 437 (Aristobulus III); *AJ* 20. 121–3 (Cumanus and Samaritans); on the Sanhedrin, see Chapter 8; Acts 23: 6–9.
39. Berenice: Joseph. *BJ* 2. 310, 314 (in 66 CE); relationship to Agrippa: Joseph. *AJ* 20. 145; Juv. 6. 156–60 (trans. Ramsay); wealth: Joseph. *Vit.* 119; Berenice and Justus: *Vit.* 342–3.
40. On Agrippa and Festus: Acts 25: 12–26: 32.
41. Acts 21: 30–34 (tribune).
42. Joseph. *AJ* 20. 158 (Aristobulus); 19. 362 (Agrippa I in Rome); 20. 211 (Neronias); on coins: Y. Meshorer, *A Treasury of Jewish Coins from the Persian Period to Bar Kokhba* (Jerusalem and Nyack, NY, 2001), no. 129; Joseph. *BJ* 2. 250–51 (vices of Nero).

## CHAPTER TEN: ROMANS AND JEWS

1. Erotian, in M. Stern (ed.), *Greek and Latin Authors on Jews and Judaism,* 3 vols. (Jerusalem, 1974–84), vol. 1, p. 446; Columella, *Rust.* 3. 8. 2.
2. Hor. *Sat.* 1. 5. 100 (credulity); Pers. 5. 179–84 (trans. Ramsay, amended Stern); Petron. *Sat.* 102; Pompeius Trogus ap. Just. *Epit.* 36. 2. 14; Seneca, *De Superstitione,* ap. August. *De civ. D.* 6. 11; Philo, *Spec. Leg.* 361. On all these texts, see P. Schäfer, *Judeophobia: Attitudes Toward the Jews in the Ancient World* (Cambridge, Mass., 1997).
3. Joseph. *AJ* 14. 215; cf. M. Pucci Ben Zeev, *Jewish Rights in the Roman World* (Tübingen, 1998), 107–18. See in general on the Jews in the city of Rome, H. J. Leon, *The Jews of Ancient Rome* (Philadelphia, 1960); L. V. Rutgers, *The Jews in Late Ancient Rome: Evidence of Cultural Interaction in the Roman Diaspora* (Leiden, 1995).
4. Philo, *Spec. Leg.* 160–61 (Sejanus); Cass. Dio 60. 6. 6 (meetings prohibited by Claudius); expulsion in 19 CE: Tac. *Ann.* 2. 85; Suet. *Tib.* 36; Joseph. *AJ* 18. 81–4; in general, E. S. Gruen, *Diaspora: Jews Amidst Greeks and Romans* (Cambridge, Mass., and London, 2002).
5. Suet. *Claud.* 25. 4; Acts 18: 2; Joseph. *AJ* 19. 290 (on Claudius); Cass. Dio 60. 6. 6; for a very different interpretation of the evidence, H. D. Slingerland, *Claudian Policymaking and the Early Imperial Repression of Judaism at Rome* (Atlanta, 1997).

6. Gruen, *Diaspora,* 38–41.
7. Acts 28: 17–28; Rom. 1: 7 (greeting); 16: 3 (Priscilla and Aquila); Joseph. *Vit.* 16.
8. Z. Yavetz, "Latin Authors on Jews and Dacians," *Historia* 47 (1998), 77–107; Varro ap. August. *De Consensu Evangelistarum* 1. 22. 30; August. *De civ. D.* 4. 31.
9. Cic. *Prov. cons.* 5. 10–12.
10. Cic. *Flac.* 28. 67, 69.
11. August. *De civ. D.* 6. 11. Gruen, *Diaspora,* 44, notes that "what Seneca himself meant remains obscure." On an Egyptian connection: Yavetz, "Latin Authors," 87; on date of composition: K. Münschel, *Senecas Werke* (Leipzig, 1922), 80; but note the date 40–41 CE proposed by R. Turcan, *Sénèque et les religions orientales* (Brussels, 1967), 12–14, 21–4; on persecution of Christians in Rome in 64 CE, see Chapter 13.
12. On these Roman attitudes to Jews before 70 CE, see Gruen, *Diaspora,* 52–3; on Jews as different in maintaining distinctiveness: D. Noy, *Foreigners at Rome: Citizens and Strangers* (London, 2000).
13. Joseph. *AJ* 18. 257–8 (Apion); 18. 264 (Gaius' statue); *BJ* 7. 50–51 (sacrifice test in Antioch); 7. 58–60 (Collega); see pp. 440–41.
14. Joseph. *Ap.* 2. 282; Sen. *Ep.* 108. 22.
15. August. *De civ. D.* 6. 11; on proselytes, Philo, *Spec. Leg.* 4. 177–8; see the (maximizing) arguments by L. H. Feldman, *Jew and Gentile in the Ancient World* (Princeton, 1993), with more cautious arguments by B. McGing "Population and Proselytism: How Many Jews Were There in the Ancient World?," in J. R. Bartlett (ed.), *Jews in the Hellenistic and Roman Cities* (London, 2002), 88–106. On Romans and the Jerusalem Temple: Joseph. *BJ* 5. 562–3 (gifts by Augustus); *AJ* 16. 14 (hecatomb sacrificed by Agrippa); sacrifice for emperor: *BJ* 2. 197, 408–21; *Ap.* 2. 77; Philo, *Spec. Leg.* 157.

### CHAPTER ELEVEN: THE ROAD TO DESTRUCTION, 37 BCE–70 CE

1. Joseph. *AJ* 17. 149–63.
2. Ibid. 17. 187.
3. Ibid. 17. 221, 252–3, 262, 264 (Sabinus).
4. Herod's troops: Joseph. *AJ* 17. 266, 269–70; *BJ* 2. 52; disturbances in 4 BCE: Joseph. *AJ* 17. 271–98.
5. Tac. *Hist.* 5. 9; Joseph. *Ap.* 1. 34–5.
6. Cass. Dio 54. 36. 2 (Dalmatia in 10 BCE); 56. 16. 3 (Bato); opposition to census: Joseph. *AJ* 18. 3–4, 23; *BJ* 2. 118; Acts 5: 37; Luke 2: 1, 3.
7. Joseph. *BJ* 2. 196–201; Tac. *Hist.* 5. 9.
8. Philo, *Leg.* 303; Joseph. *BJ* 2. 176–7; Tac. *Hist.* 5. 9.
9. Tac. *Hist.* 5. 9; Joseph. *AJ* 2. 97–8; Acts 5: 36.
10. Joseph. *AJ* 20. 112 ("twenty thousand"); *BJ* 2. 228–9; *AJ* 20. 114–17.
11. Tac. *Ann.* 12. 54; on Cumanus and the Samaritans, see pp. 360–61.
12. Joseph. *BJ* 2. 264, 253 (Eleazar), 254–7 (sicarii); *AJ* 20. 163–4 (murder of Jonathan); on "deceivers and impostors": Joseph. *BJ* 2. 258–9; *AJ* 20. 168.
13. "The Egyptian": Joseph. *BJ* 2. 261–3; *AJ* 20. 170–72; Acts 21: 38 (see above, p. 352); charlatan under Festus: Joseph. *AJ* 20. 188.
14. Joseph. *BJ* 2. 265 (looting); 7. 259–61 (class warfare); on debt: M. Goodman, *The Ruling Class of Judaea* (Cambridge, 1987), 57–8; on faction struggles within the elite, ibid., chapter 9.
15. Joseph. *BJ* 2. 273–5 (Albinus), 277–8 (Florus); Tac. *Agr.* 6. 2.
16. On Caesarea: Joseph. *AJ* 20. 173; *BJ* 2. 266; *AJ* 20. 183–4; Florus: Joseph. *BJ* 2. 280–81; Florus' wife: *AJ* 20. 252.

17. Joseph. *AJ* 20. 214.

18. Joseph. *BJ* 6. 300–309 (Jesus b. Ananias); J. S. McLaren, *Turbulent Times? Josephus and Scholarship on Judaea in the First Century* C.E. (Sheffield, 1998) (on the dangers of hindsight).

19. Joseph. *AJ* 18. 8–9, 23, 25; 20. 102; *BJ* 2. 433–4, 442–3.

20. On the messianic oracle: Joseph. *BJ* 6. 311–13; Tac. *Hist.* 5. 13; Suet. *Vesp.* 4. 5; eschatological hopes in 70 CE: Joseph. *BJ* 6. 283, 285; on early Christians, see Chapter 13.

21. Mark 12: 16; on coins issued by the procurators: *RPC* vol. 1, nos. 4954–72; for Tyrian shekels, *RPC* vol. 1, pp. 655–8.

22. Joseph. *AJ* 14. 186, 188; M. Pucci Ben Zeev, *Jewish Rights in the Roman World: The Greek and Roman Documents Quoted by Josephus Flavius* (Tübingen, 1998); T. Rajak, "Was There a Roman Charter for the Jews?," *JRS* 74 (1984), 107–23.

23. For the contrasting fortunes of Jews in Alexandria and Asia, see E. S. Gruen, *Diaspora: Jews Amidst Greeks and Romans* (Cambridge, Mass., and London, 2002), chapters 2–3.

24. Joseph. *AJ* 17. 324–38 (false Alexander).

25. Philo, *Flacc.* 27–8 (Agrippa unobtrusive); Joseph. *Ap.* 2. 35–6; *BJ* 2. 487; H. A. Musurillo, *The Acts of the Pagan Martyrs* (Oxford, 1954); Joseph. *AJ* 19. 285 (Claudius' edict).

26. On Claudius' letter to Jews and Greeks in Alexandria, see above, p. 118; diaspora pogroms in 66 CE: Joseph. *BJ* 2. 457–98.

27. Joseph. *BJ* 2. 301–8.

28. On Josephus' career in these years, see S. J. D. Cohen, *Josephus in Galilee and Rome: His Vita and Development as a Historian* (Leiden, 1979).

29. Joseph. *AJ* 17. 300 (deputation in 4 BCE); *BJ* 2. 409 (end of loyal sacrifices).

30. Cass. Dio 66. 4. 3; Joseph. *BJ* 6. 356–7 (Adiabeneans).

31. Joseph. *BJ* 2. 487–98.

32. Ibid. 2. 477–80.

33. Joseph. *Vit.* 25; *BJ* 2. 458–60 (provocation by Jerusalem rebels), 457 (Caesarea massacre); *AJ* 19. 357–8, 364–6.

34. Joseph. *BJ* 7. 47–62.

35. Tac. *Hist.* 2. 1–2.

36. Smallwood, *Docs. . . . Gaius,* no. 70 (a) and (d) (Vindex coins); Plin. *Ep.* 919 (epitaph of Verginius Rufus).

37. Smallwood, *Docs. . . . Gaius,* no. 72 (b) (Galba coins); Suet. *Nero* 48. 1, 3; 49. 1, 3–4.

38. Suet. *Galb.* 19. 2–20. 1.

39. Tac. *Hist.* 2. 47.

40. Suet. *Vesp.* 4. 5.

41. Ibid. 5. 4, 6; 6. 2–4.

42. Suet. *Vit.* 17.

43. For a clear narrative of the civil war in terms of Roman politics, see K. Wellesley, *The Long Year* A.D. *69* (London, 1975).

44. Joseph. *BJ* 7. 5–16 (parade); 6. 46 (immortality).

45. Ibid. 6. 241.

46. Sulpicius Severus, *Chronica* 2. 30. 6–7 (trans. Stern).

47. Joseph. *BJ* 6. 252–9, 261–6 (trans. Thackeray).

48. Philostr. *VA* 6. 29.

## CHAPTER TWELVE: REACTIONS, 70–312 CE

1. Joseph. *BJ* 6. 442 (lament); on portents: *BJ* 6. 289–300; Tac. *Hist.* 5. 13. 1.

2. *DJD* vol. 2, no. 19 (on the date, Y. Yadin, in *IEJ* 15 [1965], 119, n. 112); *4 Ezra* 5. 23, 25–30; 6. 25.

3. Joseph. *Ap.* 2. 193–4; M. Goodman, "Sadducees and Essenes after 70 CE," in S. E. Porter, P. Joyce and D. E. Orton (eds.), *Crossing the Boundaries* (Leiden, 1994), 347–56; R. J. Bauckham, "Josephus' Account of the Temple in 'Contra Apionem' 2. 102–109," in L. H. Feldman and J. R. Levison (eds.), *Josephus'* Contra Apionem (Leiden, 1996), 327–47.

4. J. Neusner, *The Development of a Legend: Studies on the Traditions Concerning Yohanan ben Zakkai* (Leiden, 1970); *m. Sukk.* 3. 12 (Sukkot); Joseph. *BJ* 6. 250, 268 (parallels between destructions); *b. Gitt.* 6b.

5. Joseph. *BJ* 7. 122–34, 139–57 (trans. Thackeray); for a sophisticated hypothesis about the complex publication history of this part of Josephus' work, see S. Schwartz, "The Composition and Publication of Josephus's *Bellum Iudaicum* Book 7," *Harv. Theol. Rev.* 79 (1986), 373–86.

6. M. Beard, J. North and S. Price (eds.), *Religions of Rome*, 2 vols. (Cambridge, 1998), vol. 1, pp. 132–4 (on *evocatio*); D. Barag, "Brickstamp Impressions of the Legio X Fretensis," *Bonner Jahrbücher* 167 (1967), 244–67.

7. Joseph. *BJ* 7. 160–62; F. Millar, "Last Year in Jerusalem: Monuments of the Jewish War in Rome," in J. Edmondson, S. Mason and J. B. Rives (eds.), *Flavius Josephus and Flavian Rome* (Oxford, 2005), 101–28; *BM Coins, Rom. Emp.* vol. 2, nos. 31–44 (JUDAEA CAPTA); *ILS* 264 (inscription in Circus Maximus); G. Alföldy, "Eine Bauinschrift aus dem Colosseum," *ZPE* 109 (1995), 195–226; on Jewish tax: Joseph. *BJ* 7. 218; Cass. Dio 66. 7. 2; *CPJ* vol. 2, nos. 160–229 (ostraka from Edfu).

8. Joseph. *BJ* 6. 418, 420; *Vit.* 419–21.

9. Joseph. *BJ* 7. 163 (Herodium), 164, 196–209 (Machaerus); on Masada: Joseph. *BJ* 7. 252–401 (citation from *BJ* 7. 318).

10. Plin. *HN* 5. 15 (73).

11. Joseph. *BJ* 7. 252 (Flavius Silva), 323–36, 341–88 (speeches of Eleazar), 399 (survivors).

12. Joseph. *Vit.* 422.

13. Joseph. *BJ* 3. 443; 7. 23–4; Cass. Dio 66. 15. 3–4.

14. For a different view, see D. Goodblatt, *The Monarchic Principle: Studies in Jewish Self-Government in Antiquity* (Tübingen, 1994), chapters 5–6.

15. Joseph. *BJ* 7. 17; H. M. Cotton, "A New Inscription from Caesarea Maritima and the Local Elite from Caesarea Maritima," in L. V. Rutgers (ed.), *What Athens Has to Do with Jerusalem: Essays in Honor of Gideon Foerster* (Leuven, 2002), 383, 385; Luke 24: 13.

16. On the collection of the tax in Egypt, see *CPJ* vol. 2, no. 421 (list of taxpayers in Arsinoe in 73 CE, giving ages).

17. Joseph. *BJ* 409–16 (Alexandria), 421–36 (Leontopolis), 442–51 (Cyrene).

18. Joseph. *Vit.* 424–5; on Antioch: *BJ* 7. 54–61, 107–10.

19. Joseph. *Vit.* 423, 425; on Jews as *testes veritatis*: J. Juster, *Les Juifs dans l'empire romain*, 2 vols. (Paris, 1914), vol. 1, pp. 227–30; J. Cohen, *Living Letters of the Law: Ideas of the Jew in Medieval Christianity* (London, 1999), chapter 1.

20. Julian. *Adversus Galilaeos* 306B.

21. Suet. *Dom.* 2. 1–2.

22. Ibid. 2. 1 (participation in triumph over Judaea); *RIC* vol. 2, p. 189, no. 280 (coins); Suet. *Dom.* 12. 2.

23. Cass. Dio 67. 14. 1–2; Joseph. *Ap.* 2. 125–6; M. Goodman, "The Fiscus Judaicus and Gentile Attitudes to Judaism in Flavian Rome," in J. Edmondson, S. Mason and J. Rives (eds.), *Flavius Josephus and Flavian Rome* (Oxford, 2005), 167–77.

24. Suet. *Dom.* 23. 1; on coins in general: D. C. A. Shotter, "The Principate of Nerva: Some Observations on the Coin Evidence," *Historia* 32 (1983), 215–26.

25. *Fiscus Iudaicus* coins: *RIC* vol. 2, p. 227, no. 58; p. 228, no. 82; M. Goodman, "The Meaning of 'Fisci Iudaici Calumnia Sublata' on the Coinage of Nerva," in S. J. D. Cohen and

J. Schwartz (eds.), *Josephus and the Varieties of Ancient Judaism: Louis H. Feldman Jubilee Volume* (Leiden, 2007), 81–9.

26. Joseph. *Ap.* 2. 293–4; L. Troiani, *Commento storico al Contra Apione di Giuseppe* (Pisa, 1977), 26–9 (on date); 5 *Sibyllines* 40–41; *Ep. Barn.* 16. 3–4, citing Isa. 49: 17; cf. J. Carleton Paget, *The Epistle of Barnabas* (Tübingen, 1994), 17–30.

27. Shotter, "Principate of Nerva"; for this argument, see M. Goodman, "Trajan and the Origins of Roman Hostility to the Jews," *P&P* 182 (2004), 3–29.

28. Suet. *Dom.* 23. 1; *RIC* vol. 2, p. 223, nos. 2–3 (coins); Plin. *Pan.* 8. 1; on the conspiracy: W. Eck, "An Emperor is Made: Senatorial Politics and Trajan's Adoption by Nerva in 97," in G. Clark and T. Rajak (eds.), *Philosophy and Power in the Graeco-Roman World* (Oxford, 2002), 211–26.

29. Joseph. *BJ* 3. 298–300, 304–5.

30. Ibid. 4. 366, 592–604; Tac. *Hist.* 2. 76. 1; G. Alföldy, "Traianus Pater und die Bauinschrift des Nymphäums von Milet," *Rev. Ét. Anc.* 100 (1998), 367–99.

31. Plin. *Pan.* 9. 2; 58. 3; 89. 1–2; on deification of Traianus: *BM Coins, Rom. Emp.* vol. 3, no. 498.

32. *CPJ* vol. 2, no. 194 (Dosarion).

33. *CPJ*, vol. 2, nos. 195–229 (tax receipts); F. Lepper and S. S. Frere, *Trajan's Column* (Gloucester, 1988); Smallwood, *Docs. . . . Nerva*, no. 50 (coins with Armenia legend); Cass. Dio 68. 17. 1 (cf. F. A. Lepper, *Trajan's Parthian War* [Oxford, 1948]).

34. Cass. Dio 68. 32. 1–2; Euseb. *Hist. eccl.* 4. 2. 1–5.

35. *CPJ* vol. 2, no. 438, lines 1–9.

36. *CPJ* vol. 2, no. 443, col. 2, lines 4–9.

37. On confiscations of Jewish property: *CPJ* vol. 2, nos. 447–9; on lucky escape: App. *Arabicus Liber*, F19 (in M. Stern [ed.], *Greek and Latin Authors on Jews and Judaism*, 3 vols. [Jerusalem, 1974–84], vol. 2, pp. 185–6).

38. App. *B Civ.* 2. 13 (90) (Pompey's tomb); Arr. *Parth.* ap. *Suda* (in Stern [ed.], *Greek and Latin Authors*, vol. 2, p. 152); G. Luederitz, *Corpus jüdischer Zeugnisse aus der Cyrenaika* (Wiesbaden, 1983), nos. 17, 19, 22–5; *CPJ* no. 450 (festival at Oxyrhynchus); Cass. Dio 68. 32. 3.

39. S. Applebaum, *Jews and Greeks in Ancient Cyrene* (Leiden, 1979); M. Goodman, "Diaspora Reactions to the Destruction of the Temple," in J. D. G. Dunn (ed.), *Jews and Christians* (Tübingen, 1992), 27–38.

40. Euseb. *Hist. eccl.* 4. 2. 5 (Lusius Quietus); B. Isaac and I. Roll, "Judaea in the Early Years of Hadrian's Reign," *Latomus* 38 (1979), 54–66.

41. A. R. Birley, *Hadrian: The Restless Emperor* (London, 1997); Beard, North and Price (eds.), *Religions of Rome*, vol. 1, pp. 257–9 (temple to Roma).

42. D. J. Breeze and B. Dobson, *Hadrian's Wall*, 3rd edn. (London, 1987); *BM Coins, Rom. Emp.*, vol. 3, nos. 1628–71 (ADVENTUS coins).

43. F. Millar, *The Roman Near East, 31 BC–AD 337* (Cambridge, Mass., and London, 1993), 106 (Jerash arch); on Tel Shalem inscription, W. Eck and G. Foerster, "Ein Triumphbogen für Hadrian im Tal von Beth Shean bei Tel Shalem," *JRA* 12 (1999), 294–313; G. W. Bowersock, "The Tel Shalem Arch and P. Nahal Hever/Seiyal 8," in P. Schäfer (ed.), *The Bar Kokhba War Reconsidered* (Tübingen, 2003), 171–80.

44. *BM Coins, Rom. Emp.* vol. 3, nos. 493–4; Cass. Dio 69. 12. 1.

45. SHA *Hadr.* 14. 2; M. Goodman, "Trajan and the Origins of the Bar Kokhba War," in Schäfer (ed.), *Bar Kokhba War Reconsidered*, 28–9.

46. 5 *Sibyllines* 397–402, 408–13 (Temple), 162–3, 166–70 (trans. Collins) (Rome), 1–50 (survey of Latin history).

47. L. Kadman, *Coins of Aelia Capitolina* (Jerusalem, 1956); Y. Meshorer, *The Coinage of Aelia Capitolina* (Jerusalem, 1989); N. Belayche, *Judaea—Palaestina: The Pagan Cults in Roman*

*Palaestina* (*Second to the Fourth Century*) (Tübingen, 2001); Cass. Dio 69. 12. 1–13. 3 (trans. Cary).

48. P. Schäfer, "Bar Kokhba and the Rabbis," in Schäfer (ed.), *Bar Kokhba War Reconsidered*, 1–22; App. *Syr.* 50. 252–3; Fronto, *De Bello Parthico* 2 (in Stern [ed.]), *Greek and Latin Authors*, vol. 2, p. 177).

49. G. S. Alexsandrov, "The Role of 'Aqiba in the Bar Kokhba rebellion," in J. Neusner, *Eliezer ben Hyrcanus*, vol. 2 (Leiden, 1973), 422–36; P. Schäfer, "Rabbi Aqiva and Bar Kokhba," in W. S. Green (ed.), *Approaches to Ancient Judaism*, vol. 2 (Ann Arbor, 1980), 113–30; L. Mildenberg, *The Coinage of the Bar Kokhba War* (Aarau, 1984); Y. Yadin, *Bar-Kokhba* (London, 1971), 126.

50. Apollodorus of Damascus, *Poliorcetica* (in Stern [ed.], *Greek and Latin Authors*, vol. 2, p. 136); Cass. Dio 69. 13. 2 (Severus); W. Eck, "The Bar Kokhba Revolt: The Roman Point of View," *JRS* 89 (1999), 76–89; A. Kloner and B. Zissu, "Hiding Complexes in Judaea: An Archaeological and Geographical Update on the Area of the Bar Kokhba Revolt," in Schäfer (ed.), *Bar Kokhba War Reconsidered*, 181–216; Y. Shahar, "The Underground Hideouts in Galilee and Their Historical Meaning," ibid., 217–40; Cass. Dio 69. 13. 1–2.

51. Mildenberg, *Coinage;* Y. Meshorer, *A Treasury of Jewish Coins from the Persian Period to Bar Kokhba* (Jerusalem and Nyack, NY, 2001), 135–65.

52. *y. Taan.* 68d (Venice ed.=P. Schäfer *et al., Synopse zum Talmud Yerushalmi* (Tübingen, 1991–), vol. 2, p. 261, ll. 43–6), but note that P. Schäfer, *Der Bar Kokhba Aufstand* (Tübingen, 1981), 168–9, argues that Rabbi Akiva should be excised from the text.

53. Cass. Dio 69. 14. 1–3.

54. For the evidence of Roman commemoration of the revolt, but a different interpretation of its significance, see Eck, "The Bar Kokhba Revolt," 76–89; Justin. *1 Apol.* 1. 1; 47. 4–6; Isa. 64: 10 (Hebrew); 1: 7; Justin. *Dial. Trypho* 16; Euseb. *Hist. eccl.* 4. 6. 3 (Ariston), 4 (Eusebius).

55. Quint. *Inst.* 3. 7. 21; Tac. *Hist.* 5. 5; 4. 1; Flor. *Epitoma* 1. 40. 30; M. F. Smith, "Excavations at Oinoanda 1997: The New Epicurean Texts," *Anatolian Studies* 48 (1998), p. 132, III, line 7–IV, line 2.

56. Kadman, *Coins,* 46, 73; E. Stern (ed.), *The New Encyclopedia of Archaeological Excavations in the Holy Land,* 4 vols. (Jerusalem, 1993), vol. 2, pp. 759–67; J. Magness, "In the Footsteps of the Tenth Roman Legion in Judaea," in A. M. Berlin and J. A. Overman (eds.), *The First Jewish Revolt: Archaeology, History and Ideology* (London and New York, 2002), 189–212; memorial medallion: Kadman, *Coins,* no. 87.

57. Amm. Marc. *Res Gestae* 22. 5. 5; SHA *Ant. Pius* 5. 4; *Sev.* 16. 7 (Caracalla); Jer. *Chron.* p. 211, lines 19–20 (=*GCS* 7, *Eusebius,* ed. Helm).

58. Matt. 24: 1–2 (prophecy by Jesus of Temple destruction); Amm. Marc. *Res Gestae* 23. 1. 2–3; Gregorius Nazianzenus, *Orat.* 5 (=*Adversus Julianum imperatorem II*), 3–4.

59. *b. Sanh.* 74a.

60. S. Schwartz, *Imperialism and Jewish Society, 200 B.C.E. to 640 C.E.* (Princeton, 2001) (on abandonment of Jewishness).

61. See M. Hadas-Lebel, *Jérusalem contre Rome* (Paris, 1990), 460–82; on Edom: Gen. 25: 36; 36: 8.

62. *b. Ber.* 61b; *y. Ber.* 9: 5; discussion in D. Boyarin, *Dying for God: Martyrdom and the Making of Christianity and Judaism* (Stanford, Calif., 1999), chapter 4.

63. Dan. 7–12; Joseph. *AJ* 10. 267–81; cf. *Mekilta de-Rabbi Ishmael Bahodesh* 9. 31–41 (Lauterbach).

64. *b. Gitt.* 56b.

65. 1 Sam. 5: 2–7; E. R. Goodenough, *Jewish Symbols in the Greco-Roman Period,* 13 vols. (New York, 1953–68), vol. 11, no. 334; for a more detailed interpretation of the frescoes as religious polemic, see J. Elsner, "Cultural Resistance and the Visual Image: The Case of Dura Europos," *C Phil.* 96 (2001), 269–304.

66. *CIJ* no. 972 (dedication); Dan. 11: 34; Jerome, *In Danielem* (iv) 11. 34/35 (=*CCSL* 75 A, p. 924, lines 228–30); SHA *Alex. Sev.* 22. 4 (privileges); 51.7; Ulpian in *Dig.* 50. 2. 3. 3.

67. *b. Gitt.* 59a.

68. *y. Meg.* 3. 2, 74a (Venice)=Schäfer *et al.*, *Synopse* vol. 2, p. 297, lines 23–8; S. J. D. Cohen, "The Conversion of Antoninus," in P. Schäfer (ed), *The Talmud Yerushalmi and Graeco-Roman Culture*, vol. 1 (Tübingen, 1998), 141–71; *y. Shebi.* 6. 1, 36d (Venice)=Schäfer *et al.*, *Synopse*, vol. 1/3–5, p. 266, lines 20–21.

69. L. H. Feldman, "Some Observations on Rabbinic Reaction to Roman Rule in Third-Century Palestine," *Hebrew Union College Annual* 63 (1992), 39–81; on citizenship: Cass. Dio 78. 9. 5.

70. Origen, *Ep. ad Afric.* 20. (14), lines 7–13 (ed. de Lange, p. 566).

71. See M. Goodman, "The Roman State and the Jewish Patriarch in the Third Century," in L. I. Levine (ed.), *The Galilee in Late Antiquity* (New York and Jerusalem, 1992), 127–39.

72. See D. Noy, *Jewish Inscriptions of Western Europe*, vol. 2: *The City of Rome* (Cambridge, 1995); L. V. Rutgers, *The Jews in Late Ancient Rome: Evidence of Cultural Interaction in the Roman Diaspora* (Leiden, 1995).

73. On Josephus' self-portrayal: M. Goodman, "Josephus as Roman Citizen," in F. Parente and J. Sievers (eds.), *Josephus and the History of the Greco-Roman Period* (Leiden, 1994), 329–38.

74. On Cresces Sinicerius: *JIWE*, vol. 2, no. 491.

75. Modestinus in *Dig.* 48. 8. 11; SHA *Sev.* 17. 1; Paulus, *Sent.* 5. 22. 3–4.

76. Tac. *Hist.* 5. 5; Cass. Dio 37. 17. 1.

77. Cass. Dio 37. 17. 1.

78. Ibid. 37. 17. 3.

## CHAPTER THIRTEEN: THE GROWTH OF THE CHURCH

1. *Infancy Gospel of Thomas* 1. 1; 4. 1 (from W. Schneemelcher and R. McL. Wilson [eds.], *New Testament Apocrypha*, 2nd edn. [Cambridge, 1991], vol. 1, p. 444).

2. *Coptic Gospel of Thomas* 1, 114 (from Schneemelcher and Wilson, *New Testament Apocrypha*, vol. 1, pp. 117, 129).

3. Justin, *2. Apol.* 10. 1; *Acts of John* 101 (from Schneemelcher and Wilson, *New Testament Apocrypha*, vol. 2, pp. 185–6) (composed between 150 and 250 CE).

4. Joseph. *AJ* 18. 63–4 (the text was altered in antiquity by Christian copyists, but it is probable that at least some of the original words written by Josephus have been preserved); Tac. *Ann.* 15. 44.

5. For this procedure in studying the historical Jesus, see E. P. Sanders, *Jesus and Judaism* (London and Philadelphia, 1985).

6. Acts 2: 41 (3,000 souls); 5: 36–9 (Gamaliel).

7. 1 Cor. 9: 16; Rom. 11: 25–32; 15: 9–27.

8. See M. Goodman, *Mission and Conversion: Proselytizing in the Religious History of the Roman Empire* (Oxford, 1994), chapter 5.

9. 1 Cor. 12: 28–9; Origen, *C. Cels.* 3. 9. 2–8 (ed. Borret); *The Acts of the Scillitan Martyrs 12* in H. A. Musurillo, *The Acts of the Christian Martyrs* (Oxford, 1972), 88; Paul's vision: 1 Cor. 9: 1; 15: 8–10.

10. Tatianus, *Ad Gr.* 29; Justin, *2 Apol.* 1. 2.

11. Apostates: Plin. *Ep.* 10. 96; Lucian, *De mort. Peregr.* 16.

12. See M. Goodman, "The Persecution of Paul by Diaspora Jews," in M. Goodman, *Judaism in the Roman World: Collected Essays* (Leiden, 2007), 145–52.

13. Matt. 10: 34–5, 37.

14. Acts 4: 32.

15. Justin, *2 Apol.* 2. 11, 15–18.

16. *Epistula ad Diognetum* 5. 6; cf. R. Stark, *The Rise of Christianity: A Sociologist Reconsiders History* (Princeton, 1996).

17. Acts 2: 46; 10: 11–17; 1 Cor. 9: 20–21; Acts 21: 20–26; Joseph. *AJ* 20. 200 (James); Rom. 15: 7–9.

18. M. Goodman, "Modeling the 'Parting of the Ways,' " in A. H. Becker and A. Y. Reed (eds.), *The Ways that Never Parted: Jews and Christians in Late Antiquity and the Early Middle Ages* (Tübingen, 2003), 119–29; M. Taylor, *Anti-Judaism and Early Christian Identity: A Critique of the Scholarly Consensus* (Leiden, 1995); J. M. Lieu, *Image and Reality: The Jews in the World of the Christians in the Second Century* (Edinburgh, 1996).

19. Justin, *Dial. Trypho* 47.

20. 1 Thess. 2: 15; G. N. Stanton, *A Gospel for a New People: Studies in Matthew* (Edinburgh, 1992), 97–8; *Mart. Pol.* 13. 1; Melito, *Peri Pascha* 72 (505–7), 81 (582–8), 92 (673–7) (trans. Hall).

21. Justin, *Dial. Trypho* 11, 130; Gal. 6: 16.

22. A. Harnack, *Marcion: The Gospel of the Alien God,* trans. J. E. Steely and L. D. Bierma (Durham, NC, 1990); Gal. 4: 22–4.

23. Justin, *1 Apol.* 1. 1.

24. Tert. *Apol.* 18. 8; J. M. Lieu, *Christian Identity in the Jewish and Graeco-Roman World* (Oxford, 2004); on pagan names for Jews, M. Stern (ed.), *Greek and Latin Authors on Jews and Judaism,* 3 vols. (Jerusalem, 1974–84), index.

25. Euseb. *Hist. eccl.* 3. 1. 2 (Peter); 2. 25. 5 (Paul); Rev. 17: 5; Tatianus, *Ad Gr.* 28 (trans. Whittaker); Melito in Euseb. *Hist. eccl.* 4. 26. 7; Luke 23: 4, 22; Acts 25: 8.

26. Min. Fel. *Oct.* 10. 2; Joseph. *Ap.* 2. 258–9; *Epistula ad Diognetum* 5; Matt. 22: 21; Tert. *Apol.* 5. 6; Euseb. *Hist. eccl.* 5. 5. 2.

27. Tert. *Apol.* 50. 12 ("good governors"); 9. 6 ("panting for . . . blood"); Euseb. *Hist. eccl.* 4. 3. 1; Melito in Euseb. *Hist. eccl.* 4. 26. 5–6; Euseb. *Hist. eccl.* 5. 1 (Lyons).

28. Tac. *Ann.* 15. 44; Suet. *Nero* 16. 2.

29. J. B. Rives, "The Decree of Decius and the Religion of Empire," *JRS* 89 (1999), 135–54; W. H. C. Frend, *Martyrdom and Persecution in the Early Church* (Oxford, 1965).

30. *Mart. Pol.* 9. 2; 12. 1; Plin. *Ep.* 10. 96–7 (trans. Radice).

31. On trophies of Peter and Paul: Euseb. *Hist. eccl.* 2. 25. 5–7; M. Beard, J. North and S. Price (eds.), *Religions of Rome,* 2 vols. (Cambridge, 1998), vol. 1, pp. 268–9; vol. 2, p. 347; on calendars: ibid., vol. 2, pp. 74–6; Tert. *Apol.* 50. 13.

32. Plin. *Ep.* 10. 96; Tac. *Ann.* 15. 44; Joseph. *BJ* 7. 50–51 (Jews in Antioch); Suet. *Nero* 16.

33. Acts 11: 26; Rom. 1: 7; Acts 26: 28; 1 Pet. 4: 16.

34. Tac. *Ann.* 15. 44; Ign. *Eph.* 11; *Magn.* 4; 10 (*Christianismos*); *Phld.* 6; *Did.* 12. 1–5; *The Acts of Justin and Companions* A. 3. 4, in Musurillo, *Acts,* 44 (Justin); Euseb. *Hist. eccl.* 5. 1. 20 (Sanctus).

35. Lact. *De mort. Pers.* 44. 5–6, 9.

36. Euseb. *Vit. Const.* 1. 28.

37. Acts 15: 2, 4–31; Euseb. *Hist. eccl.* 6. 43. 11–12 (Cornelius).

38. A. Hastings, "150–550," in A. Hastings (ed.), *A World History of Christianity* (London, 1999), 32–3.

39. *Cod. Iust.* 1. 9. 3; Euseb. *Vit. Const.* 3. 18. 2, 4 (trans. Cameron and Hall) (date of Easter); N. H. Baynes, *Constantine the Great and the Christian Church,* 2nd edn. (London, 1972).

40. *Cod. Theod.* 9. 40. 2 (branding); Euseb. *Hist. eccl.* 9. 9. 5, 7.

41. Euseb. *Vit. Const.* 2. 60. 2 (trans. Cameron and Hall) (idolatry); 4. 28 (charity); *Cod. Iust.* 5. 26. 1 (concubines); *Cod. Theod.* 9. 24. 1. 1 (nurses); *P Oxy.* 3759, lines 37–9 (Sundays).

42. Joseph. *Ap.* 2. 167, 179, 193; Euseb. *Oratio* 3. 5–7.

43. Euseb. *Vit. Const.* 4. 60. 3–4 (trans. Cameron and Hall).


CHAPTER FOURTEEN: A NEW ROME AND A NEW JERUSALEM

1. Amm. Marc. *Res. Gestae* 14. 6. 4–5.

2. G. F. Snyder, *Ante Pacem: Archaeological Evidence of Church Life Before Constantine,* 2nd edn. (Macon, Ga., 2003); R. Krautheimer, *Rome: Profile of a City, 312–1308* (Princeton, 1980); for Constantine as competing with Maxentius, see E. D. Hunt, "Imperial Building at Rome: The Role of Constantine," in K. Lomas and T. Cornell (eds.), *"Bread and Circuses": Evergetism and Municipal Patronage in Roman Italy* (London, 2003), 105–24.

3. Euseb. *Hist. eccl.* 9. 9. 10–11 ("saving sign" and statue); *CIL* vol. 6, no. 1139 (inscription on arch).

4. Socrates, *Hist. eccl.* 1. 16. 1 (ed. Hansen); *Publii Optatiani Porphyrii Carmina,* ed. L. Müller, 4. 5. 5–6 *(altera Roma)*; G. Dagron, *Naissance d'une capitale: Constantinople et ses institutions de 330 à 451* (Paris, 1974).

5. Euseb. *Vit. Const.* 3. 48–9 (trans. Cameron and Hall); Zos. 2. 31. 2–3; Euseb. *Vit. Const.* 4. 36. 1, 3–4 (trans. Cameron and Hall) (letter to Eusebius); *Vita S. Danielis Stylitae* 10 (ed. Delehaye, p. 12, line 13).

6. Cic. *Flac.* 28 (66–9); on Jews in fourth-century Byzantium, C. Roth *et al.* (eds.), *Encyclopaedia Judaica* (Jerusalem, 1971), vol. 5, p. 918.

7. Lactant. *De mort. pers.* 48. 3, 6 (edict of Milan); L. V. Rutgers, *The Jews in Late Ancient Rome: Evidence of Cultural Interaction in the Roman Diaspora* (Leiden, 1995).

8. Lactant. *De mort. pers.* 34. 4–5 (Galerius).

9. M. Beard, J. North and S. Price (eds.), *Religions of Rome,* 2 vols. (Cambridge, 1998), vol. 2, pp. 67, 75.

10. *Mosaicarum et Romanarum Legum Collatio* 6. 7. 1 (divine law); 1. 1. 1 (Moses); 7. 1. 1 (priority); 16. 1. 1 (divine scripture); 12. 1. 1–2. 1 (incendiarism); in general, see Rutgers, *Jews in Late Ancient Rome,* 213–53.

11. Euseb. *Vit. Const.* 3. 33. 1–2 (trans. Cameron and Hall).

12. Euseb. *Onomasticon;* E. D. Hunt, *Holy Land Pilgrimage in the Later Roman Empire,* AD 312–460 (Oxford, 1982), 148–9; Euseb. *Mart. Pal.* 11. 9–12.

13. Euseb. *Hist. eccl.* 4. 26. 14 (on Melito); on Alexander: *Hist. eccl.* 6. 11. 2; 6. 39. 2–3; Rev. 21: 10–11, 22–4 (and on Jewish writings about the new Jerusalem, see Chapter 4); J. E. Taylor, *Christians and the Holy Places: The Myth of Jewish-Christian Origins* (Oxford, 1993).

14. *Nicaea Canon* 7; Euseb. *Vit. Const.* 3. 25; 26. 2–3, 7; 28; 33. 3; 36. 1–2; 40 (trans. Cameron and Hall).

15. Hunt, *Holy Land Pilgrimage,* 37–40; on the site of the Holy Sepulchre, A. J. Wharton, *Refiguring the Post-Classical City: Dura Europos, Jerash, Jerusalem and Ravenna* (Cambridge, 1995), 88–91; on 13 September, E. D. Hunt, "Constantine and Jerusalem," *Journal of Ecclesiastical History* 48 (1997), 405–24.

16. *Itinerarium Burdigalense* (*CCSL* 175) 591. 4 (statues); J. Wilkinson, "Christian Pilgrims in Jerusalem During the Byzantine Period," *Palestine Exploration Quarterly* 108 (1976), 75–101; Jer. *Commentariorum in Esaiam* 1. 2. 9 (*CCSL* 73, p. 33).

17. Zos. 5. 8. 2; O. Irsai, "Historical Aspects of the Christian-Jewish Polemic Concerning the Church of Jerusalem in the Fourth Century," unpublished Ph.D. thesis, Hebrew Univer-

sity of Jerusalem, 1993 (in Hebrew); J. Elsner, "The *Itinerarium Burdigalense:* Politics and Salvation in the Geography of Constantine's Empire," *JRS* 90 (2000), 181–95; *Itinerarium Burdigalense* (*CCSL* 175) 549. 1–5 (title); 572. 4 (Hannibal); 578. 1 (Apollonius); description of Jerusalem: 589. 7–8, 589. 11–590. 6, 591. 1–3, 592. 5–593. 1, 595. 2–4, 598. 4–9.

18. *Itinerarium Burdigalense* (*CCSL* 175) 591. 4–5; *Bereshit Rabba* 32. 10 (ed. Albeck, p. 296); 81. 4; S. Safrai, "The Holy Congregation in Jerusalem," *Scripta Hierosolymitana* 23 (1972), 62–78; on Eutychius, see Irsai, "Historical Aspects," 53–76.

19. Epiph. *Adv. haeres.* 30. 11. 9; 30. 12. 1, 4–9; on patriarch: ibid. 30. 4. 3–4; 30. 11. 1; on reasons for the silence of the rabbis, see M. Goodman, "Palestinian Rabbis and the Conversion of Constantine to Christianity," in P. Schäfer and C. Hezser (eds.), *The Talmud Yerushalmi and Graeco-Roman Culture,* vol. 2 (Tübingen, 2000), 1–9; attacks on apostates: *Cod. Theod.* 16. 8. 1 (329 CE); *Const. Sirmondiana* 4 (335 CE).

20. S. Schwartz, *Imperialism and Jewish Society, 200 B.C.E. to 640 C.E.* (Princeton, 2001); on Essenes and the sun: Joseph. *BJ* 2. 128–9, 148–9; *Sifre on Deuteronomy* 49 (ed. Horovitz-Finkelstein, p. 114) (on God as fire).

21. Julian. *Or.* 4; on *Theos Hypsistos:* S. Mitchell, "The Cult of Theos Hypsistos between Pagans, Jews and Christians," in P. Athanassiadi and M. Frede (eds.), *Pagan Monotheism in Late Antiquity* (Oxford, 1999), 81–148; H. Erbse, *Theosophorum Graecorum Fragmenta* (Leipzig, 1995), 8 (Oenoanda oracle); M. Goodman, "The Jewish Image of God in Late Antiquity," in R. Kalmin and S. Schwartz (eds.), *Jewish Culture and Society under the Christian Roman Empire* (Leuven, 2003), 133–45; M. Wallraff, *Christus Verus Sol: Sonnenverehrung und Christentum in der Spätantike* (Münster, 2001) (Constantine and the sun god); Jewish references to *Theos Hypsistos:* Philo, *Spec. Leg.* 278; Joseph. *AJ* 16. 163.

22. J. M. Reynolds and R. Tannenbaum, *Jews and Godfearers at Aphrodisias* (Cambridge, 1987); on the Temple site: Y. Eliav, *God's Mountain: The Temple Mount in Time, Place, and Memory* (Baltimore, 2005). For scepticism about recent theories that there was a revival of priestly power in the fifth and sixth centuries, see Schwartz, *Imperialism,* 273, n. 86; on the inscription: H. M. Cotton and J. J. Price, "A Bilingual Tombstone from Zo'ar (Arabia)," *ZPE* 134 (2001), 277–83; on the dates on the Zo'ar inscriptions more generally: S. Stern, *Calendar and Community* (Oxford, 2001), 87–91.

23. J. W. Drijvers, *Cyril of Jerusalem: Bishop and City* (Leiden, 2004); Cyril of Jerusalem, *Epistula ad Constantium* 4, 6; Matt. 24: 30; Cyril of Jerusalem, *Fifteenth Catechetical Lecture* 22.

24. Jer. *In Sophoniam* 1. 15. 16 (*CCSL* 76A, p. 673, lines 669–84).

25. *t. Sot.* 15. 12–14 (memorials of Jerusalem); *Shemot Rabbah* 15. 21; last sentence from E. Schürer, rev. G. Vermes *et al., The History of the Jewish People in the Age of Jesus Christ,* 3 vols. (Edinburgh, 1973–87), vol. 1, p. 557; it was added by the revisers, Geza Vermes and Fergus Millar, to Schürer's original ending of the narrative of Jewish history up to 135 CE. I have cited it here as an acknowledgement of all that I owe to both of them for all they have taught me over many years.

## EPILOGUE: THE ORIGINS OF ANTISEMITISM

1. For a good summary of scholarship on the origins of antisemitism in antiquity, see P. Schäfer, *Judeophobia: Attitudes Toward the Jews in the Ancient World* (Cambridge, Mass., 1997).

2. Cass. Dio 66. 7. 2.

3. Acts 5: 40, 42.

4. John 11: 50; see G. Vermes, *The Passion* (London, 2005).

5. M. Hess, *Rom und Jerusalem, die letzte Nationalitätsfrage* (Leipzig, 1862); the citation is from M. Hess, *Rome and Jerusalem,* trans. M. J. Bloom (New York, 1958), 8.

# FURTHER READING

Accessible general histories of the early Roman empire can be found in C. M. Wells, *The Roman Empire,* 2nd edn. (London, 1992); M. Goodman, *The Roman World, 44 BC–AD 180* (London and New York, 1997); G. Woolf (ed.), *Cambridge Illustrated History of the Roman World* (Cambridge, 2003); M. T. Boatwright, D. Gargola and R. J. A. Talbert, *The Romans: From Village to Empire* (Oxford, 2005). On Jews and Judaism in the first centuries CE, see S. J. D. Cohen, *From the Maccabees to the Mishnah,* 2nd edn. (Louisville, Ky., 2006); E. P. Sanders, *Judaism: Practice and Belief, 63 BCE–66 CE* (London, 1992). On early Christianity, the best introduction remains H. Chadwick, *The Early Church,* 2nd edn. (London, 1993); more detailed surveys can be found in P. F. Esler (ed.), *The Early Christian World,* 2 vols. (London and New York, 2000), and H. Chadwick, *The Church in Ancient Society: From Galilee to Gregory the Great* (Oxford, 2001).

# INDEX

## A NOTE ABOUT THE AUTHOR

Martin Goodman has divided his intellectual life between the Roman and Jewish worlds. He has edited both the *Journal of Roman Studies* and the *Journal of Jewish Studies*. He has taught Roman History at Birmingham and Oxford Universities, and is currently Professor of Jewish Studies at Oxford. He is a Fellow of Wolfson College, Oxford, and of the Oxford Centre for Hebrew and Jewish Studies. In 1996 he was elected a Fellow of the British Academy. In 2002 he edited the *Oxford Handbook of Jewish Studies*, which was awarded a National Jewish Book Award for Scholarship. He lives with his family in Birmingham.

## A NOTE ON THE TYPE

The text of this book was set in Bembo, a facsimile of a typeface cut by Francesco Griffo for Aldus Manutius, the celebrated Venetian printer, in 1495. The face was named for Pietro Cardinal Bembo, the author of the small treatise entitled *De Aetna* in which it first appeared. Through the research of Stanley Morison, it is now generally acknowledged that all old style type designs up to the time of William Caslon can be traced to the Bembo cut. The present-day version of Bembo was introduced by the Monotype Corporation of London in 1929. Sturdy, well-balanced, and finely proportioned, Bembo is a face of rare beauty and great legibility in all of its sizes.

*Composed by North Market Street Graphics, Lancaster, Pennsylvania*
*Printed and bound by Berryville Graphics, Berryville, Virginia*
*Book design by Robert C. Olsson*